Lecture Notes in Artificial Intelligence   6076

Edited by R. Goebel, J. Siekmann, and W. Wahlster

Subseries of Lecture Notes in Computer Science

W0227565

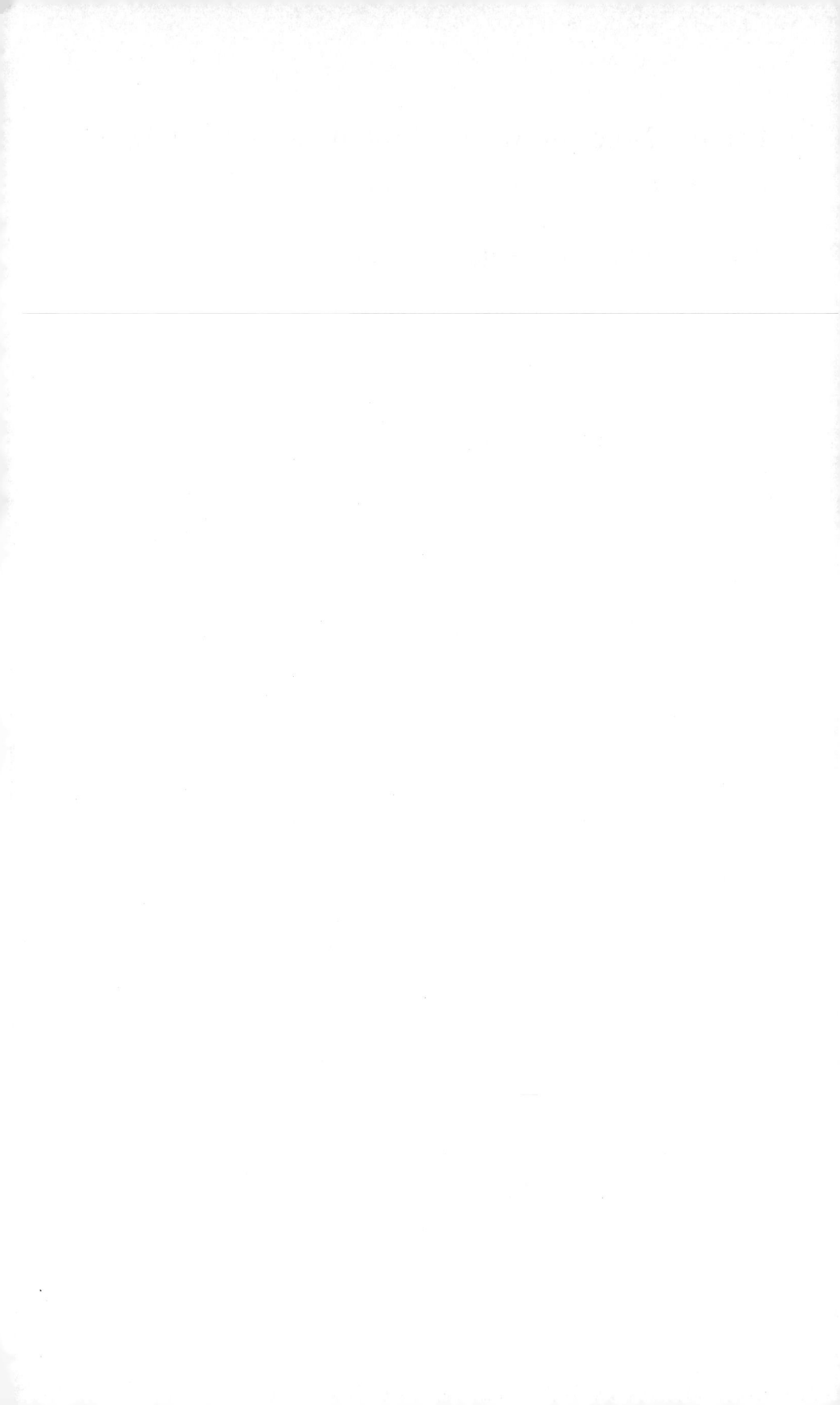

Manuel Graña Romay   Emilio Corchado
M. Teresa Garcia-Sebastian (Eds.)

Hybrid Artificial Intelligence Systems

5th International Conference, HAIS 2010
San Sebastián, Spain, June 23-25, 2010
Proceedings, Part I

 Springer

Series Editors

Randy Goebel, University of Alberta, Edmonton, Canada
Jörg Siekmann, University of Saarland, Saarbrücken, Germany
Wolfgang Wahlster, DFKI and University of Saarland, Saarbrücken, Germany

Volume Editors

Manuel Graña Romay
Facultad de informatica UPV/EHU
San Sebastian, Spain
E-mail: manuel.grana@ehu.es

Emilio Corchado
Universidad de Salamanca, Spain
E-mail: escorchado@usal.es

M. Teresa Garcia-Sebastian
Facultad de informatica UPV/EHU
San Sebastian, Spain
E-mail: mariateresa.garcia@ehu.es

Library of Congress Control Number: Applied for

CR Subject Classification (1998): I.2, H.3, F.1, H.4, I.4, I.5

LNCS Sublibrary: SL 7 – Artificial Intelligence

ISSN	0302-9743
ISBN-10	3-642-13768-7 Springer Berlin Heidelberg New York
ISBN-13	978-3-642-13768-6 Springer Berlin Heidelberg New York

springer.com

© Springer-Verlag Berlin Heidelberg 2010
Printed in Germany

Typesetting: Camera-ready by author, data conversion by Scientific Publishing Services, Chennai, India
Printed on acid-free paper   06/3180

Preface

The 5th International Conference on Hybrid Artificial Intelligence Systems (HAIS 2010) has become a unique, established and broad interdisciplinary forum for researchers and practitioners who are involved in developing and applying symbolic and sub-symbolic techniques aimed at the construction of highly robust and reliable problem-solving techniques, and bringing the most relevant achievements in this field. Overcoming the rigid encasing imposed by the arising orthodoxy in the field of artificial intelligence, which has led to the partition of researchers into so-called areas or fields, interest in hybrid intelligent systems is growing because they give freedom to design innovative solutions to the ever-increasing complexities of real-world problems. Noise and uncertainty call for probabilistic (often Bayesian) methods, while the huge amount of data in some cases asks for fast heuristic (in the sense of suboptimal and ad-hoc) algorithms able to give answers in acceptable time frames. High dimensionality demands linear and non-linear dimensionality reduction and feature extraction algorithms, while the imprecision and vagueness call for fuzzy reasoning and linguistic variable formalization. Nothing impedes real-life problems to mix difficulties, presenting huge quantities of noisy, vague and high-dimensional data; therefore, the design of solutions must be able to resort to any tool of the trade to attack the problem. Combining diverse paradigms poses challenging problems of computational and methodological interfacing of several previously incompatible approaches. This is, thus, the setting of HAIS conference series, and its increasing success is the proof of the vitality of this exciting field.

This volume *of Lecture Notes on Artificial Intelligence* (LNAI) includes accepted papers presented at HAIS 2010 held in the framework of the prestigious "Cursos de Verano of the Universidad del Pais Vasco" at the beautiful venue of Palacio de Miramar, San Sebastián, Spain, in June 2010.

Since its first edition in Brazil in 2006, HAIS has become an important forum for researchers working on fundamental and theoretical aspects of hybrid artificial intelligence systems based on the use of agents and multi-agent systems, bioinformatics and bio-inspired models, fuzzy systems, artificial vision, artificial neural networks, optimization models and alike.

HAIS 2010 received 269 technical submissions. After a rigorous peer-review process, the International Program Committee selected 133 papers which are published in these conference proceedings. In this edition emphasis was put on the organization of special sessions. Fourteen special sessions, containing 84 papers, were organized on the following topics:

- Real-World HAIS Applications and Data Uncertainty
- Computational Intelligence for Recommender Systems
- Signal Processing and Biomedical Applications
- Methods of Classifiers Fusion
- Knowledge Extraction Based on Evolutionary Learning

- Systems, Man, and Cybernetics by HAIS Workshop
- Hybrid Intelligent Systems on Logistics
- Hybrid Reasoning and Coordination Methods on Multi-Agent Systems
- HAIS for Computer Security
- Hybrid and Intelligent Techniques on Multimedia
- Hybrid ANNs: Models, Algorithms and Data
- Hybrid Artificial Intelligence Systems Based on Lattice Theory
- Information Fusion: Frameworks and Architectures

The selection of papers was extremely rigorous in order to maintain the high quality of the conference, and we would like to thank the Program Committee for their hard work in the reviewing process. This process is very important for the creation of a conference of high standard, and the HAIS conference would not exist without their help.

The large number of submissions is certainly not only testimony to the vitality and attractiveness of the field but an indicator of the interest in the HAIS conferences themselves.

As a follow-up of the conference, we anticipate further publication of selected papers in special issues scheduled for the following journals:

- *Information Science,* Elsevier
- *Neurocomputing,* Elsevier
- *Journal of Mathematical Imaging and Vision,* Springer
- *Information Fusion,* Elsevier
- *Logic Journal of the IPL,* Oxford Journals

HAIS 2010 enjoyed outstanding keynote speeches by distinguished guest speakers:

- Gerhard Ritter, University of Florida (USA)
- Mihai Datcu, Paris Institute of Technology, Telecom Paris (France)
- Marios Polycarpou, University of Cyprus (Cyprus)
- Ali-Akbar Ghorbani, University of New Brunswick (Canada)
- James Llinas, Universidad Carlos III de Madrid (Spain)
- Éloi Bossé, Defence Research and Development Canada (DRDC Valcartier) (Canada)

We would like to fully acknowledge support from the GICAP Group of the University of Burgos, the BISISTE Group from the University of Salamanca, the GIC (www.ehu.es/ccwintco), Vicerrectorado de Investigación and the Cursos de Verano of the Universidad del Pais Vasco, the Departamento de Educación, Ciencia y Universidades of the Gobierno Vasco, Vicomtech, and the Ministerio de Ciencia e Investigación. The IEEE Systems, Man & Cybernetics Society, through its Spanish chapter, and the IEEE-Spanish Section also supported this event. We also want to extend our warm gratitude to all the Special Session Chairs for their continuing support to the HAIS series of conferences.

We wish to thank Alfred Hoffman and Anna Kramer from Springer for their help and collaboration during this demanding publication project. The local organizing team (Alexandre Manhaes Savio, Ramón Moreno, Maite García Sebastian, Elsa Fernandez, Darya Chyzyk, Miguel Angel Veganzones, Ivan Villaverde) did a superb job. Without their enthusiastic support the whole conference burden would have crushed our frail shoulders.

June 2010   Emilio Corchado
                                                                   Manuel Graña

Organization

Honorary Chair

Carolina Blasco   Director of Telecommunication, Regional Goverment of Castilla y León (Spain)

María Isabel Celáa Diéguez   Consejera de Educación del Gobierno Vasco (Spain)

Marie Cottrell   Institute SAMOS-MATISSE, Universite Paris 1 (France)

Daniel Yeung   IEEE SMCS President (China)

General Chairs

Emilio Corchado   University of Salamanca (Spain)

Manuel Graña   University of the Basque Country (Spain)

International Advisory Committee

Ajith Abraham   Norwegian University of Science and Technology (Norway)

Carolina Blasco   Director of Telecommunication, Regional Goverment of Castilla y León (Spain)

Pedro M. Caballero   CARTIF (Spain)

Andre de Carvalho   University of São Paulo (Brazil)

Juan M. Corchado   University of Salamanca (Spain)

José R. Dorronsoro   Autonomous University of Madrid (Spain)

Mark A. Girolami   University of Glasgow (UK)

Petro Gopych   Universal Power Systems USA-Ukraine LLC (Ukraine)

Francisco Herrera   University of Granada (Spain)

César Hervás-Martínez   University of Córdoba (Spain)

Tom Heskes   Radboud University Nijmegen (The Netherlands)

Lakhmi Jain   University of South Australia (Australia)

Samuel Kaski   Helsinki University of Technology (Finland)

Daniel A. Keim   Computer Science Institute, University of Konstanz (Germany)

Isidro Laso   D.G. Information Society and Media (European Commission)

Witold Pedrycz   University of Alberta (Canada)

Xin Yao   University of Birmingham (UK)

Hujun Yin   University of Manchester (UK)

Michal Wozniak   Wroclaw University of Technology (Poland)

Publicity Co-chairs

Emilio Corchado	University of Salamanca (Spain)
Manuel Graña	University of the Basque Country (Spain)

Program Committee

Manuel Graña	University of the Basque Country (Spain) *(PC Co-chair)*
Emilio Corchado	University of Salamanca (Spain) *(PC Co-chair)*
Agnar Aamodt	Norwegian University of Science and Technology (Norway)
Jesús Alcalá-Fernández	University of Granada (Spain)
Rafael Alcalá	University of Granada (Spain)
José Luis Álvarez	University of Huelva (Spain)
Davide Anguita	University of Genoa (Italy)
Bruno Apolloni	Università degli Studi di Milano (Italy)
Antonio Aráuzo-Azofra	University of Córdoba (Spain)
Estefania Argente	University of Valencia (Spain)
Fidel Aznar	University of Alicante (Spain)
Jaume Bacardit	University of Nottingham (UK)
Antonio Bahamonde	University of Oviedo (Spain)
Javier Bajo	Universidad Pontifícia de Salamanca (Spain)
John Beasley	Brunel University (UK)
Bruno Baruque	University of Burgos (Spain)
Joé Manuel Benítez	University of Granada (Spain)
Ester Bernadó	Universitat Ramon Lull (Spain)
Richard Blake	Norwegian University of Science and Technology
Juan Botía	University of Murcia (Spain)
Prof Vicente Botti	Universidad Politécnica de Valencia (Spain)
Robert Burduk	Wroclaw University of Technology (Poland)
José Ramón Cano	University of Jaén (Spain)
Cristóbal José Carmona	University of Jaén (Spain)
Blanca Cases	University of the Basque Country (Spain)
Oscar Castillo	Tijuana Institute of Technology (Mexico)
Paula María Castro Castro	Universidade da Coruña (Spain)
Jonathan Chan	King Mongkut's University of Technology Thonburi (Thailand)
Richard Chbeir	Bourgogne University (France)
Enhong Chen	University of Science and Technology of China (China)
Camelia Chira	University of Babes-Bolyai (Romania)
Sung-Bae Cho	Yonsei University (Korea)
Darya Chyzhyk	University of the Basque Country (Spain)
Juan Manuel Corchado	University of Salamanca (Spain)
Emilio Corchado	University of Salamanca (Spain)

Rafael Corchuelo	University of Seville (Spain)
Guiomar Corral	University Ramon Lull (Spain)
Raquel Cortina Parajon	University of Oviedo (Spain)
Carlos Cotta	University of Málaga (Spain)
José Alfredo F. Costa	Universidade Federal do Rio Grande do Norte (Brazil)
Leticia Curiel	University of Burgos (Spain)
Alfredo Cuzzocrea	University of Calabria (Italy)
Keshav Dahal	University of Bradford (UK)
Theodoros Damoulas	Cornell University (UK)
Ernesto Damiani	University of Milan (Italy)
Bernard De Baets	Ghent University (Belgium)
Enrique de la Cal	University of Oviedo (Spain)
Javier de Lope Asiain	Universidad Politécnica de Madrid (Spain)
Marcilio de Souto	Universidade Federal do Rio Grande do Norte (Brazil)
María José del Jesús	University of Jaén (Spain)
Ricardo del Olmo	University of Burgos (Spain)
Joaquín Derrac	University of Granada (Spain)
Nicola Di Mauro	University of Bari (Italy)
António Dourado	University of Coimbra (Portugal)
Richard Duro	University of Coruña (Spain)
Susana Irene Díaz	University of Oviedo (Spain)
José Dorronsoro	Universidad Autónoma de Madrid (Spain)
Pietro Ducange	University of Pisa (Italy)
Talbi El-Ghazali	University of Lille (France)
Aboul Ella Hassanien	University of Cairo (Egypt)
Marc Esteva	Artificial Intelligence Research Institute (Spain)
Juan José Flores	University of Michoacana (Mexico)
Alberto Fernández	Universidad Rey Juan Carlos (Spain)
Alberto Fernández	University of Granada (Spain)
Elías Fernández-Combarro Álvarez	University of Oviedo (Spain)
Elsa Fernández	University of the Basque Country (Spain)
Nuno Ferreira	Instituto Politécnico de Coimbra (Portugal)
Richard Freeman	Capgemini (Spain)
Rubén Fuentes	Universidad Complutense de Madrid (Spain)
Giorgio Fumera	University of Cagliari (Italy)
Bogdan Gabrys	Bournemouth University (UK)
João Gama	University of Porto (Portugal)
Matjaz Gams	Jozef Stefan Institute Ljubljana (Slovenia)
Jun Gao	Hefei University of Technology (China)
TOM Heskes	Radboud University Nijmegen (The Netherlands)
Isaías García	University of León (Spain)
José García	University of Alicante (Spain)
Salvador García	University of Jaén (Spain)
Neveen Ghali	Azhar University (Egypt)

Adriana Giret	Universidad Politécnica de Valencia (Spain)
Jorge Gómez	Universidad Complutense de Madrid (Spain)
Pedro González	University of Jaén (Spain)
Petro Gopych	Universal Power Systems USA-Ukraine LLC (Ukraine)
Juan Manuel Górriz	University of Granada (Spain)
Maite García-Sebastián	University of the Basque Country (Spain)
Manuel Graña	University of the Basque Country (Spain)
Maciej Grzenda	Warsaw University of Technology (Poland)
Arkadiusz Grzybowski	Wroclaw University of Technology (Poland)
Jerzy Grzymala-Busse	University of Kansas (USA)
Anne Håkansson	Stockholm University (Sweden)
Saman Halgamuge	The University of Melbourne (Australia)
José Alberto Hernández	Universidad Autónoma del Estado de Morelos (Mexico)
Carmen Hernández	University of the Basque Country (Spain)
Francisco Herrera	University of Granada (Spain)
Álvaro Herrero	University of Burgos (Spain)
Sean Holden	University of Cambridge (UK)
Vasant Honavar	Iowa State University (USA)
Vicente Julián	Universidad Politécnica de Valencia (Spain)
Konrad Jackowski	Wroclaw University of Technology (Poland)
Yaochu Jin	Honda Research Institute Europe (Germany)
Ivan Jordanov	University of Portsmouth (UK)
Ulf Johansson	University of Borås (Sweden)
Juha Karhunen	Helsinki University of Technology (Finland)
Frank Klawonn	University of Applied Sciences Braunschweig/Wolfenbuettel (Germany)
Andreas König	University of Kaiserslautern (Germany)
Mario Köppen	Kyushu Institute of Technology (Japan)
Rudolf Kruse	Otto-von-Guericke-Universität Magdeburg (Germany)
Bernadetta Kwintiana	Universität Stuttgart (Germany)
Dario Landa-Silva	University of Nottingham (UK)
Soo-Young Lee	Brain Science Research Center (Korea)
Lenka Lhotská	Czech Technical University in Prague (Czech Republic)
Hailin Liu	Guangdong University of Technology (China)
Otoniel López	Universidad Autónoma de Madrid (Spain)
Karmele López	University of the Basque Country (Spain)
Teresa Ludermir	Universidade Federal de Pernambuco (Brazil)
Julián Luengo	University of Granada (Spain)
Wenjian Luo	University of Science and Technology of China (China)
Núria Macià	Universitat Ramon Llull (Spain)
Kurosh Madani	University of Paris-Est Creteil (France)
Ana Maria Madureira	Instituto Politécnico do Porto (Portugal)

Roque Marin	University of Murcia (Spain)
Yannis Marinakis	Technical University of Crete (Grece)
José Fco. Martínez-Trinidad	INAOE (Mexico)
José Luis Martínez	University of Castilla - La Mancha (Spain)
Jacinto Mata	University of Huelva (Spain)
Giancarlo Mauri	University of Milano-Bicocca (Italy)
David Meehan	Dublin Institute of Technology (Ireland)
Gerardo M. Méndez	Instituto Tecnológico de Nuevo León (Mexico)
Abdel-Badeeh M. Salem	Ain Shams University (Egypt)
Masoud Mohammadian	University of Canberra (Australia)
José Manuel Molina	University Carlos III of Madrid (Spain)
Claudio Moraga	European Centre for Soft Computing (Spain)
Marco Mora	Universidad Católica del Maule (Spain)
Ramón Moreno	University of the Basque Country (Spain)
Susana Nascimento	Universidade Nova de Lisboa (Portugal)
Martí Navarro	Universidad Politécnica de Valencia (Spain)
Yusuke Nojima	Osaka Prefecture University (Japan)
Alberto Ochoa	Juarez City University/CIATEC (Mexico)
Albert Orriols	University Ramon LLull (Spain)
Rubé Ortiz	Universidad Rey Juan Carlos (Spain)
Vasile Palade	Oxford University (USA)
Stephan Pareigis	Hamburg University of Applied Sciences (Germany)
Witold Pedrycz	University of Alberta (Canada)
Elzbieta Pekalska	University of Manchester (UK)
Carlos Pereira	Universidade de Coimbra (Portugal)
Antonio Peregrín	University of Huelva (Spain)
Lina Petrakieva	Glasgow Caledonian University (UK)
Gloria Phillips-Wren	Loyola College in Maryland (USA)
Han Pingchou	Peking University (China)
Camelia Pintea	University of Babes-Bolyai (Romania)
Julio Ponce	Universidad Autónoma de Aguascalientes (Mexico)
Khaled Ragab	King Faisal University (Saudi Arabia)
José Ranilla	University of Oviedo (Spain)
Javier Ramírez	University of Granada (Spain)
Romain Raveaux	La Rochelle University (France)
Carlos Redondo	University of León (Spain)
Raquel Redondo	University of Burgos (Spain)
Bernadete Ribeiro	University of Coimbra (Portugal)
Ramón Rizo	University of Alicante (Spain)
Peter Rockett	University of Sheffield (UK)
Adolfo Rodríguez	University of León (Spain)
Rosa M. Rodríguez Maraña	University of León (Spain)
Katya Rodriguez-Vázquez	Universidad Nacional Autónoma de México (Mexico)
Fabrice Rossi	TELECOM ParisTech (France)
António Ruano	University of Algarve (Portugal)
Ozgur Koray Sahingoz	Turkish Air Force Academy (Turkey)

Wei-Chiang Samuelson Hong	Oriental Institute of Technology (Taiwan)
Luciano Sánchez	University of Oviedo (Spain)
José Santamaría	University of Jaén (Spain)
Alexandre Savio	University of the Basque Country (Spain)
Mrs. Fatima Sayuri Quezada	Universidad Autónoma de Aguascalientes (Mexico)
Gerald Schaefer	Aston University (UK)
Robert Schaefer	AGH University of Science and Technology (Poland)
Javier Sedano	University of Burgos (Spain)
Leila Shafti	Universidad Autónoma de Madrid (Spain)
Dragan Simic	Novi Sad Fair (Serbia)
Konstantinos Sirlantzis	University of Kent (UK)
Dominik Slezak	University of Regina (Canada)
Cecilia Sönströd	University of Borås (Sweden)
Ying Tan	Peking University (China)
Ke Tang	University of Science and Technology of China (China)
Nikos Thomaidis	University of the Aegean (Greece)
Alicia Troncoso	Universidad Pablo de Olavide de Sevilla (Spain)
Eiji Uchino	Yamaguchi University (Japan)
Roberto Uribeetxeberria	Mondragon University (Spain)
José Valls	University Carlos III of Madrid (Spain)
Miguel Ángel Veganzones	University of the Basque Country (Spain)
Sebastian Ventura	Universidad de Córdoba (Spain)
José Luis Verdegay	University of Granada (Spain)
José Ramón Villar	University of Oviedo (Spain)
José Ramón Cano	University of Jaén (Spain)
Krzysztof Walkowiak	Wroclaw University of Technology (Poland)
Guoyin Wang	Chongqing University of Posts and Telecommunications (China)
Michal Wozniak	Wroclaw University of Technology (Poland)
Zhuoming Xu	Hohai University (China)
Ronald Yager	Iona College (US)
Hujun Yin	The University of Manchester (UK)
Constantin Zopounidis	Technical University of Crete (Greece)
Huiyu Zhou	Brunel University (UK)
Rodolfo Zunino	University of Genoa (Italy)
Urko Zurutuza	Mondragon University (Spain)

Special Session Committees

Real-World HAIS Applications and Data Uncertainty

José Ramón Villar	University of Oviedo (Spain)
André Carvalho	University of São Paulo (Brazil)
Camelia Pintea	University of Babes-Bolyai (Romania)

Eduardo Raúl Hruschka	University of São Paulo (Brazil)
Oscar Ibañez	European Centre for Soft Computing (Spain)
Paula Mello	University of Bologna (Italy)
Javier Sedano	University of Burgos (Spain)
Adolfo Rodríguez	Universidad de León (Spain)
Camelia Chira	University of Babes-Bolyai (Romania)
José Ramón Villar	University of Oviedo (Spain)
Luciano Sánchez	University of Oviedo (Spain)
Luis Oliveira	University of Oviedo (Spain)
María del Rosario Suárez	University of Oviedo (Spain)
Carmen Vidaurre	Technical University of Berlin (Germany)
Enrique de la Cal	University of Oviedo (Spain)
Gerardo M. Méndez	Instituto Tecnológico de Nuevo León (Mexico)
Ana Palacios	University of Oviedo (Spain)
Luis Junco	University of Oviedo (Spain)

Signal Processing and Biomedical Applications

Juan Manuel Górriz	University of Granada (Spain)
Carlos G. Putonet	University of Granada (Spain)
Elmar W. Lang	University of Regensburg (Germany)
Javier Ramírez	University of Granada (Spain)
Juan Manuel Gorriz	University of Granada (Spain)
Manuel Graña	University of the Basque Country (Spain)
Maite García-Sebastián	University of the Basque Country (Spain)
Alexandre Savio	University of the Basque Country (Spain)
Ana María Pefeito Tome	University of Aveiro (Portugal)
Elsa Fernández	University of the Basque Country (Spain)
Isabel Barbancho	University of Málaga (Spain)
Diego Pablo Ruiz Padillo	University of Granada (Spain)
Fermín Segovia Román	University of Granada (Spain)
Ingo Keck	University of Regensburg (Spain)
Manuel Canton	University of Almeria (Spain)
Miriam Lopez Perez	University of Granada
Rosa Chaves Rodríguez	University of Granada (Spain)
Roberto Hornero	University of Valladolid (Spain)
Andres Ortiz	University of Malaga (Spain)
Diego Salas-Gonzalez	University of Granada (Spain)
Ignacio Álvarez	University of Granada (Spain)
Ignacio Turias	University of Cadiz (Spain)
Jose Antonio Piedra	University of Almeria (Spain)
Maria del Carmen Carrión	University of Granada (Spain)
Roberto Hornero	University of Valladolid
Ruben Martín	University of Seville (Spain)

Methods of Classifiers Fusion

Michal Wozniak	Wroclaw University of Technology (Poland)
Álvaro Herrero	University of Burgos (Spain)
Bogdan Trawinski	Wroclaw University of Technology (Poland)
Giorgio Fumera	University of Cagliari (Italy)
José Alfredo F. Costa	Universidade Federal do Rio Grande do Norte (Brazil)
Konrad Jackowski	Wroclaw University of Technology (Poland)
Konstantinos Sirlantzis	University of Kent (UK)
Przemyslaw Kazienko	Wroclaw University of Technology (Poland)
Bruno Baruque	University of Burgos (Spain)
Jerzy Stefanowski	Poznan University of Technology (Poland)
Robert Burduk	Wroclaw University of Technology (Poland)
Michal Wozniak	Wroclaw University of Technology (Poland)
Emilio Corchado	University of Salamanca (Spain)
Igor T. Podolak	Jagiellonian University (Poland)
Vaclav Snasel	VSB-Technical University of Ostrava (Czech Republic)
Elzbieta Pekalska	University of Manchester (UK)
Bogdan Gabrys	Bournemouth University (UK)

Knowledge Extraction Based on Evolutionary Learning

Sebastián Ventura	University of Córdoba (Spain)
Amelia Zafra	University of Córdoba (Spain)
Eva Lucrecia Gibaja	University of Córdoba (Spain)
Jesus Alcala-Fernández	University of Granada (Spain)
Salvador García	University of Jaén (Spain)
Mykola Pechenizkiy	Technical University of Eindhoven (The Netherlands)
Pedro González	University of Jaén (Spain)
Antonio Peregrin	University of Huelva (Spain)
Rafael Alcalá	University of Granada (Spain)
Cristóbal Romero	University of Córdoba (Spain)
Ekaterina Vasileya	Technical University of Eindhoven (The Netherlands)

Systems, Man, and Cybernetics by HAIS Workshop

Emilio Corchado	University of Salamanca (Spain)
Juan M. Corchado	University of Salamanca (Spain)
Álvaro Herrero	University of Burgos (Spain)
Bruno Baruque	University of Burgos (Spain)
Javier Sedano	University of Burgos (Spain)
Juan Pavón	University Complutense Madrid (Spain)
Manuel Graña	University of the Basque Country (Spain)
Ramón Rizo	University of Alicante (Spain)

Richard Duro   University of A Coruña (Spain)
Sebastian Ventura   University of Córdoba (Spain)
Vicente Botti   Polytechnical University of Valencia (Spain)
José Manuel Molina   University Carlos III of Madrid (Spain)
Lourdes Sáiz Barcena   University of Burgos (Spain)
Francisco Herrera   University of Granada (Spain)
Leticia Curiel   University of Burgos (Spain)
César Hervás   Univesity of Córdoba (Spain)
Sara Rodríguez   University of León (Spain)

Hybrid Intelligent Systems on Logistics

Camelia Chira   Babes-Bolyai University (Romania)
Alberto Ochoa Zezzati   Juarez City University (Mexico)
Arturo Hernández   CIMAT (Mexico)
Katya Rodríguez   UNAM (Mexico)
Fabricio Olivetti   University of Campinas (Brazil)
Gloria Cerasela Crisan   University of Bacau (Romania)
Anca Gog   Babes-Bolyai University (Romania)
Camelia-M. Pintea   Babes-Bolyai University (Romania)
Petrica Pop   North University Baia-Mare (Romania)
Barna Iantovics   Petru Maior University Targu-Mures (Romania)

Hybrid Reasoning and Coordination Methods on Multi-agent Systems

Martí Navarro Yacer   Universidad Politécnica de Valencia (Spain)
Javier Bajo   Universidad Pontificia de Salamanca (Spain)
Juan Botía   Universidad de Murcia (Spain)
Juan Manuel Corchado   Universidad de Salamanca (Spain)
Luís Búrdalo   Universidad Politécnica de Valencia (Spain)
Stella Heras   Universidad Politécnica de Valencia (Spain)
Vicente Botti   Universidad Politécnica de Valencia (Spain)
Vicente J. Julián   Universidad Politécnica de Valencia (Spain)
Rubén Ortiz   Universidad Rey Juan Carlos (Spain)
Rubén Fuentes   Universidad Complutense de Madrid (Spain)
Adriana Giret   Universidad Politécnica de Valencia (Spain)
Alberto Fernández   Universidad Rey Juan Carlos (Spain)
Marc Esteva   IIIA-CSIC (Spain)
Carlos Carrascosa   Universidad Politécnica de Valencia (Spain)
Martí Navarro   Universidad Politécnica de Valencia (Spain)

HAIS for Computer Security (HAISfCS)

Álvaro Herrero   University of Burgos (Spain)
Emilio Corchado   University of Salamanca (Spain)

Huiyu Huiyu Zhou	Queen's University Belfast (UK)
Belén Vaquerizo	University of Burgos (Spain)
Cristian I. Pinzón	University of Salamanca (Spain)
Dante I. Tapia	University of Salamanca (Spain)
Javier Bajo	Pontifical University of Salamanca (Spain)
Javier Sedano	University of Burgos (Spain)
Juan F. De Paz Santana	University of Salamanca (Spain)
Sara Rodríguez	University of Salamanca (Spain)
Raquel Redondo	University of Burgos (Spain)
Leticia Curiel	University of Burgos (Spain)
Bruno Baruque	University of Burgos (Spain)
Ángel Arroyo	University of Burgos (Spain)
Juan M. Corchado	University of Salamanca (Spain)

Hybrid and Intelligent Techniques on Multimedia

Adriana Dapena Janeiro	Universidade da Coruña (Spain)
José Martínez	Universidad Autónoma de Madríd (Spain)
Otoniel López	Miguel Hernandez University (Spain)
Ramón Moreno	University of the Basque Country (Spain)
Manuel Graña	University of the Basque Country (Spain)
Eduardo Martínez	University of Murcia (Spain)
Javier Ruiz	Polytechnic University of Catalonia (Spain)
José Luis Martínez	Universidad de Castilla-La Mancha (Spain)
Daniel Iglesia	Universidade da Coruña (Spain)
Elsa Fernández	University of the Basque Country (Spain)
Paula Castro	Universidade da Coruña (Spain)

Hybrid ANN: Models, Data Models, Algorithms and Data

César Hervás-Martinez	University of Córdoba (Spain)
Pedro Antonio Gutiérrez	University of Córdoba (Spain)
Francisco Fernández-Navarroi	University of Córdoba (Spain)
Aldo Franco Dragoni	Università Politecnica delle Marche (Italy)
Ángel Manuel Pérez-Bellido	University of Alcalá (Spain)
Daniel Mateos-García	University of Alcalá (Spain)
Francisco Fernández-Navarro	University of Córdoba (Spain)
Germano Vallesi	Università Politecnica delle Marche (Italy)
José C. Riquelme-Santos	University of Sevilla (Spain)
Sancho Salcedo-Sanz	University of Alcalá (Spain)
Ekaitz Zulueta-Guerrero	University of the Basque Country (Spain)
Emilio G. Ortíz-García	University of Alcalá (Spain)
Kui Li	Xidian University (China)
Liang Yu	(China)
Alicia D'Anjou	University of the Basque Country (Spain)
Francisco José Martínez-Estudillo	University of Córdoba (Spain)

Juan Carlos Fernández	University of Córdoba (Spain)
Lin Gao	Hefei University of Technology (China)
Javier Sánchez-Monedero	University of Cordoba (Spain)

Hybrid Artificial Intelligence Systems Based on Lattice Theory

Vassilis Kaburlasos	Technological Educational Institution of Kavala (Greece)
Cliff Joslyn	Pacific Northwest National Laboratory (USA)
Juan Humberto Sossa Azuela	Centro de Investigación en Computación (Mexico)
Angelos Amanatiadis	Technological Educational Institution of Kavala (Greece)
George Papakostas	Democritus University of Thrace (Greece)
Gonzalo Urcid	National Institute of Astrophysics, Optics and Electronics (Mexico)
Peter Sussner	State University of Campinas (Brazil)
Radim Belohlavek	Palacky University (Czech Republic)
Theodore Pachidis	Technological Educational Institution of Kavala (Greece)
Vassilis Syrris	Aristotle University of Thessaloniki (Greece)
Anestis Hatzimichailidis	Technological Educational Institution of Kavala (Greece)
Gonzalo Aranda-Corral	University of Huelva (Spain)
Kevin Knuth	University at Albany (USA)
Manuel Graña	University of the Basque Country (Spain)
Gerhard Ritter	University of Florida (USA)
Lefteris Moussiades	Technological Educational Institution of Kavala (Greece)
Isabelle Bloch	Ecole Nationale Supérieure des Télécommunications (France)

Information Fusion: Frameworks and Architectures

José Manuel Molina López	University Carlos III (Spain)
Javier Bajo	University of Salamanca (Spain)
Jose M. Armingol	University Carlos III (Spain)
Juan A. Besada	Universidad Politécnica de Madrid (Spain)
Miguel A. Patricio	University Carlos III (Spain)
Arturo de la Escalera	University Carlos III (Spain)
Eloi Bosse	Defence R&D Canada (Canada)
Jesus Garcia	University Carlos III (Spain)
Jose M. Molina	University Carlos III (Spain)
Antonio Berlanga	University Carlos III (Spain)
James Llinas	University Carlos III (Spain)
Ana M. Bernardos	Universidad Politécnica de Madrid (Spain)

Local Organizing Committee

Manuel Graña	University of the Basque Country (Spain)
Darya Chyzhyk	University of the Basque Country (Spain)
Elsa Fernández	University of the Basque Country (Spain)
Maite García-Sebastián	University of the Basque Country (Spain)
Carmen Hernández Gómez	University of the Basque Country (Spain)
Alexandre Manhães Savio	University of the Basque Country (Spain)
Ramón Moreno	University of the Basque Country (Spain)
Miguel Angel Veganzones	University of the Basque Country (Spain)
Iván Villaverde	University of the Basque Country (Spain)

Table of Contents – Part I

Table of Contents – Part II

Y-Means: An Autonomous Clustering Algorithm

Ali A. Ghorbani and Iosif-Viorel Onut*

Faculty of Computer Science, University of New Brunswick, Fredericton, Canada

Abstract. This paper proposes an unsupervised clustering technique for data classification based on the K-means algorithm. The K-means algorithm is well known for its simplicity and low time complexity. However, the algorithm has three main drawbacks: dependency on the initial centroids, dependency on the number of clusters, and degeneracy. Our solution accommodates these three issues, by proposing an approach to automatically detect a semi-optimal number of clusters according to the statistical nature of the data. As a side effect, the method also makes choices of the initial centroid-seeds not critical to the clustering results. The experimental results show the robustness of the Y-means algorithm as well as its good performance against a set of other well known unsupervised clustering techniques. Furthermore, we study the performance of our proposed solution against different distance and outlier-detection functions and recommend the best combinations.

Keywords: Clustering, Data mining, K-means, Machine learning, Unsupervised learning.

1 Introduction

The fundamental challenge of unsupervised classification techniques is to mine similarities among the data points in order to identify a finite set of categories or clusters that best describes the given data. The application of such techniques are unlimited, and are currently used in domains such as health, medicine, Web, security, marketing and finance.

This paper is a complete re-engineering, extensive improvement, and extension to a new *dynamic* clustering method named Y-means [8]. Y-means is an unsupervised clustering technique for data classification. During the training phase, Y-means groups the observed existing data into different classes based on their similarity. During the training, Y-means learns the classes of data that exist in the training set. Based on the learned experience, at run time, the algorithm will distribute the incoming data into the already learned classes.

The Y-means algorithm is based on K-means, but manages to improve some of K-means' shortcomings by automatically adjusting the number of clusters based on the statistical nature of the data. This makes the standard clustering

---

* Dr. Iosif-Viorel Onut is currently with the Center for Advanced Studies, IBM, Ottawa, Canada.

M. Graña Romay et al. (Eds.): HAIS 2010, Part I, LNAI 6076, pp. 1–13, 2010.

state not relevant and not critical to the final set of clusters that Y-means produces. The proposed solution also eliminates the degeneracy problem by deleting the empty clusters. Finally, Y-means produces multi-center clusters as a better representation of the distribution of the dataset, compared to the single-center clusters produced by K-means.

The rest of this paper is organized as follows. The next section presents various techniques and algorithms that are currently used in this area. Next, the detail design of the proposed algorithm as well as various types of distance and outlier detection functions that we used are presented in Section 3. Section 4 presents the experimental results of Y-means algorithm. Finally, last section presents the conclusions and future work.

2   Background Review

There are two common types of classification techniques: the supervised and the unsupervised ones. The supervised learning methods, such as Multilayer Perceptron (MLP) [16], Support Vector Machine (SVM) [2], Decision Tree [22], to name a few, use extra data to establish models by mapping inputs to the known outputs (i.e., known classes). On the other hand, the unsupervised learning techniques, such as K-Nearest Neighbor [3], K-means [17], C-Means [5], CLUSTERING [15], Expectation Maximization (EM) [4], SOM [12], to name a few, do not have the knowledge of the extra mapping data, and they have to extract/mine it during the learning process.

Unsupervised learning techniques, in particular clustering methods, use data mining to achieve high inter-object similarity within each cluster while maintaining a low inter-cluster similarity. For instance, K-means partitions a collection of objects into a number of clusters by assigning them to their closest clusters based on a distance measure such as Euclidian distance [17]. The centroid of each cluster is computed as the mean vector of all the cluster members. However, the user needs to decide the number of the clusters to be created, (k), and their initial centroid.

The K-means algorithm is well known for its simplicity and low time complexity. However, the algorithm has three main drawbacks: dependency on the initial centroids, dependency on the number of clusters, and degeneracy [23]. Thus, different selections of the initial centroids often lead to different clustering results. This is mainly because K-means is based on the mean squared error and converges to a local minima [11]. This can be easily seen if the initial centroids are not well separated. The second shortcoming of K-means is the dependency on the number of initial centroids, k. This requirement is hard to meet when the distribution of data is unknown, since obtaining an optimal initial k is an NP-hard problem [23]. Finally, degeneracy happens when at the end of the clustering some of the clusters are empty. This is an undesirable result, since empty clusters are meaningless in the context of classification.

To overcome the degeneracy problem, Hansen et. al. [10] proposed H-means+, an enhanced K-means, which searches the non-empty clusters for objects that may be good candidates to replace the centroids of the existing empty clusters. Portnoy et. al. proposed another method to improve the K-means algorithm by automatically computing the final number of clusters [21]. The algorithm requires the user to define an upper bound value W for the maximum width of a cluster. Dan Pelleg and Andrew Moore proposed in 2000 the X-means algorithm[20], an improvement of the original K-means algorithm, which uses Bayesian Information Criterion for cluster splitting and kd-trees for speed improvement. Even though their method performs faster and better than the original K-means, it requires the user to select a range of possible values for the final number of clusters, and does not solve the degeneracy problem.

3   Y-Means Algorithm

Y-means is based on the K-means algorithm. The main difference between the two is Y-means' ability to autonomously decide the number of clusters based on the statistical nature of the data. This makes the number of final clusters that the algorithm produces a self-defined number rather than a user-defined constant as in the case of K-means. This overcomes one of the main drawbacks of K-means since a user-defined k cannot guarantee an appropriate partition of a dataset with an unknown distribution, a random (and possibly improper) value of initial k usually results in poor clustering.

One unrealistic solution to this problem is to find an appropriate number of clusters by trying all possible initial values for k in the K-means algorithm. Obviously this is unrealistic for a large dataset due to its time complexity. Our aim is to obtain a (semi-)optimal k by exploiting the statistical properties of the data. For instance, if the granularity of the clusters is too coarse for the given data distribution (i.e., the initial value of k is too small), the algorithm splits some of the clusters to make them finer. Conversely, if the clusters are too fine for the given data distribution (i.e., the initial value of k is too large), the algorithm will merge contiguous clusters to form larger ones. Our experiments show that by using a sequence of splitting, deleting and merging the clusters, even without the knowledge of the distribution of data, Y-means can determine an appropriate value of final k, which is independent of the initial k.

Figure 1 depicts the flowchart of the Y-means algorithm. To remove the effect of dominating features due to the feature-range differences, the dataset is first normalized. Next, the standard K-means algorithm is run over the training data. Due to the fact that the final number of clusters is independent of initial k, this number can be chosen randomly at the beginning of the clustering. Moreover, the selection of the k initial centroids is again independent of the final results. In Y-means one can simply choose the first k objects from the dataset as the first k centroids. The standard K-means algorithm uses Euclidian distance as a distance function; however, we have tested Y-means using five different distance functions as described in Section 3.1. Next, once the K-means process is completed, the algorithm checks for possible empty clusters and deletes them. The simple deletion of empty clusters is more feasible in this context since it

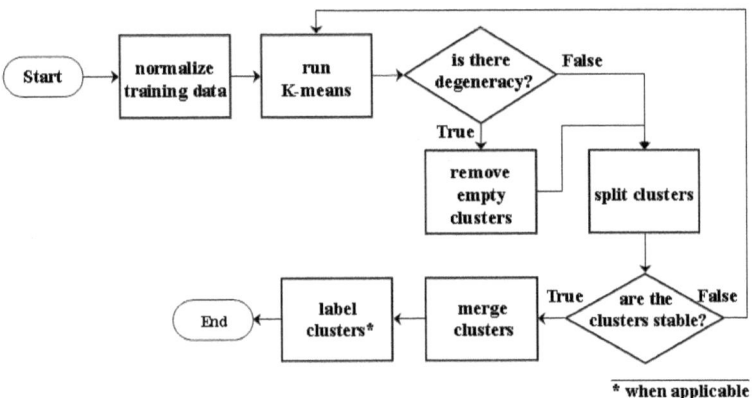

Fig. 1. The flowchart of the Y-means algorithm

means that no objects are close to the empty centroid, hence it does not help to the clustering of the dataset. In the subsequent phase, the Y-means algorithm checks each of the existing clusters for possible outliers. An outlier is an object that is far from the majority of the objects in a cluster. Each identified outlier is removed from its current cluster and forms a new cluster. We have used multiple outlier detection functions during our experiments as explained in Section 3.2.

The newly created centroids / clusters may attract objects from their immediate proximity, and thus a new K-means process is needed for the whole data set to be clustered again. In this way the course clusters are split into finer clusters, which iteratively will modify the original value k. The previously described tasks (except data normalization) are repeated until the number of detected clusters are stable (i.e., no new clusters are formed in the last iteration). One of the final stages of the algorithm is a merging process. This process will merge close-enough adjacent clusters together to form larger clusters. However, to allow arbitrary cluster shapes (e.g., spatial chains) the centroids of the newly merged clusters are kept intact. Consequently, after the merging process the algorithm produces multi-center clusters, which better map the given data. The details of merging process is explained in Section 3.3.

Cluster labeling is the final step of the Y-means algorithm. The labeling step is domain-dependent, and can be used only when it is applicable to the given dataset. Moreover, since Y-means is an unsupervised clustering technique the labels must be determined heuristically. For instance, in the case of intrusion detection, the labeling can be done based on the cluster size. If no heuristics can be applied to label a given data, this step can be skipped. Section 4.1 explains two of the labeling techniques that we used for intrusion detection problems; however, when choosing a dataset from a different domain (e.g., Iris dataset) the labeling step can be omitted. The following four subsections describe in detail each of the main tasks of Y-means algorithm.

3.1 Performing Standard K-Means

In the first step of the K-means algorithm [17], k centroids are randomly chosen from the data set. Next, all points in the dataset are assigned to their closest centroid. The original algorithm uses Euclidian distance as distance function between a point and a centroid. In the third step, the centroids are updated as being the mean value of all its members. Finally, in the last step, the centroids are checked, and if they changed, the previous two steps are recursively called until the centroids are stable. The time complexity of the K-means algorithm is $O(mkn)$, where m is the number of iteration until the convergence happens, k is the number of centroids, and n is the number of elements to be clustered.

Our implementation of K-means uses the same technique, but we have tried different distance functions namely Minkowski, Chebyshev, Canberra, and Pearson's Coefficient of Correlation distance metrics.

3.2 Splitting Clusters

The reasoning behind splitting the already existing clusters comes as a natural process when dealing with points that may belong to different distributions. Those points could end up in the same cluster if that particular cluster is the closest one to those points. Thus, we believe, it is vital for a clustering algorithm to check the composition of its clusters and accommodate possible splitting candidates (i.e., outliers). In statistics, an outlier is a point that is so far away from the expected distribution that it seems to be created as the consequence of a separate process. The idea of determining outliers comes from the theory of robust regression and outlier detection [9].

The Y-means algorithm iteratively identifies outliers and converts them to new centroids. As depicted in Fig. 1, it invokes K-means each time when the set of centroids changes. Let $\mathcal{O}_{pc}(P_j, C_l)$ be an boolean outlier detection function:

$$\mathcal{O}_{pc}(P_j, C_l) = \begin{cases} true & \text{if } P_j \text{ is an outlier in } C_l \\ false & \text{otherwise} \end{cases} \qquad \forall j, \forall l : \ j \in [1, n], l \in [1, k],$$

where n is the number of elements in the dataset and k is the number of centroids.

The Y-means algorithm uses this function to detect a single outlier per iteration for each cluster. If the cluster does not have any outlier then its centroid remains the same, otherwise a splitting occurs for that cluster (we restrict the outliers detected in one iteration to only one per cluster because chances are that after re-clustering, some of the old cluster's population will be attracted to the newly created cluster). Figure 2 depicts a simple scenario where the set of objects are partitioned into three clusters. Out of these clusters, the composition of cluster C_1 seems to be of two distributions. This is a plausible situation if $\mathcal{D}_{pc}(P_j, C_l) < \mathcal{D}_{pc}(P_j, C_2)$ and $\mathcal{D}_{pc}(P_j, C_l) < \mathcal{D}_{pc}(P_j, C_3)$, where $\mathcal{D}_{pc}$ is the distance between point j, P_j, and cluster center C_l . The figure clearly depicts that being the closest to one cluster does not necessarily mean that the point belongs to that cluster. If that is the case, then $\mathcal{O}_{pc}(P_j, C_l)$ is true, and the cluster will be divided into two parts as seen in Fig. 2(b). The newly created cluster

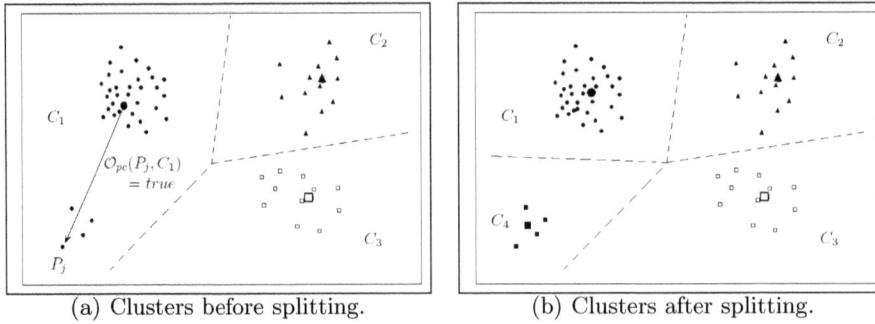

(a) Clusters before splitting.   (b) Clusters after splitting.

Fig. 2. Cluster Splitting scenario example

will have C_4 as its centroid after a new run of K-means. Hence, the accuracy of outlier identification process is essential to the accuracy of the final result. We have experimented with different outlier-identification techniques as described next in this section.

Radius based metric. The first and most graphically intuitive approach to this problem would be to try to construct a threshold around each cluster, which will be the radius of a circle. Every point within that circle will belong to the given cluster while any point outside the circle will be considered as an outlier. It is vital for this threshold to be based on the statistical properties of each cluster. Such a threshold, while different from cluster to cluster, will best represent its corresponding cluster and can be calculated autonomously. To statistically define this threshold, we consider two of the most popular statistical rules as follows:

The Empirical Rule is a statistical rule which is derived from experiments and observations. Assuming normal distribution, according to this rule, approximately 68.26%, 95.44%, 99.73%, 99.994%, and 99.99994% of the objects lie within one, two, three, four, and five standard deviations from the mean, respectively. The theorem is mathematically defined as $\mathbf{Z}_n = \frac{\sum_{i=1}^{n}(x_i) - n\mu}{\sigma\sqrt{n}}$. Walpole et al. [24] demonstrated that if $n \geq 30$, the normal approximation of the Central Limit Theorem is good regardless of the shape of the initial population, while for $n < 30$, the approximation is good only if the shape of the initial population is not far from a normal distribution.

The Chebyshev's inequality. The most important asset of this rule [24,7] is that it provides a quantitative value as shown below

$$P(|X - \mu| \geq m\sigma) \leq \frac{1}{m^2}, \qquad \forall m > 0, m \subset \mathbb{R}, \tag{1}$$

where X is a random variable, with an expected value μ and a finite standard deviation σ. The theorem states that the probability of a value X to be more than $m\sigma$ apart from the μ is less than or equal to $1/m^2$. Despite its loose bounds, the theorem is very useful because it applies to any kind of distribution. For instance, when $m = 5$ the theorem states that 96% of the populations is within 5σ.

Based on the above two statistical rules, the radius based metric is defined as:

$$\mathcal{O}_{pc}(P_j, C_l) = \begin{cases} true & \text{if } |P_j - C_l| > 5\sigma \\ false & \text{otherwise} \end{cases} \quad \forall j, \forall l \quad | \quad j \in [1, n], l \in [1, k],$$

Therefore, any object that lies outside 5σ of a cluster is considered as an outlier, and as a consequence a possible candidate for a new centroid.

We have also used Mahalanobis [18] and Tukey's [6] metrics in the implementation and analysis of Y-means.

3.3 Merging Clusters

Merging adjacent clusters comes as a natural process of recognizing similar or close characteristics among clusters. Let us first consider the simple scenario of merging two clusters (see Fig. 3). Similar to the splitting case, a merging threshold must further be computed. Furthermore, the threshold needs to be automatically computed and must best represent the statistical distributions of each cluster. An approach would be to define a function based on the σ of each cluster. Recall from Section 3.2 that based on Empirical Rule and Chebyshev's inequality there is a quantitative relationship between cluster's σ and its population. Let us define a boolean merge function of two clusters $\mathcal{M}_{cc}$ as:

$$\mathcal{M}_{cc}(C_j, C_l) = \begin{cases} true & \text{if } \mathcal{D}_{cc}(C_j, C_l) \le \alpha(\sigma_{C_j} + \sigma_{C_l}) \\ false & \text{otherwise} \end{cases} \quad \forall j, \forall l \mid j, l \in [1, k], l \neq j,$$

where C_j & C_l are the two cluster candidates for merging and α is a real number.

The previously defined formula states that two clusters C_j and C_l are merged if the distance between their centroids is less than or equal to a threshold. The threshold is dependent on the σ of the two clusters and can be seen as $\alpha\sigma_{C_j} + \alpha\sigma_{C_l}$. The smaller the α is, the fewer clusters will be merged; conversely, the higher the α is the more clusters will be merged. However, if $\alpha > 5$, the merging may not be a good solution since, from Chebyshev's inequality, at most 4% of the cluster's points are outside 5σ. Another arguable value might be $\alpha = 1.414213562$ since at most 50%

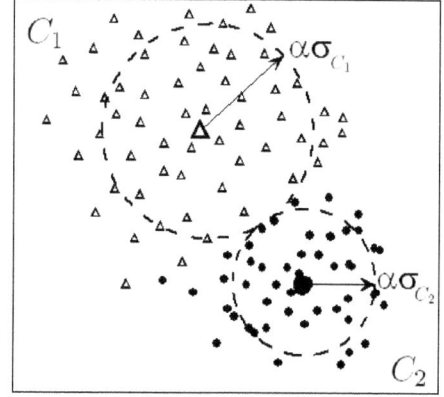

Fig. 3. Merging two adjacent clusters

of the population lies outside 1.414213562σ, and having anything more than that might be an artificial linking. Our experiments show an optimal threshold value for merging of 0.6σ (see Sec. 4.2 for details). Once the set of clusters to be merged are identified, the actual merging process needs to start. There are two main methods of merging clusters: *fusing* and *linking*. The first approach is to combine all the centroids that need to be merged into a new centroid that will become their mean, while the second technique is to keep the centroids as they are, but mark them as belonging to the same cluster.

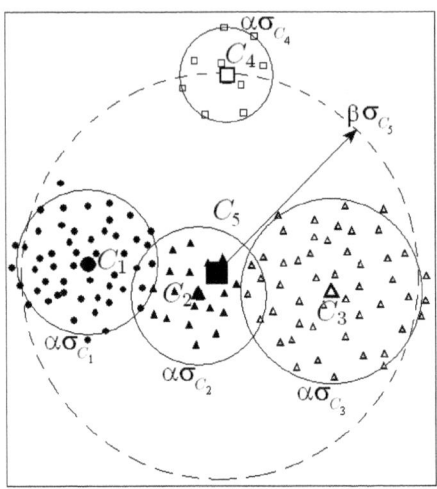

Let us consider the scenario depicted in Fig. 4, where there are four clusters (C_1, C_2, C_3, and C_4) before the merging process. Furthermore, let us consider $\mathcal{M}_{cc}(C_1, C_2) = true$, and $\mathcal{M}_{cc}(C_2, C_3) = true$. This means that the three clusters must be merged together. By using the fusing technique a new cluster, C_5, will be created as a result of merging the three candidate clusters. Naturally after reclustering, the σ_{C_5} will be higher than any of the standard deviations of the previously three merged clusters. Thus, there is a possibility that the newly computed $\alpha\sigma_{C_5}$ could be very close to another cluster (e.g., C_4), which in turn triggers further merging. This scenario may not be desirable, since as depicted in Fig. 4, cluster C_4 is very

Fig. 4. Fusing versus linking clusters

different from the other three individual clusters. Conversely, if linking approach is used, the three clusters (i.e., C_1, C_2, and C_3) will preserve their shape, but will be treated as a single cluster. In this case, cluster C_4 will not be merged with the rest of the clusters.

Y-means uses the linking technique since it proves to best model the data. This is mainly because the clusters merged this way can form different shapes (e.g. spatial chains) and are not restricted to only Gaussian shapes. Furthermore, this approach also saves computational time since the centroids remain the same and no reclustering is needed.

4   Experimental Results

The Y-means algorithm presented in the previous section has been tested using KDD Cup 1999 dataset. The primary aim of this testing was to determine the usefulness of Y-Means in automatically cluster network data into normal and intrusion classes.

The KDD99 dataset is based on a subset of the DARPA Intrusion Detection Evaluation Data Set released in 1998 by MIT Lincoln Laboratory [13,19]. The original dataset was captured from a simulated military network environment, and consists of a wide variety of real attacks. The last feature of the dataset represents the real connection label. This label can be either *normal* or *attack name*, and is not used during the training of the algorithm.

4.1   Labeling Clusters

The final stage of the Y-means algorithm is the labeling stage. The next two subsections describe two of the most commonly used labeling techniques in the intrusion detection domain.

Size based labeling. The size based labeling technique is one of the first and most common labeling techniques used in intrusion detection. This technique involves the setting of a threshold as follows:

$$\mathcal{L}_c(C_l) = \begin{cases} intrusion & \text{if } n_{C_l} \leq \tau \\ normal & \text{otherwise} \end{cases} \begin{cases} \forall \, l : l \in [1, k], \tau \subset \mathbb{R}^+, \\ \tau \in [\min_{\forall j}(n_{C_j}), \max_{\forall j}(n_{C_j})], j \in [1, k], \end{cases}$$

where $\mathcal{L}_c(C_l)$ is the labeling function, and τ represents the labeling threshold. The threshold τ is usually a user defined variable.

Distance based labeling. The distance based labeling technique assumes that the anomalous clusters are usually distant from the normal ones [1]. Let us define the inter-cluster distance of cluster C_l as [1]:

$$\text{ICD}_c(C_l) = \frac{\sum_{j=1}^{k} \mathcal{D}_{cc}(C_l, C_j)}{k - 1} \quad \forall l, \forall j \quad : \quad l, j \in [1, k], l \neq j, \tag{2}$$

where $\mathcal{D}_{cc}(C_l, C_j)$ is any of the distance functions mentioned in Section 3.1. There are two ways of setting the threshold between normal and abnormal clusters. The first approach is to define a real value as a threshold and consider anything that is further distant than the chosen threshold as abnormal clusters. The second approach is to set the threshold as a percentage value against the distances of other clusters.

4.2   Performance Measurements

We evaluate the performance of Y-means against different outlier detection techniques and point to point distance functions. The main reason behind this was to observe the degree of dependency that Y-means has on different distance functions that are used, as well as to empirically suggest the most suitable functions to be used. We have selected three outlier detection metrics (i.e., Mahalanobis, Tukey and Radius Based), six point to point distance metrics (i.e., Manhattan, Euclidian, Minkowski of order 3, Chebyshev, Canberra, and Pearson's Coefficient of Correlation), and two labeling techniques (i.e., size based and distance based). Figure 5 shows the final number of clusters that Y-means produces, as well as the number of K-means iterations it takes for the algorithm to converge.

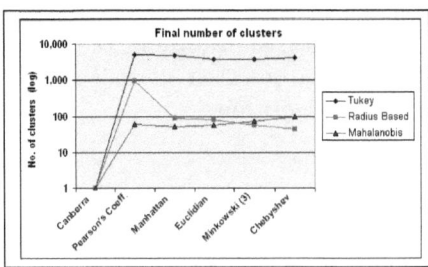
(a) The final number of clusters.

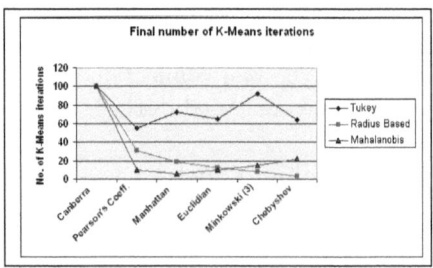
(b) The final number of K-means iterations.

Fig. 5. Y-Means performance while considering multiple point to point and outlier functions

Figures 6 and 7 show the average performance of our algorithm for each of the studied metrics while using different merging factors. Consequently, each point in Fig. 6 is computed as the average performance of each outlier detection technique over all the distance functions. Similarly, each point in Fig. 7 depicts the average performance of a distance metric while used with different outlier detection techniques. Furthermore, for each metric presented in both figures we report two curves, one obtained by using the size based labeling while the other one obtained by using the distance based labeling (see Sec. 4.1)

The Tukey's metric for outlier detection (see Fig. 6) has the best and also worse performance for the two different labeling techniques. This is explained by the number of clusters that this method produces (i.e., roughly 8000 as depicted in Fig. 5). In this case, even if the number of clusters is high, once the distance based labeling technique is used, this becomes irrelevant since all that would matter is how distant are those clusters from the rest. However, in the case of size based labeling the high number of clusters would make the final result less accurate since most of the clusters will have only a few elements, which will be considered ab-

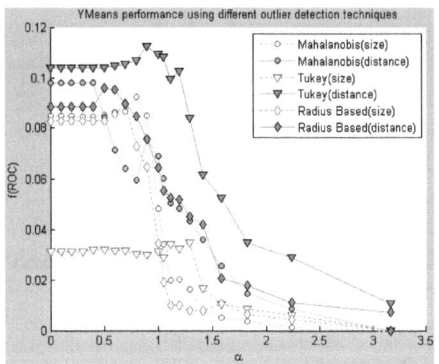

Fig. 6. Y-means performance using different outlier detection techniques and multiple merging α factors

normal. The Mahalanobis metric tends to mostly outperform the radius based metric, regardless of the used labeling technique. This is explained by the fact that Mahalabonis metric takes into consideration the covariance matrix of the cluster when computing the outlier. Note that as α increases, the performance of Y-means remains the same up to $\alpha = 0.5$. It generally increases when $\alpha \in [0.5, 0.6]$ and drastically decreases afterwards. This leads us to the conclusion that it is useful to merge clusters that are closer than 0.5 standard deviations. This would presumably decrease the number of final clusters while keeping the overall accuracy constant or slightly increasing it (see Figures 6 and 7).

In the case of point to point distances, it is seen that the best and also the worse performances are obtained when using the Pearson's Coefficient of Correlation metric to compute the distances between points. As explained earlier, this method uses the covariance and variance matrixes when computing the distance. This makes the method to create cleaner and more accurate clusters. However, the size of those clusters cannot be successfully used to identify abnormal behaviors, but rather their position (Fig. 7). Another interesting fact is that

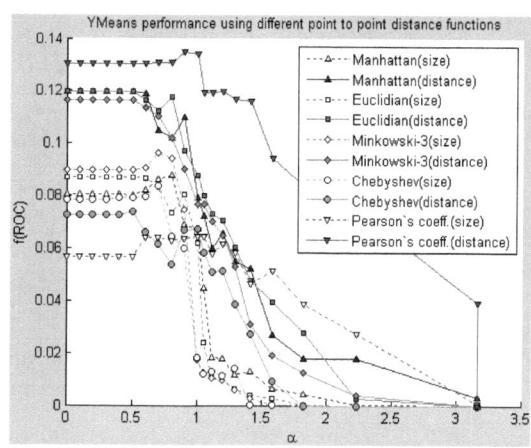

Fig. 7. Y-means performance using different point to point distance techniques and multiple merging α factors

increasing the order of Minkowski's metric will increase the performance of the classifier.

4.3 Performance against Other Algorithms

To evaluate Y-means against other unsupervised clustering algorithms we used the same dataset and two labeling techniques as in the previous cases. We have conducted our experiments using four known unsupervised clustering algorithms such as Expectation Maximization (EM) [4], K-means [17], Self Organizing Maps (SOM) [12], and Improved Competitive Learning Network (ICLN) [14]. Since none of the above four mentioned techniques automatically extract the number of clusters from the dataset, we used 50 as an initial value, as this appeared to produce the best results for the KDD Cup 99 dataset. The individual tuning parameters used for the selected algorithms were *minimum allowable standard deviation of* 1^{-6} for the EM method, *cluster stability threshold of* 0.01 for the K-means method, a 5x10 *hexagonal grid* using the *Gaussian neighborhood function* and a *learning rate of* 0.01 for the SOM method, a *minimum update rate of* 0.01 combined with a *reward rate of* 0.1 and a *punish rate of* 0.01 for the ICLN method. Finally, for Y-means we used a *cluster stability threshold of* 0.01 combined with a *merging factor* $\alpha = 0.6$. For our comparison to be fair, we used the *Euclidian Distance* as a point to point distance and the *Radius Based* outlier detection technique in Y-means. This would represent an average performance for our technique.

Figure 8 shows the ROC curves for all the tested clustering techniques. As in the previous cases, it is easily seen that the distance based labeling technique has higher accuracy than the size based one. However, in both cases, the results produced by Y-means stay in the lead. This is highly visible in the case of distance based labeling, while being the second best (after SOM) in the case of distance based labeling.

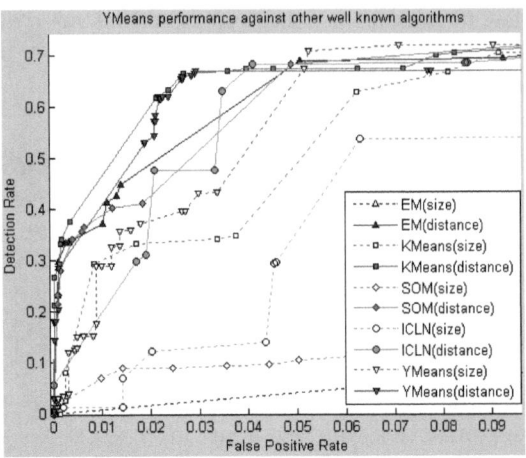

Fig. 8. Y-means performance against four well known algorithms

5   Conclusions

This paper presents a new unsupervised clustering algorithm for data classification. Y-means algorithm is based on the well known K-means algorithm, but manages to overcome three of the major shortcomings that K-means has (i.e., dependency on the initial centroids, dependency on the number of clusters, and the cluster degeneracy). Moreover, the final output of the algorithm is a collection of single- and multi-center clusters that are created based on the statistical properties of the current dataset, as opposed to K-means that uses single-center clusters and where the final number of clusters is a user defined variable. Experimental results show that Y-means has a very good performance compared with four well known unsupervised algorithms, such as EM, K-means, SOM, and ICLN. Furthermore, we also analyzed the overall performance of our algorithm using different point to point distances and outlier detection functions. The outcomes of this study provide to the user initial guidelines regarding the most suitable tuning combinations for Y-means. Our future work will mostly concentrate on various ways to improve not only the performance of the algorithm but also the speed of the clustering.

References

1. Chan, P.K., Mahoney, M.V., Arshad, M.H.: Managing cyber threats: Issues, approaches, and challenges. In: Learning Rules and Clusters for Anomaly Detection in Network Traffic, ch. 3, pp. 81–99. Springer, Heidelberg (2005)
2. Cortes, C., Vapnik, V.: Support-vector networks. Machine Learning 20(3), 273–297 (1995)
3. Cover, T., Hart, P.G.: Nearest neighbor pattern classification. IEEE Transactions on Information Theory IT-13(1), 21–27 (1967)

4. Dempster, A.P., Laird, N.M., Rubin, D.B.: Maximum likelihood from incomplete data via the em algorithm. Journal of the Royal Statistical Society, Series B 39(1), 1–38 (1977)
5. Dunn, J.C.: A fuzzy relative of the isodata process and its use in detecting compact well-separated clusters. Journal of Cybernatics 3(1), 32–57 (1973)
6. Frigge, M., Hoaglin, D.C., Iglewicz, B.: Some implementations of the boxplot. The American Statistician 43(1), 50–54 (1989)
7. Gibson, H.R.: Elementary statistics. William C. Brown Publishers, Dubuque (1994)
8. Guan, Y., Belacel, N., Ghorbani, A.A.: Y-means: a clustering method for intrusion detection. In: Proceedings of the Canadian Conference on Electrical and Computer Engineering, Montreal, Canada, May 2003, pp. 1083–1086 (2003)
9. Han, J., Kamber, M.: Data mining: Concepts and techniques. Morgan Kaufmann Publishers, New York (2001)
10. Hansen, P., Mladenovi, N.: J-means: a new local search heuristic for minimum sum-of-squares clustering. Pattern Recognition 34(2), 405–413 (2002)
11. Jain, A.K., Dubes, R.C.: Algorithms for cluster data. Prentice Hall, Englewood Cliffs (1988)
12. Kohonen, T.: Self-organizing map. Springer, Heidelberg (1997)
13. MIT Lincoln Laboratory, Intrusion detection evaluation data set DARPA1998 (1998), http://www.ll.mit.edu/IST/ideval/data/1998/1998_data_index.html
14. Lei, J.Z., Ghorbani, A.: Network intrusion detection using an improved competitive learning neural network. In: Proceedings of The Second Annual Conference on Communication Networks and Services Research (CNSR), pp. 190–197 (2004)
15. Lin, Y., Shiueng, C.: A genetic approach to the automatic clustering problem. Pattern Recognition 34(2), 415–424 (2001)
16. Lippman, R.P.: An introduction to computing with neural networks. Proceedings of the ASSP Magazine 4(2), 4–22 (1987)
17. MacQueen, J.: Some methods for classification and analysis of multivariate observations. In: Proceedings of the Fifth Berkeley Symposium on Mathematical Statistics and Probability, vol. 2(1), pp. 281–297 (1967)
18. Mahalanobis, P.: On the generalized distance in statistics. Proceedings of the National Instute of Science (India) 2(1), 49–55
19. University of California Irvine, Knowledge discovery and data mining dataset KDD 1999 (1999), http://kdd.ics.uci.edu/databases/kddcup99/task.html
20. Pelleg, D., Moore, A.: X-means: Extending k-means with efficient estimation of the number of clusters. In: Proceedings of the Seventeenth International Conference on Machine Learning, pp. 727–734. Morgan Kaufmann, San Francisco (2000)
21. Portnoy, L., Eskin, E., Stolfo, S.J.: Intrusion detection with unlabeled data using clustering. In: Proceedings of ACM CSS Workshop on Data Mining Applied to Security, DMSA 2001, November 2001. ACM, New York (2001)
22. Quinlan, J.: Induction of decision trees. Machine Learning 1(1), 81–106 (1986)
23. Spath, H.: Clustering analysis algorithms for data reduction and classification of objects. Ellis Horwood, Chichester (1980)
24. Walpole, R.E.: Elementary Statistical Concepts, 2nd edn. Macmillan, Basingstoke (1983)

A Survey and Analysis of Frameworks and Framework Issues for Information Fusion Applications

James Llinas

Chair of Excellence,
Group of Applied Artificial Intelligence, Universidad Carlos III de Madrid, Av. de la
Universidad Carlos III, 22, 28270 Colmenarejo, Madrid (Spain)
james.llinas@uc3m.es

Abstract. This paper was stimulated by the proposed project for the Santander Bank-sponsored "Chairs of Excellence" program in Spain, of which the author is a recipient. That project involves research on characterizing a robust, problem-domain-agnostic framework in which Information Fusion (IF) processes of all description, to include artificial intelligence processes and techniques could be developed. The paper describes the IF process and its requirements, a literature survey on IF frameworks, and a new proposed framework that will be implemented and evaluated at Universidad Carlos III de Madrid, Colmenarejo Campus.

1 Introduction

Before discussing Frameworks for Information Fusion (IF) applications, it is appropriate to discuss what is meant by Information Fusion. In particular, we are focused on automated IF but allow in this characterization that humans may play a role in the process. In this work, we define at the highest level of abstraction the notion that IF is an information process, embodied largely in software (one type of IF process that we focus on) but admitting various human roles in the process . The main products of the IF process are estimates of dynamic real-world conditions of interest, where the estimates are formed from the following four classes of input: Observational data, A priori knowledge based models of the dynamic world being observed , Real-time learned knowledge and models that are derived from streaming observational data or other information in an inductive mode, and Contextual data and information, which may be both dynamic (e.g. weather) and relatively static (road networks), and must of course be accessible. This contextual information is the data and information usually considered as reflective of the "ambient" environment, information that surrounds the problem-space of interest but not from the problem-space of interest itself. Such information can both constrain the interpretation of fused estimates as well as aid in the formation of those estimates. (Note however that in some cases such as Ambient Intelligence applications, estimation of the problem context is the central focus of the fusion process.) Additional characteristics of the IF process are as follows: 1) A process that has extensive stochastic aspects, driven by a wide range of uncertainties inherent to the four classes above, 2) For these dynamic, real-time, streaming-data

M. Graña Romay et al. (Eds.): HAIS 2010, Part I, LNAI 6076, pp. 14–23, 2010.

applications, the algorithms and/or reasoning logics need to have a recursive nature with some ability to predict forward in time, and 3) A process that ideally is implemented as an adaptive, feedback-control type process to improve IF operations in runtime (e.g., by adaptively managing the sensors).

2 Functional and Process Characterization

The term "fusion" is used in IF to convey the notion of a sort of merging, but fusion operations are done with the purpose of achieving a combined estimate that is both more accurate and of reduced uncertainty. In general, it can be assumed that the inputs to the process are from multiple, disparate observational sources as well as contextual information. The initial functional requirement is called "Common Referencing" (sometimes called "Alignment") which is a function that converts the input formats and semantic content to a common framework. Once this function is completed, the data are sent to a Data Association function whose purpose is eventually to allocate or assign the data to different estimation processes that are estimating attributes regarding the various entities of the world situational state. The assigned data are then provided to the State Estimation function, which can be thought to "digest" the assigned data to fuse their effects onto the estimated state. Figure 1 shows the nature of this functional flow:

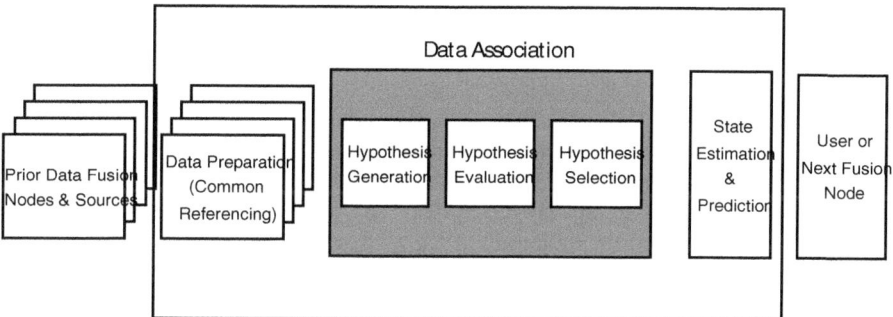

Fig. 1. Standard Fusion Functional Node

In Fig. 1, we see the Data Association process enlarged to show its three steps; in this description, the term "hypothesis" is used to mean an association hypothesis, where a candidate data item (e.g., an observation) is hypothesized to be associated to some entity in the situational space. The three functional steps are: 1) Hypothesis Generation: here, at process design-time, an enumeration of possible sources of measurements is made, 2) Hypothesis Evaluation: here, the "closeness" of any measurement to an entity is scored 3) Hypothesis Selection: here, it is typical that an "Assignment Problem" has to be solved to deal with the many-to-many possible input-to-entity associations; this is a combinatoric optimization problem well-known in Operations Research and from which the IF community has used and modified a number of solution strategies . Note that a realistic IF process will have multiple such Nodes in its

16   J. Llinas

architecture. This means that the input to any Node in such an architecture can not only be typical input data (observations for example) but also estimates coming out of a preceding node in the architectural flow. Similarly, a Node's state estimate output can flow to another Node or to an end user, or to some other system process.

In conjunction with and in addition to this functional, nodal characterization, the overall IF process is often described by the notional model below in Figure 2 [1]; it is important to understand that this model is a pedagogical model, not a process flow or to be taken as a serious architectural statement[1]. It is a characterization of the "levels" of IF processing from the point of view of layers of complexity

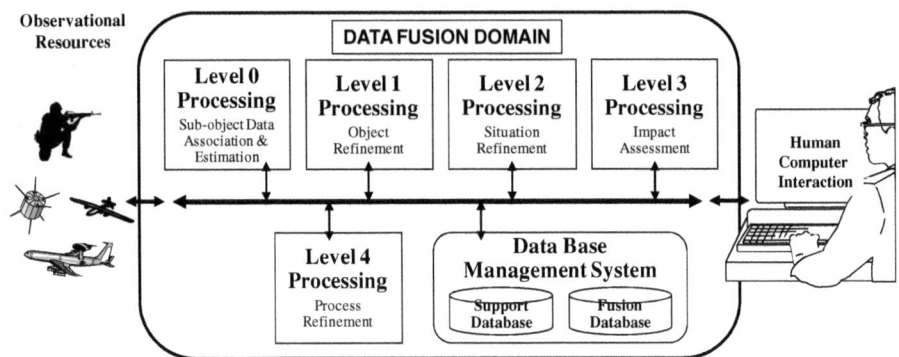

Fig. 2. Notional IF Process Diagram [1]

As noted above, the "Levels" of IF processing shown in Fig. 2 represent a layered view of state estimation complexity, from low (Level 0) to high (Level 3). It is also important to note that the above Fusion Node functions of Fig. 1 exist within any and all of the fusion Levels in any process model. Although not strictly true, the Levels can be seen as related to the assembly of the components of the world or situational state estimate, first determining the abstract sub-object elements (Level0), then the attributes of the single entities in the situation (Level 1), then the attributes of the aggregated entities, events, and behaviors that comprise what is usually called a situation (Level 2). Level 3 focuses on Impacts, and can be seen as estimating threat conditions in a military type application or a crisis condition in a natural disaster environment, or an impending collision in a transportation application.

IF processes and algorithms have proven to be extraordinarily flexible and extensible across disparate applications; for example, research at UC3M as well as at UPM in Spain has spanned the following domains: 1) Air and ground object traffic surveillance and monitoring at airport operations, 2) Video surveillance in various settings such as railway stations, 3) Context-aware and Ambient Intelligence systems, and 4) Intelligent Vehicle Systems. The Framework project at UC3M was established in part to avoid re-engineering and re-building IF processes for such disparate domains and applications.

---

[1] This IF model is typically called the "JDL" model as it was developed by the Joint Directors of Laboratories in the U.S. Defense Department in the 1980's; see [1].

3 Frameworks for Information Fusion

The word "Framework" is a somewhat fuzzy term, and this too needs to be clarified or at least its locally-defined usage made clear in any discussion addressing the term. Dictionary definitions include: "a conceptual structure intended to serve as a support or guide for the building of something that expands the structure into something useful", to name a few. Here, we take this definition in the sense that a framework is an abstraction, *not populated by domain-specific components*; that is, we argue that inclusion of domain-specific elements converts the framework into a "useful" structure. Since IF as we define above is a process enabled in software, our focus is also on Software Frameworks. Definitions of Software Frameworks are often in the same spirit as the general definition we choose to use, that is [2]: "an abstraction in which common code providing generic functionality can be selectively overridden or specialized by user code providing specific functionality". Frameworks however are very difficult to make totally domain-agnostic, and do need to consider the domain of interest in their design, but this should be done in a way that can accommodate a broad range of specific applications in the domain-space. We point out that [3], there is a notion of "inversion of control" in a framework, in that the control flow of an application based on the framework is provided by the framework itself, not the application.

3.1 Publications on Fusion Frameworks—A Review

Table 1 shows a summary of a number of papers drawn from the literature [4-19] that address IF framework concepts and issues. Five out of the sixteen papers listed however do not offer a framework construct in the sense of a process flow and control architecture, but just discuss issues. Several of the papers (4, 6, 9, 10, 14, 18) do offer such constructs but in each of these the framework concept is often domain-specific, although many good ideas are offered. Some of these ideas are integrated into the framework concept that we offer below. Space limitations do not permit the needed extended summary review of these works but we see a few key points: 1) oriented graphs are attractive structures for IF frameworks, 2) data stream management design principles may be important for streaming data applications, 3) use of the canonical Fusion Node functions is attractive in its generality, 4) powerful sensor-fusion nodes are attractive but are a factor largely for wireless applications, 5) agent or blackboard-based framework architectures seem to be the topologies of choice for higher-level fusion estimation, and 6) frameworks need to accommodate both contextual information as well as hard and soft information. One aspect of a Framework typically overlooked in these papers is the critically-important aspect of adaptive feedback and dynamic process control; recall the remark above about control inversion in that the Framework imputes the process control onto any application.

Table 1. Summary of a Sampling of IF Framework Literature

Paper [Ref]	Framework Focus	Cited advantages	Disadvantages/issues
[4]	Real-time applications	--Oriented-graph architecture --GUI-based algorithm selection	--Currently limited to Level 1 type functions --Does not discuss requirement to have algorithmic performance profiles
[5]	Intelligent auto apps	--Employs data stream mgmt techniques	--Automotive-application specific
[6]	Development suite vs a framework	--Object oriented --Plug-in modules --Uses Fusion Node	--Focused only on Level 1 --Details not shown
[7]	Significant human involvement in a toolkit concept	No specific IF substructure	No specific IF substructure
[8]	Target recognition apps	--Easier knowledge base management --Simple inter-knowledge source comms	--Possible truth maintenance system requirement
[9]	Networked/distributed Sensor/Fusion nodes	--Agent approach; use COABS grid approach	--Mostly Level 1 oriented, only numerical operations
[10]	Embedded-system apps	--Presumes powerful individual sensor nodes --Somewhat BB-like --All fusion Levels	--Fusion abstracted as holistic process; no substructure --No within-node framework
[11]	IF system and process specification	No process framework offered	No process framework offered
[12]	Wireless ad hoc sensor networks	--Automatically managed placement of fusion services --Fusion API for fusion functions and data flow --Fusion as directed task graph	--No consideration of Distributed IF issues such as OOSM and incest --Optimization is largely directed to network factors balanced against fusion performance
[13]	Use of IF for integrating disparate DB data sets	No process framework offered	No process framework offered
[14]	Framework abstraction for ambient intelligence type apps	--Only framework paper that addresses multi-modal inputs,	--Restricted range of application domains
[15]	Overview of several major fusion architectures	No process framework offered	No process framework offered
[16]	Robust, fusion-based simulation environment	--Flexible structure, inherent modularity	--Mainly focused on Naval apps
[17]	Mathematical characterization of humans interacting with fusion processes	No process framework offered	No process framework offered

Table 1. (*continued*)

[18]	Software pattern characterization	--SOA for extensibility. --Trickle-up software design pattern to decouple data management from fusion --Zone pattern provides a view of the relationship and roles between functions	--Performance impacts --Requires common data schemas and definitions to support late binding and orchestration data mgmt and fusion operations --Imputes software overhead --Complexity --Configuration mgmt
[19]	High-level fusion for Army-type, force-on-force military engagements	--Incorporates contextual aspects --Focused on high-level fusion --Multi-agent approach --Incorporates IPB methodology	--Militarily-specific (totally committed to IPB method flow) --Really a robust point design for force-on-force high-level fusion

3.2 One Possible Framework Approach

We take a position in promoting our Framework approach (shown in Fig 3) derived from the works of Bowman [20, 21], Steinberg [22], and in part from our own work [23], along with some of the above key points drawn from the literature. It is important to note that this paper is confined to a Centralized Framework; addressing the Distributed Information Fusion Framework topic will be the subject of a companion effort at UC3M. The front-end of the Framework is shown as having both Hard (electronic, physics-based) sensors and Soft (human observers) sensors, since modern defense applications have shown human observations to be critical, although it can be said that human-generated observations are also important to many other applications. These raw observational data enter into a detection, semantic labeling, and flow control composite function. Here, the raw data are processed by sensor-specific detection or fused-detection operations where the observations are in effect qualified according to these detection criteria. In conjunction with detection, the observations are semantically labeled, since detection operations often occur in the signal-processing, mathematical domain rather than the semantic domain. These are crucially-important steps, since there is no subsequent processing or erroneous processing if the detection process is either done poorly or incorrectly[2]. In our opinion, not enough attention is paid to the consideration of detection fusion opportunities, yet there are textbooks on this subject [24]. Semantic labeling can also involve complex automated processes, such as automatically labeling detected image entities with correct semantic labels. Once the best-qualified detections have been achieved, there is the question of assigning them to the various Fusion Nodes; we see this as requiring Flow Control logic. Note that the Flow Control logic will send observations to the fusion Level most appropriate to the semantic nature of the observation; e.g., a radar observation of position and velocity to a Kalman Filter at Level 1 and an event observation to a situational estimator at Level 2. The point is that observations are not necessarily

---

[2] Many fusion-based estimation algorithms have detection probability Pd as an important parameter, i.e., with better estimation resulting from higher Pd.

sequentially processed through the Levels, and Flow Control is a very important aspect that can be driven by a variety of application-specific parameters.

We show a function module called Problem Space Characterization Logic below the detection operations. To adaptively manage a system with a library of alternative algorithms that address a generically-common problem space (e.g., object tracking problems), knowledge of the performance bounds of any library algorithm in terms of an *observable* set of parameters needs to be known. With such knowledge, an intelligent algorithm manager—we see this as part of the InterNodal Adaptive Logic—can terminate a currently-operating algorithm and invoke the better algorithm for the current problem-space condition. An important point here is that the problems-space complexity parameters need to be observable by the system sensor set. Note too that this knowledge may also be Contextually-dependent, so we have Contextual information also feeding this knowledge base and control logic.

As in Bowman [20, 21], Dastner [6] and in our own work, we believe in the ubiquity of the Fusion Node construct (Fig. 1 above) in asserting that every IF process has its roots in the three functions of Common Referencing, Data Association, and State Estimation. Taking this as a given, it can be argued that any fusion Level of the JDL type can be formed as an interlaced multi-Fusion Node construct. Bowman [20] defines this type structure as a tree of such Nodes, and in his case including interwoven Resource Management (RM) nodes[3]. Regarding feedback, we immediately assert that the framework should show adaptive Internodal feedback to allow (or perhaps require) that the Nodes share and exploit information if possible. One can see this in traditional Level 1 fusion for tracking and identification usually done in two separate Fusion Nodes; kinematics are of course helpful for identification, and identification is helpful for example to know an object's feasible dynamic motion. In turn, an adaptive Inter-Level feedback process is also shown, allowing situational estimates to feedback their estimates to other levels; an example of this would be a situational estimate that would suggest that maneuvering behaviors could be expected, informing Level 1 object tracking logic that would open the tracking gates to capture the diverging measurements occurring upon the maneuver, i.e., as a maneuver-anticipation strategy instead of the (generally too-late) post-maneuver detection strategies often employed in tracking systems.

Note that all control loops need to define stopping criteria that terminate the otherwise-endless looping; that requirement is shown by the triangles in Fig 3. Another loop is shown coincident with the output layers of Levels 1-3, which incorporates a Value or Quality-driven strategy for the output or final estimates and employs that logic to adaptively control the Hard and Soft sensor system in conjunction with its agility. Note that sensor control can be either in the sense of space-time pointing of sensors or by controlling various sensor operating parameters such as waveform or power level (or yet other parameters, as modern sensors are very agile).

---

[3] A frequently-contentious point in IF process design is the distinction between "Process Refinement" or Level 4 in the JDL model (Fig 2 above) and Resource Management. Our position is that while Process Refinement may entail use of resources, the RM term has too broad an implication for what is meant by Level 4 in the original IF model.

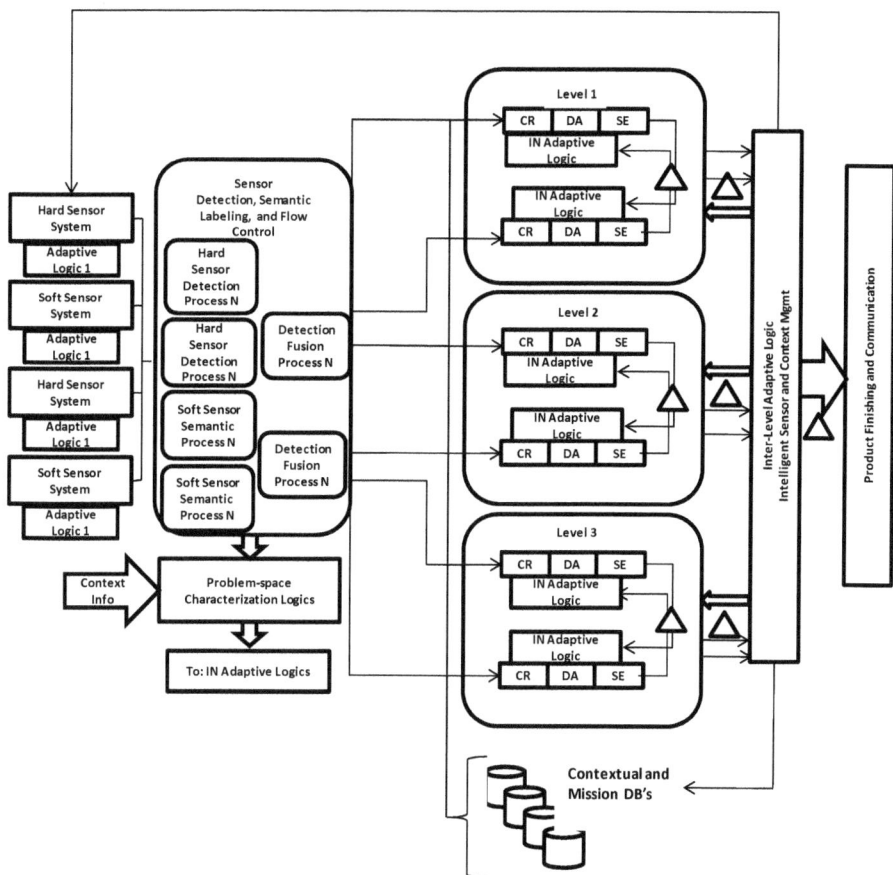

Fig. 3. Proposed Information Fusion Framework (Top-Level View)

3.3 Summary and Conclusions

While a number of efforts have been made to define a robust, extended-domain IF Framework, our review of past works indicates that (according to the Framework definitions described within the paper) no such Framework has been well-defined. Building in part on the Fusion Node concept that has stood the test of broad application, and also anchoring on adaptivity, we have characterized a proposed Framework that covers all IF process functionality, and that has a broad foundation of process agility needed for domain robustness. This research is certainly not complete, and we have ideas on the sub-structure of the Framework as proposed here, that is for example the incorporation of Blackboard architectural concepts that have been explored by us [25] and others [26-29] for the higher-Level IF inferencing and estimating processes that have been well addressed by the AI community. Future prototype development and experimentation at UC3M will no doubt reveal both the correct and incorrect aspects of the details of the Framework, but we are confident that the core concepts described here will remain in the Framework.

Acknowledgement

The author gratefully acknowledges the opportunity to participate in the Banco Santander Chairs of Excellence program and for the insightful collaborations with UC3M faculty to especially include Professors Jesus Garcia Herrero and Jose Manuel Molina.

References

[1] White Jr., F.E.: Data Fusion Lexicon, Joint Directors of laboratories, Technical Panel for C3, Data Fusion Sub-Panel, Naval Ocean Systems Center, San Diego (1987)
[2] http://en.wikipedia.org/wiki/Software_framework
[3] Riehle, D.: Framework Design: A Role Modeling Approach. Ph.D. Thesis, No. 13509. Zürich, Switzerland, ETH Zürich (2000)
[4] Besada, J.A., et al.: Generic Software Architecture for Development of Data Fusion Systems. In: Proc. of Intl. Info. Fusion Conf. (July 2002)
[5] Bolles, A.: A Flexible Framework for Multisensor Data Fusion using Data Stream Management Technologies. In: Proceedings of the 2009 EDBT/ICDT Workshops, Russia (2009)
[6] Dästner, K., Kausch, T., Opitz, F.: An Object Oriented Development Suite for Data Fusion: Design, Generation, Simulation and Testing. In: 10th International Conference on Information Fusion, Quebec City (2007)
[7] Emami, D.G.: Service and Agent Oriented Framework for Information Fusion and Knowledge Management. In: GMU C4I Center-AFCEA Symposium, May 19-20 (2009)
[8] Hou, P.K., Shi, X.Z., Lin, L.J.: Generic Blackboard Based Architecture for Data Fusion. In: 26th Annual Conference of the IEEE, Industrial Electronics Society, IECON 2000 (2000)
[9] Klausner, A., Rinner, B., Tengg, A.: I-SENSE: Intelligent Embedded Multi-Sensor Fusion. In: Proceedings of the 4th IEEE International Conf. on Intelligent Solutions in Embedded Systems, WISES 2006 (2006)
[10] Kokar, M.M., Weyman, J., Tomasik, J.A.: Fusion as an Operation on Formal Systems: A Formal Framework for Information Fusion, AFOSR Final Project Report, Northeastern Univ. (April 2001)
[11] Kumar, R., et al.: DFuse: A Framework for Distributed Data Fusion. In: ACM SenSys 2003, Los Angeles, CA (2003)
[12] McDaniel, D.: An Information Fusion Framework for Data Integration. In: Thirteenth Annual Software Technology Conference STC (May 2001)
[13] Mendonça, H., et al.: A Fusion Framework for Multimodal Interactive Applications. In: Proceedings of the 2009 International Conference on Multimodal Interfaces (2009)
[14] Mirza, A.R.: Data Fusion Architectures for Sensor Platforms. In: IEEE Aerospace Conference (2008)
[15] Paradis, S., Roy, J.: An Architecture and a Facility for the Integration of All Levels of Data Fusion. In: Proceedings of the Third International Conference on Information Fusion, Paris (2000)
[16] Posse, C., White, A., Beagley, N.: Human-Centered Fusion Framework. In: IEEE Conference on Technologies for Homeland Security (2007)
[17] Rothenhaus, K.J., Michael, J.B., Shing, M.: Architectural Patterns and Auto-Fusion

[18] Sycara, K., et al.: An Integrated Approach to High-level Information Fusion. Information Fusion 10, 25–50 (2009)
[19] Walters, J.J., Julier, S.J.: A Software Framework for Heterogeneous, Distributed Data Fusion. In: 9th International Conference on Information Fusion, Florence (2006)
[20] Bowman, C.L.: The Dual Node Network (DNN) Data Fusion & Resource Management (DF&RM) Architecture. In: AIAA Intelligent Systems Conf. Chicago, USA (2004)
[21] Bowman, C.L., Steinberg, A.N.: A Systems Engineering Approach for Implementing Data Fusion Systems. In: Hall, D., Llinas, J. (eds.) Handbook of Multisensor Data Fusion, ch. 16. CRC Press, Boca Raton (2001)
[22] Steinberg, A.N., Bowman, C.L., White, F.E.: Revisions to the JDL Data Fusion Model. In: Proc. SPIE. Sensor Fusion: Architectures, Algorithms, and Applications III, vol. 3719, pp. 430–441 (1999)
[23] Llinas, J., et al.: Revisiting the JDL Data Fusion Model II. In: Proc. of the Intl. Conference on Information Fusion, Stockholm (2004)
[24] Varshney, P.: Distributed detection and data fusion, December 1996. Springer, Heidelberg (1996)
[25] Llinas, J., Antony, R.T.: Blackboard Concepts for Data Fusion Applications. Intl. Jl Pattern Recognition and Artificial Intelligence 7(2) (1993)
[26] Peers, S.M.C.: Knowledge Representation in a Blackboard System for Sensor Data Interpretation. In: Moonis, A., Mira, J., de Pobil, A.P. (eds.) IEA/AIE 1998. LNCS, vol. 1415. Springer, Heidelberg (1998)
[27] Sutton, C.: A Bayesian Blackboard for Information Fusion, Defense Technical Information Center, ADA459893 (2004)
[28] Bosse, E., Roy, J., Paradis, S.: Modeling and simulation in support of the design of a data fusion system. Information Fusion 1(2) (December 2000)
[29] Korotkiy, M., Top, J.: Blackboard-style Service Composition with Onto, SOA. In: International Conference WWW/Internet, Portugal (2007)

A Regular Tetrahedron Formation Strategy for Swarm Robots in Three-Dimensional Environment

M. Fikret Ercan[1], Xiang Li[1,2], and Ximing Liang[2]

[1] School of Electrical and Electronic Engineering, Singapore Polytechnic, Singapore
[2] School of Information Science and Engineering, Central South University, China
mfercan@sp.edu.sg, xl_huse@126.com, ananxml@mail.csu.edu.cn

Abstract. A decentralized control method, namely Regular Tetrahedron Formation (*RTF*), is presented for a swarm of simple robots operating in three-dimensional space. It is based on virtual spring mechanism and enables four neighboring robots to autonomously form a Regular Tetrahedron (*RT*) regardless of their initial positions. *RTF* method is applied to various sizes of swarms through a dynamic neighbor selection procedure. Each robot's behavior depends only on position of three dynamically selected neighbors. An obstacle avoidance model is also introduced. Final, algorithm is studied with computational experiments which demonstrated that it is effective.

Keywords: Swarm robotics, Swarm flocking, Decentralized control.

1 Introduction

Swarm robots operating on land, air or underwater has a broad range of applications such as exploration, urban search and rescue [1], [2], [10]. Deploying large number of robots, in such challenging environments, is worthy due to fault tolerance, shorter completion time and ability to cover wider areas. However, coordinating large number of robots to perform a task collectively is not trivial and it has been the main interest of swarm robotics research during the last decade. A primary challenge is to achieve a desired collective behavior that emerges from robots' interactions with each other and the environment. Such behavior is vastly displayed in nature by social animals such as birds and insects.

A desired swarm behavior is flocking where robots show a collective and coordinated movement as one body. There is a vast research in literature on flocking behavior, inspired from artificial physics to social animal behavior (see for instance [3], [4], [5]). However, most of these studies do not consider the local formation between members of swarm. Maintaining a local formation when flocking, is a significant advantage for applications, such as surveillance, data collection and exploration. Furthermore, in many flocking methods, an individual's behavior is usually depends on all its visible/sensible neighbors, which usually causes a high uncertainty in the behavior.

In this paper, we present a method, namely Regular Tetrahedron Formation (*RTF*) strategy, to achieve a flocking behavior in a three-dimensional environment. In the following, the *RTF* method will be presented together with results obtained from experimental studies.

M. Graña Romay et al. (Eds.): HAIS 2010, Part I, LNAI 6076, pp. 24–31, 2010.
© Springer-Verlag Berlin Heidelberg 2010

2 Problem Statement and Definitions

We consider a swarm of autonomous mobile robots $r_1, r_2, \ldots, r_n$ with arbitrary and discrete initial distribution. Each robot is modeled as a point which can freely move in a three dimensional space with limited range of sensing. They have no identifiers and do not share any common coordinate system. They do not retain any memory of past states or actions. They can detect the position of other robots in close proximity, but they do not communicate explicitly with them. Each robot executes the same interaction strategy, but acts independently and asynchronously from other robots.

The distance between the robot r_i's position p_i and the robot r_j's position p_j is denoted as $dist(p_i, p_j)$. Each robot has a limited sensing area, SZ, with a sensing radius described by R_s. A constant distance, d_u , is denoted where $0 < d_u < R_s$. Robot r_i can detect the positions of other robots, $\{p_1, p_2, \ldots\}$, located within its SZ, and make the set of the observed positions, O_i. In each time step, r_i selects three robots r_{s1}, r_{s2} and r_{s3} from O_i and denote their positions as p_{s1}, p_{s2} and p_{s3}, respectively. We identify r_{s1}, r_{s2} and r_{s3} the neighbors of r_i and denote the set of their positions, $\{p_{s1}, p_{s2}, p_{s3}\}$, as N_i. Lastly, $area(r_i, r_j, r_k, r_l)$ denotes the surface area of the tetrahedron formation built by the four robots, $r_i, r_j, r_k,$ and r_l, as shown in Fig.1 (a).

Definition 1. (Tetrahedron Formation, TF) Given p_i and N_i, a tetrahedron formation is defined as a set of four discrete positions $\{p_i, p_{s1}, p_{s2}, p_{s3}\}$ denoted by $TF_i = \{p_i, p_{s1}, p_{s2}, p_{s3}\}$.

Definition 2. (Regular Tetrahedron Formation, TRF) Among the TF_i, we define a regular tetrahedron formation RTF_i, provided that all the possible distance permutations are equal to d_u.

Using TF_i and RTF_i, we can define the local interaction as follows:

Definition 3. (Local Interaction) Given TF_i, the local interaction is to have r_i attempt to maintain d_u with N_i at each time instant so as to form RTF_i.

We define flocking behavior as:

Definition 4. (Defined Flocking) When robot swarm maneuver as a body in an unknown environment, robots avoid collision among themselves and obstacles while maintaining multiple local formations.

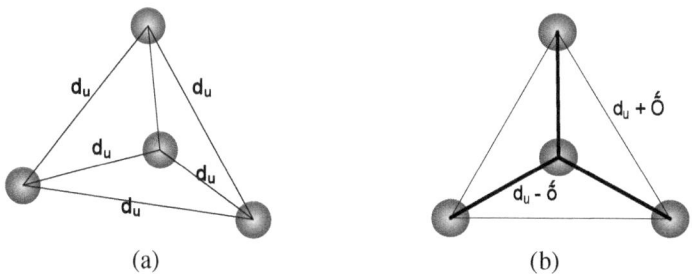

(a)   (b)

Fig. 1. a) *RTF* desired for four robots b) Unstable equilibrium in 3D space

Each robot executes the same local interaction algorithm and repeats a recursive set of operations. More specifically, at each time step, robot first detects positions of other robots (observation), then computes a local goal position using local interaction algorithm (computation), and steers towards the goal position (motion).

3   Regular Tetrahedron Formation (*RTF*) Strategy

The *RTF* strategy, which determines the basic swarm behavior, employs virtual spring mesh [6], [7]. The main advantage of our interaction strategy is that the control input of each robot is the position information of invariable number of neighbors. All the robots execute the same strategy formulated as follows:

$$\ddot{x} = u \tag{1a}$$

$$u = [\sum_{p_\alpha \in N_i} k_s \cdot (dist(p - p_\alpha) - d_u) \cdot \hat{v}_\alpha] - k_d \cdot \dot{x} \tag{1b}$$

Where x represents the Cartesian coordinates of robot's position, $\ddot{x}$ is the robot's acceleration, $\dot{x}$ is the robot's velocity. $\hat{v}_\alpha$ is the unit vector from this robot to the robot located at p_α. Control constants are the natural spring length d_u, the spring stiffness k_s, and the damping coefficient k_d. The output of each robot controller relies on the position information from only three specific neighboring robots. If we consider a minimal swarm (only four robots), then it is assumed that each robot can sense all the other robots. Each robot has an artificial spring force exerted on any one of these robots. At the point of mutual reaction, an artificial spring network is formed and it can be viewed as an undirected completed connectivity graph. For this network, the topology is fixed and $k_d > 0$. The network will eventually converge to a stationary state, where all the robots velocity will approach to zero. Intuitively, this is because the dynamics of a virtual spring are analogous to those of a real spring, in which energy is conserved. Since we ensure $k_d > 0$, there is always a damping effect acting against the motion of each robot. This forces a reduction in kinetic energy. Kinetic energy may be gained by converting potential energy stored in springs, but since springs are dissipative, the total energy in the mesh cannot increase. Since the existence of kinetic energy results in a decrease in total energy, and this energy cannot be replenished, kinetic energy must eventually reach to zero.

Lemma 1 [8]. In a spring mesh with fixed topology and $k_d > 0$, all robots eventually reach zero velocity.

Theorem 1. Given that four robots are at arbitrary and discrete positions in 3D space, under *RTF* strategy, each robot can converge to any vertex of *RT* with d_u.

Proof according to **Lemma 1**, the configuration formed by the four robots could converge to a stationary configuration, where each robot is at force-balance state. If initial configuration converges to a 2D configuration, the resulting configuration will be as shown in Fig.1-b. There exist three forces acting on each robot, and the total of the forces is zero. Some potential energy is still stored in springs and the distances between robots are not the same and equal to d_u. However, this state is unstable equilibrium. As long as initial configuration is not at this unstable state, during dynamical convergence, due to the existence of inertial disturbance in system, will not result in unstable equilibrium. If initial configuration converges to a 3D configuration, the stationary configuration is certainly a RT with a side length of d_u. Otherwise, there exist a non-zero total force acting on a robot due to the non natural length of spring. This force will enforce the robot to move in later time. Thus it will contradict the proposition given **Lemma 1**.

To verify the effectiveness of RTF strategy, experiments are conducted with four robots in BREVE simulation environment [9]. The robots are initially positioned at random and discrete positions. The parameter settings are d_u=20, k_s=0.1, and k_d=0.3. Fig.2 shows the average deviation ($adev$) of side lengths from the natural length d_u over time. We defined the $adev$ as following:

$$adev(n \cdot \Delta t) = \frac{\sum_{i=1}^{4} \sum_{j=i+1}^{4} |d_{ij}(n \cdot \Delta t) - d_u|}{6}, \quad n \in N \quad (2)$$

Here Δt is the time step determined by simulation platform; d_{ij} is the distance between robots r_i and r_j at time $n \cdot \Delta t$; N is the natural number set. Assume that the four neighboring robots are indexed as r_1, r_2, r_3, and r_4. Fig.2 shows the convergence of the four robots as a function of average deviation ($adev$) from RT. Although the $adev$ has an oscillation of about several cycles at the beginning, its magnitude approaches to zero eventually. That is, all the side lengths of the tetrahedron will eventually converge to the same value of d_u hence the four neighboring robots form a RT autonomously. If, the initial positions of the four robots are fixed, then the convergence time for a RT configuration only depends on parameters k_s and k_d. The average deviation of side lengths can be used to decide if the configuration has converged to a RT. However, it may not be adequate if we need to compute the convergence time quantitatively. As seen from Fig.2, the value of $adev$ fluctuates and finally reaches zero in 45 sec. In order to define convergence time accurately, we employ the following equation:

$$t_c(k_s, k_d) = \Delta t \cdot \min \left\{ n \left| \frac{\sum_{n}^{n+D} adev(n \cdot \Delta t)}{D} < Err, n \in N \right. \right\} \quad (3)$$

In Eq.3, D shows the time duration allowed for fluctuation (a bigger value of D means more strict convergence decision condition). Err is the tolerance of the average deviation of side lengths. Δt is the time step of simulation. It is set as 0.055 sec., which is defined by simulation platform. The other parameter settings during our experiments were D=5 and Err=0.01. We uniformly sample, six values for k_s from a range of 0.1~0.6 and ten values for k_d from a range of 0.1~1. Experiments were run 10 times, for each combination of k_s and k_d, with the same initial robot positions. The mean value of t_c is then taken as the convergence time. The optimal combination of parameters is empirically found as k_s within the range of 0.3~0.5 and k_d within 0.7~1. For all the experiments, k_s =0.3 and k_d = 0.8.

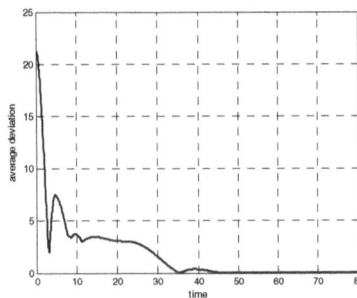

Fig. 2. Average deviation (*adev*) of side lengths vs. iteration time ($d_u = 20$)

4   The Extended *RTF* Strategy and Experimental Results

The *RTF* strategy is extended to various group sizes by executing a dynamic neighbor selection algorithm. That is, there are more than three robots in the sensing zone. Positions of these three neighbors are denoted as p_{s1}, p_{s2}, and p_{s3}. The p_{s1} is the position of the nearest robot r_{s1} from r_i. The position p_{s2} of robot r_{s2} is such that the total distance from p_i to robot p_{s1} through p_{s2} is minimal. Robot r_{s3}'s position p_{s3} makes the area of the tetrahedron built by $\{p_i, p_{s1}, p_{s2}, p_{s3}\}$ minimal. The selection rules are formulated as follows:

$$p_{s1} := \arg[\min(dist(p_i, p_\alpha))], \ p_\alpha \in O_i \tag{4}$$

$$p_{s2} := \arg[\min[dist(p_\alpha, p) + dist(p_\alpha, p_{s1})]], \ p_\alpha \in (O_i - p_{s1}) \tag{5}$$

$$p_{s3} := \arg[\min[area(p_i, p_{s1}, p_{s2}, p_\alpha)]], \ p_\alpha \in (O_i - p_{s1} - p_{s2}) \tag{6}$$

Where O_i is the observed position set of r_i with respect to local frame; O_i-p_{s1} and O_i-p_{s1}-p_{s2} are the position subsets excluding p_{s1}, p_{s1} and p_{s2} from O_i, respectively.   If p_{s2} is at the line $p_i p_{s1}$, then substitute for O_i-p_{s1} with O_i-p_{s1}-p_{s2} and repeat Eq.5; similarly, if p_{s3} is at the plane $p_i p_{s1} p_{s2}$, substitute for O_i-p_{s1}-p_{s2} with O_i-p_{s1}-p_{s2}-p_{s3} and repeat Eq.6. During the selection process, if there is still more than one candidate for p_{s1}, robot r_i determines its first neighbor by sorting the positions of the candidates in decreasing order as follows:

$$\forall p_{s1m}, p_{s2n}, \exists p_{s1m} = (p_{s1m,x}, p_{s1m,y}, p_{s1m,z}), p_{s1n} = (p_{s1n,x}, p_{s1n,y}, p_{s1n,z})$$

$$p_{s1m} > p_{s1n} \Leftrightarrow [(p_{s1m,x} > p_{s1n,x}) \vee \{(p_{s1m,x} = p_{s1n,x}) \wedge (p_{s1m,y} > p_{s1n,y})\} \tag{7}$$

$$\vee \{(p_{s1m,x} = p_{s1n,x}) \wedge (p_{s1m,y} = p_{s1n,y}) \wedge (p_{s1m,z} > p_{s1n,z})\}]$$

Here, p_{s1m} and p_{s1n} are the positions of any two candidates for p_{s1}. Similarly, if there are multiple candidates for p_{s2} or p_{s3}, robot r_i determines each of them by applying the same sorting method as described above.

An obstacle avoidance behavior, employing an artificial physics model, is also implanted to the swarm. This model mimics the interaction between a moving electron and an atom nucleus. When an electron approaches to atom nucleus, a repulsive force from the nucleus will exert on the electron, causing it to deviate from its original motion trajectory and avoid collision. Similarly, when a robot approaches to an obstacle, a repulsive force f_r will be exerted on it as shown in Fig 3. We use a repulsive velocity v_r, as described in Eq.8, to be equivalent to the repulsive force f_r. The direction of v_r is along the line drawn from the nearest point of the obstacle towards the robot. For simplicity, obstacle is considered as a closed disc, with a buffer zone of a distance d around the obstacle. The nearest point of the obstacle from the robot is denoted as O. To avoid the obstacle, robot r_i adjusts its velocity by adding v_r to its current velocity. Only if robot r_i enters into the buffer zone, there will be an equivalent repulsive velocity exerted on robot r_i, otherwise it will be not be affected. Robot r_i calculates the equivalent repulsive velocity as:

$$v_r = \frac{p_i - O}{|p_i - O|} \cdot r\left(1 - \frac{|p_i - O|}{d}\right) \cdot v_{max} \qquad (8)$$

Here, $r(x)$ is defined as a *ramp* function:

$$r(x) = \begin{cases} 0, x < 0 \\ x, x \geq 0 \end{cases} \qquad (9)$$

The maximum velocity allowed for all the robots is v_{max}. In the worst case, it is assumed that a robot has a velocity of v_{max} when it enters to the buffer zone. From the Eq.8, we see that the repulsive velocity exerted on the robot will increase from 0 to v_{max} linearly as robot approaches to obstacle. That is, at the point of impact robot will stop, as its total velocity will be zero. However, as a member of group, a robot will naturally stay away from the obstacles by following its neighbors. In other words, an individual avoids the local minimum, which is a fundamental problem in the potential field methods [4], by interacting with their neighbors.

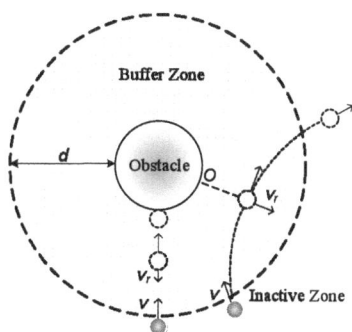

Fig. 3. Obstacle avoidance model with a single robot

For the experimental study, a number of parameters have to be set. The initial robot positions are generated randomly within a radius of 40 units in the middle of the environment; the maximum velocity, v_{max}, is set as 2 units/s; the effective sensing radius of robots is set as $R_s=60$ units, and the desired uniform distance set as $d_u=10$ units.

such as the number of robots n, the sensing radius of robot R_s, and the constant d_u. To achieve the desired collective behavior, the condition of $R_s > d_u$ holds during simulation. At the beginning, each robot can sense at least two of its neighboring robots. In Fig. 4, symbol 'o' indicates the initial and '*' indicates the final positions of the robots. The dashed lines show the trajectory trails of each robot. The simulation time, t_{sim}, for each figure is also given in figure captions.

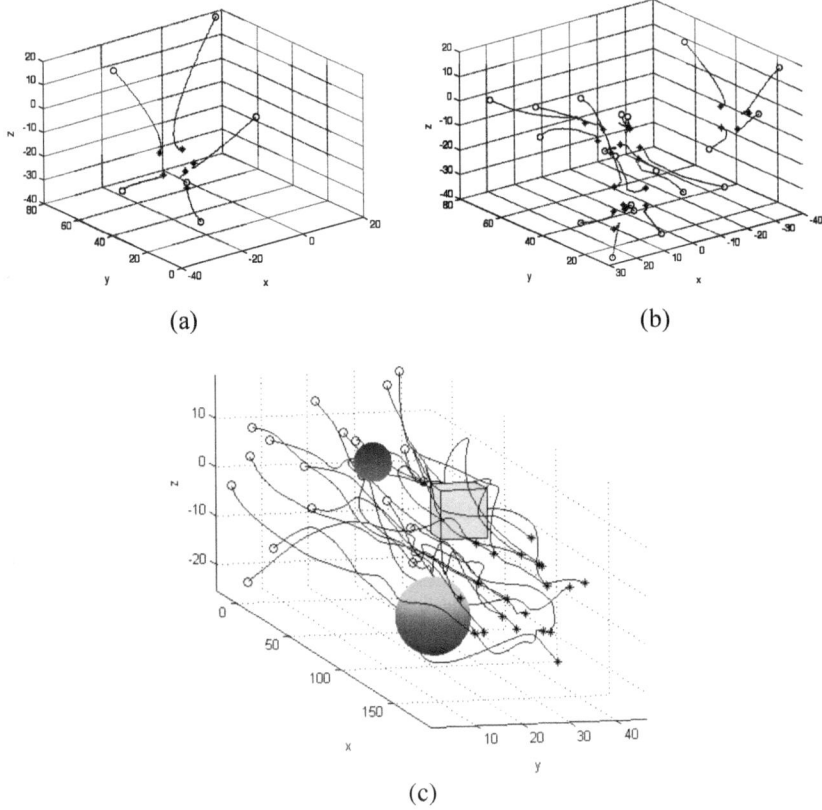

(a)   (b)

(c)

Fig. 4. a) One-aggregation, $n=6$, $t_{sim}= 31$ b) Multi-aggregation, $n=20$, $t_{sim}=36s$ c) Adaptive flocking, three obstacles, $n=20$, $t_{sim}=42s$

The minimum number of robots required is four for both *RTF* and *ERTF*. Fig.4a illustrates the aggregation as one group for six robots. If the number of robots is in the range of four to seven, one aggregation behavior is always achieved successfully regardless of the distribution of the group. The reason for this trend is apparent. Once four robots begin to aggregate, remaining robots do not have numbers to form another group separately. For a swarm containing more than seven robots, multi-aggregation may occur depending on the width of the initial distribution or the value of d_u as shown in Fig.4b. However, this could be desired for some applications such as multiple-target search and multi-location deployment. The possible number of aggregations will be in the range of $1 \sim \lfloor n/4 \rfloor$. Fig.4c shows a swarm moving towards a target (a middle point on the right hand side) in an environment populated with obstacles. It is assumed that all the robots know the target position. We observe that if the size of the obstacle is larger than d_u, swarm has a tendency to move around the obstacle as a whole. Otherwise, swarm will flock through the obstacle while individuals avoiding it on their way to target.

5 Conclusions

This study concerns with regular tetrahedron formation strategy for swarm aggregation and flocking behaviors. By integrating a dynamic neighbor selection, *RTF* strategy is expanded to large swarms where each robots' behavior determined by the position of three other neighboring robots. As calculations involve only three neighbors' position, the control strategy has less computation and depends less to the other robots. An obstacle avoidance model is also proposed. Robots, as members of swarm, can escape the local minima around the obstacle by following their neighbors. A key assumption made in this study is that robots are capable of detecting other robots' position with respect to their local frame and able to distinguish themselves from the obstacles. The resulting control strategy is suitable to realize in practice with actual robots.

References

1. Chaimowicz, L., Cowley, A., Gomez-Ibanez, D., Grocholsky, B., Hsieh, M.A., et al.: Deploying air-ground multi-robot teams in urban environments. In: Multi-Robot Systems. From Swarms to Intelligent Automata, pp. 223–234 (2005)
2. Kalantar, S., Zimmer, U.: Distributed shape control of homogenous swarms of autonomous underwater vehicles. J. Autonomous Robots 22, 37–53 (2007)
3. Turgut, A.E., Çelikkanat, H., Gökçe, F., Şahin, E.: Self-organized flocking with a mobile robot swarm. Technical Report METU-CENG-TR-2008-01, Middle East Technical University (January 2008)
4. Kim, D.H., Wang, H., Shin, S.: Decentralized control of autonomous swarm systems using artificial potential function-analytical design guidelines. J. Intel. Robot Syst. 45, 369–394 (2006)
5. Olfati-Saber, R.: Flocking for multi-agent dynamic systems: algorithm and theory. IEEE Transactions on automatic control 51, 401–420 (2006)
6. Shucker, B., Bennett, J.K.: Scalable control of distributed robotic macro sensors. In: Proc. of the7th international symposium on distributed autonomous robotic systems, DARS 2004 (2004)
7. Shucker, B., Murphey, T., Bennett, J.K.: A method of cooperative control using occasional non-local interactions. In: Proc. of IEEE Conference on Robotics and Automation (ICRA), Orlando, Florida (May 2006)
8. Shucker, B., Murphey, T., Bennett, J.K.: An approach to switching control beyond nearest neighbor rules. In: Proc. of American Control Conference (ACC) (June 2006)
9. Klein, J.: Breve: a 3D simulation environment for the simulation of decentralized systems and artificial life. In: Proc. of Artificial Life VIII, the 8th International Conference on the Simulation and Synthesis of Living Systems (2002)
10. Duro, R.J., Graña, M., de Lope, J.: On the potential contributions of hybrid intelligent approaches to multicomponent robotic system development. Information Sciences (2010) (in press)

Markovian Ants in a Queuing System

Ilija Tanackov[1], Dragan Simić[1], Siniša Sremac[1], Jovan Tepić[1],
and Sunčica Kocić-Tanackov[2]

[1] University of Novi Sad, Faculty of Technical Sciences, Trg Dositeja Obradovića 6,
21000 Novi Sad, Serbia
ilijat@uns.ac.rs, dsimic@uns.ac.rs
[2] University of Novi Sad, Faculty of Technology, Bulevar cara Lazara 1,
21000 Novi Sad, Serbia
suncicat@uns.ac.rs

Abstract. The synthesis of memoryless Markovian systems and Ant based concept with memory characteristics of deposit pheromone is the basis for the presented artificial intelligence hybrid. Only the initial elements of the system are specified in this paper by illustrating the routes of two ants. The pheromone capacity was first modelled as an exponential-type random variable. The Ant Queueing System was formed. The pheromone capacity was then used to form two independent exponential random variables. The convolution of these variables induces significant quality and quantity changes, mainly the decrease in entropy. The study also provides a possible method for dealing with stationary queueing systems when we are familiar with the state probability and the arrival rate and service rate are unknown.

Keywords: Pheromone signal, probability, convolution.

1 Introduction

High evolutionary viability of ant colonies is based on their organisational system [1]. The capability of reaching a collective decision apriori requires communication between individuals of a colony. The communication between ants of the same colony is conducted by chemical means using pheromones, infochemicals. There are several types of pheromones, like sex, alarm, trail, aggregation pheromones, etc. The pheromones can be influenced by humidity, temperature, light [2], airflow [3], characteristics of the soil [4], etc. It has been confirmed that ants, in the search for food, use several types of pheromones. A typical example is the use of three types of pheromones [5], which have different qualities and quantities. One attractive long-lasting pheromone, one attractive short-lived pheromone and one repellent [6]. Some pheromones can have two components [7]. Thereby, the attractive pheromone deposit varies depending on the food quality [8]. Social functions of ants, their age, various movement speeds, etc. can contribute to additional variations in the emission of pheromones. Chemosensory pheromone communication can be conducted without contact (olfaction) or by contact (gustation). The intensity of pheromone evaporation

M. Graña Romay et al. (Eds.): HAIS 2010, Part I, LNAI 6076, pp. 32–39, 2010.
© Springer-Verlag Berlin Heidelberg 2010

uncovers the most significant dynamic characteristic in intra-specific communication of ants. Overall, there is a great deal of factors which can cause accidental value changes of pheromones and which can affect the total entropy of information in ants' intra-communication. So far, there were no reports on the shortage of pheromones in the research of real ants. Thus, the consumption of the essential substance of ant colonies is highly optimised.

Ant colonies function successfully even under the terms of high entropy of chemosensory communication, which leads to the conclusion that individuals of a colony have an extraordinary ability to calibrate and process pheromone signals. The calibration and processing of signals are realised by the ants' sensory system. General requirements necessary to complete a quality sensor can be defined on the basis of Aristotle's principles of logic: the principle of identity, the principle of contradiction and the principle of excluded middle. In accordance with the mentioned principles of logic, a quality sensor fulfils the following conditions:

1. Sensor is sensitive to the measured signal (the principle of identity)
2. Sensor is insensitive to any other signal (the principle of contradiction)
3. Sensor does not influence the measured signal (the principle of excluded middle).

However, under the conditions of stochastic signal dynamics, even the best sensor will transfer information entropy completely onto the object of communication. Therefore, the solution for the colonies' efficiency is not in the individuals' sensors. The stochastic nature of the signal can vary with convolution of random variables.

Minimally two signals are required for the convolution of the pheromone signal. The nature of the pheromone signal is dual. The pheromone signal can be deposit and spatial [9]. The Ant System metaheuristic method, in its basic form of transition probabilities [10], accepts the dual nature of the pheromone signal. Visualisation analogy is a spatial pheromone signal.

The convolution of ants' basic pheromone capacity can be realised by diffusing one part of the basic odorant (pheromone) on a trail. The source of the odorant is an ant moving across a surface. If the odorant intensity equals ξ, its disposal causes the decomposition of the basic intensity into spatial pheromone intensity λ and deposit pheromone intensity μ. Thereby, $\xi = \lambda + \mu$ condition has been satisfied (fig. 1).

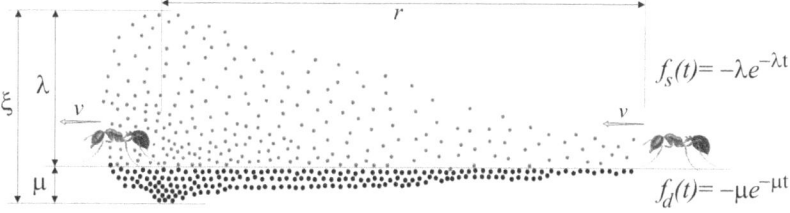

$$f_s(t) = -\lambda e^{-\lambda t}$$

$$f_d(t) = -\mu e^{-\mu t}$$

Fig. 1. Spatial and deposit fractions of the dual pheromone signal

2 Exponential Distribution

The exponential function with number e as the base, $f(x)=e^x$ has a unique equilibrium. The value of function and the arbitrary extract are identical, $f(x) = f(x)' = f(x)'' =...= e^x$. From the information theory standpoint, out of all the continuous probabilities the exponential distribution has the highest entropy. An important property of the exponential distribution is that it is memoryless. This means that if a random variable $V(x)$ is exponentially distributed $V(x)=\xi e^{-\xi x}$, its conditional probability obeys:

$$P(V > v_o + v / V > v_o) = P(V > v_o) = \frac{\int_{v_0+v}^{\infty} \xi e^{-\xi x}}{\int_{v_0}^{\infty} \xi e^{-\xi x}} = \frac{e^{-\xi(v_0+v)}}{e^{-\xi v_0}} = e^{-\xi v} \qquad (1)$$

The exponential distribution is the only continuous memoryless random distribution. If random processes in a system are described by exponential distribution, then the processes represent a special class of Markovian random processes. In such systems, the future is not conditioned by the past, but rather the temporary state, the present.

Ant based concept is a metaheuristic method of artificial intelligence. The source of intelligence in this method is based on a memory characteristic of the artificial ants' disposed pheromone. Synthesis of this memory characteristics and memoryless properties in Markovian process, was performed for systems with discrete states and discrete time [11, 12].

From the ACO convergence conditions [13] over the Poisson processes and in accordance with Palm's theorem, we come to the exponential relations among the artificial ants. The basis of relations among the real ants is pheromone communication in continual space and time. The pheromones evaporate. The evaporation of chemicals is an accidental process with most probably exponential characteristics [14, 15, 16]. By synthesising the named conditions with real and artificial ants we come to a viewpoint which justifies the use of exponential distribution in the Ant Based Concept.

3 Ant Queueing System - AQS

AQS proceeds from the assumption that the value of pheromone signal is a random variable of exponential distribution $f(l)= \xi e^{-\xi l}$ with l distance from the signal source and the intensity ξ, $\xi \geq 0$. Let the speed of the anterior ant be random and constant, and the speed of the consecutive ant proportional to the value of the received signal. If we express the distance between two consecutive ants by an integer variable X_l of the exponential function of pheromone signal $f(l)$, $X_l=INT(\xi e^{-\xi l})$, then the distance probability between the two consecutive ants equals $P(X_l)$. The probability of a unit distance X_k equals the exponential distribution integral in an interval $(k, k+1)$.

$$P(X_k) = p_k = \int_{k}^{k+1} \xi e^{-\xi l} dl = e^{-k\xi} - e^{-(k+1)\xi} = \frac{1}{e^{k\xi}} - \frac{1}{e^\xi e^{k\xi}} = \frac{1}{e^{k\xi}}\left(\frac{e^\xi - 1}{e^\xi}\right) \qquad (2)$$

The integer distance is the system's discrete state. The designed system is Markovian with discrete states and continuous intensity of the pheromone signal. The distance between two ants can be represented as a queueing system. The system's state expresses the distance value (fig. 2).

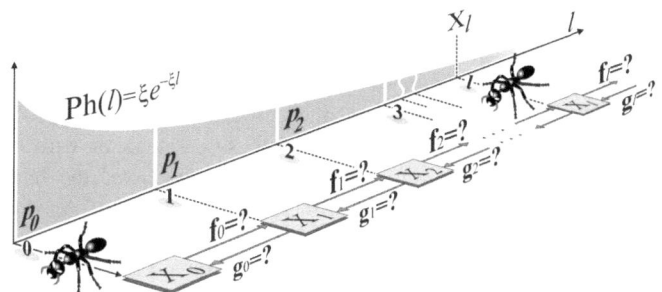

Fig. 2. Formation of the Ant Queueing System

The obtained system has an infinite number of states and has to satisfy the equation

$$\sum_{k=0}^{\infty} p_k = \sum_{k=0}^{\infty} \frac{1}{e^{k\xi}}\left(\frac{e^{\xi}-1}{e^{\xi}}\right) = \left(\frac{e^{\xi}-1}{e^{\xi}}\right)\sum_{k=0}^{\infty}\left(\frac{1}{e^{\xi}}\right)^k = 1 \qquad (3)$$

An uncommon way for the solution of queueing systems, when we are familiar with the state probabilities and the transition intensities are unknown, can be solved in the stationary mode for constant values of state probabilities. Then we have $f_k = const$ and $g_k = const$. From the differential equations starting point system we come to the following relations:

$$p_k'(t) = 0 = f_{k-1}p_{k-1} - g_{k-1}p_k - f_k p_k + g_k p_{k+1} \Leftrightarrow \frac{f_k}{g_k} = \frac{\dfrac{1}{e^{2\xi}}\left(\dfrac{e^{\xi}-1}{e^{\xi}}\right)^{-\xi}}{\dfrac{1}{e^{1\xi}}\left(\dfrac{e^{\xi}-1}{e^{\xi}}\right)} \Leftrightarrow f_k e^{\xi} = g_k \qquad (4)$$

And in general, the recurrence formula for transition intensity relations applies $f_k e^{\xi} = g_k$ $k \in (0,\infty)$. Value solution for the arrival rate and output process is an invariant of the C constant, and, in general, the queueing systems which satisfy the nature of relations $fe^{\xi} = g$, offer the defined state probabilities p_0, p_1, p_2, ... The invariant Ant Queueing System is presented in fig. 3.

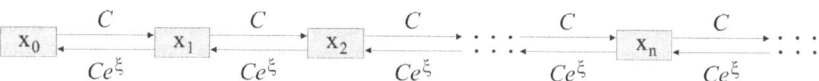

Fig. 3. Formation of the Ant Queueing System

However, at small and large constant values, the fluctuation through system states is respective, small or large. The defined AQS, as any other Queueing System has an unambiguous fluctuation. The C constant of invariant AQS has one value which needs to be estimated. Let the AQS be an ergodic system and let the starting distance between the anterior and the consecutive ant be equal to d, $l=d$. If the anterior ant is moving, the distance value with the consecutive ant is changing. As the anterior ant moves: the integer distance value d can be reduced to $(d-1)$, the integer distance value d does not change and stays d, or the integer distance value d can increase to $(d+1)$.

If the anterior ant's movement has not increased the integer distance value d, the consecutive ant with $g_{(d-1)}$ intensity traverses into $X_{(d-1)}$ state, or with $f_{(d-1)}$ intensity stays in X_d state. If the anterior ant's movement has increased the integer distance value to $(d+1)$, then the consecutive ant with g_d intensity stays in X_d state, or with f_d intensity traverses into $X_{(d+1)}$ state.

As distance is the function of pheromone signal intensity, by total probability formula, transition intensity relations will be proportional to the signal values at integer intervals. The relations are the same regardless of whether the anterior ant has changed the integer distance value or not. The transition intensity into farther f_k state and into closer g_k state equals (5). These intensities are not distance functions (memoryless), they are identical for all the states and they satisfy the nature of relations of arrival rate and service rate, $fe^{\xi}=g$. The AQS is presented in fig 4.

$$f_k = \frac{\dfrac{e^{\xi}-1}{e^{(k+1)\xi} \cdot e^{\xi}}}{\dfrac{e^{\xi}-1}{e^{k\xi} \cdot e^{\xi}} + \dfrac{e^{\xi}-1}{e^{(k+1)\xi} \cdot e^{\xi}}} = \frac{1}{e^{\xi}+1}, \qquad g_k = \frac{\dfrac{e^{\xi}-1}{e^{k\xi} \cdot e^{\xi}}}{\dfrac{e^{\xi}-1}{e^{k\xi} \cdot e^{\xi}} + \dfrac{e^{\xi}-1}{e^{(k+1)\xi} \cdot e^{\xi}}} = \frac{e^{\xi}}{e^{\xi}+1} \qquad (5)$$

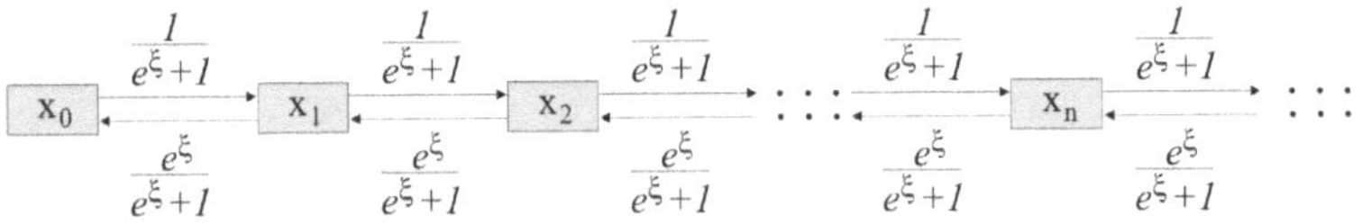

Fig. 4. Ant Queueing System-AQS

The basis of the obtained AQS is the birth and death process with the AQS constant, $C_{aqs}=(e^{\xi}+1)^{-1}$. The analogy of the birth process is the distance increase, and the analogy of the death process is the distance reduction. Thereby, the distance reduction process is the product of the birth process and the value of e^{ξ}. The mean value of the distance increase equals the arrival rate, and the mean value of the distance reduction process is the service rate. The average increase of C_{aqs} distance is performed by the anterior ant, and the average reduction of $e^{\xi}C_{aqs}$ distance is realised by the consecutive ant. If we form the ratio between the mean values of distance reduction and distance increase, we get the approach rate value or the remoteness rate value, i.e. the clusterisation factor of F_c column, which is equal to the mean value multiplier of the distance reduction $F_c=e^{\xi}\geq1$, because $\xi\geq0$. However, even with the emphasised clusterisation, the AQS cannot enter the absorbing state at zero distance. If the intensity of the pheromone signal spreading is exponential to ξ parameter, then the analogy of the average distance between two ants equals the number of clients in the system, which amounts to (6):

$$\sum_{k=0}^{\infty} kp_k = 0\left(1-\frac{1}{e^{\xi}}\right)+1\left(\frac{1}{e^{\xi}}-\frac{1}{e^{2\xi}}\right)+\ldots+k\left(\frac{1}{e^{k\xi}}-\frac{1}{e^{(k+1)\xi}}\right)+\ldots = \sum_{k=1}^{\infty}\left(\frac{1}{e^{\xi}}\right)=\frac{1}{e^{\xi}-1} \quad (6)$$

The absence of absorbing state can be explained if the AQS is seen as a system with one service channel and infinite number of queuing places. The whole structure of the queueing system stays identical. Additionally, the use of Pollaczek–Khinchin formula explains the distance reduction "delay" behind the clusterisation effects and the absence of absorbing state. The clusterisation factor logic is in accordance with the expression for calculation of the average distance between two ants [17]. Ant clusterisation is the consequence of different speeds between individuals of a colony, and it always occurs behind the slowest ant in the colony.

4 Pheromone Signal Convolution

If the basic signal is an exponentially distributed random variable (first premise), then we cannot decrease the entropy by decomposing the signal because the exponential distribution has the highest entropy (second premise). Dual signal fractions of the spatial and deposit signal stay at the level of maximum possible entropy (definiendum). This means that spatial and deposit pheromone signals have to act in accordance with the highest entropy distribution, and that is the exponential distribution. Thus, we get two signals: Spatial pheromone exponential signal $f_{sp}(l)=\lambda e^{-\lambda l}$, and deposit pheromone exponential signal $f_{de}(l)=\mu e^{-\mu l}$.

The sensory system of the consecutive ant now has the possibility to receive the spatial pheromone signal without contact (olfaction) and the deposit pheromone signal by contact (gustation). The convolution mean value is at its minimum at the half of basic pheromone capacity ξ. Since the distributions are exponential, the minimal pheromone convolution can be described by a second-order Erlang distribution with δ intensity (7), the mean value and the standard signal deviation (8), distribution function (9) and probability function of the AQS (10).

$$\left(\frac{\lambda+\mu}{\lambda\mu}\right)'_{\lambda}=\left(\frac{\lambda+\mu}{\lambda\mu}\right)'_{\mu}=0 \Leftrightarrow \lambda=\mu=\frac{\xi}{2}=\delta,\ f_{sp}(l)+f_{de}(l)=Er_2(l)=\delta^2 l e^{-\delta l} \quad (7)$$

$$E(l)=\frac{2}{\delta}=\frac{4}{\xi},\quad \sigma(l)=\frac{\sqrt{2}}{\delta}=\frac{2\sqrt{2}}{\xi} \quad (8)$$

$$F(l)=1-\sum_{n=1}^{2}e^{-\delta l}\frac{(\delta l)^{n-1}}{(n-1)!}=1-(e^{\delta l}+\delta l e^{\delta l})=1-e^{\delta l}(1+\delta l) \quad (9)$$

$$p_k=\int_{k}^{k+1}\delta^2 l e^{-\delta x}dl=1-e^{-\delta l}(1+\delta l)\Big|_{k}^{k+1}=\frac{1+k\delta}{e^{\delta k}}-\frac{1+\delta(k+1)}{e^{\delta(k+1)}} \quad (10)$$

The AQS with a minimal convolution signal and the Erlang distribution of state probability is not a Markovian system. Since we are familiar with the state probabilities, we can determine the average distance of the consecutive ants in this queueing system as well (11).

$$\sum_{k=0}^{\infty} k p_k = 0\left(\frac{1+\delta}{e^{\delta}}\right) + 1\left(\frac{1+\delta}{e^{\delta}} - \frac{1+2\delta}{e^{2\delta}}\right) + \ldots + k\left(\frac{1+k\delta}{e^{k\delta}} - \frac{1+(k+1)\delta}{e^{(k+1)\delta}}\right) + \ldots = \sum_{k=1}^{\infty}\left(\frac{1+k\delta}{e^{k\delta}}\right) =$$

$$\sum_{k=1}^{\infty}\left(\frac{1+k\delta}{e^{k\delta}}\right) = \sum_{k=0}^{\infty}\left(\frac{1+k\delta}{e^{k\delta}}\right) - 1 = \sum_{k=0}^{\infty}\left(\frac{1}{e^{k\delta}}\right) + \sum_{k=1}^{\infty}\left(\frac{k\delta}{e^{k\delta}}\right) - 1 = \frac{1}{e^{\delta}-1} + \delta\sum_{k=1}^{\infty}\left(\frac{k}{e^{k\delta}}\right) \quad (11)$$

As the inequality $\dfrac{1}{e^{\xi}-1} < \dfrac{1}{e^{\delta}-1} < \dfrac{1}{e^{\delta}-1} + \delta\sum_{k=1}^{\infty}\left(\dfrac{k}{e^{k\delta}}\right)$ applies for $\delta = \dfrac{\xi}{2}$ relations, a larger average distance is established between the consecutive ants in the system with the minimal convolution pheromone signal.

5 Discussion and Conclusion

The pheromone capacity of ants ξ without the convolution, during the exponential distribution of signal, has four times lesser value than the minimal convolution signal obtained by equal distribution of the basic pheromone capacity into spatial exponential pheromone signal and deposit exponential pheromone signal. Under the terms of minimal convolution, a smaller amount of pheromone is required to achieve the same average distance between the consecutive ants!

The relation between the exponential and Erlang distribution stands in favour of the convolution pheromone signal, which induces the decreased system entropy. The reciprocal logic offers a direct increase in the level of organisation but with the consumption reduction of the essential substance, the pheromone.

It is possible to form the Markovian AQS only in the case of two ants without the convolution signal. When there are more ants, this causes the convolution of the phase shifted exponential distributions.

Real ants use different types of multi-component pheromone with various evaporation intensities. A large number of ants, i.e. a large number of mobile signal sources with their specific features and differences form a complex convolution system. The only possible logical result of the complex convolution system is defined by the Central Limit Theorem conditions – CLT. The basis of swarm intelligence is in the CLT, and the basis of ambient intelligence is in the forming of ad hoc ant (multiagents) network with the constant CLT parameters. Even under these terms, the memoryless feature of the exponential distribution can have a crucial role in the calibration and pheromone signal processing.

References

1. Ma, S.Z., Krings, A.W.: Insect Sensory System Inspired Computing and Communications. Ad Hoc Networks 7(4), 742–755 (2009)
2. Depickère, S., Fresneau, D., Deneubourg, J.-L.: Effect of Social and Environmental Factors on Ant Aggregation: A general response? Journal of Insect Physiology 54(9), 1349–1355 (2008)

3. Garnier, G., Gautrais, J., Theraulaz, G.: The Biological Principles of Swarm Intelligence. Swarm Intelligence 1, 3–31 (2007)
4. Jeanson, R., Ratnieks, F.L.W., Deneubourg, J.L.: Pheromone Trail Decay Rates on Different Substrates in the Pharaoh's Ant. Monomorium pharaonis, Physiological Entomology 28(3), 192–198 (2008)
5. Hölldobler, B., Morgan, E.D., Oldham, N.J., Liebig, J.: Recruitment Pheromone in the Harvester Ant Genus Pogonomyrmex. Journal of Insect Physiology 47(4-5), 369–374 (2001)
6. Robinson, E.H.J., Green, K.E., Jenner, E.A., Holcombe, M., Ratnieks, F.L.W.: Decay Rates of Attractive and Repellent Pheromones in an Ant Foraging Trail Network. Insectes Sociaux 55(1), 246–251 (2008)
7. Sillam-Dussès, D., Kalinová, B., Jiroš, P., Březinová, A., Cvačka, J., Hanus, R., Šobotník, J., Bordereau, C., Valterová, I.: Identification by GC-EAD of the Two-component Trail-following Pheromone of Prorhinotermes Simplex (Isoptera, Rhinotermitidae, Prorhinotermitinae). Journal of Insect Physiology 55(8), 751–757 (2009)
8. Jackson, D., Chaline, N.: Moduluation of Pheromone Trail Strength with Food Quality in Pharaon's Ant, Monomorium Pharaonis. Animal Behaviour 74(3), 463–470 (2007)
9. Tanackov, I., Simić, D., Mihaljev-Martinov, J., Stojić, G., Sremac, S.: The Spatial Pheromone Signal for Ant Colony Optimisation. In: Corchado, E., Yin, H. (eds.) IDEAL 2009. LNCS, vol. 5788, pp. 400–407. Springer, Heidelberg (2009)
10. Teodorović, D.: Swarm Intelligence Systems for Transportation Engineering: Principles and Applications. Transportation Research Part C: Emerging Technologies 16(6), 651–667 (2008)
11. Heegaard, E.P., Sandmann, W.: Ant-based Approach for Determining the Change of Measure in Importance Sampling. In: Henderson, S.G., Biller, B., Hsieh, M.-H., Shortle, J., Tew, J.D., Barton, R.R. (eds.) Proceedings of the 2007 Winter Simulation Conference, WSC 2007, pp. 412–420 (2007)
12. Chang, H.S., Gutjahr, J.W., Yang, J., Park, S.: An Ant System Approach to Markov Decision Processes. In: Proceeding of the American Control Conference 2004, Boston, Massachusetts (2005)
13. Badr, A., Fahmy, A.: A Proof of Convergence for Ant Algorithms. Information Sciences 160(1-4), 267–279 (2004)
14. Chuntonov, K., Setina, J.: New Lithium Gas Sorbents: I. The evaporable variant. Journal of Alloys and Compounds 455(1-2), 489–496 (2008)
15. Li, M., Rouaud, O., Poncelet, D.: Microencapsulation by solvent evaporation: State of the Art for Process Engineering Approaches. International Journal of Pharmaceutics 363(1-2), 26–39 (2008)
16. Yuan, C., Lei, T., Mao, L., Liu, H., Wu, Y.: Soil Surface Evaporation Processes Under Mulches of Different Sized Gravel. CATENA 78(2), 117–121 (2009)
17. John, A., Schadschneider, A., Chowdhury, D., Nishinari, K.: Characteristics of Ant-inspired Traffic Flow. Swarm Intelligence 2, 25–41 (2008)

A Parametric Method Applied to Phase Recovery from a Fringe Pattern Based on a Particle Swarm Optimization

J.F. Jimenez[1], F.J. Cuevas[2], J.H. Sossa[1], and L.E. Gomez[1]

[1] Centro de Investigación en Computación-IPN, Unidad Profesional Adolfo-López Mateos,
Av. Juan de Dios Bátiz s/n and M. Othón de Mendizábal, Zacatenco, México,
DF. 07738, Mexico
[2] Centro de Investigaciones en Óptica A.C. Loma del Bosque #115, Col. Lomas del Campestre
C.P. 37150, León Gto. México
{jfvielma,fjcuevas}@cio.mx, hsossa@cic.ipn.mx,
sgomezb08@sagitario.cic.ipn.mx

Abstract. A parametric method to carry out fringe pattern demodulation by means of a particle swarm optimization is presented. The phase is approximated by the parametric estimation of an nth-grade polynomial so that no further unwrapping is required. On the other hand, a different parametric function can be chosen according to the prior knowledge of the phase behavior. A particle swarm is codified with the parameters of the function that estimates the phase. A fitness function is established to evaluate the particles, which considers: (a) the closeness between the observed fringes and the recovered fringes, (b) the phase smoothness, (c) the prior knowledge of the object as its shape and size. The swarm of particles evolves until a fitness average threshold is obtained. The method was able to successfully demodulate noisy fringe patterns and even a one-image closed-fringe pattern.

Keywords: Phase retrieval; Fringe analysis; Optical metrology; Particle Swarm Optimization.

1 Introduction

In optical metrology, a fringe pattern (interferogram) can be represented using the following mathematical expression:

$$I(x, y) = a(x, y) + b(x, y) \times \cos(\omega_x x + \omega_y y + \phi(x, y) + n(x, y)) \qquad (1)$$

where x, y are integer values representing indexes of the pixel location in the fringe image, $a(x,y)$ is the background illumination, $b(x,y)$ is the amplitude modulation and is $\phi(x, y)$ the phase term related to the physical quantity being measured. ω_x and ω_y are the angular carrier frequency in directions x and y. The term $n(x, y)$ is an additive phase noise. The purpose of any interferometric technique is to determine the phase term, which is related to the physical quantity, being measured. One way to calculate the phase term $\phi(x, y)$ is by using the phase-shifting technique (PST)

M. Graña Romay et al. (Eds.): HAIS 2010, Part I, LNAI 6076, pp. 40–47, 2010.

[1–5], which needs at least three phase-shifted interferograms. The phase shift among interferograms must be known and experimentally controlled. This technique can be used when mechanical conditions are met throughout the interferometric experiment.

On the other hand, when the stability conditions mentioned are not covered, many techniques to estimate the phase term from a single fringe pattern have been reported. Among them, the Fourier method [6,7], the Synchronous method [8] and the phase locked loop method (PLL) [9]. However, these techniques work well only if the analyzed interferogram has a carrier frequency, a narrow bandwidth and the signal has low noise. Moreover, these methods fail for phase calculation of a closed-fringe pattern. Additionally, the Fourier and Synchronous methods estimate the phase wrapped because of the arctangent function used in the phase calculation, so an additional unwrapping process is required. The unwrapping process is difficult when the fringe pattern includes high amplitude noise, which causes differences greater than 2π radians between adjacent pixels [10–12].

Recently, regularization [13–15] and neural networks techniques [16,17] have been used to work with fringe patterns, which contain a narrow bandwidth and noise.

In this work, we propose a technique to determine the phase $\phi(x, y)$, from a fringe pattern with a narrow bandwidth and/or noise, by parametric estimation of a global non-linear function instead of local planes in each site (x,y) as it was proposed in [13,18]. A particle swarm optimization (PSO) [19–21] is used to fit the best non-linear function to the phase from the full image not a small neighbourhood as in regularization techniques. PSO was selected to optimize the cost function instead of gradient descent technique since non-convergence problems are presented when it is used in a non-linear function fitting. Also PSO strategy reduces the possibility of falling in a local optimum. When a noisy closed fringe pattern is demodulated, neither a low-pass filter nor a thresholoding operator is required. On the other hand, regularization techniques need both of them.

2 PSO Applied to Phase Recovery

As described by Eberhart and Kennedy, PSO is an adaptive algorithm based on a social-psychological metaphor; a population of individuals (referred to as particles) adapts by returning stochastically toward previously successful regions.

The fringe demodulation problem is difficult to solve when the level of noise affecting the fringe pattern is elevated, since many solutions are possible even for a single noiseless fringe pattern. Besides, the complexity of the problem is increased when a carrier frequency does not exist (closed fringes are presented).

Given that for a closed fringe interferogram there are multiple phase functions for the same pattern, the problem is stated as an ill-posed problem in the Hadamard sense, since a unique solution cannot be obtained [22]. It is clear that image of a fringe pattern $I(x, y)$ will not change if $\phi(x, y)$ in Eq. (1) is replaced with another phase function $\hat{\phi}(x, y)$ given by

$$\hat{\phi}(x, y) = \begin{cases} -\phi(x, y) + 2\pi & (x, y) \in R, \\ \phi(x, y) & (x, y) \notin R \end{cases} \tag{2}$$

where R is an arbitrary region and k is an integer. In this work, a PSO is presented to carry out the optimization process, where a parametric estimation of a non-linear function is proposed to fit the phase of a fringe pattern. Then, the PSO technique fits a global non-linear function instead of a local plane to each pixel just like it is made with regularization techniques [13,18]. The fitting function is chosen depending on the prior knowledge of the demodulation problem as object shape, carrier frequency, pupil size, etc. When no prior information about the shape of $\phi(x, y)$ is known, a polynomial fitting is recommended. In this paper, authors have used a polynomial fitting to show how the method works.

The purpose in any application of PSO is to evolve a particle swarm of size P (which codifies P possible solutions to the problem) using update velocity and position of each particle, with the goal of optimizing a fitness function adequate to the problem to solve.

In this work, the fitness function U , which is used to evaluate the pth particle a^p in the swarm, is given by

$$U\left(a^p\right) = \alpha - \sum_{y=1}^{R-1} \sum_{x=1}^{C-1} \left\{ \left(I_N\left(x, y\right) - \cos\left(\omega_x x + \omega_y y + f\left(a^p, x, y\right)\right)\right)^2 \right.$$
$$+ \lambda \left[\left(f\left(a^p, x, y\right) - f\left(a^p, x-1, y\right)\right)^2 \right. \tag{3}$$
$$\left. \left. + \left(f\left(a^p, x, y\right) - f\left(a^p, x, y-1\right)\right)^2 \right] \right\} m\left(x, y\right),$$

where x, y are integer values representing indexes of the pixel location in the fringe image. Superindex p is an integer index value between 1 and P , which indicates the number of chromosome in the population. $I_N\left(x, y\right)$ is the normalized version of the detected irradiance at point $\left(x, y\right)$. The data were normalized in the range $[-1, 1]$. ω_x and ω_y are the angular carrier frequencies in directions x and y . Function $f(\cdot)$ is the selected fitting function to carry out the phase approximation. $R \times C$ is the image resolution where fringe intensity values are known and λ is a smoothness weight factor (it should be clear for the reader that a higher value of parameter λ implies a smoother function to be fitted). The binary mask $m(x, y)$ is a field which defines the valid area in the fringe pattern. The parameter a can be set to the maximum value of the second term (in negative sum term) at Eq. (3) in the first chromosome population, which is given by

$$\alpha = \max_p \left\{ \sum_{y=1}^{R-1} \sum_{x=1}^{C-1} \left\{ \left(I_N\left(x, y\right) - \cos\left(\omega_x x + \omega_y y + f\left(a^p, x, y\right)\right)\right)^2 \right. \right.$$
$$+ \lambda \left[\left(f\left(a^p, x, y\right) - f\left(a^p, x-1, y\right)\right)^2 \right. \tag{4}$$
$$\left. \left. \left. + \left(f\left(a^p, x, y\right) - f\left(a^p, x, y-1\right)\right)^2 \right] \right\} m\left(x, y\right),$$

parameter α is used to convert the proposal from minimal to maximal optimization since a fitness function in a PSO is considered to be a nonnegative figure of merit and profit [19].

The first term (in negative sum term) at Eq. (3) attempts to keep the local fringe model close to the observed irradiances in least-squares sense. The second term (in negative sum term) at Eq. (3) is a local discrete difference, which enforces the assumption of smoothness and continuity of the detected phase.

2.1 Particles

At the beginning of a PSO, a set of random solutions are codified in a particle swarm of size P. Each particle a is formed by the parameter function vector (possible solution) and chained string such as:

$$a = \left[a_0 | a_1 | a_2 | ... | a_n \right] \tag{5}$$

Each dimension a_i is a random real number in a defined search range $\left(\min(a_i), \max(a_i) \right)$ (the user defined maximum and minimum of a_i). These values can be initialized using prior knowledge (e.g. in the polynomial case, components x and y are related to the interferogram tilt so if a closed fringe is presented, then these values are near 0). Every dimension is generated as:

$$a_i = random(\min(a_i), \max(a_i)) \tag{6}$$

The next iterations of particles, positions and velocities are adjusted, and the function is evaluated with the new coordinates at each time-step.

2.2 Particle Velocity and Position Update

During each generation each particle is accelerated toward the particle's previous best position and the global best position. At each iteration, a new velocity value for each particle is calculated based on its current velocity, the distance from its previous best position, and the distance from the global best position. The new velocity value is then used to calculate the next position of the particle in the search space. This process is then iterated a number of times or until a minimum error is achieved.

In the inertia version of the algorithm an inertia weight, reduced linearly each generation, is multiplied by the current velocity and the other two components are weighted randomly to produce a new velocity value for this particle, this in turn affects the next position of the particle during the next generation. Thus, the governing equations are:

$$v_{id}(t+1) = \omega \cdot v_{id} + c_1 \cdot \varphi_1 \cdot \left(P_{lid} - a_{id}(t) \right) + c_2 \cdot \varphi_2 \cdot \left(P_{gd} - a_{id}(t) \right) \tag{7}$$

$$a_{id}(t+1) = a_{id}(t) + v_{id}(t+1) \tag{8}$$

where a_i is particle i's position vector, v_i is particle i's velocity vector, c_1 and c_2 are positive constants, are called acceleration coefficients, φ_1 and φ_2 are random positive numbers between 0 and 1. Some researchers have found out that setting c_1 and c_2 equal to 2 gets the best overall performance, where as ω is called inertia weight. P_l is the local best solution found so far by the i-th particle, while P_g represents the positional coordinates of the fittest particle found so far in the entire community. Once the iterations are terminated, most of the particles are expected to converge to a small radius surrounding the global optima of the search space.

2.3 PSO Convergence

The PSO convergence mainly depends on the population size. It should be clear that if we increase the population size, more chromosomes will search the global optimum and a best solution will be found in a minor number of iterations, although the processing time can be increased [19,20]. A good rule of thumb for swarm size is to choose as large a population size as computer system limitations and time constraints allow.

To stop the PSO process, different convergence measures can be employed. In this paper, we have used a relative comparison between the fitness function value of the *gbest* particle in the swarm and value a, which is the maximum possible value to get in Eq. (3). Then, we can establish a relative evaluation of uncertainty to stop the PSO as:

$$\left| \frac{\alpha - U(a^*)}{\alpha} \right| \leq \varepsilon, \tag{9}$$

where $U(a^*)$ is the fitness function value of the *gbest* particle a in the swarm in the current iteration, and ε is the relative error tolerance. Additionally, we can stop the process in a specified number of iterations, if Eq. (9) is not satisfied.

3 Experiment

The PSO based parametric method was applied to calculate phase from three different kinds of fringe patterns: shadow moiré closed fringe pattern. We used a particles swarm size equal to 100, inertia a number in the range $[0.1, 0.9]$, velocity a number in the range $[0.0001, 0.0009]$. In each particle, the coded coefficients of a fourth degree polynomial were included. The following polynomial was coded in each particle:

$$\begin{aligned} p_4(x, y) = a_0 + a_1 x + a_2 y + a_3 x^2 + a_4 xy + a_5 y^2 + a_6 x^3 + a_7 x^2 y + a_9 xy^2 \\ + a_9 y^3 + a_{10} x^4 + a_{11} x^3 y + a_{12} x^2 y^2 + a_{13} xy^3 + a_{14} y^4 \end{aligned} \tag{10}$$

so that 15 coefficients were configured in each particle inside swarm to be evolved.

3.1 Close Fringe Pattern

A low contrasted noisy closed fringe pattern was generated in the computer using the following expression:

$$I(x, y) = 127 + 63\cos(P_4(x, y) + \eta(x, y)), \tag{11}$$

where

$$
\begin{aligned}
p_4(x, y) = &-0.7316x - 0.2801y + 0.0065x^2 + 0.00036xy - 0.0372y^2 \\
&+ 0.00212x^3 + 0.000272x^2y + 0.001xy^2 - 0.002y^3 \\
&+ 0.000012x^4 + 0.00015x^3y + 0.00023x^2y^2 + 0.00011xy^3 \\
&+ 0.000086y^4
\end{aligned}
\tag{12}
$$

and $\eta(x, y)$ is the uniform additive noise in the range $\left[- 2radians, 2radians\right]$. Additionally, the fringe pattern was generated with a low resolution of 60×60. In this case, we used a parameter search range of $\left[- 1,1\right]$. The swarm of particles was evolved until the number of iterations and relative error tolerance ε was 0.05 in Eq. (9). This condition was achieved in 60s on a AMD Phemon X4-2.5 GHz computer. The fringe pattern and the contour phase field of the computer generated interferogram are shown in Fig. 1.

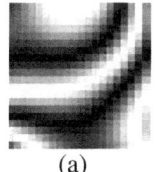  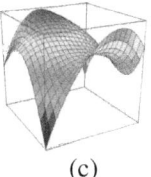

(a)   (b)   (c)

Fig. 1. (a) Original fringe pattern, (b) phase field obtained by using PSO technique and (c) phase obtained in 3D

The PSO technique was used to recover the phase from the fringe pattern. The fringe pattern and the phase estimated by PSO is shown in Fig. 1. The normalized RMS error was 0.12 radians and the peak-to-valley error was 0.94 radians. Tests are shown on Table 1, the best particle for the testers is shown on Table 2.

Table 1. Table of inertia and velocity parameters

	0.1	0.2	0.3	0.4	0.5	0.6	0.7	0.8	0.9
0.0001	2.870	3.432	3.612	3.505	3.839	3.277	2.916	2.777	2.395
0.0002	3.007	3.044	3.210	3.083	2.725	2.680	1.688	1.801	2.366
0.0003	1.665	1.875	2.565	2.559	1.576	1.708	**1.151**	1.945	2.469
0.0004	2.17	**1.738**	2.777	1.912	**1.290**	2.171	1.806	**0.567**	1.946
0.0005	1.883	1.860	2.838	1.686	1.701	2.063	1.969	0.791	1.792
0.0006	2.106	2.134	2.900	**1.086**	2.318	1.705	1.645	1.399	2.343
0.0007	1.928	1.993	**0.853**	1.168	2.019	2.270	1.772	1.428	1.828
0.0008	**0.893**	1.938	1.350	1.531	2.019	2.632	1.373	1.373	2.260
0.0009	1.536	1.911	1.436	1.773	2.407	**0.313**	1.902	0.779	**1.523**

Table 2. Patterns corresponding to the best particles

Inertia	0.1	0.2	0.3	0.4	0.5	0.6	0.7	0.8	0.9
Velocity	0.0008	0.0004	0.0007	0.0006	0.0004	0.0009	0.0003	0.0004	0.0009

4 Conclusions

A PSO based technique was applied to recover the modulating phase from closed and noisy fringe patterns. A fitness function, which considers the prior knowledge of the object being tested, is established to approximate the phase data. In this work a fourth degree polynomial was used to fit the phase.

A swarm of particles was generated to carry out the optimization process. Each particle was formed by a codified string of polynomial coefficients. Then, the swarm of particles was evolved using velocity, position and inertial.

The proposal works successfully where other techniques fail (Synchronous and Fourier methods). This is the case when a noisy, wide bandwidth and/or closed fringe pattern is demodulated. Regularization techniques can be used in these cases but the proposal has the advantage that the cost function does not depend upon the existence of derivatives and restrictive requirements of continuity (gradient descent methods). Since PSO works with a swarm of possible solutions instead of a single solution, it avoids falling in a local optimum. Additionally, no filters and no thresholding operators were required, in contrast with the fringe-follower regularized phase tracker technique.

PSO has the advantage that if the user knows prior knowledge of the object shape, then a better suited fitting parametric function can be used instead of a general polynomial function. Additionally, due to the fact that the PSO technique gets the parameters of the fitting function, it can be used to interpolate sub-pixel values and to increase the original phase resolution or interpolate where fringes do not exist or are not valid. A drawback is the selection of the optimal initial PSO parameters (such as swarm size, inertial, velocity) that can increase the convergence speed.

Acknowledgements. We wish to thank the Centro de Investigación en Computación of the I.P.N. by the support to accomplish this project as well as the Centro de Investigaciones en Optica during image recollections and tests. J. Vielma thanks CONACYT by the scholarship received to complete his doctoral studies. H. Sossa thanks the SIP-IPN under grant 20091421 for the support. H. Sossa also thanks CINVESTAV-GDL for the support to do a sabbatical stay from December 1, 2009 to May 31, 2010. Authors thank the European Union, the European Commission and CONACYT for the economical support. This paper has been prepared by economical support of the European Commission under grant FONCICYT 93829. The content of this paper is an exclusive responsibility of the CIC-IPN and it cannot be considered that it reflects the position of the European Union. Finally, authors thank the reviewers for their comments for the improvement of this paper.

References

[1] Martín, F., et al.: New advances in Automatic Reading of VLP's. In: Proc. SPC 2000 (IASTED), Marbella, España, pp. 126–131 (2000)
[2] Malacara, D., Servin, M., Malacara, Z.: Interferogram Analysis for Optical Testing. Marcel Dekker, New York (1998)
[3] Malacara, D.: Optical Shop Testing. Wiley, New York (1992)
[4] Creath, K.: In: Wolf, E. (ed.) Progress in Optics, vol. 26, p. 350. Elsevier, Amsterdam (1988)
[5] Creath, K.: In: Robinson, D., Reid, G.T. (eds.) Interferogram Analysis, p. 94. IOP Publishing, London (1993)
[6] Takeda, M., Ina, H., Kobayashi, S.: Fourier–transform method of fringe-pattern analysis for computer-based topography and interferometry. Journal of Optical Soc. of America 72, 156–160 (1981)
[7] Su, X., Chen, W.: Fourier transform profilometry: a review. Optics and Lasers in Engineering 35(5), 263–284 (2001)
[8] Womack, K.H.: Interferometric phase measurement using spatial synchronous detection. Opt. Eng. 23, 391–395 (1984)
[9] Servin, M., Rodriguez-Vera, R.: Two dimensional phase locked loop demodulation of interferograms. Journal of Modern Opt. 40, 2087–2094 (1993a)
[10] Ghiglia, D.C., Romero, L.A.: Robust two-dimensional weighted and unweighted phase unwrapping that uses fast transforms and iterative methods. J. Opt. Soc. Am. A 11, 107–117 (1994)
[11] Su, X., Xue, L.: Phase unwrapping algorithm based on fringe frequency analysis in Fourier-transform profilometry. Opt. Eng. 40, 637–643 (2001)
[12] Servin, M., Cuevas, F.J., Malacara, D., Marroquin, J.L., Rodriguez-Vera, R.: Phase unwrapping through demodulation by use of the regularized phase-tracking technique. Appl. Optics 38(10), 1934–1941 (1999)
[13] Servin, M., Marroquin, J.L., Cuevas, F.J.: Demodulation of a single interferogram by use of a two-dimensional regularized phase-tracking technique. Appl. Opt. 36, 4540–4548 (1997)
[14] Villa, J., Servin, M.: Robust profilometer for the measurement of 3-D object shapes based on a regularized phase tracker. Opt. Lasers Eng. 31, 279–288 (1999)
[15] Quiroga, J.A., Gonzalez-Cano, A.: With a Regularized Phase-Tracking Technique. Applied Optics 39(17), 2931–2940 (2000)
[16] Cuevas, F.J., Servin, M., Stavroudis, O.N., Rodriguez-Vera, R.: Multi-Layer neural network applied to phase and depth recovery from fringe patterns. Opt. Comm. 181, 239–259 (2000)
[17] Cuevas, F.J., Servin, M., Rodriguez-Vera, R.: Depth object recovery using radial Basis Functions. Opt. Comm. 163, 270 (1999)
[18] Servin, M., Marroquin, J.L., Cuevas, F.J.: J. Opt. Soc. Am. A 18, 689 (2001)
[19] Kennedy, J., Eberhart, R.C.: Particle Swarm Optimization. In: Proc. IEEE Int. Conf. on Neural Networks, Perth, pp. 1942–1948 (1995a)
[20] Kennedy, J.: The particle swarm: social adaptation of knowledge. In: IEEE International Conference on Evolutionary Computation, April 13-16, pp. 303–308 (1997)
[21] Kennedy, J., Spears, W.M.: Matching Algorithms to Problems: An Experimental Test of the Particle Swarm and Some Genetic Algorithms on the Multimodal Problem Generator. In: Proceedings of the IEEE Int'l Conference on Evolutionary Computation, pp. 39–43 (1998)
[22] Hadamard, J.: Sur les problems aux derivees partielles et leur signification physique, p. 13. Princeton University Bulletin, Princeton (1902)

Automatic PSO-Based Deformable Structures Markerless Tracking in Laparoscopic Cholecystectomy

Haroun Djaghloul, Mohammed Batouche, and Jean-Pierre Jessel

Ferhat Abbes University, Setif, Algeria
Haroun.Djaghloul@irit.fr
King Saoud University, Kingdom of Saudi Arabia
batouche@ccis.edu.sa
IRIT, Paul Sabatier University, Toulouse, France
jessel@irit.fr

Abstract. An automatic and markerless tracking method of deformable structures (digestive organs) during laparoscopic cholecystectomy intervention that uses the (PSO) behaviour and the preoperative a priori knowledge is presented. The associated shape to the global best particles of the population determines a coarse representation of the targeted organ (the gallbladder) in monocular laparoscopic colored images. The swarm behaviour is directed by a new fitness function to be optimized to improve the detection and tracking performance. The function is defined by a linear combination of two terms, namely, the human a priori knowledge term (H) and the particle's density term (D). Under the limits of standard (PSO) characteristics, experimental results on both synthetic and real data show the effectiveness and robustness of our method. Indeed, it outperforms existing methods without need of explicit initialization (such as active contours, deformable models and Gradient Vector Flow) on accuracy and convergence rate.

Keywords: Markerless tracking, Minimally Invasive Surgery, Image-guided Surgery, Evolutionary algorithms and Swarm Intelligence.

1 Introduction

Real objects tracking is an important and a very challenging research area within the field of Computer Vision. It is defined as the problem of detecting an object in the image plane and estimating its trajectory as it moves around a scene providing some of its centric information [1]. Markerless tracking task aims to recognize and track real environment without using any kind of markers.

In minimally-invasive surgery, objects tracking plays a vital role for example in computer-aided surgery and augmented reality systems. Indeed, augmented reality allows to view in transparency patient anatomical and pathological structures reconstructed preoperatively using medical images in the laparoscopic filed of view [2,3,4,5].

M. Graña Romay et al. (Eds.): HAIS 2010, Part I, LNAI 6076, pp. 48–55, 2010.

Laparoscopic cholecystectomy is actually the gold standard technique with more than 98% of all gallbladders that can be removed laparoscopically when following the described standard technique[6]. However, there is no complete medical augmented reality system that has been proposed with automatic and markerless tracking of anatomical structures and surgical instruments in the context of laparoscopic cholecystectomy.

In this study, we are interested in deformable structures tracking, mainly the gallbladder, during the laparoscopic cholecystectomy intervention. Because of the high-dimensionality problem and the complexity of anatomical structures, we use particles swarm optimization (PSO). In particular, the associated shape to the global best particles of the population determines a coarse representation of the targeted organ in laparoscopic images.

Here, a new fitness function is proposed to direct the swarm behavior and improve the detection and tracking performance. The function is defined by a linear combination of two terms, namely, the human a priori knowledge term (H) and the particle's density term (D). The a priori knowledge term best models knowledge about the targeted structure either using directly 2D sectional pre-operative medical images (CT-Scan) without 3D reconstruction or the surgery team experience. The density term makes the particle's shape as close as possible to the gallbladder image and reduces enormously sensitivity to noise although the scattered and sparse character of segmented regions.

In Section II, we provide the mathematical formula and necessary background of the proposed method to detect and track digestive organs without using markers. In Section III, we present experimental results and a comparison with some other methods that illustrate the effectiveness and performance of this method. In the last section, we present our conclusions.

2   Proposed Method

First,a statistical color model of digestive organs and surgical instruments is constructed using professional video images. Then, each organ is manually segmented and its RGB bins frequencies are stored. We call this model, the Anatomical Color Model (ACM). Also, the probability of each organ is stored in other model called the Anatomical Spatial Model (ASM). Using these two models, a preliminary pixel-wise segmentation of digestive organs is performed producing a binary image for each anatomical structure. Then, the behavior of particles swarm optimization (PSO) is used to automatically detect and track the gallbladder though the sparsity and dispersion of segmented regions in the previous step. The a priori knowledge of anatomical structures is modeled directly in the fitness function.

2.1   Pixel-Based Laparoscopic Image Segmentation

We propose to first detect digestive organs (mainly the gallbladder) using the ranking selection method which consists in an image binarization using the probabilities of the top-valued RGB bins in each anatomical color model. In laparoscopic complex scenes, this leads to many scattered regions.

2.2 PSO-Based Anatomical Structures Detection

The classical PSO (Particles Swarm Optimization) is a global search strategy for optimization problems[7]. The first version is proposed by Kennedy and Eberhart in 1995 and it is based on the social evolution simulation of an arbitrary swarm of particles based on the rules of Newtonian physic. Assuming that we have an N-dimensional problem, the basic PSO algorithm is formulated by position $x_m(t)$ and velocity $v_m(t)$ vectors representing the time evolution of (M) particles with random affected initial positions. Hence, we have:

$$x_m(t) = [x_{m_1}(t)\, x_{m_2}(t) \dots x_{m_N}(t)]^T \tag{1}$$
$$v_m(t) = [v_{m_1}(t)\, v_{m_2}(t) \dots v_{m_N}(t)]^T \tag{2}$$

In the classical and basic (PSO) version, The evolution of the swarm particles is done according to the following equations:

$$v_m(t+1) = f_{m_i}\, v_m(t) + f_{m_c}\, [D_c]_N\, (x_m(t_c) - v_m(t))$$
$$+ f_{m_s}\, [D_s]_N\, (x_{opt}(t_s) - v_m(t)) \tag{3}$$

Thus, the new position of the particle (m) is given by:

$$x_m(t+1) = x_m(t) + v_m(t+1) \tag{4}$$

Where $v_m(t)$ and $v_m(t+1)$ are, respectively, the past and the new velocity vectors of the particle (m). (f_{m_i}) is the inertia factor of the particle (m), (f_{m_c}) is its cognitive factor and (f_{m_s}) is the social factor. $[D_c]_N$ and $[D_s]_N$ are the N-dimensional diagonal matrices composed of statistically independent normalized random variables uniformly distributed between 0 and 1. (t_c) is the iteration where the particle (m) has reached its best position given by $(\hat{x}_m)$. (t_s) is the iteration where the population has found its best global value given by the coordinates of the particle (x_{opt}). It is obvious that each particle reaches its best local value before that the population elects the global best. Usually, the (PSO) algorithm is used in multi-dimensional optimization problems. In our work, we use it for detecting and tracking the gallbladder into the video-based laparoscopic cholecystectomy intervention images by minimizing the distance between the previous knowledge of its corporal surface in the 2D image plane and the density of each particle after thresholding using the (ACM). First, the greatest inner bounding disk (IBD) of each organ, mainly that of the gallbladder, is determined in the 2D UV space of the image by optimization of the following proposed criterion:

$$F_{Intra} = \beta * |1 - H| + (1 - \beta) * |1 - D| \,;\, \beta \in [0, 1] \tag{5}$$

with

$$H = \frac{\alpha}{\sum_{i,j} I_b(x)}, \tag{6}$$

and

$$D = \frac{\sum_{i,j} I_b(x)}{x_r^2},\qquad(7)$$

Where (H) denotes the impact of the priori-anatomical knowledge factor (α) and (D) the density of the (IBD) according to the count of the classified pixels and its geometric surface $(\pi * x_r^2)$ where (x_r) is its radius.

2.3 Modeling Priori Knowledge

In order to model the priori knowledge (α) associated to each organ, we propose three methods. The first and direct method consists in allowing the user to fix its value manually. This method is valuable only if the surgeon has a good experience.

Another way to determine (α) consists in building an anatomical spatial 2D model (ASM) for each organ using previous interventions videos from the largest number of different patients. This method needs to segment each organ in laparoscopic videos either manually or semi-automatically. Then, we compare segmented organ to the binary image constructed using the anatomical color model (ACM). Then, the coefficient α is computed for each organ by the sum of the Hadamard product between the two images:

$$\alpha = \sum_{i,j} (I_{statistical} \circ I_{patient}),\qquad(8)$$

The third method is based on returned information from reconstructed virtual model of the patient. However, this method needs to know a subset of camera intrinsic parameters to ensure best results. First, we suppose that a surfacic 3D model of the gallbladder is reconstructed from medical images such as ultrasound, MRI or CT-Scan. Knowing the distance between the end point of the laparoscope (L_∞) and the gallbladder surface center (G_∞) and if the gallbladder optimal plane is totally visible in the laparoscopic view, a good approximation of the priori knowledge factor (α) is given by the half of the model area in metric space (Ω_{gal}) divided by the area of elementary surface projected into one pixel (ω):

$$\alpha = \frac{\Omega_{gal}}{2 * \omega} + \epsilon,\qquad(9)$$

with,

$$\omega = \left| \overrightarrow{L_\infty G_\infty} \right| \frac{\Omega_{pixel}}{f},\qquad(10)$$

where (Ω_{pixel}) is the area of laparoscopic camera square pixel and (f) is the focal length. For simplification, we assume that $\epsilon = 0$. If the virtual gallbladder is modeled by a set of polygons P_i, we have:

$$\Omega_{gal} = \sum_i \Omega_{P_i},\qquad(11)$$

By combining "Eq. (10)" and "Eq. (11)" in "Eq. (9)", α is given so that:

$$\alpha = \frac{f * \sum_i \Omega_{P_i}}{2 * \left| \overrightarrow{L_\infty G_\infty} \right| * \Omega_{pixel}}, \tag{12}$$

Assuming that each polygon P_i is so small to cover a surfacic unity (one millimeter), we have:

$$\alpha = \frac{f}{2 * \rho^2 * \left| \overrightarrow{L_\infty G_\infty} \right|} * \nu, \tag{13}$$

where ν represents the number of polygons at millimetric precision. ρ^2 is the area of assumed squared-pixel of laparoscopic camera and it is supposed to be constant intra-operatively. According to "Eq. (13)", the parameter that changes during the intervention is $\left| \overrightarrow{L_\infty G_\infty} \right|$ because of cardio-respiratory activity and surgical instruments interaction. However, the intervention protocol states to maintain a constant distance between the end of the laparoscope and the target organ (gallbladder). Therefore, we propose to consider it as constant or that it is computed using other tracking methods such as electro-magnetic or optical systems. If medical images (MRI, CT-Scan or echography) exist with millimetric precision, the parameter ν is computed as the length of the segmented gallbladder contour in the preoperative slides. Supposing that for each preoperative image (i), the gallbladder contour length is given by (γ_i). Then, "Eq. (13)" becomes:

$$\alpha = \frac{f}{2 * \rho^2 * \left| \overrightarrow{L_\infty G_\infty} \right|} * \Gamma, \tag{14}$$

with

$$\Gamma = \sum_i \gamma_i, \tag{15}$$

If we suppose the existence of a 2D Inner Bounding Disk (IBD) with a perimeter as the contour of the gallbladder (γ_i) in the slide (i). Then:

$$\gamma_i = 2 * \pi * r_i, \tag{16}$$

Assuming that there is (n) slides that cover the targeted organ and by replacing (γ_i) in "Eq. (15)" from "Eq. (16)", we have:

$$\Gamma = 2 * n * \pi * \sum_{i=1}^{n} r_i, \tag{17}$$

By replacing (Γ) from "Eq. (17)" in "Eq. (14)", we get:

$$\alpha = \frac{n * \pi * f}{\rho^2 * \left| \overrightarrow{L_\infty G_\infty} \right|} * \sum_{i=1}^{n} r_i, \tag{18}$$

By putting

$$v = \frac{n * \pi * f}{\rho^2 * \left| \overrightarrow{L_\infty G_\infty} \right|}, \tag{19}$$

and

$$P = \sum_{i=1}^{n} r_i, \tag{20}$$

Then, α is given by:

$$\alpha = v * P \tag{21}$$

3   Experimental Results and Discussion

In order to validate the proposed method, we applied it on different medical images modalities (laparoscopic, CT-Scan or MRI). In our experiments we have used a particles population with an initial size of ($N_{pop} = 30$) particles and the tracking process is executed over fifty generations ($N_{Iter} = 50$). The global and local social parameters are constants and equal ($f_{m_c} = 0.4$, $f_{m_s} = 0.4$). The synthetic images are binary or grayscale images drawn by hand and are similar to real ones so that the same anatomical and spatial distributions of real organs into laparoscopic images are considered. In the figure (Fig.1 (a)) a synthetic binary image representing the gallbladder with the gbest particle ($m(N_{iter} = 50)$). In (Fig.1 (b)), the evolution of the gbest particle over time (swarm generations) showing the effectiveness of the optimization (F_{intra}).

The comparative study shows that the proposed method outperforms other segmentation and tracking methods (such as traditional active contour models [8], balloon-based [9] and gradient vector flow based deformable models[10]) on accuracy and convergence speed (Fig.2) without need of explicit initialization.

In (Fig.3), the method is applied to intra-operative laparoscopic image.

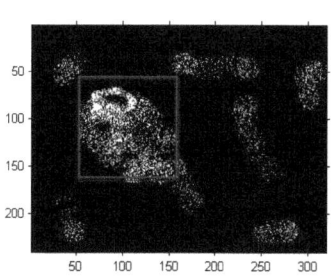

(a) Synthetic gallbladder Detection

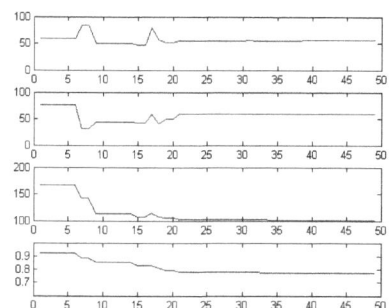

(b) Best Particle Evolution

Fig. 1. Tracking of synthetic gallbladder

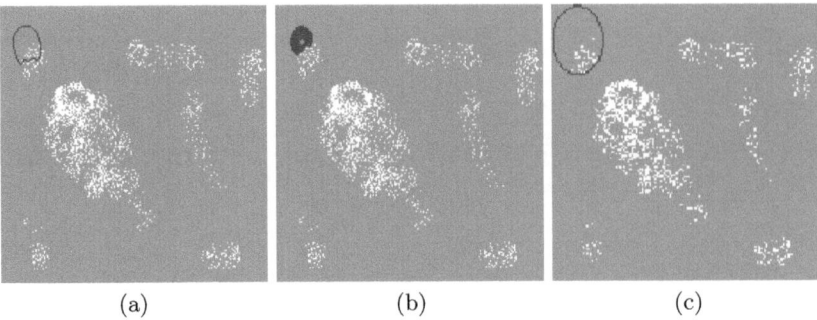

Fig. 2. Results of active contours and deformable models : (a) traditional active contour (snake); (b) balloon model; (c) Gradient Vector Flow

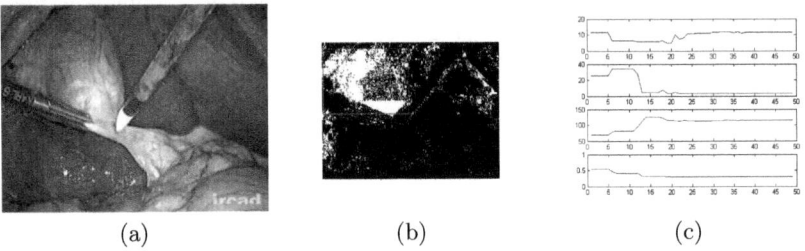

Fig. 3. PSO-based gallbladder tracking in a real laparoscopic image (IRCAD source): (a) original image; (b) PSO Tracking; (c) gbest evolution

4   Conclusion

In this paper we have presented a new multi-modal method for automatic detection and markerless tracking of the gallbladder during the laparoscopic cholecystectomy intervention. A new fitness function is proposed to direct the particles behavior for the detection and the tracking tasks of deformable structures during laparoscopic cholecystectomy intervention without using of any kind of markers or fiducials. Although, under standard PSO method limits, experiments show the effectiveness and the robustness of the proposed method for gallbladder detection and tracking in various modalities. It outperforms active contours and deformable models on accuracy and convergence speed.

References

1. Yilmaz, A., Javed, O., Shah, M.: Object tracking: A survey. ACM Computing Surveys (CSUR) 38(4), 13 (2006)
2. Soler, L., Nicolau, S., Fasquel, J.B., Agnus, V., Charnoz, A., Hostettler, A., Moreau, J., Forest, C., Mutter, D., Marescaux, J.: Virtual reality and augmented reality applied to laparoscopic and notes procedures. In: ISBI, pp. 1399–1402 (2008)

3. Nicolau, S., Pennec, X., Soler, L., Buy, X., Gangi, A., Ayache, N., Marescaux, J.: An augmented reality system for liver thermal ablation: Design and evaluation on clinical cases. Medical Image Analysis 13(3), 494–506 (2009)
4. Feuerstein, M., Mussack, T., Heining, S., Navab, N.: Intraoperative laparoscope augmentation for port placement and resection planning in minimally invasive liver resection. IEEE Transactions on Medical Imaging 27(3), 355 (2008)
5. Sugimoto, M., Yasuda, H., Koda, K., Suzuki, M., Yamazaki, M., Tezuka, T., Kosugi, C., Higuchi, R., Watayo, Y., Yagawa, Y., et al.: Image overlay navigation by markerless surface registration in gastrointestinal, hepatobiliary and pancreatic surgery. Journal of hepato-biliary-pancreatic surgery (2009)
6. Bittner, R.: The standard of laparoscopic cholecystectomy. Langenbeck's Archives of Surgery 389(3), 157–163 (2004)
7. Kennedy, J., Eberhart, R., et al.: Particle swarm optimization. In: Proceedings of IEEE International Conference on Neural Networks, vol. 4, pp. 1942–1948. IEEE, Piscataway (1995)
8. Kass, M., Witkin, A., Terzopoulos, D.: Snakes: Active contour models. International Journal of Computer Vision 1(4), 321–331 (1988)
9. Cohen, L.D.: On active contour models and balloons. CVGIP: Image Understanding 53(2), 211–218 (1991)
10. Xu, C., Prince, J.L.: Snakes, shapes, and gradient vector flow. IEEE Transactions on Image Processing 7(3), 359–369 (1998)

A Framework for Optimization of Genetic Programming Evolved Classifier Expressions Using Particle Swarm Optimization

Hajira Jabeen and Abdul Rauf Baig

National University of Computer and Emerging Sciences,
H-11/4, Islamabad, Pakistan
{hajira.jabeen,rauf.baig}@nu.edu.pk

Abstract. Genetic Programming has emerged as an efficient algorithm for classification. It offers several prominent features like transparency, flexibility and efficient data modeling ability. However, GP requires long training times and suffers from increase in average population size during evolution. The aim of this paper is to introduce a framework to increase the accuracy of classifiers by performing a PSO based optimization approach. The proposed hybrid framework has been found efficient in increasing the accuracy of classifiers (expressed in the form of binary expression trees) in comparatively lesser number of function evaluations. The technique has been tested using five datasets from the UCI ML repository and found efficient.

Keywords: Classifier Optimization, Data Classification, Genetic Programming, Particle Swarm Optimization.

1 Introduction

The potential of GP to efficiently handle the task of data classification has been recognized since its inception [1]. GP has been used for classification in several different ways. It enjoys an outstanding position amongst other classifier evolution techniques like Genetic Algorithms [2]. The GP based classifier evolution has certain advantages over other techniques. The GP evolved classifiers are transparent and comprehensible. The size and constituent elements of a GP tree are not fixed, which offers a flexible search space to probe for the best classification rule. GP is readily applicable to the data in its original form and no transformation of data is required. GP can eliminate attributes unnecessary for classification task, discarding the need of any explicit feature extraction algorithm.

In addition to above mentioned benefits, GP has a well known drawback of increase in population complexity during evolution. In case of classifier evolution one is always interested in evolving simple and comprehensible classifiers because larger trees tend to over fit the training data. On the other hand complex population adds more computation time. These factors raise the need of reducing the computation yet maintain the benefits of flexible classification methodology.

M. Graña Romay et al. (Eds.): HAIS 2010, Part I, LNAI 6076, pp. 56–63, 2010.

In this paper we have proposed a method to optimize the classifier expressions using Particle Swarm Optimization. The classifier expression is an arithmetic expression trained to output a positive real value for one class and negative real value for the other, in binary classification problems. This method has been extensively investigated in the literature [3-5] and found efficient for classification tasks. Our framework proposes addition of weights associated with all the attributes and constants (all leaf nodes) present in a classifier and optimize the values of these weights to achieve better classification accuracy.

The proposed method is efficient in terms of classification accuracy and lesser number of function calls. The proposed framework:-

- Uses a new hybrid classification methodology
- Avoid bloat by limiting the generations for evolution
- Achieve compatible classification results

After a brief introduction in Section 1, Section 2 discusses work relevant to GP based classification and different optimization techniques in GP. Section 3 presents and explains the work done by authors. Obtained results are organized and discussed in Section 4. Section 5 concludes the findings and future work is discussed.

2 Literature Review

GP has been an area of interest for various researchers during the previous years. It had been applied to solve various problems, one of those being data classification. Several methods have been proposed to tackle data classification using GP. They can be broadly categorized into three different types. The first is evolution of classification algorithms using GP. This includes simple algorithms like decision trees which[6,7], or complex algorithms like neural networks [8-10], autonomous systems [11], rule induction algorithms [12], fuzzy rule based systems and fuzzy Petri nets [13], [10]. In the second method GP is used to evolve classification rules[14-18]. The rule based systems include, atomic representations proposed by Eggermont [19] and SQL based representations proposed by Freitas [20]. Tunsel [21], Berlanga [22] and Mendes [23] introduced evolution of fuzzy classification rules using GP. The third method is evolution of discriminating classification expressions. Arithmetic expressions use (real or integer value) attributes of data as variables in the expressions and output a real value that is mapped to class decision. For multiclass problems the real output of expressions are applied thresholds. The methods include static thresholds [24], [25], dynamic thresholds [26], [25] and slotted thresholds [3]. Another method for multiclass classification is binary decomposition or one versus all method. In this method N classifiers are evolved for N class classification problem. Where, each classifier is trained to recognize samples belonging to one class and reject samples belonging to all other classes. Binary decomposition methods have been explored in [4], [5].

Particle Swarm Optimization algorithm has been originally formulated by Kennedy and Eberhart in 1995 [27]. It is efficient at solving optimization problems by modeling the sociological principle of animal groupings during their movements. The algorithm usually operates upon set of real multidimensional points scattered in the search space. These points move with certain velocity in the search space, mimicking bird's flight in search of optimal solution. The velocity of a particle in a given iteration is a function of the velocity of the previous step, its previous best position and the global best position. The algorithm has been compared with various evolutionary algorithms and found efficient in terms of faster convergence. Following are the update equations for particles in standard PSO.

$$V_{i+1} = \omega V_i + C_0 rand(0,1)(X_{lbest} - X_i) + C_1 rand(0,1)(X_{gbest} - X_i) \qquad (1)$$

$$X_{i+1} = X_i + V_i \qquad (2)$$

Where X_{gbest} is the global best or local best particle and X_{pbest} is the personal best of each particle. The values C_0 and C_1 are problem specific constants.

The Equation (1) is used to update velocity of a particle and Equation (2) is used to update the position of a particle during the PSO evolution process.

GP is a very efficient innovative technique to handle to problem of data classification but it suffers from inefficient code growth (bloat) during evolution. This increases the program complexity during the evolution process without effective increase in fitness. Another issue with GP based classification is long training time, which increases many folds with the increase in average tree size during evolution. In this paper we have proposed a method that eliminates the need of evolving GP for longer number of generations and optimizes the GP evolved intelligent structures using PSO.

3 Proposed Framework

Figure 1 shows the overview of proposed hybrid framework for classification. The first step of proposed technique is to evolve classifier expressions using GP. A classifier is an arithmetic expression trained to output a positive real value for one class and

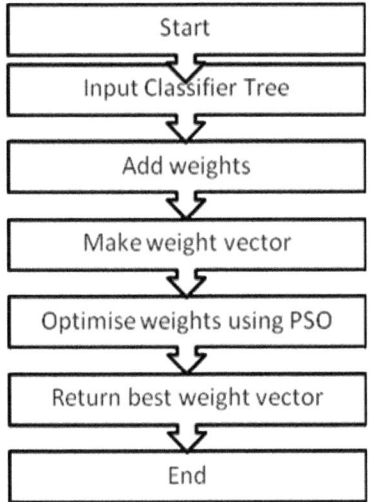

Fig. 1. Expression optimization algorithm

negative real value for the other. In order to clearly portray the efficiency of our proposed hybrid classification technique we have limited our investigation to binary classification problems in this paper.

The classification algorithm is explained as follows:-

```
Step 1. Begin
Step 2. Initialize generations to user defined value
Step 3. Select one class as 'desired' and other 'not
        desired' class
Step 4. Initialize GP-ACE population using ramped half and
        half method
Step 5. While (gen <= generations or Fit_g= 100 )
        a.  Evaluate fitness(accuracy) of each member in
            population
        b.  Find best in population and update P_Best
        c.  Fit_g=fitness(P_Best)
        d.  Perform evolutionary operators
        e.  gen = gen + 1;
Step 6. End while
Step 7. Output P_Best as classifier
Step 8. End
```

The output of above mentioned classification algorithm is a best arithmetic expression where the *fitness* of the expression is its classification accuracy.

The next step is to add weights along all the terminals present in the expression. For example consider an expression $(A_1+A_2)/A_3$ where A_1, A_2, and A_3 are attribute 1, 2 and 3 respectively. This tree will become $[(A_1*W_1) + (A_2*W_2)] / (A_3*W_3)$, after weight addition, where W_1, W_2 and W_3 are weights associated to each terminal. The weight chromosome for this tree will be $[W_1, W_2, W_3]$. Let t be the number of terminals in the classifier expression then the weight vector for it will be :-

$$[W_j] \text{ where } j=1:t \tag{3}$$

This process increases the complexity of the ACE by increasing its depth by '1'. If the number of terminals present in the tree is equal to 't' then the increase in number of nodes in tuned tree is $2't$ where t nodes are function nodes having value '*' and 't' nodes are terminal nodes having weights as their values. This method scales the input of each terminal according to its weight. Let old terminal be T_o and new terminal be T_n, then the value of new terminal would be interpreted as

$$T_{nj}=W_j*T_{oj} \text{ where } j=1:t \tag{4}$$

For the sake of optimization, a population of random weight particles is initialized. These weights are assigned random values between -1 and 1. This creates a multidimensional point in hyper space that has as many dimensions as there are weights in a GP chromosome corresponding to each terminal. PSO is used to evolve these weights for optimal values. The *fitness* of each particle is calculated by putting the values of weights in their corresponding positions and evaluating the accuracy of classifier for training data. We have used cognitive-social model that keeps track of previous best as well as the global best particle. These weight particles are evolved for optimal value for a few generations until termination criteria is fulfilled.

4 Results

The data sets used to test the proposed classification framework are taken from UCI repository. These data sets are Bupa liver disorder, Haberman's survival, Parkinson disease, Pima indians diabetes and Wisconsin breast cancer. All these datasets are real valued data sets with varying number of classes and attributes. This is to prove the effectiveness of the proposed algorithm.

Each tree in the GP evolved classifier chromosome is appended by weights at its terminals, and the weights are evolved using PSO. The results reported in this section have been averaged after tenfold cross validation. PSO has been applied ten times on each single classifier. So the results reported with PSO are averaged for 100 executions on ten different classifier expressions.

Table 1. GP Parameters

S.No	Name	Value
1	Population size	600
2	Generations	120
3	Maximum Depth	5
4	Function set	+ , - , * , / (protected division)
5	Terminal set	Attributes of data, Ephemeral constants

Table 1 lists the GP parameters used for the experimentation. Table 2 lists the parameters used for PSO. The results reported after tuning are averaged for 10 executions of PSO.

Table 2. PSO parameters

S.No	Name	Value
1	No of particles	20
2	Initial value range	[+1 , -1]
3	Number of iterations	30
4	C_1, C_2	1.49
5	W	0.7

4.1 Fitness versus Average Population Size

This is evident from various literature instances that the average population size increases during the GP evolution. In this section we have made a comparison of increase in average number of nodes in population versus average fitness of the population. This comparison has been made to show the effectiveness of proposed methodology that stops the evolutionary process earlier and increases its performance in lesser number of function evaluations. This "less" function evaluations also corresponds to the "simpler" function evaluations when keeping in mind, the graph shown below.

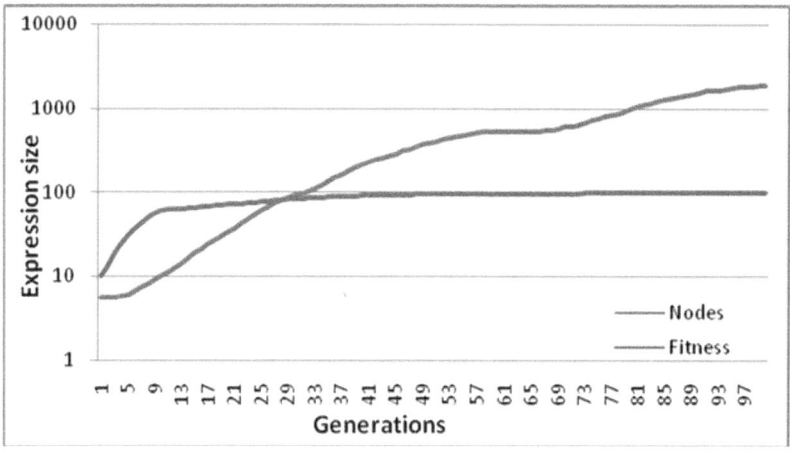

Fig. 2. Increase in expression size during evolution

4.2 Optimization Result

Table 3 presents elementary testing accuracy, after GP evolution, and accuracy achieved after PSO based optimization. We can see that PSO based optimization process has efficiently increased the accuracy of classifier expressions in considerably lesser number of function evaluations. For example in case of Bupa data the accuracy achieved by PSO is 72.38% by optimizing a classifier having 69.25% accuracy. While noting this less number of function evaluations this should also be kept in mind that more number of function evaluations in GP also corresponds to *'more complex"* evaluations due to bloat. Similar trend can be observed in other data sets as well.

Table 3. Increase in accuracy after optimization

Gen#	BUPA		HABER		PARKINSON		PIMA		WBC	
	GP	PSO	GP	PSO	GP	PSO	GP	PSO	GP	PSO
50	68.94%	**72.06%**	77.63%	**82.12%**	79.24%	**83.16%**	66.22%	**68.49%**	94.81%	**96.84%**
100	69.25%	**72.38%**	79.36%	**82.44%**	84.34%	**87.71%**	66.89%	**70.5%**	95.52%	**97.37%**

5 Conclusions

In this paper we have proposed a framework for the optimization of classifier expressions evolved by GP, it has been shown that this method tends to increase the training as well as testing accuracy of the classifiers. This method can eliminate the need for evolving GP classifiers for longer number of generations in search of better accuracy. It also helps in reducing the number of function evaluations desired for GP evolution. The more number of generations in GP also means increase in GP tree sizes over generation, making the task more complex. On the other hand, in case of PSO based optimization we can get better results in much lesser number of function evaluations at the expense of increase in depth of trees by only one level. This increase in tree complexity gives an attractive reward of increase in corresponding accuracy. Future work includes determination of optimal parameters for PSO for tuning and use of different variants of PSO for tuning.

Acknowledgements

The author Hajira Jabeen would like to acknowledge Higher Education Commission, Pakistan for providing the funding and resources for this work.

References

[1] Koza, J.R.: Genetic Programming: On the Programming of Computers by Means of Natural Selection. MIT Press, Cambridge (1992)
[2] Flockhart, I.W., Radcliffe, N.J.: GA-MINER: Parallel Data Mining with Hierarchical Genetic Algorithms. University of Edinburgh, Edinburgh (1995)
[3] Smart, W., Zhang, M.: Multiclass Object Classification using Genetic Programming. LNCS, pp. 367–376. Springer, Heidelberg (2004)
[4] Kishore, J.K., et al.: Application of Genetic Programming for Multicategory Pattern Classification. IEEE Transactions on Eolutionary Computation (2000)
[5] Bojarczuk, C.C., Lopes, H.S., Freitas, A.A.: Genetic Programming for Knowledge Discovery in Chest-Pain Giagnosis. IEEE Engineering in Medicine and Biology Magazine, 38–44 (2000)
[6] Koza, J.R.: Concept formation and decision tree induction using the genetic programming paradigm. In: Schwefel, H.-P., Männer, R. (eds.) PPSN 1990. LNCS, vol. 496, pp. 124–128. Springer, Heidelberg (1991)
[7] Li, Q., et al.: Dynamic Split-Point Selection Method for Decision Tree Evolved by Gene Expression Programming. In: IEEE Congress on Evolutionary Computation. IEEE Press, Los Alamitos (2009)
[8] Rivero, D., Rabunal, J.R., Pazos, A.: Modifying Genetic Programming for Artificial Neural Network Development for Data Mining. Soft Computing 13, 291–305 (2008)
[9] Ritchie, M.D., et al.: Genetic programming Neural Networks: A powerful bioinformatics tool for human genetics. Applied Soft Computing, 471–479 (2007)
[10] Tsakonas, A.: A comparison of classification accuracy of four genetic programming-evolved intelligent structures. Information Sciences, 691–724 (2006)
[11] Oltean, M., Diosan, L.: An Autonomous GP-based System for Regression and Classification Problems. Applied Soft Computing 9, 49–60 (2009)
[12] Pappa, G.A., Freitas, A.A.: Evolving Rule Induction Algorithms with Multiobjective Grammer based Genetic Programming. Knowledge and Information Systems (2008)
[13] Eggermont, J.: Evolving Fuzzy Decision Trees for Data Classification. In: Proceedings of the 14th Belgium Netherlands Artificial Intelligence Conference (2002)
[14] Konig, R., Johansson, U., Niklasson, L.: Genetic Programming - A Tool for Flexible Rule Extraction. In: IEEE Congress on Evolutionary Computation (2007)
[15] Engelbrecht, A.P., Schoeman, L., Rouwhorst, S.: A Building Block Approach to Genetic Programming for Rule Discovery. In: Abbass, H.A., Sarkar, R., Newton, C. (eds.) Data Mining, pp. 175–189. Idea Group Publishing (2001)

[16] Carreno, E., Leguizamon, G., Wagner, N.: Evolution of Classification Rules for Comprehensible Knowledge Discovery. In: IEEE Congress on Evolutionary Computation, pp. 1261–1268 (2007)

[17] Freitas, A.A.: A Genetic Programming Framework For Two Data Mining Tasks: Classification And Generalized Rule Induction. In: Genetic Programming, pp. 96–101. Morgan Kaufmann, CA (1997)

[18] Kuo, C.S., Hong, T.P., Chen, C.L.: Applying genetic programming technique in classification trees. Soft Computing 11, 1165–1172 (2007)

[19] Eggermont, J., Eiben, A.E., Hemert, J.I.: A comparison of genetic programming variants for data classification. In: Proceedings of the Eleventh Belgium Netherlands Conference on Artificial Intelligence, pp. 253–254 (1999)

[20] Eggermont, J., Kok, J.N., Kosters, W.A.: GP For Data Classification, Partitioning The Search Space. In: Proceedings of the 2004 Symposium on Applied Computing, pp. 1001–1005 (2004)

[21] Tunstel, E., Jamshidi, M.: On Genetic Programming of Fuzzy Rule-Based Systems for Intelligent Control. International Journal of Intelligent Automation and Soft Computing, 273–284 (1996)

[22] Berlanga, F.J., et al.: A Genetic-Programming-Based Approach for the Learning of Compact Fuzzy Rule-Based Classification Systems. In: Rutkowski, L., Tadeusiewicz, R., Zadeh, L.A., Żurada, J.M., et al. (eds.) ICAISC 2006. LNCS (LNAI), vol. 4029, pp. 182–191. Springer, Heidelberg (2006)

[23] Mendes, R.R.F., et al.: Discovering Fuzzy Classification Rules with Genetic Programming and Co-Evolution. In: Siebes, A., De Raedt, L., et al. (eds.) PKDD 2001. LNCS (LNAI), vol. 2168, pp. 314–325. Springer, Heidelberg (2001)

[24] Zhang, M., Ciesielski, V.: Genetic Programming For Multiple Class object Detection. In: Proceedings of the 12th Australian Joint Conference on Artificial Intelligence, Australia, pp. 180–192 (1999)

[25] Parrott, D., Li, X., Ciesielski, V.: Multi-objective techniques in genetic programming for evolving classifiers. In: IEEE Congress on Evolutionary Computation, pp. 183–190 (2005)

[26] Smart, W.R., Zhang, M.: Classification Strategies for Image Classification in Genetic Programming. In: Proceeding of Image and Vision Computing NZ International Conference, pp. 402–407 (2003)

[27] Kennedy, J., Eberhart, R.C.: Particle Swarm Optimization. In: IEEE International Conference on Neural Networks, pp. 1942–1948 (1995)

Developing an Intelligent Parking Management Application Based on Multi-agent Systems and Semantic Web Technologies

Andrés Muñoz and Juan A. Botía

Department of Information and Communications Engineering at University of Murcia
30100, Murcia, Spain
amunoz@um.es, juanbot@um.es

Abstract. Multi-agent systems (MAS) are being adopted in multiple areas to deal with knowledge-based applications. On the other hand, Semantic Web technologies such as OWL and SWRL have shown to be useful in managing knowledge and reasoning about it. This paper proposes an architecture based on these technologies to develop an intelligent parking management application, where agents interact to reach a consensus about the assignment of a parking area to a vehicle. Moreover, this paper tackles the inherent problem related to the rise of conflicts in MAS by means of the integration of an argumentation system called ASBO (which is part of our previous work) into the proposed architecture.

1 Introduction

The use of multi-agent systems (MAS) has demonstrated to be a natural and efficient means to deal with complex situations in distributed environments. Particularly, the situation studied in this paper is focused on developing a parking management application using agents to manage the distribution of knowledge and reach a consensus about the assignment of a parking area to a vehicle. To this end, the agents exchange proposals along with their justifications to support or oppose a specific parking area assignation. In order to be able to process this knowledge, the agents must share a common description of the domain where they are situated. Semantic Web technologies [1] are an attractive approach to model these common descriptions through ontologies and automatically execute reasoning processes over the resulting knowledge models.

The goal of this paper is to apply an architecture based on these technologies to the development of a MAS which solves the problem of assigning parking areas in an automatic and intelligent manner, by exploiting the knowledge acquired by the agents. Moreover, the rise of conflicts of knowledge –i.e. inconsistencies among the beliefs of agents– must be also taken into account when agents share their local points of view. In order to cope with conflicts of knowledge, this architecture is extended with the use of *argumentation* [8] to rationally evaluate justifications (i.e., arguments) over conflicting proposals and determine which one is the most plausible. For this purpose we utilize ASBO (Argumentation System Based on Ontologies) [6], an argumentation system developed in our previous work, which has been integrated into the proposed architecture with the aim of providing agents with argumentative capabilities.

M. Graña Romay et al. (Eds.): HAIS 2010, Part I, LNAI 6076, pp. 64–72, 2010.

Knowledge management in MAS based on the combination of argumentation and Semantic Web technologies is a recent approach. The main research line resides in detecting and resolving inconsistences among the concept and relationship descriptions of the different ontologies employed by the agents [4,2]. However, our approach is centered on assuming these concepts and relationships as the shared and accepted description model of a domain, whereas the instantiations of these elements are distributed among the agents as local pieces of knowledge. Contrarily to the shared description model, the local knowledge of each agent and the facts inferred from it are not necessarily accepted by the rest of agents. Thus, conflicts may arise among agents when they exchange their local assertions about the domain. As a result, we offer an alternative through ASBO to solve the inconsistences posed by these conflicting assertions.

The rest of this paper is structured as follows. Section 2 starts with a brief review of the most relevant Semantic Web technologies and then it introduces the proposed architecture based on these technologies to manage knowledge in MAS. In Section 3 an informal description of ASBO is given, whereas Section 4 shows the development of the parking management application through the integration of our architecture with ASBO. Finally, Section 5 summarizes the contribution of this paper.

2 An Architecture Based on Semantic Web Technologies to Manage Knowledge in MAS

The acquisition and management of knowledge by means of ontologies has been extensively tackled in the Semantic Web. One of its most prominent results is OWL [9], a standard language to model ontologies in a formal manner. Usually, OWL ontologies are divided into two disjoint sets: *TBox* and *ABox*. The former represents the scheme of the domain being modeled, and it consists of (1) concepts, which denote a set of individuals with the same characteristics, (2) binary relationships among concepts, and (3) axioms that place constraints on the concepts and relationships. Hence, the TBox can be seen as the description model of a particular domain. On the other hand, the ABox contains a set of individuals and relationships among them (generally called *assertions*). It can be seen as an extension of the model given in the TBox which represents a specific situation in the domain by instantiating concepts and relationships. Observe that it is possible to create several ABox for the same TBox, thus representing different situations for the same domain model. The key features of OWL reside in its expressiveness and the use of axioms to provide the domain model with semantics. Such semantics allow applications to infer additional information, as explained in next paragraph. OWL expressiveness depends on the version employed. In particular, we adopt the version OWL-DL which inherits the features and semantics of Description Logic [3].

Due to the formal conceptualization of a domain provided by OWL-DL ontologies, several inference processes can be automatically performed over it. One of these processes is the entailment of new knowledge based on the semantics contained in axioms. More specifically, new assertions about an individual can be inferred from the existing information associated to it. For example, suppose that a concept C is a specialization of a concept D, stated as the axiom $C \sqsubseteq D$. Then, any individual of C is automatically inferred as an individual of D. Another inference process is the consistency checking of ontologies. This process consists in the detection of contradictions among the assertions in the ABox and violations of the restrictions specified in the axioms. For instance, suppose two concepts F, G which are described as disjoint by means of the appropriate axiom. Then, the assertions $F(i), G(i)$ stating the individual i as an instance of both concepts is a violation of the restriction given by the disjoint axiom.

Besides ontologies, modeling knowledge typically involves the definition of rules, which capture conditional statements, policies, behaviours, etc. The Semantic Web also offers an alternative to express rules by means of SWRL [5], a rule language which extends OWL to include Horn-like rules. SWRL rules are in the form of an implication between a conjunction of antecedents (*body*) and consequents (*head*), meaning that whenever the conditions specified in the antecedents hold, the conditions specified in the consequent must also hold. Both conjunctions consist of *atoms* of the form $C(x)$, $R(x, y)$, $sameAs(x, y)$ and $differentFrom(x, y)$, where C is an OWL concept, R is an OWL relationship and x, y are variables, instances from the ABox or data values.

SWRL rule-based engines allows deriving new knowledge from the assertions stated in ontologies. In particular, we are interested in deriving new knowledge through the execution of rules in a forward-chaining fashion. This type of execution consists in a recursive task of triggering those rules which antecedents are fulfilled, thus generating a set of conclusions, and then checking if more rules can be triggered due to the addition of these inferred conclusions. The execution stops when no more rules can be triggered. The knowledge used to evaluate rules and decide whether their antecedents are fulfilled or not stems from assertions in the ABox. Hence, the ABox can be seen as the input knowledge base for the rule-based inference process.

The combination of OWL-DL ontologies and SWRL rules offers an expressive model to capture knowledge in a wide range of domains. Here we propose an architecture based on this combination to manage knowledge in MAS as depicted in Figure 1. In the architecture there is available an OWL-DL ontology O representing a particular domain, which is imported by the agents. The TBox of O is seen as the vocabulary of the domain to be shared by all agents. In this manner, they can "speak" the same language using the TBox as the common description model of the domain. On the other hand, the ABox of O could be used in two directions with respect to this TBox. Firstly, an ABox

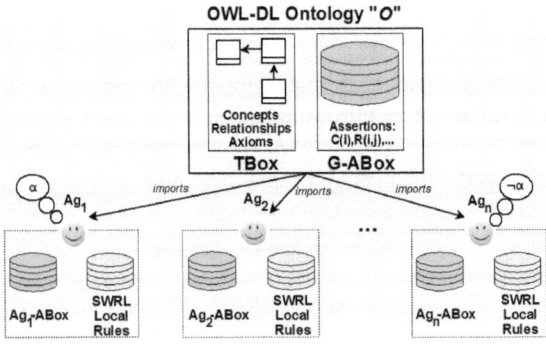

Fig. 1. An architecture based on Semantic Web technologies to manage knowledge

shared by all agents could contain assertions representing global knowledge in the MAS (*G-ABox* in Figure 1). It is seen as facts in the domain which are known and accepted by all agents. Secondly, each agent could have its own ABox containing local assertions to keep its particular (and incomplete) view of the state of affairs (Ag_i-*ABox* in Figure 1). Finally, each agent represents its expertise knowledge (e.g., policies) through a local set of SWRL rules defined with elements from O.

In this paper it is assumed that the knowledge in the G-ABox complements the local knowledge of each agent's Ag_i-ABox so as the union of the assertions of both knowledge bases is consistent. Additionally, it is also assumed that the knowledge inferred by an agent from this union and the execution of its local rules is consistent as well. However, this inferred knowledge could raise conflicts with the knowledge maintained by other agents in the MAS. An example of this kind of conflict is shown in Figure 1, where Ag_1 maintains the assertion α and Ag_n keeps the assertion $\neg\alpha$. The mechanism for solving these conflicts will be revised in the next section.

3   Solving Conflicts of Knowledge through ASBO

In the architecture proposed in Section 2 conflicts arise whenever an agent Ag_i proposes an assertion α to an agent Ag_j which maintains the assertion $\neg\alpha$, or when Ag_j maintains an assertion β and its union with α violates any restriction given by an axiom of the ontology O. In both cases, the consistency checking process performed by Ag_j ends with an invalid state. An alternative to solve these conflicts resides in integrating ASBO into the agents. ASBO is an argumentation system based on ontologies developed in our previous work, which main goal is to enable agents to automatically solve conflicts of knowledge by means of exchange of arguments in a dialectical fashion. Here an informal account of the argumentation process performed in ASBO is presented.

In the first place ASBO enables an agent to automatically build arguments for each assertion derived during the rule-based inference explained in Section 2. An argument in ASBO is defined as $\langle \phi, S \rangle$, where ϕ is the conclusion, i.e. the assertion being justified, and $S=(\Phi, r)$ is the support set of ϕ, i.e. a set of ABox assertions Φ and a SWRL rule r such as Φ is the minimal set that fulfills the atoms in the antecedent of r so as the atom in its consequent is instantiated to ϕ (we assume SWRL rules with only one atom in the consequent). Letters U and V denote ASBO arguments in the next paragraphs.

The structure of ASBO arguments is implemented by means of an OWL-DL ontology and shared by all agents. In this manner, agents can instantiate this structure to build an argument and communicate it to other agents. Moreover, an agent can process an argument sent by another agent in order to detect inconsistencies between their own knowledge and the conclusion or support set of such an argument. Then, this agent can build a counterargument to attack the received argument, which in turn can be attacked by another argument, etc. In ASBO an argument $U=\langle \phi, S_U \rangle$ can attack another argument $V=\langle \varphi, S_V \rangle$ by *rebutting* or *undercutting* it. In the first case, the union of their conclusions ϕ and φ produces an inconsistency in the agent's ABox. In the second case, the union of ϕ and one assertion of S_V produces the inconsistency.

Apart from the notion of attack between a pair of arguments, in ASBO is also defined a relationship of *defeat* to indicate if the attacked argument is invalidated by its counterargument. Thus, U defeats V in two manners. The first one occurs when U undercuts

V, since this attack invalidates a premise needed by V to support its conclusion. The second case happens when U rebuts V and besides (a) U is preferred to V according to some criteria and (b) V does not undercut U. It is possible to define several types of criteria to decide which argument is more plausible when they are rebutting each other. There are two criteria implemented in ASBO: *specificity* and *agent priorities*. The first one determines that $U=\langle\phi, S_U\rangle$ is preferable to $V=\langle\varphi, S_V\rangle$ when $\Phi_V \subset \Phi_U$, such as $\Phi_V \in S_V$ and $\Phi_U \in S_U$. In words, U is better informed than V since the set of assertions in S_U contains more information than the set of assertions in S_V. On the other hand, the agent priorities criterion establishes hierarchies between agents according to their expertise or responsibility on the assertions made about an ontology concept or relationship. For example, suppose that ϕ and φ are conflicting assertions about a concept C, and U, V have been generated by agents Ag_1 and Ag_2, respectively. Suppose also that C has associated an agent priorities criterion such as Ag_1 is higher than Ag_2 in the hierarchy. Then, U is preferable than V according to this criterion.

Finally notice that the defeat relationship is defined for two arguments solely. Since a counterargument can be defeated by another argument, it is also needed a procedure to establish the eventual status of each argument on the basis of all interactions among the arguments exchanged in a MAS. In ASBO we are interested in establishing the status of the arguments which support/oppose an assertion α to decide whether it is accepted or not. To this end, the status of such arguments is determined through the development of a persuasion dialog between two agents. This kind of dialog consists of a set of performatives and a protocol which regulates the exchange of assertions and arguments between a proponent (i.e., the agent proposing α) and an opponent (i.e, the agent attacking α) with the aim of convincing each other about accepting (or rejecting) α. The performatives given in ASBO allow agents to propose, challenge, accept and reject assertions and arguments, whereas the protocol dictates the rules of commencement, development and termination of persuasion dialogs. As the dialog progresses, the agents build a dialectical tree which gathers all the exchanged utterances and the interactions among arguments. When the dialog finishes, the tree is evaluated by means of an algorithm to obtain the status of the root, which contains the utterance proposing α. If the root is found to be accepted (*in*), the proponent wins the dialog and α is accepted, returning the arguments which support it. If the root is found to be not accepted (*out*), the opponent wins the dialog and α is not accepted. It is also possible to find the root as *undecided* when the status of the arguments supporting/attacking α cannot be determined. In this case, the acceptance of α is left as unknown.

The structure of ASBO arguments and formal definitions of their relationships of attack and defeat can be found elsewhere [6]. For a detailed specification of the persuasion dialog developed in ASBO the reader is referred to [7].

4   An Intelligent Parking Management Application

A real application has been developed through the combination of the architecture proposed in Section 2 and ASBO. Such an application is being developed as a part of the project "SEISCIENTOS" (see *http://www.grc.upv.es/600/*) and it consists in a parking management system (PMS) which aim is to control the access to the parking areas (PA) of the University of Murcia (UMU). The PMS architecture together with the decision process for assigning parking areas are explained here.

UMU parking areas are divided into *Priority-PA*, which are near the buildings but they have a small number of spaces; and *NoPriority-PA*, which have a large number of spaces but they are farther from the buildings. Priority-PA are reserved for vehicles considered as preferential by the PMS (*PriorityVcl* henceforth), which a priori are those owned by high-position UMU personnel (e.g., deans) and disabled people who are part of the staff. On the other hand, NoPriority-PA are used by vehicles considered as no preferential (*NoPriorityVcl* henceforth), which are those owned by the rest of UMU staff and visitors. These kinds of vehicles are labeled as "*UMU-NP*" and "*Visitor*", respectively. However, they could be classified as PriorityVcl if it is proved that either the driver is a visitor with a preferential parking profile (e.g., a visitor who owns a disability parking card) or she is a "UMU-NP" staff who has an imminent event according to her agenda (e.g., a researcher who has an important meeting with the UMU board members and she is late). The definitions of the different types of vehicles, PAs, profiles, etc. and their relationships are modeled using an OWL-DL ontology called "PMS Ontology".

The PMS architecture is depicted in Figure 2. This architecture is distributed in such a manner that the vehicles' information is separately managed from the PA's information. The former is processed by the VCL agent, which goal is to assign the nearest PA for each incoming vehicle. To this end, VCL uses the GPS data and the driver's profile provided by the vehicle's on-board computer. On the other hand, the PA's information is controlled by the PRK agent, which goal is to assign a PA to an incoming vehicle according to the priority levels of both elements. In this case, PRK maintains a database with the license plate numbers of the UMU staff vehicles and manages the state of the PAs (i.e., number of free spaces and priority level). Due to each agent may assign a different PA for the same vehicle according to their local knowledge and goals, they start a decision process in order to reach a consensus about the correspondent PA. Observe the use of both agents to manage the separation of knowledge and goals (expressed through rules) in the architecture. The next paragraphs explain the use of the PMS Ontology to enable the distribution of knowledge and the development of the decision process.

Regarding the distribution of knowledge, Figure 2 shows the disposal of the PMS Ontology where the TBox contains the vocabulary describing the types of vehicles, PAs, etc., which is shared by the VCL and PRK agents. Apart from the TBox, this

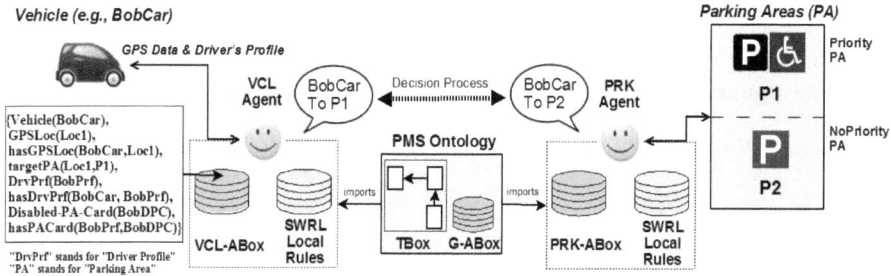

Fig. 2. Elements of the PMS distributed architecture

ontology contains a shared G-ABox populated with assertions representing the available PAs and the parking assignations already established. In relation to the agents, PRK maintains its local knowledge about PAs (i.e., number of free spaces and priority level) by means of assertions stated in the PRK-ABox with the shared vocabulary. Moreover, this agent employs the SWRL rules given below to allocate a vehicle in a PA according to the matching between their priorities (rules $R\_Priority$-PA and $R\_NoPriority$-PA) and to classify it as NoPriorityVcl (rule $R\_Visitor$, only the case for visitor vehicles is shown here). Note that the relationship $parking(?v, ?p)$ indicates that the vehicle $?v$ is assigned to the PA $?p$:

$R\_Priority$-PA : $PriorityVcl(?v) \wedge Priority$-$PA(?p) \Rightarrow parking(?v, ?p)$
$R\_NoPriority$-PA : $NoPriorityVcl(?v) \wedge NoPriority$-$PA(?p) \Rightarrow parking(?v, ?p)$
$R\_Visitor$: $Visitor(?v) \Rightarrow NoPriorityVlc(?v)$

Analogously, VCL manages the GPS data and driver's profile as local knowledge in the VCL-ABox, also expressed using the shared vocabulary given in the TBox. Likewise, this agent keeps the following rules to infer a parking access assignment according to the GPS location data (rule $R\_GPSParking$) and to classify a visitor vehicle as PriorityVcl when the driver owns a disabled parking card (rule $R\_Disabled$, where $DrvPrf$ stands for "Driver Profile"):

$R\_GPSParking$: $Vehicle(?v) \wedge GPSLoc(?g) \wedge PA(?p) \wedge hasGPSLoc(?v, ?g) \wedge$
$\wedge\, targetPA(?g, ?p) \Rightarrow parking(?v, ?p)$
$R\_Disabled$: $Visitor(?v) \wedge DrvPrf(?d) \wedge Disabled$-$PA$-$Card(?c) \wedge$
$\wedge\, hasDrvPrf(?v, ?d) \wedge hasPACard(?d, ?c) \Rightarrow PriorityVcl(?v)$

Let us now see the decision process to assign a PA to the incoming vehicle $BobCar$. To execute this process, VCL and PRK use an implementation of ASBO by means of a tool called ORE-AS (see *http://sourceforge.net/projects/ore-as/*) to exchange their proposals and arguments through a persuasion dialog as described in Section 3. Suppose for this scenario that the G-ABox contains the assertions $\{PA(P1), PA(P2)\}$ indicating the available PAs. Moreover, the PRK agent maintains the local assertions $\{Priority$-$PA(P1), NoPriority$-$PA(P2)\}$ in its PRK-ABox, as shown in Figure 2 (suppose that both PAs have free spaces). When $BobCar$ enters the UMU campus, it sends its GPS data ($Loc1$) and driver's profile ($BobPrf$, which has associated the disabled parking card $BobDPC$) to VCL. All this information is transformed to assertions in VCL-ABox (see list of assertions in Figure 2, on the left-hand side of VCL-ABox). VCL calculates $P1$ as the nearest PA according to the GPS data received (this fact is stated through the relationship $targetPA(Loc1, P1)$). Based on this GPS data, VCL generates the following argument for supporting $P1$ as the PA to be assigned to $BobCar$:

U_{VCL_1}=$[parking(BobCar, P1), (\{Vehicle(BobCar), GPSLoc(Loc1), PA(P1),$
$hasGPSLoc(BobCar, Loc1), targetPA(Loc1, P1)\},$
$R\_GPSParking)]$

Now, VCL starts the ASBO persuasion dialog by claiming $parking(BobCar, P1)$ (see Figure 3). Then, PRK asks for reasons about this proposal and VCL answers with argument U_{VCL_1}. After receiving this argument, PRK checks its vehicle license database and it discovers that $BobCar$ is a visitor vehicle. Using this information and

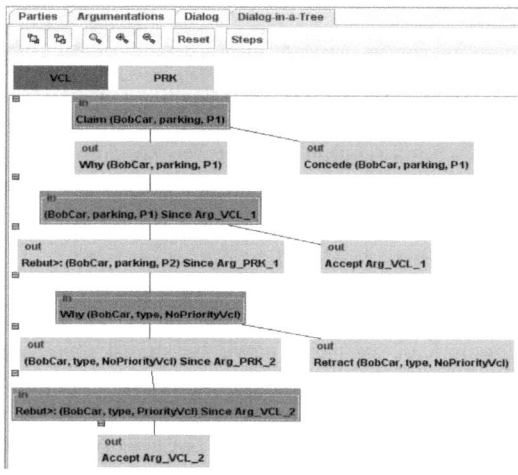

Fig. 3. Persuasion dialog between VCL and PRK about BobCar (ORE-AS snapshot)

rule $R\_Visitor$, PRK classifies $BobCar$ as a NoPriorityVcl (see argument U_{PRK_2} below). Such a classification leads PRK to build the argument U_{PRK_1} which concludes $parking(BobCar, P2)$ according to the priorities of both elements:

$U_{PRK_1}=[parking(BobCar,P2),\quad(\{NoPriorityVcl(BobCar),NoPriorityPA(P2)\},$
$\qquad\qquad\qquad\qquad R\_NoPriority\text{-}PA)]$
$U_{PRK_2}=[NoPriorityVcl(BobCar),(\{Visitor(BobCar)\},R\_Visitor)]$

PRK detects that U_{VCL_1} and U_{PRK_1} rebut each other, since the PMS Ontology states that the relationship $parking$ can only have one PA associated to the same vehicle. Moreover, this agent is the ultimate responsible for assigning PAs, which is represented by its rank being higher than VCL's rank in the agent priorities criterion about $parking$. As a result, U_{PRK_1} defeats U_{VCL_1}. PRK sends argument U_{PRK_1} to VCL, which computes the same defeating result among both arguments. Consequently, the only alternative for VCL to attack U_{PRK_1} is to undercut its support set. Then, this agent asks for reasons about the assertion $NoPriorityVcl(BobCar)$ in such a support set and PRK answers U_{PRK_2}. Thus, VCL agent discovers that $BobCar$ is a visitor vehicle from the support set of U_{PRK_2}. Using this information and the disabled parking card associated to the driver's profile, VLC builds the next argument:

$U_{VCL_2}=[PriorityVcl(BobCar),\{Visitor(BobCar),DrvPrf(BobPrf),Disabled\text{-}$
$\qquad\qquad PA\text{-}Card(BobDPC),hasDrvPrf(BobCar,BobPrf)$
$\qquad\qquad hasPACard(BobPrf,BobDPC)\},R\_Disabled)]$

In this case VCL detects that U_{VCL_2} and U_{PRK_2} rebut each other since $Priority\text{-}Vcl$ and $NoPriorityVcl$ are disjoint concepts in the PMS Ontology. Besides, U_{VCL_2} is more specific than U_{PRK_2} since its support set contains more information that U_{PRK_2}'s support set, and the agent priorities criterion is not applied here. Therefore, U_{VCL_2} defeats U_{PRK_2} and it also undercuts (and defeats) U_{PRK_1}. VCL sends U_{VCL_2} to PRK which computes the same defeating interactions with its own arguments. PRK does not find any assertion to attack in the support set of U_{VCL_2} (it checks that Bob's profile and his disabled parking card are authentic and valid) and it eventually accepts such an argument. As PRK does not have more arguments to support $NoPriorityVcl(BobCar)$, it retracts its proposals and accepts the VCL's initial claim $parking(BobCar, P1)$. As a result $BobCar$ is given authorization to enter $P1$. This persuasion dialog is entirely shown in Figure 3 through a snapshot of the implementation of ASBO in the agents.

5   Conclusions and Future Work

Multi-agent systems and Semantic Web technologies can be combined giving as a result an architecture to automatically manage knowledge in distributed environments. Since the appearance of conflicts is an inherent problem of such environments, we extend the resulting architecture with an argumentation system called ASBO which enables agents to rationally deal with conflicts. ASBO is part of our previous work and its features are informally introduced here. In this paper we exploit the integration of all these technologies to develop an intelligent parking management application. The next steps in this line are directed to develop new situations in the PMS, evaluate the performance of the proposed architecture in this application and extend its usage in other applications.

Acknowledgments. This work has been supported by the Research Projects TSI-020302-2009-43 and TIN2008-06441-C02-02 through the Fundación Séneca within the Program "Generación del Conocimiento Científico de Excelencia" (04552/GERM/06), Murcia, Spain, and by the Spanish Ministerio de Ciencia e Innovación under the FPU grant AP2006-4154.

References

1. Berners-Lee, T., Hendler, J., Lassila, O.: The Semantic Web. Scientific American 284(5), 34–43 (2001)
2. Black, E., Hunter, A., Pan, J.Z.: An Argument-Based Approach to Using Multiple Ontologies. In: Godo, L., Pugliese, A. (eds.) SUM 2009. LNCS, vol. 5785, pp. 68–79. Springer, Heidelberg (2009)
3. Baader, F., et al. (eds.): The Description Logic Handbook: Theory, Implementation, and Applications. Cambridge University Press, Cambridge (2003)
4. Gómez, S.A., Chesñevar, C.I., Simari, G.R.: Reasoning with Inconsistent Ontologies through Argumentation. Journal of Applied Artificial Intelligence 1(24), 102–148 (2009)
5. Horrocks, I., Patel-Schneider, P.F., Boley, H., Tabet, S., Grosof, B., Dean, M.: SWRL: A Semantic Web Rule Language combining OWL and RuleML. W3C Recommendation (2004)
6. Muñoz, A., Botía, J.A.: ASBO: Argumentation System Based on Ontologies. In: Klusch, M., Pěchouček, M., Polleres, A. (eds.) CIA 2008. LNCS (LNAI), vol. 5180, pp. 191–205. Springer, Heidelberg (2008)
7. Muñoz, A., Botía, J.A.: A Formal Model of Persuasion Dialogs for Interactions among Argumentative Software Agents. Journal of Physical Agents 3(3) (2009)
8. Rahwan, I., Simari, G. (eds.): Argumentation in Artificial Intelligence. Springer Series, New York (2009)
9. van Harmelen, F., McGuinness, D.L. (eds.): OWL Web Ontology Language Overview. World Wide Web Consortium (W3C) Recommendation (2004)

Linked Multicomponent Robotic Systems: Basic Assessment of Linking Element Dynamical Effect

Borja Fernandez-Gauna, Jose Manuel Lopez-Guede, and Ekaitz Zulueta

Computational Intelligence Group, Universidad del Pais Vasco
www.ehu.es/ccwintco

Abstract. The Linked Multicomponent Robotic Systems are characterized by the existence of a non-rigid linking element. This linking element can produce many dynamical effects that introduce perturbations of the basic system behavior, different from uncoupled systems. We show through a simulation of a distributed control of a hose tranportation system, that even a minimal dynamical feature of the hose (elastic forces opposing stretching) can produce significant behavior perturbations.

1 Introduction

Controlling wheeled mobile robots to follow a predefined path is a well-known problem that has been approached in a broad set of ways: smoothed bang-bang controllers [7], PID and adaptive controllers [5], fuzzy controllers [11,8], tracking-error model-based predictive controllers [6], or through dynamic feedback linearization [10]. Some authors have taken the path following problem one step further to that of keeping multi-robot formations along the path [13], but very little literature exists nowadays about the constraints imposed in physically linked multi-robot systems [3,14,2]. We assume as the cooperative control paradigm the works of [12], although for lack of space we will not be able to detail here our formulation of the distributed controller being simulated.

A Linked Multicomponent Robotic System (L-MCRS) [1] is a collection of robotic units coupled through a passive non-rigid element, such as a hose or a cable. It is our working hypohesis that this passive connection imposes dynamic contraints to the robot dynamics and transmits non-linear dynamical forces among robots. That means that definite effects can be observed that differentiate the L-MCRS from a collection of uncoupled robotic units. We assume as the problem paradigm the transportation of a hose. The basic question is: does the hose introduce any perturbation on the behavior of the system under the command of (distributed) controller? To show that the definitive answer is yes, we introduce the simplest dynamical effect of the hose: it behaves as a spring when it is streched longer than its nominal length. Simulations show this effect clearly.

This paper is organized as follows: in Section 2 we give the system definition, including the dynamical description and the two performance measures of the individual and overall system behavior, that will quantify the observed effects.

M. Graña Romay et al. (Eds.): HAIS 2010, Part I, LNAI 6076, pp. 73–79, 2010.

Section 3 gives some hints about the definition of the distributed control, which can not be given in full detail here. Section 4 shows the results of the conducted simulation experiments. Finally, some conclusions are given in Section 5.

2 System Definition

Consider the problem of an elastic hose fixed to some wheeled mobile robots that are moving following a known path so that there are L meters long hose segments between every pair of consecutive robots. To avoid the hose interfering the robots' motion, a L meters Euclidian distance between consecutive pairs of robots is desired. Our simulation will focus on the effects caused by elastic traction forces between robots that appear when the distance between consecutive robot units is larger than L, and how the whole system behavior is affected.

2.1 Definitions and Restrictions

The path followed by the robot units will be defined as a function of the travelled distance s:
$$\boldsymbol{H}(s) = (h^x(s), h^y(s))$$
The usual path tracking approach will be assumed: each robot will use a reference or virtual robot along the path and its controller will try to minimize the error between its position and the reference. The ith robot's bi-dimensional position will be denoted as $\boldsymbol{P_i} \equiv [P_i^x \; P_i^y]$, and the position of its reference will be derived from its position along the path (s_i) using the previously defined function: $\boldsymbol{H}(s_i)$.

We can then define $d(s, L)$ as the function that returns the minimum value greater than s that fullfills $|\boldsymbol{H}(s) - \boldsymbol{H}(d(s,L))| = L$. That is, the index along the path for the nearest point ahead that is L distant from $\boldsymbol{H}(s)$.

For a predefined path to be travelled keeping a fixed distance L between a pair of robots, a sufficient condition can be set: $d(s, L)$ must be a continuous monotically increasing function defined for every value of s.

For generalization purposes, we further define in a recursive manner:

$$e(s, L, i) \begin{cases} s & i = 0 \\ e(d(s, L), L, i - 1) & else \end{cases} \tag{1}$$

2.2 Dynamical Model

The most basic model of the effect of the linking element is to introduce an elastic traction force due to hose stretching. The robots are assumed to be powerful enough so that any other hose-related forces can be neglected. The elastic force acts when Euclidean distance among robots grows bigger than the nominal linking element size.

For the basic motion of the robots, a simple dynamic model can be used: $\dot{V}_i^y = \frac{F_i^x}{m}$ and $\dot{V}_i^y = \frac{F_i^y}{m}$, where m is the mass of the robots, V_i^x and V_j^y represent the components of the the ith vehicle's velocity vector, F_i^x and F_i^y represent the components of the force vector applied on the ith vehicle in the x and y axis by its locomotor system. The elastic traction force T_i between i^{th} and $(i+1)^{\text{th}}$ robots are modelled as a clamped spring neglecting compression forces. Therefore, the linking element has no effect if the Euclidean distance between two robots is less than L:

$$T_i^x = K \cdot \max(0, |\boldsymbol{P}_i - \boldsymbol{P}_{i+1}| - L) \cdot \cos(\beta_i),$$
$$T_i^y = K \cdot \max(0, |\boldsymbol{P}_i - \boldsymbol{P}_{i+1}| - L) \cdot \sin(\beta_i),$$

where K is the spring constant and β_i is the angle of the segment connecting the ith and $(i+1)^{\text{th}}$ robots relative to the x-axis. Including these terms into our dynamic model, we obtain:

$$\dot{V}_i^x = \frac{F_i^x - T_{i-1}^x + T_i^x}{m}, \tag{2}$$
$$\dot{V}_i^y = \frac{F_i^y - T_{i-1}^y + T_i^y}{m}.$$

The expected position for the ith robot can then be calculated as:

$$\dot{P}_i^x = V_i^x, \tag{3}$$
$$\dot{P}_i^y = V_i^y.$$

2.3   System Performance Measures

We need to define a system performance measurement-function so that we can compare the performance of the system with and without the hose dynamics. Two functions have been used to measure individual error:

Mean square Euclidian distance error between robots (e_i^{dis}):

$$e_i^{dis} = \frac{\int_0^t (|\boldsymbol{P}_i - \boldsymbol{P}_{i+1}| - L)^2}{t}$$

Mean square Euclidian distance error between robots and their desired position (e_i^{pos}):

$$e_i^{pos} = \frac{\int_0^t (|\boldsymbol{P}_i - \boldsymbol{H}(\boldsymbol{s_i})|)^2}{t}$$

Using these two functions, system error has been measured as the sum of the mean square deviations: $e^{dis} = \sum_{i=0}^{n-2} e_i^{dis}$ and $e^{pos} = \sum_{i=0}^{n-1} e_i^{ref}$.

3   Consensus-Based Control Approach

In[12] two basic consensus-based methodologies are described to approach distributed multi-vehicle cooperation problems: with and without an optimization objective. In the first case, an objective is desired to be optimally achieved while in the second, only cooperation among the individuals is desired. The first approach has been applied on the reference level, so that the references to be followed by the robots are controlled in a cooperative way. The essence of the methodology can be summarized in four steps: (a) defining the cooperation objective and constraints, (b) defining the coordination variables and coordination functions[9], (c) designing a centralized cooperation scheme and (d) building a consensus-based distributed cooperation scheme.

Two ways to represent the system state are proposed in [12]: as a group-level reference state or as individual local vehicle states. The first implies that individual control decisions can be derived from a group-level set of variables, while the second assumes that each individual acts according to the states of its neighbors. For the purposes of this work, the former can be used, denoting as ξ the base-position of the robot formation, this is, the desired position of the last robot. Using the previously defined function 1, the desired position for each robot can be expressed as $e(\xi, L, i)$, where i is the zero-based index of a robot in the formation.

Due to lack of space we can not describe in detail the cooperative control implemented in the simulation. It has been defined so as to minimize an objective function $J_{obj} = \sum_{i=0}^{n-1} J_{cf,i}$, defined in terms of local objective functions at each robot $J_{cf,i} = \int_0^t (s_i - e(\xi, L, i))^2 dt$, subject to the constraint $J_{const} = \sum_{i=0}^{n-2} |[H(s_i) - H(e(\xi, L, i))] - [H(s_{i+1}) - H(e(\xi, L, i+1))]|$. The minimization leads to a distributed control where each local control rule takes the form of a PID controller.

4   Simulation Experimental Results

Our goal is to measure the individual performance impact on linked MCRSs performance in comparison to non-linked MCRSs and, for that purpose, each of the simulated robots was assigned a maximum force output F_i^{max} and its output force vector was then clamped so that the individual performance could be individually affected. An experiment was conducted with 5 robots travelling along the path represented in figure 1 keeping a fixed separation of $L = 0.2m$ between every consecutive pairs. The system was first simulated including the hose dynamic model ($K^s = 40Nm$) and then without it ($K^s = 0Nm$), so the performance impact due to the physical link could be quantified. In the simulation experiment the last robot was made the weakest. $F_0^{max} = 2.5N$ and $F_1^{max} = F_2^{max} = F_3^{max} = F_4^{max} = 5N$. The results are presented in table 1 and figure 2.

Table 1 shows that the poor individual performance of the last robot ($i = 0$) doesn't affect the individual performance of the remaining robot units when no

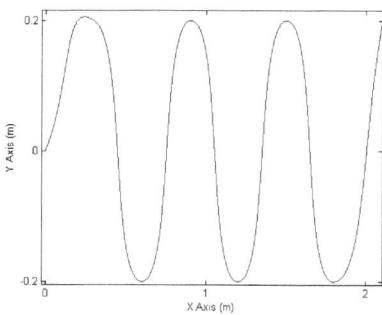

Fig. 1. Nominal path followed by the robot units

Table 1. Simulation experiment results

		Local robot performances					Global	
	i	0	1	2	3	4	System performance	
$K = 0$	e_i^{dis}	0.0102	0.0000	0.0000	0.0000		e^{dis}	0.0104
	e_i^{pos}	0.0103	0.0002	0.0002	0.0001	0.0002	e^{pos}	0.0111
$K = 40$	e_i^{dis}	0.0000	0.0000	0.0000	0.0000		e^{dis}	0.0000
	e_i^{pos}	0.0100	0.0069	0.0025	0.0015	0.0007	e^{pos}	0.0216

elastic force due to the physical link is present ($K^s = 0$), and e_i^{dis} and e_i^{pos} remains constant ($e_i^{dis} = 0.000$ and $e_i^{pos} \simeq 0.002$ for all $i = 1, ..., 4$).

When there is some elastic force due to hose stretching ($K^s = 40$), e_0^{dis} drops to zero as could be expected because the model used avoids separations between robots bigger than L. As the last robot moves slower than the rest and the dynamic model tries to keep distance between robots under L, the rest of the robots are forced to go slower so that the maximum segment length is respected, and that makes them unable to follow their references without the physic link. The system error e^{pos} grows from 0.0111 to 0.0216, which implies a 95% error growth due to the hose dynamics.

Figures 2a and 2c represent the Reference-Position error ($|P_i - P_{i+1}|$) for $K^s = 0$ and $K^s = 40$ respectively. The traction effect can be clearly seen if both figures are compared: while the former shows that the error for the last does not influence the rest, the latter shows how error between references and robots is spread. Nearest neighbors show the poorest individual performance. The Position-Reference distance oscillates as the references go faster at the curves to compensate the change in the growth of the euclidian distance between robots, and oscillations get closer to zero as time goes on, due to the Integrative component of the Proportional-Integrative controller used. Observing figs. 2b and 2d, one can easily see how the hose propagates trough the whole system the local perturbations of the behavior of robot units.

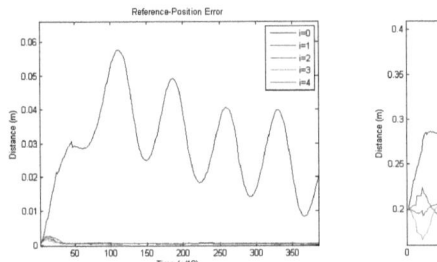

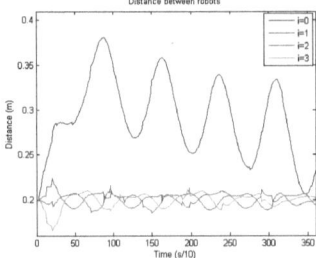

(a) Reference position error without linking element elastic force
$K = 0$

(b) Error on the distance between
robots with no linking element elastic force $K = 0$

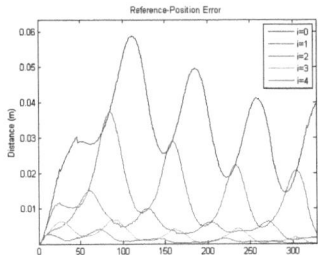

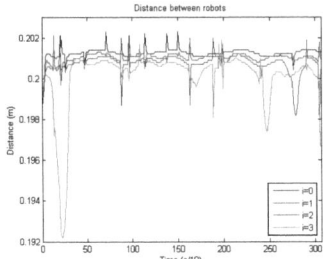

(c) Position error when there is
linking element elastic force involved

(d) Error in the distance between
robots when there is a linking element elastic force $K = 40N$

Fig. 2. Errors in the system with and without linking element elastic force

5   Conclusions

The basic question addressed in this paper is: there is any definite effect due to
the existence of a flexible linking element between robot units? To give an answer
we have introduced one of the simplest models: an elastic hose that introduces
an elastic traction force when stretched longer than its nominal value. Otherwise
the hose does not have any effect. Through a simulation of a collection of robots
following a given path we observe that even this simplified model of the hose
dynamics can introduce significant perturbations in the system's behavior. It is
our conclusion that further work must be devoted to this kind of systems to
fully explore their behaviors, and to prepare the grounds for its exploitation in
some applications and complex environments. We will also like to explore the
feasibility of hierarchical analysis and formulation of the problem [4].

References

1. Duro, R.J., Graña, M., de Lope, J.: On the potential contributions of hybrid intelligent approaches to multicomponent robotic system development. Information
   Sciences (2010) (in press)

2. Echegoyen, Z., Villaverde, I., Moreno, R., Graña, M., d'Anjou, A.: Linked multi-component mobile robots: modeling, simulation and control. In: Robotics and Autonomous Systems (submitted 2010)
3. Echegoyen-Ferreira, Z.: Contributions to Visual Servoing for Legged and Linked Multicomponent Robots. PhD thesis, UPV/EHU (2009)
4. Graña, M., Torrealdea, F.J.: Hierarchically structured systems. European Journal of Operational Research 25, 20–26 (1986)
5. Huang, L.: Speed control of differentially driven wheeled mobile robots: Model-based adaptive approach. Journal of Robotic Systems 22(6), 323–332 (2005)
6. Klancar, G., Skrjanc, I.: Tracking-error model-based predictive control for mobile robots in real time. Robotics and Autonomous Systems 55, 460–469 (2007)
7. Koh, K.C., Cho, H.S.: A smooth path tracking algorithm for wheeled mobile robots with dynamic constraints. Journal of Intelligent and Robotic Systems 24, 367–385 (1999)
8. Liu, N.: Intelligent path following method for nonholonomic robot using fuzzy control. In: Second International Conference on Intelligent Networks and Intelligent Systems (2009)
9. McLain, T.W., Beard, R.W.: Coordination variables, coordination functions, and cooperative timing missions. AIAA Journal of Guidance, Control, & Dynamics 28(1), 150–161 (2005)
10. Oriolo, G., De Luca, A., Vendittelli, M.: Wmr control via dynamic feedback linearization: Design, implementation, and experimental validation. IEEE Trans. Control Systems Technology 10(6), 835–852 (2002)
11. Raimondi, F.M., Melluso, M.: A new fuzzy robust dynamic controller for autonomous vehicles with nonholonomic constraints. Robotics and Autonomous Systems 52, 115–131 (2005)
12. Ren, W., Beard, R.W.: Distributed Consensus in Multi-Vehicle Cooperative Control: Theory and Applications. Springer, Heidelberg (2007)
13. Shi-Cai, L., Da-Long, T., Guang-Jun, L.: Formation control of mobile robots with active obstacle avoidance. Acta Automatica Sinica 33(5), 529–535 (2007)
14. De La Nava, I.V.: On Computational Intelligence Tools for Vision Based Navigation of Mobile Robots. PhD thesis, UPV/EHU (2009)

Social Simulation for AmI Systems Engineering

Teresa Garcia-Valverde, Emilio Serrano, and Juan A. Botia

University of Murcia*
{mtgarcia,emilioserra,juanbot}@um.es

Abstract. This paper propose the use of multi-agent based simulation
(MABS) to allow testing, validating and verifying Ambient Intelligence
(AmI) environments in a flexible and robust way. The development of
AmI is very complex because of this technology must often adapt to contextual information as well as unpredictable and changeable behaviours.
The concrete simulation is called Ubik and is integrated into the AmISim
architecture which is also presented in this paper. This architecture deals
with AmI applications in order to discover defects, estimate quality of
applications, help to make decisions about the design, etc. The paper
shows that Ubik and AmISim provide a simulation framework which can
test scenarios that would be impossible in real environments or even with
previous AmI simulation approaches.

1 Introduction

Ambient Intelligence (AmI) is a new vision in which people are surrounded by
intelligent embedded objects within an environment that is able to recognize and
to respond to different individuals [4]. The contextual information and ubiquitous
computing are the base of AmI. From ubiquitous computing, AmI environments
have many non-intrusive and invisible devices communicated and integrated into
the environment. These devices generate information about the environment,
users and changes in both of them; generating a context-aware environment.
With this contextual information, services and applications in AmI systems are
able to adapt to changes.

The development of AmI environments becomes a difficult process because of
the high variety of scenarios, heterogeneous devices, different sources of information, changing contexts, unpredictable and changeable behaviours, adaptation to
users etc. In these situations, the design and development of a framework that
allows testing, validating and verifying AmI environments with a flexible and
robust model is necessary. There are some proposals about real home environments to test AmI environments, such as AwareHome Project [8] or Adaptative

---

* This research work is supported by the Spanish Ministry of Science and Innovation
under the grants AP2007-04269 and AP2007-04080 of the FPU program and in the
scope of the Research Projects TSI-020302-2009-43, TIN2008-06441-C02-02, through
the Fundación Séneca within the Program "Generación del Conocimiento Científico
de Excelencia" (04552/GERM/06).

M. Graña Romay et al. (Eds.): HAIS 2010, Part I, LNAI 6076, pp. 80–87, 2010.
© Springer-Verlag Berlin Heidelberg 2010

House [10]. Using real environments supposes a considerable economical investment for deployment of devices all over the area and installation and tuning
of applications. Besides, using real environments to test is unfeasible in many
situations, for example, in an emergency situation.

In order to approach the problems derived of these requirements, several simulators in related fields to AmI have been developed. However, these simulators
are focused in just a part or only a few parts of an AmI environment. Examples exists which are focused in devices and their communications under AmI
constraints [12] or in simulation of sensors, actuators, and the environment, but
without simulation of context or adaptation to it, such as the ubiquitous computing simulator of Reynolds et. al [13].

Regarding ubiquitous computing, there are well-known simulation tools as
Ubiwise[1] or TATUS[5]. Both Ubiwise and TATUS use first person shooter
games. This feature provides to the simulator usability in the experimentation.
However, these games limit the number of individuals in the environment, their
relations, individuals or group behaviours, etc. A multi-agent based simulation,
like Ubik, supports a considerably high number of individuals and more flexibility
for simulation and study of social behaviours. There are some works that have
followed these multi-agent based approaches (e.g. [14]). However, these works
should support a common framework for adding contextual information easily,
reusing it, interpreting it and reasoning on the context[11]. Without an entire
context model, providing adaptative and intelligent services is unfeasible.

There are some proposals which explicitly use a context-aware model. For example, QuakeSim [2] is a tool which interactively simulates context information
in real time. However, this work is more focused in the agent model. We propose
in this work a multi-agent based simulation that takes into account all features regarded with AmI systems and integrates them in a common framework:
AmISim. AmISim is a simulator of entire AmI environment which uses Ubik[1], a
Multi-agent based simulation (MABS) for multi-agent models of social systems.
MABS allows designing flexible AmI environments like complex systems.

The next section describes the solution and architecture proposed. Section
3 shows a scenario which simulates an emergency situation and the adaptative
strategy of evacuation of several workers in an office building. Finally, in section
4 some conclusions are given.

2   Simulation of AmI Environments and Users

AmI environments have many non-intrusive and invisible devices communicated
and integrated into the environment. These devices generate information about
the environment, users and changes in both of them. With this information,
services and applications in AmI systems are able to adapt to changes. In order
to design a full AmI simulator that provides all described requirements, the
following features must be considered in an AmI simulator: *the environment
model*, *the agent model*, *the context model* and *the adaptation model*. In this

---

[1] http://ants.dif.um.es/staff/emilioserra/Ubik/

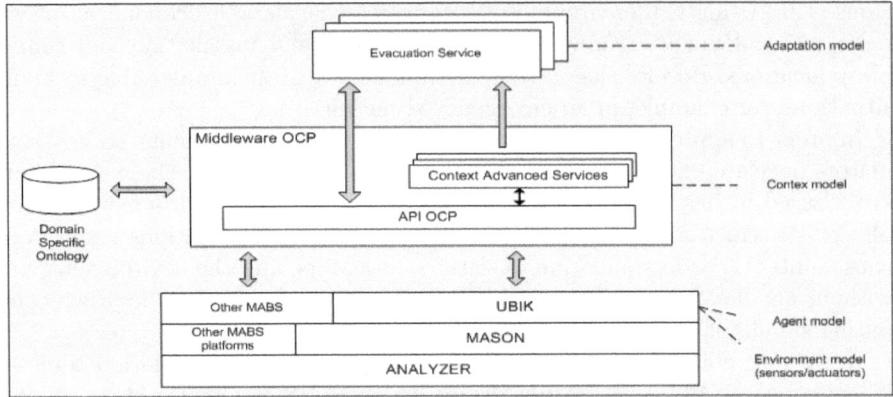

Fig. 1. AmISim architecture

work, AmISim has been modelled from these features. Next section presents the design and the architecture of AmISim.

2.1   AmISim

The architecture of *AmISim* is depicted in Fig. 1. The architecture covers the four models of social simulation in AmI: environment, agent, context and adaptation.

In the architecture, the environment model and the agent model are in the low level and they simulated to and using MASON[2] social simulation platform. In the mid level the context model can be found. OCP (Open Context Platform) [11] and a domain specific ontology are used for modelling the contextual information in this level. OCP is a middleware which provides support for management of contextual information and merging of information from different sources. Finally, in the upper level is the adaptation model. Several applications or services which use contextual information for adapting to the environment and users can be located in this level. This allocation in levels allows keep separated ones levels to others. So, it is possible obtain a hybrid system, where, some levels are integrated in a real environment. For example, some real sensors could be deploying in a real building or, like in our case, where the model context is entirely real.

The sensors in the environment model simulate data continuously calculated from several features of the sensors. These sensors send these data to OCP, i.e., they are the producers of OCP. OCP manages these data for generating contextual information and it stores them in its historical ontology. Then, the contextual information is available for the applications or services of the adaptation model, i.e., the consumers of OCP. They can use the context for offering services adapted to the environment. This is the ascending flow of information in the system, but there is another descending flow of information. There may

---

[2] MASON, http://cs.gmu.edu/eclab/projects/mason/

be services that can generate new useful contextual information (for example, a service of machine learning) that is stored by OCP or services that can generate orders to the actuators for influencing in the environment. The next sections describe each model that composes the system in depth.

Environment model and agent model. The environment model describes the physical world, design buildings, complex objects, sensors, actuators, the communications, etc. This model must be flexible and configurable. This model in this work is focused in work places (i.e. an office building), but it can be simulated in a large number of scenarios thanks to the flexibility of Ubik. The physical scenario can be configured with a different number of rooms, windows, doors, stairs, etc.

Other important factor in a simulator for AmI environments, as we mentioned above, is the model of sensors and actuators, because they allow sensing context and acting on it. Sensors and actuators can have a wide range of features and properties. In this work, the approach for modelling these devices only describes their most fundamental features. We defined a set of features which allow setting several different behaviours for sensors and actuators. However, other features can be added easily thanks to the design philosophy of MASON. This simulation platform was designed with the intention that a JAVA programmer can easily add new features, rather than a simulation specific complex platform [9].

Both sensors and actuators can be wearable or static, and they can generate data in periodical intervals or just only sporadically. Each of these features can be configured for the simulation setting. Its usual range of data, its scope, the probability or frequency of its occurrences, the probability that unusual data are produced, etc. can be configured too. In this work, actuators are considered in a similar way that sensors, but they have some particular properties, for example, the effect of an action in the environment.

Typically simulators used in AmI or similar environments used to forget or simplify the agent model. However, AmI is focussed on users, their experiences and interactions. So, the agent model is a fundamental goal in a simulator of this kind. Because of this, Ubik proposes multi-agent models of social systems for achieving this goal. MABS is employed in disparate fields as sociology, biology, physics, chemistry, ecology, economy, etc [3]. The common point within the broad application domain of MABS is that in every situation, there is a real interest in learning from the simulation to improve their own effectiveness [6]. The existence of people with this profile is more than noticeable in the field of AmI. So, Ubik has capabilities to test, verify and validate AmI systems in order to discover defects, estimate quality of the designed model or helping when making decisions about the design of devices, adaptative applications, information services or other elements in the environment model.

Each user in Ubik is simulated with an agent. Agents in Ubik have several features, both physical and related to behaviour. So, it is possible to define the age, role in his organization, velocity of movement, etc. and other features like its duty, its leadership skills or its happiness, for example. Besides, it is possible to configure the different agent's states, for example, working or running, and the actions that can be performed on the environment. All these features compose the behaviour of an agent in Ubik. Like in the model of sensors and actuators, other behavioural features can be added easily.

Context model. The context model gathers, merges, interprets, reasons and stores the contextual information, i.e., all relevant information that surrounds the environment and the users. Contextual information must be represented in a specific model for using it. In this work, the context model is realized by the middleware of OCP. OCP is a middleware which provides support for management of contextual information and it models contextual information for classifying situations of interest and triggering off the relevant actions at each moment. The middleware OCP represents the information in an ontological model and interprets it using SWRL rules[7].

Ontologies are key for building AmI systems because they allow a common framework for sharing knowledge, interoperating between agent and devices and reasoning about contextual information. In OCP a generic OWL-based ontology is used and this ontology is refined with the domain specific ontology. The ontology contains a historic of contextual information. Some applications or services require the history of the context. For example, for temporal reasoning, predicting future actions or locations, learning behaviour of the users, etc. However, there are applications can not store this information (e.g., a mobile device with memory constraints), and the middleware must provides this service.

OCP is a middleware for the management of contextual information in which the applications can consume or produce information. The OCP API captures the raw information from devices and provides contextual information thanks to the ontology, which maintains information for applications and obtains new information through inference and merging context. Besides, the applications can generate contextual information by using rule-based inference and produce new useful contextual information for OCP. Moreover, OCP provides a set of context advanced services. These services are specialized services which provide elaborate information from the contextual information in the ontology or in the historic of the ontology using the OCP API. These services deliver a more efficient and scalable access to applications and external services.

Adaptation model. This is the most flexible model in AmISim. It consists of all applications and services that are offered to the environment. Both services and applications use contextual information from the context model for adapting to the environment and offer personalized and proactive services to the environment and agents. A service or application in the adaptation model is composed of two parts. On the one hand, it has an API for accessing and using the context model. On the other hand, it has the specific adaptation logic. So, to add a new application in the system it is necessary that it has the two components.

The API of the adaptation model behaves like an interface between the context model (realized by OCP) and the adaptation logic in the adaptation model. This API is responsible for extracting contextual information that the application or service needs and for converting it to the format used by this one, for example, in OWL format or in a numeric value for providing the number of individuals in a specific place. But this API is not specific for each service, a service or application can use an API from other services or applications if performs the operations which it needs.

The use of APIs allows providing the needed information to the adaptation logic and this provides it with a great flexibility. The API abstracts to the adaption logic from the rest of the system, and this abstraction allows introducing any adaptation mechanism. So, it is possible to design the adaptation logic by semantic SWRL rules, reinforcement learning or mining data stream techniques, machine learning methods using the historical contextual information, etc.

3   An Example

In this section we apply AmISim in an emergency scenario example. In the scenario we have deployed an AmI system with sensors and actuators in an office building where a critical situation is produced. In concrete, we simulate a fire emergency. Such scenarios can not be tested in a real environment, but we can also simulate a scenario of a crisis response with AmISim. In this case, we are going to simulate the evacuation for a fire in a building with several floors, rooms, corridors, stairs and elevators where a lot of individuals are working.

Each user is represented by an agent and has some features than differentiates it from the rest. Each feature can be set with different weight for assigning it more or less importance and each agent has a level of damage which will reduce depending on the level of risk of the zones that crosses in the evacuation and the time. So, an agent is defined by its physical and behavioural features. The *velocity* and the *age* are the physical features of an agent. The psychical features are the *duty* (influenced by the *level of risk* of the action orders him by the system), the *imitation* (agent acts according to other agents) and the *panic* (if an agent suffers a panic attack, she will keep immobile).

The agents move through the environment. The environment model is defined by a grid which represents the building (Fig. 2) where the number of windows, doors and the number and kind of sensors and actuators are configurable. In this scenario there are three kinds of sensors[3]: (1) RFID sensors for the location of individuals, (2) sensors to measure the intensity of fire in a zone of the building, (3) sensors for detecting if a door or a window is opened. The actuators[4], must give orders from the system to the agents for the evacuation or for realizing certain actions (showing a message or using a voice sound).

The environment changes dynamically due to fire. A simple fire model is used. The intensity of fire is increased in a factor β every x seconds in a specific zone if the intensity of fire is greater than 0, i.e., the fire has already reached this zone. When the intensity of fire reaches a certain threshold α in a zone, the fire is spread with minimum intensity to the neighbouring zones and so on. In the case

---

[3] Gray hexagons in Fig. 2.
[4] Black hexagons in Fig. 2.

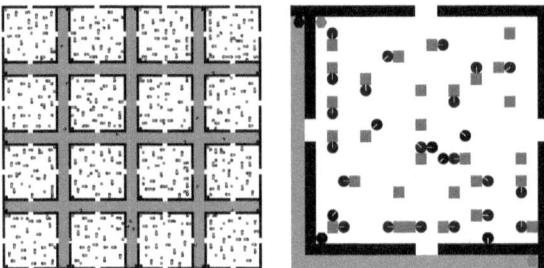

Fig. 2. On the left, a floor in AmISim with 400 agents. On the right, the zoom in the upper right corner of the floor.

of walls and closed doors, the spread of fire is produced with a greater threshold than the normal. So, the actions of agent will reduce the fire hazard.

This simulated information from sensors is extracted, interpreted and stored in the specific ontology from the context model. The interpretation of data is realized by the domain specific ontology and by SWRL rules that infer the information. When the information changes, the context model is stored in the historic. Besides, the context model in this scenario offers an advanced context service for providing the number of individuals in a specific place. This service is needed because of the realization of this task by the adaptation model would be inefficient and non-scalable.

According to the information in the context model, the adaptation model fits the evacuation strategy. This strategy is based in the Dijkstra algorithm. However, the cost of a node in our scenario is given by the risk in this zone (intensity of fire). So, the strategy finds the shortest and less danger path. Besides, when a stairs is congested, the algorithm removes this destination of its set of possible destinations. We can know if a stair is congested thanks to the context advanced service of the context model. So, jams in the exits can be avoided. When the optimal path has been determined, it is communicated to the actuators for the notification. The adaptation model uses SWRL rules for determining these notifications. Only the agents in the scope of actuators can receive the orders, the rest remains walking randomly until they are in this scope. When the agents perceive the notifications, they follow them and leave the building.

4   Conclusions and Future Work

We have discussed the requirements of an AmI simulator. AmI environments require a lot of information about users, environment, changes, etc., i.e., the contextual information. The contextual information allows applications and services to adapt to the changing environment. Then, we propose AmISim, a MABS for AmI environment which satisfies these requirements.

AmI simulation allows recreating real environments, testing different settings, learning individual or group behaviours of agents, adapting applications to the environment, designing strategies trial-and-error over critical scenarios, etc. So, AmISim provides a simulation framework which can test scenarios that would be impossible in real environments. For example, we have proved AmISim in an emergency scenario and we have showed that it is feasible setting the physical environment and strategies for an adequate evacuation. In future work will focus on testing our simulator using more real examples and evaluating the applied methodology for testing, validation and verification in these scenarios.

References

1. Barton, J.J., Vijayaraghavan, V.: Ubiwise: A ubiquitous wireless infrastructure simulation environment, Tech. Report hpl2002-303. HP Labs (2002)
2. Bylund, M., Espinoza, F.: Testing and demonstrating context-aware services with quake iii arena. Communications of the ACM 45(1), 46–48 (2002)
3. Drogoul, A., Vanbergue, D., Meurisse, T.: Multi-agent based simulation: Where are the agents? In: MABS, pp. 1–15 (2002)
4. Ducatel, K., Bogdanowicz, M., Scapolo, F., Leijten, J., Burgelman, J.C.: Scenarios for ambient intelligence in 2010. Technical report, ISTAG, The Information Society Technology Advisory Group (2001)
5. Lewis, D., O'Donnell, T., O'Sullivan, D., O'Neill, E., Klepal, M., Pesch, D.: A testbed for evaluating human interaction with ubiquitous computing environments. In: TRIDENTCOM 2005, pp. 60–69. IEEE Computer Society, Los Alamitos (2005)
6. Gilbert, N., Troitzsch, K.G.: Simulation for the Social Scientist. Open University Press, Stony Stratford (2005)
7. Horrocks, I., Patel-Schneider, P.F., Boley, H., Tabet, S., Grosof, B., Dean, M.: Swrl: A semantic web rule language combining owl and ruleml. Technical report (2004)
8. Kidd, C.D., Orr, R., Abowd, G.D., Atkeson, C.G., Essa, I.A., MacIntyre, B., My-natt, E., Starner, T.E., Newstetter, W., et al.: The Aware Home: A Living Laboratory for Ubiquitous Computing Research. LNCS, pp. 191–198. Springer, Heidelberg (1999)
9. Luke, S., Cioffi-Revilla, C., Panait, L., Sullivan, K.: Mason: A new multi-agent simulation toolkit. In: Proceedings of Swarmfest Workshop (2004)
10. Mozer, M.C.: The neural network house: An environment that adapts to its inhabitants. In: Proceedings of the American Association for Artificial Intelligence Spring Symposium on Intelligent Environments, pp. 110–114 (1998)
11. Nieto, I., Botía, J.A., Gómez-Skarmeta, A.F.: Information and hybrid architecture model of the ocp contextual information management system (2006)
12. Litz, L., Gabel, O., Reif, M.: Ncs testbed for ambient intelligence. In: 2005 IEEE International Conference on Systems, Man and Cybernetics, vol. 1, pp. 115–120 (2005)
13. Cahill, V., Reynolds, V., Senart, A.: Requirements for an ubiquitous computing simulation and emulation environment. In: InterSense 2006, p. 1. ACM, New York (2006)
14. O'grady, M., Liu, Y., O'hare, G.: Scalable context simulation for mobile applications, pp. 1391–1400 (2006)

Automatic Behavior Pattern Classification for Social Robots

Abraham Prieto, Francisco Bellas, Pilar Caamaño, and Richard J. Duro

Integrated Group for Engineering Research, Universidade da Coruña, Spain
{abprieto,fran,pcsobrino,richard}@udc.es

Abstract. In this paper, we focus our attention on providing robots with a system that allows them to automatically detect behavior patterns in other robots, as a first step to introducing social responsive robots. The system is called AN-PAC (Automatic Neural-based Pattern Classification). Its main feature is that ANPAC automatically adjusts the optimal processing window size and obtains the appropriate features through a dimensional transformation process that allow for the classification of behavioral patterns of large groups of entities from perception datasets. Here we present the basic elements and operation of AN-PAC, and illustrate its applicability through the detection of behavior patterns in the motion of flocks.

Keywords: motion pattern analysis, behavior detection, cognitive developmental robotics, social robots, artificial neural networks.

1 Introduction

Researchers in the autonomous robotics field have been increasing their interest in the social aspects of the architectures they design [1][2]. Robots that operate completely isolated from the behavior of other robots, performing simple or complex tasks, but assuming that their environment will be modified only by themselves, have been studied for decades [3][4]. Such assumptions are not realistic if fully autonomous robots that perform their tasks taking into account there are other "inhabitants" in environment where they are placed are to be obtained. That is, robotic architectures must include concepts like attention, learning by observation, behavior detection, imitation and so on, to really understand what is happening in the environment [5].

Cognitive developmental robotics (CDR) is one of the most promising approaches in autonomous robotics, and tries to obtain open-ended, autonomous learning systems that continually adapt to their environment, as opposed to the classical tendency of constructing robots that carry out particular, predefined tasks [6]. The basic concept behind CDR is "physical embodiment", that allows structuring information through interactions with the environment and other robots. CDR uses a developmental model that starts from the fetal sensorimotor mapping in the womb and moves up to social behavior learning through body representation, motor skill development, and spatial perception. One of the key aspects of CDR is the autonomous development of social behaviors such as early communication, action execution and understanding, vocal imitation, joint attention, and empathy development.

M. Graña Romay et al. (Eds.): HAIS 2010, Part I, LNAI 6076, pp. 88–95, 2010.

Hence, the cognitive developmental model must include some kind of description of the events occurring in the environment that are not due to the actions the robot applies. The problem is how to acquire and represent such information in an autonomous way so that the robot can use it to guide its behavior depending on the behavior of its "neighbors". This topic has been studied extensively, starting from the work of Kuniyoshi [7][8], who carried out several experiments with real robots in topics like behavior matching by observation or imitation, being one of the pioneers in the CDR approach. In multirobot systems, tracking multiple targets is a fundamental task for mobile robot teams [9][10]. A typical example is the Robocup competition, where an autonomous detection of the other team's behavior is very relevant to adapt a team's strategy [11]. Although all of these approaches have provided clear improvements, the autonomous detection of behaviors in multi-robot systems is an open topic with several aspects that remain unsolved where authors present different techniques and approaches continuously [12][13].

In this work, we propose a neural based pattern analysis system that can be incorporated to the control system of an autonomous robot allowing it to classify behavior patterns in other robot teams within its environment. This system is called ANPAC (Automatic Neural-based Pattern Classification) and its main contribution is that it automatically adjusts the processing window size and the preprocessing parameters, thus obtaining the appropriate features and reducing the amount of sensorial information required as much as permitted by the desired accuracy, allowing for an adaptive data classification strategy in very large data sets.

2 Automatic Neural-Based Pattern Classification

The objective of the system is to classify the type of motion a multitude of agents is performing as a whole. To attempt to obtain an Artificial Neural Network whose inputs are the trajectories of A agents (being A in the order of tens or hundreds) which are each represented by some type of encoding (deviation angles, positions, or whatever) for t instants of time (usually tens) would result in an ANN with $A x t$ inputs (hundreds or thousands) and would be very hard to train. On the other hand, to characterize the motion of a group, it is usually only necessary to sample some individuals (the sampling window) and, in reality, not all the points of the trajectory would be needed, just some representation of it in terms of features that contains enough information to be able to discriminate between the desired categories with the desired discrimination level. The system will automatically establish the minimum number of individuals to sample and the minimum set of features to obtain these discrimination levels. In fact, it obtains these parameters as it trains the network for the classification task. The approach has been called Automatic Neural-based Pattern Classification system (ANPAC).

A simple block diagram of the ANPAC system proposed here is displayed in Fig. 1. The first block (left) represents the high dimensional *input dataset*, which consists of a data matrix that must include some type of representation of the behavior of the robots to be analyzed. In this case, we will focus our attention on motion patterns, that is, the data matrix is made up of the trajectories followed by the set of robots, which must be classified in terms of behavior patterns. In the applications section, we will describe a particular example with a possible representation of such trajectories.

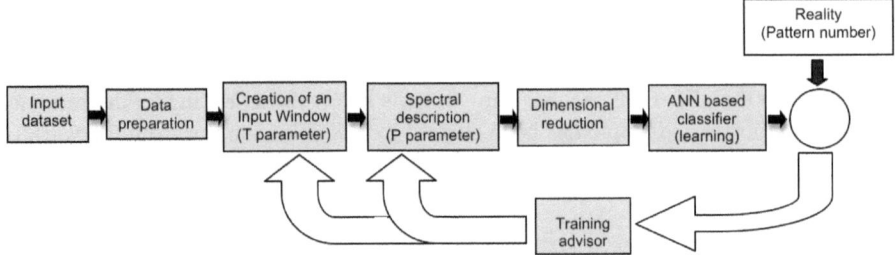

Fig. 1. Block diagram of the ANPAC system

The processing of the trajectories matrix starts with a *data preparation* stage. At this point the matrix values are normalized in order to make them independent of the velocity of the robots and scaled to the adequate input range of the ANN that performs the classification. To this end, the set of vectors that make up the trajectories matrix are put through a Principal Component Analysis (PCA) module that determines the principal components of the data and rewrites the values of each vector in terms of the projections over them (the principal components obtained). This stage results in no information loss as we are calculating all of the components, but now we have a representation of the original matrix that is ordered in terms of variance.

For a **T** robot set, we have a **TxN** matrix where **N** is the number of principal components considered as necessary in order to better describe the trajectories without redundant information. It would obviously be very cumbersome to use all of these values for all the samples as inputs to the classifier and we must seek some type of description of these matrices in terms of features or descriptors so that the number of inputs is manageable. This is the objective of the component description procedure. This description can be made for each of the **T** values representing the values of each principal component for each trajectory and, as they are arranged in terms of descriptive importance; more features may be used to describe the first component than the second and so on. In addition, not all of the components are usually necessary in order to attain the discrimination degree one needs for a given application, and thus, the minimum number of descriptors, **P**, as well as which **P** descriptors, out of the possible descriptors for the **N** possible principal components we take, need to be determined. These descriptor values will be the inputs to the classification ANN. Depending on the complexity and variability of the behavior, the number of parameters required for an adequate description will vary. The module for the extraction of trajectory descriptors works on **T** trajectory windows extracted from the initial matrix. The size robot group is determined by the adviser concurrently with parameter **P**. The optimal values for **P** and **T** are attained through a simple rule-based advisor whose input is the evolution of the discrimination error in the classification as the classification ANNs are being trained. Its outputs are the new values for **T** and **P**.

Consequently, the main problem here is how to produce a set of descriptors in such a way that when more are required, and thus the inputs of the ANN are increased, the ANN does not have to be trained all over again. To address this problem we have chosen an incremental approach. In the following two subsections we describe the way trajectory vectors are combined and incrementally described, how the advisor works, and finally provide some data on how the RBF adapts to these changes.

2.1 Incremental Description

We start with a window of **T** vectors with **N** components in each vector. Thus, to put it another way, for each component we have a cluster of **T** values coming from each of the vectors of the robots and these should be reduced to a set of incremental descriptors. Once converted, we will have a two-dimensional matrix, one dimension corresponding to the principal components and another to the cluster descriptors.

This procedure starts by sorting the **T** values and creating an ordered one-dimensional vector with them. The first descriptor is the average value of the vector, which is quite a coarse measure but very representative in many cases. The second descriptor is obtained by selecting the sub-vector of size **T/2** -within the original vector- that displays the smallest variation in angle values (as the components of the vector are ordered, this is the minimum value between the first and last element of the subvector) and the average of this subvector is the second descriptor. Note that this value represents the **T/2** most similar values, indicating a specific component.

For the third descriptor and onwards the procedure varies a little, but it follows the same general rule. First we select the subvector with **T/3** elements and minimum variation, then we remove this subvector from the original one and we select again the minimum variation subvector of size **T/3** from the remaining original vector of size **2T/3**. In general, for the n-th descriptor we select the minimum variation sub-vector with size **T (n-2)/n**, then we remove this subvector from the original one and finally we select a minimum variation vector of size **T/n** from the remaining **2T/n** sized original vector. More formally, the descriptors represent the average of the subvector of size **1/n** between percentile **(n-2)/n** and percentile **(n-1)/n**, considering the percentiles in terms of frequency/mode instead of using the real value.

		Components				
		1	2	3	4	5
Descriptors	1	1	2	4	7	11
	2	3	5	8	12	
	3	6	9	13		
	4	10	14			
	5	15				

Fig. 2. One possible order in which the **P** descriptors may be taken to provide the ANN inputs

Once the initial matrix is converted into an incremental two-dimensional matrix of cluster descriptors, it is necessary to define a criterion to select which values are input to the ANN as the description of the cluster. That is, we have to choose **P** values to represent the cluster accurately but trying to use a minimal representation for the discrimination level we are trying to achieve. **P** is determined by the advisor and thus, here we have to select **P** elements from this matrix. Essentially, it is necessary to arrange the elements of the matrix in terms of significance. Fig. 2 displays the order selected based on both the experience of several trials with different ordering criteria and preserving a balance between accuracy and group characterization.

2.2 Training Advisor and ANN Classification

The tuning or advisory module modifies the parameters of the first stage after evaluating the evolution of the classification error. This tuning system operates in the classification space and not in terms of other more classical parameters such as mean squared error or others. Thus, the appropriate measure should be the Discrimination level (DL), which is the average proportion of misclassified samples.

To perform its task, the training advisor uses a search algorithm to guide the modification of the dimensional reduction parameters ($\mathbf{P}$) and the input window size ($\mathbf{T}$). It is structured as a set of rules: it uses a random initial search direction and maintains it while the global discrimination error level decreases. If the error level increases, a new random advance direction is selected. In addition, to provide extra exploratory capabilities, a small probability of changing the direction selected for the algorithm is added.

The classification is carried out in ANPAC using a variable size Radial Basis Function ANN that was chosen over other options due to their good behavior over this type of problems. Nevertheless, the topology of the network is not a crucial issue in this case and the methodology presented may be applied using other types of networks as well.

The objective is to allow the system to modify the number of inputs during the training procedure (to adapt it to the changing number of descriptors, $\mathbf{P}$, that are considered as the advisor changes) without the need to restart the learning process from scratch. Obviously, if one directly introduces new inputs in a trained network, the results are unpredictable and may imply having to restart training. The descriptors of the window data have been chosen so as to provide a gradually more detailed view of the trajectories data. Consequently, whenever an increase of the number of parameters takes place, that is, new inputs come to bear on the network; these parameters add information to previous lower resolution descriptors and, consequently, their influence can be smoothed by introducing neurons and weights for them that are the same as for their originators. This leads to very little distortion on the operation of the network.

Additionally, in order to smooth even further the consequences of these modifications, several coefficients are introduced to gradually increase the effect of the new inputs on the hidden layers. These new attenuated inputs need to be trained in the same way as the old ones, and, consequently, the training algorithm must be modified in this direction. When the number of neurons is decreased, the process is the same, the redundant inputs and synapse connections are smoothly removed and the training is adapted to its new configuration. The rate of increase or decrease of the transition coefficients values has been regulated to reduce the sharp transitory increase of the error.

The different experiments performed have shown that this variable size network allows an automatic adjustment of the number of inputs without having to reset the training process. In addition, we have observed that varying the dimensionality of the search space during training often accelerates convergence and improves the precision of the resulting network.

3   Motion Patterns in Flocks

An illustrative example of the ANPAC capabilities in behavior pattern analysis in robots, we have applied it in the automatic detection of flock movements. This example is based in the well-known Reynold's boids [14], a group of virtual agents that using a simple computational model carry out a coordinated animal motion such as bird flocks and fish schools. We have modeled the basic boids system in a more general way, contemplating it as a complex system that is influenced by three forces that make up its resulting movement: an *external* force (due to an external acceleration field that is generated by the environment and varies with time), a *collective* force (due to a set of local interaction rules that follow the same structure as the original Reynold's rules) and an *individual* force (implying that each boid follows a variable trajectory). These three force components can affect each boid to a different degree, resulting in behaviors that are a combination of the three basic ones: ordered (only external force), complex (only collective force) or chaotic (only individual force).

In Fig. 3 we have represented 4 different behavior patterns that can be created with the combination of these three forces, and that are examples of the type of detection the social robot we are designing must carry out. Fig. 3a corresponds to a chaotic behavior that is a consequence of using only individual force, with random values in positions and velocities in the boids. Fig. 3b corresponds to a combination of the external and individual components, resulting in a combination between ordered and chaotic behaviors. Fig. 3c shows an organized behavior obtained using only the external component. Finally, in Fig. 3d we have used a combination of the external and collective components, providing a typical flock behavior that follows the external force line, that is, a complex but ordered behavior pattern.

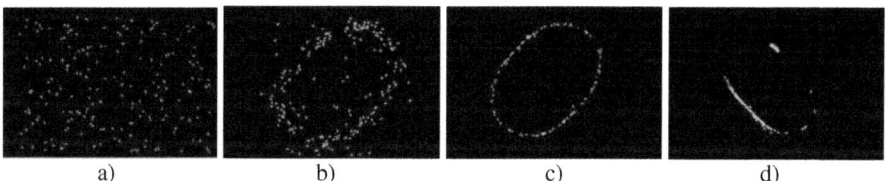

a)   b)   c)   d)

Fig. 3. Examples of different flock behaviors obtained combining the three basic forces

The motion of a group of boids was recorded for a fixed number of time steps (N) to obtain a matrix with 2xTxN real numbers (x and y components of the T trajectories). This representation was then converted into a representation showing the deviation of the trajectory of each boid with respect to the average of the group. As the boids all move at the same speed, an angle provides the information on this deviation for each instant, thus resulting in a TxN matrix. This was the initial data set presented to the ANPAC system.

To simplify the analysis of the results, we have divided the experiment in three parts corresponding to the combination of the three previously explained forces in groups of two. First, we have executed the ANPAC system using a fixed valued of 0.1 in the individual force and varying the external and collective components from 0 to 1. This way, we can analyze the obtained behavior using only one output in the ANN.

In this case, the created behaviors range from purely ordered to purely complex, and the ANPAC system must classify them properly and adjust the number of boids required to achieve such successful classification. In Fig. 4 (top-left) we show the variation with time in the discrimination error together with the variation of the P and T values. The system is stopped once it reaches stable values, in this case, around step 800. As shown we obtain a discrimination error of 0.06 around training step 500, which implies a discrimination level of 94%. In this case, the parameters T and P are automatically adjusted by ANPAC to values of 15 and 6 respectively. This means that the system needs 15 boids and 6 input values to the neural network (features) to discriminate with 94% accuracy between these behavior patterns. As commented before, this adaptive response is the main contribution of this approach, providing real autonomy to the robot while maximizing the computational efficiency.

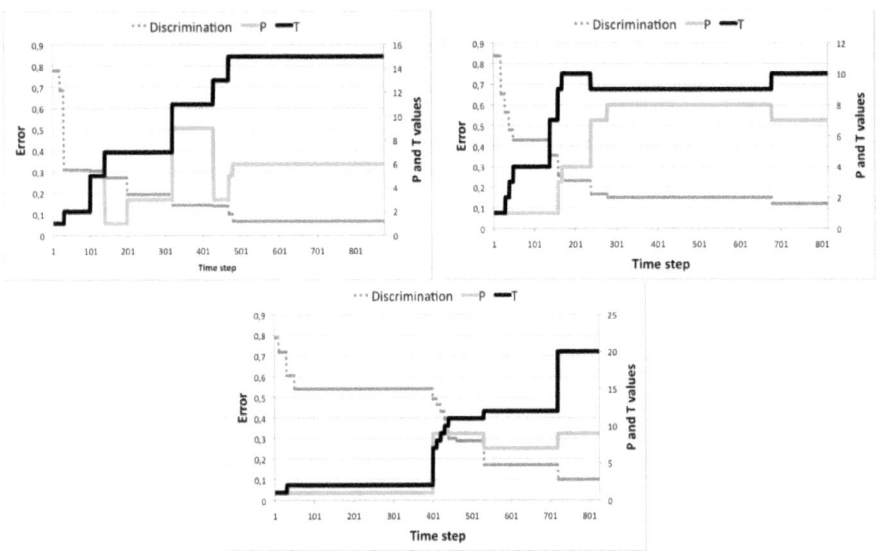

Fig. 4. Evolution of the discrimination error together with the P and T values fixing the individual (top-left), external (top-right) and collective (bottom) forces

Fig. 4 (top-right) shows the equivalent curves but in the case we fix the external force to 0.1 and vary the other two components. Now, the resulting behaviors will vary from complex to chaotic. As we can see, we obtain a global reliable discrimination level of 89% (error value in 0.11) around training step 700, which is again a successful result but denotes that this combination of parameters imply the more complex behaviors to be discriminated. The values of the T and P parameters are now stable at 10 and 7 in this case. Finally, in Fig. 4 (bottom) we have the results when fixing the collective force contribution to 0.1 and vary the individual and external components, corresponding to behaviors ranging from ordered to chaotic. Now the discrimination level reaches the 90% at training step 700. This level is achieved with 21 boids in the window (T parameter) and with a P value of 11. The global results shown in Fig. 4 show that the ANPAC system is able to automatically adjust the parameters that characterize the boids' trajectories. This allows for a successful discrimination of behavior patterns in the flock.

4 Conclusions

The ANPAC system presented in this paper is an approach to allow a simple training procedure for artificial neural network based classifier systems that have to deal with behavior datasets of large collections of individuals and which imply large numbers of inputs in the networks. ANPAC automatically adjusts a sampling size over the data set dividing it into windows that are characterized through a set of automatically generated parameters. These windows and parameter sets are the optimal possible for a given discrimination degree and allow adjusting of the number of inputs to the network as training progresses through an incremental strategy that does not distort the training process. The approach presented has been tested on a synthetic problem involving the classification of boid motion patterns and the results have been very satisfactory.

References

1. Sam Ge, S., Mataric, M.: Preface. International Journal of Social Robotics 1, 1–2 (2009)
2. Duffy, B.R.: Fundamental Issues in Affective Intelligent Social Machines. The Open Artificial Intelligence Journal 2, 21–34 (2008)
3. Bekey, G.A.: Autonomous Robots, From Biological Inspiration to Implementation and Control. The MIT Press, Cambridge (2005)
4. Arcady Meyer, J., Husbands, P., Harvey, I.: Evolutionary robotics: A survey of applications and problems. In: Husbands, P. (ed.) EvoROB/EvoRobot 1998. LNCS, vol. 1468, pp. 1–21. Springer, Heidelberg (1998)
5. Breazeal, C.L.: Designing Sociable Robots. MIT Press, Cambridge (2002)
6. Asada, M., Hosoda, K., Kuniyoshi, Y., Ishiguro, H., Inui, T., Yoshikawa, Y., Ogino, M., Yoshida, C.: Cognitive Developmental Robotics: A Survey. IEEE Transactions on Autonomous Mental Development 1(1), 12–34 (2009)
7. Kuniyoshi, Y.: Fusing autonomy and sociability in robots. In: Proceedings of the First International Conference on Autonomous Agents, pp. 470–471 (1997)
8. Kuniyoshi, Y.: Behavior Matching by Observation for Multi-Robot Cooperation. In: Proceedings of the Seventh International Symp. on Robotics Research, pp. 343–352 (1996)
9. Isler, V., Spletzer, J., Khanna, S., Taylor, C.: Target tracking with distributed sensors: the focus of attention problem. In: Proceedings IROS 2003 (2003)
10. Parker, L.: Distributed algorithms for multi-robot observation of multiple moving targets. Autonomous Robots 12(3), 231–255 (2002)
11. Bruce, J., Balch, T., Veloso, M.: Fast and inexpensive color vision for interactive robots. In: Proceedings IROS 2000 (2000)
12. Roduit, P., Martinoli, A., Jacques, J.: Quantitative Method for Comparing Trajectories of Mobile Robots Using Point Distribution Models. In: Proc. of the 2007 IEEE/RSJ Int. Conf. on Intelligent Robots and Systems (IROS 2007), pp. 2441–2448 (2007)
13. Stroupea, A., Balch, T.: Value-based action selection for observation with robot teams using probabilistic techniques. Robotics and Autonomous Systems 50, 85–97 (2005)
14. Reynolds, C.: Flocks, herds and schools: A distributed behavioral model. In: SIGGRAPH 1987: Proc.14th Annual Conf. on Computer Graphics and Interactive Techniques, pp. 25–34 (1987)

Healthcare Information Fusion Using Context-Aware Agents

Dante I. Tapia[1], Juan A. Fraile[2], Ana de Luis[1], and Javier Bajo[2]

[1] Departamento de Informática y Automática, University of Salamanca,
Plaza de la Merced s/n, 37008 Salamanca, Spain
[2] Pontifical University of Salamanca, c/ Compañía 5, 37002 Salamanca, Spain
{dantetapia,adeluis}@usal.es, {jafraileni,jbajope}@upsa.es

Abstract. Context aware systems have evolved into complex information systems capable of providing large quantities of information obtained from network sensors with heterogeneous characteristics. This article proposes a multi-agent system that monitors patients and maintains a permanent fix on their location within a given context. The system uses information provided by sensors distributed throughout the environment. The system agents take the information they receive and fuse it to improve the decisions and actions involved in their processing. The multi-agent system implements a SOA-based platform, which allows heterogeneous Wireless Sensor Networks to communicate in a distributed way. This article presents the evaluation of the solutions provided by the agents through the information flow for the organization.

Keywords: Information Fusion, Context-Awareness, Multi-Agent Systems, Healthcare.

1 Introduction

There is currently a considerable variety of sensors that can observe user contexts. The diversity of characteristics: observable parameters, temporal and sample scales, means of acquisition, etc., is a source of practical problems that, if they are to be solved, must be clearly understood [2]. Within the user context, the high level of dynamism is tied to important restrictions and factors to consider. Data fusion can improve the perception of the context information and solve some of these problems. These methods seek to widen the observational space, increase the contextual and temporal coverage, reduce ambiguities, and supplant any shortcomings in any individually considered contextual observations [2].

The search for effective and non-invasive solutions within a user context brings us to context-aware systems. These systems store and analyze all of the relevant information that surrounds and forms part of the user context. The user's preferences, taste, location, frame of mind, activities, surroundings, vital signs, as well as the room temperature and lighting conditions, etc., comprise the information that can be classified as the initial context information, and can be easily captured from the user's residence. The information is usually acquired through sensors located in different Wireless Sensor Networks (WSN). The current trend for displaying information to

M. Graña Romay et al. (Eds.): HAIS 2010, Part I, LNAI 6076, pp. 96–103, 2010.

system users, given the large number of small and portable devices, is through an arrangement of distributed heterogeneous systems and WSN. In this regard, multi-agent systems [6] facilitate the development of context-aware environments in the home. Multi-agent systems have been studied recently as monitoring systems [4] for the medical care [6] of sick and dependent individuals in their home [6] [8]. These systems provide continual support in the daily life of these individuals, predicting potentially dangerous situations and managing the physical and cognitive assistance of each person [1]. Taking these solutions into account, it is logical to conclude that multi-agent systems facilitate the design and development of home care environments [1] and improve the services currently available, incorporating new functionalities. Multi-agent systems add a high level of abstraction regarding to the traditional distributed computing solutions.

This article presents the HealthCare Context-Aware Computing (HCCAC) multi-agent architecture, which is capable of supervising and monitoring persons in healthcare contexts. The goal of HCCAC is to provide solutions for the wellbeing of its users, by incorporating itself indistinguishably into their daily lives. HCCAC integrates CBR-BDI [6] agents that are capable of learning beyond their initial knowledge, interacting autonomously with their environment. The coordination process among agents should organize the flow of information in such a way that the communication between the different agents, each equipped with a sensor, and the agent that incorporates the information, can be translated into an optimal use of global resources. HCCAC uses the Services laYers over Light PHysical devices (SYLPH) platform [4]. SYLPH is based on a Service-Oriented Architecture (SOA) model for integrating heterogeneous Wireless Sensors Networks (WSNs) into HealthCare systems. The communication between the agents and the devices takes place with wireless technologies like ZigBee [4], while Radiofrequency Identification (RFID) is used for identification [11]. These technologies provide the structure that is required for supporting the communication needs for the system agents with devices and data handling equipment. The simple integration and interaction between intelligent agents, sensors and devices is what led us to propose the integration of HCCAC architecture and SYLPH.

The remainder of the paper is structured as follows: section 2 presents the problem description. Section 3 describes how HCCAC and SYLPH have been used to provide a robust wireless infrastructure and a detailed analysis of information fusion performed by the system. Finally, section 4 presents the results and conclusions obtained.

2   Background and Problem Description

The concept laid out in this article is the union of two systems: a multi-Agent HCCAC system [5] which receives a variety of different information from multiple sensor networks managed by the SYLPH platform [4]. The multi-agent system combines the information received into an integrated data base in order to better handle the information and more effectively act on the network sensors. Integrated information systems generally process very heterogeneous information. When the HCCAC system presents its information diagram to an agent that is requesting certain results, it must omit the variety of integrated information that the system has assembled.

Consequently, the HCCAC system has two fundamental tasks: (i) to integrate a known set of data sources that refer to a diagram of individual data and (ii) to generate a new unified diagram, based on individual diagrams, that is complete, summarized and comprehensible.

Recent years have given way to a number of multi-agent architectures that utilize data merging to improve their output and efficiency. Such is the case with Castanedo et al., [3] amplify the CS-MAS architecture to incorporate dynamic data fusion through the use of an autonomous agent, locally fused within the architecture. This agent is created dynamically by a centrally fused agent. These agents work in conjunction with the agents that control and manage the sensors to capture information. Therefore, at any given moment, there may be several locally fused autonomous agents that can generate duplicate information. There are also systems, such as that presented by Pfeffer et al. [10], which are based on the use of agents to supervise objectives within a dynamic environment. This system performs data fusion at the level where agents supervise objectives. The agents do not provide a coordinated approach in the supervision of objectives and, as a result, can make important objectives susceptible to attacks. The system attempts to avoid these attacks by creating supervising teams, but the information still remains dispersed among each of the supervisor agents. Other models, such as the one presented by Liu et al. [7] attempt to avoid the collision and inconsistency of data by using an information fusion method. The model is formed by two agents and three levels of data fusion that attempt to locate the most optimal and non-redundant data model. This system [7] focuses exclusively on fusing information without taking the data sources into account. It is also true that there are a number of systems, such as HiLIFE [11], which cover all of the phases related to information fusion by specifying how the different computational components can work together in one coherent system. These phases can range from the data fusion algorithms that operate in heterogeneous networks, to the computational methods that combine low and high level information, and dynamically manage intelligent sensors to acquire additional data. HiLIFE has also been integrated into the RETSINA [11] multi-agent system, which provides an agile and sophisticated reasoning mechanism using the information fused by HiLIFE.

The aforementioned studies clearly focus on information fusion with regards to multi-agent systems. There are data fusion models that obtain an optimized and efficient diagram. Few systems attempt to combine information fusion with information gathering components. Those that have attempted, do so through the union of two systems that have been developed independently, as is the case with HiLIFE and RETSINA [11]. Our study would like to go one step further and, in addition to capturing information from multiple sensor networks, equip each agent with data fusion capabilities so that they can structure the information they receive both consistently and without redundancy.

3 The Healthcare Monitoring System

This section describes the main features of a monitoring system that integrates the HCCAC [5] and SYLPH [4] platforms aimed at improving healthcare of dependent people. The HCCAC system is based on a multi-agent architecture that is comprised

of various types of intelligent agents [5]. The primary agent in HCCAC is the Interpreter Agent, which is integrated into the system. The purpose of this agent is to provide solutions for the wellbeing of the user through the use of action plans based on
the information provided by the WSN sensors. The most important characteristics of
the system are: (i) the Interpreter Agent has reasoning capability; it can analyze and
reason the context data gathered by the system and provide proactive solutions, (ii)
the Interpreter Agent can easily adapt to the context within which it acts, (iii) gather
sensor data and messages from other agents in order to provide efficient solutions and
(iv) the Interpreter Agent performs a data fusion with the information received. The
system uses several WSNs in order to automatically gather context information.
Based on the data received by the WSNs, the Interpreter agent fuses, evaluates and
reasons the data in order to develop action plans and initiate events that affect the
sensors that are also connected in the WSNs.

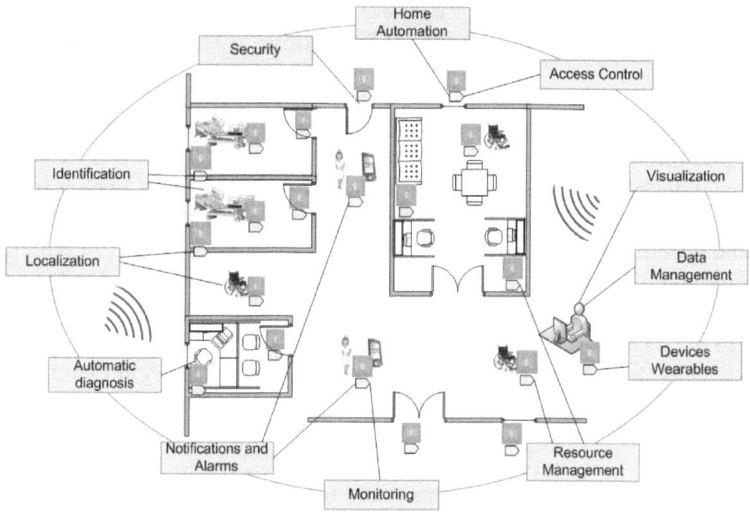

Fig. 1. WSN at healthcare facility

Figure 1 shows the basic communication and infrastructure schema of the monitoring system. A network of ZigBee devices has been designed to cover each patient to
be monitored. Each of the monitored patients carries a ZigBee remote control that
incorporates a button which can be pressed in event of needing remote assistance or
urgent help. Moreover, there are a set of ZigBee sensors that obtain information about
the environment (e.g. light, smoke, temperature, doors' states, etc.) in which the user
lives and that physical response to the changes (e.g. light dimmers, fire alarms or door
locks). Each of these ZigBee nodes includes a C8051F121 microcontroller and a
CC2420 IEEE 802.15.4 radiofrequency transceiver. Each of the ZigBee and Bluetooth
devices are connected as nodes within the SYLPH platform. Each of the nodes is
controlled by a Provider agent in the HCCAC system, which is in charge of gathering
the information from the sensor, applying the first filtering process to the information
received, and sending the information to the Interpreter agent.

There is also a computer and mobiles connected to a remote healthcare monitoring center via Internet. Alerts generated by the Interpreter Agent can be forwarded from the patients' homes to the caregivers in the remote center, allowing them to communicate with patients in order to check possible incidences. These alerts can be, for instance, the detection of a patient's fall or a high smoke level in the patient's home. This computer acts as device to control the Interpreter Agent and ZigBee master node through a physical wireless interface (e.g. a ZigBee network adapter as a ZigBee USB (Universal Serial Bus) dongle or a ZigBee node connected through the computer's USB port). The computer is also the master node of a Bluetooth network formed by the sensors working as slave nodes. At the SYLPH level, the computer performs as a SYLPH Gateway so that it connects both WSNs each to other.

The following subsection provides a detailed explanation of the information that is obtained from the environment, how it is fused, stored, and finally, how it is processed and represented.

3.1 Obtaining and Merging Context Information

The Interpreter agent performs a detailed analysis of the information that it received in order to generate efficient solutions. The capabilities of the Interpreter agent can be analyzed as follows. To begin, the Interpreter agent administers and fuses the information, and distributes tasks among the remaining system agents, which in turn communicate with the Interpreter agent to transmit any changes in the context, tasks, or additional specific user information, which is then updated by the Interpreter agent. The Interpreter agent manages all cases of inserting, deleting and updating each user. It controls the connection and disconnection of the users to the system. It continually calculates the location of the users, informing where each one is located. Additionally, it is responsible for optimizing the task planning prior to any event that may require a new plan, such as with the number of system users, or when there is a change in the condition of the context, for example, a sudden change in temperature, or a gas or water leak.

Figure 2, which provides a diagram of the Interpreter agent, describes the information that it gathers and manages its protocols, activities, permission and responsibilities. The Interpreter agent has a context-aware belief base in which it stores all events that constitute its knowledge base. It structures these beliefs and relates them within the context-aware environment and with the user. The beliefs may include: (i) the location of the user taken from a RFID chip carried by the user, and transmitted by the location sensors to the system, (ii) the exterior temperature captured from web services, (iii) the interior temperature gathered from ZigBee temperature sensors connected to the WSN, (iv) the illumination gathered from the ZigBee light sensors connected to the WSN, and (v) the level of smoke taken from the ZigBee smoke detectors connected to a WSN. All of these data are initially captured and filtered by the HCCAC system provider agents. The provider agents send this information to the Interpreter agent, which stores and processes it. When the Interpreter agent received this information during the fusion process, it can do one of three things: (i) accept the information, because it is completely coherent and non-redundant, and therefore useful for reasoning and actions within the environment, (ii) reject it because it is duplicate information that the agent already contains and is therefore disposable, or

```
Scheme: Interpreter Agent

Description: Manages the database and distributes the tasks among the remaining
agents in the system.

Attributes:
User - Location – Temperature – Gas Control – Fluid Control - LocationGPS – Light
Control – Smoke Control – Preferences - OnOffDevice

Protocols and Activities:
ConsultBD, UpdateBD, Make Planning, Send Planning, Discharge Conection, User
Disconnection, Access Control, Response Context Request, Get User List, Generate
Context Change, Alert Response, Change Conditional Context, Information Request,
Location Request, Terminal Discharge, Terminal Cancel.

Permits:
Update (User | Terminal | Location | Planning | Login | Alert)

Responsabilities:
Interpreter = (ConsultBD | UpdateBD | Make Planning | Send Planning | Discharge
Login | User Disconnection | Access Control | Response Context Request | Get User
List | Generate Context Change | Alert Response | Change Conditional Context |
Information Request | Location Request | Terminal Discharge | Terminal Cancel)
```

Fig. 2. Diagram of the Interpreter agent

(iii) refine the information, which is useful but cannot be stored as is, and requires a specific type of processing. One example of refining information is when the Interpreter agent receives the same status information from a particular sensor. In this case, the Interpreter agent does not store all the information it receives; instead it groups it according to periods of time in which the sensor status has not changed.

All actions are structured through Java objects, which represent beliefs. These objects each have a name and attributes that have simple or multiple values, according to the type of information that the attribute stores. For example, an object that represents the information from the smoke detector will have an attribute with a simple value that indicates whether the fire alarm should or should not sound, and another object that represents the information for the temperature will have an attribute with a multiple value that indicates a range of temperature within specific periods of time. The beliefs base also incorporates the concept of data bases related to objects. The language for queries related to objects, Object Constraing Language (OCL) used in the HCCAC system, can recover subsets of context-aware beliefs. The filtering conditions for beliefs represent an expression of a particular state, for example one or more than one belief. Once the condition is satisfied, an internal event is generated, and this event activates a plan or gives way to adopting a new set of objectives. In the Interpreter agent, beliefs represent changes in the state of the sensors installed within the context-aware environment. This makes it possible to easily add new types of sensors that can assist in the daily tasks of the user, or to add a new state for a given sensor to a task plan at a future time. All of the task plans and actions plans specific to the Interpreter agent contribute towards achieving the final objective.

4 Conclusions and Future Work

Services for health and wellbeing promote healthy behavior, encourage preventative care, and help users to solve inconveniences within a health context in an effective manner. All health services established within a healthcare context are based on a close and trusting relationship between the user and the health service [9]. Additionally, these services have to be transparent for the users so that the support offered is imperceptible to the user. All of these services can be achieved after passing through a number of internal steps that are hidden from the user. One of these steps is the fusion of information gathered from the healthcare context. Data fusion is the final step in the process of integrating data. First the individual profiles are collected, and then duplicate information is identified [2]. Of all the integration systems presented in section 2, only a few are truly capable of managing contradictory or redundant data. The intelligent agent system presented in this article is capable of generating an integrated and efficient diagram that does not contain duplicated information. This is possible because the Interpreter agent receives the structured information through the provider agents. The provider agents perform the initial filter of information from the information received through the sensors. As a result, the multi-agent system assigns tasks among the different agents so that the process of information fusion is quick and simple, while consuming minimal system resources. The multisensory fusion of healthcare data contributes to a global comprehension of the actions and process involved in the monitoring of dependent individuals.

Regarding the monitoring system described, the next step consists of developing this proposal and implementing it in a real scenario. Moreover, additional future work will focus on testing the system in different environments and looking for feedback to adjust and improve the proposed solution. That is our next challenge.

Acknowledgments. This work was supported by the MICINN project TIN2009-13839-C03.

References

1. Bajo, J., Fraile, J.A., Corchado, J.M., Pérez-Lancho, B.: The THOMAS Architecture in Home Care Scenarios: A case study. Expert Systems with Applications 37(5), 3986–3999 (2010)
2. Bleiholder, J., Naumann, F.: Data Fusion. ACM Computing Surveys (CSUR), Article 1, 41(1) (2008)
3. Castanedo, F., García, J., Patricio, M.A., Molina, J.M.: Data fusion to improve trajectory tracking in a Cooperative Surveillance Multi-Agent Architecture. Elsevier, Article in Press (2009), doi:10.1016/j.inffus.2009.09.002
4. Corchado, J.M., Bajo, J., Tapia, D.I., Abraham, A.: Using Heterogeneous Wireless Sensor Networks in a Telemonitoring System for Healthcare. IEEE Transactions on Information Technology in Biomedicine. Special Issue: Affective and Pervasive Computing for Healthcare (2009) (in Press)
5. Fraile, J.A., Bajo, J., Corchado, J.M.: Applying Context-Aware Computing in Dependent Environments. In: Mira, J., Ferrández, J.M., Álvarez, J.R., de la Paz, F., Toledo, F.J. (eds.) IWINAC 2009. LNCS, vol. 5602, pp. 85–94. Springer, Heidelberg (2009)

6. Fraile, J.A., Bajo, J., Corchado, J.M.: Multi-Agent Architecture for Dependent Environments. In: Providing Solutions for Home Care. Inteligencia Artificial. Special Issue 7th Ibero-American Workshop in Multi-Agent Systems, vol. 42, pp. 36–45 (2009), ISSN: 1137-3601
7. Liu, Y.-H., Wang, S.-Z., Du, X.-M.: A multi-agent information fusion model for ship collision avoidance. In: 2008 International Conference on Machine Learning and Cybernetics, vol. 1, pp. 6–11 (2008)
8. Muñoz, M.A., Gonzalez, V.M., Rodriguez, M., Favela, J.: Supporting context-aware collaboration in a hospital: an ethnographic informed design. In: Proceedings of Workshop on Artificial Intelligence, Information Access, and Mobile Computing 9th International Workshop on Groupware, CRIWG 2003, Grenoble, France, pp. 330–334 (2003)
9. Pierce, L.L., Steiner, V.L., Khuder, S.A., Govoni, A.L., Horn, L.J.: The effect of a Web-based stroke intervention on carers' well-being and survivors' use of healthcare services. Disability & Rehabilitation, Editorial Board Members 31(20), 1676–1684 (2009)
10. Pfeffer, A., Das, S., Lawless, D., Ng, B.: Factored reasoning for monitoring dynamic team and goal formation. Information Fusion. Science Direct 10(1), 99–106 (2009)
11. Sycara, K., Glinton, R., Yu, B., Giampapa, J., Owens, S., Lewis, M., Grindle, L.T.C.C.: An integrated approach to high-level information fusion. Information Fusion 10(1), 25–50 (2009)

Multivariate Discretization for Associative Classification in a Sparse Data Application Domain

María N. Moreno García, Joel Pinho Lucas, Vivian F. López Batista, and M. José Polo Martín

Department of Computing and Automatic, University of Salamanca, Salamanca, Spain
mmg@usal.es

Abstract. Associative classification is becoming a promising alternative to classical machine learning algorithms. It is a hybrid technique that combines supervised and unsupervised data mining algorithms and builds classifiers from association rules' models. The aim of this work is to apply these associative classifiers to improve estimation precision in the project management area where data sparsity involves a major drawback. Moreover, in this application domain, most of the attributes are continuous; therefore, they must be discretized before generating the rules. The discretization procedure has a significant effect on the quality of the induced rules as well as on the precision of the classifiers built from them. In this paper, a multivariate supervised discretization method is proposed, which takes into account the predictive purpose of the association rules.

1 Introduction

The major advances obtained lately in the field of data mining come from the hybridization of diverse techniques, since the research into the improvement of single algorithms is not producing great results. On the other hand, the success of data mining methods depends on the application domain. Issues such as the amount of data available for the training process or the number and type of the attributes have a significant influence on the precision of the predictive models. Project management is an application field where the machine learning methods do not give satisfactory results since the available dataset is usually small and most of the attributes are continuous. This is one of the reasons why these methods are not widely used for making software estimations and the classic methods are still being applied. The development of hybrid techniques can contribute to replacing traditional software estimation methods by new data mining approaches.

The most usual software characteristics to be estimated are software size and project effort or cost. In this study we try to take advantage of data mining methods in order to obtain reliable software size estimations that can be used later in project effort and cost estimation. Our aim is to find the proper combination of techniques for solving the most important drawbacks found in the project management field, which are responsible for the low precision of classical machine learning algorithms.

The main problem we have to deal with is the sparsity of the dataset due to the low number of available examples for inducing the predictive models against the great

M. Graña Romay et al. (Eds.): HAIS 2010, Part I, LNAI 6076, pp. 104–111, 2010.

number of possible attribute values. Traditional machine learning methods yield poor results with sparse datasets; therefore, it is necessary to find a method slightly sensitive to the sparsity in order to obtain good estimations in this application domain. Because of the successful results provided by association rules in other kinds of estimations, also in the project management field [13], we attempt a classification based on association, which is a machine learning technique that combines concepts from classification and association. Such methods work with discrete attributes, but most of the attributes involved in software size estimation are continuous. This is another problem that arises in the software project application domain, which means it is necessary to carry out a discretization process prior to the application of the data mining algorithms. Association analysis is one of the data mining areas where discretization has most relevance. Association rules can only be generated from discrete attributes; thus, an adequate discretization process has a significant impact on the quality of the rules. Association analysis is considered an unsupervised data mining method, unlike classification, which is a supervised technique. The first is mainly used in the area of knowledge discovery in databases, whereas classification is applied for predictive purposes. Traditionally, both kinds of techniques have been used to solve different kinds of problems. However, recent studies show that knowledge discovery algorithms, such as association rule mining techniques can be successfully used for building accurate and efficient classifiers [8] [11] [12] called associative classifiers.

The rest of the paper is organized as follows. Section 2 includes a review of relevant works in the literature concerning associative classification and discretization. In Section 3 the proposed discretization algorithm is described. The experimental study is presented in section 4 and conclusions are given in section 5.

2 Related Work

The concept of association between items was introduced by Agrawal and col. and put into practice in their well known Apriori algorithm [1]. Since then, association rule induction has been the object of numerous works in the literature. Most of them are focused on simplifying the rule set and improving the algorithm performance. In recent years, association rules have been used for classification purposes and thus a new data-mining approach has emerged: associative classification.

Several proposals of associative classification have been reported recently: CBA (Classification Based in Association) [8], CPAR (Classification based on Predictive Association Rules) [19], MCAR (Multi-class Classification based on Association Rules) [15] and CMAR (Classification based on Multiple class-Association Rules) [6]. Associative classification rule mining generates association rules having only one attribute, the class, in their consequent term. Therefore, such rules can be used to classify examples: in order to classify an item, its attribute values are matched to every rule's antecedents. The attribute value of the consequent term (from one or more selected rules) will be the predicted class. Usually, the classification model is presented as an ordered list of rules obtained by a rule ordering mechanism [17]. In the CBA algorithm [8] the rules are ordered following their confidence values. The MCAR algorithm considers in addition the support of the rules. The CMAR algorithm uses all the rules that match the example to be classified instead of using just one rule.

The class is selected from the group whose elements hold the highest correlation value according to the weighted χ2 measure. In a similar way, the CPAR algorithm divides rules into groups, but uses the "k" best rules that represent each class, instead of using all the rules that match the example to be classified. Then, Laplace Accuracy is used as the only measure to select the group and to perform the classification.

Association rule algorithms work with discrete attributes, therefore a discretization process is required before generating the rules. This is a critical task in classification and knowledge discovery, which should be adapted to the data mining methods in order to improve the induced models. Several discretization approaches are available [9]. They can be classified into supervised and unsupervised techniques. The former are usually applied with knowledge discovery algorithms while the latter are used by machine learning algorithms. The performance of such algorithms is significantly affected by the discretization process.

Two simple unsupervised techniques commonly used are equal-width and equal-frequency, which consist of creating a specified number of intervals with the same size or with the same number of records, respectively. The purpose of the discretized data and the statistical characteristics of the sample to be treated should be kept in mind when one of these algorithms is selected. For example, equal-width discretization yields poor results when the sample distribution is not uniform, but is more suitable for obtaining coherent and comprehensible intervals of values for certain attributes such as age, lines of code, etc., for a better interpretation of the results. Supervised methods, used mainly in classification problems, consider entropy measures. These are often embedded within machine learning algorithms such as those of decision trees induction. In these cases, the supervised discretization considers class information for generating the intervals while unsupervised discretization does not. The intervals obtained are those that best discriminate the classes. One well-known supervised method is the one proposed by Fayyad and Irani [5], which is an entropy-based multi-interval discretization procedure.

On the other hand, discretization can also be univariate or multivariate. Univariate binning quantifies one continuous attribute at a time while multivariate discretization concurrently considers multiple attributes, that is, the threshold values of the intervals are searched simultaneously for all continuous attributes. Though univariate discretization is used more and is simpler than the multivariate one, the latter has more advantages, particularly in the discovery of association rules since all available attributes are concurrently involved in the mining process. Multivariate discretization allows obtaining interdependences between attributes that can improve the quality of the association rules, especially when they are used for classification. This is the scenario of our work, in which we use association rules for building a classifier.

Attribute discretization methods for mining association rules have been treated in the literature. Nearly everyone takes the support factor of the rules as the main feature for splitting the attribute values into intervals. In [14] the measure of "partial completeness", based on confidence and support factors, is defined for quantifying the information lost by partitioning quantitative attributes. Values are fine-partitioned and then, adjacent intervals are combined if necessary. Lian et al. [7] introduce the concept of "density" to capture the characteristics of quantitative attributes and propose an efficient procedure to locate "dense regions" for mining association rules. The density of the regions representing rules is a measure used to evaluate the interestingness of the rules instead of using support and confidence. An alternative to the conversion of continuous attributes into discrete data is to consider the distribution of the continuous data, via standard statistical measures such as mean and variance [2]. Recently, several partition methods based on the fuzzy set theory have been proposed [16]. The mined rules are expressed in linguistic terms, which are more natural and understandable. In these works either both the antecedent and consequent parts of the rules are formed by a single item or the consequent part is not fixed. In our case the consequent part must be fixed because it is the class attribute and the antecedent part is an itemset. Thus, a multivariate discretization that considers all the attributes is more suitable.

3 Proposed Method for Associative Classification

The reason for using associative classification instead of classical machine learning algorithms such as Bayesian Networks or decision trees is the low precision that the latter provide with sparse datasets. We use the concept of sparsity as the inverse of density, which refers to the ratio between the number of records and the number of distinct values of the attributes. Our case study is located in the project management context, where the number of available records is usually scarce, there are many attributes and most of them take continuous values. Our aim is to demostrate that, in this application domain, associative classification combined with a proper discretization procedure overcomes other classification methods including hybrid approaches such as multiclassifiers.

We propose a multivariate discretization algorithm based on clustering (CBD, Clustering Based Discretization) in order to manage quantitative attributes. When the number of available attributes is large, a previous selection process is carried out, taking into account the classification purpose of the associative model. In this way, the selected attributes are those with higher values of purity, a measure that informs us as to how well the attribute discriminates the classes. It is based on the amount of information (entropy) provided by the attribute [10].

The proposed clustering technique, the CBD algorithm, was applied for discretizing the selected attributes simultaneously, including the label attribute. Clusters of similar records were built by using the iterative k-means algorithm with a Euclidean distance metric [9]. The clusters were built giving more weight to the class attribute. This is a supervised way of obtaining the best intervals for classification. The distribution of attribute values in the clusters was used for carrying out the discretization according to the following procedure, based on the method proposed by us for mining conventional quantitative association rules without classification purpose [13]:

1. The number of intervals for each attribute is the same as the number of clusters. If m is the mean value of the attribute in the cluster and σ is the standard deviation, the initial interval boundaries are $(m - \sigma)$ and $(m + \sigma)$.
2. For adjacent intervals i and $i+1$:
    If $(m_i > m_{i+1} - \sigma_{i+1})$ or $(m_{i+1} < m_i + \sigma_i)$ the two intervals are merged into one:
    $(m_i - \sigma_i)$, $(m_{i+1} + \sigma_{i+1})$
    else
        the cut point between intervals i and $i+1$:
        $(m_{i+1} - \sigma_{i+1} + m_i + \sigma_i)/2$

In this way continuous attributes are transformed into discrete ones. Then, an associative classification algorithm can be applied. Its results are significantly influenced by the discretization procedure as we can verify in next section.

4 Experimental Study

The proposed method was validated with data from 42 software projects. The aim was to estimate software size (LOC) from other attributes measured in early activities of the life cycle. The dataset containing 42 examples and 12 attributes was obtained from experiments carried out by Dolado [4]. The first step is to search the best attributes for discriminating LOC by calculating their cumulative purity, a measure of the purity of partitioning the data when more than one attribute is used. The attributes found by means of Mineset, a Silicon Graphics tool [10], were: RELATION (total number of relations), NTRNSMKII (number of transactions MKII), OPT-MENU (total number of menu choices), DATAELEMENT (total number of data elements) and OUTMKII (number of total ouputs) with a cumulative purity of 97.95%. These attributes were discretized by means of the CBD algorithm and the discrete values were used as the input to the associative classification method. In order to obtain profitable results, taking into account the problem domain and the distribution of values of the LOC attribute, we considered five clusters to start the CBD procedure in order to generate the suitable intervals of values for the selected attributes. The class attribute was weighted over the other attributes in the clustering process with the intention of directing the splitting to the most suitable intervals for the later associative classification.

In order to validate the proposed Clustering Based Discretization (CBD) procedure, the dataset was treated with several classification methods including multiclassifiers. These are hybrid approaches whose superiority over classical classifiers has been demonstrated in many research works. In this study, the precision obtained by applying such methods with continuous data (except the class attribute) was analyzed. In addition, several associative classification methods were applied with discretized data by means of different discretization algorithms. We used 10-fold cross validation. The comparative study of the results is summarized in Figure 1.

We applied Bayes Net, the decision tree J4.8 and two multiclassifiers, Bagging with RepTree [3] and Staking with CeroR [18]. Several base classifiers were used for building the multiclassifiers but we only report the most precise ones. These methods require a discrete class attribute; therefore we split the LOC values into five equal width intervals in order to maintain some consistency with the proposed method, since five was the number of intervals provided by the CBD algorithm.

CBA and CMAR were the associative classification methods selected for the study since both our experience and the literature have demonstrated their superiority over other methods. Usually CMAR has more predictive precision than CBA at the expense of a higher computational cost. In this case study the computational cost of both methods was similar, given the reduced size of the dataset. CMAR was applied with data discretized by means of four different algorithms: equal width, equal frequency, Fayyad and Irani method, and the proposed CBD procedure. To apply the Fayyad and Irani method, five equal width intervals of LOC were used since the algorithm works

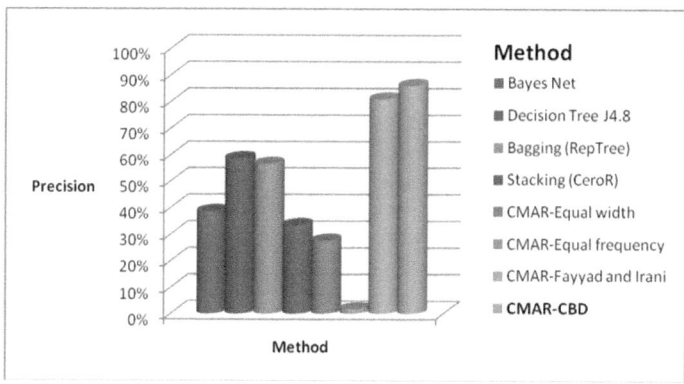

Fig. 1. Precision obtained by different methods

Table 1. Summary of the results

CLASSIFICATION METHOD	PRECISION
Bayes Net	38.46%
Decision Tree J4.8	58.97%
Bagging (RepTree)	56.41%
Stacking (CeroR)	33.33%
CMAR-Equal width	27.50%
CMAR-Equal frequency	1.67%
CMAR-Fayyad and Irani	80.83%
CMAR-CBD	**85.83%**

with nominal class attributes. CMAR was executed with a minimum support of 10% and a minimum confidence threshold of 75%.

Figure 1 and Table 1 show the improvement in the accuracy achieved by the method proposed in this work in an application domain consisting of a sparse dataset. The reduced number of available records can be the cause of the very poor results provided by traditional classifiers. In this context, even robust methods such as multi-classifiers cannot overcome the individual classifiers. CMAR gives better results than non-associative classification methods with two out of four discretized datasets, those obtained by applying the Fayyad and Irani method and the procedure proposed in this work, the CBD algorithm. The latter provided the highest precision, 85.83%, a very good result bearing in mind the sparse dataset and the low precision achieved by classical classifiers and multiclassifiers. Although the precision differences given by CMAR with CBD and the Fayyad and Irani method are not very significant, the last method has the drawback that it works with nominal class attributes while CBD does not, but it discretizes all attributes simultaneously, including the class. Furthermore, CBD achieves better precision with a lower number of rules. These results also demonstrate the great influence of the discretization procedure on the accuracy of the predictions provided by associative classification methods.

5 Conclusions

Most machine learning methods are very vulnerable to the characteristics of the data-set they are applied to. Sparsity is one of the factors that produce the worst negative effects on their precision. In this work a hybrid approach is proposed in order to deal with that problem in the project management field. In this application domain there are a large amount of available attributes representing the factors that influence the variable to be predicted; however, the number of projects where the attributes are gathered from is very low. This fact leads to a great sparsity of the dataset and there-fore, to low precision on the part of classification methods. We applied associative classification in order to deal with that drawback because these methods are less vul-nerable to sparsity than others. Moreover, the presence of continuous quantitative attributes becomes an additional problem because these algorithms require discrete attributes as input. Thus, we have proposed a multivariate supervised discretization procedure, CBD, especially indicated for classification problems. The combination of CBD and the CMAR associative classification method was applied for software size estimation from a dataset comprising the drawbacks mentioned above. The case study demonstrated that our proposal widely surpasses the classic supervised learning methods, including other hybrid approaches such as multiclassifiers. The experiments also demonstrate the great influence of the discretization procedure on the accuracy of the associative classification methods.

References

1. Agrawal, R., Imielinski, T., Swami, A.: Mining associations between sets of items in large databases. In: Proc. of ACM SIGMOD Int. Conference on Management of Data, Washinton, DC, pp. 207–216 (1993)
2. Aumann, Y., Lindell, Y.: A statistical theory for quantitative association rules. Journal of Intelligent Information Systems 20(3), 255–283 (2003)
3. Breiman, L.: Bagging predictors. Machine Learning 24(2), 123–140 (1996)
4. Dolado, J.J.: A validation of the component-based method for software size estimation. IEEE Transactions on Software Engineering 26(10), 1006–1021 (2000)
5. Fayyad, U.M., Irani, K.B.: Multi-interval discretization of continuous valued attributes for classification learning. In: Proc. of the Thirteenth International Joint Conference on Arti-cial Intelligence, IJCAI 1993, Chambery, France, pp. 1022–1027 (1993)
6. Li, W., Han, J., Pei, J.: CMAR. Accurate and efficient classification based on multiple class-association rules. In: Proc. of the IEEE International Conference on Data Mining (ICDM 2001), California, pp. 369–376 (2001)
7. Lian, W., Cheung, D.W., Yiu, S.M.: An efficient algorithm for dense regions discovery from large-scale data streams. Computers & Mathematics with Applications 50, 471–490 (2005)
8. Liu, B., Hsu, W., Ma, Y.: Integration classification and association rule mining. In: Proc. of 4th Int. Conference on Knowledge Discovery and Data Mining, New York, pp. 80–86 (1998)
9. Liu, H., Hussain, F., Tan, C.L., Dash, M.: Discretization. An enabling technique. Data Mining and Knowledge Discovery 6, 393–423 (2002)
10. Mineset user's guide, v. 007-3214-004, 5/98, Silicon Graphics (1998)

11. Moreno, M.N., García, F.J., Polo, M.J.: Mining interesting association rules for Prediction in the Software Project Management Area. In: Kambayashi, Y., Mohania, M., Wöß, W. (eds.) DaWaK 2004. LNCS, vol. 3181, pp. 341–350. Springer, Heidelberg (2004)
12. Moreno, M.N., Miguel, L.A., García, F.J., Polo, M.J.: Building knowledge discovery-driven models for decision support in project management. Decision Support Systems 38(2), 305–317 (2004)
13. Moreno, M.N., Ramos, I., García, F.J., Toro, M.: An association rule mining method for estimating the impact of project management policies on software quality, development time and effort. Expert Systems with Applications 34(2), 522–529 (2008)
14. Srikant, R., Agrawal, R.: Mining quantitative association rules in large relational tables. In: Proc. of ACM SIGMOD Conference, Montreal, Canada, pp. 1–12 (1996)
15. Thabtah, F., Cowling, P., Peng, Y.: MCAR: multi-class classification based on association rule. In: Proc. of the International Conference on Computer Systems and Applications (AICCSA 2005), Washington, USA, p. 33-I. IEEE, Los Alamitos (2005)
16. Verlinde, H., De Cock, M., Boute, R.: Fuzzy versus quantitative association rules. A fair data-driven comparison. IEEE Transactions on Systems, Man, and Cybernetics - Part B. Cybernetics 36, 679–684 (2006)
17. Wang, Y., Xin, Q., Coenen, F.: A novel rule ordering approach in classification association rule mining. In: Perner, P. (ed.) MLDM 2007. LNCS (LNAI), vol. 4571, pp. 339–348. Springer, Heidelberg (2007)
18. Wolpert, D.H.: Stacked Generalization. Neural Networks 5, 241–259 (1992)
19. Yin, X., Han, J.: CPAR. Classification based on predictive association rules. In: Proc. of SIAM International Conference on Data Mining (SDM 2003), pp. 331–335 (2003)

Recognition of Turkish Vowels by Probabilistic Neural Networks Using Yule-Walker AR Method

Erdem Yavuz[1] and Vedat Topuz[2]

[1] Research Asst. Istanbul Commerce University Engineering and Architecture Faculty,
Küçükyalı, 34840, İstanbul, Turkey
Ph.: (+90) 216 48918 88; Fax: (+90) 216 489 97 14
eyavuz@iticu.edu.tr
[2] Asst. Prof. Dr. Marmara University Vocational School of Technical Sciences, Göztepe,
34722, İstanbul, Turkey
Ph.: (+90) 216 418 25 04; Fax: (+90) 216 418 25 05
vtopuz@marmara.edu.tr

Abstract. In this work, recognition of vowels in Turkish Language by probabilistic neural networks is implemented using a spectral analysis method. Power spectral density of the phones obtained from speakers is estimated. Then weighted power spectrum is calculated after power spectral density of that phone is passed through a number of band pass filters. In this way, estimated power spectrums of the phones which are obtained from speakers approximate to a mel scale. Mel scale coefficients obtained, form the feature vector of the phone that is pronounced. These feature vectors constitute the database of the related speaker. Thus and so, every speaker has its own database. When it comes to recognize a phone pronounced by a speaker later, a probabilistic neural network model is created using the database belonging to that speaker. The feature vector of the phone which is to be recognized is computed as mentioned above. In this study, speaker-dependent recognition of Turkish vowels has been realized with an accuracy rate of over 95 percent.

Keywords: Vowel recognition, spectral analysis, probabilistic neural networks.

1 Introduction

Speaking is a natural and efficient way of communication among people. Automatic speech recognition and speech synthesis by machines have attracted much attention in the last 50 years. First studies in this area were done in 1952 by Davis, Biddulph and Balashek [1]. Together with the considerable developments in statistical modeling regarding speech recognition, today in the world automatic speech recognition systems are used widely in many fields, requiring human-machine interaction such as handling incoming calls to call centers and query-based information systems (current travel information, weather forecast supply) [2]. Automatic speech recognition systems also can provide great convenience for people with disabilities.

For languages such as English and Japanese speech recognition systems have been developed and many of these systems are used in different applications in real life.

M. Graña Romay et al. (Eds.): HAIS 2010, Part I, LNAI 6076, pp. 112–119, 2010.
© Springer-Verlag Berlin Heidelberg 2010

But to say the same thing is unlikely for Turkish Language. Efforts to develop speech recognition systems for Turkish Language have so far been limited. There are many reasons for this. The most important one is that unlike the Indo-European languages, Turkish is an agglutinative. For languages that have agglutinative morphology, such as Turkish, Finnish, or Hungarian, it is possible to produce thousands of forms for a given root word [3]. This reveals the very large vocabulary [4].

Methods used in speech recognition systems vary according to the characteristics of the targeted language. Turkish is an agglutinative language and many suffixes can be added to the end of a Turkish word. For this reason, it is difficult to develop a word-based speech recognition system for Turkish Language [5]. Thus, if Turkish speech recognition systems are to be developed, this system makes more sense to be syllable-based or phoneme-based. One of the most important factors affecting the success of the recognition system is the unit used in speech recognition systems. If the unit used is large in size, such as words, then distinctive sound features included in that unit will be enough and thus the success of speech recognition systems will be high. On the other hand, this situation brings to dealing with large vocabulary. If the unit used in the speech recognition system is small in size, for example, phoneme or syllable, limited size of the database is concerned. The disadvantage of phoneme-based and syllable-based recognition systems is that the start and end points of phonemes and syllables within spelling of a word are somewhat difficult to detect.

In this study, recognition of vowels in Turkish Language by probabilistic neural networks has been implemented using spectral analysis methods. This paper represents general structure of the system developed, its application and results.

2   Speech Signal Preprocessing

Preprocessing is a process of preparing speech signal for further processing. The spectrum of speech signal shows a downward trend, whereby frequencies in the upper part of the spectrum are attenuated [6]. To perform an accurate analysis, audio signal spectrum must be smoothed first. To perform this operation, first order high pass filter is used generally. This filter is used for emphasizing high frequency components. Transfer function of this filter is shown in equation (1).

$$H(z) = 1 - \alpha z^{-1} \tag{1}$$

α in the equation is a constant and usually varies between 0.9 and 1. Result of the filtering process is shown in Figure 1. In this example, α is chosen to be 0.95.

An important problem in speech processing is to detect the moments of speaking in a noisy environment. This problem is generally called "endpoints detection" [7]. During audio recording, ambient noise is sensed by the microphone and this noise will be present in the speech signal acquired. Non-silent part of the speech must be separated from the ambient noise. Algorithms developed by Rabiner and Sambur or other algorithms in the literature can be used to determine endpoints of isolated words. The scope of this study is limited to vowels. So, determining endpoints of vowels which are recorded in a noisy environment is relatively easier than determining endpoints of words that begin with a consonant.

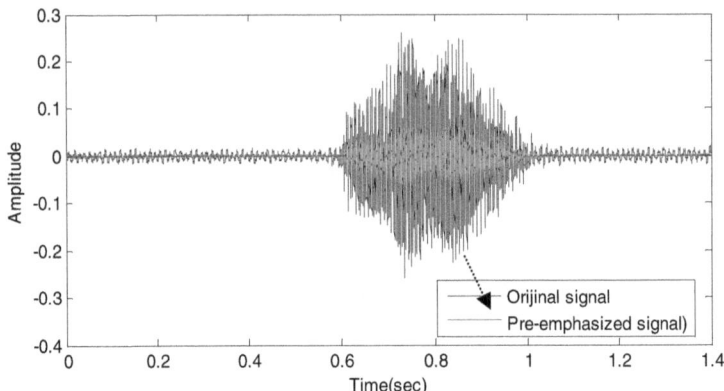

Fig. 1. Waveform of the spelling of the vowel "o" by a speaker: original signal (the dark color), and pre-emphasized signal (the light color)

Informative graphics about determining endpoints of a vowel spelling are shown in Figure 2. Audio signal is first segmented into 5 milisecond frames and average magnitude difference value of each segment is computed. Average magnitude difference value of non-segmented audio signal is computed as well and this value is set to be the average magnitude threshold value.

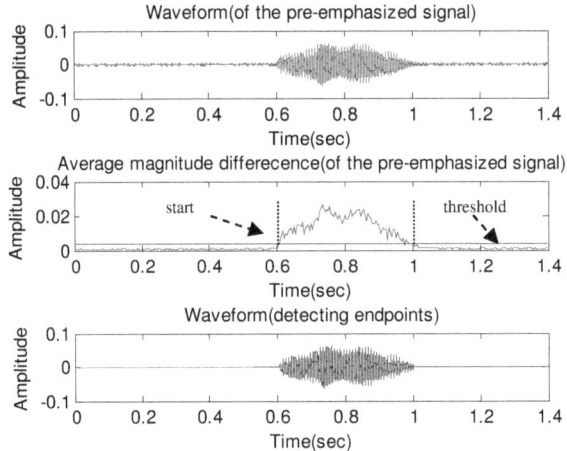

Fig. 2. Detecting endpoints of the spelling of a vowel (namely, aforementioned vowel "o")

First segment that has an average magnitude value greater than the threshold value is assumed to be the starting point of that audio signal. Last segment that has an average magnitude value greater than the threshold value is assumed to be the end point of that audio signal. So, endpoints of vowel spellings are computed in this simple way.

Because of physical constraints, vocal tract shape generally changes fairly slowly with time and tends to be constant over short time intervals (about 10-20 ms) [6]. A reasonable approximation is to divide speech signal into frames of equal length. Before making any frequency analysis, each frame of signal is multiplied by a tapered window (generally **Hamming** or **Hanning** window). If windowing were not applied, spurious high-frequency components would be introduced into the spectrum [6]. Analysis window length should be short enough to give the required time resolution and should at the same time be long enough to provide sufficient frequency resolution. A common compromise is to use 20-25 ms window [6]. In this study, sounds are recorded at a sampling frequency of 16 KHz and window length is chosen as 20 ms. Therefore, according to these two parameters the window length (also frame length) turns out to be 320 samples. Windowing process applied on a frame of speech signal is shown in Figure 3.

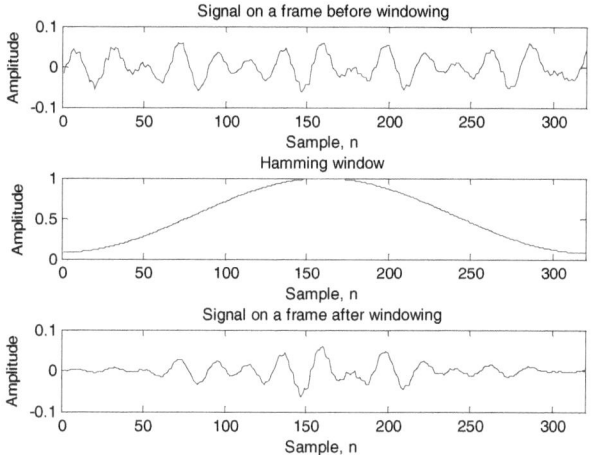

Fig. 3. Illustration of windowing process applied to a frame

3 Feature Extraction

After preprocessing the speech signal, it is necessary to represent it with less data, i.e. to create feature vectors from it. It is difficult to understand the content of the signal by looking at the waveform (in time domain). Important information is in the frequency, phase and amplitude values of sinusoidal components that make up the speech signal [8]. Fourier transform can be used in order to represent the speech signal with less data and also to obtain more meaningful information. Power spectral density (PSD) estimation means computing power spectrum of the signal. Frequency content of the signal is characterized by power spectral density. Spectral estimation methods are categorized into two groups: parametric methods and non-parametric methods [9]. In nonparametric methods, the PSD is estimated directly from the signal itself [10]. Parametric methods are those in which the PSD is estimated from a signal that is assumed to be output of a linear system driven by white noise. These methods are sometimes referred to as autoregressive *(AR)* methods. AR methods are good at adequately describing spectra of data which is peaky.

Data in many practical signals such as speech signal tend to have a spectrum that is peaky. So, AR methods are very suitable for this type of signals. AR methods that are used to estimate spectrums of signals, in the Signal Processing Toolbox of MATLAB are: Yule-Walker, Burg, Covariance, and Modified Covariance.

In this study, Yule-Walker spectral estimation algorithm is used. Using Yule-Walker algorithm, a 14th order AR model is defined and spectral contents of signals are computed by this model. Estimating power spectral density of a vowel spelling using Yule-Walker algorithm is shown in Figure 4. Red straight line shown in Figure 4-a is a threshold value which is obtained by multiplying average value of the power spectrum by 1.4. By taking the part of the spectrum above the threshold and discarding the rest of it, new power spectrum is obtained which can be called "derived power spectrum". Derived power spectrum obtained is shown in Figure 4-b.

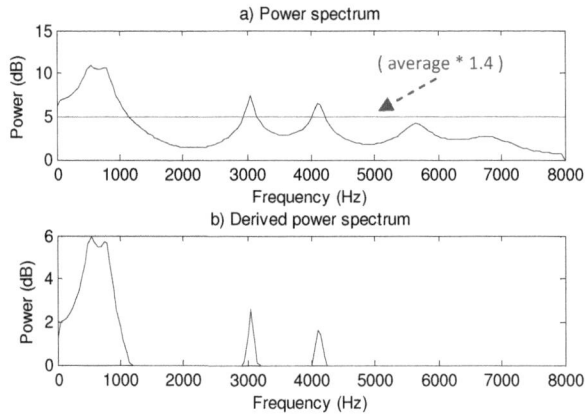

Fig. 4. Estimating power spectrum using Yule-Walker algorithm

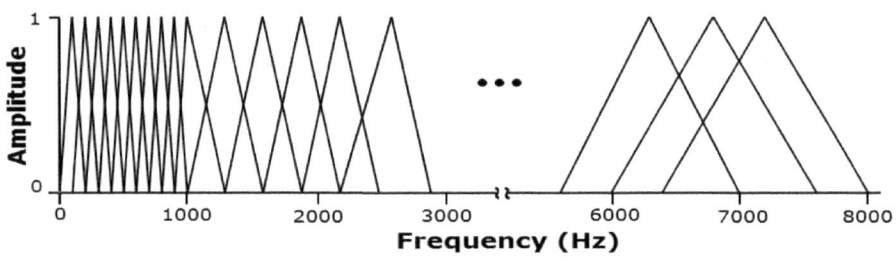

Fig. 5. Triangular filters of the type suggested by Davis and Mermelstein (in 1980) for transforming the output of a Fourier Transform onto a mel scale

Psycophysical studies show that the frequency resolving power of human ear is of logarithmic fashion [6]. In the light of this information, a filter bank with a number of channels is involved. Bandwidth and spacing of these channels increase with frequency motivated by psycophysical studies of the frequency resolving power of human ear. Triangular filters, which were suggested by Davis and Mermelstein in 1980, used to transform the output of Fourier transform onto a mel scale are shown in Figure 5. Approximately 20 channels are used for speech with a 4 kHz bandwith [6]. A few channels can be added for higher-bandwidth signals.

In this study, the power spectrum shown in Figure 4-b is passed through a filter bank with 27 channels. Lower and upper frequencies of these filter channels are given in Table 1. As seen in the table, center frequencies of the filters are spaced equally on a linear scale up to 1 kHz, and equally o a logarithmic scale above 1 kHz. A coefficient is computed for each filter by summing the result which is obtained by passing the power spectrum through that band-pass filter. This process is done for each filter and eventually 27 coefficients are obtained. These coefficients make up the feature vector.

Table 1. Lower and upper frequency values of channels of the filter bank used

Cnannel #	Lower-Upper Frequencies (Hz - Hz)	Channel #	Lower-Upper Frequencies (Hz - Hz)	Channel #	Lower-Upper Frequencies (Hz - Hz)
1	0 - 200	10	900 - 1100	19	2800 - 3600
2	100 - 300	11	1000 - 1400	20	3200 - 4000
3	200 - 400	12	1200 - 1600	21	3600 - 4400
4	300 - 500	13	1400 - 1800	22	4000 - 5000
5	400 - 600	14	1600 - 2000	23	4400 - 5400
6	500 - 700	15	1800 - 2200	24	5000 - 6200
7	600 - 800	16	2000 - 2600	25	5400 - 6600
8	700 - 900	17	2200 - 2800	26	6200 - 7600
9	800 - 1000	18	2600 - 3200	27	6600 - 8000

4   Classification

This section gives the details of classification process in the vowel recognition system. The objective of this process is to match a vowel spelling to one of the eight vowels in Turkish Language (which are "a", "e", "i", "ı", "o", "ö", "u", and "ü"). This proposes a classification problem. Neural networks are exploited to solve this problem.

The network model used in the solution to this classification problem is shown in Figure 6. Probabilistic neural networks, which are a kind of radial basis networks, can be used to solve classification problems.

In the feature extraction stage, a vowel spelling is processed so as to be represented with a feature vector that consists of 27 coefficients. In this network model, first layer computes distances from the input vector to the training inputs and creates a new vector. The resultant vector indicates how close the input is to a training input. The second layer sums these contributions to each class of inputs to produce its net output

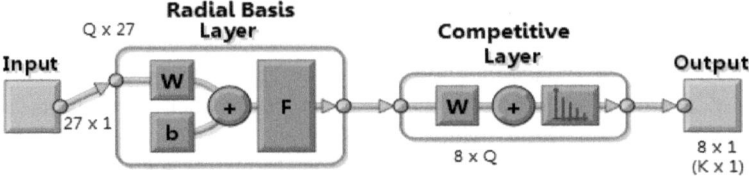

Q= number of inputs/targets pair = number of neurons in layer 1
K= number of classes of input data = number of neurons in layer 2

Fig. 6. The probabilistic neural network model used

as a vector of probabilities. Finally, the compete function on the output of second layer selects the maximum of these probabilities, and produces 1 for one vowel and 0s for the rest.

Each speaker is asked to give the pronunciation of all vowels three times in order for training the neural network. Normal, short and long pronunciations of vowels are collected. A training set that has a size of Q x 27 is formed after audio recordings collected for training are passed through the preprocessing and feature extraction stages respectively. As three sets of pronunciation (of eight vowels) are collected for training, the value of Q here automatically becomes 24. This can be seen in Table 2, which shows the training set for a speaker.

For testing purposes, 800 utterances of vowels were collected from 20 speakers (10 females, 10 males) within the range of 25-50 years old. The average recognition rate is 96.5 % for the testing set.

Table 2. Training set for a speaker

							TRAINING SET													
		INPUT										TARGET								
		FEATURE VECTOR COEFFICIENTS										VOWELS								
		C1	C2	C3	C4	C5	...	C23	C24	C25	C26	C27	a	e	i	ı	o	ö	u	ü
NORMAL	1	0	0	0,03	0,13	0,28	...	0	0	0	0	0	1	0	0	0	0	0	0	0
	2	0,03	0,05	0,09	0,15	0,24	...	0	0,12	0,1	0	0	0	1	0	0	0	0	0	0
	3	0,16	0,27	0,42	0,44	0,21	...	0	0	0	0	0	0	0	1	0	0	0	0	0
	4	0,24	0,39	0,57	0,89	0,92	...	0	0,34	0,07	0,32	0,08	0	0	0	1	0	0	0	0
	5	0,31	0,44	0,52	0,64	0,84	...	0	0	0	0	0	0	0	0	0	1	0	0	0
	6	0,1	0,15	0,19	0,26	0,39	...	0	0,04	0,05	0	0	0	0	0	0	0	1	0	0
	7	0,52	0,74	0,84	0,97	1	...	0	0	0,01	0,1	0	0	0	0	0	0	0	1	0
	8	0,18	0,29	0,41	0,56	0,42	...	0	0	0,01	0,04	0	0	0	0	0	0	0	0	1
SHORT	9	0,05	0,08	0,11	0,15	0,23	...	0	0	0	0	0	1	0	0	0	0	0	0	0
	10	0,02	0,04	0,08	0,14	0,25	...	0	0	0	0	0	0	1	0	0	0	0	0	0
	11	0,12	0,23	0,39	0,44	0,19	...	0	0	0,18	0,23	0	0	0	1	0	0	0	0	0
	12	0,07	0,13	0,2	0,32	0,56	...	0	0,01	0,21	0,26	0,01	0	0	0	1	0	0	0	0
	13	0,24	0,34	0,4	0,51	0,67	...	0	0	0	0	0	0	0	0	0	1	0	0	0
	14	0,05	0,09	0,15	0,25	0,42	...	0	0	0	0	0	0	0	0	0	0	1	0	0
	15	0,53	0,71	0,72	0,73	0,75	...	0	0,22	0,47	0,47	0,02	0	0	0	0	0	0	1	0
	16	0,15	0,23	0,3	0,35	0,26	...	0	0	0	0	0	0	0	0	0	0	0	0	1
LONG	17	0,15	0,22	0,27	0,35	0,47	...	0	0	0,06	0,06	0	1	0	0	0	0	0	0	0
	18	0	0	0,01	0,09	0,26	...	0	0	0,05	0,1	0	0	1	0	0	0	0	0	0
	19	0,22	0,38	0,59	0,52	0,21	...	0	0,02	0,33	0,04	0	0	0	1	0	0	0	0	0
	20	0,24	0,37	0,49	0,66	0,62	...	0	0,04	0,34	0,02	0	0	0	0	1	0	0	0	0
	21	0,35	0,49	0,54	0,62	0,72	...	0	0	0	0	0	0	0	0	0	1	0	0	0
	22	0,11	0,17	0,21	0,29	0,41	...	0	0	0	0	0	0	0	0	0	0	1	0	0
	23	0,66	0,9	0,95	0,99	1	...	0	0	0	0	0	0	0	0	0	0	0	1	0
	24	0,24	0,39	0,57	0,67	0,39	...	0	0	0	0	0	0	0	0	0	0	0	0	1

5 Conclusion

This paper has illustrated the speaker-dependent recognition of vowels by a probabilistic neural network. In the feature extraction stage, power spectral density estimation is used which is a type of spectral analysis methods. A probabilistic neural network model which is a kind of radial basis networks is used to recognize an unknown vowel spelling. In this study, speaker-dependent recognition of Turkish vowels has been realized with an accuracy rate of over 95 percent. We have demonstrated that Yule-Walker AR method can be used to recognize the Turkish vowels with acceptable results. The coefficient of 1.4 that is used in calculating the derived power spectrum which is utilized to create the feature vector has emerged as a result of a number of iterations. When this coefficient is chosen to be smaller (especially less than 1.2), the recognition rate is observed to be negatively affected.

References

1. Davis, K.H., Biddulph, R., Balashek, S.: Automatic Recognition of Spoken Digits. J. Acoust. Soc. Am. 24(6), 637–642 (1952)
2. Juang, B.H., Rabiner, L.R.: Automatic Speech Recognition – A Brief History of the Technology Development (2004)
3. Shibatani, M., Bynon, T.: Approaches to Language Typology, p. 5. Oxford University Press, Oxford (1999)
4. Tunalı, V.: A Speaker Dependent, Large Vocabulary, Isolated Word Speech Recognition System For Turkish. MSc Thesis, Marmara University Institute For Graduate Studies In Pure And Applied Sciences, Departmant of Computer Engineering, İstanbul, Turkey (2005)
5. Can, B.: Bir Hece-Tabanlı Türkçe Sesli İfade Tanıma Sisteminin Tasarımı Ve Gerçekleştirimi. Master Tezi, Hacettepe Üniversitesi Fen Bilimleri Enstitüsü, Bilgisayar Mühendisliği Bölümü, Ankara, Türkiye (2007)
6. Holmes, J., Holmes, W.: Speech Synthesis and Recognition. Taylor & Francis, London (2001)
7. Rabiner, L.R., Sambur, M.R.: An Algorithm for Determining the Endpoints of Isolated Utterances. The Bell System Technical Journal 54(2), 297–315 (1975)
8. Aşlıyan, R.: Design and Implementation of Turkish Speech Engine, Ph.D. Thesis, Dokuz Eylül University Graduate School of Natural And Applied Sciences, Turkey (2008)
9. Priestley, M.B.: Spectral Analysis and Time Series. Academic Press, London (1991)
10. Stoica, P., Moses, R.: Introduction to Spectral Analysis. Prentice Hall, Upper Saddle River (1997)

A Dynamic Bayesian Network Based Structural Learning towards Automated Handwritten Digit Recognition

Olivier Pauplin and Jianmin Jiang

Digital Media & Systems Research Institute
University of Bradford, United Kingdom
o.pauplin@bradford.ac.uk, j.jiang1@bradford.ac.uk
http://dmsri.inf.brad.ac.uk/

Abstract. Pattern recognition using Dynamic Bayesian Networks (DBNs) is currently a growing area of study. In this paper, we present DBN models trained for classification of handwritten digit characters. The structure of these models is partly inferred from the training data of each class of digit before performing parameter learning. Classification results are presented for the four described models.

1 Introduction

Bayesian Networks (BNs) [1][2][3], also called Belief Networks or Probabilistic Networks, allow to represent probability models in an efficient and intuitive way. Their temporal extension, Dynamic Bayesian Networks (DBNs) [4][5], have been recently applied to a range of different domains. A natural way to use them is to represent temporal cause-and-effect relationships between events. In that case, the DBN can be seen as a knowledge base for diagnostic and prediction [6]. Another kind of application exploits the ability of DBNs to be trained to detect patterns. They have been used in speech recognition [7] as a flexible and efficient extension of Hidden Markov Models. In video or image analysis, DBNs can be used to detect specific actions, with applications such as sport event detection [8], meeting activity segmentation [9] (also based on prosodic and lexical features), and surveillance and tracking [10]. For most of these tasks, the observed information used as an input for the DBN is made of pre-extracted features (various colour statistics, motion intensity of tracked points...), however it is also possible to use low-level data such as image pixels, as shown for instance by the application of DBNs to character recognition [11].

In this paper, we perform handwritten digit recognition using DBN models whose structure have been partly automatically learned from the training set of data. Complete structure learning is tractable for BNs or DBNs with complete data [12][13][14], but becomes rapidly intractable for DBNs with numerous nodes and with the presence of hidden nodes. To overcome this problem, we adopted a mixed approach where some links of the graph are learned independently from the final structure of the model, and are then completed with additional nodes

M. Graña Romay et al. (Eds.): HAIS 2010, Part I, LNAI 6076, pp. 120–127, 2010.

and links. The paper is organised as follow: in section 2, we briefly introduce BNs and DBNs, their main properties and the main ideas behind parameter learning in DBNs. We then describe the four kinds of DBN models we built to conduct the experiments. Section 3 contains the description of the experiments, and the results. Section 4 concludes this paper.

2   Dynamic Bayesian Networks

2.1   General Remarks

A Bayesian Network is a Directed Acyclic Graph (DAG) in which each node represents a random variable and quantitative probability information. Directed links (arrows) connect pairs of nodes. Node X is said to be the parent of node Y if there is an arrow from X to Y. The meaning of that link can be expressed in the following way: "X has a direct influence on Y". Influence is quantified by Conditional Probability Tables (CPT, for discrete nodes) or Conditional Probability Densities (CPD, for continuous nodes) associated with each node, which contain the conditional probabilities of the random variable for each combination of values of its parents. Nodes that do not have parents are associated with a prior probability instead of a conditional probability.

Given a set of random variables $(X_1, ..., X_n)$, the value of every entry in the full joint probability distribution is given by equation 1. A key aspect of BNs is that the equation can be written in a simplified form which is easily deduced from the topology of the network. The joint probability distribution in a BN is given by equation 2, where $Parents(X_i)$ denotes the parents of X_i.

$$P(X_1, ..., X_n) = P(X_1) \cdot \prod_{i=2}^{n} P(X_i|X_{i-1}, ..., X_1) \tag{1}$$

$$P(X_1, ..., X_n) = \prod_{i=1}^{n} P(X_i|Parents(X_i)) \tag{2}$$

Dynamic Bayesian Networks are an extension of static BNs to temporal events occurring at discrete times t. The graph of a DBN is built by juxtaposing several instances of a single BN, each instance of the BN (or time slice of the DBN) corresponding to a value of t. The complete network is obtained by adding directed links between slices (inter-slice links), in the direction of the time flow. Two assumptions are widely used in order to simplify the modelling:

- The Markov order of the DBN is equal to 1: the states at t only depend on states at t and $t - 1$;
- The DBN is stationary: its structure and parameters (conditional and prior probabilities) are the same for all $t \geq 2$ (provided the first time slice is $t = 1$).

DBNs can be used to perform inference, training and pattern detection tasks on data sets. Inference is the computation of the posterior probability of a query variable in the network, given the values of observed variables. Inference can be exact or approximate [4], approximate inference being the only feasible solution for large networks. One advantage of using DBNs over BNs is that the stationarity assumption allows to apply efficient inference algorithms (an unrolled DBN treated as a static BN would require much more computational power).

A detailed description of parameter and structure learning is beyond the scope of this article (see [15][16][17] for more details). For a discrete node related to a single random variable, learning the parameters means finding the conditional probabilities of the random variable for each different combination of values of its parents. For a continuous Gaussian node, the same principle applies except that two parameters have to be determined in each case: the mean and the standard deviation of the Gaussian distribution. Learning the parameters with complete data can be done by applying the principle of Maximum Likelihood, i.e. trying to find the set of parameters $\{\theta_1, ..., \theta_m\}$ that maximises the likelihood $P(d_1, ..., d_p | \theta_1, ..., \theta_m)$ where $\{d_1, ..., d_p\}$ is a set of observed data. When some variables are hidden (or data is incomplete), the Expectation-Maximisation (EM) algorithm can be used to learn the DBN parameters: using inference as a subroutine, it computes the expected values of the hidden variables given the current parameter values and the data, then it uses the inferred values as if they were observed values and applies the principle of Maximum Likelihood. Those steps are iterated until no improvement of the likelihood is achieved.

2.2   The Proposed Model Designs

The DBN models we present in this study have their structure partly based on inter-slice links learned from data. We have built and tested the following four models.

Model 1: Learned inter-slice links. The task of learning a DBN structure relies on the choice of a scoring function assessing how well a network "matches" a set of data. That scoring task can be performed by using the Bayesian Information Criterion (BIC score) [17], which combines the likelihood of the data according to a network with a penalty intended to avoid learning a network with too high a complexity (the absence of penalty would lead in most cases to learning the completely connected network). Learning the structure of DBNs from incomplete data may be done using the Structural EM algorithm (SEM) [18], but remains computationally challenging for complex networks.

The BIC score for a graph G and a set of complete data D is given by:

$$BIC = \log P(D|G, \hat{\Theta}) - \frac{\log N_s}{2} N_p \qquad (3)$$

where:

- $\hat{\Theta}$ is the set of parameters for G that maximises the likelihood of D,
- N_s is the number of data sample in D,
- N_p is the dimension of G or number of free parameters, which is equal to the number of parameters in the case of complete data.

Based on this approach, Model 1 is made of a structure whose only links are inter-slice links between evidence nodes, learned from the complete data. Structure learning is performed separately for each class of character, using a random subset of 500 digits per class extracted from our training set (the MNIST database, presented in section 3). The evidence nodes (or observed nodes) of the DBN observe values from a column of pixels of a digit image, i.e. node E_i^t observes the value of the pixel at the intersection of line i and column t. That approach may lead to DBNs with a number of nodes such that the task of inference and learning would be difficult. In order to reduce the number of parameters of our models, we normalised the digit images to the size 14 pixels $\times$ 14 pixels, from an original size of 28×28. Other limitations arise from the structure learning method used, which requires that all nodes are discrete and observed. That allows to find the optimal set of parents for each node separately. Therefore, digit images are binarised before learning the structure, with a threshold of half the maximum value of a pixel. The maximum number of parents per node is fixed to 7 in order to only learn the most useful links, and all parents of a node in time slice $t + 1$ belong to time slice t. For each node, the selected combination of parents is the one that corresponds to the highest BIC score according to the data.

An example of DBN structure from this model is presented in Fig. 1(a). For a given digit image, each pixel value is observed once, so the unrolled DBN has $t_{max} = 14$ time slices (one per column of an image), each time slice containing 14 evidence nodes (one per pixel of a column).

Model 2: Learned inter-slice links and hidden node. Fig. 1(b) shows the second kind of DBN structure tested. Evidence nodes are the same as previously, with the same inter-slice links and the same observations of columns of pixels. Each time slice contains an additional hidden discrete node linked to all evidence nodes of the slice, and to the hidden node in the next slice. The number of states of hidden discrete nodes is fixed to 13, as our experiments have shown no significant improvement for higher values.

Model 3: Coupled structure. The coupled structure (Fig. 1(c)) is obtained by linking two DBNs from the previous model, one observing a column of pixels per time slice, the second observing a line of pixels per time slice. The two hidden nodes are discrete and have 13 states. The inter-slice links between evidence nodes observing lines (E_i^t, $i = 15..28$) have been learned in the same way as those between evidence nodes observing columns (E_i^t, $i = 1..14$), but separately.

Model 4: Learned inter- and intra-slice links, and hidden node. This model (Fig. 1(d)) is based on Model 2, with additional intra-slice links between evidence nodes. Intra-slice links have been learned from the data in the same way as inter-slice links, i.e. using the BIC score, and a different set of intra-slice links has been learned for each class of data. To avoid cycles in the graph, intra-slice links were made to follow the constraint according to which E_i^t can only be a parent of E_j^t if $i < j$.

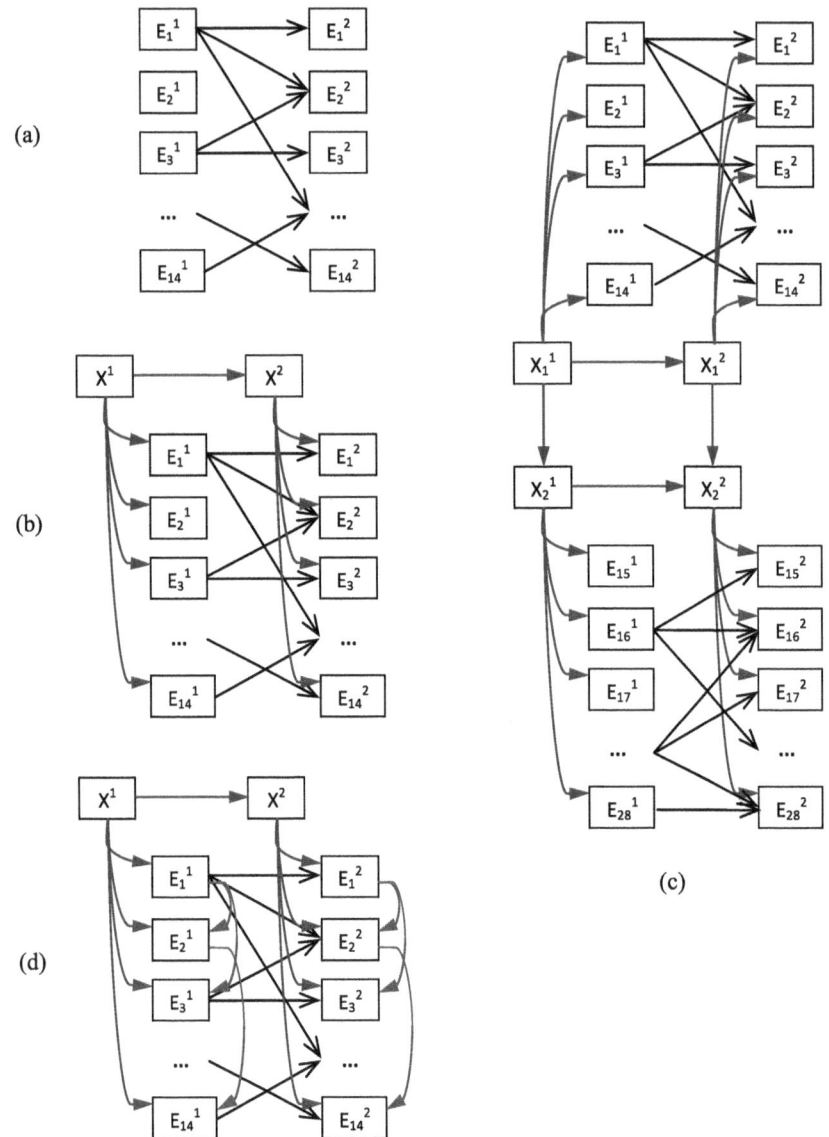

Fig. 1. The first two time slices of four DBN architectures. The complete unrolled DBNs have $t_{max} = 14$ time slices. E_i^t is the evidence node number i in time slice t, and X_j^t is the hidden node number j in time slice t (X^t if there is only one hidden node per time slice). (a) Model 1: A DBN made of evidence nodes only, with inter-slice links learned from the data (columns of pixels). (b) Model 2: Same evidence nodes as in (a), with one hidden node per slice, connected to every evidence nodes of the slice. (c) Model 3: A DBN observing columns and lines of pixels coupled through hidden nodes. (d) Model 4: Same as Model 2, completed with intra-slice links learned from the data. The links between evidence nodes are shown as an example, and they are different for each class of data.

3 Experiments and Results

The data we used is extracted from the MNIST database of handwritten digits [19], which contains a training set of 60000 examples of characters, and a test set of 10000 examples. Fig. 2 shows a few examples of characters from the MNIST database.

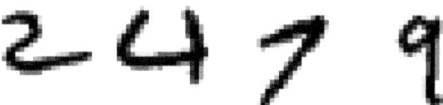

Fig. 2. Examples of characters extracted from classes 2, 4, 7 and 9 of the original MNIST database (size 28×28). Our experiments used images resized to 14×14.

The experiments have been conducted with the BayesNet Toolbox for Matlab [20], which provides source code to perform numerous operations on BNs and DBNs. The DBN parameters are learned using the EM algorithm mentioned in section 2. Our training set was made by randomly extracting 500 samples of data per class (5000 samples in total) from the MNIST training set. For recognition, we used a total of 2000 samples of data randomly extracted from the MNIST test set. Images were resized to half their initial size to reduce the number of parameters in the models; image size reduction also results in information loss, which may hamper the learning and recognition tasks.

For each of the four models presented in section 2.2, experiments were conducted using discrete (binary) evidence nodes with binary images, and using Gaussian evidence nodes. For the latter case, pixel values have been scaled from the interval [0,255] to [0,1]. During each of these eight experiments, one DBN was trained for each class of data, with the particular links previously learned from that class of data; then each digit of our test set was tested with the DBNs of the ten classes and assigned to the class whose DBN gave the highest log-likelihood.

The results are summarised in table 1. For each model, it can be seen that Gaussian evidence nodes provide an important improvement for this application compared to discrete ones. The hidden node in Model 2 resulted in significantly better results than those obtained with Model 1, but the additional intra-slice links (Model 4) brought only a marginal improvement compared to Model 2. The coupled architecture of Model 3 gave the best results for both kinds of evidence nodes, and reached an average recognition rate of 93.3% with Gaussian evidence nodes; the corresponding standard deviation of the recognition rate of the different classes is 3.4 percentage points. Digits from classes 1 and 0 were the most correctly classified by Model 3 (Gaussian evidence nodes) with recognition rates of respectively 98.3% and 97.2%, while classes 7 and 4 have the lowest recognition rates, respectively 87.5% and 89.1%, both of them being most of the time mistakenly labelled as 9.

In [11], tests of several HMM and DBN models on the original MNIST database are reported, with recognition rates ranging from 87.4% (Horizontal HMM), to

Table 1. Recognition rates (%) of handwritten digits

	Model 1	Model 2	Model 3	Model 4
Discrete evidence nodes	67.7	69.6	74.8	71.2
Gaussian evidence nodes	81.0	90.2	93.3	90.6

94.9% for the best DBN. The same study reported SVMs provided a recognition rate of 96.1%. However, our results are not readily comparable as they are obtained using reduced images (4 times less observations), which inevitably lowers the information available for learning and recognition.

4 Conclusion

In this paper we have presented a task of handwritten digit recognition using Dynamic Bayesian Networks. The observations of our models were columns and lines of pixels, with up to 28 evidence nodes and 2 hidden nodes per time slice. Four DBN models with different structures have been tested. The structure was partly learned from the training set of data, separately for each class of digit. We used a trade-off between complete automatic structure learning and manual heuristic search for an efficient structure, by learning inter- and intra-slice links between evidence nodes from data before incorporating them with hidden discrete nodes. For each model, experiments were conducted with binary and Gaussian evidence nodes, the latter giving much better results.

DBNs offer a great range of possibilities and there is much scope for exploration and improvement. As we have seen, this application leads to a certain disparity between the recognition rates of the different classes. Future work could be to perform a two-step learning, where the first step would be dedicated to detecting which class is the most difficult to classify, and the second step would focus on improving the DBN structure of the class identified during the first step, using not only the training data of that class but also the data of other classes in order to find the most discriminative links.

Acknowledgment

The authors wish to acknowledge the financial support for the research work supported by the MICIE project under the European Framework-7 Programme (Contract No: 225353).

References

1. Kelly, D.L., Smith, C.L.: Bayesian inference in probabilistic risk assessment–The current state of the art. Reliability Engineering & System Safety 94 (2008)
2. de Campos, L.M., Castellano, J.G.: Bayesian network learning algorithms using structural restrictions. International Journal of Approximate Reasoning 45 (2006)

3. Russell, S., Norvig, P.: Artificial Intelligence, A Modern Approach, 2nd edn. Prentice Hall, Englewood Cliffs (2003)
4. Murphy, K.P.: Dynamic Bayesian Networks: Representation, Inference and Learning, PhD dissertation, UC Berkeley, Computer Science Division (July 2002)
5. Mihajlovic, V., Petkovic, M.: Dynamic Bayesian Networks: A State of the Art, CTIT technical reports series, TR-CTIT-34 (2001)
6. Kao, H.-Y., Huang, C.-H., Li, H.-L.: Supply chain diagnostics with dynamic Bayesian networks. Computers & Industrial Engineering 49 (2005)
7. Daoudi, K., Fohr, D., Antoine, C.: Dynamic Bayesian networks for multi-band automatic speech recognition. Computer Speech & Language 17 (2003)
8. Huang, C.-L., Shih, H.-C., Chao, C.-Y.: Semantic analysis of soccer video using dynamic Bayesian network. IEEE Transactions on Multimedia 8 (2006)
9. Dielmann, A., Renals, S.: Automatic Meeting Segmentation Using Dynamic Bayesian Networks. IEEE Transactions on Multimedia 9 (2007)
10. Zajdel, W., Cemgil, A.T., Kröse, B.J.A.: Dynamic Bayesian Networks for Visual Surveillance with Distributed Cameras. In: Havinga, P., Lijding, M., Meratnia, N., Wegdam, M. (eds.) EUROSSC 2006. LNCS, vol. 4272, pp. 240–243. Springer, Heidelberg (2006)
11. Likforman-Sulem, L., Sigelle, M.: Recognition of degraded characters using dynamic Bayesian networks. Pattern Recognition 41 (2008)
12. Tsamardinos, I., Brown, L.E., Aliferis, C.F.: The max-min hill-climbing Bayesian network structure learning algorithm. Machine Learning 65 (2006)
13. Pinto, P.C., Nagele, A., Dejori, M., Runkler, T.A., Sousa, J.M.C.: Using a Local Discovery Ant Algorithm for Bayesian Network Structure Learning. IEEE Transactions on Evolutionary Computation 13 (2009)
14. Rajapaksea, J.C., Zhoua, J.: Learning effective brain connectivity with dynamic Bayesian networks. NeuroImage 37 (2007)
15. Pearl, J.: Probabilistic Reasoning in Intelligent Systems: Networks of Plausible Inference, 2nd edn. Morgan Kaufman, Los Altos (1988)
16. Ghahramani, Z.: Learning Dynamic Bayesian Networks. In: Giles, C.L., Gori, M. (eds.) IIASS-EMFCSC-School 1997. LNCS (LNAI), vol. 1387, p. 168. Springer, Heidelberg (1998)
17. Friedman, N., Murphy, K., Russell, S.: Learning the Structure of Dynamic Probabilistic Networks. In: Conference on Uncertainty in Artificial Intelligence, UAI 1998 (1998)
18. Friedman, N.: Learning Belief Networks in the Presence of Missing Values and Hidden Variables. In: International Conference on Machine Learning (1997)
19. LeCun, Y., Cortes, C.: The MNIST database of handwritten digits (1998), http://yann.lecun.com/exdb/mnist/
20. Murphy, K.P.: BayesNet Toolbox for Matlab, http://people.cs.ubc.ca/~murphyk/Software/BNT/bnt.html (last updated 2007)

A Dual Network Adaptive Learning Algorithm for Supervised Neural Network with Contour Preserving Classification for Soft Real Time Applications

Piyabute Fuangkhon and Thitipong Tanprasert

Distributed and Parallel Computing Research Laboratory, Assumption University
592 Soi Ramkamhang 24, Ramkamhang Road, Hua Mak, Bangkapi, Bangkok 10240 TH
piyabutefng@au.edu, t_tanprasert@yahoo.com

Abstract. A framework presenting a basic conceptual structure used to solve adaptive learning problems in soft real time applications is proposed. Its design consists of two supervised neural networks running simultaneously. One is used for training data and the other is used for testing data. The accuracy of the classification is improved from the previous works by adding outpost vectors generated from prior samples. The testing function is able to test data continuously without being interrupted while the training function is being executed. The framework is designed for a parallel processing and/or a distributed processing environment due to the highly demanded processing power of the repetitive training process of the neural network.

Keywords: Supervised Neural Network; Outpost Vector; Contour Preserving Classification; Feed-forward Back-propagation; Soft Real Time Applications.

1 Introduction

It is known that repetitive feeding of training samples is required for allowing a supervised learning algorithm to converge. If the training samples effectively represent the population of the targeted data, the classifier can be approximated as being generalized. However, there are many times when it is impractical to obtain such a truly representative training set. Many classifying applications are acceptable with convergence to a local optimum. As a consequence, this kind of application needs occasional retraining when there is sliding of actual context locality.

Assuming a constant system complexity, when the context is partially changed, some new cases are introduced while some old cases are inhibited. The classifier will be required to effectively handle some old cases as well as new cases. Assuming that this kind of situation will occur occasionally, it is expected that the old cases will age out, the medium-old cases are accurately handled to a certain degree, and new cases are most accurately handled. Since the existing knowledge is lost while retraining new samples, an approach to maintain old knowledge is required. While the typical solution uses prior samples and new samples on retraining, the major drawback of this approach is that all the prior samples for training must be maintained.

M. Graña Romay et al. (Eds.): HAIS 2010, Part I, LNAI 6076, pp. 128–135, 2010.
© Springer-Verlag Berlin Heidelberg 2010

In soft real time applications where new samples keeps coming for both training and testing process but the deadline is desirable, the adaptive learning algorithm must be able to train data and test data simultaneously. With only one supervised neural network [18], [19], training and testing process cannot be executed at the same time.

In this paper, a framework for solving adaptive learning problems by supervised neural network is proposed for soft real time applications. The framework based on [18], [19] improves the accuracy of the classification by adding outpost vectors generated from prior samples and uses two neural networks for training data and testing data simultaneously. Research works related to this paper are in the field of adaptive learning [1], [2], [3], [4], [5], [6], [7], [8], [9], [10], [11], [12], [13], [14], [15], incremental learning [16], contour preserving classification [17], distributed and parallel neural network [20], [21], [22].

Following this section, section 2 describes the proposed framework. Section 3 describes the experimental results. Section 4 discusses the conclusion of the paper.

2 Framework

A proposed framework consists of two supervised neural networks which are processed simultaneously to solve adaptive learning problems in soft real time applications. The first supervised neural network called *"train-network"* is used in training process and the second supervised neural network called *"test-network"* is used in the testing process.

Figure 1 presents the proposed framework. It shows the details of how the final training set is constructed and how the dual network adaptive learning algorithm works. There are three parameters in [18], [19] but there are four parameters in the proposed framework: *new sample rate (α), outpost vector rate for new samples (β), decay rate (γ), and outpost vector rate for prior samples (δ)*. The outpost vector rate for prior samples is added to sharpen the boundary between classes of prior data. The function of each parameter is as followings.

Firstly, the new sample rate (α) is the ratio of the number of selected new samples over the number of arriving new samples. It determines the number of selected new samples to be included in the final training set. Using larger new sample rate will cause the network to learn new knowledge more accurately. When new sample rate is greater than 1.0, some new samples will be repeatedly included in the final training set. The number of selected new samples is calculated by formula:

$$nns = \alpha \times ns .$$

(1)

where   nns   is the number of selected new samples,
         α   is the new sample rate $[0, \infty)$,
         ns   is the number of new samples

Secondly, the outpost vector rate for new samples (β) is the ratio of the number of generated outpost vectors over the number of selected new samples. It determines the number of outpost vectors generated from new samples to be included in the final training set. Using larger outpost vector rate for new samples will sharpen the boundary of classes of new data. When outpost vector rate for new samples is greater than

1.0, duplicated locations in a problem space will be assigned to outpost vectors. The number of outpost vectors generated from new samples is calculated by formula:

$$novns = \beta \times ns .$$ (2)

where   novns   is the number of outpost vectors,
         β is the outpost vector rate (new samples) $[0, \infty)$,
         ns   is the number of new samples

Thirdly, the decay rate (γ) is the ratio of the number of decayed prior samples over the number of selected new samples. It determines the number of decayed prior samples to be included in the final training set. The larger decay rate will cause the network to forget old knowledge slower. When decay rate is greater than 1.0, more than one instance of some prior samples will be included in the decayed prior sample set. The number of decayed prior samples is calculated by formula:

$$ndc = \gamma \times ps .$$ (3)

where   ndc   is the number of selected prior samples,
         γ is the decay rate $[0, \infty)$,
         ps   is the number of prior samples

Lastly, the outpost vector rate for prior samples (δ) is the ratio of the number of generated outpost vectors over the number of prior samples. It determines the number of outpost vectors generated from prior samples to be included in the final training set. Using larger outpost vector rate for prior samples will sharpen the boundary of classes of prior data. When outpost vector rate for prior samples is greater than 1.0, duplicated locations in the problem space will be assigned to the outpost vectors. The number of outpost vectors generated from prior samples is calculated by formula:

$$novps = \delta \times ps .$$ (4)

where   novps   is the number of outpost vectors,
         δ is the outpost vector rate (prior samples) $[0, \infty)$,
         ps   is the number of prior samples

After the generation of selected new sample set, outpost vector set generated from new samples, decayed prior sample set, and outpost vector set generated from prior samples, these sets are then combined (UNION) to form the final training set for training process. After the final training set is constructed, the train-network will be trained with the final training set. The training will be repeated if the performance of the train-network is lower than the goal. When the performance of the train-network meets the goal, the train-network will be turned into the test-network which will be used for testing process. The previous test-network if any will be discarded. The training will start again when a specified number of new samples have been collected. Both train-network and test-network will run simultaneously to solve adaptive learning problems in soft real time applications. Figure 2 presents the algorithm of the training process. The statement in [18], [19] that sets the new sample set as a dummy decayed prior sample set in the first training session is removed.

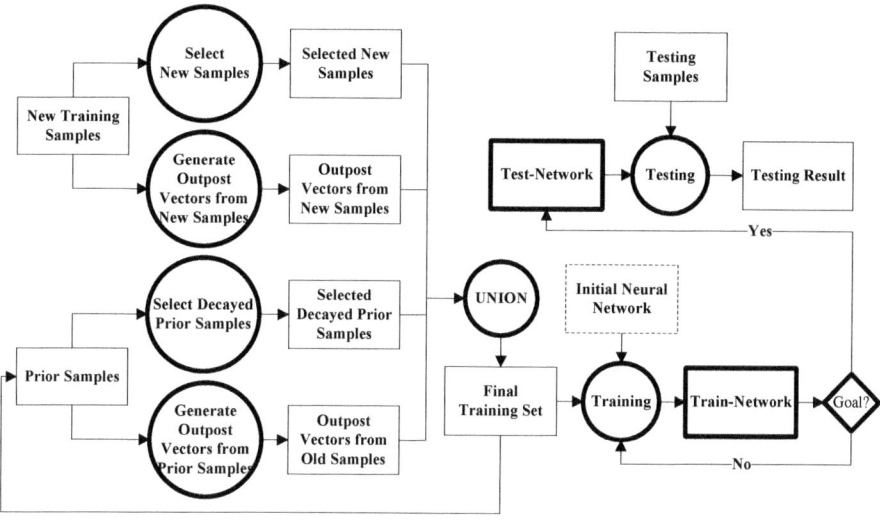

Fig. 1. Proposed Framework

```
1  for each training session
2    Construct selected new sample set by
3      Calculate nns by (1)
4      Randomly select samples from new sample set
5    Construct outpost vector set for new samples by
6      Calculate novns by (2)
7      Generate outpost vectors from new sample set
8    Construct decayed prior sample set by
9      Calculate ndc by (3)
10     Randomly select samples from prior sample set
11   Construct outpost vector set for prior samples by
12     Calculate novps by (4)
13     Generate outpost vectors from prior sample set
14   Construct final training set by
15     UNION   ( selected new sample set,
                 outpost vector set for new samples,
                 decayed prior sample set,
                 outpost vector set for prior samples )
16   Initialize train-network
17   repeat
18     Train train-network with final training set
19   until (performance of train-network meets the goal)
20   Set train-network as test-network
21   Set final training set as prior sample set for the next training
     session
22 end for
```

Fig. 2. Algorithm for the Training Process

The time complexity of the training process includes the time complexity of the final training set generation and the time complexity of the repetitive training.

The time complexity of the final training set generation is computed from the time complexity of the selected new sample set generation, the outpost vector set (new samples) generation, the decayed prior sample set generation, and the outpost vector set (prior samples) generation. Given that n_A is the number of new samples of class A, n_B is the number of new samples of class B, n_{Aps} is the number of prior samples of class A, and n_{Bps} is the number of prior samples of class B,

- The time complexity of the selected new sample set generation is $O(n_A+n_B)$.
- The time complexity of the outpost vector (new samples) set generation is $O(n_A n_B)$.
- The time complexity of the decayed prior sample set generation is $O(n_{Aps}+n_{Bps})$.
- The time complexity of the outpost vector (prior samples) set generation is $O(n_{Aps} n_{Bps})$.

Therefore the total time complexity of the final training set construction is $O(n_A n_B)+O(n_{Aps} n_{Bps})$.

The time complexity of the repetitive training is computed from the time complexity of the selected training function $O(x)$ and the number of times the training function is repeated $O(1)$. Therefore the total time complexity of the repetitive training is $O(x)$.

In total, the time complexity of the training process including the time complexity of the final training set generation and the time complexity of the repetitive training is $O(n_A n_B)+O(n_{Aps} n_{Bps})+O(x)$.

Larger new sample set and parameters will increase the size of the final training set causing the time for training set construction to be increased. However, the time spent for final training set generation is generally insignificant compared to the massive computation of the repetitive training of the supervised neural network. By using two neural networks, the capability of training data and testing data simultaneously is available for solving adaptive learning problems in soft real time applications.

3   Experimental Results

The experiments were conducted and tested with the 2-dimension partition problem. The distribution of samples was created in limited location of 2-dimension donut ring as shown in Figure 3. This partition had three parameters: *Inner Radius (R1), Middle Radius (R2) and Outer Radius (R3)*. The class of samples depended on geometric position. There were two classes of data which were designed as one (1) and zero (0). Class 0 covers the area from 0 to Inner Radius (R1) and from Middle Radius (R2) to Outer Radius (R3) and Class 1 covers the area from Inner Radius (R1) to Middle Radius (R2).

The context of the problem was assumed to shift from an angular location to another while maintaining some overlapped area between consecutive contexts as shown in Figure 4. The set numbers identify the sequence of training and testing sessions.

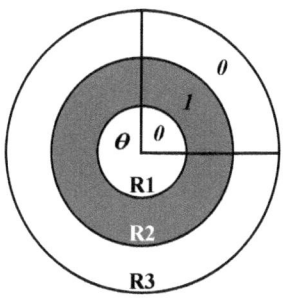

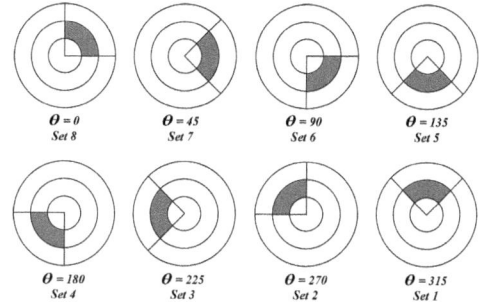

Fig. 3. Shape of Partition Area   **Fig. 4.** Shifting of Problem Context

In the experiment, the data set was separated into 8 training sets (Set 1 to 8) and 8 testing sets (Ratios of Gap and Random are 5:0, 5:5, 5:10, 10:0, 10:5, 10:10, 10:15, 10:20). Each set consisted of 400 samples. Each training set was used to generate a new training set consisting of selected new samples, outpost vectors generated from new samples, selected decayed prior samples, and outpost vectors generated from old samples.

The size of new training set was determined by the number of current samples and the decay rate. Figure 5a and Figure 5b present the sample final training sets of the old algorithm [18], [19] and the proposed framework having $\alpha = 1.0$, $\beta = 0.5$, $\gamma = 4.0$, $\delta = 0.0$ and $\alpha = 1.0$, $\beta = 0.5$, $\gamma = 2.0$, $\delta = 1.0$ respectively. The final training sets in Figure 5a consisted of 2,200 samples including 400 selected new samples (1.0×400), 200 outpost vectors (new samples) (0.5×400), 1,600 selected decayed prior samples (4.0×400), and no outpost vector (prior samples) ($0.0\times1,600$). The final training sets in Figure 5b consisted of 2,200 samples including 400 selected new samples (1.0×400), 200 outpost vectors (new samples) (0.5×400), 800 selected decayed prior samples (2.0×400), and 800 outpost vectors (prior samples) (1.0×800).

The first final training set was trained with the feed forward back-propagation neural network (*train-network*) with the following parameters: network size = [10 1]; transfer function for hidden layer = "logsig"; transfer function for output layer = "logsig"; max epochs = 500; goal = 0.001. After the train-network was turned into test-network, the test-network started testing service while the second final training set was being generated. The second final training set was then trained and turned into *test-network*. The previous test-network was discarded. This training process was repeated until all final training sets were trained completely.

Figure 6 presents the testing results of the old algorithm and the proposed framework with 8 testing sets. The testing results show that the proposed framework yields lower error rate for classification than the old algorithm. When the experiment was conducted in a multi-programmed uni-processor system, the time spent during the training and testing of the old algorithm and the proposed was the same because of the thread switching. However, in a multiprocessor system, one processor executed the training function as one thread while another processor executed the testing function as another thread simultaneously. The testing serviced without delay while the training function was being executed.

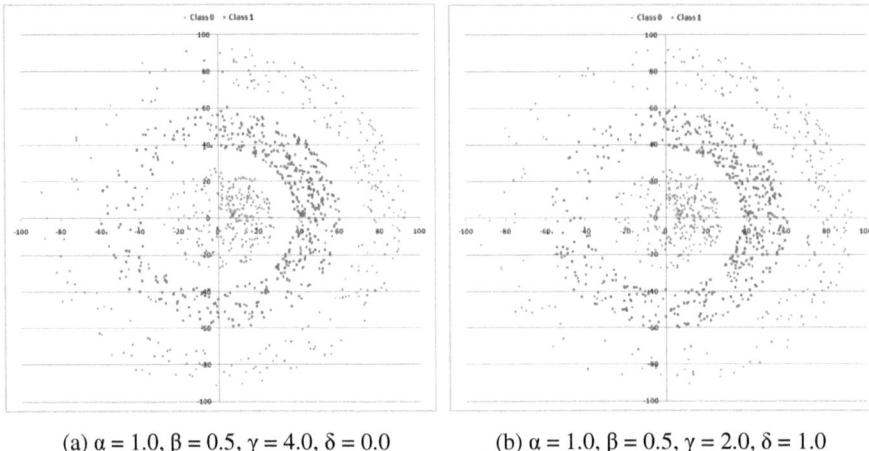

(a) α = 1.0, β = 0.5, γ = 4.0, δ = 0.0   (b) α = 1.0, β = 0.5, γ = 2.0, δ = 1.0

Fig. 5. Final Training Sets of Old Algorithm [18], [19] and Proposed Framework Respectively

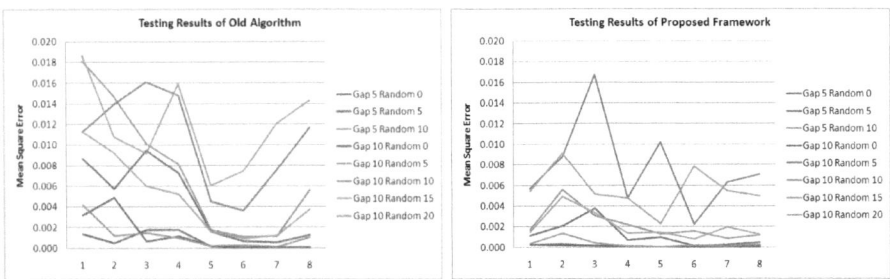

Fig. 6. Testing Results of Old Algorithm [18], [19] and Proposed Framework Respectively

4   Conclusion

A framework for solving adaptive learning algorithms in soft real time applications is proposed. The framework based on [18], [19] consists of two supervised neural networks running simultaneously. One is used for training data and the other is used for testing data. The accuracy of the classification is improved from the previous works by adding outpost vectors generated from prior samples. In a multi-programmed uniprocessor system where the training function and testing function share the same processor, the time spent during the training and testing of the old algorithm and the proposed is the same. However, in multiprocessor system, one processor can execute the training function while another processor can execute the testing function simultaneously. The testing can service without delay while the training function is being executed. When the training function takes very long time, the proposed framework will show its true performance.

References

1. Tanprasert, T., Kripruksawan, T.: An approach to control aging rate of neural networks under adaptation to gradually changing context. In: ICONIP 2002, pp. 174–178 (2002)
2. Tanprasert, T., Kaitikunkajorn, S.: Improving synthesis process of decayed prior sampling technique. In: INTECH 2005, pp. 240–244 (2005)
3. Burzevski, V., Mohan, C.K.: Hierarchical growing cell structures. In: ICNN 1996, pp. 1658–1663 (1996)
4. Fritzke, B.: Vector quantization with a growing and splitting elastic network. In: ICANN 1993, pp. 580–585 (1993)
5. Fritzke, B.: Incremental learning of locally linear mappings. In: ICANN 1995, pp. 217–222 (1995)
6. Martinez, T.M., Berkovich, S.G., Schulten, K.J.: Neural gas network for vector quantization and its application to time-series prediction. IEEE Transactions on Neural Networks 4(4), 558–569 (1993)
7. Chalup, S., Hayward, R., Joachi, D.: Rule extraction from artificial neural networks trained on elementary number classification tasks. In: Proceedings of the 9th Australian Conference on Neural Networks, pp. 265–270 (1998)
8. Craven, M.W., Shavlik, J.W.: Using sampling and queries to extract rules from trained neural networks. In: ICML 1994, pp. 37–45 (1994)
9. Setiono, R.: Extracting rules from neural networks by pruning and hidden-unit splitting. Neural Computation 9(1), 205–225 (1997)
10. Sun, R., Peterson, T., Sessions, C.: Beyond simple rule extraction: Acquiring planning knowledge from neural networks. In: WIRN Vietri 2001, pp. 288–300 (2001)
11. Thrun, S., Mitchell, T.M.: Integrating inductive neural network learning and explanation based learning. In: IJCAI 1993, pp. 930–936 (1993)
12. Towell, G.G., Shavlik, J.W.: Knowledge based artificial neural networks. Artificial Intelligence 70(1-2), 119–165 (1994)
13. Mitchell, T., Thrun, S.B.: Learning analytically and inductively. In: Mind Matters: A Tribute to Allen Newell, pp. 85–110 (1996)
14. Fasconi, P., Gori, M., Maggini, M., Soda, G.: Unified integration of explicit knowledge and learning by example in recurrent networks. IEEE Transactions on Knowledge and Data Engineering 7(2), 340–346 (1995)
15. Tanprasert, T., Fuangkhon, P., Tanprasert, C.: An improved technique for retraining neural networks in adaptive environment. In: INTECH 2008, pp. 77–80 (2008)
16. Polikar, R., Udpa, L., Udpa, S.S., Honavar, V.: Learn++: An incremental learning algorithm for supervised neural networks. IEEE Transactions on Systems, Man, and Cybernetics 31(4), 497–508 (2001)
17. Tanprasert, T., Tanprasert, C., Lursinsap, C.: Contour preserving classification for maximal reliability. In: IJCNN 1998, pp. 1125–1130 (1998)
18. Fuangkhon, P., Tanprasert, T.: An incremental learning algorithm for supervised neural network with contour preserving classification. In: ECTI-CON 2009, pp. 470–473 (2009)
19. Fuangkhon, P., Tanprasert, T.: An adaptive learning algorithm for supervised neural network with contour preserving classification. In: Deng, H., Wang, L., Wang, F.L., Lei, J. (eds.) Artificial Intelligence and Computational Intelligence. LNCS (LNAI), vol. 5855, pp. 389–398. Springer, Heidelberg (2009)
20. Calvert, D., Guan, J.: Distributed artificial neural network architectures. In: HPCS 2005, pp. 2–10 (2005)
21. Seiffert, U.: Artificial neural networks on massively parallel computer hardware. In: ESANN 2002, pp. 319–330 (2002)
22. Yang, B., Wang, Y., Su, X.: Research and design of distributed training algorithm for neural networks. In: ICMLC 2005, pp. 4044–4049 (2005)

The Abnormal vs. Normal ECG Classification Based on Key Features and Statistical Learning

Jun Dong[1], Jia-fei Tong[1], and Xia Liu[2]

[1] Suzhou Institute of Nano-technology and Nano-bionics,
Chinese Academy of Sciences, 215125, China
[2] Shanghai Ruijin Hospital, 200025, China
jdong2010@sinano.ac.cn, tongjiafei@126.com, liuxia9110@yahoo.com.cn

Abstract. As cardiovascular diseases appear frequently in modern society, the medicine and health system should be adjusted to meet the new requirements. Chinese government has planned to establish basic community medical insurance system (BCMIS) before 2020, where remote medical service is one of core issues. Therefore, we have developed the "remote network hospital system" which includes data server and diagnosis terminal by the aid of wireless detector to sample ECG. To improve the efficiency of ECG processing, in this paper, abnormal vs. normal ECG classification approach based on key features and statistical learning is presented, and the results are analyzed. Large amount of normal ECG could be filtered by computer automatically and abnormal ECG is left to be diagnosed specially by physicians.

Keywords: ECG, Classification, Features, Support Vector Machine, Statistical Learning.

1 Introduction

It's well to know that cardiovascular diseases have become one of the most frequent and dangerous problems in modern society, and it is much more difficult to take immediate measures to help the patient without real time ECG (electrocardiogram) information. Therefore, remote ECG monitor/diagnosis system, which will be a kind of key requirement of the BCMIS (basic community medical insurance system) to be established before 2020 by the Chinese government, is necessary.

Traditional ECG monitors are divided into two sorts: general monitor at hospital and Holter which can be used to record ECG data for 24 hours or more. The recorded data can be displayed and analyzed by physicians through special computer system.

Our solution [1,2] is the "remote network hospital system" as shown in Fig. 1. It includes a belted detector, smart phone, data server, diagnosis terminal and short/long distance wireless modules. We have developed the wireless ECG monitor which has been licensed by the Shanghai Food and Drug Administration in China in 2006. The ECG acquired in dynamic environments through the belted detector is received, stored, displayed and analyzed by the smart phone.

M. Graña Romay et al. (Eds.): HAIS 2010, Part I, LNAI 6076, pp. 136–143, 2010.

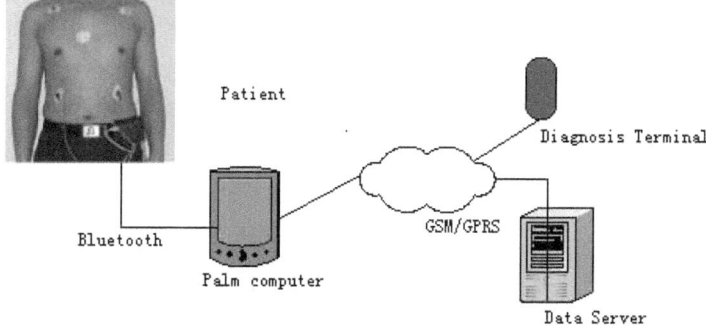

Fig. 1. Architecture of the remote network hospital system

GSM/GPRS is used between the mobile phone and server, in contrast to the Bluetooth communication used between the detector and smart phone. Remote diagnosis terminals (e.g. PC) with more functions than the smart phone are used to examine ECG.

When real time ECG arrives at the data server, the server will inform an identified physician whose responsibility is to response in time. If he or she is not in the office, the ECG can be browed with his/her mobile phone, and then diagnose the ECG through the man-machine interface and send back treatment instructions.

Originally, the physicians who are in charge of taking response in according to server request have to spend much time for distinguishing abnormal vs. normal ECG. It will be more efficient if normal ECG can be recognized automatically by computer and abnormal ECG left to be diagnosed specially by physicians. It's better when the monitor can make some decision on common cardiovascular diseases automatically. But academic researches on this issue focused on test by the aid of MIT/BIH where only lead II ECG is ready, and the classification did not meet the requirements in practice. We are intended to solve the classification problem by statistical learning here, and put forward the approach to emphasize the real course when physicians thinking about the ECG to get conclusion. Therefore, we select features (see section 2) according to experienced physicians. No other work focuses on them as we did.

2   Basic Approaches and Data

In general, computer-aided ECG diagnosis includes preprocess, features recognition and classification processes. We have got more results when concerning imagery thinking and morphology features in recognition phase [3~5]. Theoretically, many mathematics methods could be used to classify. Recently statistical learning approaches such as support vector machine (SVM) are paid more attentions on. Several ECG classification works with SVM can be found,

Table 1. ECG features set I and set II for classification

number	23 features(set I)	14 feature(set II)
1	P wave	√
2	R wave	√
3	R wave start point	√
4	R wave end point	
5	T1 wave	√
6	T2 wave	√
7	P wave start point	
8	P wave end point	
9	T wave start point	
10	T wave end point	
11	PP	√
12	QRS	√
13	PR	√
14	ST	√
15	QT	√
16	RR	√
17	TT	
18	P	√
19	T	
20	Total beat	√
21	T1 T2	
22	ST	
23	PR	√

such as multiclass support vector machine with the error correcting output codes [6], combining the SVM network with preprocessing methods yielding two neural classifiers [7], and SVM classifier designed by a perturbation method [8] etc.

We use both Bayesian and SVM methods to analyses and compare each other. Basic contents can be found in references [9,10], only calculating steps are listed in the following section.

Open source tool–ECGPuwave [11] is used to extract features, as demonstrated in table1 1 (second column), from 1 to 10 are amplitude features, and from 11 to 23 are interval features (set I).

The number of features is very important which will influence execution time. So we manage to decrease the features number. On the other hand, too few features mean they can't represent the general ECG situation. Therefore we have to find balance point among them. In fact, some features are not used practically by physicians for diagnosing common diseases. We make conclusion on the number through experienced physicians, and got most important 14 features (third column, set II) from physicians' experience.

3   Bayesian Classifier

The steps for Bayesian classifier are as following.

(1)Assume train data set
$x = (x_1, x_2, ..., x_n)$ each x_i owns m features:
$x_i = (x_{i1}, x_{i2}, ..., x_{im}), i = 1, ..., n$
(2)Total classifications are noted as $w = (w_1, w_2, ..., w_c)$. Samples number is
n,among which $n_1, n_2, ..., n_c$ belongs to $w_1, w_2, ..., w_c$ respectively. Then prior
probability is

$$P(w_i) = \frac{n_i}{n}, i = 1, 2, ..., c. \tag{1}$$

(3)Mean vector is

$$\mu_i = (\mu_{i1}, \mu_{i2}, ..., \mu_{im}), i = 1, ..., c, \mu_{ij} = \frac{1}{n_i} \sum_{k=1}^{n_i} x_{kj}, j = 1, ..., m. \tag{2}$$

Covariance matrix is

$$\sum = (\Sigma_1, \Sigma_2, ..., \Sigma_c), \Sigma_i = \frac{1}{n_i} \sum_{k=1}^{n_i} (x_k - \mu_i)(x_k - \mu_i)^T, i = 1, ..., c. \tag{3}$$

(4) Calculate similar condition probability density function for each classification with each data. With teat data $y = (y_1, y_2, ..., y_m)$ assume similar condition
probability density obey multivariate normal distribution, then similar condition
probability density function is

$$p(y|w_i) = \frac{1}{(2\pi)^{d/2}|\sum_i|^{1/2}} \exp\{-\frac{1}{2}(y - \mu_i)^T \sum_i^{-1}(y - \mu_i)\}, i = 1, ..., c. \tag{4}$$

(5) According to (2), (4) and

$$p(w_i|y) = \frac{p(y|w_i)p(w_i)}{\sum_i p(y|w_i)p(w_i)} \tag{5}$$

The post-probability of each classification could be calculated.
(6) If $p(w_i|y) > p(w_j|y), \forall j \neq i$, then test data y belongs to the ith classifica-
tion.

MIT-BIH Arrhythmia Database on lead II [12] is used, with 36369 normal
beats and 6875 abnormal for training, while 42741 normal beats and 8330 abnormal beats for testing.

The definitions of true positive (TP) vs. false positive (FP), and of true
negative (TN) vs. false negative (FN) are conventional. Accordingly, the following definitions can be applied when examining the performance of detection
algorithms:

$$\begin{aligned} Sensitivity(SE) = [TP/(TP + FN)]\% \\ Specificity(SP) = [TN/(TN + FP)]\% \end{aligned} \tag{6}$$

Table 2. Bayesian classifier results

Features	SE	SP	GCR
set I	70.90	93.84	90.10
set II	64.80	93.06	87.07

$$General\ correctness\ rate(GCR) = (TP+TN)/(TP+FN+TN+FP)\%. \quad (7)$$

The results are shown in table 2. SE, SP and GCR are represented with percent (%). As we can see, for setI, although SP is a little better than that with set II, but SE is better more, which is more important for our target.

4   SVM Classifier

The steps for SVM classifier are as following.

(1)assuming trained set $T = \{(x_1, y_1), ..., (x_n, y_n)\} \in (X \times Y)^n$, where $x_i \in X = R^n$ Each x_i owns m feature: $x_i = (x_{i1}, x_{i2}, ..., x_{im}), i = 1, ..., n$, $y_i \in Y = \{-1, +1\}, i = 1, 2, ..., n$. If x_i is normal, then $y_i = +1$, otherwise $y_i = -1$.

(2)Select suitable kernel $K(x_i, y_j)$ and punishment parameter C.

$$K(x_i, x_j) = \exp(-\|x_i - x_j\|^2/2\delta^2), \quad (8)$$

where δ should be determined as prior condition, RBF is selected here.

(3)The object function of quadric programming optimization [13]:

$$W(\alpha) = \frac{1}{2}\sum_{i=1}^{n}\sum_{j=1}^{n} y_i y_j \alpha_i \alpha_j K(x_i, x_j) - \sum_{j=1}^{n}\alpha_j, \quad (9)$$

s.t.$\sum_{i=1}^{n} y_i\alpha_i = 0, 0 \le \alpha_i \le C, i = 1, 2, ..., n$,

$$Get\ optimized\ solution\ \alpha^* = (\alpha_1^*, \alpha_2^*, ..., \alpha_n^*)^T. \quad (10)$$

(4)Select sub-variable α_j^* among α^* satisfying $0 < \alpha_j^* < C$,

$$b^* = y_j - \sum_{i=1}^{n} y_i\alpha_i^* K(x_i, x_j). \quad (11)$$

(5)With test data Z, construct decision function

$$f(z) = sgn(\sum_{i=1}^{n} y_i\alpha_i^* K(z, x_i) + b^*). \quad (12)$$

It's normal when $f(z)=+1$ while abnormal when $f(z)=-1$.

MIT-BIH Arrhythmia Database (lead II) is used too. 101837 beats of 45 records are selected. With some unrecognized beats being ignored, 94315 beats

Table 3. $C = 8000$ with set I

γ	0.01	0.03	0.05	0.09	1	10	50	100
SP	98.85	99.24	99.29	99.27	98.62	99.48	99.96	99.99
SE	89.7	91.98	93.3	93.88	94.87	89.23	60.65	38.86
GCR	97.36	98.06	98.31	98.39	98.01	97.81	93.55	90.02

Table 4. $C = 8000$ with set II

γ	0.01	0.03	0.05	0.09	1	10	50	100
SP	84.42	88.63	90.38	91.87	94.43	94.20	89.10	81.22
SE	97.73	98.30	98.55	98.69	98.93	98.36	99.29	99.65
GCR	94.90	96.25	96.82	97.25	97.97	97.48	97.13	95.74

Table 5. $\sigma = \frac{\sqrt{2}}{2}$ with set I

C	0.01	0.05	0.1	1	10	100	1000	5000
SP	99.90	99.45	99.39	99.36	99.35	99.24	98.95	98.75
SE	35.89	76.13	84.07	91.56	94.37	95.03	94.68	94.96
GCR	89.46	95.65	96.89	98.09	98.54	98.55	98.25	98.13

Table 6. $\sigma = \frac{\sqrt{2}}{2}$ with set II

C	0.01	0.05	0.1	1	10	100	1000	5000
SP	43.53	76.75	82.75	90.10	92.43	93.34	94.00	94.26
SE	98.65	98.14	98.23	98.57	98.93	99.07	99.07	98.93
GCR	86.96	93.61	94.95	96.77	97.55	97.86	97.99	97.94

are ready, among which 79110 beats are normal and 15205 beats are abnormal separately.

Open source SVM tool Libsvm is selected here. Two parameters, C and δ should be determined first of all. So two kinds of experiments are designed: C is fixed with 8000 and δ is fixed with $\frac{\sqrt{2}}{2}$. In Libsvm, $\gamma = \frac{1}{2\delta^2}$ is set for RBF. Several results are demonstrated in table 3 to table 6 respectively.

As the tables show, when C is fixed, as γ increased, the correctness is improved. The result is optimized when $\gamma = 1$. On the other hand, when δ is fixed, as C increased, the correctness for normal beats is down till $C = 1$. Then the correctness for abnormal beats is up fast.

Table 7 is the compared results with reference [6] with same data set, where 90 normal beats and 270 abnormal beats are used for training, while 90 normal beats and 270 abnormal beats are used for testing. RBF is selected with $\gamma = 3.125$, and $C = 80$.

Table 7. Compared results with reference [6]

	SE	SP	GCR
set I	99.63	100	99.72
set II	100	100	100
Reference [6]	99.25	98.89	98.61

Table 8. Compared results with reference [7]

	SE	SP	GCR
set I	99.63	99.30	99.59
set II	99.73	99.25	99.57
Reference [7]	97.19	97.80	95.91

Table 9. Compared results with reference [8]

	SE	SP	GCR
set I	99.63	100	99.72
set II	99.63	100	99.72
Reference [8]	97.20	100	98.10

Table 8 is the compared results with reference [7] with same data set, where 17 features are selected, and 2000 normal beats and 4690 abnormal beats are used for training, while 2000 normal betas and 4095 abnormal beats are used for testing. RBF is selected with $\gamma = 2$ and $C = 100$.

Table 9 is the compared results with reference [8] with same data set, where 18 features are selectedand 180 normal beats and 540 abnormal beats are used for training, while 90 normal betas and 270 abnormal beats are used for testing. RBF is selected with $\gamma = 0.5$ and $C = 100$.

5   Conclusions

The advantages of Bayesian classifier lies in: the algorithm is simple and stable. That means its robustness is good. But the conditions such as prior probability and condition probability density functions make it's not convenient to be used in practice. On the other hand, SVM needs only limited samples, give global optimized solution avoiding the local optimized problem using neural network. At the same time, its generalization capability is good. However, to select the kernel function is an intractable issue. Furthermore, large train set is left unsolved.

We have developed special ECG database [14] for test, and deployed the classification software module in remote server center of medicine school of Shanghai Jiaotong University, China. When the algorithm being transformed to embedded system such as wireless ECG monitor, the computational complexity will be discussed in detail.

Now large amount of normal ECG have been filtered by computer automatically and abnormal ECG is left to be diagnosed specially by physicians in "remote network hospital system". We are managing to combine several classifiers to get better results.

Acknowledgments. Sponsored by Program of Shanghai Chief Scientist (07X D14203), Shanghai Basic Key Research Project (08JC1409100).

References

1. Dong, J., Zhu, H.H.: Mobile ECG Detector through GPRS/Internet. In: Tsymbal, A. (ed.) Proceeding of IEEE 17th CBMS, pp. 485–489. IEEE Computer Society Press, Los Alamitos (2004)
2. Dong, J., Xu, M., Zhu, H.H., Lu, W.F.: Wearable ECG Recognition and Monitor. In: Alexey, T. (ed.) Proceeding of IEEE 18th CBMS, pp. 413–418. IEEE Computer Society Press, Los Alamitos (2005)
3. Dong, J., et al.: The Creation Process of Chinese Calligraphy and Emulation of Imagery Thinking. IEEE Intelligent Systems 23(6), 56–62 (2008)
4. Dong, J., Xu, M., Zhan, C.M., Lu, W.F.: ECG Recognition and Classification: Approaches, Problems and New Method. Journal of Biomedical Engineering 24(6), 1224–1229 (2007) (in Chinese)
5. Dong, J., Zhang, J.W.: Experience-based Intelligence Simulation in ECG Recognition. In: CIMCA 2008, Austria, pp. 796–801 (2008)
6. Übeyli, E.D.: ECG Beats Classification Using Multiclass Support Vector Machines with Error Correcting Output Codes. Digital Signal Processing 17, 675–684 (2007)
7. Osowski, S., Hoai, L.T., Markiewicz, T.: Support Vector Machine based Expert System for Reliable Heartbeat Recognition. IEEE Transactions on Biomedicine Engineering 51(4), 582–589 (2004)
8. Acır, N.: A Support Vector Machine Classifier Algorithm Based on a Perturbation Method and Its Application to ECG Beat Recognition Systems. Expert Systems with Applications 31, 150–158 (2006)
9. Theodoridis, S., Koutroumbas, K.: Pattern Recognition, 3rd edn. Electronic Industry Press, Beijing (2006) (in Chinese)
10. Wang, L.P., Shen, M., Tong, J.F., Dong, J.: An Uncertainty Reasoning Method for Abnormal ECG Detection. In: IEEE Second International Symposium on IT in Medicine & Education, Ji'nan, China, pp. 1091–1096 (2009)
11. MIT-BIH ECGPuwave Tool,
   http://www.physionet.org/physiotools/ecgpuwave
12. MIT-BIH Arrhythmia Database,
   http://www.physionet.org/physiobank/database/mitdb
13. Deng, N.Y., Tian, Y.J.: The New Approach in Data Mining-Support Vector Machine, pp. 335–341. Sciences Press, Beijing (2004) (in Chinese)
14. Zhang, J.W., Dong, J.: The Chinese Cardiovascular Diseases Database and its Management Tool. In: 10th IEEE Bioinformatics and Bioengineering. IEEE Press, New York (2010) (accepted)

Classification of Wood Pulp Fibre Cross-Sectional Shapes

Asuka Yamakawa[1] and Gary Chinga-Carrasco[2]

[1] Department of chemical engineering, Norwegian University of
Science and Technology (NTNU), NO-7491 Trondheim, Norway
[2] Paper and Fibre Research Institute (PFI),
Hogskoleringen 6B, NO-7491 Trondheim, Norway

Abstract. This work presents a comparison of two statistical approaches
for automatic classification of fibre shapes, i.e. Canonical Discriminant
Analysis (CDA) and Mahalanobis Discriminant Analysis (MLDA). The
discriminant analyses were applied to identify and classify several fibre
cross-sectional shapes, including e.g. intact, collapsed, touching and fibrillated fibres. The discriminant analyses perform differently, giving clear in-
dications of their suitability for classifying a given group of fibre elements.
Compared to CDA, MLDA was more reliable and relatively stable.

1 Introduction

Wood pulp fibres are most important within several industry sectors, being an
important component in e.g. paper products, fibre-based composites and most
recently as a source of sugar for biofuel production. Wood pulp fibres may thus be
industrially processed for achieving specific properties depending on the target
application.

It is most desirable to characterize the effect of different processes and treatments on the fibre structure as this may affect several end-use properties of a
given material. Scanning electron microscopy (SEM) has proven to be suitable
for assessment of cross-sectional dimensions of wood pulp fibres [7] [9]. However,
the quantification is demanding and may require the intervention of an operator
for performing subjective evaluation of fibre cross-sectional elements.

Computerized image analysis is a powerful tool to edit and process digital
images of wood pulp fibres [6] [2] [9]. According to [3] the main challenge in
the automatic quantification of wood pulp fibre dimensions, in images containing
a large amount of fibres, is not the extraction of data from single fibre elements
or the automatic post-processing (editing), but the identification of a given fibre
that may need a specific post-processing. Discriminant analysis is a statistical
method to obtain the discriminant function which best separate two or more
classes of objects or events. Such approach may be part of a data mining and
decision support system, which may form the basis for automatic classification,
processing any quantification of fibre cross-section.

The purpose of the study is to verify the suitability of the two statistical
approaches for classifying fibre cross-sectional elements. It is the intention to

M. Graña Romay et al. (Eds.): HAIS 2010, Part I, LNAI 6076, pp. 144–151, 2010.

find an automatic classification based on several shape descriptors. Such an approach will secure the objectivity and reduce the subjectivity involved in manual quantification of wood pulp fibre dimensions.

2   Materials and Methods

2.1   Preparation and Image Acquisition

Market thermo-mechanical pulp (TMP) fibres were applied in this study. The TMP process disrupts the fibre wall structure, thus creating the series of particular cross-sectional shapes. To secure a proper cross-sectional characterization, the fibre were aligned and freeze-dried. The TMP fibres were embedded in epoxy resin (Epofix, Struers) and cured for 24 hrs. The blocks were hand-held ground and automatically polished. For details see [9].

Cross-sectional images of the pulp fibres were acquired with a Hitachi S-3000 variable pressure SEM, using a solid stage backscatter detector. The magnifications was 150×. The acceleration voltage was 5 kV. The size of the images was 2560×1920 pixels with a resolution 0.31 μm. The working distance was 8–10 mm. Images containing totally some 2000 objects were acquired.

2.2   Image Processing and Analysis

The public domain ImageJ program [8] [1] was applied for image processing and analysis. The original greylevel images were thresholded automatically. The cross-sectional fibre shapes were quantified with the Shape descriptor plugin [10].

The cross-sectional fibres are classified based on several shape descriptors (Table 1). The fibres were classified into three groups by the number of lumens (no lumen, single lumen, multiple lumens). In the "no lumen group", there were three kinds of fibre shapes, split, touching and discontinuity (Fig.2). The "single lumen group" also consists of three kinds of fibres, intact, intact with shoulders

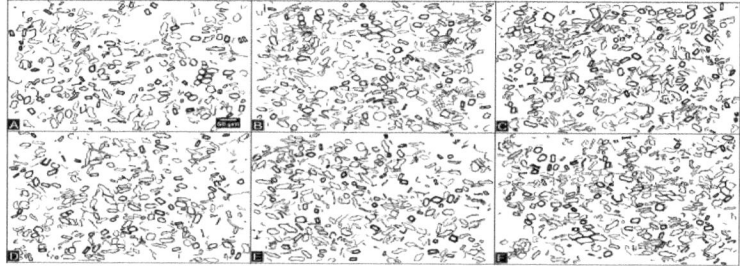

Fig. 1. SEM cross-sectional images of TMP fibres. Images A-E were used as data for training. Image F was used for verifying the generated discriminant functions. Bar = $50\mu m$.

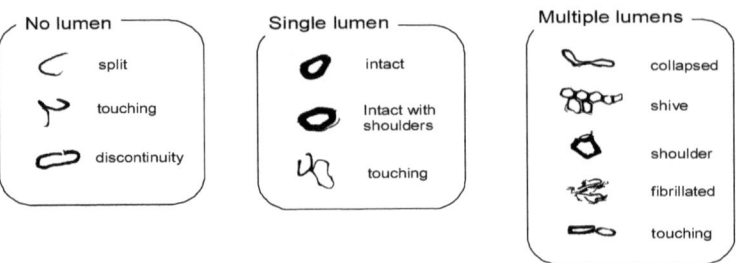

Fig. 2. Some typical shapes in the no-lumen, single lumen and multiple lumens groups

and touching. Five shapes were included in the "multiple lumens group", i.e. collapsed, shive, shoulder, fibrillated and touching. Discriminant analyses were applied to the fibre elements in each group to classify them by their corresponding shapes.

2.3   Shape Description

Several shape descriptors were measured for each object with the Shape descriptor plugin (Table 1). For clarification purposes, the left and center pictures in Fig.3 exemplify the convex area and the best fitting ellipse approximation.

Table 1. Shape discriptors

Shape descriptor	$\frac{Formula}{Description}$	Shape descriptor	$\frac{Formula}{Description}$
Area ratio	$\frac{Area(exc.lumen)}{Area(inc.lumen)}$	Solidity	$\frac{Area}{Convex\,Area}$
Form Factor	$\frac{4\pi \cdot Area(inc.lumen)}{perimeter^2}$	Convexity	$\frac{Convex\,Perimeter}{Perimeter}$
Roundness	$\frac{4 \cdot Area(inc.lumen)}{\pi \cdot Majoraxis^2}$	Circularity	$\frac{4\pi \cdot Area(exc.lumen)}{perimeter^2}$
Aspect ratio	$\frac{Majoraxis}{Minoraxis}$		

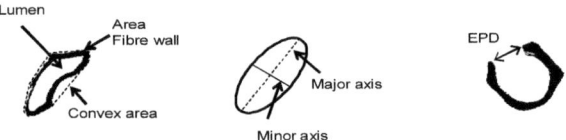

Fig. 3. Schematic representation of cross-sectional fibre elements. The convex area is given by the dotted lines in the left picture. The corresponding best fitting ellipse is given in the center. The distance between two end points of a fibre element is marked in the right side.

In addition, the distance between two endpoints (EPD) (Fig.3 right) and two variables related to the EPD (EPD/Perimeter and EPD/Majoraxis) were calculated for each given fibre element without lumen.

3 Discriminant Analysis

3.1 Canonical Discriminant Analysis (CDA)

Canonical discriminant analysis is one of multiple discriminant analyses that classify objects into three or more categories using continuous or dummy categorical variables as predictors.

Let us consider a set of features $\boldsymbol{x}_{n_c}^c = (x_{n_c 1}^c, x_{n_c 2}^c, \cdots, x_{n_c I}^c)$ $(n_c = 1, \cdots, N_c)$ for each sample of an object with known class c $(c = 1, 2, \cdots, C)$. Here N_c and I represent the number of the samples in class c and the dimension of the feature vector respectively. Consider a problem to determine the best class in C for a new observation $\boldsymbol{x}' = (x_1', x_2', \cdots, x_I')$.

Let be arbitrary coefficients $a_1^c, a_2^c, \cdots, a_I^c$ corresponding to I explanatory variables $x_1^c, x_2^c, \cdots, x_I^c$. The linear function $z_{n_c}^c$ is defined as

$$z_{n_c}^c = a_1^c x_{n_c 1}^c + a_2^c x_{n_c 2}^c + \cdots + a_I^c x_{n_c I}^c \qquad (n_c = 1, 2, \cdots, N_c) \qquad (1)$$

The total sum of squares (S_T) that represents the variance of $z_{n_c}^c$ is decomposed with the "between classes scatter matrix" S_B and "within classes scatter matrix" S_W as follows:

$$S_T = S_B + S_W \qquad (2)$$

$$S_B = \sum_{c=1}^{C} N_c (\overline{z^c} - \overline{z})^2, \qquad S_W = \sum_{c=1}^{C} \sum_{n_c=1}^{N_c} (z_{n_c}^c - \overline{z^c})^2$$

where $\overline{z^c}$ is the mean in class c and $\overline{z}$ is the overall mean of the data sample. To best discriminate the C classes by z is equal to maximize the ratio between S_B and S_W as follows:

$$\boldsymbol{max.} \qquad J(\boldsymbol{a}) = \frac{S_B}{S_W}$$

$$= \frac{\boldsymbol{a}' B \boldsymbol{a}}{\boldsymbol{a}' W \boldsymbol{a}} \qquad (3)$$

where

$$B = (b_{pq}), \qquad b_{pq} = \sum_{c=1}^{C} N_c (\overline{x_p^c} - \overline{x_p})(\overline{x_q^c} - \overline{x_q})$$

$$W = (w_{pq}), \qquad w_{pq} = \sum_{c=1}^{C} \sum_{n_c=1}^{N_c} (x_{pn_c}^c - \overline{x_p^c})(x_{qn_c}^c - \overline{x_q^c})$$

$$\boldsymbol{a} = (a_1, a_2, \cdots, a_I)' \qquad (p = 1, \cdots, I, \quad q = 1, \cdots, I)$$

From $\partial J(\boldsymbol{a})/\partial \boldsymbol{a} = 0$, we obtain the eigenvalue problem

$$(B - \lambda W)\boldsymbol{a} = 0 \tag{4}$$

The eigenvector corresponding to the ith eigenvalue is represented as $\boldsymbol{a}_i = (a_{i1}, a_{i2}, \cdots, a_{iI})'$ $(i = 1, \cdots, r)$ and the vector elements are called canonical variables. The liner combination with the first eigenvector is called the first canonical variate.

3.2 Mahalanobis Discriminant Analysis (MLDA)

Classification based on Mahalanobis distance is one of the most common discriminant analyses [4] [11]. Consider which class x belongs to, class A or B in Fig.4 and Fig.5. The gray circles in the figures represent the probability distributions of the objects in each class. The simplest method is to calculate the distances between the object x and the centers of each class and assign it to the shortest distance class.

- If $d_A^2 - d_B^2 < 0$ then x belongs to A

- If $d_A^2 - d_B^2 \geq 0$ then x belongs to B

In Fig.4, d_A (the distance between the center in the class A and x) is somewhat shorter than d_B(the distance between the center in the class B and x). Consequently x is assigned to the class A. On the other hand, it is not advisable to take the (Euclidean) distances into account in Fig.5 because the variances of the objects in class A and B are different. While the probability that x belongs to the class A is nearly zero because the objects in the class A gather around the center, there is some probability that the class B contains x because the probability distribution widely spreads. Therefore distance based on correlations between variables is necessary. Considering the correlations, in general, the distance in the above rules are defined as

$$d_{(c)}^2 = (\boldsymbol{x} - \overline{\boldsymbol{x}^c})'(S^c)^{-1}(\boldsymbol{x} - \overline{\boldsymbol{x}^c}) \tag{5}$$

$$S^c = (S_{pq}^c), \qquad S_{pq}^c = \frac{1}{N_c} \sum_{n_c=1}^{N_c} (x_{n_c p}^c - \overline{x_p^c})(x_{n_c q}^c - \overline{x_q^c})$$

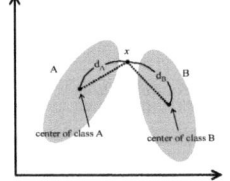

Fig. 4. Data distribution1

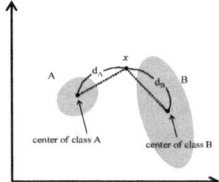

Fig. 5. Data distribution2

$$\overline{\boldsymbol{x}^c} = \frac{1}{N_c} \sum_{n_c=1}^{N_c} \boldsymbol{x}_{n_c}^c \qquad (c = 1, 2, \cdots, C \quad p = 1, \cdots, I, \quad q = 1, \cdots, I)$$

The distance $d_{(c)}^2$ is called Mahalanobis' generalized distance.

4   Results

The total population of fibre elements consisted of 2000 objects with various shapes (Fig.1). Apparent lumens that were smaller than 20 pixels were closed. After classifying the objects by the number of lumens (no lumen, single lumen and multiple lumens groups), the first five images were used for training data to generate discriminant functions(Fig.1A-E) and the last image was used for verifying the discriminant functions (Fig.1F). With two kinds of discriminant analyses, MLDA and CDA, the objects in each group were classified by their corresponding shapes.

For instance, considering the first five cross-sectional images, the fibre elements having a single lumen consisted of 269 intact, 211 intact with shoulders and 128 touching objects. Based on the 608 objects, discriminant functions were generated by MLDA and CDA to classify the mixed objects into three classes (intact, intact with shoulders and touching). Moreover 132 mixed fibre elements in the sixth cross-sectional image were discriminated with the same functions. In the same manner, discriminant functions for no and multiple lumens objects were calculated, based on 895 and 150 training data. 212 and 22 checking data were used for the verification of the models, respectively. In each case, the 2-13 explanatory variables were chosen empirically for generating the discriminant functions. MLDA classified the data into two classes in the procedure, that is $n-1$ steps are needed to partition data into n classes. On the other hand, data were classified into n classes by CDA in one single step.

The number of the training data and the error ratios of the training and checking data are shown in Table 2. There are not big difference between the error rations of the training and checking data, except for the multiple lumen group by MLDA. This means that the reproductivity of the discriminant functions is good. However, the error ratio of the checking data by MLDA is about twice than that of the training data in the multiple lumens group. This seems to imply an overfitting problem because the data was classified into 5 classes despite having only 150 training data in the multiple lumens group. On the other hand, the error

Table 2. Error ratios

	# of training data	MLDA		CDA	
		training	checking	training	checking
No lumen	608	21.8 %	25.5 %	23.2 %	26.4 %
Single lumen	895	17.3 %	15.9 %	20.1 %	25.8 %
Multiple lumens	150	16.0 %	31.8 %	50.7 %	50.0 %

Table 3. Classification. Some fibre elements that were correctly classified or misclassified.

		Correctly classified	Misclassification by MLDA	Misclassification by CDA
no lumen	Discontinuity fibres			
	Split fibres			
	Touching fibres			
single lumen	Intact fibres			
	Shoulder fibres			
	Touching fibres			
multiple lumens	Touching fibres			
	Collapsed fibres			
	Shive fibres			
	Shoulder fibres			
	Fibrillated fibres			

ratios of the training and checking data in the multiple lumens group by CDA are nearly the same and high. This may be due to the poor linear regression models since the five discriminant functions were generated with few training data in one single step.

Table 3 shows the misclassified examples in the checking data. In the discontinuity class, some discontinuity fibres with a shoulder were difficult to classify well. Intact fibre objects were well-recognized by MLDA. However intact fibres with small shoulders were not recognized well (Table 3). There are several common misrecognized objects. For instance, the two common fibres are shown in the shive class in the multiple lumen group. However the third object in the shive fibre class misclassified by CDA, was recognized as a touching object by MLDA although both of them are errors. Though there was one collapsed fibre in the checking data, no object was chosen in the collapsed class by MLDA. It was misclassified in the touching class by MLDA and well-recognized by CDA.

5   Conclusion

We have applied MLDA and CDA, to two dimensional image data to classify them by their shapes. We have discussed the advantages and disadvantages of each approach by direct comparison of the results. CDA is easier to handle and for understanding the data structures because it classifies data into several classes in one single step and shows canonical variates. On the other hand, although it takes time to deal with MLDA because we have to choose explanatory variables empirically, their reliability is higher and relatively stable. Therefore we adopt MLDA for our future works. Proper shape classification will be a major advantage for post-processing fibre cross-sections correctly. Such post-processing include e.g. 1) opening collapsed fibre, 2) separating touching fibre and 3)rounding fibre with shoulders. The approach presented in this study will thus form the basis for developing automatic procedures for quantifying wood fibre cross-sectional dimensions and shapes, as influenced by industrial processes in the pulp and paper industry.

Acknowledgement

The financial support from the WoodWisdom-Net project, WoodFibre3D, is gratefully acknowledged.

References

1. Abramoff, M.D., Magelhaes, P.J., Ram, S.J.: Image Processing with Image. J. Biophotonics Int. 11(7), 36–42 (2004)
2. Chan, B.K., Jang, H.F., Seth, R.S.: Measurement of fibre wall thickness by confocal microscopy and image analysis. Appita J. 5(3), 229 (1998)
3. Chinga-Carrasco, G., Lenes, M., Johnsen, P.O., Hult, E.-L.: Computer-assisted scanning electron microscopy of wood pulp fibres: dimensions and spatial distributions in a polypropylene composite. Micron 40(7), 761–768 (2009)
4. McLachlan, G.J.: Discriminant Analysis and Statistical Pattern Recognition. John Wiley & Sons, New York (2004)
5. Graña, M., Torrealdea, F.J.: Hierarchically structured systems. European Journal of Operational Research 25, 20–26 (1986)
6. Kibblewhite, R.P., Bailey, D.G.: Measurement of fibre cross-section dimensions using image processing. Appita J. 41(4), 297–303 (1988)
7. Kure, K.-A., Dahlqvist, G.: Development of structural fibre properties in high intensity refining. Pulp. Paper Can. 99(7), 59–63 (1998)
8. Rasband, W.: ImageJ (1997), http://rsb.info.nih.gov/ij
9. Reme, P.A., Johnsen, P.O., Helle, T.: Assessment of fibre transverse dimensions using SEM and image analysis, J. Pulp. Pap. Sci. 28(4), 122–128 (2002)
10. Syverud, K., Chinga, G., Johnssen, P.O., Leirset, I., Wiik, K.: Analysis of lint particles from full-scale printing trials. Appita J. 60(4), 286–290 (2007)
11. Bow, S.-T.: Pattern Recognition and Image Preprocessing. Marcel Dekker, New York (2002)

A Hybrid Cluster-Lift Method for the Analysis of Research Activities

Boris Mirkin[1,2], Susana Nascimento[3], Trevor Fenner[1], and Luís Moniz Pereira[3]

[1] School of Computer Science, Birkbeck University of London, London, WC1E 7HX, UK
[2] Division of Applied Mathematics, Higher School of Economics, Moscow, RF
[3] Computer Science Department and Centre for Artificial Intelligence (CENTRIA),
Faculdade de Ciências e Tecnologia, Universidade Nova de Lisboa, Caparica, Portugal

Abstract. A hybrid of two novel methods - additive fuzzy spectral clustering and lifting method over a taxonomy - is applied to analyse the research activities of a department. To be specific, we concentrate on the Computer Sciences area represented by the ACM Computing Classification System (ACM-CCS), but the approach is applicable also to other taxonomies. Clusters of the taxonomy subjects are extracted using an original additive spectral clustering method involving a number of model-based stopping conditions. The clusters are parsimoniously lifted then to higher ranks of the taxonomy by minimizing the count of "head subjects" along with their "gaps" and "offshoots". An example is given illustrating the method applied to real-world data.

1 Introduction

The last decade has witnessed an unprecedented rise of the concept of ontology as a computationally feasible tool for knowledge maintenance. For example, the usage of Gene Ontology [5] for interpretation and annotation of various gene sets and gene expression data is becoming a matter of routine in bioinformatics (see, for example, [14] and references therein).

To apply similar approaches to less digitalized domains, such as activities of organizations in a field of science or knowledge supplied by teaching courses in a university school, one needs to distinguish between different levels of data and knowledge, and build techniques for deriving and transforming corresponding bits of knowledge within a comprehensible framework.

The goal of this paper is to present such a framework, utilizing a pre-specified taxonomy of the domain under consideration as the base. In general, a taxonomy is a rooted-tree-like structure whose nodes correspond to individual topics in such a way that the parental node's topic generalizes the topics of its children's nodes. We concentrate on the issue of representing an organization or any other system under consideration, in terms of the taxonomy topics. We first build profiles for its constituent entities in terms of the taxonomy and then thematically generalize them.

To represent a functioning structure over a taxonomy is to indicate those topics in the taxonomy that most fully express the structure's working in its relation to the taxonomy. It may seem that conventionally mapping the system to all nodes related to topics involved in the profiles within the structure would do the job, but it is not the case - such a

M. Graña Romay et al. (Eds.): HAIS 2010, Part I, LNAI 6076, pp. 152–161, 2010.

mapping typically represents a fragmentary set of many nodes without any clear picture of thematic interrelation among them. Therefore, to make the representation thematically consistent and parsimonious, we propose a two-phase generalization approach. The first phase generalizes over the structure by building clusters of taxonomy topics according to the functioning of the system. The second phase generalizes over the clusters by parsimoniously mapping them to higher ranks of the taxonomy determined by a special parsimonious "lift" procedure. It should be pointed out that both building fuzzy profiles and finding fuzzy clusters are research activities well documented in the literature; yet the issues involved in this project led us to develop some original schemes of our own including an efficient method for fuzzy clustering combining the approaches of spectral and approximation clustering [10].

We apply these constructions to visualize activities of Computer Science research organizations. We take the popular ACM Computing Classification System (ACM-CCS), a conceptual four-level classification of the Computer Science subject area as a pre-specified taxonomy for that. An earlier stage of this project is described in [11]. This work extends the additive clustering model described in [11] to fuzzy additive clustering by using the spectral decomposition of our similarity matrix and extracting clusters one by one, which allows to draw a number of model-based stopping conditions. Found clusters are lifted to higher ranks in the ACM taxonomy and visualised via a novel recursive parsimonious lift method.

The rest of the paper is organized as follows: Section 2 introduces taxonomy-based profiles, Section 3 describes a new spectral fuzzy clustering method for deriving fuzzy clusters from the profiles, Section 4 introduces our parsimonious lift method to generalize found clusters to higher ranks in a taxonomy tree. Section 5 presents the application of the proposed cluster-lift method to a real world case.

2   Taxonomy-Based Profiles: Why Representing over the ACM-CCS Taxonomy?

In the case of investigation of activities of a university department or center, a research team's profile can be defined as a fuzzy membership function on the set of leaf-nodes of the taxonomy under consideration so that the memberships reflect the extent of the team's effort put into corresponding research topics.

In this case, the ACM Computing Classification System (ACM-CCS)[1] is used as the taxonomy. ACM-CCS comprises eleven major partitions (first-level subjects) such as *B. Hardware, D. Software, E. Data, G. Mathematics of Computing, H. Information Systems*, etc. These are subdivided into 81 second-level subjects. For example, item *I. Computing Methodologies* consists of eight subjects including *I.1 SYMBOLIC AND ALGEBRAIC MANIPULATION, I.2 ARTIFICIAL INTELLIGENCE, I.5 PATTERN RECOGNITION*, etc. They are further subdivided into third-layer topics as, for instance, *I.5 PATTERN RECOGNITION* which is represented by seven topics including *I.5.3 Clustering, I.5.4 Applications*, etc.

Taxonomy structures such as the ACM-CCS are used, mainly, as devices for annotation and search for documents or publications in collections such as that on the ACM portal [1]. The ACM-CCS tree has been applied also as: a gold standard for ontologies derived by web mining systems such as the CORDER engine [17]; a device for

determining the semantic similarity in information retrieval [8] and e-learning applications [18,4]; and a device for matching software practitioners' needs and software
researchers' activities [3].

Here we concentrate on a different application of ACM-CCS – a generalized representation of a Computer Science research organization which can be utilized for analysis and planning purposes. Obviously, an ACM-CCS visualized image can be used for
overviewing scientific subjects that are being developed in the organization, assessing
the scientific issues in which the character of activities in organizations does not fit
well onto the classification – these can potentially be the growth points, and help with
planning the restructuring of research and investment.

In our work, fuzzy profiles are derived from either automatic analysis of documents
posted on the web by the teams or by explicitly surveying the members of the department. To tackle this, and also to allow for expert evaluations, we developed an interactive
E-Survey tool of Scientific Activities-ESSA (available at https://copsro.di.fct.unl.pt/),
that provides two types of functionality: i) collection of data about ACM-CCS based
research profiles of individual members; ii) statistical analysis and visualization of the
data and results of the survey on the level of a department. The respondent is asked
to select up to six topics among the leaf nodes of the ACM-CCS tree and assign each
with a percentage expressing the proportion of the topic in the total of the respondent's
research activity for, say, the past four years. The set of profiles supplied by respondents forms an $N \times M$ matrix F where N is the number of ACM-CCS topics involved
in the profiles and M the number of respondents. Each column of F is a fuzzy membership function, rather sharply delineated because only six topics may have positive
memberships in each of the columns.

3 Representing Research Organization by Fuzzy Clusters of ACM-CCS Topics

3.1 Deriving Similarity between ACM-CCS Research Topics

We represent a research organization by clusters of ACM-CCS topics to reflect thematic
communalities between activity profiles of members or teams working on these topics.
The clusters are found by analyzing similarities between topics according to their ap-
pearances in the profiles. The more profiles contain a pair of topics i and j and the
greater the memberships of these topics, the greater is the similarity score for the pair.

There is a specific branch of clustering applied to similarity data, the so-called relational fuzzy clustering [2]. In the framework of 'usage profiling' relational fuzzy clustering is a widely used technique for discovering different interests and trends among
users from Web log records. In bioinformatics several clustering techniques have been
successfully applied in the analysis of gene expression profiles and gene function prediction by incorporating gene ontology information into clustering algorithms [6].

In spite of the fact that many fuzzy clustering algorithms have been developed already, the situation remains rather uncertain because they all involve manually specified
parameters such as the number of clusters or threshold of similarity, which are subject
to arbitrary choices. This is why we come up with a version of approximate clustering

modified with the spectral clustering approach to make use of the Laplacian data transformation, which has proven an effective tool to sharpen the cluster structure hidden in the data [7]. This combination leads to a number of model-based parameters as aids for choosing the right number of clusters.

Consider a set of V individuals ($v = 1, 2, \cdots, V$), engaged in research over some topics $t \in T$ where T is a pre-specified set of scientific subjects. The level of research effort by individual v in developing topic t is evaluated by the membership f_{tv} in profile f_v ($v = 1, 2, \cdots, V$).

Then the similarity $w_{tt'}$ between topics t and t' can be defined as the inner product of profiles $f_t = (f_{tv})$ and $f_{t'} = (f_{t'v})$, $v = 1, 2, \cdots, V$, modified by individual weights.

To make the cluster structure in the similarity matrix sharper, we apply the spectral clustering approach to pre-process the similarity matrix W using the so-called Laplacian transformation [7]. First, an $N \times N$ diagonal matrix D is defined, with (t, t) entry equal to $d_t = \sum_{t' \in T} w_{tt'}$, the sum of t's row of W. Then unnormalized Laplacian and normalized Laplacian are defined by equations $L = D - W$ and $L_n = D^{-1/2} L D^{-1/2}$, respectively. Both matrices are semipositive definite and have zero as the minimum eigenvalue. The minimum non-zero eigenvalues and corresponding eigenvectors of the Laplacian matrices are utilized then as relaxations of combinatorial partition problems [16,7]. Of comparative properties of these two normalizations, the normalized Laplacian, in general, is considered superior [7].

Yet the Laplacian normalization by itself cannot be used in our approach below because our method relies on maximum rather than minimum eigenvalues. To pass over this issue, the authors of [12] utilized a complementary matrix $M_n = D^{-1/2} W D^{-1/2}$ which relates to L_n with equation $L_n = I - M_n$ where I is the identity matrix. This means that M_n has the same eigenvectors as L_n, whereas the respective eigenvalues relate to each other as λ and $1 - \lambda$, so that the matrix M_n can be utilized for our purposes as well. We prefer using the Laplacian pseudoinverse transformation, Lapin for short, defined by

$$L_n^-(W) = \tilde{Z}\tilde{\Lambda}^{-1}\tilde{Z}'$$

where $\tilde{\Lambda}$ and $\tilde{Z}$ are defined by the spectral decomposition $L_n = Z\Lambda Z'$ of matrix $L_n = D^{-1/2}(D - W)D^{-1/2}$. To specify these matrices, first, set T' of indices of elements corresponding to non-zero elements of Λ is determined, after which the matrices are taken as $\tilde{\Lambda} = \Lambda(T', T')$ and $\tilde{Z} = Z(:, T')$. The choice of the Lapin transformation can be explained by the fact that it leaves the eigenvectors of L_n unchanged while inverting the non-zero eigenvalues $\lambda \neq 0$ to those $1/\lambda$ of L_n^-. Then the maximum eigenvalue of L_n^- is the inverse of the minimum non-zero eigenvalue λ_1 of L_n, corresponding to the same eigenvector. The inverse of a λ near 0 could make the value of $1/\lambda$ quite large and greatly separate it from the inverses of other near zero eigenvalues of L_n. Therefore, the Lapin transformation generates larger gaps between the eigen-values of interest, which suits our one-by-one approach described in the next section well.

Thus, we utilize further on the transformed similarity matrix $A = L_n^-(W)$.

3.2   Additive Fuzzy Clusters Using a Spectral Method

We assume that a thematic fuzzy cluster is represented by a membership vector $u = (u_t)$, $t \in T$, such that $0 \leq u_t \leq 1$ for all $t \in T$, and an intensity $\mu > 0$ that expresses the extent of significance of the pattern corresponding to the cluster, within the organization under consideration. With the introduction of the intensity, applied as a scaling factor to u, it is the product μu that is a solution rather than its individual co-factors.

Our additive fuzzy clustering model involves K fuzzy clusters that reproduce the pseudo-inverted Laplacian similarities $a_{tt'}$ up to additive errors according to the following equations:

$$a_{tt'} = \sum_{k=1}^{K} \mu_k^2 u_{kt} u_{kt'} + e_{tt'}, \qquad (1)$$

where $u_k = (u_{kt})$ is the membership vector of cluster k, and μ_k its intensity.

The item $\mu_k^2 u_{kt} u_{kt'}$ expresses the contribution of cluster k to the similarity $a_{tt'}$ between topics t and t', which depends on both the cluster's intensity and the membership values. The value μ^2 summarizes the contribution of intensity and will be referred to as the cluster's weight.

To fit the model in (1), we apply the least-squares approach, thus minimizing the sum of all $e_{tt'}^2$. Since A is definite semi-positive, its first K eigenvalues and corresponding eigenvectors form a solution to this if no constraints on vectors u_k are imposed. On the other hand, if vectors u_k are constrained to be just 1/0 binary vectors, the model (1) becomes of the so-called additive clustering [15,9].

We apply the one-by-one principal component analysis strategy for finding one cluster at a time. Specifically, at each step, we consider the problem of minimization of a reduced to one fuzzy cluster least-squares criterion

$$E = \sum_{t,t' \in T} (b_{tt'} - \xi u_t u_{t'})^2 \qquad (2)$$

with respect to unknown positive ξ weight (so that the intensity μ is the square root of ξ) and fuzzy membership vector $u = (u_t)$, given similarity matrix $B = (b_{tt'})$.

At the first step, B is taken to be equal to A. Each found cluster changes B by subtracting the contribution of the found cluster (which is additive according to model (1)), so that the residual similarity matrix for obtaining the next cluster will be $B - \mu^2 u u^T$ where μ and u are the intensity and membership vector of the found cluster. In this way, A indeed is additively decomposed according to formula (1) and the number of clusters K can be determined in the process.

Let us specify an arbitrary membership vector u and find the value of ξ minimizing criterion (2) at this u by using the first-order condition of optimality:

$$\xi = \frac{\sum_{t,t' \in T} b_{tt'} u_t u_{t'}}{\sum_{t \in T} u_t^2 \sum_{t' \in T} u_{t'}^2},$$

so that the optimal ξ is

$$\xi = \frac{u'Bu}{(u'u)^2} \qquad (3)$$

which is obviously non-negative if B is semi-positive definite.

By putting this ξ in equation (2), we arrive at

$$E = \sum_{t,t' \in T} b_{tt'}^2 - \xi^2 \sum_{t \in T} u_t^2 \sum_{t' \in T} u_{t'}^2 = S(B) - \xi^2 \left(\mathbf{u}'\mathbf{u}\right)^2,$$

where $S(B) = \sum_{t,t' \in T} b_{tt'}^2$ is the similarity data scatter.

Let us denote the last item by

$$G(u) = \xi^2 \left(\mathbf{u}'\mathbf{u}\right)^2 = \left(\frac{\mathbf{u}'B\mathbf{u}}{\mathbf{u}'\mathbf{u}}\right)^2, \tag{4}$$

so that the similarity data scatter is the sum:

$$S(B) = G(u) + E \tag{5}$$

of two parts, $G(u)$, which is explained by cluster (μ, u), and E, which remains unexplained.

An optimal cluster, according to (5), is to maximize the explained part $G(u)$ in (4) or its square root

$$g(u) = \xi \mathbf{u}'\mathbf{u} = \frac{\mathbf{u}'B\mathbf{u}}{\mathbf{u}'\mathbf{u}}, \tag{6}$$

which is the celebrated Rayleigh quotient, whose maximum value is the maximum eigenvalue of matrix B, which is reached at its corresponding eigenvector, in the unconstrained problem.

This shows that the spectral clustering approach is appropriate for our problem. According to this approach, one should find the maximum eigenvalue λ and corresponding normed eigenvector z for B, $[\lambda, z] = \Lambda(B)$, and take its projection to the set of admissible fuzzy membership vectors.

According to this approach, there can be a number of model-based criteria for halting the process of sequential extraction of fuzzy clusters:

1. The optimal value of ξ (3) for the spectral fuzzy cluster becomes negative.
2. The contribution of a single extracted cluster becomes too low, less than a prespecified $\tau > 0$ value.
3. The residual scatter E becomes smaller than a pre-specified ϵ value, say less than 5% of the original similarity data scatter.

More details on the method referred to as ADDI–FS, including its application to affinity and community structure data along with experimental comparisons with other fuzzy clustering methods, are described in [10].

4   Parsimonious Lifting Method

To generalize the contents of a thematic cluster, we lift it to higher ranks of the taxonomy so that if all or almost all children of a node in an upper layer belong to the cluster, then the node itself is taken to represent the cluster at this higher level of the ACM-CCS taxonomy. Such lifting can be done differently, leading to different portrayals of the cluster on ACM-CCS tree depending on the relative weights of the events taken into account. A major event is the so-called "head subject", a taxonomy node covering (some of) leaves belonging to the cluster, so that the cluster is represented by a set of head subjects. The penalty of the representation to be minimized is proportional to the number of head subjects so that the smaller that number the better. Yet the head subjects cannot be lifted too high in the tree because of the penalties for associated events, the cluster "gaps" and "offshoots".

The gaps are head subject's children topics that are not included in the cluster. An offshoot is a taxonomy leaf node that is a head subject (not lifted).

The total count of head subjects, gaps and offshoots, each weighted by both the penalties and leaf memberships, is used for scoring the extent of the cluster misfit needed for lifting a grouping of research topics over the classification tree. The smaller the score, the more parsimonious the lift and the better the fit. Depending on the relative weighting of gaps, offshoots and multiple head subjects, different lifts can minimize the total misfit.

5   An Application to a Real World Case

Let us illustrate the approach by using the data from a survey conducted at the Centre of Artificial Intelligence, Faculty of Science & Technology, New University of Lisboa

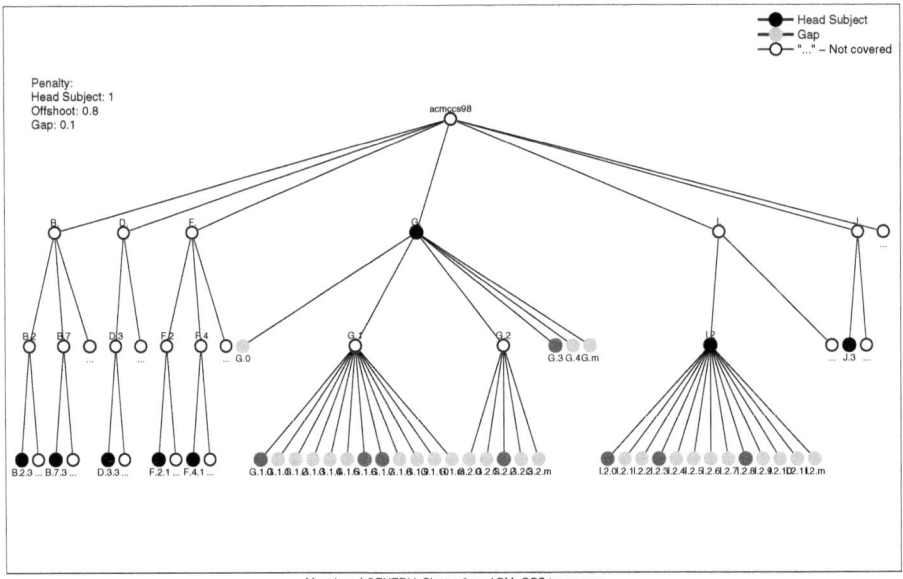

Mapping of CENTRIA Cluster 2 on ACM–CCS taxonomy

Fig. 1. Mapping of CENTRIA cluster 2 onto the ACM-CCS tree with penalties $h = 1$, $o = 0.8$ and $g = 0.1$

(CENTRIA-UNL). The survey involved 16 members of the academic staff of the Centre who covered 46 topics of the third layer of the ACM-CCS.

With the algorithm ADDI-FS applied to the 46×46 similarity matrix, two clusters have been sequentially extracted, after which the residual matrix has become definite negative (stopping condition (1)). The contributions of two clusters total to about 50%. It should be noted that the contributions reflect the tightness of the clusters rather than their priority stand. Cluster 1 is of pattern recognition and its applications to physical sciences and engineering including images and languages, with offshoots to general aspects of information systems. In cluster 2, all major aspects of computational mathematics are covered, with an emphasis on reliability and testing, and with applications in the areas of life sciences. Overall these results are consistent with the informal assessment of the research conducted in the research organization. Moreover, the sets of research topics chosen by individual members at the ESSA survey follow the cluster structure rather closely, falling mostly within one of the two.

Figure 1 shows the representation of CENTRIA's cluster 2 in the ACM-CCS taxonomy with penalties of $h = 1$, $o = 0.8$, and $g = 0.1$. Increasing the gap penalty g from 0.1 to 0.2 would lead to a different parsimonious generalization in which the head subject 'G' is decomposed into a number of head subjects on lower ranks of the hierarchy.

6   Conclusion

We have described a hybrid method for representing aggregated research activities over a taxonomy. The method constructs fuzzy profiles of the entities constituting the structure under consideration and then generalizes them in two steps. These steps are:

(i) fuzzy clustering research topics according to their thematic similarities, ignoring the topology of the taxonomy, and

(ii) lifting clusters mapped to the taxonomy to higher ranked categories in the tree.

These generalization steps thus cover both sides of the representation process: the empirical – related to the structure under consideration – and the conceptual – related to the taxonomy hierarchy.

This work is part of the research project *Computational Ontology Profiling of Scientific Research Organization* (COPSRO), main goal of which is to develop a method for representing a Computer Science organization, such as a university department, over the ACM-CCS classification tree.

In principle, the approach can be extended to other areas of science or engineering, provided that such an area has been systemised in the form of a comprehensive concept tree. Potentially, this approach could lead to a useful instrument for comprehensive visual representation of developments in any field of organized human activities.

The research described in this paper raises a number of issues related to all main aspects of the project: data collection, thematic clustering and lifting. On the data collection side, the mainly manual e-survey ESSA tool should be supported by an automated analysis and rating of relevant research documents including those on the internet. The ADDI-FS method, although already experimentally proven competitive to a number of existing methods, should be further explored and more thoroughly investigated. The issue of defining right penalty weights for cluster lifting should be addressed. Moreover, further investigation should be carried out with respect to the extension of this approach to more complex than taxonomy, ontology structures.

Acknowledgments

The authors are grateful to CENTRIA-UNL members that participated in the survey. Igor Guerreiro is acknowledged for developing software for the ESSA tool. Rui Felizardo is acknowledged for developing software for the lifting algorithm with interface shown in Figure 1. This work has been supported by grant PTDC/EIA/69988/2006 from the Portuguese Foundation for Science & Technology. The support of the individual research project 09-01-0071 "Analysis of relations between spectral and approximation clustering" to BM by the "Science Foundation" Programme of the State University – Higher School of Economics, Moscow RF, is also acknowledged.

References

1. ACM Computing Classification System (1998),
   http://www.acm.org/about/class/1998 (Cited September 9, 2008)
2. Bezdek, J., Keller, J., Krishnapuram, R., Pal, T.: Fuzzy Models and Algorithms for Pattern Recognition and Image Processing. Kluwer Academic Publishers, Dordrecht (1999)
3. Feather, M., Menzies, T., Connelly, J.: Matching software practitioner needs to researcher activities. In: Proc. of the 10th Asia-Pacific Software Engineering Conference (APSEC 2003), p. 6. IEEE, Los Alamitos (2003)
4. Gaevic, D., Hatala, M.: Ontology mappings to improve learning resource search. British Journal of Educational Technology 37(3), 375–389 (2006)
5. The Gene Ontology Consortium: Gene Ontology: tool for the unification of biology. Nature Genetics 25, 25–29 (2000)
6. Liu, J., Wang, W., Yang, J.: Gene ontology friendly biclustering of expression profiles. In: Proc. of the IEEE Computational Systems Bioinformatics Conference, pp. 436–447. IEEE, Los Alamitos (2004), doi:10.1109/CSB.2004.1332456
7. von Luxburg, U.: A tutorial on spectral clustering. Statistics and Computing 17, 395–416 (2007)
8. Miralaei, S., Ghorbani, A.: Category-based similarity algorithm for semantic similarity in multi-agent information sharing systems. In: IEEE/WIC/ACM Int. Conf. on Intelligent Agent Technology, pp. 242–245 (2005), doi:10.1109/IAT.2005.50
9. Mirkin, B.: Additive clustering and qualitative factor analysis methods for similarity matrices. Journal of Classification 4(1), 7–31 (1987)
10. Mirkin, B., Nascimento, S.: Analysis of Community Structure, Affinity Data and Research Activities using Additive Fuzzy Spectral Clustering, Technical Report 6, School of Computer Science, Birkbeck University of London (2009)
11. Mirkin, B., Nascimento, S., Pereira, L.M.: Cluster-lift method for mapping research activities over a concept tree. In: Koronacki, J., Wierzchon, S.T., Ras, Z.W., Kacprzyk, J. (eds.) Recent Advances in Machine Learning II, Computational Intelligence Series, vol. 263, pp. 245–258. Springer, Heidelberg (2010)

12. Ng, A., Jordan, M., Weiss, Y.: On spectral clustering: analysis and an algorithm. In: Ditterich, T.G., Becker, S., Ghahramani, Z. (eds.) Advances in Neural Information Processing Systems, vol. 14, pp. 849–856. MIT Press, Cambridge (2002)
13. Graña, M., Torrealdea, F.J.: Hierarchically structured systems. European Journal of Operational Research 25, 20–26 (1986)
14. Skarman, A., Jiang, L., Hornshoj, H., Buitenhuis, B., Hedegaard, J., Conley, L., Sorensen, P.: Gene set analysis methods applied to chicken microarray expression data. BMC Proceedings 3(Suppl. 4), S8 (2009), doi:10.1186/1753-6561-3-S4-S8
15. Shepard, R.N., Arabie, P.: Additive clustering: representation of similarities as combinations of overlapping properties. Psychological Review 86, 87–123 (1979)
16. Shi, J., Malik, J.: Normalized cuts and image segmentation. IEEE Transactions on Pattern Analysis and Machine Intelligence 22(8), 888–905 (2000)
17. Thorne, C., Zhu, J., Uren, V.: Extracting domain ontologies with CORDER. Tech. Reportkmi-05-14, pp. 1–15. Open University (2005)
18. Yang, L., Ball, M., Bhavsar, V., Boley, H.: Weighted partonomy-taxonomy trees with local similarity measures for semantic buyer-seller match-making. Journal of Business and Technology 1(1), 42–52 (2005)

Protein Fold Recognition with Combined SVM-RDA Classifier

Wiesław Chmielnicki[1] and Katarzyna Stąpor[2]

[1] Jagiellonian University, Faculty of Physics,
Astronomy and Applied Computer Science
[2] Silesian University of Technology, Institute of Computer Science
`wieslaw.chmielnicki@uj.edu.pl`
`http://www.fais.uj.edu.pl`

Abstract. Predicting the three-dimensional (3D) structure of a protein is a key problem in molecular biology. It is also an interesting issue for statistical methods recognition. There are many approaches to this problem considering discriminative and generative classifiers. In this paper a classifier combining the well-known Support Vector Machine (SVM) classifier with Regularized Discriminant Analysis (RDA) classifier is presented. It is used on a real world data set. The obtained results improve previously published methods.

Keywords: Support Vectore Machine, Statistical classifiers, RDA classifier, protein fold recognition.

1 Introduction

Protein structure prediction is one of the most important goals pursued by bioinformatics. Proteins manifest their function through these structures so it is very important to know not only sequence of amino acids in a protein molecule, but also how this sequence is folded. The successful completion of many genome-sequencing projects has meant the number of proteins without known 3D structure is quickly increasing.

There are several machine-learning methods to predict the protein folds from amino acids sequences proposed in literature. Ding and Dubchak [5] experiments with Support Vector Machine (SVM) and Neural Network (NN) classifiers. Shen and Chou [9] proposed ensemble model based on nearest neighbour. A modified nearest neighbour algorithm called K-local hyperplane (HKNN) was used by Okun [14]. Nanni [13] proposed ensemble of classifiers: Fishers linear classifier and HKNN classifier.

There are two standard approaches to the classification task: generative classifiers use training data to estimate a probability model for each class, then test items are classified by comparing their probabilities under these models. The discriminative classifiers try to find the optimal frontiers between classes based on all samples of the training data set.

M. Graña Romay et al. (Eds.): HAIS 2010, Part I, LNAI 6076, pp. 162–169, 2010.

This paper presents a classifier which combines the SVM (discriminative) classifier with statistical RDA (generative) classifier. The SVM technique has been used in different application domains and has outperformed the traditional techniques. Contrary to traditional techniques, which try to minimize empirical risk (the classification error on the training data) SVM minimizes the structural risk (the classification error on never before seen data).

However, the SVM is a binary classifier but the protein fold recognition is a multi-class problem. There are many methods proposed to deal with this issue One of the first and well-known methods is one-versus-one strategy with max-win voting scheme. In this strategy every binary classifier votes for the preferred class and the voting table is created. Originally a class with maximum number of votes is recognized as the correct class.

However some of these two-way classifiers are unreliable. The votes from these classifiers influence the final classification result. In this paper there is a strategy presented to assign a weight (which can be treated as a measure of reliability) to each vote based on values of the discriminant function from RDA classifier.

The rest of this paper is organized as follows: Section 2 introduces the database and the feature vectors used is these experiments, Section 3 describes the method of combining the classifiers and Section 4 presents experimental results and conclusions.

2   The Database and Feature Vectors

Using machine-learning methods entails the necessity to find out databases with representation of known protein sequences and its folds. Then this information must be converted to the feature space representation.

2.1   Database

In experiments described in this paper two data sets derived from SCOP (Structural Classification of Proteins) database are used. The detailed description of these sets can be found in Ding and Dubchak [5]. The training set consists of 313 protein sequences and the testing set consists of 385 protein sequences. These data sets include proteins from 27 most populated different classes (protein folds) representing all major structural classes: α, β, α/β, and $\alpha + \beta$. The training set was based on PDB_select sets (Hobohm et al. [18], Hobohm and Sander [19]) where two proteins have no more than 35% of the sequence identity. The testing set was based on PDB-40D set developed by Lo Conte et al. [8] from which representatives of the same 27 largest folds are selected. The proteins that had higher than 35% identity with the proteins of the training set are removed from the testing set.

2.2   Feature Vectors

In our experiments the feature vectors developed by Ding and Dubchak [5] were used. These feature vectors are based on six parameters: Amino acids composition (C), predicted secondary structure (S), Hydrophobity (H), Normalized van der Waals volume (V), Polarity (P) and Polarizability (Z). Each parameter corresponds to 21 features except Amino acids composition (C), which corresponds to 20 features. The data sets including these feature vectors are available at http://ranger.uta.edu/~chqding/protein/. For more concrete details, see Dubchak et al. [6], [7]. In this study the sequence length was added to the Amino acids composition (C) vector and the feature vectors based on these parameters were used in different combinations creating vectors from 21D to 126D.

3   The Proposed Combined Classifier

The discriminative classifiers are based on minimum error training, for which the parameters of one class are trained on the samples of all classes. For statistical classifiers, the parameters of one class are estimated from the samples of its own class only. Therefore the characteristics of these kinds of classifiers differs in several respects.

The discriminative classfiers give higher accuracies than statistical ones when there is enough training samples, but however the accuracy of regularized statistical classfiers (such as RDA) are more stable and when training data set is small they generalize better.

Additionally statistical classifiers are resistant to outliers, whereas discriminative ones are susceptible to outliers because their decision regions tend to be open [28]. For more detailed discussion see Liu and Fujisawa [27].

In protein fold recognition problem we have very small training data sets because the number of proteins with known 3D structure is relatively small. So our motivation was to combine the properties of both types of classifiers.

3.1   The SVM Classifier

The Support Vector Machine (SVM) is a well known large margin classifier proposed by Vapnik [10]. The basic concept behind the SVM classifier is to search an optimal separating hyperplane, which separates two classes. The decision function of the binary SVM is presented as:

$$f(x) = sign\left(\sum_{i=1}^{N} \alpha_i y_i K(x_i, x) + b\right) , \tag{1}$$

where $0 \leq \alpha_i \leq C, i = 1, 2, \ldots, N$ are nonnegative Lagrange multipliers, C is a cost parameter, that controls the trade off between allowing training errors and forcing rigid margins, x_i are the support vectors and $K(x_i, x)$ is the kernel function.

The SVM is a binary classifier but the protein fold recognition is a multi-class problem Generally, there are two types of approaches to this problem. One of them is considering all classes in one optimization. The second approach is to cover one n-class problem into several binary problems.

There are many methods proposed in literature, such as one-versus-others, one-versus-one strategies, DAG (Directed Acyclic Graph), ADAG (Adaptive Directed Acyclic Graph) methods (Platt et al. [20]), (Kijsirikul et al. [22]), BDT (Binary Decision Tree) approach (Fei and Liu [21]), DB2 method (Vural and Dy [11]), pairwise coupling (Hasti and Tibshirani [24]) or error-correcting output codes (Dieterich and Bakiri [25]). In our classifier we use the first and well-known method: one-versus-one strategy with max-win voting scheme.

The LIBSVM library version 2.89 was used in our research (Chang and Lin, [3]). Although the implementation of this library includes one-versus-one strategy for the multi category problems only the binary version of the classifier was used. LIBSVM provides a choice of build-in kernels i.e. Linear, Polynomial. Radial Basis Function (RBF) and Gausian. The RBF kernel:

$$K(x_i, x) = -\gamma \|x - x_i\|^2, \gamma > 0 , \tag{2}$$

gave the best results in our experiments.

The parameters C and γ must be chosen to use the SVM classifier with RBF kernel. It is not known beforehand which C and γ are the best for one problem. Both values must be experimentally chosen, which was done by using a cross-validation procedure on the training data set. The best recognition ratio 58.7% was achieved using parameters values $g = 0.1$ and $C = 128$.

In one-versus-one strategy with max-win voting scheme the two-way classifiers are trained between all possible pairs of classes. Every binary classifier votes for the preferred class and in this way the voting table is created. Originally a class with maximum number of votes is recognized as the correct class.

However some of these two-way classifiers are unreliable. The votes from these classifiers influence the final classification result. In our method there is a strategy presented to assign a weight to each vote. The weight is based on the values of the discriminant function from RDA classifier as described below.

3.2   The RDA Classifier

Quadratic discriminant analysis (QDA) [23] models the likelihood of class as a Gaussian distribution and then uses the posterior distributions to estimate the class for a given test vector. This approach leads to discriminant function:

$$d_k(x) = (x - \mu_k)^T \Sigma_k^{-1}(x - \mu_k) + \log |\Sigma_k| - 2 \log p(k) , \tag{3}$$

where x is the test vector, μ_k is the mean vector, Σ_k covariance matrix and $p(k)$ is prior probability of the class k. The Gaussian parameters for each class can be estimated from the training data set, so the values of Σ_k and μ_k are replaced in formula (3) by its estimates $\hat{\Sigma}_k$ and $\hat{\mu}_k$.

However, when the number of training samples n is small compared to the number of dimensions of the training vector the covariance estimation can be ill-posed. The approach to resolve the ill-posed estimation is to regularize covariance matrix. First the covariance matrix Σ_k can be replaced by their average (pooled covariance matrix) i.e. $\hat{\Sigma} = \sum \hat{\Sigma}_k / \sum \hat{N}_k$ which leads to Linear Discriminant

Analysis (LDA). This assumes that all covariance matrices are similar. It is very limited approach so in Regularized Discriminant Analysis (RDA) (Friedman [26]) each covariance matrix can be estimated as:

$$\hat{\Sigma}_k(\lambda) = (1 - \lambda)\hat{\Sigma}_k + \lambda\hat{\Sigma} \,, \tag{4}$$

where $0 \le \lambda \le 1$. The parameter λ controls the degree of shrinkage of the individual class covariance matrix estimate toward the pooled estimate.

In our experiments we decide to use selection algorithm to find better feature vector for RDA classifier. The best selection method is to check all possible feature combinations. However, the number of them is far to high to use such an algorithm, but the features used in our experiments are based on parameters C, S, H, V, P, Z (as described in section 2) that create six feature sets containing 21 values each, so all combination of these sets can be considered. The total number of these combinations is 63, so the brute force algorithm can be used. The best combination (63D feature set based on C, S, P parameters) was found using cross-validation on the training data set.

The next step was to find the best parameter value for regularization. There is no universal value of λ for all classification problems. This value must be experimentally chosen using cross-validation procedure on the training data set In our experiment we find that $\lambda = 0.8$ gave the best results.

The RDA classifier uses a table of values of discriminant functions $d_k(x)$ and assigns a test vector to a class with minimal value of this function. Using this algorithm the recognition ratio 55,6% was achieved.

3.3   The Combined SVM-RDA Classifier

It is easy to notice that the bigger value of the discriminant function for the class the smaller probability that the vector belongs to this class. Let us consider a SVM binary classifier that deals with i-th and j-th class. Assume that this classifier assigns the vector x to the class i. Then the difference with $d_i(x)$ and $d_{min}(x) = \min\{d_k(x)\}$, $k = 1, 2, \ldots, n$ can be treated as a measure of reliability such a classifier. Formally this measure will be the weight of the vote and can be defined as:

$$1 - \frac{d_i(x) - d_{min}(x)}{d_{min}(x)} \,. \tag{5}$$

Then each vote from every binary classifier has its weight. The maximum value of the weight is 1 for the vote that assigns the vector to the class with minimum value of the discriminant function. We can notice that the weight is 0 when the value of the discriminant function for the test vector is twice the minimal and will be negative for bigger values. We can avoid this effect restricting the values to the $[0, 1]$ inteval but it has no influence on the final results.

All votes have its weights, so now they are not equally treated as in one-versus-one strategy. The protein with maximum number of votes (which is now a real number) is classified as the correct class. The recognition rate using this method is 61,8%.

4   Results and Conclusions

In this paper we present a combined generative/discriminative classifier. The proposed classifier uses the information provided by generative classifier, to improve recognition rate of the discriminative one. The combined SVM-RDA classifier achieves better result (61,8%) than the SVM (58,7%) or RDA (55,6%) classifiers alone.

The accuracy measure used in this paper is the standard Q percentage accuracy (Baldi et al., [1]). Suppose there is $N = n_1 + n_2 + \ldots + n_p$ test proteins, where n_i is the number of proteins which belongs to the class i. Suppose that c_i of proteins from n_i are correctly recognised (as belonging to the class i). So the total number of $C = c_1 + c_2 + \ldots + c_p$ proteins is correctly recognized. Therefore the total accuracy is $Q = C/N$.

The results achieved using the proposed strategies are promising. The recognition rates obtained using these algorithms (55,6% - 61,8%) are comparable to those described in literature (48.8% - 61.2%). The obtained results are very

Table 1. Comparison among different methods

Method	Recognition ratio
SVM [5]	56.0%
HKNN [14]	57.4%
DIMLP-B [15]	61.2%
RS1_HKNN_K25 [13]	60.3%
RBFN [16]	51.2%
MLP [17]	48.8%
SVM-RDA (this paper)	61.8%

encouraging. Our results improved the recognition ratio achieved by other methods proposed in literature but however some extra experiments are needed especially to consider other approaches to the multi-class SVM.

References

1. Baldi, P., Brunak, S., Chauvin, Y., Andersen, C., Nielsen, H.: Assessing the accuracy of prediction algorithms for classification: an overview. Bioinformatics 16, 412–424 (2000)
2. Prevost, L., Qudot, L., Moises, A., Michel-Sendis, C., Milgram, M.: Hybrid generative/discriminative classifier for unconstrained character recognition. Pattern Recognition Letters 26, 1840–1848 (2005)
3. Chang, C.C., Lin, C.J.: LIBSVM: a library for support vector machines (2001), Software available at http://www.csie.ntu.edu.tw/~cjlin/libsvm
4. Chothia, C.: One thousand families for the molecular biologist. Nature 357, 543–544 (1992)

5. Ding, C.H., Dubchak, I.: Multi-class protein fold recognition using support vector machines and neural networks. Bioinformatics 17, 349–358 (2001)
6. Dubchak, I., Muchnik, I., Holbrook, S.R., Kim, S.H.: Prediction of protein folding class using global description of amino acid sequence. Proc. Natl. Acad. Sci. USA 92, 8700–8704 (1995)
7. Dubchak, I., Muchnik, I., Kim, S.H.: Protein folding class predictor for SCOP: approach based on global descriptors. In: Proceedings ISMB (1997)
8. Lo Conte, L., Ailey, B., Hubbard, T.J.P., Brenner, S.E., Murzin, A.G., Chotchia, C.: SCOP: a structural classification of protein database. Nucleic Acids Res. 28, 257–259 (2000)
9. Shen, H.B., Chou, K.C.: Ensemble classifier for protein fold pattern recognition. Bioinformatics 22, 1717–1722 (2006)
10. Vapnik, V.: The Nature of Statistical Learning Theory. Springer, New York (1995)
11. Vural, V., Dy, J.G.: A hierarchical method for multi-class support vector machines. In: Proceedings of the twenty-first ICML, Banff, Alberta, Canada, July 4-8, p. 105 (2004)
12. Wang, L., Shen, X.: Multi-category support vector machines, feature selection and solution path. Statistica Sinica 16, 617–633 (2006)
13. Nanni, L.: A novel ensemble of classifiers for protein fold recognition. Neurocomputing 69, 2434–2437 (2006)
14. Okun, O.: Protein fold recognition with k-local hyperplane distance nearest neighbor algorithm. In: Proceedings of the Second European Workshop on Data Mining and Text Mining in Bioinformatics, Pisa, Italy, pp. 51–57, September 24 (2004)
15. Bologna, G., Appel, R.D.: A comparison study on protein fold recognition. In: Proceedings of the ninth ICONIP, Singapore, November 18-22, vol. 5, pp. 2492–2496 (2002)
16. Pal, N.R., Chakraborty, D.: Some new features for protein fold recognition. In: Kaynak, O., Alpaydın, E., Oja, E., Xu, L. (eds.) ICANN 2003 and ICONIP 2003. LNCS, vol. 2714, pp. 1176–1183. Springer, Heidelberg (2003)
17. Chung, I.F., Huang, C.D., Shen, Y.H., Lin, C.T.: Recognition of structure classification of protein folding by NN and SVM hierarchical learning architecture. In: Kaynak, O., Alpaydın, E., Oja, E., Xu, L. (eds.) ICANN 2003 and ICONIP 2003. LNCS, vol. 2714, pp. 1159–1167. Springer, Heidelberg (2003)
18. Hobohm, U., Sander, C.: Enlarged representative set of Proteins. Protein Sci. 3, 522–524 (1994)
19. Hobohm, U., Scharf, M., Schneider, R., Sander, C.: Selection of a representative set of structures from the Brookhaven. Protein Bank Protein Sci. 1, 409–417 (1992)
20. Platt, J.C., Cristianini, N., Shawe-Taylor, J.: Large Margin DAGs for Multiclass Classification. In: Proceedings of Neural Information Processing Systems, NIPS 1999, pp. 547–553 (2000)
21. Fei, B., Liu, J.: Binary Tree of SVM: A New Fast Multiclass Training and Classification Algorithm. IEEE Transaction on Neural Networks 17(3) (2006)
22. Kijsirikul, B., Ussivakul, N.: Multiclass support vector machines using adaptive directed acyclic graph. In: Proceedings of IJCNN, pp. 980–985 (2002)
23. Fukunaga, K.: Introduction to Statistical Pattern Recognition, 2nd edn. Academic Press, New York (1990)
24. Hastie, T., Tibshirani, R.: Classification by pairwise coupling. Annals of Statistics 26(2), 451–471 (1998)
25. Dietterich, T.G., Bakiri, G.: Solving multiclass problems via error-correcting output codes. Journal of Artificial Intelligence Research 2, 263–286 (1995)

26. Friedman, J.H.: Regularized Discriminant Analysis. Journal of the American Statistical Association 84(405), 165–175 (1989)
27. Liu, C.L., Fujisawa, H.: Classification and Learning for Character Recognition: Comparison of Methods and Remaining Problems. In: Proc. Int. Workshop on Neural 21 Networks and Learning in Document Analysis and Recognition, Seoul, Korea (August 2005)
28. Gori, M., Scarselli, F.: Are multilayer perceptrons adequate for pattern recognition and verification? IEEE Trans. Pattern Anal. Mach. Intell. 20(11), 1121–1132 (1998)

Data Processing on Database Management Systems with Fuzzy Query

İrfan Şimşek[1] and Vedat Topuz[2]

[1] Msc. Sultançiftliği Primary School, Çekmeköy, 34788, Istanbul, Turkey
Ph.: (+90) 216 312 13 81; Fax: (+90) 216 429 29 10
irfansimsek@gmail.com
[2] Asst. Prof. Dr. Marmara University Vocational School of Technical Sciences, Göztepe,
34722, Istanbul, Turkey
Ph.: (+90) 216 418 25 04; Fax: (+90) 216 418 25 05
vtopuz@marmara.edu.tr

Abstract. In this study, a fuzzy query tool (SQLf) for non-fuzzy database management systems was developed. In addition, samples of fuzzy queries were made by using real data with the tool developed in this study. Performance of SQLf was tested with the data about the Marmara University students' food grant. The food grant data were collected in MySQL database by using a form which had been filled on the web. The students filled a form on the web to describe their social and economical conditions for the food grant request. This form consists of questions which have fuzzy and crisp answers. The main purpose of this fuzzy query is to determine the students who deserve the grant. The SQLf easily found the eligible students for the grant through predefined fuzzy values. The fuzzy query tool (SQLf) could be used easily with other database system like ORACLE and SQL server.

Keywords: Fuzzy logic, fuzzy query, database.

1 Introduction

Database management systems have made a significant progress in terms of functionality and performance since they were first designed in the 1960s. However, the query systems of relational database management systems, which are widespread today, are based on two-value logic. In this logic, an entry either meets the criteria or not. After the querying criteria, it creates sets whose boundaries are certain. This is in contradiction with our natural thinking method, because we are unable to differentiate some objects in our daily lives in such a certain way. For example, a person does not suddenly become short or tall because of a couple of millimeters difference [1-6]. In order to define these situations, using fuzzy logic will be beneficial to simplify the query and get a more correct report.

Today's database management systems are advanced in terms of performance and functionality and almost all of them have their own high-level query systems. However, these query systems work with precise values or value intervals. [7-9].

M. Graña Romay et al. (Eds.): HAIS 2010, Part I, LNAI 6076, pp. 170–177, 2010.
© Springer-Verlag Berlin Heidelberg 2010

The fuzzy set theory, proposed by L.A. Zadeh, aims at processing the indefinite and vague information. In other words, the concept of fuzziness refers to the state of ambiguity which stems from the lack of certainty. The fuzzy logic and the fuzzy set theory play an important role for vague knowledge display and almost all of our expressions in the daily language contain fuzziness. (cold-hot, rich-poor, short-long etc.) [10-13]. Ambiguity plays an important role in human thinking style, especially in communication, inference, and in identifying and abstracting figures; and the importance of the fuzzy theory appears at this point. When we wish to transform the user interfaces which enable us to communicate with machines into a human-oriented style, the fuzzy theory becomes an effective tool at our hands [14].

The fuzzy query provides us with the ability to evaluate imprecise data and use expressions such as "old" or "rich" which do not imply certain quantities. The fuzzy query provides the nearest data to us, if what we search for does not exist. This is a very beneficial feature especially if we do not have absolute information or the information we have is not quantitative [9, 15-17].

2 "SQLf" Fuzzy Query Software

The SQLf Software was written by taking into consideration the software designed to make fuzzy queries on database management systems such as SummarySQL and FuzzyQuery. The Figure 1 shows the relationship between the SQLf software's browser, php and database server. The task of the SQLf software is to make both classical and fuzzy queries on non-fuzzy database systems and report the results. The software was encoded in PHP programming language. It is available on the web and the address is *http://www.fuzzyquery.com.*

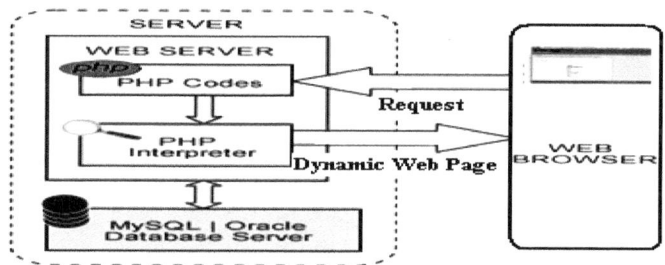

Fig. 1. Relationship between the SQLf Software's Browser, Php and Database Server

The components of the software are as follows:

1. The graphical interface that interacts with the user
2. Making connection settings to the database management system
3. Defining the criteria necessary for the query (Criteria Definition)
4. Defining fuzzy sets for table fields (Fuzzy Sets)
5. Monitoring the impact of hedges on the current fuzzy sets (Hedges)
6. Creating precise and fuzzy queries from the defined criteria (Query Design)

7. Controlling the queries created and determining the desired fields on the result table (Query Control)
8. Displaying the result table and the query statistics after running the controlled query according to the desired fields (Query Run)

The software is composed of two main sections as shown in figure 2, namely the fuzzying and query.

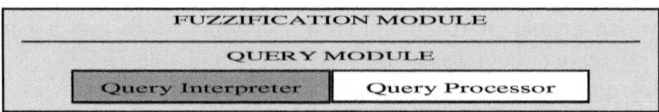

Fig. 2. Main Parts of Systems

The fuzzification module: Since the database folder on which query is made is not fuzzy, firstly a fuzzying operation is needed. To this end, the user is shown the fields of the desired folder and then s/he is enabled to define fuzzy sets for the fields s/he desired. There is no restriction about which fields the user can fuzzy. Fuzzying is generally made for the fields containing quantitative data. Fuzzy sets are defined as the sets of pairs of elements and degrees of membership. In order to reuse the definitions, a set database was formed in which all the entered information is stored.

The query module: The query processor steps in, after the defined queries are controlled. The general structure of the query processor is demonstrated in the Figure 3, finds the matching degree of each entry and produces a report accordingly.. Unlike the classical processing, the matching degree of the query is not either 0 or 1, but it is a number between 0 and 1.

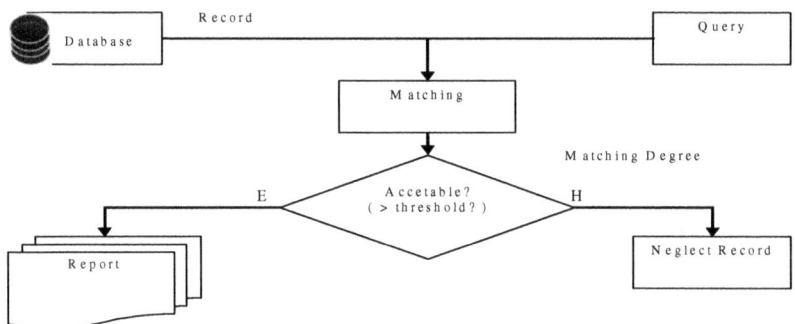

Fig. 3. Essence of Database Querying

3   Example: Marmara University Food Grant

Performance of SQLf was tested with Marmara University student's food grant data. The students filled a form which describes their social and economical positions for the food grant request on the web. This form consists of questions which have fuzzy and crisp answers. The SQLf easily found the eligible students for grants with predefined fuzzy values. Fuzzy query tool (SQLf) was designed to work not only with this database, but also with other databases.

3.1 The Assessment Table

The Food Grant Database consists of three tables; namely student information, family information and contact information. Since our aim is to find the students who deserve the food grant, we will conduct the assessment on the family information table which contains the student's living conditions, the state of family, and the other received grants.

Table 1 shows the family information table's field names, field types and other features of fields. The fields which will be assessed in this table and the characteristics of these fields in terms of the information they contain are as follows:

Table 1. Family Information Table

Field Name	Field Type	Empty	Default	Explanation
Id	int(11)	No		Student ID
stOfPa	tinyint(4)	No		State of parents (1-3) as a numerical value
numCh	int(11)	No		Number of children in the family
numChAttSch	int(11)	No		Number of children attending school.
fathOcc	tinyint(11)	No		Father's occupation (1) Private, (2) Self-Employed,(3)Public,(4) Unemployed.
mothOcc	tinyint(11)	No		Mother's occupation
stFamHou	tinyint(4)	No		State of house in which the family stay (1-4) as a numerical value.
netInc	decimal(10)	No		Sum of the family's net income
scho1	varchar(20)	Yes	NULL	Names of the scholarships that the
scho2	varchar(20)	Yes	NULL	student receive, if any
scho3	varchar(20)	Yes	NULL	
noScho	tinyint(6)	No		Whether the student receives scholarship from another institution as 1 and 0
stHouse	tinyint(4)	No		State of the house in which the student currently stay (1-6) as a numerical value

3.2 Defining Fuzzy Sets

Before defining the criteria, constitution of the fuzzy sets is needed for the fuzzy criteria. The fuzzy sets constituted are placed at the fsql_fsets table in the MySQL database to be used later. The fuzzy sets constituted for our application sample are shown in Table 2.

Table 2. Food Grant Fuzzy Sets Table

Field (field name)	fsname (fuzzy set name)	fsetForm (formal information)	fsalpha (Alpha cut coefficient)	fmin (minimum data)	Fmax (maximum data)
netInc	poor	decline	0	0	1000
stOfPa	bad	l.increasing	0	1	3
numChAttSch	very	growth	0	0	20
numCh	very	growth	0	0	20
fathOcc	bad	growth	0	1	4
mothOcc	bad	growth	0	1	4
stFamHou	bad	decline	0	1	4
estHouse	bad	decline	0	1	6

3.3 Preparing the Criteria

After constituting the fuzzy sets, the criteria should be prepared in order to use these fuzzy sets in our query. The criteria are divided into two categories; namely the precise qualitative expressions and the fuzzy qualitative expressions. The processing steps for the fields for which criteria will be prepared are as follows:

1. The "Criteria Definition" section should be visited.
2. The relevant field should be selected from the fields section.
3. Since fuzzy qualitative expressions will be constituted, the fuzzy operator (@) should be selected from the operators section.
4. We do not need to select any switcher for our application sample. Thus, the expression of <none> should be selected from the Hedges section.
5. From the value section, the set, which we have constituted from the "Fuzzy Sets" section before, should be selected..

Figure 4 shows the fuzzy qualitative expressions prepared for the application sample. Totally four fuzzy qualitative expressions have been prepared.

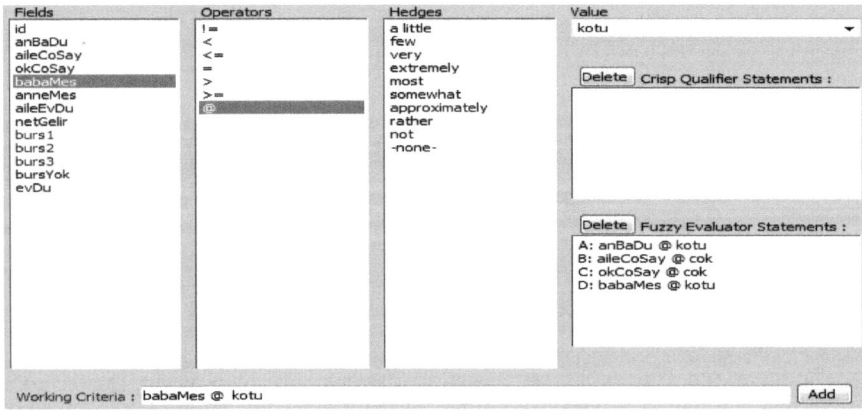

Fig. 4. Criteria Definition Sections

3.4   Constituting the Queries from the Prepared Criteria

By connecting the simple fuzzy qualitative expressions prepared in the "Criteria Definition" section with AND or OR in the "Create Query" section, complex fuzzy qualitative expressions are constituted. The figure 5 shows the complex fuzzy qualitative expressions constituted for the application sample.

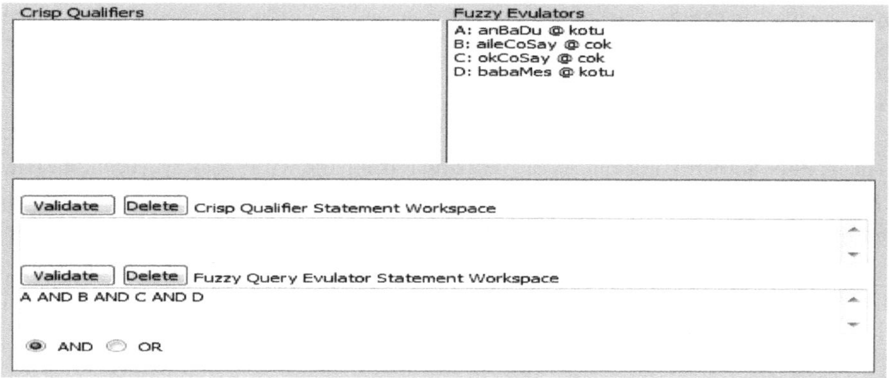

Fig. 5. Query Design Sections

The query sentence can either be a simple single sentence, or a complex sentence consisting of several simple sentences connected with AND or OR. If such a complex sentence is the case, the matching degrees of each sub-sentence are calculated for each entry and thus the overall matching degree is obtained. The entries whose matching degrees are above a defined lower limit are written on the output folder. The sentence or sub-sentences may not be fuzzy. In this case, the operators such as =, >, >=, <, <= etc. and constant values are used in the query, instead of switchers and fuzzy sets.

Fig. 6. Query Control Sections

3.5 Controlling the Queries

Figure 6 shows Query Control sections. The "Query Control" section should be visited in order to control the SQL and SQLf expressions which appear after approving the expressions connected in the "Query Design" section. In this section, the user not only controls the expressions but also defines the settings for the result report. The boundary value is also determined in this section. We defined it as 0.2 in our application sample. It means that, after the query, those whose degrees of membership are below 0.2 will be ignored during the reporting.

3.6 Running the Queries and the Result Table

The results shown by Table 3 are obtained from the "Run Query" section. After the query, 88 out of 3645 people are listed. In this table μ(grant) field shows the fuzzy deserve level of grant according student ID and other information which are used in fuzzy query. μ(grant) values could be between 0 and 1 and 1 value means that student completely deserved the grant. A part of the result table is presented in Table 3.

Table 3. Result Table

μ(grant)	ID	stHouse	stFamHou	numCh	numChAttSch	netInc
0.86	2282	1	1	3	3	265
0.82	2301	1	1	3	3	300
0.778	2610	2	1	4	4	170
0.777	1704	2	2	5	5	200
0.776	1590	2	2	3	3	245

4 Conclusion

This paper proposes a fuzzy query languages (fuzzy relational calculus and fuzzy relational algebra) based on the relational database query languages. This is an application of the fuzzy set theory and the fuzzy logic was carried out by developing an interface which renders possible to query on any relational database with query sentences similar to the sentences used in the daily language. Complex fuzzy query sentences including hedges and crisp values could be constituted.

Efficiency of application is shown with student food grant problem. This is an example of relational database which have crisp and fuzzy fields. Hence, it is not convenient to say who deserved food grant easily. Therefore all applicant student food grant deserved degree was found as a fuzzy membership value. Consequently this developed application could be used to query any relational database which has crisp or fuzzy fields.

References

1. Mutlu, T.: A Fuzzy Query Tool For Non-Fuzzy Databases, Master Thesis, Istanbul Technical University Information Sciences Institute, Istanbul (1996)
2. Bahadır, A.: Flexible Querying in Standard Database Systems With Fuzzy Set Approach, Master Thesis, Istanbul Technical University Information Sciences Institute, Istanbul (1999)
3. Andersen, T., Christiansen, H., Larsen, H.L.: Flexible Query Answering System, pp. 45–61, 187-209, 247-277. Kluwer Academic Publishers, Boston (1997)
4. Zadeh, L.A., Kacprzyk, J.: Fuzzy Logic for the Management of Uncertainty, pp. 645–672. Wiley, New York (1992)
5. Kacprzyk, J., Ziolkowski, A.: Database Queries with Fuzzy Linguistic Quantifiers. IEEE Transactions on Systems, Man and Cybernetics SMC-16(3), 474–478 (1986)
6. Takahashi, Y.: A Fuzzy Query Language for Relational Databases. IEE Transactions on Systems, Man and Cybernetics 21(6), 1576–1579 (1991)
7. Rasmussen, D., Yager, R.R.: SummarySQL–A Fuzzy Tool For Data Mining. Intelligent Data Analysis 1(1-4), 49–58 (1997)
8. Rasmani, K.A., Shen, Q.: A Data-Driven Fuzzy Rule-Based Approach for Student Academic Performance Evaluation. Applied Intelligence 23(3), 305–319 (2006)
9. Zadeh, L.A.: Knowledge Representation in Fuzzy Logic. IEEE Transactions on Knowledge and Data Engineering 1(1), 89–100 (1989)
10. Klir, G.J., Yuan, B.: Fuzzy Sets and Fuzzy Logic Theory and Applications, pp. 379–388. Prentice Hall, New Jersey (1995)
11. Tanaka, K.: An Introduction to Fuzzy Logic for Practical Applications, pp. 68–75. Springer, New Jersey (1996)
12. Ross, J.T.: Fuzzy Logic with Engineering Applications, pp. 52–75. McGraw Hill Inc, New York (2004)
13. Kosko, B.: Fuzzy Engineering, pp. 18–24. Prentice Hall, New Jersey (1997)
14. Zongmin, M.: Fuzzy Database Modeling of Imprecise and Uncertain Engineering Information, pp. 137–155. Springer, New York (2006)
15. Zimmermann, H.J.: Fuzzy Sets, Decision Making, and Expert Systems, pp. 125–134. Kluwer Academic Publishers, Boston (1987)
16. Terano, T., Asai, K., Sugeno, M.: Fuzzy Systems Theory and Its Applications. Academic Press, San Diego (1992)
17. Şen, O.N.: Oracle SQL, SQL*PLUS, PL/SQL and Database Management, Beta Impression Publication Distributor, Istanbul, pp. 85–90 (2000)

A Hybrid Approach for Process Mining: Using From-to Chart Arranged by Genetic Algorithms

Eren Esgin[1], Pinar Senkul[2], and Cem Cimenbicer[2]

[1] Middle East Technical University, Informatics Institute
[2] Middle East Technical University, Computer Engineering Department,
065531 Ankara, Turkey
eesgin@ii.metu.edu.tr, senkul@ceng.metu.edu.tr,
e1247519@metu.edu.tr

Abstract. In the scope of this study, a hybrid data analysis methodology to business process modeling is proposed in such a way that; From-to Chart, which is basically used as the front-end to figure out the observed patterns among the activities at realistic event logs, is rearranged by Genetic Algorithms to convert these derived raw relations into activity sequence. According to experimental results, acceptably good (sub-optimal or optimal) solutions are obtained for relatively complex business processes at a reasonable processing time period.

Keywords: From-to Chart, Genetic Algorithms (GA), Process Mining, Business Process Modeling (BPM), Event Logs.

1 Introduction

Even though contemporary information systems are intensively utilized in enterprises, their actual impact in automating complex business processes is still constrained by the difficulties encountered in the design phase [6]. Reference model is influenced by the personal perceptions, because of the lack of deep knowledge about the domain on hand [1]. As a result, crucial discrepancies between process design and process enactment are emerged and reference models for target business process tend to be rather incomplete, subjective and at a too high level [2,3]. Process mining is proposed a remedy to these discrepancies by mining interesting patterns from the event logs and discovering the business process model automatically [6,7,8,9,10,11].

A new approach for process mining is based on using From-to Chart for analyzing the event logs [2]. This approach consists of two components: *From-to Chart* and *process flow branch discovery* [2]. From-to Chart is an analytical tool, which is basically used in monitoring material handling routes between operations, machines, departments or work centers on the production floor [3]. The underlying methodology inherits this tool from facility layout domain and implements it in a distinct field, i.e. business process modeling, as the basic bookkeeping material in monitoring transitions among activities occurred in process instances and figuring out if there exists any specific order of the occurrences for representing in process model [2]. As the

M. Graña Romay et al. (Eds.): HAIS 2010, Part I, LNAI 6076, pp. 178–186, 2010.
© Springer-Verlag Berlin Heidelberg 2010

second component, process flow branch discovery is a type of process mining algorithm, which is used to distill behavioral process knowledge from a set of real time execution with respect to several evaluation metrics (e.g. support–confidence framework and modified lift) and convert these distilled patterns into process model. In this work, proposed approach is further improved by using genetic algorithms for rearranging the From-to Chart. In the previous work, this rearrangement was performed by a permutative approach, which led to an exponential increase in execution time. Hence we aimed to improve the prior version of the approach in terms of total processing time with *Genetic Algorithms* (GA), which are adaptive methods used to solve search and optimization problems [12].

This paper is organized as follows: Section 2 includes the related work. Section 3 describes basic concepts about From-to Chart. Section 4 introduces the proposed approach. In Section 5, the application of the presented approach on a real case is described. Finally, Section 6 includes the concluding remarks.

2 Related Work

In [6], Aalst et al. highlights the process mining usage in analysis and improvement of process flexibility. It proposes the enrichment of obtained event logs with semantic information. Consequently process mining techniques can capture the reactive and stimulus entities for the change in event logs. Likewise [6], [7] aims to handle both case and control-flow perspectives in an integrated fashion. While production workflow is strongly process-oriented, the case handling paradigm basically concentrates on the case itself, which is the fundamental object to be produced.

The idea of applying process mining in the context of workflow management was first introduced in [8]. In this study, two issues are handled. The first issue is to discover a workflow graph generating activities appearing in a given workflow log. The second issue is to find the definitions of the relation conditions.

Cook and Wolf have investigated similar issues in the context of software engineering process. In [9], they describe three methodologies for process discovery ranging from the purely algorithmic to purely statistical: RNET, KTAIL and MARKOV.

In [10], Weijters and Aalst propose a rediscovery technique to deal with noise and to validate workflow processes by uncovering and measuring the discrepancies between the prescriptive models and actual process executions. Detecting concurrency appears as one of the fundamental concerns. Therefore AND/OR connectors are aimed to be explicitly distinguished in the process model. Moreover, local and global metrics are proposed to find explicit representations for a broad range of process models. These metrics are revised in [1]. In [11], the proposed method, named alpha algorithm, seeks to rediscover sound Workflow nets. Given such an algorithm, it is aimed to find the class of workflow nets which can be rediscovered. As a way of representation, it generates concrete Petri nets for a broad range of process models rather than a set of dependency relation between events like in [10].

As a GA implementation in facility layout problem (FLP), Sarker et al. attempts to handle locating multiple identical machines in a linear layout, which is called tertiary assignment problem (TAP) in [14]. It is attempted to solve this problem type by identifying sets of identical machines which may be partitioned into individual, unique machines. In order to relax the underlying FLP and provide approximate solutions, amoebic matrix is implemented.

3 Basic Concepts

The basic From-to Chart is a square, symmetric matrix for summarizing material handling between related operations, machines, departments or work centers on the production floor with high volume production rate [4]. Actually minimizing the material handling cost is the most considered objective, since between 15% - 70% of the total production cost can be attributed to material handling [15]. This analytical technique is useful for several purposes including designing relative locations of operations, demonstrating material flow patterns and showing degree of self-sufficiency of each operation for better arrangement to reduce handling, costs, distances, production control problems, etc. [3]. Major use cases encountered at From-to Chart are visualized in Figure 1:

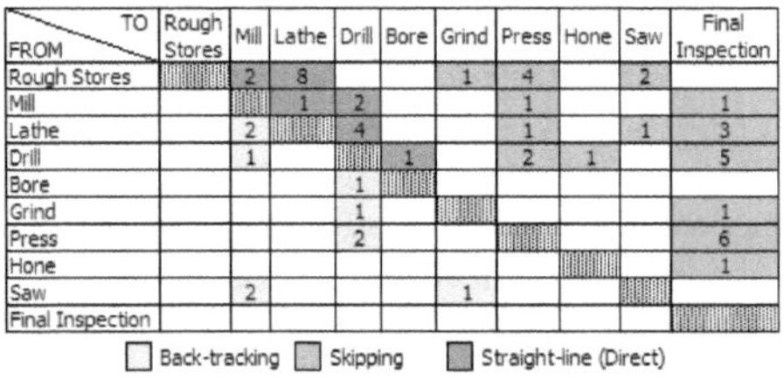

TO / FROM	Rough Stores	Mill	Lathe	Drill	Bore	Grind	Press	Hone	Saw	Final Inspection
Rough Stores		2	8			1	4		2	
Mill			1	2			1			1
Lathe		2		4			1		1	3
Drill		1			1		2	1		5
Bore				1						
Grind				1						1
Press				2						6
Hone										1
Saw		2				1				
Final Inspection										

☐ Back-tracking ☐ Skipping ■ Straight-line (Direct)

Fig. 1. Major Use Cases at From-to Chart

From-to Chart is a descriptive material to reduce a large volume data into a workable formation such that; the construction of a From-to Chart does not result directly in the solution of a layout problem [4]. On the other hand, a more quantitative approach to minimize material handling is obtained by taking *moments* of the accumulated score at each element around the diagonal and aiming for the lowest moment total at From-to Chart as stated in [2]. The number of elements away from the diagonal is used as the moment arm. Objective function to minimize the total moment of from-to chart is formulated as follows:

$$Min\ Z = \sum_{i=1}^{N}\sum_{j=1}^{N} f_{ij} \times |j - i| \times p \tag{1}$$

In this formula, f_{ij} indicates total move from operation i to operation j, $|j - i|$ is the distance from operation i to operation j, and p is the back-tracking penalty point assigned to each entry below the diagonal. Back-tracking penalty point is *doubled* to enforce the model towards a straight line arrangement [5]. Therefore, p is determined as follows:

$$p = \begin{cases} 1 & \text{when } j \geq i \\ 2 & \text{when } i > j \end{cases}$$

4   From-to Chart Based Process Discovery: Using Genetic Algorithms for Rearrangement

4.1   Constructing From-to Chart from Event Logs

The starting point of the proposed methodology is the creation of a FROMTOCHART table by retrieving the activity type labels from the event logs and populating FROM-TOCHART table. For populating the table, event logs are arranged by process instance identifier (e.g. caseID) and then ordered by timestamp in ascending order. Then, predecessor and successor are parsed for each transition in process instances (cycles) and the current score at (predecessor,successor)th element in FROMTOCHART table is incremented by one.

4.2   Evaluating the Scores at From-to Chart

At traditional From-to Chart implementation, total score of each element is directly taken into consideration in rearrangement of the matrix. However in the proposed methodology, it is aimed to eliminate the effect of *weak* scores on finding the fittest activity sequence by pruning down them prior to rearrangement.

Basically there are three evaluation metrics used in the proposed methodology: *confidence for from-to chart* (confidence FTC), *support for from-to chart* (support FTC) and *modified lift* [2]. These metrics act as the major stick yard to control the level of robustness and complexity of the discovered process model from large amounts of data. While formulating these metrics, the original formations in association rule mining are taken as the basis [2].

4.3   Rearranging From-to Chart

This operation is the *engine component* of proposed methodology, which aims to find out the activity sequence with the minimum total moment value at FROMTOCHART table. The mapping of basic GA notations into the business process modeling domain is such that; a *chromosome* possessed by an individual is represented as an activity sequence and each *gene* position in this chromosome corresponds to a unique activity type. The coarse-grained GA stages are implemented as follows:

i. Initialization. Initial population can be generated with or without a *schema*. Holland's *schema theorem* explains the power of the GA in terms of how schemata are processed [13].

In the case of non-schema application, a Permutation class randomly generates the candidate chromosomes, which are encoded according to activity type domain alphabet. On the other hand if the initial population is generated according to the schema, the schema has to be constructed firstly. In order to construct the schema, a *transition top-list*, which holds *top n scores*[1] that are retrieved from the From-to Chart, is instantiated. Afterwards, a top-down search is performed at the transition top-list in order to

---

[1] The length of the transition top list, n, is formulated as $|\text{activity type domain}|^2 \times 0.2$. The stereotype 0.2 is based on *Pareto Principle* (also known as *80-20 rule*).

construct the schema. As a result, a non-intermittent schema[2] with the maximum length of $|$ `activity type domain` $|$ $/3$ is constructed.

ii. Fitness Score Calculation. As far as GA are concerned, it is better to have higher fitness scores to provide more opportunities especially in selection stage. Therefore the inverse of the objective function is used as the denominator of the fitness function to search for the minimum moment. The numerator of the fitness function is set to the total scores that are marked at the From-to Chart.

$$f(z) = \frac{\sum_{i=1}^{N} \sum_{j=1}^{N} score_{ij}}{\sum_{i \in chromosome\,Z} \sum_{j \in chromosome\,Z} score_{ij} \times |j - i| \times p} \qquad (2)$$

Because of the moment notation, the maximum value for the fitness function, $f(z)$, is 1 (i.e. all transitions at From-to Chart are straight-line type).

iii. Selection. A hybrid method, which is composed of *pure* and *elitist* selection, is implemented. Pure selection is a kind of random selection type where the individual i has a probability of `FitnessScore`$_i$/$\sum$`FitnessScore` to be selected as a parent to mate. On the other hand, elitist selection keeps a projected ratio of the best fitted individuals at each iteration of the algorithm. The default ratio for elitist selection is 0.10.

iv. Crossover. Actually crossover is not always applied to all pairs of parents selected for mating such that, a default likelihood of crossover is set to p_c=0.80. If the crossover is not applied, the offspring are produced by simply duplicating the parents. Otherwise, a single crossover gene position, which is in the [1, `chromosomeLength`] interval, is randomly selected and chromosome subsets are exchanged according to this gene position.

v. Mutation. Mutation independently alters each gene value at the offspring chromosome with relative small probability (typically p_m=0.02). In higher order domain alphabets, in which binary coding is not appropriate, mutation and crossover framework may cause problems with chromosomes legality, e.g. multiple copies of a given activity type may occur at the offspring. Therefore we propose an alternative mutation scheme that automatically swaps the duplicate activity type with a randomly selected unobserved value. Hence a uniform chromosome that satisfies the chromosome legality is reproduced.

vi. Population Convergence. As a termination condition, if the fitness scores of at least 95% of the individuals in the last population are in the *convergence band*[3], no more new population is generated. The default value for convergence ratio is 0.15.

---

[2] The constructed schema does not include any undefined # bits. Therefore the *length* and *order* characteristics of the underlying schema are equal.

[3] The interval of convergence band is determined as [(1-convergenceRatio),1].

4.4 Extracting Relations

Although the fittest activity sequence is the backbone of discovered process model, it is limited to sequential behavior. In this aspect, this operation aims to extract one-to-one and one-to-many relations among activities by concentrating on the evaluated scores in FROMTOCHART table. Evaluated scores are the essential metrics to determine whether the underlying transition is worth to be visualized in process model such that;

a. Positive score at $(i,j)^{th}$ element highlights that the transition represented by this element is significant with respect to evaluation metric(s). Therefore successor of the transition (i.e. activity j) is added to successive activity list of activity i.

b. Negative or zero-valued score indicates that the underlying transition is challenged by evaluation metric(s). Therefore this element is neglected in constructing process model operation.

5 Case Study: Discovering Credit Card Application Business Process

Credit card application business process consists of ten activity types: "receive applications", "check completeness", "get more information", "check loan amount", "perform checks for large amount", "perform checks for small amount", "make decision", "notify acceptance", "notify rejection" and "deliver credit card". Table 1 shows the initial state of FROMTOCHART table for this business process logs. Note that recApp activity is denoted as the initiator activity.

Table 1. Initial State of FROMTOCHART Table

	recApp	chkCom	getInf	chkLoan	perChkLar	perChkSma	makDec	notAcc	notRej	delCrCrd	Row Total
recApp	0	333	0	0	0	0	0	0	0	0	333
chkCom	0	0	335	333	0	0	0	0	0	0	668
getInf	0	335	0	0	0	0	0	0	0	0	335
chkLoan	0	0	0	0	320	13	0	0	0	0	333
perChkLar	0	0	0	0	0	0	320	0	0	0	320
perChkSma	0	0	0	0	0	0	13	0	0	0	13
makDec	0	0	0	0	0	0	0	147	186	0	333
notAcc	0	0	0	0	0	0	0	0	0	147	147
notRej	0	0	0	0	0	0	0	0	0	0	0
delCrCrd	0	0	0	0	0	0	0	0	0	0	0

Table 2. Final State of FROMTOCHART Table

	recApp	chkCom	getInf	chkLoan	perChkLar	perChkSma	makDec	notAcc	notRej	delCrCrd	Calculated Support Threshold	Calculated Confidence Threshold
recApp	0	333	0	0	0	0	0	0	0	0	83.25	83.25
chkCom	0	0	335	333	0	0	0	0	0	0	83.25	167
getInf	0	335	0	0	0	0	0	0	0	0	83.25	83.75
chkLoan	0	0	0	0	320	0	0	0	0	0	83.25	83.25
perChkLar	0	0	0	0	0	0	320	0	0	0	83.25	80
perChkSma	0	0	0	0	0	0	0	0	0	0	83.25	3.25
makDec	0	0	0	0	0	0	0	147	186	0	83.25	83.25
notAcc	0	0	0	0	0	0	0	0	0	147	83.25	36.75
notRej	0	0	0	0	0	0	0	0	0	0	83.25	0
delCrCrd	0	0	0	0	0	0	0	0	0	0	83.25	0

Calculated Support Threshold = 0.25 * 333 (number of process instances in training dataset)
Calculated Confidence Threshold = 0.25 * row total of underlying initiator activity

After FROMTOCHART table is created and parsed transitions in activity streams are populated to this table, scores are evaluated with respect to support and confidence thresholds (support FTC=0.25 and confidence FTC=0.25). Table 2 shows the final state of FROMTOCHART table.

After scores are evaluated, GA engine reproduces activity sequences starting with recApp activity and then calculates fitness score for these activity sequences according to proposed population size (populationSize=80) and maximum number of iterations (maxIterationNum=250) settings. For instance, the first generated activity sequence *chr1* is {recApp, chkCom, getInf, chkLoan, perChkLar, perChkSma, makDec, notAcc, notRej, delCrCrd}. Fitness score for this activity sequence is calculated as follows:

$$Moment_{recApp} = 333 \times 1$$
$$Moment_{chkCom} = 335 \times 1 + 333 \times 2$$
$$Moment_{getInf} = 335 \times 1 \times 3$$
$$Moment_{chkLoan} = 320 \times 1$$

$$Moment_{perChkLar} = 320 \times 2$$
$$Moment_{makDec} = 147 \times 1 + 186 \times 2$$
$$Moment_{notAcc} = 147 \times 2$$

$$Total\ moment = 4112 \qquad fitness\ score_{chr1} = \frac{2482}{4112} \cong 0.604$$

Since the activity perChkSma increments the moment arm of activity makDec at the row belonging to perChkLar activity, it has to be shifted to the end of activity sequence. Hence the fittest (and optimum) activity sequence is obtained as {recApp, chkCom, getInf, chkLoan, perChkLar, makDec, notRej, notAcc, delCrCrd, perChkSma} with a 0.684 fitness score.

After rearrangement of FROMTOCHART table, relations are extracted according to positive scores at FROMTOCHART table. Consequently, dependency/frequency graph, which is a kind of finite state machine that visually converts the fittest activity sequence (*genotype*) into the to the discovered process model (*phenotype*), is constructed as shown in Figure 2.

For this data set, the ratio of transitions in testing dataset that are visualized in the dependency/frequency graph (i.e. recall rate of the discovered process model) is 98.89%. Additionally, all extracted relations have corresponding complements in testing dataset (i.e. precision of the discovered process model is 100%) and a 43.59% improvement[4] is achieved in total processing time.

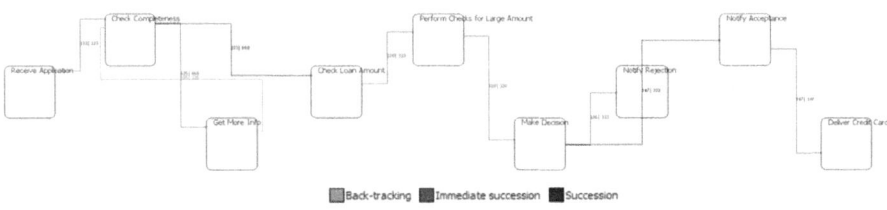

Fig. 2. Discovered Relations in Dependency/Frequency Graph Form

---

[4] Proposed GA approach decrements total processing time to 44 seconds. For the simplified version of the underlying business process (i.e. some of the activity types are eliminated), the processing time for the prior approach is approximately 78 seconds.

According to the experimental results, relatively large *population size* and *schema application* positively affect the performance of GA implementation. Moreover reasonable *mutation probability* (e.g. $p_m=0.02$) enables undirected jumps to abandon the local optimal regions and move to slightly different areas at the search space.

6 Conclusion

In this study, we improve a hybrid approach for deriving patterns among activities from event logs. The novelty of this methodology resides in the fact that; an analytical tool from facility layout domain is adapted to a new problem domain and is used as the baseline to monitor behaviors among activities observed in business process. Besides, the time performance of the method is further improved by using GA for rearrangement of the From-to Chart.

The activity sequence, which is rearranged in a straight-line form by developed GA engine in an acceptable processing time, constitutes the backbone of discovered process model without sacrificing from accuracy. As the future work, the developed GA engine can be adapted to Skeleton-based Facility Layout Problems (FLPs), if required material routings are available.

References

[1] Mǎruşter, L., Weijters, A.J.M.M.T., van der Aalst, W.M.P., van den Bosch, A.: Process Mining: Discovering Direct Successors in Process Logs. In: Lange, S., Satoh, K., Smith, C.H. (eds.) DS 2002. LNCS, vol. 2534, pp. 364–373. Springer, Heidelberg (2002)

[2] Esgin, E., Senkul, P.: Hybrid Approach to Process Mining: Finding Immediate Successors of a Process by Using From-to Chart. In: Int. Conf. on Machine Learning and Applications, pp. 664–668 (2009)

[3] Apple, J.M.: Material Handling Systems Design. The Ronald Press Company, New York (1972)

[4] Francis, R.L., McGinnis, L.F., White, J.A.: Facility Layout and Location: An Analytical Approach. Prentice Hall, New Jersey (1992)

[5] Meyers, F.E., Stephens, M.P.: Manufacturing Facilities Design and Material Handling. Pearson Prentice Hall, New Jersey (2005)

[6] van der Aalst, W.M.P., Gunther, C., Recker, J., Reichert, M.: Using Process Mining to Analyze and Improve Process Flexibility. In: Proc. of BPMDS 2006 (2006)

[7] Gunther, C.W., van der Aalst, W.M.P.: Process Mining in Case Handling Systems. In: Proc. of Multikonferenz Wirtschaftsinformatik 2006 (2006)

[8] Agrawal, R., Gunopulos, D., Leymann, F.: Mining Process Models from Workflow Logs. In: Schek, H.-J., Saltor, F., Ramos, I., Alonso, G. (eds.) EDBT 1998. LNCS, vol. 1377, p. 469. Springer, Heidelberg (1998)

[9] Cook, J.E., Wolf, A.L.: Discovering Models of Software Processes from Event-Based Data. ACM Transactions on Software Engineering and Methodology (TOSEM) 7(3), 215–249 (1996)

[10] Weijters, A.J.M.M., van der Aalst, W.M.P.: Rediscovering Workflow Models from Event-Based Data Using Little Thumb. Integrated Computer-Aided Engineering 10(2), 151–162 (2003)

[11] van der Aalst, W.M.P., Weijters, A.J.M.M., Maruster, L.: Workflow Mining: Discovering Process Models from Event Logs. Transaction on Knowledge and Data Engineering 16(9), 1128–1142 (2004)

[12] Dianati, M., Song, I., Treiber, M.: An Introduction to Genetic Algorithms and Evalution Stragies. Univ. of Waterloo, Canada

[13] Beasley, D., Bull, D.R., Martin, R.R.: An Overview of Genetic Algorithms: Part 1. Fundamentals. University Computing 15(2), 58–69 (1993)

[14] Sarker, B.R., Wilbert, E.W., Hogg, G.R.: Locating Sets of Identical Machines in a Linear Layout. Annals of Operations Research 77, 183–207 (1998)

[15] Yamamoto, H., Qudeiri, J.A., Yamada, T., Rizauddin, R.: Production Layout Design System by GA with OOEM. Artificial Life and Robotics 13(1), 234–237 (2008)

Continuous Pattern Mining Using the FCPGrowth Algorithm in Trajectory Data Warehouses

Marcin Gorawski and Pawel Jureczek

Silesian University of Technology, Institute of Computer Science,
Akademicka 16, 44-100 Gliwice, Poland
{Marcin.Gorawski,Pawel.Jureczek}@polsl.pl

Abstract. This paper presents the FCP-Tree index structure and the new algorithm for continuous pattern mining, called FCPGrowth, for Trajectory Data Warehouses. The FCP-Tree is an aggregate tree which allows storing similar sequences in the same nodes. A characteristic feature of the FCPGrowth algorithm is that it does not require constructing intermediate trees at recursion levels and therefore, it has small memory requirements. In addition, when the initial FCP-Tree is built, input sequences are split on infrequent elements, thereby increasing the compactness of this structure. The FCPGrowth algorithm is much more efficient than our previous algorithm, which is confirmed experimentally in this paper.

1 Introduction

Frequent pattern mining is used in many applications to detect recurring situations. In this paper we address the problem of the efficient exploration of frequent continuous patterns which allow preserving the spatial continuity of the regions of interest in a regular grid. The FCPGrowth algorithm presented in the paper can detect frequent continuous routes of objects, which in turn can be used for a more detailed analysis of objects' behaviours. It is worth noting that the algorithm may also be used in other fields of computer science. Moreover, the FCP-Tree (Frequent Continuous Pattern Tree) is used as the underlying data structure for that algorithm. The tree is also called a aggregate tree, since it can aggregate similar sequences in the same nodes.

In the research literature, we can find a lot of algorithms which can be used (directly or indirectly) to explore continuous patterns. In the beginning, we should mention the GSP algorithm ([1]) which belongs to Apriori-like algorithms and has many versions which improve its performance. The Apriori-like algorithms have applications in many fields of computer science, including the analysis of trajectories of objects. For example, the paper [2] shows how to transform trajectory points into corresponding sequences of regions. Those regions (polygons) can have practically any shape. The sequences of regions are explored by the Apriori-iAll algorithm. Although the performance of Apriori-like algorithms is sufficient

M. Graña Romay et al. (Eds.): HAIS 2010, Part I, LNAI 6076, pp. 187–195, 2010.
© Springer-Verlag Berlin Heidelberg 2010

for most applications, in a data warehouse more efficient methods of exploration are necessary. The authors of the paper [3] proposed the PrefixSpan-based algorithm for continuous patterns mining. In the paper [4], a tree data structure called an aggregation tree is presented, which store sequences of Web pages visited by users. That tree is used to store similar sequences in the same nodes and thus the size of data to be analyzed can be reduced. The aggregation tree is also known as the prefix tree – it should be noted that other names are also used. The authors of [5] extended the aggregation tree with the auxiliary data structure (header table) which stores the links to tree nodes containing the same label. In the paper [6] frequent patterns are explored by using the WAP-Tree index. The algorithm from [6] can generate patterns which contain the same recurring items, however, in contrast to our index, resulting patterns do not preserve the continuity of elements. The authors of [7], based on WAP-Tree, developed a new SMAP-Mine algorithm and SMAP-Tree i CMAP-Tree index structures, respectively for mining sequential and continuous patterns associated with mobile services. Another structure which is worth mentioning is FLWAP-Tree [8]. That structure stores, in the header table, pointers to the first occurrence of the node with a given label in a branch of the prefix tree. Hierarchical solutions are considered in [12]. In [9] a new method of exploration was presented, which can find the complete moving paths of objects, including cyclic, non-cyclic and backward patterns. In comparison to the work discussed above, our algorithm looks for patterns in a database set, in which a single sequence does not contain repetitions of elements. Thanks to this assumption, we do not need to create a prefix tree in a recursive call.

The organization of the paper is as follows. Section 2 introduces the definition of the continuous pattern. In Section 3 we describe how we explore the continuous patterns. Section 4 presents pseudocodes of algorithms described in Section 3 and Section 5 shows the performance results. Section 6 provides a summary of the paper.

2   Continuous Sequential Patterns

In the remainder of this paper the following points are assumed:

1. Each element occurs only once in a sequence, i.e. the element is unique in a given sequence. For example, the sequence A→ B→ A→ C is not appropriate here because the element A occurs twice. This assumption is not rigorous, since in the case of trajectories of objects, after mapping those trajectories into sequences of regions, there are rarely sequences which contain repeated elements. For example, if someone is going to travel by car, they chooses the shortest route using a satellite navigation system.

2. Since we analyze continuous sequences of regions of interest for the regular grid, we want to preserve the continuity of sequences – this assumption refers to the spatial continuity. It is due to the fact that we map the entire sequence by means of regions of the grid and the omission of any element of this sequence interrupts the spatial continuity (see Figure 1).

Fig. 1. A continuous sequence of regions of interest

In view of these assumptions we introduce the following definitions:

Definition 1. *Definition of containment*
   Given two sequences $X = \langle b_1 b_2 \ldots b_m \rangle$ *and* $Y = \langle a_1 a_2 \ldots a_n \rangle$, *where* $m \leq n$, *the sequence* X *is a continuous subsequence of* Y *if there exists an integer* i *such that* $a_1 = b_i, a_2 = b_{i+1}, \ldots, a_n = b_{i+n-1}$, *and if for any two elements* b_i *and* b_j *($i \neq j$) we have* $b_i \neq b_j$.

Definition 2. *Definition of support*
   Given a set of sequences $S = \{s_1, s_2, \ldots, s_m\}$, *the support of a pattern* s *is defined as follows:*
   $sup(s) = |\{s_i | s \subseteq s_i\}|/m$ *for* $1 \leq i \leq m$.

Definition 3. *Definition of frequent sequence*
   A sequence s *is frequent in* S *if it has a support equal to or greater than the user-specified threshold minsup:*
   $sup(s) \geq minsup$.

3   FCP-Tree Index and FCPGrowth Algorithm

The FCP-Tree index is built by using the transformed input sequences. In the first step of the prefix tree construction algorithm, we count the support for each distinct element of the sequences. Next, those elements whose supports are less than the minimum support *minsup* are removed. In the second step, continuous subsequences are inserted into the prefix tree. It should be noted that the input sequence is split on infrequent elements and then the resulting continuous subsequences are added to the prefix tree – infrequent elements are automatically removed from the resulting sequences. As a consequence of this approach long sequences can be divided into shorter parts. Since the sequences are split on infrequent elements, the correctness of the generated patterns is preserved. It results from the fact that an infrequent element cannot occur in any pattern and interrupts the continuity of elements. Frequent elements are inserted into the header table and indicate the beginnings of the compressed sequences.

Example. Table 1 shows the input sequences and the sequences obtained from them after the initial preprocessing. The elements of the input sequences have the following supports: A:2, B:5, C:3, F:3, G:4, I:1, J:2, K:2, Z:1. When we assume $minsup = 2$, elements I and Z will be infrequent, as a result of which the first and the third sequences will be divided into subsequences.

Table 1. The division of input sequences into subsequences

No.	Input sequences	Transformed sequences
1	A→ G→ F→ I→ B	A → G→ F, B
2	A→ G→ F→ J→ K	A→ G→ F→ J→ K
3	C→ G→ Z→ B	C→ G, B
4	B→ G→ F	B→ G→ F
5	B→ C→ J→ K	B→ C→ J→ K
6	B→ C→ J	B→ C→ J

The following figure (Figure 2) shows a prefix tree which was created by using the first four sequences from Table 1. At the beginning of the tree building process the header table is created, and when sequences are inserted, the respective pointers to the appropriate nodes of the tree are added to it. The insertion of a sequence into the prefix tree starts at its root node which we denote as *null* according to the generally accepted convention. This node is a virtual root node of the tree.

Example. Given the sequence B→ C→ J→ K we check if the root of the tree contains on the list of their children the node with the label B. Since the node exists, we increase the support of this node by 1 and, recursively, check if the successive element of the sequence is in the list of children of B. In our case, the node labeled with C is not found, therefore, it is necessary to create it, add to the appropriate list in the table header and set its support value to 1. Because the newly created tree node has no children, we repeat the described process for the last two elements (respectively J and K) of the sequence. The resulting tree is shown in Figure 3.

It is easy to notice that the smaller the minimum support value is, the longer subsequence are added to the prefix tree. On the contrary, the greater the minimum support value the more infrequent elements and greater probability of occurrence of shorter subsequences.

After building the FCP-Tree, we recursively traverse it for each frequent element of the header table at a given level of recursion, the selection order of items from this table does not affect the generated patterns. Mining frequent patterns is performed by the FCPGrowth algorithm. In the FCPGrowth algorithm we make use of the observation that in each recursion, we must only check if the total support for each element situated directly behind an element from the header table is equal to or greater than *minsup*. Figure 3 presents a prefix tree with a header table which indicates the beginnings of compressed continuous sequence. Each item in the header table has the form *label:support* where *label* denotes a frequent element and *support* expresses how often this element appears in the sequences. In addition, each item has a list of pointers which point to elements with a given label in the prefix tree. When the FCPGrowth algorithm chooses the element G from the header table (Figure 3), it stores the element in the result set, adds this element at the end of the current prefix, and counts the

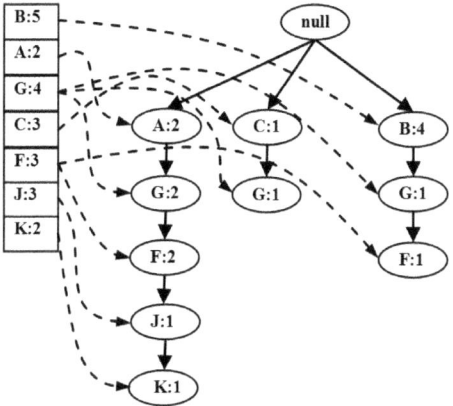

Fig. 2. Building the FCP-Tree

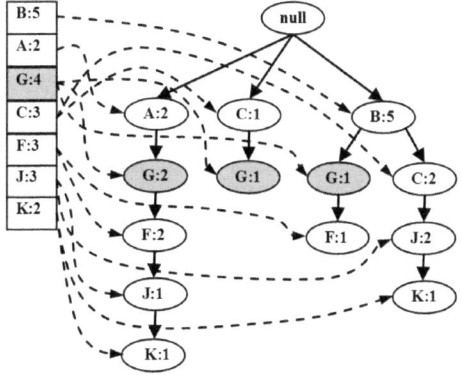

Fig. 3. Final FCP-Tree

support for every element which occurs in the prefix tree directly behind G. In our example, there only exists the element F which has the total support equal to 3. Since there exists at least one frequent element, a new header table, new item for the element F and list of pointers for the corresponding nodes in the prefix tree are created. Please note that the list contains only pointers to nodes in the branches of the prefix tree where the element F occurs directly behind G. Then, the FCPGrowth algorithm is called recursively for the newly created header table and prefix <G>. The next iteration is shown in Figure 4. Because there are no frequent elements behind F, the FCPGrowth algorithm ends.

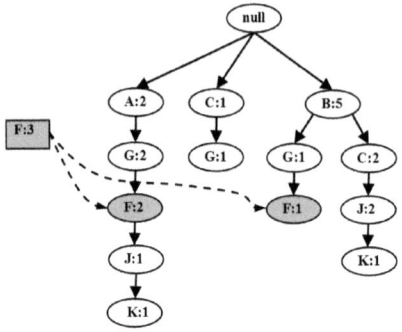

Fig. 4. FCPGrowth algorithm

4 Pseudocodes

In this section we describe the FCP-Tree and FCPGrowth algorithms.

Algorithm 1. algorithm for mining frequent continuous patterns
1.Scan the sequence database S once and find all frequent elements of the sequences. 2.Scan the sequence database S again and build the FCP-Tree index according to Algorithm 2. 3.Call the FCPGrowth algorithm for the FCP-Tree.

According to Algorithm 1, in the initial step we find the support for each unique element appearing in the analyzed sequences. The support of an element is the number of sequences containing that element in the sequence database S. An element is considered to be frequent if its support sup is at least equal to the minimum support $minsup$ specified by the user. During the second scan sequences are inserted into the tree according to the Algorithm 2. After constructing the FCP-Tree, we called the FCPGrowth algorithm.

Algorithm 2. FCP-Tree building algorithm

---

1)Create the FCP-Tree root and insert all frequent elements of the sequences into the header table. In the table header, each of those elements has a list of nodes in which this element appears. In the beginning, the lists are empty.

2) For each sequence s do the following:

a) Set the current node n to the root of the FCP-Tree and the pointer p to the first element of sequence s.

b) Check if the current element p in the sequence s is frequent, if so, go to step c), if not, go to step d).

c) Check if the node n has among its children an element pointed by p. If so, increase its support by 1, set the current node n to the child and go to step e), if not, go to step f).

d) If the pointer p indicates the last element of the sequence, go to the next sequence in S and to step a). Otherwise, set the pointer p to the next element of the sequence s, the current node n to the root of the FCP-Tree and go to step b).

e) If the pointer p points to the last element in the sequence, go to the next sequence in S and to step a). Otherwise, set the pointer p to the next element of the sequences s and go to step b).

f) Create a new node w for the element pointed to by p, increase its support by 1 and set the current node n to the newly created node w. In addition, add w to the header table and go to step e).

The first call of the FCPGrowth algorithm is for the empty prefix.

Algorithm 3. FCPGrowth algorithm

---

1) For each frequent item e stored in the header table do the following:

a) Add the element e at the end of *prefix*. Add the created pattern to the result set.

b) Create a new header table on the basis of a node list *nl* which is associated with an element e of the header table.

c) If the new header table is not empty, call the FCPGrowth algorithm for this header table and *prefix*.

d) Remove the last element of the prefix.

---

5   Experiments

The trajectories have been generated by the generator [10]. The performance of the FCPGrowth algorithm is compared to the VAES algorithm [11] which is one of fastest algorithms for mining continuous patterns. All algorithms were written in Java (JDK1.6) and the experiments were carried out on a computer with with Intel Core Duo E6550 2.33GHz and 4GB of RAM and running Windows 7.

Figure 5 presents running times for the FCPGrowth and VAES algorithms for different numbers of trajectories and minimum support *minsup*. Figure 6 shows detailed performance results for the FCPGrowth algorithm.

As you can see the FCPGrowth algorithm is always more efficient than the VAES algorithm. For the both algorithms, the increase in the number of sequences increases the running time. In the case of the FCPGrowth algorithm

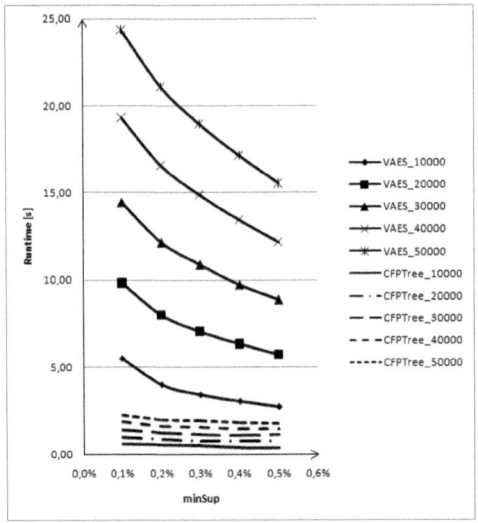

Fig. 5. FCPGrowth vs.VAES

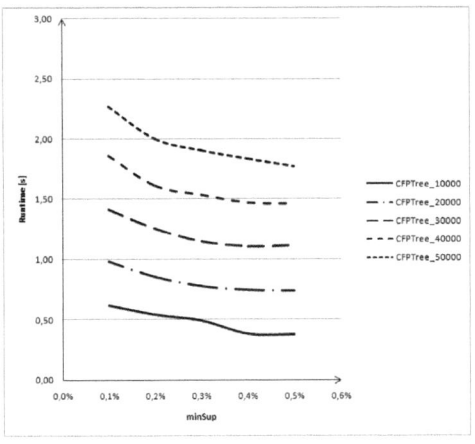

Fig. 6. Performance of FCPGrowth

this increase is partly due to an increase in the number of sequences which are inserted into the FCP-Tree. The advantage of FCPGrowth over VAES results from aggregation of sequences in the FCP-Tree.

6   Conclusion

The paper presents the FCPGrowth algorithm for continuous pattern mining, which is based on the FCP-Tree. The FCP-Tree is an aggregate tree that allows storing similar sequences in the same nodes. In the paper we also compared the performance of the FCPGrowth and VAES algorithms. In the future work, we will implement the other types of queries, e.g. queries for mining maximal and closed patterns. We will also use a version of the FCP-Tree for supporting updates in data.

References

1. Srikant, R., Agrawal, R.: Mining Sequential Patterns: Generalizations and Performance Improvements. In: 5th Int. Conf. on Extending Database Technology, pp. 3–17 (1996)
2. Lee, J.W., Paek, O.H., Ryu, K.H.: Temporal moving pattern mining for location-based service. Journal of Systems and Software 73, 481–490 (2004)
3. Yuan, H., Zhang, Y., Wang, C.: A Novel Trajectory Pattern Learning Method Based on Sequential Pattern Mining. In: Proc. of the Second Int. Conference on Innovative Computing, Informatio and Control, p. 472 (2007)
4. Spiliopoulou, M., Faulstich, L.C.: WUM: A tool for web utilization analysis. In: Atzeni, P., Mendelzon, A.O., Mecca, G. (eds.) WebDB 1998. LNCS, vol. 1590, pp. 184–203. Springer, Heidelberg (1999)
5. Han, J., Pei, J., Yin, Y.: Mining Frequent Patterns without Candidate Generation. In: Proc. of the 2000 ACM SIGMOD Int. Conf. on Management of Data, pp. 1–12 (2000)
6. Pei, J., Han, J., Mortazavi-Asl, B., Zhu, H.: Mining Access Patterns Efficiently from Web Logs. In: Proc. of Pacific-Asia Conf. on Knowledge Discovery and Data Mining, pp. 396–407 (2000)
7. Tseng, V.S., Lin, K.W.: Efficient mining and prediction of user behavior patterns in mobile web systems. Information and Software Technology, 357–369 (2006)
8. Tang, P., Turkia, M.P., Gallivan, K.A.: Mining web access patterns with first-occurrence linked WAP-trees. In: Proc. of the 16th Int. Conf. on Software Engineering and Data Engineering, pp. 247–252 (2007)
9. Tseng, S., Chan, W.C.: Mining complete user moving paths in a mobile environment. In: Proc. of the Int. Workshop on Databases and Software Engineering (2002)
10. Brinkhoff, T.A.: A Framework for Generating Network-Based Moving Objects. Geoinformatica, 153–180 (2002)
11. Gorawski, M., Jureczek, P.: A Proposal of Spatio-Temporal Pattern Queries. In: The 4th Int. Conf. on Complex Intelligent and Software Intensive Systems Geoinformatica, pp. 587–593 (2009)
12. Graña, M., Torrealdea, F.J.: Hierarchically structured systems. European Journal of Operational Research 25, 20–26 (1986)

Hybrid Approach for Language Identification Oriented to Multilingual Speech Recognition in the Basque Context

N. Barroso[1], K. López de Ipiña[2], A. Ezeiza[2], O. Barroso[1], and U. Susperregi[1]

[1] Irunweb Enterprise, Auzolan 2B – 2, Irun, 20303 Spain
{nora,odei,unai}@irunweb.com
[2] Departamento de Ingeniería de Sistemas y Automática
Grupo de Inteligencia Computacional
Escuela Politécnica Universidad del País Vasco/Euskal Herriko Unibertsitatea
Plaza de Europa1, Donostia, 20008
{karmele.ipina,aitzol.ezeiza}@ehu.es

Abstract. The development of Multilingual Large Vocabulary Continuous Speech Recognition systems involves issues as: Language Identification, Acoustic-Phonetic Decoding, Language Modelling or the development of appropriated Language Resources. The interest on Multilingual Systems arouses because there are three official languages in the Basque Country (Basque, Spanish, and French), and there is much linguistic interaction among them, even if Basque has very different roots than the other two languages. This paper describes the development of a Language Identification (LID) system oriented to robust Multilingual Speech Recognition for the Basque context. The work presents hybrid strategies for LID, based on the selection of system elements by Support Vector Machines and Multilayer Perceptron classifiers and stochastic methods for speech recognition tasks (Hidden Markov Models and n-grams).

Keywords: Automatic Speech Recognition, Multilingual System, Large Vocabulary Continuous Speech Recognition, Under-resourced Languages, Cross-lingual strategies.

1 Introduction

Automatic Speech Recognition (ASR) is a broad research area that absorbs many efforts from the research community. Indeed, many applications related to ASR have progressed quickly in recent years, but these applications are generally very language-dependent. Specifically the development of Large Vocabulary Continuous Speech Recognition (LVCSR) systems involves issues as: Acoustic-Phonetic Decoding, Language Modelling or the development of appropriated Language Resources. It is also significant to highlight that the demand of multilingual systems in human-computer interfaces is growing and automatic Language Identification (LID) is becoming increasingly important for the speech community as a fundamental tool to rich theses systems. Research in this field has been active for several years, but work is most often conducted only on telephone speech.

M. Graña Romay et al. (Eds.): HAIS 2010, Part I, LNAI 6076, pp. 196–204, 2010.

In this sense, the use of multilingual Broadcast News (BN) data is also interesting for LID. In last decade BN transcription systems have been developed for several languages [1,2,3], and LID would become a useful component for them. This is essential for channels which broadcast in several languages, but also for monolingual where often appear other languages, foreign terms or cross-lingual data. In some cases an utterance containing two or more languages and code-switching speech is required [4].

The interest on Multilingual Systems arouses in the Basque Country because there are three official languages in use (Basque, Spanish, and French), and there is much cross-lingual interaction among them, even if Basque has very different roots than the other two languages. Indeed, the speakers tend to mix words and sentences in the three languages in their discourse, and the acoustic interactions among the three languages and among the Basque dialects are fairly interesting from the researchers' point of view. Although there is much work to do with Basque Speech Recognition alone [5,6]. In fact, the statistical nature of the approaches used in Automatic Speech Recognition (ASR) requires a great quantity of language resources in order to perform well. For under-resourced languages which are mostly from developing countries, those resources are available in a very limited quantity because of its economic interest and the lack of standardized automatic processing tools. In this situation, language data collection is a challenging task and requires innovative approaches and tools [3,7]. Therefore, the development of a robust system is a much tougher task for under-resourced languages, even if they count with powerful languages beside it. The main goal of our project is the development of Multilingual LVCSR systems in the Basque context. Nowadays, in particular, this work is oriented to Basque Broadcast News (BN) because most of the mass media use Spanish, French, and/or Basque, and many of them have shown their interest in the development of these kind of systems for their media. Thus, the three languages have to be taken into account to develop efficient ASR and LID systems in this field. Next section describes the features of the languages. Section 3 presents the resources and methods to develop the LID system. Section 4 analyzes the experimentation and finally, some conclusions and future work are given in section 5.

2   Phonetic Features of the Languages

The analysis of the features of the chosen languages is a crucial issue because they have a clear influence on both the performance of the Acoustic-Phonetic Decoding (APD) and on the vocabulary size of the system. In order to develop the APD, an inventory of the sounds of each language was necessary. Table 1 summarises the sound inventories for the three languages expressed in the SAMPA notation. In order to get an insight of the phoneme system of these three languages, we would like to remark some of the features mentioned above. On the one hand, Basque and Spanish have very similar vowels and in some dialects Basque and French have similarities. In comparison to Basque or Spanish, French has a very much richer vocal system. On the other hand, some of the consonants that are rare in French such as "L" (i.e. Feuille) are very common in Basque or Spanish. Therefore, a cross-lingual Acoustic Model could be very useful in these cases. Another special feature in this experiment is the richness of affricates and fricatives present in Basque. These sounds will be very difficult to differ and the cross-lingual approach won't work for them, but it has to be said that even native Basque speakers don't make differences among some affricates and fricatives.

Table 1. Sound Inventories for Basque, French and Spanish in the SAMPA notation

Sound Type	Basque	French	Spanish
Plosives	p b t d k g c	p b t d k g	p b t d k g
Affricates	ts ts´ tS		ts
Fricatives	gj jj f B T D s s´ S x G Z v h	f v s z S Z	gj jj F B T D s x G
Nasals	m n J	m n J N	m n J
Liquids	l L r rr	l R	l L r rr
Vowel glides	w j	w H j	w j
Vowels	i e a o u @	i e E a A O o u y 2 9 @ e~ a~ o~ 9~,	i e a o u

3 Resources and Methods

3.1 Resources

The basic resources used in this work have been mainly provided from two Broadcast News sources [6]. On the one hand, the Basque Public Radio-Television group (EITB) has provided us with videos of their Broadcast News in Basque and Spanish. On the other hand, Infozazpi irratia, a new trilingual (Basque, French, and Spanish) digital radio station which currently emits only via Internet has provided audio and text data from their news bulletins. The texts have been processed to create XML files which include information of distinct speakers, noises, and sections of the speech files and transcriptions. The transcriptions for Basque also include morphological information such as each word's lemma and Part-Of-Speech tag. Resources Inventory is described in Table 2.

3.2 Methods

Various information sources can be exploited in order to identify a given language: acoustic, phonetic, phonotactic, lexical, etc. Automatic Language Identification (LID) may be based on different types and combinations of these information sources. Their modelling requires specific resources, knowledge and corpora, for each language. Acoustic-phonetic and lexical approaches typically make use of language-dependent acoustic phone models, language-dependent phone bigrams, and for a lexical approach, a more or less comprehensive vocabulary for each language [8,9,10,11]. In this work we will use language-dependent acoustic phone models with language-dependent phone bigrams taken into account several rules for the cross-lingual utterances. Many projects have been developed with several European languages [12], but Basque has fewer resources than many of them. In order to decrease the negative

Table 2. Resources Inventory: Broadcast News (video, audio), Transcription of broadcast-XML files, textual databases and lexical elements

Language	Broadcast Video/hh:mm:ss	Broadcast Audio/hh:mm:ss	Transcription XMLhh:mm:ss	Textual Database
EU	6:37:00	18:00:00	12:00:00	8M
FR	-	2:58:00	2:58:00	2M
ES	9:35:00	12:34:00	12:34:00	4M
Total	16:12:00	33:12:00	33:12:00	14M

impact that the lack of resources has in this area, the alternative surges in the form of cross-lingual Acoustic Modelling [2].

Wheatley et al. [13] already suggested the idea to train phone models for a new language using other languages and they implemented a number of different metrics for measuring similarities among cross-language phonetic models. The idea behind cross-lingual speech recognition is to transfer existing resources of Acoustic Models to a target language without using a speech database in this target language [2]. This way the usage of a complete speech database in the target language can be avoided. Therefore, it seems an interesting alternative for Basque language, and this paper tackles this issue developing a baseline Acoustic-Phonetic Decoder for each of the three languages in order to compare them and to facilitate further experiments on future cross-lingual Acoustic Modelling.

Hidden Markov Models (HMMs) are, undoubtedly, the most employed core technique for Automatic Speech Recognition (ASR) but we are still far from achieving highperformance ASR systems [1,2,7]. In this sense, several Machine Learning based proposals can be found in the bibliography [14,15,16,17] in order to deal with this problem. Most of them are hybrid techniques of HMMs, Support Vector Machines (SVMs), and Neural Networks (NNs). SVMs solution relies on maximizing the distance between the samples and the classification border. This distance is known as the margin and, by maximizing it, they are able to generalize unseen patterns. This maximum margin solution allows the SVM to outperform most nonlinear classifiers in the presence of noise, which is one of the longstanding problems in ASR [14]. Thus, we propose a hybrid approach based on SVMs, Multilayer Perceptrom (MP) and SC-HMMs, taken into account the high level of noise in the database.

In a first stage the input signal is transformed and characterized with a set of 13 Mel Frequency Cepstral (MFCC), energy and their dynamic components, taken into account the high level of noise in the signal. The frame period was 10 milliseconds, the FFT uses a Hamming window and the signal had first order pre-emphasis applied using a coefficient of 0.97. The filter-bank had 26 channels. In a second stage new feature vectors based on Gaussian histograms of the MFCCs, energy and their dynamics components (295 parameters: 3 of energy and 3 MFCC based Gaussian histograms) have been generated in order to carry out afterwards the sublexical unit selection. One the other hand one of the main issues in ASR is the development of robust Acoustic-Phonetic Decoders (APDs) that transform the acoustic signal in sequences of sublexical units (phone, syllables or tri-phones). In the present work the optimum set of sublexical units is select from the sound inventories by Support Vector Machine (SVM) and Multilayer Perceptrom classifiers. Finally each acoustic sublexical unit will be model into the APD by a Semi-Continuous Hidden Markov Model (SC-HMM) for both LID and Multilingual LVCSR.

The Multilingual LVCSR system we propose has two stages. First the LID system selects the language of the utterance and sends the information to the Multilingual LVCSR system. Then the appropriated recognition elements are chosen for ASR tasks: sublexical units (phones, tri-phones or syllables), lexical units (words, non-words, sub-words or morphemes), vocabulary (concatenations of sublexical units, SC-HMMs) and Language Model (n-grams). Finally the Multilingual LVSCSR system extracts the message from the speech signal.

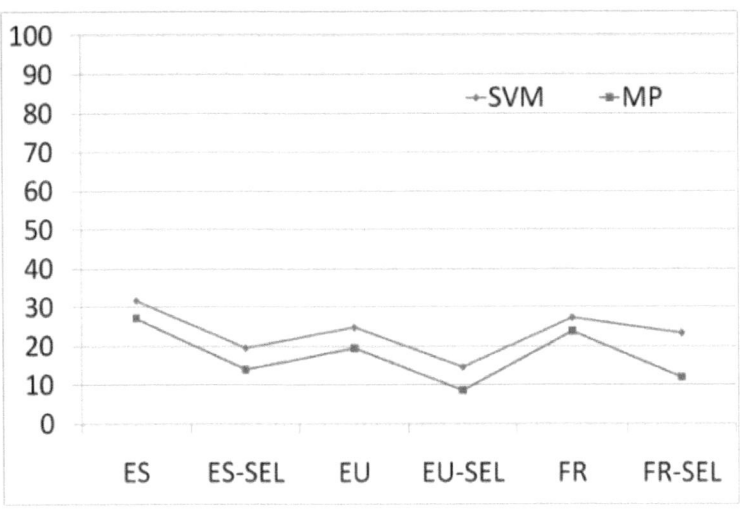

Fig. 1. Phone Error Rate (PER) with *Original* and *Selection* sublexical unit sets and both classifiers, SVM and MP, for the three languages: Basque, Spanish and French (*EU, ES, FR*)

In the designed LID approach, a Parallel Phone Recognizer followed by Language Modeling (PPRLM) [18,19], will be used. The main objective of PPRLM is to model the frequency of occurrence of different sublexical unit sequences in each language. This system has three stages. First, a phone recognizer takes the speech utterance and outputs the sequence of sublexical units corresponding to it. Then, the sequence of sublexical units is used as input to a Language Model (LM) module. In recognition, the LM module scores the probability that the sequence of sublexical units corresponds to the language. Finally a *Maximum Likelihood* based Language Decision System (LDS) select the language. It can create several phone recognizers modeled for different languages. Our PPRML system will use the SC-HMMs of the previously selected sublexical units and bi-grams.

4 Experimentation

4.1 Selection of Sublexical Units

The preliminary experimentation stage we have performed has consisted in the selection of sublexical units by Machine Learning classifiers. First balanced sample sets of the sublexical units based on the sound inventories (table 1) are created, the so-called *Original* (ES, EU, FR). Then new sublexical unit proposals are generated by SVM and MP classifiers. Finally the unit selection is based on results of Phone Error Rate (PER), confusion matrices and linguistic criteria. During this process the units with highest PER and confusion, and linguistically close are fused taking also into account the general PER of all sublexical units. The new unit sets are the so-called *Selection* (ES-SEL, EU-SEL, FR-SEL).

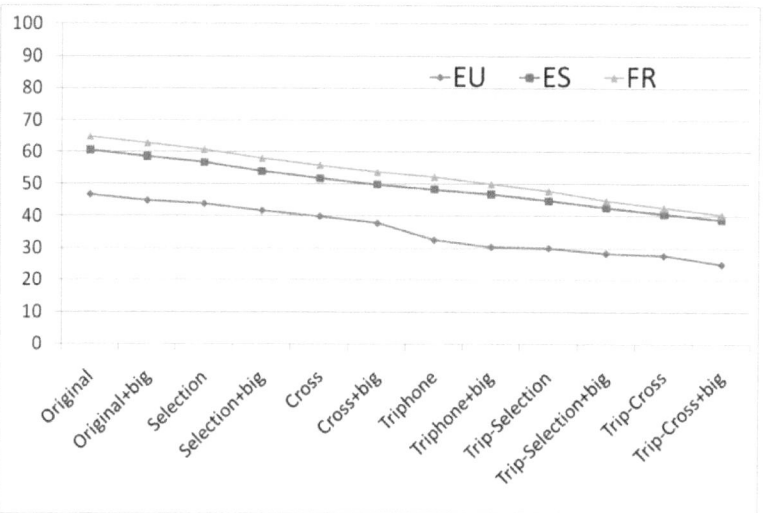

Fig. 2. PER in ASR (SC-HMMs, n-grams) with different sublexical units sets (*Original, Selection and Tri-phones*), free-gram, bi-grams and cross-lingual approach for the three languages

Figure 1 presents PER values with all analyzed sublexical units. Results show that *Selection* proposals outperformer the *Original* ones about %10 for both paradigms. It is obvious that PER in ASR (SC-HMMs and n-grams, figure 2) is lower for Basque than for Spanish and French. This can be explained with three main reasons: the simple vowel structure in Basque and Spanish eases the overall recognition of phones; the mean noise level in French is also higher and there is a relevant appearance of cross-lingual elements in Spanish and French. The second set of tests has consisted in using tri-phones, phone based bi-grams and cross-lingual strategies. The results show that tri-phones improve previous performance around %8 and cross-lingual techniques around %3 (figure 2).

4.2 LID Experimentation

In this experimentation the PPRLM LID system is composed by three parallel APD and two kinds of LMs: free grammar or bi-grams. The set of sublexical units used are: *Original, Selection and Tri-phones*. Besides, some cross-lingual approaches have been included. The test is composed by 1000 sentences from Infozazpi radio in the three languages (Basque, Spanish and French).

The obtained results are presented in figure 3 (LID error rate). It is obvious that the recognition is much better for Basque and French than for Spanish. This can be explained with some reasons:

1. Basque obtains the best PER values (figure 2) because of its robust APD.
2. Despite of French has poor PER results (due to the language complexity) the acoustically great different with regard to Spanish and Basque produces an optimum LID performance.

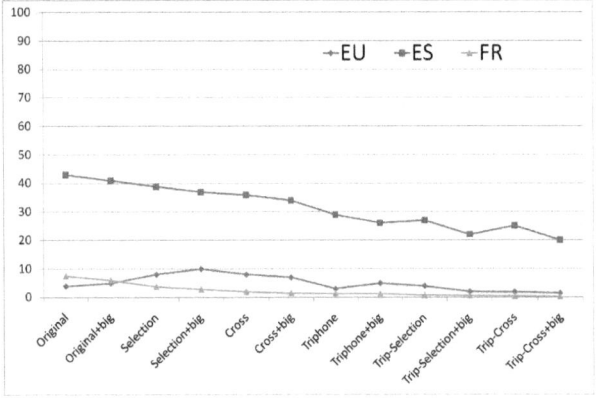

Fig. 3. LID error rate with different sets of sublexical units (*Original, Selection and Tri-phones*), LMs (free gram and bi-gram) and cross-lingual approach for *EU, ES* and *FR sets.*

3. We have also to highlight that the acoustic difference among languages produces certain stability in French recognition taken into account the scant appearance of Basque utterances with French influence.
4. Spanish and Basque have a close influence between them due to their acoustic similarities mainly in vowels. Figure 3 shows the evolution of LID error rate for both languages. As Spanish improves its performance, Basque tends to perform worse. Finally both languages reach stability.

Best and most stable results are obtained for *Tri-phones, Selection* and cross-lingual approaches. In summary, the developed LID system obtains for the three languages satisfactory and stable results regarding to LID error rate (figure 3) and Equal Error Rate (EER), about %6, %19 and %4 for Basque, Spanish and French respectively.

5 Concluding Remarks

The final goal of the project is to develop a Multilingual Large Vocabulary Continuous Speech Recognition (LVCSR) system in the Basque context for Spanish, French and Basque. In order to develop a real-life multi-purpose system that could be useful for difficult recognition tasks, we have chosen a Broadcast News Speech Database with many speakers, environments, and noises. The present work describes the development of a Language Identification (LID) system oriented to robust Multilingual Speech Recognition for the Basque context. The hybrid system is based on the selection of sublexical units by Support Vector Machines and Multilayer Perceptron classifiers and stochastic methods for ASR tasks (SC-HMM and n-grams). Our new sublexical unit proposals and the use of tri-phones and cross-lingual approaches improve considerably the system performance. Three languages achieve an optimum and stable recognition rate despite of the problem complexity. Obtained results will be improved in our ongoing work with robust matrix covariance estimation and robustness methods, new cross-lingual methodologies and including Basque dialects with French influence.

Acknowledgements. This work has been partially supported by the Basque Goverment, SAIOTEK 2007 plan and from the Spanish Ministerio de Ciencia y Tecnología, project TSI2006-14250-C02-01.

References

1. Schultz, T., Kirchhoff, N.: Multilingual Speech Processing. Elsevier, Amsterdam (2006)
2. Schultz, T., Waibel, A.: Multilingual and Crosslingual Speech Recognition. In: Proceedings of the DARPA Broadcast News, Workshop (1998)
3. Seng, S., Sam, S., Le, V.B., Bigi, B., Besacier, L.: Which Units For Acoustic and Language Modeling For Khmer Automatic Speech Recognition. In: 1st International Conference on Spoken Language Processing for Under-resourced languages Hanoi, Vietnam (2008)
4. Dau-Cheng, L., Ren-Yuan, L.: Language Identification on Code-Switching Utterances Using Multiple Cues. In: Proc. of Interspeech 2008 (2008)
5. Lopez de Ipiña, K., Graña, M., Ezeiza, N., Hernández, M., Zulueta, E., Ezeiza, A., Tovar, C.: Selection of Lexical Units for CSR of Basque. In: Sanfeliu, A., Ruiz-Shulcloper, J. (eds.) CIARP 2003. LNCS, vol. 2905, pp. 244–250. Springer, Heidelberg (2003)
6. Barroso, N., Ezeiza, A., Gilisagasti, N., Lopez de Ipiña, K., López, A., López, J.M.: Development of Multimodal Resources for Multilingual Information Retrieval in the Basque context. In: Proccedings of Interspeech 2007, Antwerp, Belgium (2007)
7. Le, V.B., Besacier, L.: Automatic speech recognition for under-resourced languages: application to Vietnamese language. IEEE Transactions on Audio, Speech, and Language Processing 17(8), 1471–1482 (2009)
8. Li, H., Ma, B.: A Phonotactic Language Model for Spoken LID. ACL (2005)
9. Ma, B., Li, H.: An Acoustic Segment Modeling Approach to Automatic Language Identification. In: Proc. Interspeech 2005, Lisbon, Portugal, pp. 2829–2832 (2005)
10. Matejka, P., Schwarz, P., Cernocky, J., Chytil, P.: Phonotactic LID using High Quality Phoneme Recognition. In: Proc. Interspeech 2005, Lisbon, Portugal, pp. 2237–2240 (2005)

11. Nagarajan, T., Murthy, H.A.: Language Identification, Using Parallel Syllable-Like Unit Recognition. In: Proc. ICASSP, pp. I-401 – I-404 (2004)
12. Vandecatseye, A., Martens, J.P., Neto, J., Meinedo, H., Garcia-Mateo, C., Dieguez, F.J., Mihelic, F., Zibert, J., Nouza, J., David, P., Pleva, M., Cizmar, A., Papageorgiou, H., Alexandris, C.: The COST278 pan-European Broadcast News Database. In: Proceedings of LREC 2004, Lisbon, Portugal (2004)
13. Wheatley, B., Kondo, K., Anderson, W., Muthusamy, Y.: An evaluation of Cross-Language Adaptation for Rapid HMM Development in a New Language. In: International Conference on Acoustics, Speech, and Signal Processing, Adelaine, pp. 237–240 (1994)
14. Padrell, J., Martín-Iglesias, D., Díaz-de-María, F.: Support Vector Machines for Continuous Speech Recognition. In: 14th European Signal Processing Conference (EUSIPCO 2006), Florence, Italy, September 4-8 (2006)
15. Ganapathiraju, A., Hmaker, J., Picone, J.: Hybrid SVM/HMM architectures for speech recognition. In: Proc. of the International Conference on Spoken Language Processing, vol. 4, pp. 504–507 (2000)
16. Smith, N., Gales, M.: Speech recognition using SVMs. In: Advances in Neural Information Processing Systems, vol. 14. MIT Press, Cambridge (2002)
17. Cosi, P.: Hybrid HMM-NN architectures for connected digit recognition. In: Proc. of the International Joint Conference on Neural Networks, vol. 5 (2000)
18. Ambikairajah, L., Choi, E.: Robust language identification based on fused phonotactic information with MLKSFM ICME. In: 2009 IEEE International Conference on pre-classifier, Multimedia and Expo. (2009)
19. Graña, M., Torrealdea, F.J.: Hierarchically structured systems. European Journal of Operational Research 25, 20–26 (1986)

An Approach of Bio-inspired Hybrid Model for Financial Markets

Dragan Simić[1,2], Vladeta Gajić[1], and Svetlana Simić[3]

[1] University of Novi Sad, Faculty of Technical Sciences, Trg Dositeja Obradovića 6,
21000 Novi Sad, Serbia
dsimic@uns.ac.rs,itil@uns.ac.rs
[2] Novi Sad Fair, Hajduk Veljkova 11, 21000 Novi Sad, Serbia
dsimic@novosadskisajam.rs
[3] University of Novi Sad, Faculty of Medicine, Hajduk Veljkova 1,
21000 Novi Sad, Serbia
dsimic@eunet.rs

Abstract. Biological systems are inspiration for the design of optimisation and classification models. Applying various forms of bio-inspired algorithms may be a very high-complex system. Modelling of financial markets is challenging for several reasons, because many plausible factors impact on it. An automated trading on financial market is not a new phenomenon. The model of bio-inspired hybrid adaptive trading system based on technical indicators usage by grammatical evolution and moving window is presented in this paper. The proposed system is just one of possible bio-inspired system which can be used in financial forecast, corporate failure prediction or bond rating company.

Keywords: Bio-inspired, financial markets, grammatical evolution.

1 Introduction

Biological systems are a notable source of inspiration for the design of optimisation and classification algorithm, and all of the methodologies have their metaphorical roots in models on biological and social processes. Biologically inspired algorithms do not seek to perfectly imitate the complex workings of these systems; rather they draw metaphorical inspiration from them in order to create mathematical algorithms, which can be used in an attempt to solve hard, real-world problems, such as modelling financial markets. A brief overview of some of these bio-inspired individual technologies is provided in the following section while the challenges in the modelling of financial markets are presented in Section 3. Section 4 presents biological analogy of grammatical evolution system. The Section 5 describes index trading system uses by grammatical evolution. Section 6 presents bio-inspired hybrid adaptive trading system usage by grammatical evolution and moving window. Section 7 concludes the paper and provides notes on future work.

M. Graña Romay et al. (Eds.): HAIS 2010, Part I, LNAI 6076, pp. 205–212, 2010.

2 Bio-inspired Models

Artificial neural networks (ANNs) are modelling methodology whose inspiration arises from a simplified model of the way the human brain operates. ANNs can be used to construct models for the purposes of prediction, classification and clustering. ANNs are a non-parametric modelling tool, developed directly from data, and for financial forecasting as presented in [1].

Evolutionary algorithms draw inspiration from the processes of biological evolution which breed solutions to problems. The algorithm commences by creating initial population of potential solutions, and these are iteratively improved over many generations. In successive iterations of the algorithm, fitness-based selection takes place within the population of solutions among the selected solutions, in an attempt to uncover even better solutions over multiple generations. Bio-inspired models that employ an evolutionary approach include genetic algorithms (GA), genetic programming (GP), evolutionary strategies and evolutionary programming. The model for quantitative bankruptcy prediction based on GA is shown in [2] and usage by GP in [3]. A significant recent addition to these methodologies is grammatical evolution (GE), an evolutionary automatic programming methodology.

The social models are drawn from swarm metaphor. Two popular variants of swarm models exist, those inspired by the flocking behaviour of birds and fish, and those inspired by the behaviour of social insects such as ants. The essence of these systems is that they exhibit flexibility, self-organisation, and communication between individual members of the population. In general two models that are inspired-by-nature are presented in [4]; particular ant colony optimisation and particle swarm optimisation models for credit risk assessment and audit qualifications. Further, development of accurate behaviour of honey bees for financial decisions based on financial classification models involves the selection of the appropriate independent variables which are relevant for the problem at hand. An approach of proposed method combined with the nearest neighbour optimisation algorithm is tested in a financial classification task. The proposed honey bee method and other inspired-by-nature algorithms such as particle swarm optimization algorithm, an ant colony optimization, a genetic algorithm and a taboo search algorithm are tested in a financial classification task involving credit risk assessment [5].

Human immune system is a highly complex system, comprised of an intricate network of specialised tissues, organs, cells and chemical molecules. The natural immune system has capabilities to recognise, destroy and remember almost unlimited number of foreign bodies, and also to protect the organism from misbehaving cells in body. Artificial immune systems draw inspiration from the workings of the natural immune system, and these characteristics have been implemented and used for the prediction of bankruptcy of companies [6].

A review of expert systems and evolutionary computing for financial investing from early 1990s to mid-2000s is presented in [7]. It may be noted that the tendency was, in the early nineties, to use expert systems tools but, in later period, evolutionary computation tools become predominant. However, the most common financial application area in both periods was financial accounting. One predominant trend in the latest research is to merge both knowledge-based and evolutionary approaches.

3   Challenges in the Modelling of Financial Markets

Modelling of financial markets is challenging for several reasons. Many plausible factors that impact financial markets include interest rates, exchange rates, and the rate of economic growth. There is no hard theory as to how exactly these factors effect prices of financial assets, partly because the effects are complex, non-linear and time-lagged. A change in interest rates may impact on the foreign exchange rate for currency, in turn affecting the level of imports and exports of that country.

Another difficulty that arises in financial modelling is that unlike modelling of physical systems, a controlled experiment cannot be conducted in this case. Only one simple path through time is available for the examination, as we only have one history of market events. Additionally, some factors which can have effect on financial markets are inherently unpredictable, such as earthquakes, the weather, or political events [8]. Taken together, these difficulties imply that market movements can never be accurately predicted.

4   Grammatical Evolution

Grammatical Evolution is an evolutionary algorithm that can evolve *computer programs*, *rule sets* or more generally *sentences* in any language [9]. Rule sets could be diverse as a regression model or a trading system for financial markets. Rather than representing the programs as syntax trees, a *linear genome* representation is used in conjunction with grammar.

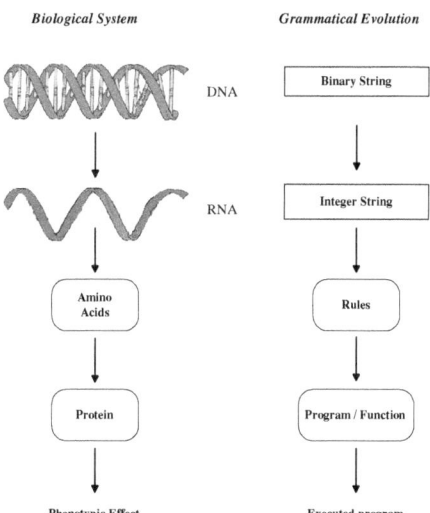

Fig. 1. Comparison between biological genetic system and the grammatical evolution system

The GE system (fig. 1) is inspired by the biological process of generating protein from the genetic material of the biological organisms. The genetic material (DNA, deoxyribonucleic acid) contains the information required to produce specific proteins at different points along the molecule. Consider DNA to be a string of building blocks called nucleotide. Groups of three nucleotides, called codons, are used to specify the building blocks of proteins. These protein building blocks are known as amino acids, and sequence of these amino acids is determined by the sequence of codons on the DNA strand.

In order to generate protein, the nucleotide in the sequence is first transcribed into a slightly different format, a sequence elements on a molecule known RNA (ribonucleic acid). Codons within the RNA molecule are then translated to determine the sequence of amino acids that are contained within the protein molecule.

The result of the expression of the genetic material as proteins in conjunction with environmental factors is the phenotype. In GE, the phenotype is a sentence(s) in some language (a program in the C programming language) that is generated from the genetic material. This is unlike the standard method of generating a solution directly in an evolutionary algorithm by explicitly encoding the solution within the genetic material.

5   Index Trading Using Grammatical Evolution

There are number of reasons to suppose that the use of an evolutionary automatic programming (EAP) approach such as grammatical evolution can provide fruitful in the financial domain. EAP methodologies facilitate the use of complex fitness functions including discontinuous, non-differentiable functions. This is of particular importance in the financial domain as the fitness criterion may be complex, usually requiring balancing and risk. Another useful feature of EAP is that it produces human-readable rules that have the potential to enhance understanding of the problem domain.

An application of grammatical evolution to construct a simple trading system based on technical indicators is presented in this section. The technical indicators can be broadly grouped into four categories: (1) moving average indicators; (2) momentum indicators; (3) range indicators; (4) oscillators. In the creation of the treading system using technical indicators, the challenge is to select indicators, their associated parameters, and to combine indicators to produce a trading signal. The first three of the above groupings of indicators are defined in the grammar and are used to evolve the trading systems.

The rules evolved by GE are used to generate three signals for each day of the training or test periods: *Buy*, *Sell* or *Do Nothing*. A variant on the trading methodology developed in [10] is applied. If a *Buy* signal is indicated, a fix investment of €1,000 is a made in the market index. This position is closed at the end of a fixed ten-day period. On the production of a *Sell* signal, an investment of €1,000 is sold short and again this position is closed out after ten-day period. This gives rise to a maximum potential investment of €10,000 at any point in time and the potential loss on individual short sales is in theory infinite but in practice is unlikely to exceed the investment of €1,000. The profit or loss on each transaction is calculated taking into account one-way trading cost of 0.2% and allowing a further 0.3% for slippage.

To allow comparison of returns generated by the trading system with those of a *buy-and-hold* investment strategy, the total return generated by the developed trading system is a combination of its trading return and the risk-free rate of return generated on uncommitted funds.

The values of the market indices change substantially over the training and testing periods. The training data set was composed of 440 days, and the remaining data is divided into five hold-out samples totalling 2125 trading days. Before the trading rules were constructed, these values were normalised using a two-phase pre-processing. Initially the daily values were transformed by dividing them by a 75-day lagged moving average and then normalised using linear scaling into range 0 to 1.

The grammar used to create the trading systems includes function definitions of moving average, momentum and trading range, permitting the inclusion of technical indicators using these functions in the generated trading systems.

The daily signals generated by the trading system are post processed using following rule:

$Buy = Value < 0.33$
$Do\ Nothing = 0.33 >= Value < 0.66$
$Sell = 0.66 >= Value$

A key decision is construction of a trading system which will determine what fitness measure should be adopted. A simple fitness measure such as the profitability of the system both in and out of sample or the *excess return* in a trading strategy is against *buy-and-hold* strategy, where the fitness measure used in the evolutionary process is defined as the '*excess return*', is incomplete, as it fails to consider the risk of the trading system.

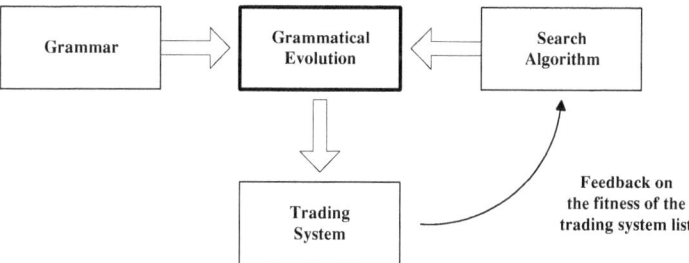

Fig. 2. GE system with plug-in inputs, the search (genetic) algorithm and the grammar

The risk of the trading system can be estimated in variety of ways. One method is to consider market risk, defined here as the risk of loss of funds due to an adverse market movement. A measure of this risk is provided by the maximum *drawdown* (the maximum cumulative loss) of the system during a training test period. This measure of risk can be added into the fitness function in a variety of formats including (*return/maximum drawdown*) or (*return − x (maximum drawdown*). Each fitness function will encourage the evolution of trading systems with good return to risk characteristics by discriminating against *high-risk/high-reward* trading rules. In the second version of the fitness functions, *x* represents a *tuning parameter*. As the value of *x* is increased, the evolved trading systems become more conservative. In this example the second version of the fitness function is used, and the value of x is set to one.

The trading system evolved by grammatical evolution (fig. 2) demonstrates better risk performance then the benchmark *buy-and-hold* strategy. The risk of the benchmark *buy-and-hold* portfolio generated by the technical trading rules increases the risk because it maintains fully invested position at all times in the market.

In this trading system simple exit strategy, which automatically closed trading positions after ten days, was adopted. Therefore, in essence, the grammar was designed to evolve good trading position '*entry*' strategies. The current model could easily be extended to also evolve the exit strategy by making appropriate modifications to the grammar.

6   Adaptive Trading Using Grammatical Evolution

Rather than employing a single fixed training period, the trading system continues to retrain as new data becomes available using a variant on the *moving window* approach. This permits the system to adapt to dynamic market conditions, while maintaining a memory of good solutions that worked well in past market environments. The system can also adjust the size of the position it takes in the market depending on the strength of the trading signal produced.

The trading system developed is based on moving averages. Simple extensions to the grammar, embedding other technical indicators, would permit the evolution of more complex sets of technical trading rules.

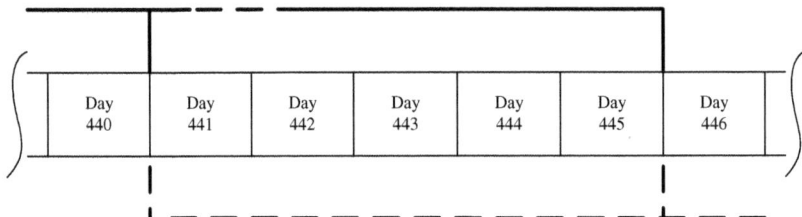

Fig. 3. The initial population of trading rules (days 1-440), the best of rules is used to trade *live*, the trading window is moved forward five days in the current population of rules

An initial training period is set aside on which the population of proposed trading rules was trained, with the aim that a competent population is evolved after a certain number of generations, (G). The system then goes '*live*', and begins to trade (fig. 3). The trading system takes the best performing rule from the initial trading period, and uses this rule to trade for each of the following x days. After x days have elapsed, the *training window* moves forward in the time-series by x days, and the current population of trading rules is retrained over the new data window for the number of generations g, where $g < G$. This training process embeds both memory and adaptive capability in the trading system, as good past trading rules serve as a starting point for trading system adaptation.

The value of g relative to that of x determines the *memory/adaptiveness balance* in the trading system. A small value of g means that memory is emphasised over adaptation, as new data have relatively less chance to influence the trading rules. The value of g needs not to be fixed, and could itself adopt over time. In periods of rapid market change a trading system with *long memory* could be a disadvantage, whereas in stabile periods a longer memory could be well advantageous. The length of the *trading/retraining window (x)* also impacts the adaptiveness of the trading system. If x large, the trading rules are altered less frequently, each adaptive *step* during retraining will tend to be larger. The *moving window* training process of the first 440 days data is used to create the initial population of trading rules. Data from days 1-75 is reserved to allow the evolved rules to use moving averages of up to a maximum lag of 75 days. The trading rules are trained on the data for days 76-440, for 100 (G) generations. The trading rule, which generates the best return over the trading period, then is used to trade *live* for the next 5 days (x). The training window is then moved forward to include these 5 days, and the population of trading rules is adapted by retraining it for 2 or 10 (g) generations in the *training/live* trading process.

The hybrid trading system adopts more complex *entry strategy*, and a *variable size* investment is made, depending on the strength of the trading signal. The amount invested for each signal is:

$$Amount\,invested = \frac{Size\,of\,trading\,signal}{Maximum\,trading\,signal} * 1000 \tag{1}$$

The stronger the signal the greater the amount invested, subject to the maximum investment amount of €1,000. Signal received from a trading rule oscillate around a pivot of zero. Signals greater than zero constitute a *Buy* signal, those less than zero constitute a *Sell* signal. To allow the system to decide how much to invest on the given trade using the above rule, the maximum size of the trading signal must be determined, and do this in an adaptive manner. Initially, it is posted in the maximum signal as being the size of the first buy signal generated by the system. If a signal is subsequently generated that it is stronger than this, the maximum trading signal is reset to the new amount. If the sum to be invested is greater than the cash available, the model will invest the cash available reduced by costs of the transactions. Upon receiving a *Sell* signal all positions are closed.

7   Conclusion and Future Work

Biological systems are inspiration for the design of optimisation and classification models and highly complex systems. A significant recent addition to bio-inspired methodologies is grammatical evolution, an evolutionary automatic programming methodology, which can be used to evolve financial trading system.

This paper illustrates the modelling of an adaptive trading system, a model of bio-inspired hybrid adaptive trading system based on technical indicators usage by grammatical evolution and *moving window*. This permits the system to adapt to dynamic market conditions, while maintaining a memory of good solutions that worked well in past market environments.

A particular benefit of adopting a population-based approach to developing trading rules is that multiple rules are uncovered. Rather than implementing a trading system, which relies on single rule, where the best rule is found, an obvious strategy is to diversify trading across a number of the better trading rules. There are several methods of implementing this approach. The simplest is to allocate funds to each rule and trade them independently. Another approach is to implement a multi-stage model, which takes the trading signals produced by several rules, combines them, and produces a final trading signal. A variant on this approach is to create a series of *families* of trading rules, using GE or an alternative methodology, where each *family* is trading using non-homogeneous inputs. The prediction from the best rule from each *family* could then be used as input to a second-stage model, which produces the final trading signal. Periodically the entire system could be retrained, and new trading rules created.

Presented model for financial markets is not only limited to this case study but it can be applied to other business activities as well as financial forecasting, corporate failure prediction or bond rating company.

References

1. Walczak, S.: An Empirical Analysis of Data Requirements for Financial Forecasting with Neural Networks. Journal of Management Information Systems 17(4), 203–222 (2001)
2. Kim, M.J., Han, I.: The Discovery of Experts' Decision Rules from Quantitative Bankruptcy Data Using Genetic Algorithms. Expert System Application (25), 637–646 (2003)
3. Alfaro-Cid, E., Sharman, K., Esparcia-Alcázar, E.: A Genetic Programming Approach for Bankruptcy Prediction Using a Highly Unbalanced Database. In: Giacobini, M. (ed.) EvoWorkshops 2007. LNCS, vol. 4448, pp. 169–178. Springer, Heidelberg (2007)
4. Marinakis, Y., Marinaki, M., Doumpos, M., Zopounidis, C.: Ant Colony and Particle Swarm Optimisation for Financial Classification Problems. Expert Systems with Applications 36(7), 10604–10611 (2009)
5. Marinaki, M., Marinakis, Y.M., Zopounidis, C.: Honey Bees Mating Optimization Algorithm for Financial Classification Problems. Applied Soft Computing 10(3), 806–812 (2010)
6. Singh, R., Sengupta, R.N.: Bankruptcy Prediction Using Artificial Immune Systems. In: de Castro, L.N., Von Zuben, F.J., Knidel, H. (eds.) ICARIS 2007. LNCS, vol. 4628, pp. 131–141. Springer, Heidelberg (2007)
7. Rada, R.: Expert Systems and Evolutionary Computing for Financial Investing. Expert Systems with Applications 34(4), 2232–2240 (2008)
8. Simić, D., Simić, S.: An Approach to Efficient Business Intelligent System for Financial Prediction. Soft Computing 11(12), 1185–1192 (2007)
9. O'Neill, M., Ryan, C.: Grammatical Evolution. IEEE Transactions Evolutionary Computation 5(4), 349–358 (2001)
10. Brock, W., Lakonishok, J., LeBaron, B.: Simple Technical Trading Rules and the Stochastic Properties of Stock Returns. Journal of Finance 47(5), 1731–1764 (1992)

Interactive and Stereoscopic Hybrid 3D Viewer of Radar Data with Gesture Recognition

Jon Goenetxea, Aitor Moreno, Luis Unzueta,
Andoni Galdós, and Álvaro Segura

Vicomtech. Mikeletegi Pasealekua 57, Parque Tecnológico 20009, Donostia-San
Sebastián, Spain
{jgoenetxea,amoreno,lunzueta,agaldos,asegura}@vicomtech.org
http://www.vicomtech.es

Abstract. This work presents an interactive and stereoscopic 3D viewer of weather information coming from a Doppler radar. The hybrid system shows a GIS model of the regional zone where the radar is located and the corresponding reconstructed 3D volume weather data. To enhance the immersiveness of the navigation, stereoscopic visualization has been added to the viewer, using a polarized glasses based system. The user can interact with the 3D virtual world using a Nintendo Wiimote for navigating through it and a Nintendo Wii Nunchuk for giving commands by means of hand gestures. We also present a dynamic gesture recognition procedure that measures the temporal advance of the performed gesture postures. Experimental results show how dynamic gestures are effectively recognized so that a more natural interaction and immersive navigation in the virtual world is achieved.

Keywords: Stereo Visualization, Weather Doppler Radar, Gesture Recognition, Human-Computer Interaction, Hybrid System.

1 Introduction

The display of meteorological data is being utilised in several fields. From the meteorological research centres to the broadcast networks, the weather information has been utilised to show their users or audience some visual conceptions of the large amount of raw information. For years, 2D maps and diagrams have been used to represent temperatures and surface pressures forecasting, results from the predictive models. Also, meteorologists need to access and visualize historical data for their reports [12].

The increment in the number of weather stations and the introduction of advanced weather instruments such as weather radar or wind profilers provides a huge amount of new data that requires an adaptation of the existing visualization methods or the creation of new ones in order to allow users to understand it. Specifically, data acquired by weather radars cannot be easily represented in a traditional 2D figure and therefore, lot of previous scientific works have researched about how the weather radar information could be represented in 3D [1,3].

M. Graña Romay et al. (Eds.): HAIS 2010, Part I, LNAI 6076, pp. 213–220, 2010.
© Springer-Verlag Berlin Heidelberg 2010

214 J. Goenetxea et al.

In this work, an interactive and immersive hybrid 3D viewer to visualize complete weather radar volumes is presented (Fig. 1). As the radar scans depend totally of the surrounding terrain, it is important for the presented 3D viewer to display correctly the radar scan over a digital terrain model (DEM) of the territory. Additionally, interactive methods have been added to help the user to navigate through the 3D world, by moving the virtual camera in the 3D space, and between different radar scans (time), allowing to custom and interactive animations of weather radar scans.

A Nintendo Wiimote and a Nunchuk [7], but extensible to other tracking systems, are used for navigating and giving commands by means of dynamic gestures. Integrated acceleration sensors allow us to interact with the system using a wireless device (except Wiimote-Nunchuck connection), fulfilling all the technical requirements with a low cost. In section 3, a dynamic gesture recognition procedure suitable for this platform is presented, which is able to measure the temporal advance of the performed gesture postures. Experimental results on gesture recognition are shown in section 4. Finally, we discuss the obtained results and conclude with the future work derived from this study.

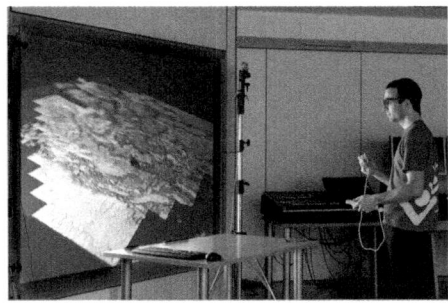

Fig. 1. The stereoscopic 3D viewer controlled with the Wiimote and Nunchuk [7]

2 3D Representation and Visualization

A fully interactive viewer requires a 3D virtual world, which is composed of two main elements: i) a 3D model coming from the weather radar data and ii) the terrain where the weather radar is located. The most common used techniques to integrate terrain and radar data involve the overlapping of 2D images: a terrain image where colors represent the height and image of the weather radar [5]. Usually, this image is typically represented as a 2D image in the form of either PPI (plan position indicator) or CAPPI (constant altitude PPI) [2].

This kind of 2D representations loses most of the semantics of the radar scan, since it is impossible to display all the hidden information and the relationships between several 2D images and the 3D terrain. From a geometrical point of view, all the samples referring to a given radar scan can be mapped in a set of concentric cones.

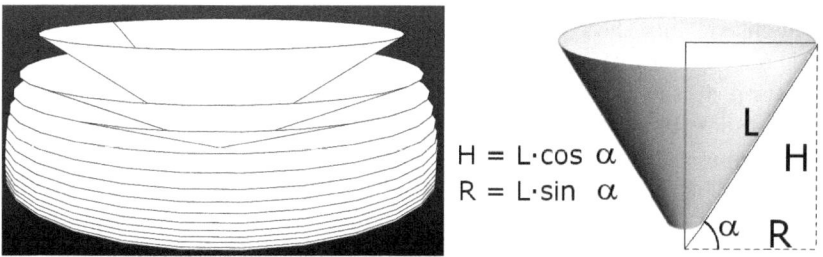

$$H = L \cdot \cos \alpha$$
$$R = L \cdot \sin \alpha$$

Fig. 2. An approximated 3d model is created by using a set of concentric cones. The radius and height of each cone is calculated from the metadata of the radar scan.

The geometry of the weather radar data is approximated as a set of concentric 3D cones (Fig. 2), with the radar located in their common vertex [6]. The height and radius of each of the cones are determined by the elevation angle of such scan.

The visualization of the weather radar data is achieved by texturing those cones. Such textures are created by applying a predetermined color map to the input data (Fig. 3), which transforms an input grey value (coming directly from the weather radar) into a 32-bit color (RGBA) [4]. Any other transformation of the textures, like subsampling or mipmapping, is left to the graphical hardware through the OpenGL API. The resulting 3D visualization of the radar data using this representation is highly fast and interactive.

In this work, we use the weather radar data provided by the radar located in Mount Kapildui (Basque Country, Spain). The 3D model of the whole Basque Country is based on a highly detailed digital elevation model and a set of properly adjusted high resolution orthophotographs, provided by the Basque Government. This large amount of data has been prepared and transformed into a PagedLOD model, ready to be loaded and rendered by the OpenSceneGraph graphics library

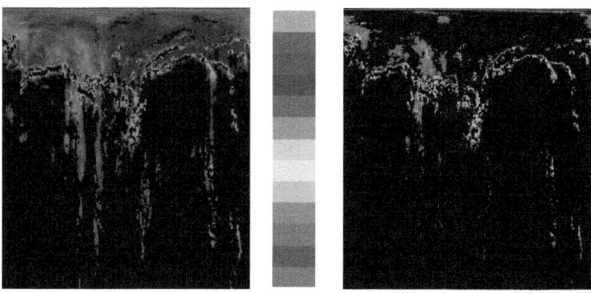

Fig. 3. Color mapping of a single scan of the weather radar. A colored RGBA texture (on the right) is created by appling a transfer function (shown in the middle) to the scalar data (on the left). The black area in the texture corresponds to the alpha channel, allowing a proper 3D visualization of the scene when all the textures of the set of concentrical cones are rendered together.

at interactive frame rates. The terrain data and the radar scans are correctly georeferenced, since the radar data includes the corresponding UTM coordinates and therefore, a seamless visualization of the 3D terrain model and the radar information at the same time is achieved without major inconveniences. The union of radar and topographic data clearly highlights the presence of ground clutter around the highest mountain ranges.

The interactive visualization of a single radar volume merged with the 3D geographic model enhances the understanding of the data. With such viewer, the user can navigate through the 3D world and inspect the radar data and its relationship with the terrain (mountains, valleys). With the visualization of a sequence of consecutive radar volumes, the user knowledge is increased dramatically, since the temporal axis gives additional information to the viewer. Hidden information in the full set of sequential 2D slides, which compose the radar scans, emerges when several data are visualized in an animated way. Some of most appealing retrieved information refers to the evolution of the rain clouds, the visual inspection of the trajectories of the storms and the effect of the mountains in the evolution of the rain clouds.

The animation support requires to have a quite large amount of consecutive radar data, which will be loaded in runtime. As the data amount could be randomly huge, it is not feasible to precalculate all the 3D model of the radar scans. Therefore, a fast on-demand construction of the 3D models is required.

3   Interaction through Dynamic Gesture Recognition

The navigation through the 3D world in our system is achieved using the Nintendo Wiimote [7] and its IR bar as a 3D mouse controller. The variation in depth is estimated by triangulating a pair of IR beams emitted by the bar projected onto the Wiimote IR sensor. To enhance the immersiveness of the navigation, stereoscopic visualization has been added to the viewer, using polarized glasses.

In this system, there are 7 actions that the user can do apart from navigating through the 3D world: *play, stop, rewind, fast forward* and *restart* the current animation, and also go to *previous* and *next* animations. This could be done by clicking on their corresponding buttons, but in order to obtain a more natural interaction with the system, dynamic hand gestures captured by the Nintendo Nunchuk's [7] triaxial accelerator have been used (Fig. 4).

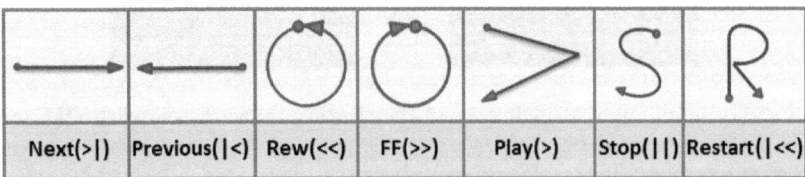

Fig. 4. The dynamic gestures used to be performed with the Nunchuk [7]

There are recent works that have used this triaxial accelerator for gesture recognition. Schlomer et al. [9] used HMM for training and recognizing gestures and achieved an average recognition rate of 90% with 5 different gestures and 6 users (a total of 450 performances). Unzueta et al. [10] focused their work more on the *segmentation* task and used a simple spatio-temporal k-NN procedure for the recognition which did not handle explicitly *time warping* (see [8] for a review on gesture recognition). Nevertheless, they attained a recognition of 99% with 10 different gestures and a total of 200 performances done by a single user.

In this case, the number of states used to represent a gesture is the needed minimal amount without a noticeable degradation in its shape. We propose to resample gestures using a cubic spline. For that, the first derivatives of the start and the end points must be defined. We estimate these using the following equations (where f is a feature, t the time instant and n the number of states):

$$\frac{\partial f_j^{(t-(n-1))}}{\partial t} = f_j^{(t-(n-2))} - f_j^{(t-(n-1))}, \text{ and } \frac{\partial f_j^{(t)}}{\partial t} = f_j^{(t)} - f_j^{(t-1)} \qquad (1)$$

The algorithm presented in this work uses a positive temporal advance counter. It is based in the algorithm presented for Mena et al. [11], and is adapted and optimised to work with different users, taking in account gesture styles, and to be used in real time environments. Fig. 5 depicts the procedure. The database is composed of N performances of the 7 gestures and all of them are resampled using a cubic spline in order to have the same number of postures.

When a new potential gesture is captured, the nearest correspondences with respect to all database gesture postures are obtained. In this way, two measurements can be obtained: i) the mean minimal distance with respect to each database gesture and ii) the temporal advance of the nearest postures. The temporal advance is measured with a voting system that increases the count only when the nearest posture index is over the previous one. This allows also handling with time warping. Multiplying this count by the inverse of the mean nearest distance allows the system to automatically decide the label corresponding to the performed gesture, as the highest score will correspond to the most similar gesture of the database both in space and time. An Euclidean distance is used, for its simplicity and the good experimental results obtained with it.

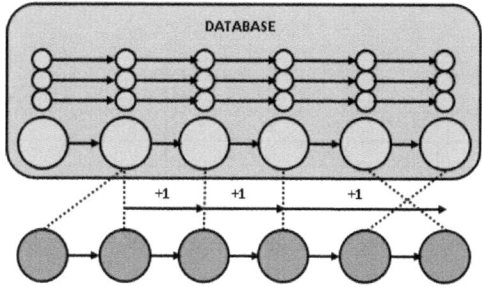

Fig. 5. Nearest posture temporal advance procedure

4   Experimental Results

For the gesture recognition test, 5 different people perform 20 repetitions of the 7 gestures (a total of 700 samples). In our experiments, in our experiments using 15 states for all gestures we obtain satisfactory results. Each user defines the gesture performance period pressing a button, so the system captures frames while the gesture button is pressed. Then, the sequence is evaluated by the classifier.

In order to determine the performance of the algorithm, the leave-one-out procedure is used in the same way as [9,10]. Recognition results per gesture and person are shown in Fig. 6. These reveal that the recognition rate is greater than 95% in the person differentiation, and greater than 96% for each gesture. On the other hand, the confusion matrix (Fig. 7) shows that the overall correct recognition rate is greater than 96%.

Fig. 8 shows two examples of a correct and an incorrect gesture matching for the recognition of *start* and *previous* gestures respectively (only the four best candidates are shown). In the former case, both the temporal advance votes and the inverse distances for the *start* candidate are far away from the rest and therefore their combination clearly makes the system decide the correct option. However, this does not happen in the other case, especially because of the closer distances to the *next* gesture candidate, but also due to its higher temporal advance at the end of it. The latter is a consequence of an incorrect segmentation of the gesture during the performance.

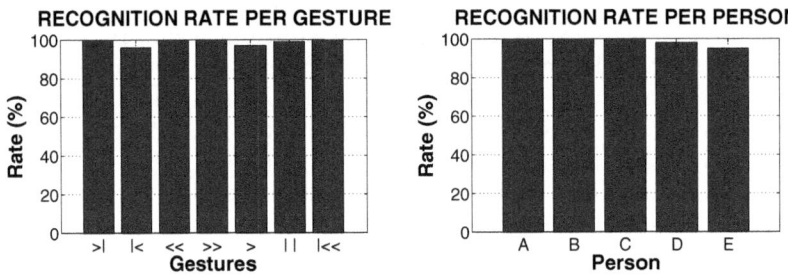

Fig. 6. Recognition rate per gesture and person

Asigned Class	Real Class						
	>|	>>	||	>	|<	<<	|<<
>|	100	0	0	1	3	0	0
>>	0	100	0	0	0	0	0
||	0	0	99	0	0	0	0
>	0	0	0	97	1	0	0
|<	0	0	0	1	96	0	0
<<	0	0	1	0	0	100	0
|<<	0	0	0	1	0	0	100

Fig. 7. Overall Confusion Matrix

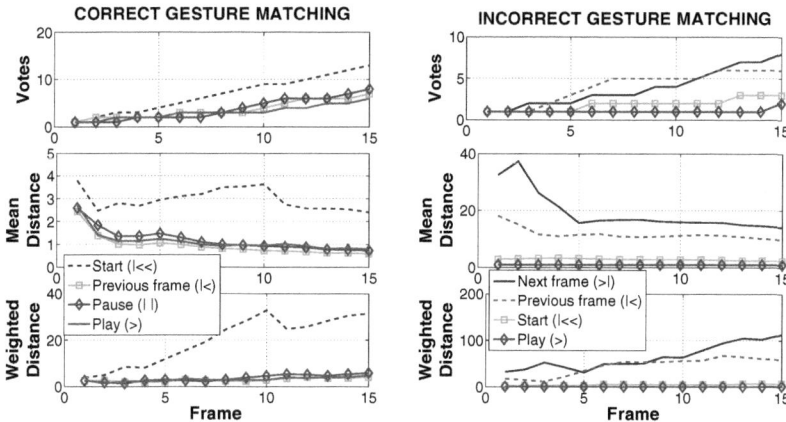

Fig. 8. Correct and incorrect matching of gestures during the recognition process

5   Conclusions and Future Work

We have presented an interactive and stereoscopic hybrid 3D viewer, which enhances the user experience respect to the traditional 2D format, by rendering a whole and animated dataset of radar data georeferenced to the place where the Doppler radar is located.

We have also presented a dynamic gesture recognition procedure used for interacting with the weather animations by means of hand gestures with the Nunchuk [7]. We have shown that our gesture recognition procedure outperforms previous approaches attaining recognition rates over 95% for a wide range of gestures and performers (a total of 700 samples).

Future work will focus on the automatic segmentation of the gestures in order to avoid erroneous manual segmentations that can lead to incorrect recognitions. More meteorological information like wind fields, temperatures, precipitation and other weather instruments will also be added to let the users find visual correlations between the whole collection of instruments and data. In order to take better data and samples, filtering and noise reduction algorithms will be taken into account [13,14].

Acknowledgments. This work has been funded by the Basque Government's ETORTEK Project research programs.

References

1. Del Greco, S., Ansari, S.: Radar Visualization and Data Exporter Tools to Support Interoperability and the Global Earth Observation System of Systems (GEOSS), from the National Oceanographic and Atmospheric Administration's (NOAA's) National Climatic Data Center (NCDC). In: ASCE Conf. Proc., vol. 316, p. 390 (2008)

2. James, C.N., Brodzik, S.R., Edmon, H., Houze Jr., R.A., Yuter, S.E.: Radar data processing and visualization over complex terrain. Wea. Forecasting 15, 327–338 (2000)
3. Maki, M., Miyachi, H.: Visualization of Doppler Radar Data - Three-Dimensional Images of Snow Bands. Report of the National Research Institute for Earth Science and Disaster Prevention 62, 1–13 (2001)
4. Ginn, E.W.L.: From PPI to Dual Doppler Images - 40 Years of Radar Observations at the Hong Kong Observatory. In: Proceedings of the 32nd Session of the ESCAP/WMO Typhoon Committee, Seoul, Republic of Korea (1999)
5. Toussaint, M., Malkomes, M., Hage, M., Hller, H., Meischner, P.: A real time data visualization and analysis environment, scientific data management of large weather radar archives. First European conference on radar meteorology, Physics and Chemistry of the Earth, Part B: Hydrology, Oceans and Atmosphere 25(10-12), 1001–1003 (2000)
6. Chen, P., Wu, L.: 3D Representation of Radar Coverage in Complex Environment. IJCSNS International Journal of Computer Science and Network Security 7(7), 139–145 (2007)
7. Nintendo Wii^{TM}console, at http://www.wii.com/
8. Mitra, S., Acharya, T.: Gesture Recognition: A Survey. IEEE Transactions on Systems, Man, and Cybernetics, Part C: Applications and Reviews 37(3), 311–324 (2007)
9. Schlömer, T., Poppinga, B., Henze, N., Boll, S.: Gesture Recognition with a Wii Controller. In: Proceedings of the Second International Conference on Tangible and Embedded Interaction (TEI 2008), Bonn, Germany, pp. 11–14 (2008)
10. Unzueta, L., Mena, O., Sierra, B., Suescun, Á.: Kinetic Pseudo-Energy History for Human Dynamic Gestures Recognition. In: Perales, F.J., Fisher, R.B. (eds.) AMDO 2008. LNCS, vol. 5098, pp. 390–399. Springer, Heidelberg (2008)
11. Mena, O., Unzueta, L., Sierra, B., Matey, L.: Temporal Nearest End-Effectors for Real-Time Full-Body Human Actions Recognition. In: Perales, F.J., Fisher, R.B. (eds.) AMDO 2008. LNCS, vol. 5098, pp. 269–278. Springer, Heidelberg (2008)
12. Trafton, J.G., Trickett, S.B.: A new model of graph and visualization usage. In: Proceedings of the Twenty-Third Annual Conference of the Cognitive Science Society, pp. 1048–1053 (2001)
13. Zhou, H., Hu, H.: Reducing Drifts in the Inertial Measurements of Wrist and Elbow Positions. IEEE Transactions on Instrumentation and Measurement, 575–585 (2010)
14. Pons, J.L., Rocon, E., Ruiz, A.F., Moreno, J.C.: Upper-Limb Robotic Rehabilitation Exoskeleton: Tremor Suppression. In: Kommu, S.S. (ed.) Rehabilitation, pp. 453–470 (2007), ISBN 978-3-902613-04-2

Recognition of Manual Actions Using Vector Quantization and Dynamic Time Warping

Marcel Martin[1], Jonathan Maycock[2],
Florian Paul Schmidt[2], and Oliver Kramer[3]

[1] Bioinformatics for High-Throughput Technologies, Computer Science 11,
TU Dortmund, Germany
[2] Neuroinformatics Group, Cognitive Interaction Technology Center of Excellence,
Bielefeld University, Germany
[3] Algorithms Group, International Computer Science Institute, Berkeley, CA, USA

Abstract. The recognition of manual actions, i.e., hand movements, hand postures and gestures, plays an important role in human-computer interaction, while belonging to a category of particularly difficult tasks. Using a Vicon system to capture 3D spatial data, we investigate the recognition of manual actions in tasks such as pouring a cup of milk and writing into a book. We propose recognizing sequences in multi-dimensional time-series by first learning a smooth quantization of the data, and then using a variant of dynamic time warping to recognize short sequences of prototypical motions in a long unknown sequence. An experimental analysis validates our approach. Short manual actions are successfully recognized and the approach is shown to be spatially invariant. We also show that the approach speeds up processing while not decreasing recognition performance.

1 Introduction

Manual intelligence plays an important role in human-computer interaction and robotics, see Ritter *et al.* [12]. Hands are the most important manipulators in a human's interaction with the environment. Therefore, the precise recognition of manual actions will be an essential part of human-computer interaction. Data can be captured from multiple sources, e.g., acceleration sensors, cameras, gloves or, as in our scenario, a visual marker system. A quantization of the high-dimensional sequences simplifies the analysis. In the following, we introduce a hybrid approach based on *vector quantization* (VQ) and *dynamic time warping* (DTW) [15]. In Section 2, we summarize related work in the fields of DTW and recognition of manual actions. In Section 3, we introduce our manual action recognition system. In Section 4, we present experimental results from a scenario of daily manual actions such as picking up a book or pouring milk into a cup. We concentrate on the selection of the most relevant features and on a comparison of runtimes of different algorithms for the VQ step.

M. Graña Romay et al. (Eds.): HAIS 2010, Part I, LNAI 6076, pp. 221–228, 2010.

2   Related Work

Gesture recognition is often done in two steps. In the segmentation step, candidates for gestures are identified. Keogh *et al.* [7] propose a theoretical segmentation framework that can be applied. Non-gestures may be recognized with the approach by Lee *et al.* [9]. In the second step, identified segments are classified. Ekvall and Kragic [4] use Hidden Markov Models to model the hand posture sequence during a grasping task. They improve the recognition rate of their system by using data from the entire sequence, not only the final grasp. Caridakis *et al.* [2] introduced an approach for the recognition of gestures based on hand trajectories. Visual data is recorded with a camera and translated by a real-time image processing module while a self-organizing map (SOM) [8] discretizes the spatial information, and a Markov approach models the temporal information. The approach is not location invariant. Gavrila *et al.* [5] consider the recognition of human movements as a classification problem involving the matching of a test sequence with several reference sequences representing prototypical activities. The data is captured using a moving light display system. After extracting joint angles as features, they use DTW to match the movement patterns. Stiefmeier *et al.* [14] have proposed a method for online and real-time spotting and classification of gestures in a wearable and ubiquitous computing scenario with body-worn sensors. Continuous motions are aggregated to trajectory segments and transformed into direction vectors. Equidistantly distributed codebook vectors quantize the features and dynamic programming is used for sequence matching. Recently, Chang *et al.* [3] explored how to methodically select a minimal set of hand posture features from optical marker data for grasp recognition. Starting with 31 markers, they used supervised feature selection to reduce the feature set of surface marker locations on the hand for grasp classification of individual hand postures. They found that a reduced feature set of only five markers was able to retain at least 92% of the accuracy of classifiers trained on the full set of markers. However, in contrast to the work presented here, they only considered the classification of a hand posture at a single point in time.

3   Gesture Recognition System

After raw Vicon data has been recorded, we recognize manual actions in three steps. First, motion features are computed and normalized. Second, the high-dimensional features are mapped onto symbols using VQ. Third, the sequence of symbols, which can be seen as a string, is analyzed with DTW.

3.1   Vicon

Vicon is a digital optical motion capture system that allows high-precision 3D object tracking [1]. Our setup is a purposefully built cage (length 2.1 m, width 1.3 m, height 2.1 m) that has 14 MX3+ cameras capturing at 200 frames per second. The table on which the experiment was carried out has a height of 1.0 m. Reflective markers were placed near the tips of each of the fingers, on each of the knuckles, and on the back of the hand (Fig. 1).

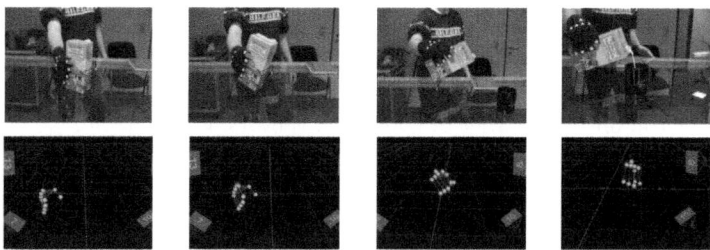

Fig. 1. Example of manual action scenario: a carton of milk is grasped, picked up, and milk is poured into a cup; lower figures show the corresponding visualization of the markers in Nexus [1], a software program from Vicon

3.2   Feature Computation and Preprocessing

Vicon delivers a stream of 33-dimensional vectors x_1 to x_n consisting of 3D positional data for the 11 markers on the hand. As preprocessing step, we reduce the sampling rate from 200 Hz to 20 Hz by averaging over ten adjacent samples to produce one new sample. This does not degrade performance later, but reduces computation time, which is quadratic in the length of the sequences.

We require that a gesture made twice in different locations or facing different directions is considered the same (spatial invariance and invariance under rotations around the (upwards pointing) z axis). Euclidean coordinates are unsuitable, but the following features fulfill the requirement: F1: The angle between the x-y-plane and the axis going through the index finger knuckle and baby finger knuckle markers (inclination of the hand); F2: the distance between the thumb tip and the index finger tip markers. The following two features are computed for either all markers or just the five fingertip markers: F3: The magnitudes of the velocities; F4: the angles between successive velocity vectors. We also calculate the barycenter of all markers or the fingertip markers only and derive the following features: F5: The velocity of the z coordinate of the barycenter; F6: the average distance of the five finger tip markers to the barycenter; F7: the magnitude of the velocity of the barycenter; F8: the magnitude of the velocity of the barycenter projected onto the x-y-plane ("ground speed"); F9: the angle between successive barycenter velocity vectors.

After feature extraction, the features need to be normalized. We tested two methods: Variance normalization ensures that the mean of each dimension is zero and the variance is one. Range normalization modifies each dimension such that the minimum is zero and the maximum is one.

3.3   Feature Quantization

After feature extraction and normalization, the next step is the quantization of the high-dimensional feature vectors. In this paper, VQ is the process of mapping feature vectors to a set of representational codebook vectors $c_1, \ldots, c_K$. The codebook vectors are distributed in feature space in a training step by one of the techniques described below. After training, new feature sequences are quantized by computing the closest codebook vector for each feature vector. This can be interpreted as translating the high-dimensional sequences of feature vectors into strings over the finite alphabet of codebook vectors. Quantization is an essential part of our approach since it allows for faster computation in the following matching procedure. We also assume that a VQ algorithm allows for a smoother quantization than dividing the feature space into grids or distributing codebook vectors equidistantly. Instead, VQ algorithms adapt to the data and therefore capture the intrinsic structure of the data.

We make use of three approximation techniques to distribute the codebook vectors in feature space. K-means clustering [10] minimizes the distances between K codebook vectors and all samples in training set $\mathcal{T}$ by iteratively repeating two steps. The first step assigns each data sample $\boldsymbol{x}_i$ to the closest codebook vector $\boldsymbol{c}_j$, and the next step computes a new codebook vector as the average of all assigned data samples. Similarly, SOMs [8] distribute K neurons in the data space. Here, codebook vectors $\boldsymbol{c}_j$ are neural weight vectors $\boldsymbol{w}_i$. In the training phase, for each data sample $\boldsymbol{x}_i$, the closest neural weight vector $\boldsymbol{w}_j$ is computed and its weights as well as the weights $\boldsymbol{w}_k$ of the neighbor neurons are pulled into the direction of $\boldsymbol{x}_i$ by $\boldsymbol{w}_k' = \boldsymbol{w}_k + \eta \cdot h(\boldsymbol{w}_j, \boldsymbol{w}_k) \cdot (\boldsymbol{x} - \boldsymbol{w}_k)$, where η is the learning rate and h is the neighborhood function that defines the distance to the weight vector $\boldsymbol{w}_j$ of the winner neuron on the map of neurons. This map is an artificial topology of neurons, typically arranged as a chain or on a grid. The growing neural gas (GNG) by Martinetz [11] is closely related to the SOM, but defines the neighborhood $h(\cdot)$ in data space.

Our program is written in Python using the GNG implementation given in the Modular toolkit for Data Processing (MDP) v2.5 [16], a K-means implementation given in SciPy [6] (module `scipy.cluster.vq`), and our own SOM implementation.

3.4 Dynamic Time Warping

DTW can be used to compute a distance between two sequences s and t of length n and m that are mostly the same but differ by local time distortions. DTW was initially developed for the task of speech recognition, but has since been applied to many domains in which multidimensional linear sequences are observed. The problem is to find a correspondence of each sequence element s_i of s to an element t_j of t and vice versa such that the (weighted) sum of distances between corresponding elements is minimized. This sum is the DTW distance. Since the sequences represent time series data, the correspondences must be monotonic. For example, when s_i corresponds to t_j, then s_{i+1} must correspond to a $t_{j'}$ where $j' \geq j$.

We first define a distance $d(i, j)$ between single sequence elements: For K-means and the GNG, $d(i, j)$ is the Euclidean distance between the codebook vectors assigned to s_i and s_j. For the SOM, $d(i, j)$ is the distance on the SOM grid between the two neurons assigned to s_i and s_j. Without VQ, let $d(i, j) :=$ $\|t_j - s_i\|$.

One advantage of using VQ is that we can pre-compute all values of $d(i, j)$, which gives a large speed-up in the following algorithm.

To solve the DTW problem, we use this recursion algorithm by Sakoe and Chiba [13]:

$$g(i,j) = \min \begin{cases} g(i-1,j-2) + 2d(i,j-1) + d(i,j), \\ g(i-1,j-1) + 2d(i,j), \\ g(i-2,j-1) + 2d(i-1,j) + d(i,j) \end{cases}, \quad \begin{matrix} i = 1,\ldots,n, \\ j = 1,\ldots,m \end{matrix} \quad (1)$$

where $d(i, j)$ is a distance between s_i and t_j and $g(i, j)$ is the non-normalized DTW distance between the sequence prefixes $s_{1,\ldots,i}$ and $t_{1,\ldots,j}$. We let $g(i, j) = \infty$ when $i < 1$ or $j < 1$. $g(i, j)$ can be computed with dynamic programming.

The initial condition in Sakoe and Chiba's paper is $g(1, 1) = 2d(i, j)$, and their normalized DTW distance is $DTW(s,t) = \frac{g(n,m)}{n+m}$. The sequences are therefore compared from end to end. To allow that s may start anywhere within t, we change the initial condition to $g(1, j) = 2d(1, j) \forall j = 1,\ldots,m$. To allow s to end anywhere, the new DTW distance is $DTW'(s,t) = \frac{g(n,m')}{n+m'}$, where $m' = \mathrm{argmin}_{j=1,\ldots,m} g(n, j)$. m' is the position at which s ends within t. To find out the start position, we introduce table h. If $h(i, j) = k$, the optimal path through (i, j) starts at position k in sequence t. The initial conditions are $h(1, j) = j \forall j = 1,\ldots,m$. $h(i, j)$ is either $h(i-1, j-2)$, $h(i-1, j-1)$, or $h(i-2, j-1)$, depending on which term in (1) is minimal.

4   Experimental Analysis

We now present an experimental evaluation of our approach. We recorded everyday actions similar to the scenario depicted in Fig. 1, which were carried out on four objects (cup, milk carton, pen and book). These recordings serve as *reference manual actions* and constitute the *training data*. The actions are: 1) Open book, 2) Pick up pen, 3) Write in the book, 4) Put down the pen, 5) Close book, 6) Pick up milk carton, 7) Simulate pouring milk into cup, 8) Put milk back in original position, 9) Pick up cup and bring to mouth to simulate drinking, 10) Put cup back in original position, and 11) Bring hand back to original position. We then recorded seven long sequences of manual actions that, among other unknown motions, contain variations of the reference actions. The sequences vary in order and orientation to allow an analysis of spatio-temporal dependencies of our technique. For clarity, we illustrate two of the seven sequences: Seq. 1 consists of all the above steps in the order given. In Seq. 5, all four objects were rotated about the z-axis and the cup and the milk carton positions were swapped. The sequence of actions then matched Seq. 1 except that actions 9) and 10) were not carried out. We recorded each sequence three times for a total of 21 sequences. The first seven sequences comprise the *validation data* and the 14 remaining sequences comprise the *test data*. The sequences of the validation data contain 66 known manual actions in total. Those of the test data contain 132 known actions.

For all three quantization algorithms, we chose parameters in the following way to limit the codebook size to 100 vectors, which we found to yield a reasonable quantization: For GNG training, we set the maximum number of codebook vectors to 100. We observed that around 70 were used. For K-means clustering, the number of cluster centers was also set to 100. 64 clusters were found to be nonempty. In case of the SOM, we used a 2-dimensional 10×10 grid.

In this paper, we assume that we know which actions occur in each trial and that each action occurs at most once. This is not an inherent limitation of our approach since preliminary experiments suggest that a properly chosen DTW distance threshold to decide if the action occurs can make the approach fully usable in practice, which will be subject of future work. To measure how well our program finds a gesture, we use the following score function. Let the interval (b_p, e_p) be the predicted location of the found action and let (b_t, e_t) be the true location of the action. We define the (relative) *overlap* $o(b_t, e_t, b_p, e_p) := \frac{\max\{\min\{e_p, e_t\} - \max\{b_p, b_t\}, 0\}}{\max\{b_p - e_p, b_t - e_t\}}$. The overlap is 100% when both intervals are the same and decreases as they move apart. It is zero when the intervals are disjoint.

Evaluation Algorithm. A single run of the program consists of the following steps. 1) Load the reference motions; 2) Compute normalized features and train a VQ algorithm; 3) Load either validation or test data and compute normalized features; 4) Convert references and action sequences to symbol sequences using the trained VQ algorithm; 5) For each manual action sequence, search for each known action and record the overlap o; 6) Report the average overlap $\hat{o}$ and how often o was at least 50%, 75%, and 90%.

4.1   Feature Selection

To find the best feature sets, we ran the program on the validation data using all $2^9 - 1$ possible nonempty feature sets, but without VQ. For each set, we test variance and range normalization and compute features F3–F9 from either all or only the fingertip markers (a total of $4 \cdot (2^9 - 1)$ runs). We then looked at the feature sets with the best average overlap $\hat{o}$ (Tab. 4.1). All of them contain F1 and F2. F3 was never used and F4 only once. F5–F9 seem to overlap in the sense that at least one of them can be dropped without detriment.

For the following experiments, we pick the following feature sets (underlined in Tab. 4.1). Feature set A is the best in Tab. 4.1: variance normalization, fingertip markers only, features F1, F2, F5, F6, F8, and F9. Feature set B is at position 5 in Tab. 4.1 in terms of overlap, but it achieved the highest number of overlaps of at least 90% and contains only four features: variance normalization, all markers, features F1, F2, F8, and F9. Feature set C is at position 15, but also reached a high number of overlaps of at least 90% with only four features: range normalization, all markers, features F1, F2, F6, and F9.

Table 1. Best feature sets among all 2044 possible nonempty feature set/normalization/marker combinations, without VQ. V: Variance normalization; R: Range normalization; T: fingertip markers; A: all markers. The n_x rows indicate how often $\hat{o}$ was at least $x\%$ (within 66 actions).

$\hat{o}$ [%]	79.66	78.3	78.07	77.93	77.79	77.73	77.68	77.64	77.61	77.58	77.48	77.41	77.39	77.34	77.3	77.16	77.1	77.08	76.98
rank	1	2	3	4	5	6	7	8	9	10	11	12	13	14	15	16	17	18	19
norm.	V	V	V	V	V	V	V	R	V	R	V	V	R	R	R	V	R	V	R
markers	T	T	A	A	A	A	A	A	T	T	A	A	A	T	A	A	A	A	A
F1	×	×	×	×	×	×	×	×	×	×	×	×	×	×	×	×	×	×	×
F2	×	×	×	×	×	×	×	×	×	×	×	×	×	×	×	×	×	×	×
F3																			
F4																×			
F5	×	×	×			×	×		×		×					×	×	×	
F6	×	×	×	×		×	×	×	×		×	×		×	×	×	×	×	
F7		×		×		×	×	×	×	×	×		×	×				×	×
F8	×		×	×	×	×	×	×		×		×	×			×	×	×	×
F9	×	×		×	×	×	×	×	×	×	×	×	×	×	×				
n_{90}	14	13	12	14	19	12	10	14	16	12	13	13	17	15	21	18	16	8	12
n_{75}	46	44	42	43	43	44	43	42	44	44	43	44	41	44	44	42	42	45	40
n_{50}	65	64	65	64	64	64	64	65	63	63	64	64	65	63	60	64	61	62	64

4.2 Comparison of Vector Quantization Approaches

Using the three chosen feature sets, we ran the evaluation program on the test data set with enabled VQ to compare the approaches in terms of runtime and recognition accuracy (Tab. 2).

Table 2. Comparison of K-means, SOM, and GNG recognition accuracy, overall runtime and time spent for DTW, using three feature sets with high recognition rate. Evaluation was done on the test data set. *time* is total runtime in seconds. *DTW* is the runtime only for the DTW step in seconds.

Feat. set	No VQ			GNG			SOM			K-means		
	$\hat{o}$ [%]	time	DTW	$\hat{o}$ [%]	time	DTW	$\hat{o}$ [%]	time	DTW	$\hat{o}$ [%]	time	DTW
A	70.35	148.2	133.2	68.94	43.6	17.5	72.23	231.0	16.3	70.45	41.0	25.1
B	69.45	151.6	131.8	66.76	46.5	17.0	60.02	220.3	16.7	66.46	48.0	26.1
C	64.02	167.5	147.6	63.99	44.1	16.4	62.09	242.7	16.4	63.27	46.7	26.5

The recognition accuracies are almost the same for no VQ, the GNG, and K-means. Only the SOM shows slightly worse recognition results for feature sets B and C. We observe significant savings in terms of DTW runtime when the VQ methods are used. The overall runtime is reduced by more than two thirds in the cases of GNG and K-means. In case of the SOM, the increased total runtime is due to a long training time because of the non-optimized implementation.

5 Summary and Outlook

Our experimental analysis reveals that our approach can recognize the manual actions of a small set of everyday actions, while a VQ preprocessing step can lead to significant savings in runtimes. We will extend the approach in various ways. To analyze inter-subject differences, we will enrich the experimental data and record manual actions using different subjects. A further task is to find reliable indicators to decide whether a certain gesture we are looking for occurs at all (in any form). Furthermore, we will extend the framework to a general framework for the recognition of manual action sequences and related multidimensional dynamic data that allows the integration of various preprocessing steps, vector quantization and string matching algorithms.

References

1. Vicon motion capture system, http://www.vicon.com/
2. Caridakis, G., Karpouzis, K., Drosopoulos, A., Kollias, S.: SOMM: Self organizing Markov map for gesture recognition. Pattern Recogn. Lett. 31(1), 52–59 (2009)
3. Chang, L.Y., Pollard, N.S., Mitchell, T.M., Xing, E.P.: Feature selection for grasp recognition from optical markers. In: Proc. of the IEEE/RSJ Int. Conf. on Intelligent Robots and Systems, pp. 2944–2950 (2007)
4. Ekvall, S., Kragic, D.: Grasp recognition for programming by demonstration. In: Proc. IEEE Int. Conf. Robotics and Automation, pp. 748–753 (2005)
5. Gavrila, D.M., Davis, L.S.: 3-D model-based tracking and recognition of human movement. In: Proc. Int. Work. on Face and Gesture Recognition, Zurich, Switzerland (1995)
6. Jones, E., Oliphant, T., Peterson, P., et al.: SciPy: Open Source scientific tools for Python (2001-2010)
7. Keogh, E.J., Chu, S., Hart, D., Pazzani, M.J.: An online algorithm for segmenting time series. In: Proc. of the 2001 IEEE Int. Conf. on Data Mining, pp. 289–296 (2001)
8. Kohonen, T.: The self-organizing map. Proc. IEEE 78(9), 1464–1480 (1990)
9. Lee, H.-K., Kim, J.H.: An HMM-based threshold model approach for gesture recognition. IEEE Trans. Pattern Anal. Mach. Intell. 21, 961–973 (1999)
10. Lloyd, S.P.: Least squares quantization in PCM. IEEE Trans. Inform. Theor. 28(2), 129–137 (1982)
11. Martinetz, T., Schulten, K.: A neural-gas network learns topologies. Artificial Neural Networks, 397–402 (1991)
12. Ritter, H., Robert, H., Röthling, F., Steil, J.J.: Manual intelligence as a Rosetta Stone for robot cognition. In: ISRR (December 2007)
13. Sakoe, H., Chiba, S.: Dynamic programming algorithm optimization for spoken word recognition. IEEE Trans. Acoust. Speech Signal Process. 26, 43–49 (1978)
14. Stiefmeier, T., Roggen, D.: Gestures are strings: Efficient online gesture spotting and classification using string matching. In: Proc. of 2nd Int. Conf. on Body Area Networks, BodyNets (2007)
15. Wendemuth, A.: Grundlagen der stochastischen Sprachverarbeitung, Oldenbourg (2004)
16. Zito, T., Wilbert, N., Wiskott, L., Berkes, P.: Modular toolkit for Data Processing (MDP): a Python data processing frame work. Frontiers in Neuroinformatics 2, 8 (2008)

Protecting Web Services against DoS Attacks: A Case-Based Reasoning Approach

Cristian Pinzón[1, 2], Juan F. De Paz[2], Carolina Zato[2], and Javier Pérez[2]

[1] Universidad Tecnológica de Panamá, Av. Manuel Espinosa Batista, Panama
[2] Departamento Informática y Automática, Universidad de Salamanca, Plaza de la Merced s/n, 37008, Salamanca, Spain
`{cristian_ivanp,fcofds,carol_zato,jbajope}@usal.es`

Abstract. The real-time detection is a key factor to detect and block DoS attacks within Web services. DoS attacks can be generated for different techniques that take advantage of points vulnerable within Web services. This paper describes a novel proposal based on a real time agent to classify user requests and detect and block malicious SOAP messages. The classification mechanism is based on a Case-Base Reasoning (CBR) model, where the different CBR phases are time bounded. Within the reuse phase of the CBR cycle is incorporated a mixture of experts to choose the most suitable technique of classification depending on the feature of the attack and the available time to solve the classification. A prototype of the architecture was developed and the results obtained are presented in this study.

Keywords: DoS attacks, Web Service, Multi-agent System, CBR.

1 Introduction

Since web services are a combination of a variety of technologies such as SOAP, HTTP, and XML, they are vulnerable to different type of attacks. One of the threats that is becoming more common within web services environments and jeopardizes the availability factor is denial of service attack (DoS) [1-2]. Some security mechanism such as traditional layer 2-4 firewalls and even application level firewalls are no longer viewed as an effective way for providing a solution to this new threat.

The real-time detection is an important requirement for security systems, mainly when the threats are related with DoS attacks. With systems requiring a response to be given before a specific deadline, as determined by the system needs, it is essential that the execution times for each of the tasks carried out by the system are predictable and able to guarantee a correct execution within the time needed for the given response. This article presents a novel proposal to cope with DoS attacks, but unlike existing solutions [1-5] our proposal takes into account the different mechanisms that can lead to a DoS attack within Web services for example (Recursive Payloads, XML Injection, SQL Injection, etc). In addition, our proposal is based on a real time classifier agent that incorporates a mixture of experts to choose a specific technique of classification depending on the feature of the attack and the available time to solve the classification. The internal structure of the agent is based on the Case-Base Reasoning

M. Graña Romay et al. (Eds.): HAIS 2010, Part I, LNAI 6076, pp. 229–236, 2010.
© Springer-Verlag Berlin Heidelberg 2010

(CBR) model [6], with the main difference being that the different CBR phases are time bounded, thus enabling its use in real time.

The rest of the paper is structured as follows: section 2 presents the problem that has prompted most of this research work. Section 3 shows a general view of the temporal bounded CBR used as deliberative mechanism in the classifier agent. Section 4 explains in detail the classification model designed. Finally, the conclusions and results of our work are presented in section 5.

2   Denial of Service Attacks Description

Recently the availability of web services has been threatened by a well known and studied type of attack known as denial of service (DoS). With XML the risk of a DoS attack being carried out increases considerably. The most common message protocol for Web Services is SOAP, an XML based message format. Such a SOAP message is usually transported using the HTTP protocol. The DoS attacks at the web services level generally take advantage of the costly process that may be associated with certain types of requests. Table 1 presents the types of DoS attack analyzed within this study.

Table 1. Types of attacks

Types of Attacks	Description
Recursive Payloads	A message written in XML can harbor as many elements as required, complicating the structure to the point of overloading the parser.
Oversize Payloads	It reduces or eliminates the availability of a web service while the CPU, memory or bandwidth are being tied up by a massive mailing with a large payload.
Buffer overflow	This attack targets the SOAP engine through the Web server. An attacker sends more input than the program can handle, which can cause the service to crash.
XML Injection	Any element that is maliciously added to the XML structure of the message can reach and even block the actual Web service application.
SQL Injection	An attacker inserts and executes malicious SQL statements into XML
XPath Injection	An attacker forms SQL-like queries on an XML document using XPath to extract an XML database.

A DoS attack mechanism can affect the availability of web services to a greater or lesser degree depending on the complexity of the type of attack used and the target component of the attack. It is important to understand that the focus of our proposal centers on the classification of web service requests through SOAP messages. Finally, there are several initiatives within this field: [1-5]. However, the main disadvantage common to each of these approaches is their low capacity to adapt themselves to the changes in the patterns, which reduces the effectiveness of these methods when slight variations in the behaviours of the known attacks occur or when new attacks appear. Moreover, most of the existing approaches are based on a centralized perspective. Because of this and the focus on performance aspects, centralized approaches can become a bottleneck when security is broken, causing a reduction of the overall performance of the application. In addition, none of these approaches considers the limitations or restrictions in the response time.

3   Temporal-Bounded Case-Based Reasoning

A real time agent is one that is able to support tasks that should be performed within a restricted period of time [7]. Intelligent agents may use a lot of reasoning mechanisms to achieve these capabilities, including planning techniques or Case-Based Reasoning (CBR) techniques. The main assumption in CBR is that similar problems have similar solutions [8]. If we want to use CBR techniques as a reasoning mechanism in real-time agents, it is necessary to adapt these techniques to be executed so that they guarantee real-time constraints. In real-time environments, the CBR phases must be temporally bounded to ensure that solutions are produced on time, giving the system a temporally bounded deliberative case-based behavior.

As a first step, we propose a modification of the classic CBR cycle, adapting it so that it can be applied in real-time domains. First, we group the four reasoning phases that implement the cognitive task of the real-time agent into two stages defined as: the learning stage, which consists of the revise and retain phases; and the deliberative stage, which includes the retrieve and reuse phases. Each phase will schedule its own execution time. These new CBR stages must be designed as an anytime algorithm, where the process is iterative and each iteration is time-bounded and may improve the final response.

In accordance with this, our Time Bounded CBR cycle (TB-CBR) will operate in the following manner. The TB-CBR cycle starts at the learning stage, checking if there are previous cases waiting to be revised and possibly stored in the case-base. In our model, the solutions provided at the end of the deliberative stage will be stored in a solution list while a feedback about their utility is received. When each new CBR cycle begins, this list is accessed and while there is enough time, the learning stage of those cases whose solution feedback has been recently received is executed. If the list is empty, this process is omitted. After this, the deliberative stage is executed. The retrieval algorithm is used to search the case-base and retrieve a case that is similar to the current case (i.e. the one that characterizes the problem to be solved). Each time a similar case is found, it is sent to the reuse phase where it is transformed into a suitable solution for the current problem by using a reuse algorithm. Therefore, at the end of each iteration of the deliberative stage, the TB-CBR method is able to provide a solution for the problem at hand, although this solution can be improved in subsequent iterations if the deliberative stage has enough time to perform them.

4   Classifier Real-Time Agent Based on CBR Approach

This section presents an agent specially designed to incorporate an adaptation of the previously mentioned TB-CBR model as a reasoning engine in which the learning phase is eliminated since it is now performed by human experts. The TB-CBR agent utilizes a global case base, which avoids any duplication of the content of any information compiled from the cases or any information contained in the results of the analysis. Tables 2, 3 and 4 show the structure of the cases. Table 2 shows the fields recovered from the analysis of the service request headers. Table 3 shows the fields associated with the analysis of the service requests that were obtained after the analysis performed by the parser application.

Table 2. Header Fields

Fields	Type	Variable
IDService	Int	h_1
Subnet mask	String	h_2
SizeMessage	Int	h_3
NTimeRouting	Int	h_4
LengthSOAPAction	Int	h_5
TFMessageSent	Int	h_6

Table 3. Definition of Fields Recovered by the Parser

Description	Fields	Type	Variable
Number of header elements	NumberHeaderElement	Int	p_1
Number of elements in the body	NElementsBody	Int	p_2
Greatest value associated to the nesting elements	NestingDepthElements	Int	p_3
Greatest value associated to the repeated tag within the body	NXMLTagRepeated	Int	p_4
Greatest value associated with the leaf nodes among the declared parents	NLeafNodesBody	Int	p_5
Greatest value of the associated attributes among the declared elements	NAttributesDeclared	Int	p_6
Type of SQL command	Command_Type	Int	p_7
Number of times that the AND operator appears in the string	Number_And	Int	p_8
Number of times that the OR operator appears in the string	Number_Or	Int	p_9
Number of times the Group By function appears	Number_GroupBy	Int	p_{10}
Number of times that the Order By function appears	Number_OrderBy	Int	p_{11}
Number of times that the Having function appears	Number_Having	Int	p_{12}
Number of Literals declared in the string	Number_Literals	Int	p_{13}
Number of times that the Literal Operator Literal expression appears	Number_LOL	Int	p_{14}
Length of the SQL string	Length_SQL_String	Int	p_{15}
Greatest value associated with the length of the string among the elements or attributes within the body	LengthStringValueBody	Int	p_{16}
Total number of incidences during the parsing process	TotalNumberIncidenceParsing	Int	p_{17}
Reference to an external entity	URIExternalReference	Int	P_{18}
Number of variables declared in hte XPath expression	XPathVariablesDeclared	Int	P_{19}
Number of elements affected in the consulted node	XpathNumberElementAffected	Int	p_{20}
Number of literals declared in the XQuery Statement	XPathNumberLiteralsDeclared	Int	p_{21}
Number of times the And operator appears in the XQuery Statement	XPathNumberAndOperator	Int	p_{22}
Number of time the Or operator appears in the XQuery statement.	XPathNumberOrOperator	Int	p_{23}
Number of functions declared in the XQuery Statement	XPathNumberFunctionDeclared	Int	p_{24}
Lentgh of the XQuery Statement in a SOAP message	XPathLenghtStatement	Int	p_{25}
Cost of processing time (CPU)	CPUTimeParsing	Int	p_{26}
Cost of memory size (KB)	SizeKbMemoryParser	Int	p_{27}

From the information contained in the Tables 3 it is possible to obtain the global structure of the cases. In this way, the information of each case can be represented by the following tuple:

$$c = \left(\{ h_i \,/\, i = 1...6 \} \cup \{ p_j \,/\, j = 1...27 \} \cup \{ x_{lm} \,/\, l = 1...6, m = 1...2 \} \right) \qquad (1)$$

Where l represents the set of attacks showed in Table 1; for each the values X_l, the first of the values stores the probability of attack achieved for the associated technique, whilst the second of the parameters stores whether it really was an attack.

When the system receives a new request, the TB-CBR agent performs an analysis that can determine whether it is an attack, in which case it identifies the type of attack. The following sections describe the different stages of the deliberative stage for the TB-CBR.

- **Retrieve:** The retrieval time for the cases depends on the size of the cases in the case base. If the size is known, it is easy to predict how much execution time will be used to recover the cases. The asymptotic cost is linear ($O(n)$). The cases that have been retrieved during this phase are selected according to the information obtained from the headers of the packages of the HTTP/TCP-IP transport protocol from the new case. The information retrieved corresponds to the service description fields, and the service requestor's subnet mask. Assuming that the newly introduced case is represented by c_{n+1}, the case c_{n+1} is defined by the following tuple: $c_{n+1} = \left(\{ h_i \,/\, i = 1...6 \} \right)$. The new case does not initially contain information related to the parser since it would be necessary to analyze the content of the message.

$$c_{.h_1 h_2} = f_s(C) = \{ c_{j.h_1 h_2} \in C \,/\, c_{j.h_1} = c_{n+1 \cdot h_1} \cap c_{j.h_2} = c_{n+1 \cdot h_2} \} \qquad (2)$$

where $c_{j.hl}$ represents the case j and h_l, a property that is determined according to the data shown in Table 2, C represents the set of cases, and f_s the retrieval function. In the event that the retrieved set is empty, the process continues with the retrieval of the messages only without considering the subnet mask.

- **Reuse:** Each type of attack in our proposal (except for Xpath and SQL Injection attacks) can be analyzed by two different techniques. The first is known as the Light technique and is usually a detection algorithm with a low temporal cost, but of low quality as well. On the other hand, using a Heavy technique, the result of the analysis is much more exact, but it requires a much higher amount of execution time. Using these techniques to analyze an attack allows the real time agent to apply the one that is best suited to its needs, without violating the temporal restrictions that should be considered when executing the deliberative stages. In order to determine which is the set of techniques that provides the best solution, it is necessary for the length and quality associated with each technique to be predictable, as seen from a global perspective that includes all possible combinations of techniques.

The different techniques that the classifier agent executes once the optimal combination of techniques has been determined include a set of common inputs that are represented by p_c and are defined as follows: $p_c = \{ p_1, p_{28}, p_{29}, p_2, p_3, p_4, p_5, p_6, p_{16}, p_{17}, p_{26}, p_{27} \} k$. The remaining entries vary according to the techniques used, which is specified for each one. Table 4 shows the information of the different techniques used for each of the attacks. In Additions, the different fields associated with each of the attacks for the Heavy techniques are detailed. The Light techniques only use the fields that refer to the request headers, specifically the following fields $\{h3, h4, h5, h6\}$.

Table 4. Techniques Associated with the Attacks and Variables of the Heavy Techniques

Types of Attacks	Light Techniques	Heavy Techniques	Variables / Heavy Techniques
Oversize Payload	Decision Tree	N. Network	$\{h_3, h_4, h_5, h_6, p_c\}$
Recursive Parsing	Naïve Bayes	N. Network	$\{h_3, h_4, h_5, h_6, p_c\}$
Buffer Overflow	Decision tree	N. Network	$\{h_3, h_4, h_5, h_6, p_c\}$
XML Injection	SMO	N. Network	$\{h_3, h_4, h_5, h_6, p_c\}$
SQL Injection		N. Network	$\{p_8, p_9, p_{10}, p_{11}, p_{12}, p_{13}, p_{14}, p_{15}\} \cup \{h_3, h_4, h_5, h_6, p_c\}$
Xpath Injection		N. Network	$\{p_{19}, p_{20}, p_{21}, p_{22}, p_{23}, p_{24}\} \cup \{h_3, h_4, h_5, h_6, p_c\}$

In addition to the light techniques displayed in Table 4, there is a global neural network that contains each of the inputs listed in the column variables/Heavy Techniques for the type of attack. This network will be used in those situations where the response time is critical and it is not possible to check each case individually.

At the end of the Reuse stage of the CBR cycle, the optimal output is selected, corresponding to the maximum values provided by each of the experts, so that if any exceeds a given threshold, the service request is considered to be an attack, and classified as such. Once the analysis is complete, if an attack has been detected, the service request is rejected and is not sent to the respective provider. Subsequently, the result of the analysis is evaluated by a human expert through the Revise and Retain phase, if it is necessary to store the case associated with the request.

5 Results and Conclusion

This article has described a new approach to protect web services environments against DoS attacks. In order to validate the initial prototype, we proposed a benchmark case study that used description 3 from the web services, designed especially for testing. The service requests were initiated from an agent specifically developed for that task and these were classified by a classifier real-time agent. The description for each of these services was used to build by hand a set of tests to validate the effectiveness of our Classifier real-time agent. The set of test was developed to determine whether the use of the mixture of experts was able to improve the detection and subsequent classification of the attack mechanisms.

Prior to initiating the tests, the attack classification mechanisms were analyzed for each use of a Light or Heavy technique. The analysis demonstrated that the use of Heavy techniques provided a better classification, but with a greater temporal cost. Although this result was expected and logical, the tests were performed in order to empirically prove the execution times in the worst case for each of the different techniques. The time was used to determine which set of techniques should be applied so as to not exceed the deadline, which was not exceeded in any of the executions.

The first test compares a series of results obtained for the different type of attacks and classification techniques. In order to perform these tests, 1500 requests were generated, of which 750 were legal and 750 illegal, distributed in groups of 125, 125, 125, 125, 100 and 150 for each type of attack: Oversize Payload, Recursive Parsing, Buffer Overflow, XML Injection, Xpath Injection and SQL Injection, respectively.

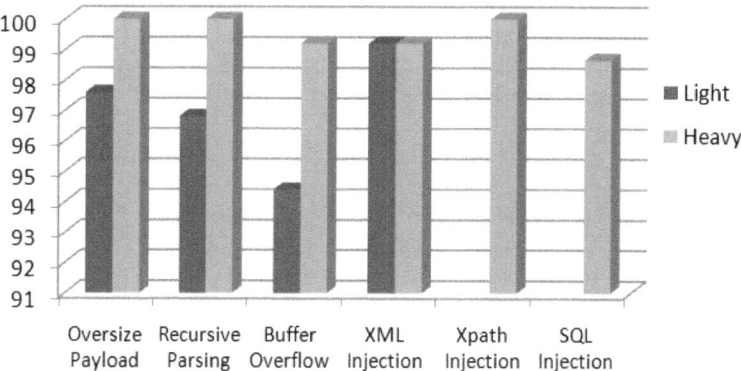

Fig. 1. Percentage of attacks correctly classified

The classification techniques indicated in Table 4 were applied to each type of attack. Figure 1 lists the percentage of attacks correctly classified for light and heavy techniques. It is clear that the light techniques have a lower rate of correctness than the heavy techniques for the different attacks for which they are available.

Once the rate of correctness was analyzed, we proceeded to analyze the results with regards to execution time. A second set with a total of 1500 available queries were used to analyze the execution time. We replicated and analyzed 30,000 execution to calculate the average execution time. The final result is shown in Figure 2, which shows that the execution time for the neural network to perform its estimates is much greater than the other techniques.

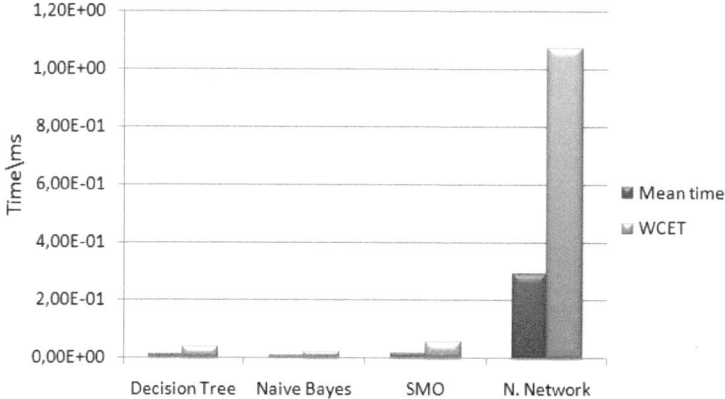

Fig. 2. Average time and Worst Case Estimated Time (WCET)

The results are promising and allow us to conclude that our approach can be considered as a solid alternative to detect and block DoS attacks in web service environments. However, there is still much work to be done, especially with regards to checking the validity of our approach in heterogeneous real environments. These are our next challenges.

Acknowledgments. This work has been supported by the Spanish Ministry of Science and Innovation TIN 2009-13839-C03-03 and The P.E.P. 2006-2010 IFARHU-SENACYT-Panama.

References

1. Gruschka, N., Jensen, M., Luttenberger, N.: A Stateful Web Service Firewall for BPEL. In: IEEE International Conference on Web Services, pp. 142–149 (2007)
2. Im, E.G., Song, Y.H.: An Adaptive Approach to Handle DoS Attack for Web Services. In: Kantor, P., Muresan, G., Roberts, F., Zeng, D.D., Wang, F.-Y., Chen, H., Merkle, R.C. (eds.) ISI 2005. LNCS, vol. 3495, pp. 634–635. Springer, Heidelberg (2005)
3. Chonka, A., Zhou, W., Xiang, Y.: Defending Grid Web Services from XDoS Attacks by SOTA. In: EEE International Conference on Pervasive Computing and Communications, vol. 6, pp. 1–6. IEEE Computer Society, Los Alamitos (2009)
4. Padmanabhuni, S., Singh, V., Kumar, K.M.S., Chatterjee, A.: Preventing Service Oriented Denial of Service (PreSODoS): A Proposed Approach. In: IEEE International Conference on Web Services (ICWS 2006), pp. 577–584. IEEE Computer Society, Los Alamitos (2006)
5. Ye, X.: Countering DDoS and XDoS Attacks against Web Services. In: IEEE/IFIP International Conference on Embedded and Ubiquitous Computing, vol. 1, pp. 346–352. IEEE Computer Society, Los Alamitos (2008)
6. De Paz, J.F., Rodríguez, S., Bajo, J., Corchado, J.M.: Case-based reasoning as a decision support system for cancer diagnosis: A case study. International Journal of Hybrid Intelligent Systems 6(2), 97–110 (2009)
7. Julian, V., Botti, V.: Developing real-time multi-agent systems. Integrated Computer-Aided Engineering 11(2), 135–149 (2004)
8. Corchado, J.M., Laza, R., Borrajo, L., Yáñez, J.C., Luis, A.D., Valiño, M.: Increasing the Autonomy of Deliberative Agents with a Case-Based Reasoning System. International Journal of Computational Intelligence and Applications 3, 101–118 (2003)

Ranked Tag Recommendation Systems Based on Logistic Regression*

J.R. Quevedo, E. Montañés, J. Ranilla, and I. Díaz

Computer Science Department
University of Oviedo
{quevedo,montaneselena,ranilla,sirene}@uniovi.es

Abstract. This work proposes an approach to tag recommendation based on a logistic regression based system. The goal of the method is to support users of current social network systems by providing a rank of new meaningful tags for a resource. This system provides a ranked tag set and it feeds on different posts depending on the resource for which the user requests the recommendation. The performance of this approach is tested according to several evaluation measures, one of them proposed in this paper (F_1^+). The experiments show that this learning system outperforms certain benchmark recommenders.

1 Introduction

Tagging can be defined as the process of assigning short textual descriptions, called tags, to information resources, which allow the user to organize the content. This becomes very popular and helpful for large-scale systems such as Folksonomies. A Folksonomy [3] is a collection of resources entered by users in posts. Each post consists of a resource and a set of keywords, so-called tags, attached to it by a user. Generally, the resource is specific to the user who added it to the system, but all users are invited to label it with tags.

This paper proposes an approach to tag recommendation based on a learning process. The work starts from the hypothesis that a learning process improves the performance of the recommendation task. It explores several information to feed on the learner. It also analyzes the fact that recent posts are more useful and suitable to recommend new tags.

The remainder of the paper is structured as follows. Section 2 presents background information about tag recommendation in social networks. Our approach is put in context in Section 3 while the proposed method is provided in Section 4. Section 5 details some novel performance evaluation metrics. Finally Section 6 shows the results and Section 7 draws the work conclusions.

---

* This work was supported by the Spanish Ministerio de Educación y Ciencia and the European Regional Development Fund [TIN2007-61273].

M. Graña Romay et al. (Eds.): HAIS 2010, Part I, LNAI 6076, pp. 237–244, 2010.

2   Related Work

Different approaches have been proposed to support users during the tagging process depending on the purpose for which they were built. Some of them makes recommendations by analyzing tag co-occurrences or studies graph-based approaches.

Jäschke et al. [5] adapt a user-based collaborative filtering as well as a graph-based recommender built on top of FolkRank. Basile et al. [1] propose a smart TRS able to learn from past user interaction as well as the content of the resources to annotate. Katakis et al. [6] model the automated tag suggestion problem as a multi-label text classification task. Sigurbjornsson et al. [8] present the results by means of a tag characterization focusing on how users tags photos of `Flickr` and what information is contained in the tagging.

Most of these systems require information associated with the content of the resource itself [1]. Others simply suggest a sets of tags as a consequence of a classification rather than providing a ranking of them [6]. Some of them require a large quantitative of supporting data [8]. The proposal of this work avoids these drawbacks through a novel approach which establishes a tag ranking by a machine learning approach based on Logistic Regression.

3   Tag Recommender Systems (TRS)

A folksonomy is a tuple $F := (\mathcal{U}, \mathcal{T}, \mathcal{R}, \mathcal{Y})$ where $\mathcal{U}$, $\mathcal{T}$ and $\mathcal{R}$ are finite sets, whose elements are respectively called users, tags and resources, and $\mathcal{Y}$ is a ternary relation between them, i. e., $\mathcal{Y} \subseteq \mathcal{U} \times \mathcal{T} \times \mathcal{R}$, whose elements are tag assignments (posts). When a user adds a new or existing resource to a folksonomy, it could be helpful to recommend him/her relevant tags.

TRS usually take the users, resources and the ratings of tags into account to suggest a list of tags to the user. According to [7] a TRS can briefly be formulated as a system that takes as input a given user $u \in \mathcal{U}$ and a resource $r \in \mathcal{R}$ and produces a set $\mathcal{T}(u, r) \subset \mathcal{T}$ of tags as output. Jäschke et al. in [5] define a post of a folksonomy as a user, a resource and all tags that this user has assigned to that resource. This work slightly modifies this definition in the sense that it restricts the set of tags to the tags used simultaneously to tag a resource by a user.

There exist some simple but frequently used TRS [5] based on providing a list of ranked tags extracted from the set of posts connected with the current annotation.

- MPT (Most Popular Tags): For each tag t_i, the posts with t_i are counted and the top tags (ranked by occurrence count) are utilized as recommendations.
- MPTR (Most Popular Tags by Resource): For a resource r_i it is counted for every tag in every posts they occur together with r_i. The tags occurring most often together with r_i are then proposed as recommendations.
- MPTU (Most Popular Tags by User): For a resource r_i it is counted for each tag in how many posts they occur together with r_i. In addition, for a

user u_i it is counted for every tag in every posts they occur together with u_i. The tags occurring most often together with either r_i or u_i are taken as recommendations.

- MPTRU (Most Popular Tags by Resource or User): For a resource r_i it is counted for each tag in how many posts they occur together with r_i. In addition, for a user u_i it is counted for every tag in how many posts they occur together with u_i. The tags occurring most often together with either r_i or u_i are taken as recommendations.

The introduction of a learning system is expected to improve the performance of them.

4   Learning to Recommend

This section depicts the whole procedure followed in order to provide a user and a resource with a set of ranked tags. These recommendations are based on a learning process that learns how the users has previously tagged resources. The core of the method is a supervised learning algorithm based on logistic regression [2]. This paper studies different training sets built according to the user and resource for whom the recommendations are provided.

The key points of the system are the following

- The training set depends on each test set and it is built specifically for each of them.
- Several training sets are built according to different criteria and afterwards compared and evaluated.
- The learning system adopted was LIBLINEAR [2], which provides a probabilistic distribution before the classification. This probability distribution is exerted to rank the tags, taking as most suitable tag the one with highest probability value.
- The tags of the ranking will be all that appear in the categories of each training set. This entails that some positive tags of a test post might not be ranked.

4.1   Definition of the Test Set

The traditional approach splits the data into training and test sets at the beginning. Afterwards, a model is inferred using the training set and it is validated thanks to the test set [6]. In this paper, the methodology used is quite different in the sense that the training and test sets are not fixed. The test set is randomly selected and afterwards an *ad hoc* training set is provided to each test post.

According to the definition of a folksonomy in Section 3, it is composed by a set of posts. Each post is formed by a user, a resource and a set of tags, i.e., $p_i = (u_i, r_i, \{t_{i_1}, \ldots, t_{i_k}\})$

Each post of a folksonomy is candidate to become a test post. Each test post is then turned into as many examples as tags used to label the resource. Therefore, post p_i is split into k test examples

$$e_1 = (u_i, r_i, t_{i_1}) \ldots e_k = (u_i, r_i, t_{i_k}) \tag{1}$$

4.2   Definition of the Training Set

Whichever learning system strongly depends on the training set used to learn. This work dynamically selects an *ad hoc* training set from the N most recent posts posted *before* the test post. This parameter N is experimentally fixed.

This characteristic makes the TRS to suggest the on-fashion folksonomy tags and it produces a more scalable system, since the number of posts in the training set does not increase according to the number of posts posted before the test post. This characteristic makes solving the problem by the learning system feasible.

Therefore, the choice of the training set for a given test post is reduced to define the criteria the posts must satisfy to be included in the training set. This work studies different criteria.

Approach 1. TR Let $p_i = (u_i, r_i, \{t_{i_1}, \ldots, t_{i_k}\})$ be a test post. Let $\mathcal{R}_{u_i}$ be the subset of posts associated to a resource r_i and

$$\mathcal{R}^t_{r_i} = \{p_i / p_i \in \mathcal{R}_i \text{ and it was posted before } t\}.$$

TR approach selects as training set the N most modern posts of $\mathcal{R}^{d_i}_{r_i}$, being d_i the date when p_i was posted.

Approach 2. TU Let $p_i = (u_i, r_i, \{t_{i_1}, \ldots, t_{i_k}\})$ be a test post. Let $\mathcal{P}_{u_i}$ be the personomy (the subset of posts posted by a user constitutes the so-called personomy) associated to a user u_i and

$$\mathcal{P}^t_{u_i} = \{p_i / p_i \in \mathcal{P}_{u_i} \text{ and it was posted before } t\}$$

TU approach selects as training set the N most modern posts of $\mathcal{P}^{d_i}_{u_i}$, being d_i the date when p_i was posted.

Approach 3. TRU The above training sets do not take into account that the learned model which is used after a resource is presented to the user. Hence, this approach proposes to go further and to add as training examples those concerning with the resource for which the recommendations are demanded. The examples whose tags have been previously assigned to the resource by the user to whom the recommendations are provided are removed because it has no sense to recommend a user the tags he had previously used to label the resource.

Therefore, the training set associated to p_i is formed by

$$UR^{d_i}_{u_i, r_i} = \{\mathcal{P}^d_i \cup \mathcal{R}^d_i\} \backslash \{p_j / p_j = (u_i, r_i, \{t_1, ..., t_n\})\}$$

4.3   Example Representation

Once both the training and test sets are defined, it is necessary to transform them into a computable form understandable for a machine learning system. Therefore, we have to define the features which characterize the examples as well as the class of each example.

The features which characterize the examples are the tags previously used to tag the resource in the folksonomy. Hence, each example will be represented by a boolean vector V of size M (the number of tags of the folksonomy) where $v_j = 1$ if and only if t_j was used to tag the resource before and 0 otherwise, where $j \in 1, \ldots, M$. The class of a example will be the tag with which the user has tagged the resource in this moment.

In addition, removing redundant or non-useful features which add noise to the system is usually helpful to increase both the effectiveness and efficiency of the classifiers. The example representation based on tags as features makes possible perform a simple feature selection in the training set consisting of just keeping those tags which represent the test (this approach will be called TRUTR).

4.4   Learning System

The key point of this paper is to provide a ranked set of tags adapted to a user and a resource. Therefore, it could be beneficial a learning system able to rank the tags, indicating to the user which tag is the best and which one is the worst for the resource.

In this framework, LIBLINEAR [2] is an open source library[1] based on SVM which is a recent alternative able to accomplish multi-category classification through logistic regression, providing a probabilistic distribution before the classification. This probability distribution is exerted to rank the tags, taking as most suitable tag the one with highest probability value. In the same sense the most discordant tag will be the one with lowest probability.

This work uses the default LIBLINEAR configuration after a slight modification of the output. The evaluation in this case takes place when a resource is presented to the user.

5   Performance Evaluation

So far, no consensus about an adequate metric to evaluate a recommender is stated [5]. In ([6]) a random post for each user is picked up and afterwards they provide a set of tags for this post based on the whole folksonomy except such post. Then, they compute the F_1 as

$$F_1 = \frac{1}{|D|} \sum_{(u,r) \in D} \frac{2|\mathcal{T}^+(u,r) \cap \mathcal{T}(u,r)|}{|\mathcal{T}(u,r)| + |\mathcal{T}^+(u,r)|} \qquad (2)$$

---

[1] Available at http://www.csie.ntu.edu.tw/~cjlin/liblinear/

where D is the test set, $\mathcal{T}^+(u, r)$ are the set of tags user u has assigned to resource r (positive tags) and $\mathcal{T}(u, r)$ are the set of tags the system has recommended to user u to assign resource r.

The main drawback of this process of evaluation is that it just evaluates the performance of a classification rather that the performance of a ranking But, a TRS able to return the positive tags at the top of the ranking is obviously preferred than one that returns the positive tags at the bottom of the ranking. Hence, defining an evaluation metric able to quantify both the tags a TRS recommends and the order in which it ranks them is an expected challenge to cope with. The Area Under the ROC Curve (AUC) or Average Precision (AP) are two a priori measures to evaluate a ranking. The Normalized Discounting Cumulative Gain (NDCG) [4] is another evaluation measure for Information Retrieval (IR) systems that compute the cumulative gain a user obtains by examining the retrieval result up to a given ranked position. But, Both of them present some drawbacks in tag recommendation because the rankings to compare could not have the same number of tags and it is possible that some tags of the test never appear in the training. In fact, all of them are thought to compare permutations of a predefined set of tags.

This paper proposes an alternative which tries to overcome those drawbacks. It consists of computing the F_1 measure for all possible cutoffs of the ranking for which a positive tag is returned and to choose the highest one. It will be denoted by F_1^+ and it is defined by $F_1^+ = \max_{0 <= i <= r}(F_1)_i$ where r is the size of the ranking, that is, the number of tags returned by the system, $(F_1)_i$ is the F_1 of the classification assuming that the system has classified the first i tags as positive ones and the rest as negative ones. Notice that i ranges from 0 (which means that the system has not returned any tag as positive) to r (which means that the system has returned all the tags as positive).

Since a negative tag in the ranking does not lead to an improvement of the F_1, only computing F_1^+ for the cutoffs where a positive tag is placed is required. Hence, this metric gives an optimal position of the ranking. Notice that it does not vary if negative tags are added to the tail of the ranking, as it happens to AP. But, it takes into account all positive tags and not just the positive tags which appear on the top of the ranking, as AUC also does.

6 Experiments

The experiments were carried out over the collection bt08, which is a dataset formed by bibtex posts extracted from ECML PKDD Dicovery Challenge 2008[2]. It is extracted from Bibsonomy[3], a web-based social bookmarking and publication-sharing system that enables users to tag web documents as well as bibtex entries of scientific publications.

---

[2] http://www.kde.cs.uni-kassel.de/ws/rsdc08/
[3] http://www.bibsonomy.org

Table 1. Performance of the benchmark TRSs for bt08 dataset

	F_1^+	AUC	AP	NDCG		F_1^+	AUC	AP	NDCG
MPT	6.7%	5.8%	4.6%	6.6%	MPTU	37.2%	56.3%	28.8%	42.5%
MPTR	7.8%	5.2%	5.7%	7.7%	MPTRU	38.2%	57.9%	29.7%	43.7%

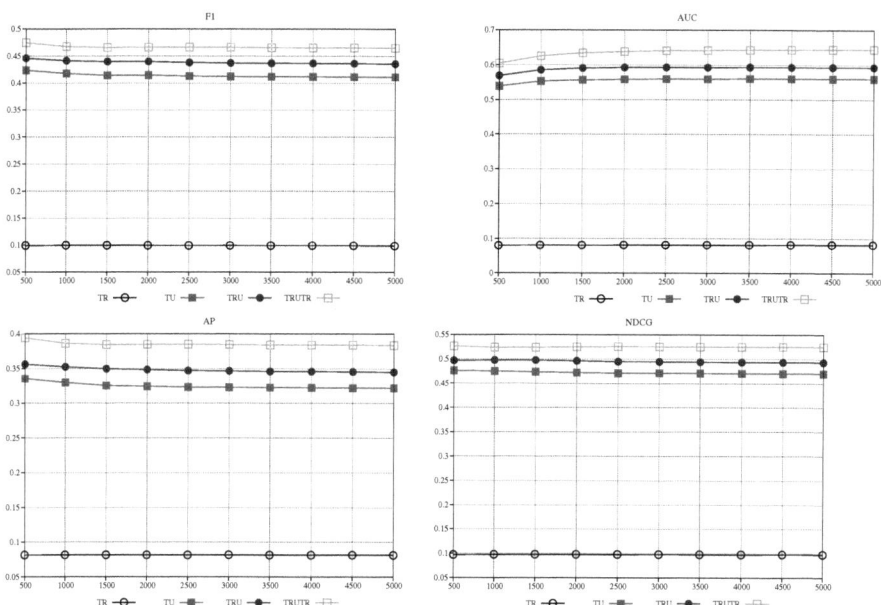

Fig. 1. F_1^+, AUC, AP and NDCG of bt08 data set

Before using the data sets, tag cleaning was made according to PKDD Discovery Challenge 2008. The number of users, tags, resources and posts of this collection is respectively $1, 206$, $29, 739$, $96, 616$ and $278, 008$.

To test the methods, 1000 test posts were randomly selected. For each one, several ranked tag sets are provided depending on the approach that builds the training set (which leads to four possible TRS: TR, TU, TRU and TRUTR) and the cardinality (N) of the training set ($N = i * 500$ with $i = 1, 2, \ldots, 10$).

Table 1 shows the behavior of the benchmark TRSs according to the evaluation metrics detailed in 5. As MPTRU seems to be better than the rest benchmark TRSs, it is considered as reference from now on.

Figure 1 respectively shows the F_1^+, the AUC, the AP and the NDCG evaluation measures for the dataset and the four ways of building the training set. Clearly, the system performance is considerably increased when the posts that the user of the test post has posted are included as training examples. Besides, adding to the training set the posts in which the resource of the test post is involved also helps to improve the effectiveness of the recommender. Furthermore, if only the tags that represent the test are kept to represent the training set formed by the posts with either the resource of the user of the test post, the performance in enhanced. These results were statistically confirmed with a paired-samples Wilcoxon test.

7   Conclusions and Future Work

This work proposes a TRS based on a novel approach which learns to rank tags from previous posts in a folksonomy using a logistic regression based system. In addition, a new evaluation measure is proposed, namely F_1^+ which overcomes the drawbacks of other ranking evaluation metrics as AUC, AP and NDCG.

The TRSs proposed are compared to the best benchmark TRS (MPTRU). The results show a significant improvement of all the TRSs with regard to MPTRU, being that with take into account test representation (TRUTR) the best of the four versions. In addition, it is possible to keep the performance without making the learning process slow down so much, since it is not necessary to add great amount of training examples. Therefore, the introduction of a learning system becomes beneficial for recommending tags. Since example and feature selection improves the performance of a learning based TRS, it would be interesting to explore new approaches in that direction as future work.

References

1. Basile, P., Gendarmi, D., Lanubile, F., Semeraro, G.: Recommending smart tags in a social bookmarking system. In: Bridging the Gep between Semantic Web and Web 2.0 (SemNet 2007), pp. 22–29 (2007)
2. Keerthi, S.S., Lin, C.J., Weng, R.C.: Trust region newton method for logistic regression. Journal of Machine Learning Research (9), 627–650 (2008)
3. Hotho, A., Jäschke, R., Schmitz, C., Stumme, G.: Trend detection in folksonomies, pp. 56–70 (2006)
4. Järvelin, K., Kekäläinen, J.: Cumulated gain-based evaluation of ir techniques. ACM Trans. Inf. Syst. 20(4), 422–446 (2002)
5. Jäschke, R., Marinho, L., Hotho, A., Schmidt-Thieme, L., Stumme, G.: Tag recommendations in folksonomies. In: Hinneburg, A. (ed.) Proceedings of LWA 2007, September 2007, pp. 13–20 (2007)
6. Katakis, I., Tsoumakas, G., Vlahavas, I.: Multilabel text classification for automated tag suggestion. In: Proceedings of ECML PKDD Discovery Challenge (RSDC 2008), pp. 75–83 (2008)
7. Marinho, L., Schmidt-Thieme, L.: Collaborative tag recommendations. In: Studies in Classification, Data Analysis, and Knowledge Organization, pp. 533–540. Springer, Heidelberg (2008)
8. Sigurbjörnsson, B., van Zwol, R.: Flickr tag recommendation based on collective knowledge. In: Proceedings of WWW 2008, pp. 327–336. ACM, New York (2008)

A Hybrid Robotic Control System Using Neuroblastoma Cultures

J.M. Ferrández[1,2], V. Lorente[2], J.M. Cuadra[4], F. delaPaz[4],
José Ramón Álvarez-Sánchez[4], and E. Fernández[1,3]

[1] Instituto de Bioingeniería, Universidad Miguel Hernández, Alicante, Spain
[2] Departamento de Electrónica, Tecnología de Computadoras y Proyectos,
Universidad Politécnica de Cartagena, Spain
[3] CIBER-BBN, Spain
[4] Departamento de Inteligencia Artificial, UNED, Spain

Abstract. The main objective of this work is to analyze the computing capabilities of human neuroblastoma cultured cells and to define
connection schemes for controlling a robot behavior. Multielectrode Array (MEA) setups have been designed for direct culturing neural cells
over silicon or glass substrates, providing the capability to stimulate and
record simultaneously populations of neural cells. This paper describes
the process of growing human neuroblastoma cells over MEA substrates
and tries to modulate the natural physiologic responses of these cells by
tetanic stimulation of the culture. We show that the large neuroblastoma
networks developed in cultured MEAs are capable of learning: establishing numerous and dynamic connections, with modifiability induced by
external stimuli and we propose an hybrid system for controlling a robot
to avoid obstacles.

Keywords: Hybrid systems, cultured neural network, induced plasticity,
robotic control.

1 Introduction

Using biological nervous systems as conventional computer elements is a fascinat-
ing problem that permits the hybridization between Neuroscience and Computer
Science. There exist many research approaches based on mimicking this bioinspired parallel processing, not only from the algorithm perspective [1,5], but
also from the silicon circuits design. These bioinspired approaches are useful for
pattern recognition applications, like computer vision or robotics, however they
are implemented over serial and artificial silicon processors with fixed and static
structure. A real biological processor with millions of biological neurons and
a huge number of interconnections, would provide much more computational
power instead of their low transition rates due to high number of computing
elements and the extraordinary network capability of adaptation and reconfiguration to unknown environments. This extraordinary capability is related with
natural unsupervised learning.

M. Graña Romay et al. (Eds.): HAIS 2010, Part I, LNAI 6076, pp. 245–253, 2010.

Our learning experiments were performed in neural cultures containing 120.000 human neuroblastoma SH-SY5Y, under the assumption that this kind of cells are able to respond electrically to external stimuli and modulate their neural firing by changing the stimulation parameters. Such cultured neuroblastoma networks showed dynamical configurations, being able to develop and adapt functionally in response to external stimuli over a broad range of configuration patterns. We are especially interested in analyzing if populations of neuroblastoma cells are able to process and store information, and if learning can be implemented over this biological structure.

The main objective is to build a hybrid system integrating biological and electronic systems to achieve a new computational structure, able of robotic guidance in an obstacle avoidance task. MEA setups have been designed for direct culturing neural cells over silicon or glass substrates, providing the capability to stimulate and record simultaneously populations of neural cells. This paper describes the process of growing human neuroblastoma cells over MEA substrates and tries to modulate the natural physiologic responses of these cells by tetanic stimulation of the culture. We show that the large neuroblastoma networks developed in cultured MEAs are capable of learning: establishing numerous and dynamic connections, with modifiability induced by external stimuli and we propose an hybrid system for controlling a robot to avoid obstacles.

2   Human Neuroblastoma Cultures

Hebbian learning describes a basic mechanism for synaptic plasticity wherein an increase in synaptic efficacy arises from the presynaptic cells repeated and persistent stimulation of the postsynaptic cell. The theory is commonly evoked to explain some types of associative learning in which simultaneous activation of cells leads to pronounced increases in synaptic strength. The N-methyl-D-aspartate (NMDA) receptor, a subtype of the glutamate receptor, has been implicated as playing a key role in synaptic plasticity in the central nervous system [3], where as dopamine receptors are involved in the regulation of motor and cognitive behaviors. For most synaptic ion channels, activation (opening) requires only the binding of neurotransmitters. However, activation of the NMDA channel requires two events: binding of glutamate (a neurotransmitter) and relief of Mg2+ block. NMDA channels are located at the postsynaptic membrane. When the membrane potential is at rest, the NMDA channels are blocked by the Mg2+ ions. If the membrane potential is depolarized due to excitation of the postsynaptic neuron, the outward depolarizing field may repel Mg2+ out of the channel pore. On the other hand, binding of glutamate may open the gate of NMDA channels (the gating mechanisms of most ion channels are not known). In the normal physiological process, glutamate is released from the presynaptic terminal when the presynaptic neuron is excited. Relief of Mg2+ block is due to excitation of the postsynaptic neuron. Therefore, excitation of both presynaptic and postsynaptic neurons may open the NMDA channels, this is closely related with Hebbian learning.

In neuroscience, long-term potentiation (LTP) is a long-lasting enhancement in signal transmission between two neurons that results from stimulating them synchronously. It is one of several phenomena underlying synaptic plasticity, the ability of chemical synapses to change their strength. As memories are thought to be encoded by modification of synaptic strength, LTP is widely considered one of the major cellular mechanisms that underlies learning and memory. The term long-term potentiation comes from the fact that this increase in synaptic strength, or potentiation, lasts a very long time compared to other processes that affect synaptic strength. Induction of LTP occurs when the concentration of calcium inside the postsynaptic cell exceeds a critical threshold. In many types of LTP, the flow of calcium into the cell requires the NMDA receptor, which is why these types of LTP are considered to be NMDA receptor-dependent. NMDA receptor-dependent LTP can be induced experimentally by applying a few trains of high-frequency stimuli to the connection between two neurons, this is called tetanization, or tetanic stimulation. So, a tetanic stimulation consists of a high-frequency sequence of individual stimulations of a neuron. It is associated with long-term potentiation, the objective of this work. High-frequency stimulation causes an increase in transmitter release called post-tetanic potentiation [2]. This presynaptic event is caused by calcium influx. Calcium-protein interactions then produce a change in vesicle exocytosis. Some studies [6] use repetitive stimulation for training neural cultures, achieving activity potentiatiation or depresion.

A human neuroblastoma SH-SY5Y cell line, that express clonal specific human dopamine receptors, and also NMDA receptors, will be the biological platform for studying learning in cultured cells. Neuroblastoma SH-SY5Y cells are known to be dopaminergic, acetylcholinergic, glutamatergic and adenosinergic, so in this line they respond to different neurotransmitters. The cells have very different growth phases, as it can be seen in Figure 1a). The cells both propagate via mitosis and differentiate by extending neurites to the surrounding area. The dividing cells can form clusters of cells which are reminders of their cancerous nature, but chemicals can force the cells to dendrify and differentiate, in some kind of neuritic growth.

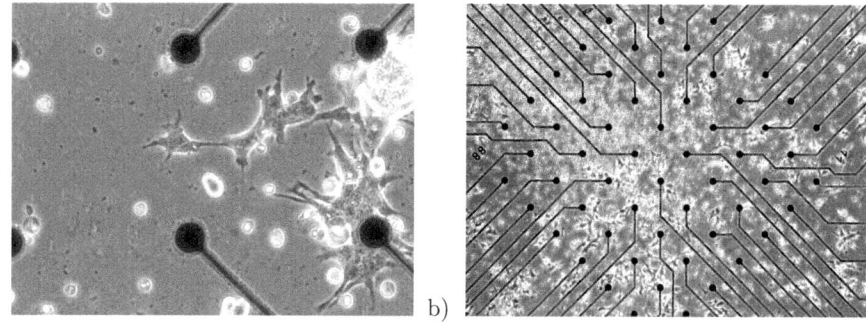

Fig. 1. a) Human neuroblastoma cells over multielectrode array. b)Biological neural network over MEA.

The neuroblastoma cultures are maintained in a 37 degree humidified incubator with 5% CO2 and 95% O2 with serum-free Neurobasal medium. Under the aforementioned conditions we were able to record stable electrophysiological signals over different days in vitro (div). The medium was replaced one-half of the medium every 5 days. At 10 div, the cells decrease their adhesion to the plate, so more of the population lost their contact with the metal elements and after 15 div, they get an embryonic configuration. So, the same neuroblastoma cells where seeded in polyethyleneimine (PEI) covered MEAs. The main drawback of this covering is that only few electrodes are covered with cells, because it stops the growing process, so we will get very limited responses from the whole electrode matrix. The choice is to have a lot of cells with strong adhesion to the electrodes a few days, or few covered electrodes with longer survival times.

3   Experimental Setup

The basic components of the proposed system are shown in Figure 2.

The substrate-embedded multielectrode array technology was used. It includes arrays of 60 Ti/Au/TiN electrodes, 30 microm in diameter, and spaced 200 microm from each other [MultiChannelSystems (MCS), Reutlingen, Germany]. A commercial 60 channel amplifier (B-MEA-1060; MCS) with frequency limits of 10–3000 Hz and a gain of 1024X was used. Stimulation through the MEA is performed using a dedicated two channel stimulus generator (MCS) able of time multiplexing the signals for stimulating the 60 electrodes in a nearly parallel process. The microincubation environment was arranged to support long-term recordings from MEA dishes by electrically heating the MEA platform to 37°C. Data were digitized using MCS analog-to-digital boards. Each channel is sampled at a frequency of 24,000 samples/sec and prepared for analysis using the MC-RACK softeware provide also by Multichannel Systems.

We use this system for remote obstacle avoidance, having the neuroblastoma culture mounted in an inverted microscope connected to the control unit, instead of having the cultures attached to the robot in an embedded system, that nowadays has many technical difficulties. The robot sends information about the environment to the computer using a bluetooth link and it has infrared sensors for detecting obstacles.

Neural spike events, embedded in the noisy signals, are detected by comparing the instantaneous electrode signals to level thresholds set for each data channel.

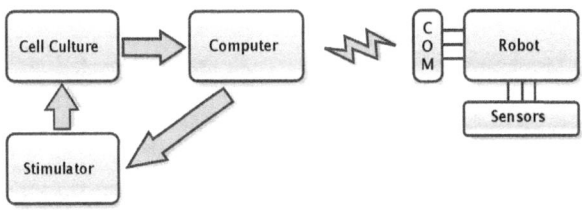

Fig. 2. Experimental Setup

The standard deviation of each data trace is used to estimate its spike threshold, a time interval of 500 ms is used to calculate it. The threshold is set as a multiple of the computed deviation, only values above will be extracted as spiking activity. The sign of the factor determines whether the spike detection level is positive or negative. A value between -1 and -4 is appropriate for most applications, in this work the threshold was set to -3. When a supra-threshold event occurs, the signal window surrounding the event was time-stamped and stored together with the state of the visual stimulus for later, offline analysis. For spike sorting we used a free program, NEV2lkit, which has been recently developed by our group and runs under Windows, MacOSX and Linux (source code and documentation is freely available [7]). NEV2lkit loads multielectrode data files in various formats (ASCII based formats, LabView formats, Neural Event Files, etc) and is able to sort extracted spikes from large sets of data. The sorting was done using principal component analysis (PCA) and performed simultaneously on many records from the same experiment.

4   Results

The cultured neuroblastoma cells establish synaptic connections. In Figure 1b) it can be seen differentiated and non-differentiated neuroblastoma cell bodies growing around the whole electrode population. The dendritic arborescence is more evident in the magnification Figure 1a) where differentiated neural cells surround the four electrodes while the rest of the cells are in their growing process. Figure 1b) corresponds to 80.000 neuroblastoma cells seeded in a no-poly-ethylene-imine (no-PEI) MEA at 2nd day in vitro (div).

The electrophysiological properties of the neuroblastoma cultures were analyzed by recording the spontaneous activity of the network. Time course of experiments was over 15 days; recordings were done using two MCS-Meas with two neuroblastoma cell cultures (but only in one the cells survived till day 15). In vitro neuroblastoma networks show spontaneously firing. The firing rates change during the culture development with marked day differences and the global rate is closely related to the age of the network.

The physiological recordings correspond to neuroblastoma cultures in the range of 1-7 div. They show bursting and spiking activity, with usually negative depolarizations. Figure 3a) shows the spiking activity of the neural population with an automatic detection level for each electrode. This is very convenient if you have multiple channels for extracting spikes.

During the neuroblastoma development, a wide range of population bursting or showing synchronized activity has been observed, according to some studies in neural cultures preparations [8]. The burst usually contains a large number of spikes at many channels, with variable duration, from milliseconds to seconds.

4.1   Tetanic Stimulation

Spontaneous activity was recorded for intervals of 3 minutes before stimulation (PRE-data), and the total number of spikes extracted was counted. The biphasic

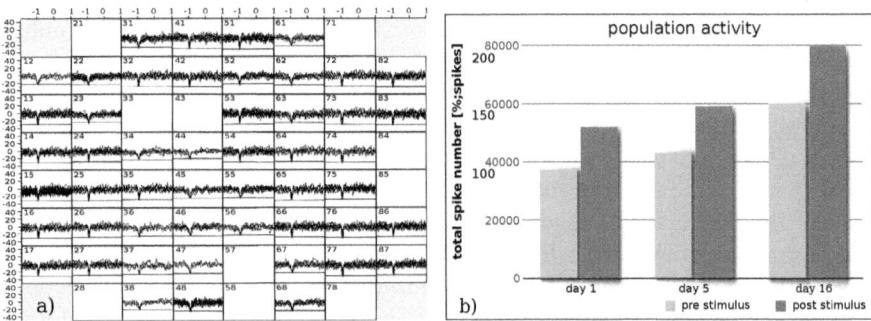

Fig. 3. a) Spontaneous neural activity detected by the multielectrode array. b) Induced neural activity by tetanization stimuli.

stimulus consists in a 10 trains of a 100 anodic-first waveform with 1 Volt amplitude delivered to all 60 electrodes in order to propagate a tetanization stimulus to the neuroblastoma culture.

Once the tetanization stimulus was applied to the whole population 5 minutes after the stimulation a 3 minutes interval was recorded (POST-data). Only neuronal signals which had at least a 2:1 signal:noise ratio were valued as "spikes". Again, the total number of spikes extracted was counted. This process was made for cultures at 1 day in vitro (div), 5 div and 16 div. Figure 3b) represents the counted spikes with bar charts for the different recordings. The conclusions from this figure are: 1) While the neuroblastoma culture is growing new connections are created, and the number of spikes increases as the culture expands over the MEA. 2) After a tetanic stimulation the cells continue with their increased spiking rate, providing a persistent change in the culture behavior. When a change in the network response lasts, such a change can be called learning.

In all the experimentation performed, tetanic stimulation was applied as training method, and the electrophysiological properties of the neuroblastoma culture change, getting a potentiation effect on the spontaneous firing, modulating in this way the culture neural activity.

4.2 Robotic Control

For controlling the direction of the robot we propose to compute the vector resulting from neural activity recorded in the human neuroblastoma culture. This vector will be provided to the robot in order to guide its movement. The sensors will detect the obstacles, and the information will be passed to the computer in order to induce a selective tetanization of the biological neural network for changing the resulting direction vector. In Figure 4a), the selected electrodes for the tetanization are shown in order to selectively induce a persistent change in the biological neural network behavior.

When the robot detects an obstacle at the left of its path, an stimulation signal will be sent to the system for tetanizing the left tissue. By tetanization of

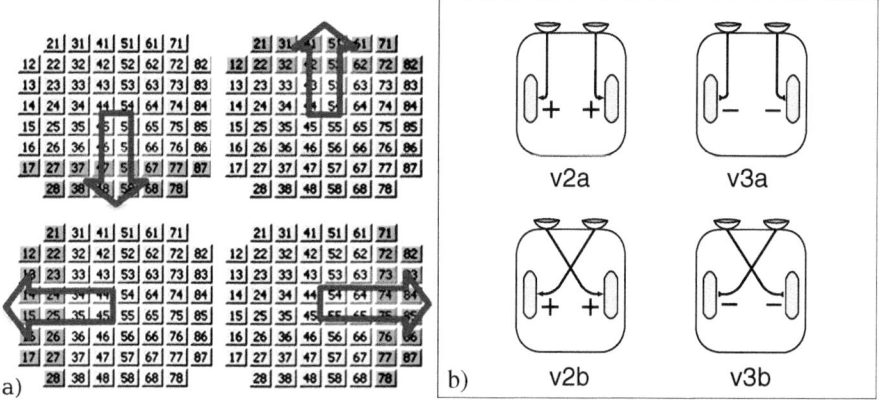

Fig. 4. a) Selective electrode tetanization. b) Simple Braitenberg's vehicles showing sensory motor connections.

the electrodes at the left part of the array, an increase in the firing rate of the neural cells laying in this area of the culture will be achieved. If each culture side is connected to the corresponding robot motor, we get a direction vector for the robot pointing to the right in this particular case.

5 Discussion

Valentino Braitenberg [4] describes the different behaviors originated by simple neural sensory motor circuits. In his experimental research, he found that very simple neural structure give rise to very complex and astonishing behaviors. These behaviors, independent from its underlying neural structure, are known as fear, anger... and so on.

The neural robotic control system proposed in this paper aims to implement Braitenberg´s vehicles. The proposed system is oriented to obstacle avoidance with the following scheme: an increase in the neural activity of lateral part of the culture will imply an increase of the speed in the corresponding robot motor, Braitenberg's vehicle v2a, see Figures 4b) and 5. If the scheme is transposed in a cross-modal connection, that is every part of the culture is connected to the opposite lateral motor, the robot behavior changes, orienting its direction to the stimulus source, Braitenberg's vehicle v2b. This behavior could be seen as attacking or pursuing the source.

If we include inhibitory connections instead of excitatory ones, the behavior also changes, Braitenberg's vehicles v3a and v3b. The obstacle-avoiding robot would decrease its speed as it approaches the source, stopping in front of it, while the source attacking robot would also decrease its speed as it reaches the source, but any perturbation on the source intensity would achieve escaping from it.

If we have two different sensory systems, one can be used for an obstacle avoidance task, while the other for detecting the source-goal. The combination

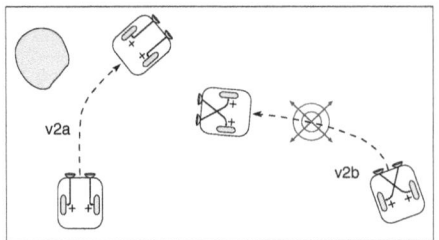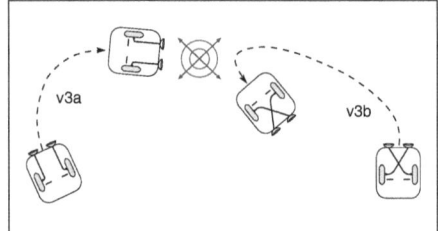

Fig. 5. Braitenberg's vehicles behaviors

of both systems would induce reaching a certain goal while avoiding obstacles, the main objective in autonomous robotics. In such scenario it is essential to define the subsystems priority: if the goal to reach is behind some obstacles, the obstacle avoidance task must impose over the reaching-goal task. This priority can be implemented by inhibiting the goal-reaching task when an obstacle is detected.

In conclusion, the first definition for building the biologically robotic control system is the number of neuroblastoma cultures to use: if two neural cultures are used, one for each sensory system, and hence for each behavior, there must exist some inhibition mechanism for blocking the neural activity of the reaching-goal culture when an obstacle is detected. On the other hand if there exist only one neural culture for both tasks, some inhibitory connections should be induced over the culture in order to define the priority system over the neural subpopulations.

The first solution, two neural cultures, is a very expensive solution, because the 64-channel registering-stimulation system has an elevate cost, and the equipment mounted over an inverted microscope. This solution should be connected to the same computer that must analyze the neural activity of each culture for implementing the inhibition strategies. In addition each culture must be stimulated using different Braitenberg principles in order to define the desired behavior task.

The second solution could be implemented training different parts of the cultures with different Braitenberg paradigms and defining inhibitory connections between both areas. This solution requires culturing, training and reading neural cells in parallel, defining different stimulation paradigms for different neural subpopulations. The main difficulty is that the growing process of the culture is not homogeneous over the Multielectrode Array, evoking distinct neural activity patterns. In this case it is needed a normalizing process for getting homogeneous activity on the electrodes, or improving the growing protocols for seeding and culturing homogeneous biological neuroblastoma networks. A third solution could consist in a hybrid system with one behavior implemented over the biological culture and the other in the hardware that is reading the neural activity, implementing a biological-silicon super-structure. The limitation is the number of electrodes available for reading/stimulating the neural tissue that in our system is 64 bidirectional electrodes. An optical stimulation of the tissue would provide much more spatial resolution, and inhibition procedures, so we are working in selective genetic programing the neuroblastoma cultures for optical stimulation, using in this way many visual processes, we call it optogenetic neuroblastoma culture.

References

1. Anderson, J.A., Rosenfeld, E.: Neurocomputing: Foundations of research. MIT Press, Cambridge (1998)
2. Antonov, I., Antonova, I., Kandel, E.R.: Activity-dependent presynaptic facilitation and hebbian ltp are both required and interact during classical conditioning in aplysia. Neuron 37(1), 135–147 (2003)
3. Bading, H., Greenberg, M.E.: Stimulation of protein tyrosine phosphorylation by nmda receptor activation. Science 253(5022), 912–914 (1991)
4. Braitenberg, V.: Vehicles: Experiments in Synthetic Psichology. MIT Press, Cambridge (1984)
5. Duro, R.J., Graña, M., de Lope, J.: On the potential contributions of hybrid intelligent approaches to multicomponent robotic system development. Information Sciences (2010) (in Press)
6. Jimbo, Y., Robinson, H.P., Kawana, A.: Strengthening of synchronized activity by tetanic stimulation in cortical cultures: application of planar electrode arrays. IEEE Transactions on Biomedical Engineering 45(11), 1297–1304 (1998)
7. Micol, D.: Nev2lkit (2006), http://nev2lkit.sourceforge.net/
8. Wagenaar, D.A., Pine, J., Potter, S.M.: An extremely rich repertoire of bursting patterns during the development of cortical cultures. BMC Neuro-science 7, 11 (2006)

Image Segmentation with a Hybrid Ensemble of One-Class Support Vector Machines

Bogusław Cyganek

AGH University of Science and Technology
Al. Mickiewicza 30, 30-059 Kraków, Poland
`cyganek@agh.edu.pl`

Abstract. In this paper an efficient method of image segmentation from large data samples is presented. Segmentation is stated as a novelty detection problem for which the one-class support vector machines (OC-SVM) are employed. However, to improve performance and scalability the input space of samples is first k-means partitioned, and then each partition is independently trained with an OC-SVM. This way a parallel structure of expert classifiers is obtained with of a small average number of support vectors and high precision.

1 Introduction

Segmentation of images belongs to one of the fundamental tasks of CV [4]. In some cases segmentation can be based on characteristic features of point samples, such as color or texture. If the samples concern one group of objects, such as road signs or human skin, then the problem can be defined as novelty detection in an image for which the OC-SVM are known to give good results [14][0][1]. However, for more complicated groups of samples better results can be obtained if the input space is first efficiently segmented and then each segment is bounded by a dedicated classifier.

The idea of building hybrid ensembles of classifiers has found much attention for years [13][10][12][8]. In this context some works were devoted to development of efficient methods of such feature selection which allow the best results of classification. For instance Kuncheva in [9] analyses a problem of data clustering *followed by* selection of the most successful classifier which is then allowed to label data in the Voronoi cell of the cluster centroid. Thus, the two steps of clustering and choosing the best classifier are separate. The recent work by Jackowski and Woźniak [6] shows an adaptive extension to the method by Kuncheva. Their main idea is to combine the two steps of clustering and selection of the best classifier into a unified evolutionary process of searching for the best division of the space *and* commitment of available classifiers. For the latter they use the backpropagation neural networks.

In this paper we propose a version of the above approach with special aim at computer vision applications. The method does image segmentation based on a preselected set of prototype data points. The input data set is proposed first to be partitioned with the k-means into a complete group of disjoint data sets. Then a novel proposition is to train each set with a single OC-SVM classifier which requires only *two* parameters to be determined. Such an ensemble of classifiers is then used for segmentation of unknown images. The proposed system is an extension to our method

M. Graña Romay et al. (Eds.): HAIS 2010, Part I, LNAI 6076, pp. 254–261, 2010.
© Springer-Verlag Berlin Heidelberg 2010

[3] which allows better accuracy, a highly parallel structure of experts, and a lower average number of support vectors. The experiments showed good results in a problem of human skin segmentation, as well as in detection of the road signs.

2   Building an Ensemble of Boundary Classifiers

Much effort has been devoted for development of efficient and accurate segmentation of color images. The first example is human skin segmentation [5][7][11]. Other example is a task of road signs detection based on characteristic colors. The solutions are based on fuzzy logic [1], OC-SVM [3], etc.

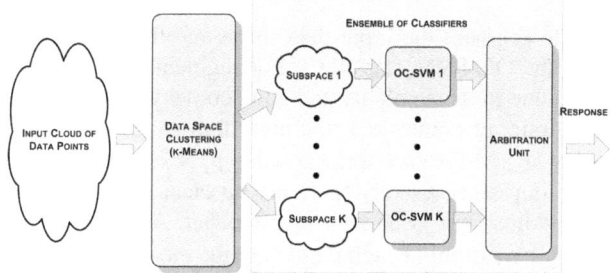

Fig. 1. Structure of the ensemble of classifiers for image segmentation

However, it was observed that for some problems the OC-SVM fits poorly to data. In such cases the hypersphere that encompasses data is either too large, which leads to the increase of the false positive rate, or it requires an excessive amount of support vectors (SVs). In the latter case the generalization abilities of the classifier are greatly reduced. Quantitatively the data fit parameter can be measured with

$$\rho_i = \frac{\# SV_i}{\# D_i}, \tag{1}$$

where $\#SV_i$ is a number of support vectors for a given data set D_i. In practice good classification results were obtained for $\rho_i < 0.1$. In turn, this parameter depends on two parameters of the OC-SVM which are width σ of the Gaussian kernel and the training parameter v, which can be found by the grid search. However, for some data sets a satisfactory ρ_i cannot be obtained due to data complexity even in the feature space.

Thus, our idea is *to split the initial data space* into separate and as compact as possible clusters and then train individual OC-SVM classifiers with each of the clusters. All of them constitute a committee machine which unique response is provided from the arbitration unit. Fig. 1 depicts a parallel architecture of the proposed system. In the case of an ensemble of classifiers the criterion (1) becomes

$$\rho = \sum_{i=1}^{M} \rho_i = \sum_{i=1}^{M} \frac{\# SV_i}{\# D_i}, \tag{2}$$

where M denotes number of members of the ensemble and each D_i is a subset of data. As will be shown in the next section, the input space D is partitioned into a set $\{D_i\}$ with an unsupervised clustering method. Thus, there are $2M$ parameters to be found. However, the problem gets complicated since those depend on partitioning of data. Therefore optimization of (2) imposes optimization of the data clustering process.

In our realization the aforementioned optimization problem was simplified. For clustering the k-means method was used [4]. The unknown is the number M of means and their initial values. The former is chosen usually on an additional knowledge or on experiments. The initial values are randomly drawn from the input data set.

3 Input Space Segmentation

Our main idea is to segment the input data space and then to use each cluster independently to train the OC-SVM classifiers. For segmentation we use the well known k-means algorithm due to its simplicity and good convergence properties.

Given a set of training points $\{x_i\}$, the algorithm starts with choice of the initial number of clusters D_i and for each a mean value μ_i is selected. In practice this is the most troublesome step since usually there are no clear criteria about the number of clusters. We will address this issue later in this paper. After initialization the method proceeds iteratively by assigning each point x_i to the closest mean μ_m in a cluster $D(i)$ in accordance with the following

$$D(i) = \arg\min_{1 \le m \le M} \|x_i - \mu_m\|_L ,\tag{3}$$

where $\|.\|_L$ denotes a chosen distance metric (most common is the Euclidean), and M is the number of clusters. Then each mean value is recomputed as follows

$$\mu_m = \frac{1}{\#D_m} \sum_{x_i \in D_m} x_i .\tag{4}$$

The above steps (3) and (4) follow until convergence state is reached, i.e. there are no changes in means and in the point assignments to the clusters.

A qualitative insight into the k-means clustering can be gained by analyzing the total sums of distances

$$S_m = \sum_{x \in D_m} \|x - \mu_m\|^2 , \text{ and } S_t = \sum_{m=1}^{M} S_m .\tag{5}$$

which should be as minimal as possible since k-means does not guarantee the globally optimal solution, though in practice it converges very fast. In other words, different starting conditions (i.e. number and positions of the means) can provide different solutions. Moreover, for a given solution it is difficult to tell whether it is optimal.

In our task the population $\{x_i\}$ denotes sample points with characteristic colors collected manually from many exemplars of real images. Although different color spaces were tried, we found out that in the segmentation stage the RGB space is the best. However, other color spaces perform better in the case of the OC-SVM classifiers, as will be discussed in the next section.

4 Boundary Description with One-Class SVM

Support Vector Machines (SVM) were proposed by V. Vapnik and collaborators [1]. However, in many problems only exemplars of one data class are available or there is a big discrepancy between number of samples in the classes. In such cases we are interested in finding a boundary of a distribution of the points from one class. Then, a test point is classified as belonging to the class if it falls inside the bounded region.

As shown by Schölkopf *et al.* [14], the single-class problem for a given set of data $\{x_i\}$ can be stated as computing such a hyperplane w (Fig. 2)

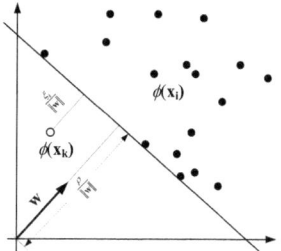

Fig. 2. The separating hyperplane in the feature space Φ. Support vectors (SV) are on the hyperplane, outliers are outside and are controlled by the slack variables ξ.

$$\langle w, x \rangle - \rho = 0 \tag{6}$$

that separates $\{x_i\}$ with *the maximal margin* from the origin. $\langle a, b \rangle$ denotes an inner product between vectors a and b. At the same time it is allowed to have some outliers in the set $\{x_i\}$. This can be accounted for as the convex optimization problem

$$\min_{w, \xi_1 \ldots \xi_N, \rho} \left[\frac{1}{2} \|w\|^2 + \frac{1}{vN} \sum_{n=1}^{N} \xi_n - \rho \right], \text{ with } \underset{1 \le n \le N}{\forall} \ \langle w, x_n \rangle \ge \rho - \xi_n, \ \ \xi_n \ge 0. \tag{7}$$

In the above ξ_n are called slack variables, N is a number of points in $\{x_i\}$, and v is a parameter that controls expected number of outliers in data. The problem (7) can be solved by means of the Lagrange multipliers. Its dual Wolfe representation is

$$\min_{\alpha_1 \ldots \alpha_N} \left[\sum_{n=1}^{N} \sum_{m=1}^{N} \alpha_n \alpha_m \langle x_n, x_m \rangle \right], \text{ with } \underset{1 \le n \le N}{\forall} \ 0 \le \alpha_n \le \frac{1}{vN}, \text{ and } \sum_{n=1}^{N} \alpha_n = 1. \tag{8}$$

In the above α_n denote the Lagrange multipliers. The solution to (8) can be obtained with e.g. the SMO algorithm [14]. It is a series of N values of α_n^* (some of which can be 0) each associated to a single data point. The points for which their corresponding $\alpha_n^* > 0$ lie on the hyperplane w and are called the support vectors (SV). The hyperplane w can be expressed as an α-weighted sum of the SVs

$$w = \sum_{n \in SVs} \alpha_n x_n, \tag{9}$$

since for all other points (other than SVs) their $\alpha_i = 0$. Thus, taking any support vector x_m a distance of the hyperplane to the origin is

$$\rho = \langle \mathbf{w}, \mathbf{x}_m \rangle = \sum_{n \in SVs} \alpha_n \langle \mathbf{x}_n, \mathbf{x}_m \rangle. \tag{10}$$

Taking above into consideration a distance of a test point $\mathbf{x}_x$ to the hyperplane is $\langle \mathbf{w}, \mathbf{x}_x \rangle$ which, if greater than ρ, indicates that a point belongs to the class, i.e. if

$$\sum_{n \in SVs} \alpha_n \langle \mathbf{x}_n, \mathbf{x}_x \rangle \geq \underbrace{\sum_{n \in SVs} \alpha_n \langle \mathbf{x}_n, \mathbf{x}_m \rangle}_{\rho}. \tag{11}$$

It is worth noting that the value of ρ used in the condition (11) can be precomputed.

The above derivations can be extended into the feature domain substituting each $\mathbf{x}$ for a certain mapping function $\Phi(\mathbf{x})$. However, we easily notice that the decision equation (11) involves exclusively an inner product between vectors. In the feature space this transforms into a kernel computation, as follows

$$K\left(\mathbf{x}_i, \mathbf{x}_j\right) = \Phi^T\left(\mathbf{x}_i\right)\Phi\left(\mathbf{x}_j\right), \tag{12}$$

which is a scalar value. In our experiments we used the Gaussian kernel

$$K_G\left(\mathbf{x}_i, \mathbf{x}_j\right) = e^{-\gamma\|\mathbf{x}_i - \mathbf{x}_j\|^2}, \tag{13}$$

where the parameter γ controls its spread. For this type of kernel it can be shown that the above derivation is equivalent to the hypersphere formulation presented by Tax *et al.* [0], which was also used in [3].

5   System Training and the Run-Time Arbitration

The goal of the system training is to achieve the best performance measured as the best accuracy and fast operation. In practice however, the accuracy factor is difficult to measure, since we lack sufficient reference data. The only available ones are samples of the points of interest. To some extend performance can be measured with (1). In other words, we found experimentally that if for some SVM (1) is greater than 0.1 then performance is usually inferior. Based on the above we propose the following optimization algorithm:

1. Select a number of clusters M, which determines number of expert OC-SVM classifiers. For practical reasons this was in the range 1-25.
   Select number of trials T.
2. For each $1 \leq m \leq M$:
   3. Do T times:
      4. Randomly select the centers μ_m and run the k-means procedure.
      5. For each partition D_i search the best parameters v and γ to train its expert OC-SVM such as to maximally separate D_i. In experiments we used the grid search over $v \in \{0.005, 0.01, 0.05\}$ and $0.001 \leq \gamma \leq 48$ in steps of 0.02.
      6. Train each OC-SVM with the best parameters found in the previous step. Compute its fitness measure (1).
      7. Compute the overall fitness measure (2) and if it is *minimal* store the whole configuration (all α and SVs).

During point testing each expert OC-SVM provides its yes/no answer. The arbitration unit, presented in Fig. 1, is responsible for selecting the final answer of the ensemble. However, it can happen that a point is classified as a positive by more than one classifier. Therefore in our system we assumed that a test point is classified as a positive one iff it is classified as a positive one *exclusively by one of the experts* in the ensemble. This leads to the best precision of the system.

6 Experimental Results

The entire system was implemented in C++ and run on the computer with the 2GB RAM and with the processor Pentium Core 2 T7600 @ 2.33GHz. Below we present results obtained in a set of 16 different images in which 11174 skin sample points were manually selected. Then all the points are k-means segmented into disjoint partitions. These partitions do not necessarily follow image boundaries. Then each partition is used to train a dedicated OC-SVM. More precisely, randomly selected 90% of a partition is used for training, whereas the rest 10% for validation. This process is repeated for iteratively changed parameters γ and ν. The best value in terms of correct answers and #SV is stored.

Table 1. Values of five partitions in our experiment: number of points in each cluster, cumulative distance in each cluster, number of support vectors necessary to bound a cluster

m, for $M=5$	$\#D_m$	S_m	#SVs
0	2956	1 428 400	9
1	2500	1 326 400	6
2	3894	1 303 600	7
3	831	700 021	8
4	993	518 922	7

Table 1 contains number of exemplars in each of the $M=5$ partitions alongside with the corresponding distance sums S_m, and with the corresponding number of the SVs.

For the same data set we also built the system for $M=1$ and $M=10$ partitions. Comparison of the performance for all three setups presents Table 2.

Table 2. Performance parameters for different number M of initial clusters

M	1	5	10
Av. #SVs	8	7	9
Av. answer time [s] per image (318x480)	1.9	2.2	3.6
Av. precision	0.77	0.89	0.94

Fig. 3 depicts operation of the system on one of the test images that was not used in training. This is checked with different number of partitions of the input data set of RGB samples. We easily notice that using more than one OC-SVM leads to better accuracy (Fig. 3b,c,d), retaining the generalization capabilities at the same time.

As alluded to previously, in our experiments the best partitioning of the initial space with the k-means algorithm was obtained in the RGB color space. However, it happened often that for the RBF OC-SVM slightly better results were obtained with the Farnsworth color space. In general this can depend on a data set and the kernel. Parameter M was in the range of 1 to 25, and T was set to 5-10. Since we assume there are only singular outliers in the training data set, the parameter v was chosen from the set of three values {0.005, 0.01, 0.05}, whereas $0.05 \le \gamma \le 64$, in steps of 0.05.

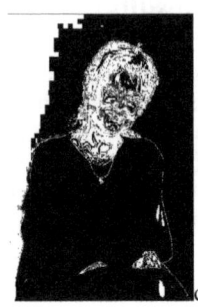

Fig. 3. Results of image segmentation for skin detection. An original 318x480 image (a). Segmentation for k=1, i.e. one expert OC-SVM (b), for k=5 (c), k=10 (d). In all variants the best training parameters γ and v were found by cross validation.

The presented method was also tested for the road signs detection problem in [3], i.e. for which M=1. For M>1 this version outperforms the method in [3], which agrees also with conclusions presented in the paper by Kuncheva [9]. In this experiment two data sets were used, one for the red signs with 6159 samples, the second with 7035 samples of yellow points.

7 Conclusions

In this paper we propose a hybrid classification system which allows classification of data belonging to one class. The method was applied and tested in the task of image segmentation based on manually selected color samples of the human skin. However, the areas of application can be much wider, such as e.g. medical or image annotation.

Based on our experiments and observation we can conclude with the following characteristics of the method.

Pros:

1. The number of clusters M can start from 1 which means only one "classical" OC-SVM;
2. Different features can be used for segmentation and different for training of the OC-SVM thus introducing an *a priori* knowledge;
3. The method naturally builds a parallel structure (possible improvement of performance);
4. System can be used for novelty detection (e.g. tumors in medical images, malfunctions of a machinery, etc.), as well as other applications such as image annotations, etc.

Cons:

1. The best configuration can depend on a data set; The number of parameters to set is $2M+1$;
2. There are not strict rules on choosing some parameters, such as M, T, and γ.
3. If well balanced positive/negative data sets are available then classical binary SVM can lead to better results [0].

Our C++ implementation have not yet taken an advantage of a highly parallel structure of the system. However, we easily notice that an average number of SVs does not increase, and sometimes even decreases, for larger M (Table 2). Therefore in parallel implementation there should be no significant run-time penalty.

Acknowledgement

This work was supported from the Polish funds for scientific research in 2010.

The author would like to express his gratitude to the reviewers for their comments, as well as to the following students who helped in preparation of the data sets: M. Dankiewicz, D. Kalicki, I. Piekarz, J. Sorocki, J. Tobijasiewicz, and Nadia Cyganek.

References

1. Boser, B., Guyon, I., Vapnik, V.: An training algorithm for optimal margin classifiers. In: Fifth Annual Workshop on Computational Learning Theory, pp. 144–152. ACM, New York (1992)
2. Cyganek, B.: Soft System for Road Sign Detection. Theory and Applications of Fuzzy Logic and Soft Computing, Advances in Soft Computing 41, 316–326 (2007)
3. Cyganek, B.: Color Image Segmentation With Support Vector Machines: Applications To Road Signs Detection. International Journal of Neural Systems 18(4), 339–345 (2008)
4. Duda, R., Hart, P., Stork, D.: Pattern Classification. Wiley, Chichester (2001)
5. Hsu, R.-L., Abdel-Mottaleb, M., Jain, A.K.: Face Detection in Color Images. IEEE PAMI 24(5), 696–707 (2002)
6. Jackowski, K., Wozniak, M.: Algorithm of designing compound recognition system on the basis of combining classifiers with simultaneous splitting feature space into competence areas. Pattern Analysis and Applications 12, 415–425 (2009)
7. Jones, M.J., Rehg, J.M.: Statistical Color Models with Application to Pixel-Level Human Skin Detection. In: IEEE Int. Conf. Pattern Recognition, vol. 1, pp. 1056–1059 (2000)
8. Kittler, J., Hatef, M., Duing, R.P.W., Matas, J.: On Combining Classifiers. IEEE PAMI 20(3), 226–239 (1998)
9. Kuncheva, L.I.: Cluster-and-selection method for classifier combination. In: Proc. 4th International Conference on Knowledge-Based Intelligent Engineering Systems & Allied Technologies (KES 2000), Brighton, UK, pp. 185–188 (2000)
10. Kuncheva, L.I.: Combining Pattern Classifiers. Wiley, Chichester (2004)
11. Phung, S.L., Bouzerdoum, A., Chai, D.: Skin Segmentation Using Color Pixel Classification: Analysis and Comparison. IEEE PAMI 27(1), 148–154 (2005)
12. Polikar, R.: Ensemble Based Systems in Decision Making. IEEE Magazine, 21–45 (2006)
13. Rastrigin, L.A., Erenstein, R.H.: Method of Collective Recognition, Energoizdat, Moscow (1981) (in Russian)
14. Schölkopf, B., Smola, A.J.: Learning with Kernels. MIT Press, Cambridge (2002); Tax, D., Duin, R.: Support Vector Data Description. Machine Learning, 45–66 (2004)

Power Prediction in Smart Grids with Evolutionary Local Kernel Regression

Oliver Kramer, Benjamin Satzger, and Jörg Lässig

International Computer Science Institute, Berkeley CA 94704, USA
{okramer,satzger,jla}@icsi.berkeley.edu
http://www.icsi.berkeley.edu/

Abstract. Electric grids are moving from a centralized single supply chain towards a decentralized bidirectional grid of suppliers and consumers in an uncertain and dynamic scenario. Soon, the growing smart meter infrastructure will allow the collection of terabytes of detailed data about the grid condition, e.g., the state of renewable electric energy producers or the power consumption of millions of private customers, in very short time steps. For reliable prediction strong and fast regression methods are necessary that are able to cope with these challenges. In this paper we introduce a novel regression technique, i.e., evolutionary local kernel regression, a kernel regression variant based on local Nadaraya-Watson estimators with independent bandwidths distributed in data space. The model is regularized with the CMA-ES, a stochastic non-convex optimization method. We experimentally analyze the load forecast behavior on real power consumption data. The proposed method is easily parallelizable, and therefore well appropriate for large-scale scenarios in smart grids.

1 Introduction

If we want to design smarter electric grids that are more adaptive or even "intelligent", the large amount of information about the grid status, e.g., current wind or solar energy production, or actual power demands of customers must be considered. Prediction is important for energy saving and cost efficient real-time decisions. An increasing infrastructure of smart meters at the level of consumers is supported by governmental laws in many countries, and is currently leading to an explosion of data about electric grids. Already today, smart meters are able to yield the consumption status of each customer every second. To be able to analyze this large amount of data, strong large-scale techniques have to be developed that allow precise predictions of power supply and power consumption behaviors, e.g., to avoid voltage band violations. For each customer, a short-, mid-, and long-term profile can be computed, leading to a precise estimation of future energy consumption habits. The development of large-scale data mining techniques in a distributed computing scenario becomes an essential challenge in smart energy grids.

A survey of methods for the prediction of power supply and demand give Alfares and Nazeeruddin [3]. They classify related methods into nine classes, from

M. Graña Romay et al. (Eds.): HAIS 2010, Part I, LNAI 6076, pp. 262–269, 2010.
© Springer-Verlag Berlin Heidelberg 2010

multiple regression to expert systems. But most methods are not parallelizable or demand a new and expensive training process if the data archive is changed. Short-term load forecasting with kernel regression has been proposed by Agarwal *et al.* [2]. They compared kernel regression to artificial neural networks, ordinary least squares and ridge regression. We will propose a more flexible kernel regression hybrid in this paper. Prediction in energy systems is not only restricted to load forecasting, but also concentrates on other properties. As an example, Nogales *et al.* [9] analyze dynamic regression and transfer function models to forecast next-day electricity prices. Lora *et al.* [7] also predict next-days prizes using a weighted nearest neighbors approach, concentrating on parameter determination, e.g., size of time series windows and number K of neighbors.

In this paper we introduce a novel hybrid regression method that we think is well appropriate to solve these tasks. It unifies kernel regression and evolutionary computation. In Section 2 we introduce evolutionary local kernel regression (ELKR), and discuss, how ELKR can be parallelized for large-scale decentralized smart grid scenarios. Section 3 shows an experimental analysis on real data of power demand in electricity grids. Finally, Section 4 summarizes the results and provides an outlook to future work.

2   Evolutionary Local Kernel Regression

2.1   The Nadaraya-Watson Estimator

Kernel regression is a non-parametric approach and allows fast estimations for reasonable bandwidth choices. It is based on the Nadaraya-Watson estimator that has been introduced by Nadaraya and Watson [8,12]. We assume that $(\mathbf{x}_1, \mathbf{y}_1), \dots, (\mathbf{x}_N, \mathbf{y}_N)$ is a set of N recorded input output values, e.g., N recorded power consumption values within a particular time period. For an unknown $\mathbf{x}'$ we like to forecast $\mathbf{f}(\mathbf{x}')$. Kernel regression is based on a density estimate of data samples with a kernel function K. A typical kernel function is the Gaussian kernel:

$$K_{\mathbf{H}}(\mathbf{z}) = \frac{1}{(2\pi)^{q/2}\det(\mathbf{H})} \exp\left(-\frac{1}{2}\left|\mathbf{H}^{-1}\mathbf{z}\right|^2\right). \tag{1}$$

The kernel density function becomes a measure for the *density* of two points $\mathbf{x}_1, \mathbf{x}_2$, if their distance $\mathbf{z} = |\mathbf{x}_1 - \mathbf{x}_2|$ is fed into the function. An essential part of kernel regression is the bandwidth h that becomes a diagonal matrix $\mathbf{H} = \mathrm{diag}(h_1, h_2, \dots, h_d)$ in case of the multivariate expression. Parameter q is scaling the Gaussian function in height, and usually set to $q = 1$. The sum of density estimates of an unknown point $\mathbf{x}$ and all data samples, multiplied with the corresponding function values, yield the Nadaraya-Watson estimate for $\mathbf{f}(\mathbf{x}; \mathbf{H})$, i.e.:

$$\mathbf{f}(\mathbf{x}; \mathbf{H}) = \sum_{i=1}^{N} \mathbf{y}_i \frac{K_{\mathbf{H}}(\mathbf{x} - \mathbf{x}_i)}{\sum_{j=1}^{N} K_{\mathbf{H}}(\mathbf{x} - \mathbf{x}_j)}. \tag{2}$$

Hence, each sample $(\mathbf{x}_i, \mathbf{y}_i)$ contributes to the prediction of the function value of $\mathbf{x}$, weighted by the normalized (denominator) kernel densities in data space.

If we assume that the results of N kernel density computations can be saved, each prediction can be computed in $\mathcal{O}(N)$. If the model is trained with regard to the bandwidth matrix $\mathbf{H}$ on the training set, it may over-adapt to the training examples, and loose the ability to generalize, an effect known as overfitting. Overfitting is likely to happen if the training set's size is small, or if the number of free parameters of a model is comparatively large. Small bandwidth values lead to an overfitted prediction function, while high values generalize too much. To avoid overfitting, Clark [5] proposed to select the bandwidth matrix $\mathbf{H}$ as result of LOO-CV. The idea of determining the optimal bandwidth matrix $\mathbf{H}$ by LOOC-CV is to apply the Nadaraya-Watson estimator, leaving out the data pair $(\mathbf{x}_i, \mathbf{y}_i)$ for each summand. The resulting error function that has to be minimized is:

$$e_{loocv} = \frac{1}{N} \sum_{i=1}^{N} \|\mathbf{y}_i - \mathbf{f}_{-i}(\mathbf{x}_i; \mathbf{H})\|_2 \tag{3}$$

$$= \frac{1}{N} \sum_{i=1}^{N} \|\mathbf{y}_i - \sum_{j \neq i} \frac{K_{\mathbf{H}}(\mathbf{x}_i, \mathbf{x}_j)}{\sum_{k \neq i} K_{\mathbf{H}}(\mathbf{x}_j, \mathbf{x}_k)} \mathbf{y}_j\|_2 \tag{4}$$

Here, $\mathbf{f}_{-i}$ denotes the Nadaraya-Watson estimator leaving out the i-th data point. All points, without the data sample $\mathbf{y}_i$ itself, contribute to the estimation of $\mathbf{f}(\mathbf{x}_i)$.

2.2   Extending Kernel Regression to ELKR

This section enhances kernel regression by the concept of locality, the evolution of kernel parameters, and minimization of the prediction error with a stochastic optimization method. The concepts are introduced in detail in the following.

Local Models. To handle multiple data space conditions in different areas of the data space, we introduce the concept of locality. Each Nadaraya-Watson model is specified by a codebook vector $\mathbf{c}_i$ from the set of codebook vectors $\mathcal{C} = (\mathbf{c}_1, \cdots, \mathbf{c}_K) \in \mathbb{R}^q$ in latent space. A data element $(\mathbf{x}_i, \mathbf{y}_i)$ is assigned to the Nadaraya-Watson model $\mathbf{f}_{k^*}(\mathbf{x}_i; \mathbf{H}_{k^*})$ with minimal distance to its codebook vector, i.e., $k^* = \arg\min_k \|\mathbf{x}_i - \mathbf{c}_k\|$. Algorithm 1 shows the pseudo-code of the approach with K local regression models, and archive $\mathfrak{A}$ of samples $(\mathbf{x}_i, \mathbf{y}_i)$, $1 \leq i \leq N$. At the beginning, the codebook vectors are randomly distributed in data space. In the training phase, the codebook vectors and the other properties of each local model are optimized, in order to adapt to local data space distributions that may afford separate bandwidths. The optimization goal is to minimize the overall data space reconstruction error of all local models, i.e., with regard to the codebook vector set $\mathcal{C}$, and the local bandwidth matrices $\mathbf{H}_k$:

$$e_{\mathrm{ELKR}} = \frac{1}{N} \sum_{i}^{N} \|\mathbf{f}_{k^*}(\mathbf{x}_i; \mathbf{H}_{k^*}) - f(\mathbf{x}_i)\|_2, \tag{5}$$

with

$$k^* = \arg\min_{k=1,\ldots,K} \|\mathbf{x}_i - \mathbf{c}_k\|. \tag{6}$$

The assignment of data samples to local models results in a significant speedup. If we assume that the data samples are on average uniformly distributed to all K models, the computation time for the prediction of one data element can be reduced to the $1/K$-th.

Algorithm 1. LOCAL KERNEL REGRESSION

Require: Archive $\mathfrak{A}$, $\mathbf{H}$, K, request $\mathbf{x}_1, \ldots, \mathbf{x}_u$
1: Initialize K local Nadaraya-Watson models
2: **for** $i = 1$ to $|\mathfrak{A}|$ **do**
3:     Assign data samples $(\mathbf{x}_i, \mathbf{y}_i)$ to closest local model
4:     Compute $\mathbf{f}(\mathbf{x}_i, \mathbf{H})$
5: **end for**

Stochastic LOO-CV. Taking into account every data sample, the computation of e_{cv} can be a computationally expensive undertaking. To accelerate the bandwidth adaptation mechanism in case of large data sets, we stochastically select at least one data element for each kernel regression model, i.e., we compute $\mathbf{f}_{-i,k}(\mathbf{x}_i; \mathbf{H}_k)$ for a randomly chosen element i. Stochastic LOO-CV may not be as strong as LOO-CV, and it will be subject to future work to analyze, how many stochastic repetitions will be necessary in practical applications to balance between overfitting and generalizations. In our scenario one repetition turned out to be sufficient for satisfying prediction capabilities, see Section 3.

CMA-ES Engine. We use the CMA-ES [6,10] for adaptation of the free parameters of the k-th model, i.e., of the codebook vector $\mathbf{c}_k$ and bandwidth matrix $\mathbf{H}_k$. Historically, covariance matrix adaptation techniques have developed from evolution strategies (ES) [4]. In each generation ES produce λ offspring solutions and select μ solutions as parents for generation $t+1$. Often, intermediate recombination is applied: for two uniformly selected parents $\mathbf{x}_1$ and $\mathbf{x}_2$, the offspring is $\mathbf{x}' := \frac{1}{2}\mathbf{x}_1 + \frac{1}{2}\mathbf{x}_2$. ES became famous for their Gaussian mutation operator with σ-self-adaptation. In case of the CMA-ES the covariance matrix of differences between a successful solution and its parents is basis of the mutation process. The CMA-ES step sizes are controlled using the derandomized cumulative pathlength control by Ostermeier *et al.* [10]. Its main idea is to construct a solution path based on the difference between a current solution and a predecessor that is c generations older. This difference is the basis of a so called evolution path. A parameter defines the number of generations taken into account, i.e., defining the exploitation of past information. For a more detailed introduction to the CMA-ES we can recommend the tutorial by Hansen [6]. The CMA-ES has two advantages. First, it belongs to the class of non-convex stochastic optimization methods and allows a flexible LOO-CV minimization with a low chance of getting trapped in local optima. Secondly, like kernel regression it is embarrassingly parallelizable, e.g., on the level of subpopulations or candidate solutions, see Section 2.3.

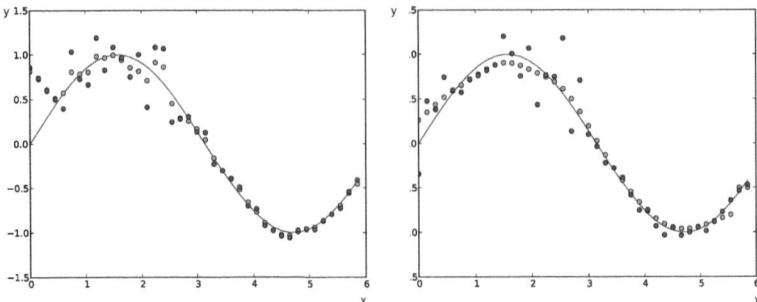

Fig. 1. Illustration of the benefits of more than one kernel regression model. The usual Nadaraya-Watson estimator with only one bandwidth (left part) and two local models (right part). The local model allows an adaptation to local noise conditions.

Illustration. Figure 1 illustrates the advantage of local Nadaraya-Watson models for a simple sinus function (indicated by line) in the interval $[0, 6]$ with two different areas of noise (red dots), i.e., $g(x) = \sin(x) + \gamma \cdot \mathcal{N}(0, 1)$, with $\gamma = 0.25$ for $x \in [0, 3[$, and $\gamma = 0.08$ for $x \in [3, 6]$. The different noise values afford different bandwidths in the two areas, i.e., the left and the right part of the function, blue dots indicate the prediction. This is not possible with only one single Nadaraya-Watson estimator (left part of Figure 1). To reduce the data space reconstruction error on average, the area with high noise overadapts to the noisy values due to a too small bandwidth. In case of local models, a smoother adaptation to local search characteristics, e.g. different degrees of noise, is possible (right part of Figure 1).

2.3   Parallelization

Evolutionary kernel regression is a method that is parallelizable in two kinds of ways, i.e, on the level of the kernel density computations of kernel regression, and on the level of the evolvement of candidate solutions or subpopulations. First, on the level of the regression method, we assume that the prediction of N_1 values has to be computed. For the sake of simplicity, we assume that each call of a kernel density function K takes one time step. Furthermore, we assume that the archive consists of N_2 data samples. The prediction of the N_1 values takes $\mathcal{O}(N_1 \cdot N_2)$ kernel function computations. For M (uniform) machines, the computation of the kernel density sum, can be distributed and parallelized by assigning the kernel density computations uniformly to M machines. If we assume only constant cost for the distribution of the archive on M machines as well as the aggregation of results of the M machines, i.e. $f(\mathbf{x}) = f_1(\mathbf{x}), \ldots, f_M(\mathbf{x})$, the parallelization results in a total runtime of $\mathcal{O}(N_1 \cdot N_2/M)$. In the distributed computing scenario of a smart grid, the assumed constants and idealizations do not apply, but have to be filled with properties of the real system, e.g., envelope delay and computational power of the real machines. Second, evolutionary methods are famous for their property to be parallelizable. The application of genetic operators such as recombination and covariance matrix based mutation, as well as the fitness computation of individuals or subpopulations can be distributed on M machines.

3   ELKR in Power Prediction Scenarios

In the following, we will apply ELKR for prediction of power demand based on real power consumption data published by the Irish state-owned company EIRGRID, see [1]. The data shows the electricity production required to meet the national electricity consumption, including system losses and generators' requirements. The power consumption is stated in mega-watt (MW) every 15 minutes. In our scenario, we have used the data about the power consumption of three succeeding Sundays in January 2010 and February 2010 to predict the power consumption of the following Sunday.

We have tested various settings for ELKR. In our experiments we use $K = 5$ local kernel regression models with Gaussian density kernel, and allow the evolvement of bandwidth matrices $\mathbf{H}_k$ based on stochastic LOO-CV. For this sake, we use a $(5, 10)$-CMA-ES, i.e, a parental population of size $\mu = 5$, and an

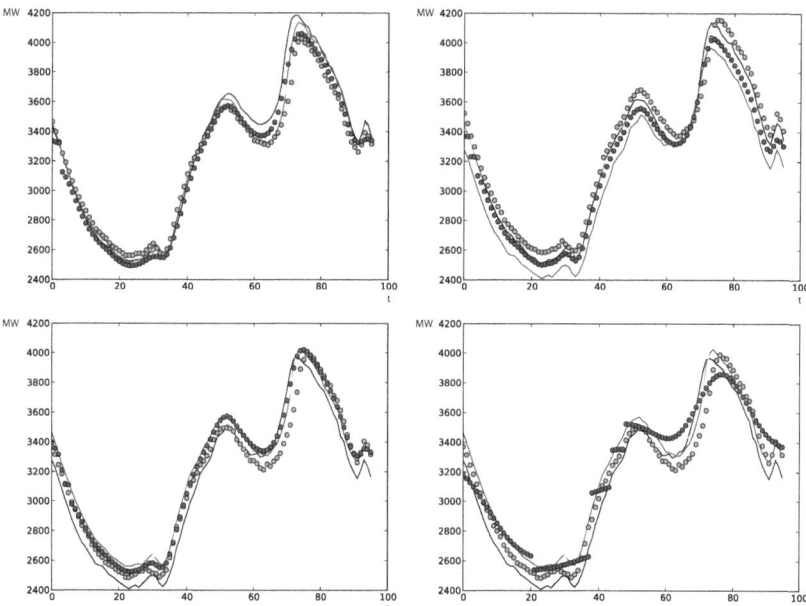

Fig. 2. Prediction of power demands (in MW) with ELKR for three Sundays in January and February 2010 ($t = 1, \ldots, 96$), each based on the previous three Sundays (colored lines). Red dots show the power prediction, blue dots show the amount of power that has been consumed. ELKR shows satisfying forecast capabilities. For comparison, the lower right part shows a run with local models, but constant bandwidth of $h_k = 5.0$.

offspring population of size $\lambda = 10$. The CMA-ES terminates after 200 fitness function evaluations, while the bandwidth is initialized with $h = 5.0$. Figure 2 shows typical runs of ELKR. The upper left part of the figure shows the power prediction of the consumption on Feb 7 based on the consumption on Sundays Jan 17, Jan 24, and Jan 31 (scenario A). The upper right part shows the prediction of Feb 14 based on Jan 24, Jan 31, and Feb 7 (scenario B). The lower left part of Figure 2 shows the prediction of the power consumption on Feb 21 based on Feb 14, Feb 7, and Jan 31 (scenario C). The colored lines show the three observed power consumption developments. In each figure, the red dots show the prediction while the blue dots show the actual power consumption that has to be predicted. In all experiments we can observe that ELKR is able to make satisfying predictions. For comparison, the lower left part shows the same prediction with a fixed bandwidth of $h = 5.0$. The regression model does not adapt to the data, but generalizes too much.

Table 1. Comparison of common kernel regression with a constant bandwidth $h = 5.0$, ELKR with $K = 5$ and CMA-ES based stochastic LOO-CV, least median square regression and backpropagation, in terms of training error e_{TR} on the archive, and error e_{TE} on the test set. For ELKR best and median values of 15 runs are shown.

	$K = 1, h = 5.0$		$K = 5$, LOO-CV				LMS		NN	
	e_{TR}	e_{TE}	best e_{TR}	med e_{TR}	best e_{TE}	med e_{TE}	e_{TR}	e_{TE}	e_{TR}	e_{TE}
A	93.89	86.88	66.91	67.39	63.88	64.44	74.08	64.78	134.67	124.51
B	91.06	118.66	58.06	60.79	104.33	104.72	57.79	105.58	104.64	154.01
C	97.44	86.00	72.43	79.58	56.04	64.00	71.95	58.79	142.95	159.31

Table 1 compares kernel regression with only one model and constant bandwidth $h = 5.0$ to ELKR with stochastic LOO-CV and CMA-ES based bandwidth optimization (200 generations). The results are measured in terms of *training* error e_{TR}, i.e., average absolute deviation from all three training data sets, and test error e_{TE} on the fourth Sunday, i.e., average absolute deviation from the test values of a fourth data set, see scenarios A-C above. In case of ELKR, the best and median results of 15 runs are shown. The experimental results show that ELKR achieves significantly better prediction accuracies on the training archive data and the test data set. Interestingly, the accuracy on the forecast data set is higher than the accuracy on the archive data in case of scenario A and C. This is probably caused by higher deviations of particular power demand curves, i.e., outliers in the archive. Furthermore, Table 1 shows a comparison to least median square regression (LMS) and a backpropagation neural network [11] (96 neurons on input, 48 neurons on hidden layer). ELKR shows competitive results to LMR, and even slightly better results on the test set, while it outperforms the backpropagation network.

4   Conclusion

In this paper we have introduced an extension of kernel regression that is based on local models, and independent stochastic optimization of the bandwidth matrices $\mathbf{H}_k$. LOO-CV can be performed without additional cost. The assignment to local models saves computations, as only the kernel regression model with the closest codebook vector is taken into account for prediction. We have shown experimentally how the model behaves on real data in a power prediction scenario. ELKR has shown significantly higher accuracies than common kernel regression or backpropagation, and competitive results to LMR. The regression as well as the evolutionary part of ELKR are easily parallelizable, and therefore well appropriate for large-scale data mining scenarios in smart grids. We plan to perform parameter studies of ELKR on real power data and also conduct experiments on other regression problems, e.g., on UCI machine learning library data sets. In this context we will concentrate on prediction problems that afford different regularizations in different parts of the data space.

Acknowledgement

The authors thank the German Academic Exchange Service (DAAD) for funding their research, and EIRGRID for the permission to use their energy data.

References

1. Download centre EIRGRID, http://www.eirgrid.com/
2. Agarwal, V., Bougaev, A., Tsoukalas, L.H.: Kernel regression based short-term load forecasting. In: ICANN, vol. (2), pp. 701–708 (2006)
3. Alfares, H., Nazeeruddin, M.: Electric load forecasting: literature survey and classifcation of methods. International Journal of Systems Science 33(1), 23–34 (2002)
4. Beyer, H.-G., Schwefel, H.-P.: Evolution strategies - A comprehensive introduction. Natural Computing 1, 3–52 (2002)
5. Clark, R.: A calibration curve for radiocarbon dates. Antiquity 46(196), 251–266 (1975)
6. Hansen, N.: The CMA evolution strategy: A tutorial. Technical report, TU Berlin, ETH Zürich (2005)
7. Lora, A.T., Santos, J.M.R., Expósito, A.G., Ramos, J.L.M., Santos, J.C.R.: Electricity market price forecasting based on weighted nearest neighbors techniques. IEEE Transactions on Power Systems 22(3), 1294–1301 (2007)
8. Nadaraya, E.: On estimating regression. Theory of Probability and Its Application 10, 186–190 (1964)
9. Nogales, F.J., Contreras, J., Conejo, A.J., Espinola, R.: Forecasting next-day electricity prices by time series models. IEEE Transactions on Power Systems 17, 342–348 (2002)
10. Ostermeier, A., Gawelczyk, A., Hansen, N.: A derandomized approach to self-adaptation of evolution strategies. Evol. Comput. 2(4), 369–380 (1994)
11. Rumelhart, D., Hintont, G., Williams, R.: Learning representations by back-propagating errors. Nature 323(6088), 533–536 (1986)
12. Watson, G.: Smooth regression analysis. Sankhya Series A 26, 359–372 (1964)

Automatic Quality Inspection of Percussion Cap Mass Production by Means of 3D Machine Vision and Machine Learning Techniques

A. Tellaeche, R. Arana, A. Ibarguren, and J.M. Martínez-Otzeta

Fundación Tekniker, Av. Otaola 20, 20600 Eibar, Gipuzkoa, Spain
{atellaeche,rarana,aibarguren,jmmartinez}@tekniker.es

Abstract. The exhaustive quality control is becoming very important in the world's globalized market. One of these examples where quality control becomes critical is the percussion cap mass production. These elements must achieve a minimum tolerance deviation in their fabrication. This paper outlines a machine vision development using a 3D camera for the inspection of the whole production of percussion caps. This system presents multiple problems, such as metallic reflections in the percussion caps, high speed movement of the system and mechanical errors and irregularities in percussion cap placement. Due to these problems, it is impossible to solve the problem by traditional image processing methods, and hence, machine learning algorithms have been tested to provide a feasible classification of the possible errors present in the percussion caps.

Keywords: 3D imaging, high speed inspection, machine learning classifiers.

1 Introduction

Nowadays, there is a big competence in the globalized market and quality inspection systems are becoming fundamental for company competitiveness.

This research has been carried out on demand of an industrial group that sells its products globally all over the world, specialized in the development and manufacturing of civil explosives and initiation systems for infrastructure industries. It is also a leading producer of hunting cartridges and powders for sporting use. The automatic quality control system developed inspects in real time the mass production of the percussion caps to be mounted in hunting cartridges for sporting use.

The errors that are suitable to appear in the percussion caps during their assembly in the production line are the following, each of them defining a class for pattern classification:

1. Percussion cap without errors
2. The central part of the cap is dented
3. The central capsule is badly mounted
4. The central capsule is inverted

M. Graña Romay et al. (Eds.): HAIS 2010, Part I, LNAI 6076, pp. 270–277, 2010.

5. There are rests of paper in the joints of the cap
6. There is no central capsule mounted
7. The central capsule is dirty
8. The external capsule is dirty or dented
9. The percussion cap is missing in the plate
10. The central capsule is mounted above tolerance
11. The central capsule is mounted below tolerance

In the actual process of fabrication, the plates are inspected manually, and samples are extracted at random for statistics. With the system developed based in 3D machine vision, 100% of percussion caps will be inspected and statistics will be carried out in real time, using the database created with all the data and measurements of the percussion caps inspected. For decision making, machine learning and pattern recognition techniques have been used. Besides the simple classifiers, a multiclassifier using voting rules has also been designed to strengthen the overall performance in making a correct classification of the errors [1,2].

This paper is organized as follows. In section 2 details are given about the 3D image acquisition system and the image processing for numerical data acquisition. In section 3 the classifiers used for this research are explained. In section 4 results are given for the classification techniques tested, and finally conclusions are presented in section 5.

2   System for 3D Image Acquisition

3d techniques have been throughly used in quality control tasks. Among them we can cite projected fringes method (PFM), electronic speckle interferometry (ESPI), the structured-lighting reflection technique (SLRT), white-light interferometry (WLI) and laser scanning methods (LSM). A review of them can be found in [3]. In this work we have used laser triangulation, a technique that has been shown to be useful in many different applications, as pavement analysis [4], quality control in construction [5] or in an industrial setting [6].

The camera used for image acquisition is a Ranger E55 model from SICK. For 3D laser triangulation, a 3B class laser line is used.

Both camera and lighting system are mounted in a linear axis to scan each plate at uniform speed. According to [7], an ordinary setup provides the maximum height resolution, where the camera is orthogonal to the object under inspection and the laser is placed in a certain angle.

Figure 1 shows the aspect of the images obtained.

In each image there are established five regions of interest (ROIs), each of them corresponding to the tentative positions on the five groups of 120 percussion caps present en each plate. Within each ROI it is performed a *model finder* operation using a synthetic model of a percussion cap [8]. By these two operations all the percussion caps in the images are perfectly located, ready to apply local image processing operations to them.

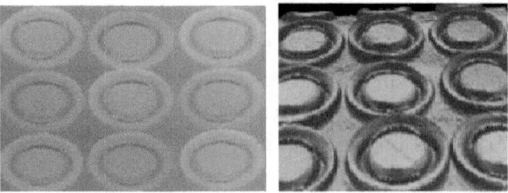

Fig. 1. Acquired 3D image from Ranger E55 and 3D interpretation of the image obtained

In the 3D image processing six line profiles are programmed for the analysis of each percussion cap, three horizontal and three vertical. The percussion caps in the image have an elliptical shape, so the parameters of the line profiles differ depending on the type of line profile, horizontal or vertical. The errors in settlement and the irregularities of the plate make very difficult to analyze the signals provided by the line profiles, and constitute a justification for using pattern recognition techniques in percussion cap error detection.

With the numerical data of a line profile corresponding to a percussion cap, several values are obtained such as the maximum and minimum values of the external capsule of the percussion cap and the maximum, minimum and mean values of the central or internal capsule of the percussion cap.

The majority of errors related to tolerance in the fabrication of the percussion caps have their definition based in measurement comparison between the height values of the central capsule and the height values of the borders of the external capsule. Other error detections are based on the divergence of the height values of the central capsule of the percussion cap. Using statistics it is possible to estimate the *regression line* of the values corresponding to the central capsule of the percussion cap [9]. With this *regression line* it is possible to estimate the height values that the central capsule should have at the points where the maximums at the beginning and ending of the percussion cap occur, taking into account the slope of the regression line. Once these maximum values are calculated, it is possible to obtain the difference among these values and the real values of both maximums.

To calculate the *regression line*, let the X axis of the values in the line profile be the independent value and the heights obtained in the line profile the dependent values. A value in the position i of the array provided in by the line profile will have an independent value in the X axis $x_i = i$ and a height value of y_i.

After calculating the covariance value between both variables, it is possible to establish the regression line correspondent to the heights in the central capsule of the percussion cap as follows:

$$y = \overline{y} + \frac{\sigma_{xy}}{\sigma_x^2}(x - \overline{x}) \tag{1}$$

For a X_M value where a maximum exists, the theoretical height of the internal central capsule at that point can be estimated:

$$y_i = \frac{\sigma_{xy}}{\sigma_x{}^2} X_M - \frac{\sigma_{xy}}{\sigma_x{}^2} \overline{x} + \overline{y} \tag{2}$$

This process is repeated for each of the six line profiles calculated in each percussion cap.

With all the values extracted from a line profile and the regression line estimated, a data vector is constructed for each of the six line profiles of a percussion cap:

$$X_i = \{x_1, x_2, \cdots x_{12}\} \tag{3}$$

Where each of the components of the vector is:

- X_1 = x coordinate where the maximum at the beginning of the percussion cap occurs.
- X_2 = x coordinate where the minimum at the beginning of the percussion cap occurs.
- X_3 = x coordinate where the maximum at the ending of the percussion cap occurs.
- X_4 = x coordinate where the minimum at the ending of the percussion cap occurs.
- X_5 = maximum height value in the central capsule of the percussion cap.
- X_6 = minimum height value in the central capsule of the percussion cap.
- X_7 = mean of height values in the central capsule of the percussion cap.
- X_8 = slope of the regression line
- X_9 = bias of the regression line
- X_{10} = mean quadratic error between the regression line values and the real values of the central capsule of the percussion cap
- X_{11} = difference between the real height value in X_1 and the theoretical value of the regression line at the same point.
- X_{12} = difference between the real height value in X_3 and the theoretical value of the regression line at the same point.

3   Machine Learning Algorithms for Pattern Recognition

In this section there will be presented the different approaches used for error classification using the vectors as input data. Three main approaches have been tested, such as statistical, with Bayesian networks, Clustering (K-NN), and Decision trees (C4.5). Finally voting techniques have been used to try to obtain optimal classification performance.

Bayesian Networks: The Bayesian networks are probabilistic graphical models that represent a set of random variables and their conditional independences via a directed acyclic graph [10,11,12,13,14]. The nodes of the Bayesian network represent the random variables, and edges represent conditional dependences, thus, nodes which are not connected represent variables which are conditionally independent of each other. Each node is associated with a probability function that takes as input a particular set of values for the parent variables of the node and gives the probability of the variable represented by the node.

For the Bayesian network formal definition, let $G = (V, E)$ be a directed acyclic graph, and let $X = (X_v)_{v \in V}$ be a set of random variables indexed by V. X is a Bayesian network with respect to G if its joint probability density function can be written as a product of the individual density functions, conditional on their parent variables:

$$p(x) = \prod_{v \in V} p(x_v | x_{pa(v)}) \tag{4}$$

Where $pa(v)$ is the set of parents of v.

k-NN algorithm: The k *nearest neighbors* algorithm is a supervised classification method used for classifying data vectors based on closest training examples in the feature space. K is a positive integer, typically small [15,16,17].

The training vectors belong to a multidimensional space. A vector i with p attributes, can be represented as follows:

$$X_i = \{x_{1i}, x_{2i}, \cdots x_{pi}\} \in X \tag{5}$$

A vector in the data space is assigned to a certain class C if this class is the most frequent one among the k closest training examples. To determine the distance between two vectors, the Euclidean distance is used. The training phase consists on aggregating each example $\langle x, f(x) \rangle$ where $x \in X$, to the database.

In the decision phase, given a x_q vector to be classified, let $x_1, \cdots, x_k$ be the k neighbors closest to x_q in the database, then:

$$\hat{f}(x) \leftarrow \mathrm{argmax}_{v \in V} \sum_{i=1}^{k} \delta(v, f(x_i)) \tag{6}$$

Where: $\delta(a, b) = 1$ if $a = b$ and 0 otherwise. $\hat{f}(x_q)$ is the most common value of f among the k nearest neighbors of x_q.

According to the literature, high values of K reduce the noise effect in the samples, but establish boundaries among similar classes. Due to this effect and the characteristics of the data vectors available, our $K - nn$ classifier works better with small values of K. Three values have been tested ($K = 1, 3, 5$), obtaining the best performance, 89.49% correctly classified instances with $K = 3$ (80.8021% for $K = 1$ and 88.4549 for $K = 5$).

C4.5 decision tree: C4.5 is an algorithm used to generate a decision tree, developed by Ross Quinlan [18]. C4.5 is an extension of ID3 algorithm, also created by Quinlan [19].

C4.5 builds decision trees analyzing the normalized information gain (7) of the available variables, measure based in entropy (8).

$$Gain(S, A) \equiv Entropy(S) - \sum_{v \in Values(A)} \frac{|S_v|}{|S|} Entropy(S_v) \tag{7}$$

Where:

S is a collection of samples, Values(A) is the set of all possible values for attribute A, and S_v is the subset of S for which attribute A has value v.

$$Entropy(S) \equiv \sum_{i=1}^{c} -p_i \, log_2 \, p_i \qquad (8)$$

Where:

p_i is the proportion of S belonging to class i.

During the tree building process, the algorithm chooses the attribute with the highest value of Information Gain for splitting the data and place it in the highest nodes of the tree structure.

Voting techniques for classifier combination: Classifier combination [1,2] is a powerful tool to improve the performance of single classifiers. The use of different paradigms can increase the recognition rates as each algorithm is able to analyze a different part of the search space. Each of the different classifiers performs an independent classification and when all the predictions are gathered a voting process is done to determine the final class of the new case. In this work, the simple classifiers have been combined using a simple voting process (Bayes Network + 3-NN + C 4.5).

4   Comparative Analysis and Performance Evaluation

To assess the validity of the different classifiers used for error detection, 1150 samples obtained from the line profiles in the percussion caps have been used. For each line profile a data vector is obtained as stated in 3. After having obtained the 1150 data vectors, each of them have been classified by experts in a class ranging from 1 to 11, attending to the possible errors exposed in the introduction. These 1150 samples previously classified are used for validation and testing of the classifiers used in this work.

4.1   Measures to Assess Validity

To assess validity, several common measures used in machine learning have been obtained for each classifier. All the measures are based in the four outcomes that can be obtained when trying to predict the classification of a certain sample: True Positive (TP), True Negative (TN), False Positive (FP) and False Negative (FN). Taking into account these four outcomes the validity measures obtained are:

1. Correctly Classified Instances (CCI): Percentage of samples correctly classified.
2. Incorrectly Classified Instances (ICI): 100% - CCI.
3. True Positive Rate (TPR): TP / (TP + FN). Also called Recall measure.
4. False Positive Rate (FPR): FP / (FP + TN)
5. Precision (P): TP / (TP + FP)
6. F-Measure (FM): Defined as (2 * Precision * Recall) / (Precision + Recall)

Table 1. Error Classification Results

	CCI	ICI	TPR	FPR	Precision	F-Meas
Bayes Net	87.58%	12.41%	0.876	0.067	0.89	0.882
3-NN	89.49%	10.50%	0.895	0.137	0.874	0.878
C4.5	**91.14%**	8.85%	0.911	0.086	0.899	0.904
BN+3NN+C4.5	**92.27%**	7.72%	0.923	0.093	0.911	0.912

4.2 Results Obtained

The table 1 shows the different results obtained with the different classifiers.

The C4.5 tree algorithm offers a performance of above 90%. This algorithm offers also a very fast execution for real time tasks.

The multiple classifiers offer in general terms a better performance than the simple ones [1]. The multiple classifier obtains the best performance of all the approaches tested.

The final decision making is carried out taking into account the six line profiles defined in each percussion cap. To classify a percussion cap having one of the possible errors, at least four out of six line profiles must provide the same error to validate the percussion cap as having that certain error. By this method the correct classification percentage is increased above the value of 95%.

5 Conclusions

Due to the nature of the installation of the 3D machine vision inspection system in the production line of percussion caps there are errors inherent to the process, such as small irregularities in the shape of the plates and small errors in the percussion caps settlement inside the plates. Because of all these problems and taking into account the accuracy demanded to the system, this problem was unfeasible to be solved applying decisions based on direct measurements. With the use of machine learning techniques it has been possible to overcome the problems exposed previously obtaining a correct classification of percussion caps of above 95%.

References

1. Kuncheva, L.I.: Combining pattern classifiers: methods and algorithms. Wiley-Interscience, Hoboken (2004)
2. Kittler, J., Hatef, M., Duin, R.P.W., Matas, J.: On combining classifiers. IEEE Transactions on Pattern Analysis and Machine Intelligence 20, 226–239 (1998)
3. Leopold, J., Gunther, H., Leopold, R.: New developments in fast 3D-surface quality control. Measurement 33(2), 179–187 (2003)
4. Li, Q., Yao, M., Yao, X., Xu, B.: A real-tyme 3D scanning system for pavement distortion inspection. Measurement Science and Technology 21(1) (2010)
5. Bosche, F.: Automated recognition of 3D CAD model objects in laser scans and calculation of as-built dimensions for dimensional compliance control in construction. Advanced engineering informatics 24(1), 107–118 (2010)

6. Picon-Ruiz, A., Bereciartua-Perez, M.A., Gutierrez-Olabarria, J.A., Perez-Larrazabal, J.: Machine vision in quality control. Development of 3D robotized laser-scanner. DYNA 84(9), 733–742 (2010)
7. Boehnke, K.: Hierarchical Object Localization for Robotic Bin Picking. PhD thesis, Politehnica University of Timisoara (2008)
8. Gonzalez, R., Woods, R.: Digital Image Processing, 3rd edn. Prentice Hall, Upper Saddle River (2008)
9. Draper, N.R., Smith, H.: Applied Regression Analysis. Probability and Statistics, 3rd edn. Wadsworth and Brooks, New york (1998)
10. Tellaeche, A., Burgos-Artizzu, X.P., Pajares, G., Ribeiro, A.: A vision-based method for weeds identification through the bayesian decision theory. Pattern Recognition 41(2), 521–530 (2008)
11. Domingos, P., Pazzani, M.: On the optimality of the simple bayesian classifier under zero-one loss. Machine Learning 29(2-3), 103–130 (1997)
12. Friedman, N., Goldszmidt, M.: Building classifiers using bayesian networks. In: Proceedings of the Thirteenth National Conference on Artificial Intelligence, pp. 1277–1284. AAAI Press, Menlo Park (1996)
13. Castillo, E., Gutierrez, J.M., Hadi, A.S.: Learning Bayesian Networks. In: Expert Systems and Probabilistic Network Models. Monographs in Computer Science, pp. 481–528. Springer, New York (1997)
14. Jensen, F.V., Nielsen, T.D.: Bayesian networks and decision graphs. In: Information Science and Statistics, 2nd edn. Springer, New York (2007)
15. Dasarathy, B.V.: Nearest Neighbor (NN) Norms: NN Pattern Recognition Classification Techniques. IEEE Computer Society Press, Los Alamitos (1991)
16. Shakhnarovich, G., Darrel, T., Indyk, P.: Nearest-Neighbor Methods in Learning and Vision. The MIT Press, Cambridge (2005)
17. Cover, T.M., Hart, P.E.: Nearest neighbor pattern classification. IEEE Trans. IT-13 1, 21–27 (1967)
18. Quinlan, J.R.: Induction of decision trees. Machine Learning, 81–106 (1986)
19. Quinlan, J.R.: C4.5: Programs for Machine Learning. Morgan Kaufmann, San Mateo (1993)

Speaker Verification and Identification Using Principal Component Analysis Based on Global Eigenvector Matrix

Minkyung Kim[1,*], Eunyoung Kim[2], Changwoo Seo[3], and Sungchae Jeon[4]

[1,2] Department of Media, Soongsil University, 511 Sangdo-dong, Dongjak-gu, Seoul Korea
pengcap@empal.com, key710503@ssu.ac.kr
[3,4] Medical & IT Fusion Research Division, Korea Electrotechnology Research Institute,
1271-19, Sa-dong, Sangnok-gu, Ansan-city, Gyeonggi-do, Korea
{cwseo,sarim}@keri.re.kr

Abstract. Prinicipal component anaysis (PCA) is one of the most general purpose feature extraction methods. A variety of methods for PCA has been proposed. Many conventional methods, however, require a larger amount of training data when the eigenvector matrix of each speaker is calculated. This paper proposes a global eigenvector matrix based PCA for speaker recognition (SR). The proposed method uses training data from all speakers to calculate the covariance matrix and uses this matrix to find the global eigenvalue and eigenvector matrix to perform PCA. During the training and testing of this method, the global PCA coefficients instead of the PCA coefficients of each speaker are used in performing PCA transformation. Compared to the PCA and the conventional methods in the Gaussian mixture model (GMM)-based speaker identification (SI) and speaker verification (SV), the proposed method shows better performance while requiring less storage space.

Keywords: Principal component analysis (PCA), Eigenvector, Speaker verification (SV), Speaker identification (SI), Gaussian mixture model (GMM).

1 Introduction

Principal component analysis (PCA) has been widely used for data analysis and dimension reduction throughout science and engineering [1,2,3]. It constructs a representation of the data with a set of orthogonal basis vectors that are the eigenvectors of the covariance matrix generated from the data, which can also be derived from eigenvalue decomposition. By projecting the data onto the dominant eigenvectors, the dimension of the original dataset can be reduced with little loss of information [4,5,6]. However, in PCA transformation based on the full data covariance matrix, a larger amount of training data for obtaining a good transformation is required.

---

* K. Sandaral.

M. Graña Romay et al. (Eds.): HAIS 2010, Part I, LNAI 6076, pp. 278–285, 2010.

To reduce complexity and improve the performance in speaker recognition, a PCA fuzzy mixture model [7] and a Gaussian mixture model (GMM) based on local PCA [8] were proposed. The PCA fuzzy mixture model was derived from the combination of the PCA and the fuzzy version of the mixture model with diagonal covariance matrices. The GMM based on local PCA first partitions the data space into several disjointed regions by vector quantization (VQ), and then performs PCA on each region. However, when calculating the eigenvalue matrix and the eigenvector matrix of each speaker, both the PCA fuzzy mixture model and the local PCA-based GMM require a large amount of speech data. However, unlike speech recognition, it is impossible for GMM-based SR method to obtain enough data on each speaker.

In this paper, to overcome these problems, we propose a global eigenvector matrix-based PCA for both SV and SI. The proposed method uses training data from all speakers to calculate the covariance matrix and then uses this matrix to find the global eigenvalue matrix and the global eigenvector matrix to perform PCA. Therefore, during the training and testing, our proposed method uses the global PCA coefficients instead of the PCA coefficients of each speaker. The transformation problem caused by the lack of training data is solved by using the normalized global eigenvector matrices obtained from all speakers. The effectiveness of the proposed method is shown by the results of the comparative experiments with both the PCA and the conventional methods.

2 Global Eigenvector Matrix Based Principal Component Analysis (PCA)

We assume that $x_s(t) \in R^N$ is an N-dimensional feature vector of the training speaker s for recognition, and that $X^S = \{X_s, s = 1, \cdots, S\}$, where $X_s = \{x_s(t), t = 1, \cdots, T_s\}$ is a set of S training speakers with length T_s. We computed the covariance matrices for the feature vectors of the total training data by the following equation as

$$\Sigma_G = E\left[(x - \gamma)(x - \gamma)^T \mid x \in R^N\right]$$
$$= \frac{1}{S}\sum_{s=1}^{S}\left\{\frac{1}{T_s}\sum_{t=1}^{T_s}(x_s(t) - \gamma)(x_s(t) - \gamma)^T\right\}, \tag{1}$$

where γ is the reference vector and T is the transpose of the matrix. The covariance matrix estimated from eq.(1) was used to find the global eigenvalue matrix and the corresponding global eigenvector matrix. The covariance matrices Σ_G of X^S are given by the eigenvalue decomposition [9] of

$$\Sigma_G = \Psi_G \Lambda_G^2 \Psi_G^T, \tag{2}$$

where Ψ_G is the matrix of global eigenvectors and $\Lambda_G^2 = diag\left(\lambda_{G,1}^2, \lambda_{G,2}^2, \cdots, \lambda_{G,N}^2\right)$ is the diagonal matrix of global eigenvalues. Since the importance of any transformed coordinate is measured by the magnitude of its eigenvalue, only the $K(N \geq K)$ principal eigenvectors, the ones associated with the largest eigenvalue, were taken. The corresponding global eigenvector matrices to the ordered global eigenvalues are given

$$\Omega_G = [\Psi_{G,1}, \Psi_{G,2}, \cdots, \Psi_{G,K}]. \tag{3}$$

Then, the eigenvector matrices were used to transform the feature vector to optimally represent the original data.

During the training and testing by the global PCA coefficients, the input feature vector for the GMM of each speaker is transformed into

$$y_s(t) = \Omega_G^T x_s(t), \tag{4}$$

where Ω_G^T is a $K \times N$ weight matrix, the rows of which are the K principal eigenvectors. The information ratio I_G, given by

$$I_G = \frac{\sum_{j=1}^{K} \lambda_{G,j}^2}{\sum_{i=1}^{N} \lambda_{G,i}^2} \tag{5}$$

reflects the information rate of the linearly transformed data in the original data [10].

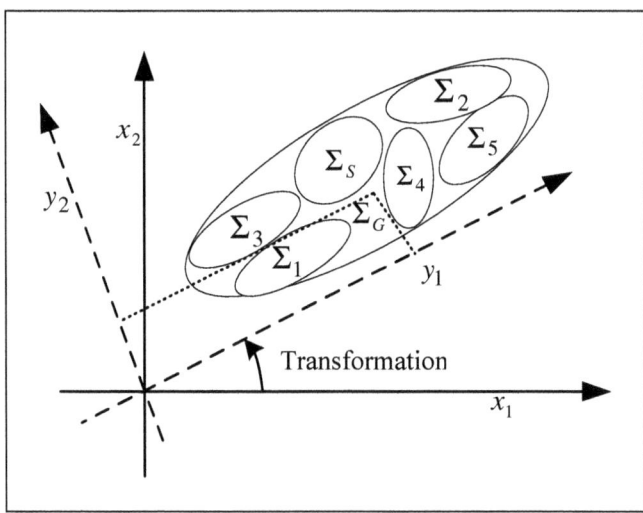

Fig. 1. Transformation of the global PCA method in two-dimensional space

Figure 1 shows the transformation of PCA based on the covariance in two-dimensional space. In Fig. 1, the small ellipses explain the covariance matrices $\{\Sigma_1, \Sigma_2, \cdots, \Sigma_S\}$ presenting the distribution of the feature vector by each speaker for the PCA, and the big ellipse, including all of the smaller ellipses, present the global covariance matrix Σ_G from the training data of all speakers. Therefore, the transformation can obtain sufficient data, regardless of the utterance length, due to the use of training data from all speakers where training data are lacking.

3 Speaker Recognition

3.1 Gaussian Mixture Model (GMM)

Let $y(t) \in R^K$ be a K-dimensional feature vector transformed by the global eigenvector matrix-based PCA. A Gaussian mixture density is defined by a weighted linear combination of M component densities as [11]

$$p(y(t) \mid \theta) = \sum_{i=1}^{M} w_i b_i(y(t)), \qquad (6)$$

where the component densities, $b_i(y(t))$, are defined by K-variate Gaussian function of the form

$$b_i(y(t)) = \frac{1}{(2\pi)^{K/2} |\Sigma_i|^{1/2}} \exp\left\{ -\frac{1}{2}(y(t) - \mu_i)^T \Sigma_i^{-1}(y(t) - \mu_i) \right\} \qquad (7)$$

with mean vector μ_i and covariance matrix Σ_i for the i-th mixture. The mixture weights w_i, furthermore satisfy the constraint $\sum_{i=1}^{M} w_i = 1$. Collectively, the parameters of speaker's density model are denoted as $\theta = \{w_i, \mu_i, \Sigma_i\}_{i=1}^{M}$.

To estimate parameters from all sequences of T vectors $Y = \{y(t), t = 1, \cdots, T\}$, the GMM likelihood can be written as

$$p(Y \mid \theta) = \prod_{t=1}^{T} p(y(t) \mid \theta). \qquad (8)$$

In general, the maximum-likelihood (ML) estimation is used to estimate the parameter θ which maximizes the likelihood of the GMM. Since the GMM likelihood of the nonlinear function is impossible to be maximized directly, the ML estimations can be possible by using the expectation-maximization (EM) algorithm iteratively [11,12]. The basic idea of the EM algorithm is, beginning with an initial model θ, to estimate a new model $\hat{\theta}$, such that $p(Y \mid \hat{\theta}) \geq p(Y \mid \theta)$. The new model then becomes the initial model for the next iteration and the process is repeated until a convergence threshold is reached.

3.2 Speaker Verification (SV)

Let $p(Y \mid \theta_s)$ and $p(Y \mid \theta_b)$ be probability density functions (PDFs) for a speaker model, and a universal background model (UBM) or a world model [13,14], respectively, in GMM. The average log-likelihood of a model is computed as

$$
\begin{aligned}
\Lambda_m(Y \mid \theta_s, \theta_b) &= \frac{1}{T} \sum_{t=1}^{T} \log \frac{p(y(t) \mid \theta_s)}{p(y(t) \mid \theta_b)} \\
&= \frac{1}{T} \sum_{t=1}^{T} \log p(y(t) \mid \theta_s) - \frac{1}{T} \sum_{t=1}^{T} \log p(y(t) \mid \theta_b) \\
&= L(Y \mid \theta_s) - L(Y \mid \theta_b)
\end{aligned}
\tag{9}
$$

Using this likelihood ratio, the decision is made as

$$
\Lambda_m(Y \mid \theta_s, \theta_b) \quad
\begin{cases}
\geq Th, & accept\,as\,spekaer, \\
< Th, & reject\,as\,imposter,
\end{cases}
\tag{10}
$$

where Th is a threshold for the decision logic.

3.3 Speaker Identification (SI)

For SI, each of S speakers is represented by GMMs, $\theta_1, \cdots, \theta_S$, respectively. The object of speaker identification is to find the speaker model that has the maximum log likelihood ratio for a given feature sequence as [11]

$$
\hat{s} = \max_{1 \leq s \leq S} \sum_{t=1}^{T} \log p(y(t) \mid \theta_s)
\tag{11}
$$

4 Experimental Results

To evaluate the performance of the proposed method (GEPCA: Global Eigenvector based PCA), SV and SI experiments were performed by using both the PCA and conventional methods. In the experiments, the speech database consisted of Korean sentences spoken by 200 speakers (100 males, 100 females) during three recording sessions (five recordings per session) for three weeks. The given Korean sentences, used by all speakers, were "yel-lora chamke (open sesame)," with short utterance length of 0.8 seconds [15]. Among the speech data, 10 utterances were used for the PCA coefficients and training, while the remaining five utterances generated in the final session were used for testing. The speech data were sampled at 11.025 kHz with 16 bits, and each frame length was 16 ms with 50% overlap. The feature vector consisted of 12-mel frequency cepstral coefficient (MFCC) and 13-delta cepstrum including differential energy [16].

Table 1. Comparison results of the number of parameters

Methods	Total Parameters
Proposed GEPCA	$S \times M(2K+1) + N \times K$
PCA	$S(M(2K+1) + N \times K)$
Conventional method	$S \times M(2N+1)$

The number of parameters required in the proposed GEPCA, PCA, and conventional methods is presented in Table 1. Even the proposed GEPCA needs extra $N \times K$ storage for the transformation, but it requires fewer parameters than does the PCA or the conventional method. For example, the proposed method ($S = 200$, $M = 32$, and $K = 20$) requires 262,900 parameters. However, the PCA ($S = 200$, $M = 32$, and $K = 20$) and the conventional method ($S = 200$, $M = 32$, and $N = 25$) require 362,400 and 326,400 parameters, respectively.

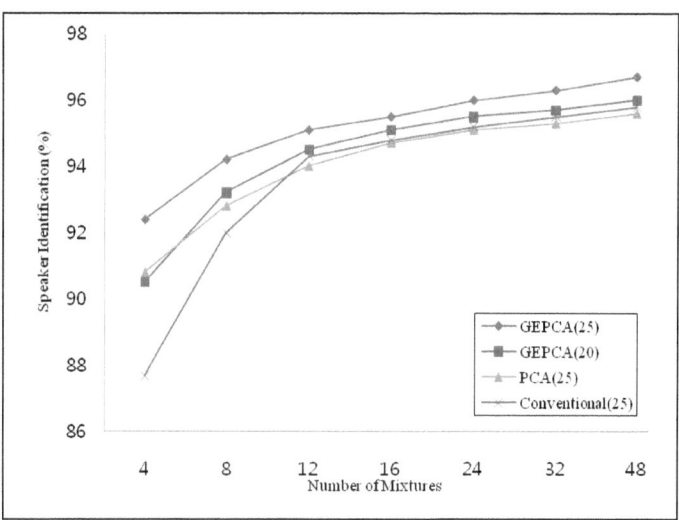

Fig. 2. Speaker identification performance (%) by the number of mixtures

Figure 2 shows the speaker identification performance for the various numbers of mixtures. The dimensions of the feature vectors for the proposed method had $N = 25$ and $K = 20$, and the PCA and conventional methods had $N = 25$. From the figure, the proposed GEPCA(25) method showed an improvement of about 1.14% and 1.67% compared with the PCA(25) and the conventional method(25), respectively, when the order of feature vector was the same. The proposed GEPCA(20) method showed an improvement of about 0.30% and 0.83% in identification performance, with lower order of feature vector, over the PCA(25) and conventional method(25), respectively.

But the PCA(25) showed worse performance than the conventional method(25) by the lack of training and test data over 12 mixtures due to the short utterance.

The experimental results based on false reject rates (FRR), false accept rates (FAR) and equal-error rates (EER) for speaker verification are shown in Table 2. The universal background model had 250 Gaussian components [14]. In the Table 2, our GEPCA(25) showed an improvement of about 0.41% and 0.59% compared with the PCA(25) and the conventional method(25), respectively, when the order of feature vector was the same. The proposed GEPCA(20) showed an improvement of about 0.06% and 0.24% in verification performance, with 26.5% and 19.5% lower complexity, over the PCA(25) and the conventional method(25), respectively. The PCA(25) showed a similar performance over the conventional method(25).

Table 2. Speaker verification errors (%) by the number of mixtures

	Mixtures								
	16			32			48		
	FRR	FAR	EER	FRR	FAR	EER	FRR	FAR	EER
Proposed GEPCA(25)	7.7	1.23	**3.43**	7.4	1.10	**3.21**	7.1	1.05	**2.89**
Proposed GEPCA(20)	8.0	1.20	**3.71**	7.8	1.25	**3.53**	7.6	1.24	**3.35**
PCA(25)	8.1	1.31	**3.85**	7.9	1.27	**3.56**	7.6	1.27	**3.37**
Convent. method(25)	8.3	1.38	**4.03**	8.2	1.39	**3.81**	7.9	1.37	**3.49**

Although the proposed method required extra steps to obtain the global eigenvector based transformation matrix from training data, the storage space for both training and testing was reduced due to the previously calculated global eigenvector based PCA coefficients. From these results, the proposed method is efficient for resolving the transformation problem caused by the lack of training data.

5   Conclusion

A global eigenvector matrix-based principal component analysis (PCA) method for both speaker verification (SV) and speaker identification (SI) is proposed. The proposed method uses training data from all speakers to find the global eigenvalue matrix and the global eigenvector matrix. The transformation problem caused by the lack of training data is solved by using the normalized global eigenvector matrices. Experimental results show that the proposed method has better performance than the PCA and conventional methods while requiring less storage space and complexity.

Acknowledgments. This research was supported by the cooperative R&D Program funded by the Korea Research Council Industrial Science and Technology, Republic of Korea.

References

1. Liu, L., He, J.: On the use of orthogonal GMM in speaker recognition. In: Int. Conf. on ASSP, pp. 845–849 (1999)
2. Tan, Y., Shi, L., Tong, W., Wang, C.: Multi-class cancer classification by total principal component regression (TPCR) using microarray gene expression data. Nucleic Acids Research 33(1), 56–65 (2005)
3. Shen, H., Huang, J.Z.: Sparse principal component analysis via regularized low rank matrix approximation. Journal of Multivariate Analysis 99, 1015–1034 (2008)
4. Ariki, Y., Tagashira, S., Nishijima, M.: Speaker recognition and speaker normalization by projection to speaker subspace. In: Int. Conf. on ASSP, pp. 319–322 (1996)
5. Jolliffe, I.T.: Principal component analysis, 2nd edn. Springer, New York (2002)
6. Tang, F., Tao, H.: Binary principal component analysis. In: British Machine Vision Conf., pp. 377–386 (2006)
7. Lee, Y., Lee, J., Lee, K.Y.: PCA Fuzzy Mixture Model for Speaker Identification. In: Liu, J., Cheung, Y.-m., Yin, H. (eds.) IDEAL 2003. LNCS, vol. 2690, pp. 992–999. Springer, Heidelberg (2003)
8. Seo, C., Lee, K.Y., Lee, J.: GMM based on local PCA for Speaker Identification. Electronics Letters 37(24), 1486–1488 (2001)
9. Golub, G.H., Loan, C.F.V.: Matrix Computations, 3rd edn. The Johns Hopkins University Press, Baltimore (1996)
10. Flury, B.N.: Common Principal Components in k Groups. J. Acoust. Soc. Am. 79(388), 892–898 (1984)
11. Reynolds, D.A., Rose, R.: Robust text-independent speaker identification using Gaussian mixture speaker models. IEEE Trans. on SAP 3(1), 72–82 (1995)
12. Dempster, A.P., Laird, N.M., Rubin, D.B.: Maximum likelihood from incomplete data via the EM algorithm. J. Roy. Stat. Soc. 39(1), 1–38 (1977)
13. Matsui, T., Furui, S.: Likelihood normalization for speaker verification using a phoneme and speaker-independent model. Speech Communication 17, 109–116 (1995)
14. Reynolds, D.A., Quatieri, T.F., Dunn, R.B.: Speaker verification using adapted Gaussian mixture models. Digit. Signal Process. 10(1-3), 19–41 (2000)
15. Seo, C., Sim, K., Kim, E., Ko, H., Lim, Y.: Speaker verification system using extended sequential probability ratio test in PDA. In: Mauthe, A., Zeadally, S., Cerqueira, E., Curado, M. (eds.) FMN 2009. LNCS, vol. 5630, pp. 188–193. Springer, Heidelberg (2009)
16. Young, S., Evermann, G., Kershaw, D., Moore, G., Odell, J., Ollason, D., Povey, D., Valtchev, V., Woodland, P.: The HTK Book (for HTK version 3.2). Cambridge University Engineering Department, Cambridge (2002)

Hybrid Approach for Automatic Evaluation of Emotion Elicitation Oriented to People with Intellectual Disabilities

R. Martínez[1], K. López de Ipiña[1], E. Irigoyen[1], and N. Asla[2]

[1] Departamento Ingeniería de Sistemas y Automática, Grupo de Inteligencia Computacional
{raquel.martinez,karmele.ipina,eloy.irigoyen}@ehu.es
[2] Departamento de Psicología Social y Metodología de las Ciencias del Comportamiento, de la
Facultad de Psicología
nagore.asla@ehu.es
Universidad del País Vasco/Euskal Herriko Unibertsitatea

Abstract. People with intellectual disabilities and elderly need physical and intellectual support to ensuring independent living. This is one of the main issues in applying Information and Communication Technology (ICT) into Assistive Technology field. In this sense the development of appropriated Intelligent Systems (ISs) offers new perspectives to this community. In our project a new IS system (LAGUNTXO) which adds user affective information oriented to people with intellectual disabilities has been developed. The system integrates a Human Emotion Analysis System (HEAS) which attempts to solve critical situations for this community as block stages. In the development of the HEAS one of the critical issues was to create appropriated databases to train the system due to the difficulty to simulate pre-block stages in laboratory. Finally a films and real sequences based emotion elicitation database was created. The elicitation material was categorized with more actual features based on discrete emotions and dimensional terms (pleasant, unpleasant). Classically the evaluation is carried out by a specialist (psychologist). In this work we present a hybrid approach for Automatic Evaluation of Emotion Elicitation databases based on Machine Learning classifiers and K-means clustering. The new categorization and the automatic evaluation show a high level of accuracy with respect to others methodologies presented in the literature.

Keywords: Automatic Evaluation, Human Emotion Management System, Human Emotion Elicitation, Machine Learning.

1 Introduction

Integrating people with intellectual disabilities into working and social environments is one of the main issues in applying Information and Communication Technologies (ICTs) into the Assistive Technology field. Particularly, it is necessary to pay special attention to the integration problem of people with intellectual disabilities. In this sense the development of appropriated Intelligent Systems (ISs) offers new perspectives to this community.

M. Graña Romay et al. (Eds.): HAIS 2010, Part I, LNAI 6076, pp. 286–293, 2010.

These devices are designed to reach the user adaptation and to obtain an interaction that allows overcoming personal disabilities, for increasing the performance, individual autonomy, working capability, personal safety and a healthy environment in work and social places. In our work a new IS system, LAGUNTXO [1], which adds user affective information oriented to people with intellectual disabilities has been developed. The system integrates a Human Emotion Analysis System (HEAS) which attempts to solve critical situations as block stages. Frequently, people with intellectual disabilities have blockage situations where they cannot take a decision or answer to a stimulus. Typically, these situations appear either when they are anxiously, or when they suffer a panic attack, or when the requirements are further than they can do. In many cases, the main objective is detecting emotional changes, instead of classifying emotions, in order to attend these situations before beginning. One of the main issues to develop the HEAS is to create databases with appropriate samples of emotion stages to train the system. In this case we need to detect block stages. Thus the first step is the emotion elicitation at laboratory trying to reproduce pre-block stages.

In section 2, human emotion survey and analysis are presented. Next, methods oriented to people with disabilities are shown. In section 4 the development of the elicitation database is described. Hybrid evaluation methods for Automatic Evaluation are presented in section 5. Finally, some concluding remarks and future outlines are pointed out.

2   Human Emotion Analysis

The human emotion is a widely studied field on neuronal process theory, as well as sociology, and cognitive process theory [2,3,4]. According to Cañamero [5], human emotion entails distinctive integrated ways of perceiving and assessing situations, processing information, and modulating and prioritizing actions. Emotion is a feeling expressed by a physiologic function like facial reactions, cardiac pulse and behavioural reactions like block situations, aggressions, crying, etc. However, many times the individual masks their emotions as a result of a cultural learning process ("socialized emotions"). Specifically, people with intellectual disabilities cover their emotions by mean of unpredictable emotional stages. Human interaction includes emotional information of the interlocutors that is transmitted explicitly through the language and implicitly through nonverbal communication. Lang et al. suggest that there are 3 systems implied in the expression of the emotions and could serve like indicators to detect the user emotions: Verbal information (user's auto-report on the perceived emotion), Conduct (registry of face and gesture expressions and paralinguistic parameters of the voice), Psycho-physiological answers (registry of cardiac rate, conductance of the skin, electro-brain answer, etc.)[6].

Therefore, a computer based system which registers and recognizes user's emotions will be necessary, to determine which basic emotions go away to measure and which are their subjective or verbal, related to conduct and psycho- physiological. For classifying emotions there is not an established model. When a person camouflages emotions a perceptible physiologic response is not produced and the classical emotion measure system cannot be used, so a different measuring system should be developed, incorporating both individual artificial emotional patterns (emotional data bases of human emotional patterns) and emotional memories (data bases of human experiences). In these patterns, the individuality of the people and the cultural components have to be considered. According to some authors, human emotions are restricted to 6, although in some cases it is possible to find experimental results classifying more than 15 emotions. This may cause confusion in the development of an automatic emotion recognition system. Furthermore, while one would expect a set of basic emotions to be consistently recognized across cultures—in other words, being universal—evidence suggests that there is minimal universality at least in the recognition of emotions from facial expressions [2,3,4,5].

3 Experimentation Methods Oriented to People with Disabilities

Since one of the main goals of the research is the development of a HEAS oriented to people with intellectual disabilities, the first step is to create appropriate human modelling and measurement of both perceptible and not perceptible emotions. Our most recent works are focused on the study and regulation of human reactions. This is a very intricate topic, since it involves human emotion detection, it requires a complex sensor configuration, and it needs many arduous experiments in order to achieve reliable results. Moreover Non Intrusive Intelligent Systems (NIIS) have to be created in order to measure biological signals in people with intellectual disabilities taking privacy and ethical issues into account. In general, the law forbids any kind of experimentation with people with intellectual disabilities in order to protect these vulnerable persons. Besides, the results obtained with a set of volunteers are difficult to extrapolate to any kind of user, including people with intellectual disabilities. We would like to remark that despite everybody could benefit of the results of research on assistive technology, accessibility and intelligent environments, the participation of people with disability in these research experiments are of lively interest, since they have many more difficulties of adaptation than other people, and they are more sensible to bad technological design.

The humanistic and ethical view is absolutely imperative. This ethical point of view should be complemented with legal considerations as well. For modelling human emotion, a previous study in laboratories producing emotion elicitation is relevant, first with people without intellectual disabilities and then with final users when the system performance would be enough robust [7].

4 Development of the Video Elicitation Database

The development of a HEAS to detect and manage block situations requires appropriate elicitation databases. Since, the goal of our elicitation process will be to induce pre-block stages respecting the ethical criteria described previously, we will analyze the elicitation techniques to create real stress, anxiously or panic attack situations.

Many emotion elicitation techniques have been studied: mental image reproductions, displaying emotional categorized films and slides, real-life techniques, autobiographical memories, hypnosis, facial postures, Velten mood induction technique, music, among others. Among them displaying emotional categorized films seems to achieve better results due to its dynamic profile [8]. Furthermore, it has been widely observed that emotional categorized films can elicit strong subjective and physiological changes. Moreover, the dynamic profile of this technique obtains an optimal artificial model of reality, conforming practical problems of real-life technique, and providing better procedures to comply with ethical issues. For that reasons, it seems to offer a very good technique emotion elicitation in laboratory, especially for specific emotional states. Films are effective stimuli to elicit emotions. A set of films to elicit specific emotions was developed in a previous study by *Gross* et al [8]. Nowadays, this set of films is been used as valid material in current studies. However in our work, some of these films were replaced for actual films after a first validation by specialists (psychologist and system developers) to test their impact in our society (table 1). Most of these films were just not valid because of: they were old films with bad imagine and sound quality; the language translation was not effective; they were movies with low emotional impact due to previous visualization. Finally the elicitation database was developed with more than 50 films. These films were selected: consulting film experts, owners from video clubs, internet forums and also looked for real facts where they gave more emotions than a film [9,10]. For the experimentation stage, 20 video clips from the database and a neutral clip to recover the emotional basal level were selected (*Gross+RF*). For the preliminary experimental stage, a questionnaire about 12 classical emotions descriptions was used, and in order to increase the participant perceptions, new emotions provided by the participants were also included. In the final experimental stage, the questionnaire to define the attributes of the database is based on discrete emotions and dimensional terms (pleasant, unpleasant) with a range from 0 (not at all, none) to 8 (extremely/a great deal).

Table 1. Description of the Video Elicitation database

	Ind-Num	Film Num	Real Scene N	Instances
Gross	5	13	1	61
Gross+RF	7	21	7	62
Gross+RF-SS	45	30	6	562

The database elements have the following attributes, extract from the questionnaires: 3 classical scales, activity, dominance and valence (*Classical* proposal); 16 emotional descriptions (*Classical* proposal and these descriptions constitute *Rottenberg* proposal) [11]; new emotional answer descriptions provides by participants such as: Boredom, Freedom, Loneliness, Fascination or Hate (*Rottenberg proposals* and new descriptions constitute New Proposal, table 2). Most of these new emotional answers are strong emotional description due to the films selection oriented to induce pre-block stage and stress limit situations. The database was classified in 7 emotions. Subsequently, the films were mounted in three groups with 10 clips each one. In order to organize appropriately the projection, it was necessary to avoid editing neither 2 clips with the same emotion, nor with the same valence [9]. Finally the developed database has 45 volunteers and more than 1000 emotional answers (table 1).

Table 2. Identification of the attributes of the database elements

Attribute	Classical	Rottenberg	New Emotional
Valence	X	X	X
Activity	X	X	X
Dominance	X	X	X
Amusement	-	X	X
Anger	-	X	X
Anxiety	-	X	X
Confusion	-	X	X
Contempt	-	X	X
Disgust	-	X	X
Embarrassment	-	X	X
Fear	-	X	X
Guilt	-	X	X
Happiness	-	X	X
Love	-	X	X
Pride	-	X	X
Sadness	-	X	X
Shame	-	X	X
Surprise	-	X	X
Unhappiness	-	X	X
Other emotion	-	-	X

5   Hybrid Approach for Automatic Evaluation

A brief manual validation of the database was carried out by specialists (psychologists and system developers) over *Gross* and Real Films (Gross+RF) sets. Figure 1 shows relevant conclusions in this validation. Analyzing the obtained values, it can be observed that the video clips used in second set obtained better values in the emotional

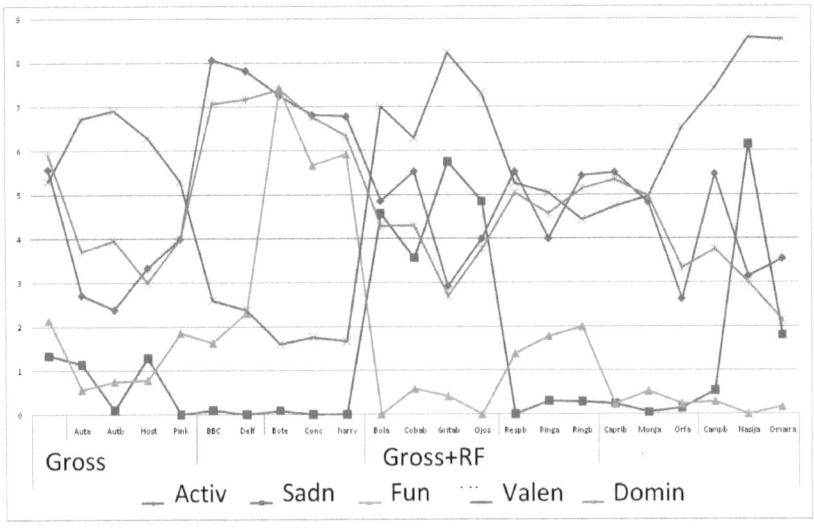

Fig. 1. Manual validation by specialists over *Gross* and *Gross+RF* sets

answer situations over the *Gross* proposal. This is due to the selection of films oriented to produce strong emotional answers to induce pre-block stage and stress limit situations. Then in order to achieve a deep and exhaustive Automatic Evaluation of the database a new methodology based on Machine Learning and unsupervised K-means clustering has been designed. This approach will also provide new emotion answer proposals to complete the previous manual validation.

The single Machine Learning paradigms used in the Automatic Evaluation are briefly introduced: C4.5, Multilayer Perceptron (MP), Naive Bayes (BN) classifiers, KNN and Support Vector Machines (SVM). The above mentioned methods have been applied over the cross-validated data sets. Each instance corresponds to an emotional answer. Three experiments were carried out (figure 2). *Gross* and *Gross+RF* have been described in section 4 and *Gross+RF-SS* is based on a subset extract from *Gross+RF* with similar size to *Gross* and created to compare appropriately the results.

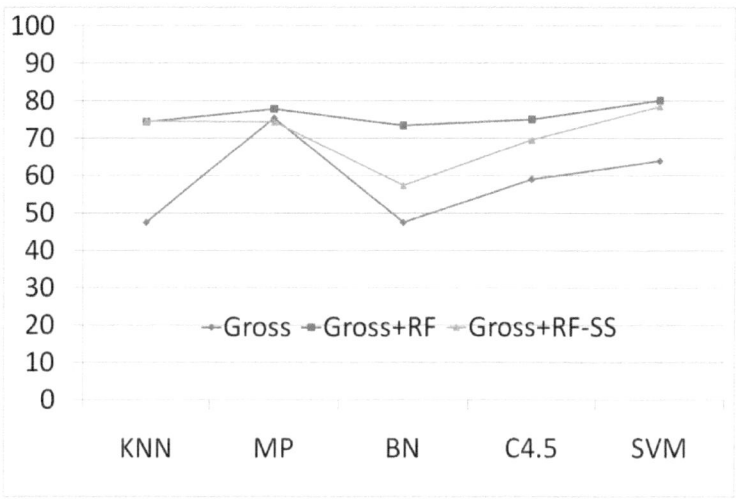

Fig. 2. 10-fold cross-validation, accuracy for *Gross*, *Gross+RF* and *Gross+RF-SS*

On the one hand, figure 2 shows the classification results obtained by the whole set of variables, for *Gross*, *Gross+RF* and *Gross+RF-SS* respectively showing accuracy for each classifier with 10-fold cross-validation. Results show a good performance for most paradigms obtaining the best accuracy for SVM. On the other hand in *Gross+RF* and *Gross+RF-SS* the accuracies outperform the previous ones in more than 10%. It must also be highlighted that the new database improves the well classified rate for all the ML paradigms, as figure 2 shows. This is due to the features of the new films selected to produce strong emotional answers oriented to induce pre-block stage and stress limit situations. On the second hand, figure 3 shows the classification results for *Gross+RF* set with *Classical, Rottenberg, Principal Components* and *New Proposal*. Figure 3 shows the best results for *New Proposal* emotion description set and poor results for *Classical* approach. Thus we can conclude that new emotional

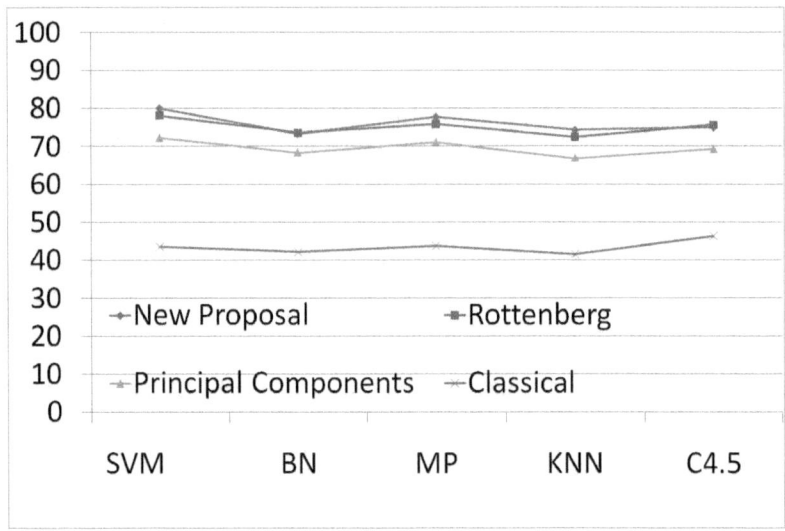

Fig. 3. 10-fold cross-validation, accuracy for Gross+RF with Classical, Rottenberg, Principal Components and New Proposal

answers descriptions contribute to introduce new relevant details about these pre-block situations. Finally some new emotional answer proposals have been generated with K-means clustering algorithm in unsupervised mode. The obtained results were analyzed by the specialist and have provided interesting information and options to model emotional answers in the future.

5 Concluding Remarks

A new Human Emotion Analysis System (HEAS) has been designed in order to prevent and regulate non-perceivable human emotions. This HEAS will enhance the Intelligent System (*LAGUNTXO*) performance [1]. Despite everybody could benefit of the results of research on assistive technology, accessibility and intelligent environments, the participation of people with disabilities in these research experiments will be of lively interest, since these persons have many more difficulties of adaptation than other people, and they are more sensible to bad technological design.

In this work, new methods and material to analyze and classify human emotions, and corresponding elicited emotions have been tested. This study has provided finding emotional changes which give the opportunity of detecting block situations in people with intellectual disabilities. The hybrid evaluation over the created elicitation material and methods indicates a high level of accuracy with respect to others classically presented in the literature. Finally, new studies are going to be performed in the future taking into account new affective resources and emotional answers proposals provided by the specialist and unsupervised clustering methods, and hierarchical methods [12].

Acknowledgements. The involved work has received financial support from the Spanish Ministerio de Ciencia y Tecnología, project TSI2006-14250-C02-01, and the Spanish Ministerio de Industria, Turismo y Comercio, project PDM-2006-178.

References

1. Conde, A., López de Ipiña, K., Larrañaga, M., Garay-Vitoria, N., Irigoyen, E., Ezeiza, A., Rubio, J.: An Intelligent Tutoring System oriented to the Integration of People with Intellectual Disabilities. In: PAAMS 2010, SMC-IEEE Workshop, Spanish Chapter, Salamanca (2010)
2. Cowie, R., Douglas-Cowie, E., Cox, C.: Beyond emotion archetypes: Databases for emotion modeling using neural networks. J. Neural Networks 18, 371–388 (2005)
3. Fragopanagos, N., Taylor, J.G.: Emotion recognition in human–computer interaction. J. Neural Networks 18, 389–405 (2005)
4. Taylor, J., et al.: Emotion and brain: Understanding emotions and modelling their recognition. J. Neural Networks 18, 313–316 (2005)
5. Cañamero, L.: Emotion understanding: From the perspective of autonomous robots research. J. Neural Networks 18, 445–455 (2005)
6. Lang, P.J., Öhman, A., Vaitl, D.: The International Affective Picture System (Photografic slides). In: University of Florida (eds.) Center for Research in Psychophysiology, Gainesville, FL (1998)
7. Ezeiza, A., Garay, N., López de Ipiña, K., Soraluze, A.: 2008 Ethical issues on the design of assistive technology for people with mental disabilities. In: Fillet, J.F. (ed.) Proceedings of the International Conference on Ethics and Human Values in Engineering (ICEHVE 2008), pp. 75–84 (2008), ISBN: 978-84-96736-42-9
8. Gross, J., Levenson, W.: Emotion Elicitation Using Films. J. Cognition and Emotion 9, 87–108 (1995)
9. Stephens, C.L.: Autonomic Differentiation of Emotions: A Cluster Analysis Approach. Technical Report, Virginia Polytechnic Institute and State University (2007)
10. Schaefer, A., Nils, F., Sanchez, X., Philippot, P.: A multi-criteria assessment of emotional films. In: Report for publication, University of Louvain (eds.) Louvain-La-Neuve, Belgium (2005)
11. Rottenberg, J., Ray, R.D., Gross, J.J.: Emotion elicitation using films. In: Coan, J.A., Allen, J.J.B. (eds.) The handbook of emotion elicitation and assessment. Oxford University Press, London (2007)
12. Graña, M., Torrealdea, F.J.: Hierarchically structured systems. European Journal of Operational Research 25, 20–26 (1986)

Fusion of Fuzzy Spatial Relations

Nadeem Salamat and El-hadi Zahzah

Université de La Rochelle
Laboratoire de Mathematiques, Images et Applications
Avenue M Crépeau La Rochelle 17042, France
{nsalamat,ezahzah}@univ-lr.fr

Abstract. Spatial relations are essential for understanding the image configuration and modeling common sense knowledge. In most of existing methods, topological, directional and distance spatial relations are computed separately as they have separate application domains. Introduction of Temporal Geographic Information System (TGIS), spatio-temporal reasoning and study of spatio-temporal relations required the computation of topological and metric spatial relations together.
In this paper the fuzzy topological and directional relations are integrated with the help of fuzzy Allen relations and directions are evaluated by specific fuzzy membership functions. A matrix of fuzzy relations is developed where the topological and directional relations are integrated for a 2D scene. Experiments are performed to validate the proposed method. The results are analyzed and interpreted from histograms.

Keywords: Topological and metric relations, Fuzzy topological relations, Fusion of spatial relations, Fuzzy directional relations, Matrix of fuzzy relations.

1 Introduction

Temporal Geographic Information System (TGIS) was introduced in recent years. This enhancement of Geographic Information System (GIS) deeply affects the present studies in GIS and need fusion of different information provided from different sensors given heterogenous data. The fusion of spatial relations will be helpful in defining the spatio-temporal relations, reasoning in many decision processus. In existing methods, topological, directional and distance spatial relations are studied separately. Beside this information, fuzzy spatial relations are also important for fuzzy reasoning, fuzzy image understanding and fuzzy change detection. Fuzzy topological relations are studied by the extended models of 9 -intersections [5,4] and Region Connected Calculus (RCC8) [13,14,16]. These topological relations are studied through the object model with intermediate boundaries or the well known *Egg-Yolk* model [2,3]. Fuzzy directional relations can be defined using the mathematical morphology as in [7] and numerical methods as in [11,10]. Fuzzy directional relations assign a degree to each cardinal direction and different methods are used to assign the degree to a cardinal direction. Another type of metric relation is the distance relations.

M. Graña Romay et al. (Eds.): HAIS 2010, Part I, LNAI 6076, pp. 294–301, 2010.

These relations provide us the distance information about the closet part of objects and a fuzzy membership function assigns a degree to the distance relation Near, Far and Far off [1]. In the approaches for finding the fuzzy directional relations, crisp objects are considered and fuzzy objects are treated by considering the Egg's boundary. Fuzzy methods for directional relations work for the limited set of topological relations. All sort of relations are essential for image understanding, modeling common sense knowledge, natural phenomenon and spatial reasoning [6]. This requirement of image understanding needs to apply different methods to find the topological, directional and distance relations between the objects and it is needed to have a single method where we can get all the required information about the spatial scene. In this work two types of fuzzy sets are used, $1D$ fuzzy sets for finding the fuzzy Allen relations and then $1D$ directional fuzzy sets for evaluating the directions in $2D$ scene. This method of using the $1D$ fuzzy sets provide us the integrated topological and directional information of a $2D$ scene. These integrated information of a $2D$ scene are represented in a matrix. Each entity of this matrix represents the percentage surface area of two objects having a topological relation in a specific direction.

This paper is structured as follows, section 2 discusses in detail the different terms and computations necessary for $1D$ Allen relations, in section 3 the fusion of topological and directional relations and their interpretation is given. Results for different configurations is given in section 4. Section 5 concludes the paper.

2   Terminology Used for Computation Fuzzy Allen Relations

2.1   Oriented Lines, Segments and Longitudinal Sections

Let A and B be two spatial objects and $(v, \theta) \in \mathbb{R}$, where v is any real number and $\theta \in [0, 2\pi]$. $\Delta_\theta(v)$ is an oriented line at orientation angle θ. $A \cap \Delta_\theta(v)$ is the intersection of object A and oriented line $\Delta_\theta(v)$. It is denoted by $A_\theta(v)$, called segment of object A and its length is x. Similarly for object B where $B \cap \Delta_\theta(v) = B_\theta(v)$ is segment and z is its length. y is the difference between the maximum value of $B \cap \Delta_\theta(v)$ and minimum of $A \cap \Delta_\theta(v)$ (for details [12]). In case of polygonal object approximations (x, y, z) can be calculated from intersecting points of line and object boundary. If there exist more than one segment, then it is called longitudinal section. In this paper all the 180 directions are considered with an angle increment of one degree and lines are drawn by $2D$ Bresenham digital line algorithm. A polygonal object approximation is taken and lines passing through the polygon vertices are taken into account.

2.2 $1D$ Allen Relations in Space

Allen [8] relations are arranged as $A = \{<, m, o, s, f, d, eq, d_i, f_i, s_i, o_i, m_i, >\}$ with meanings *before, meet, overlap, start, finish, during, equal, during_ by, finish_ by, start_ by, overlap_ by, meet_ by, and after*. All the Allen relations in space are conceptually illustrated in figure 1. These relations have a rich

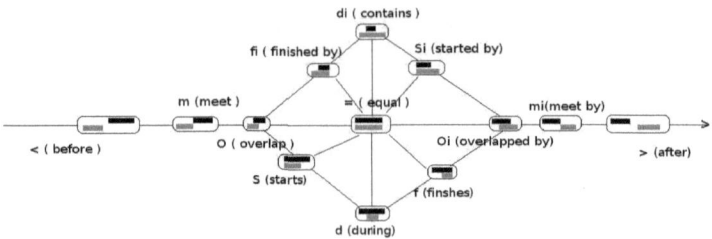

Fig. 1. Black segment represents the reference object and gray segment represents argument object

support for the topological and directional relations. In the neighborhood graph of Allen relations, three paths can be find (because we assume that objects are monolithic and don't changing size during their movement. Some possible paths are ignored due to this reason). Depending upon the neighborhood graph of Allen relations, Inverse of these relations can be divided into two categories, object commutativity and reorientation of relations. According to reorientation of a relation, we can write $A_1 = \{<, m, o, S, d, f_i, d_i, =\}$ and their inverses as $A_2 = \{>, m_i, o_i, f, d, S_i, d_i, =\}$. This shows that relations $d, =, d_i$ have their own reorientations. Region Connected Calculus - RCC8 relations are possible combination of 8 independent Allen relations in $1D$. These relations and their inverse show that the whole $2D$ space can be explored with the help of $1D$ Allen relations using oriented lines varying from $(0, \pi)$.

2.3   Fuzzification of Allen Relations

Fuzzification process of Allen relations do not depend upon particular choice of fuzzy membership function, trapezoidal membership function is used due to flexibility in shape change. Let $r(I, J)$ be Allen relation between segments I and J where $I \in A$(argument object) and $J \in B$ (reference object), r' is the distance between $r(I, J)$ and its conceptional neighborhood. We consider a fuzzy membership function $\mu : r' \longrightarrow [0, 1]$. The fuzzy Allen relations defined by Matsakis [12] are

- $f_<(I, J) = \mu_{(-\infty, -\infty, -b-3a/2, -b-a)}(y)$,
- $f_>(I, J) = \mu_{(0, a/2, \infty, \infty)}(y)$
- $f_m(I, J) = \mu_{(-b-3a/2, -b-a, -b-a, -b-a/2)}(y)$,
- $f_{mi}(I, J) = \mu_{(-a/2, 0, 0, a/2)}(y)$
- $f_{oi}(I, J) = \mu_{(-a, -a/2, -a/2, 0)}(y)$
- $f_{si}(I, J) = min(\mu_{(-(b+a)/2, -a, -a, +\infty)}(y), \mu_{(-3a/2, -a, -a, -a/2)}(y),$
  $\mu_{(z, 2z, +\infty, +\infty)}(x))$
- $f_d(I, J) = min(\mu_{(-b, -b+a/2, -3a/2, -a)}(y), \mu_{(-\infty, -\infty, z/2, z)}(x))$

where $a = min(x, z), b = max(x, z)$ and x is the length of longitudinal section of argument object A and z is the length of longitudinal section of reference object B. Most of relations are defined by one membership function like $before$, *after*,*meet*, *meet_by* and some of them are defined by more than one membership functions like $d(during)$, $d_i(during\_by)$, f ($finish$), f_i ($finished\_by$). In fuzzy set theory, sum of all the relations is one, this gives the definition for relation fuzzy *equal*. During the decomposition process of an object into segments, there can be multiple segments depending on object shape and boundary which is called longitudinal section. Different segments of a longitudinal section are at a certain distance and these distances might effect end results. Fuzzy *T-conorms* are used for fuzzy integration of available information. Here for simplicity only *T-conorm* (Fuzzy *OR* operator)is used.

$$\mu_{(OR)}(u) = max(\mu_{(A)}(u), \mu_{(B)}(u))$$

2.4   Normalized Fuzzy Histogram of Allen Relations

Histogram of fuzzy Allen relation represents total area of subregions of A and B that are facing each other in given direction θ. Mathematically it can be written as [15]

$$\int_{-\infty}^{+\infty} (\sum_{r \epsilon A} F_r(\theta, A_\theta(v), B_\theta(v))) dv = (x+z) \sum_{k=1}^{n} r(I_k, J_k)$$

where z is the area of reference object and x is area of augmented object in direction θ, n is total number of segments treated and $r(I_k, J_k)$ is an Allen relation for segments (I_k, J_k). These histograms are normalized by dividing all Allen's relations by their sum for every θ. It is represented by $\lceil F_r^{AB}(\theta) \rfloor$ where $r \in A$. $\lceil F_r^{AB}(\theta) \rfloor = \frac{F_r^{AB}(\theta)}{\sum_{\rho \in A} F_\rho^{AB}(\theta)}$. These fuzzy Allen relations are directional fuzzy numbers and can be used to define the quantitative fuzzy directional relations.

3   Fusion of Topological and Directional Relations

This section consists of two subsections where in first one it is described how different functions can be used to assess the fuzzy qualitative directions and how the different Allen relations are combined for topological and directional information fusion. In second subsection, the representation method for the fuzzy topological and fuzzy directional relations is described in detail.

3.1   Fusion of Topological and Directional Components

All these equations depicted in section 2.3 assign a numerical value to a topological spatial relation in a direction θ. To find directional contents of a topological relation, these numerical values are used with directional fuzzy sets. Directions are represented as $\{E, NE, N, NW, W, SW, S, SE\}$ with meanings *East, North_ East, North, North_ West, West, South_ West, South* and *South_ East*. To assess these fuzzy directional relations, two trigonometric membership functions $cos2\theta$ and $sin2\theta$ are used. As angle distribution is taken to the half plane so opposite Allen relations are used to define the opposite directions except the direction East and West where union of both relations are used. Mathematically these relations can be defined as

$$- f_E = \sum_{\theta=0}^{\frac{\pi}{4}} A_{r_2} \times cos^2(2\theta) + \sum_{\theta=\frac{3\pi}{4}}^{\pi} A_{r_1} \times cos^2(2\theta)$$

$$- f_W = \sum_{\theta=0}^{\frac{\pi}{4}} A_{r_1} \times cos^2(2\theta) + \sum_{\theta=\frac{3\pi}{4}}^{\pi} A_{r_2} \times cos^2(2\theta)$$

$$- f_N = \sum_{\theta=\frac{\pi}{4}}^{\frac{3\pi}{4}} A_{r_2} \times cos^2(2\theta)$$

$$- f_S = \sum_{\theta=\frac{\pi}{4}}^{\frac{3\pi}{4}} A_{r_1} \times cos^2(2\theta)$$

Where $A_{r_i} \in A_i, i = 1, 2$ given in section 2.2 and $f \in \{D, EC, PO, TPP, NTPP, TPPI, NTPPI, EQ\}$ which respectively mean Disjoint, Externally connected, Partially overlap, Tangent properpart,   Non tangent properpart, Tangent properpart inverse, Non Tangent properpart inverse, and Equal.

3.2   Interpretation of Topological and Directional Relations

The relations are manipulated in (8×8) matrix where $C(i,j)$ represents the ith topological relation in j^{th} direction. Rows are arranged in an order of $\{D, EC, PO, TPP, NTPP, TPPI, NTPPI, EQ\}$. Different directions may yield different $1D$ relations in $2D$ space and different relations may coexist along the same direction. A conclusion about the overall $2D$ relation is given below.

1. Only first row is non zero then objects have fuzzy disjoint (DC) topological relation.
2. If the first and the second rows are non zero then the overall relation in $2D$ space is fuzzy *meet EC*.
3. If there exist at least one non zero value in third row it means there exist fuzzy topological relation *overlap.* or If non zero values also exist in *TPP* along with *NTPP* (*TPPI* along with *NTPPI*) then the relation will be *TPP* (*NTPP*) in the corresponding direction.
4. Relations *PP, PPI, EQ* hold if the corresponding relation holds in all directions. A relation will hold if all elements in a row are non zero and all other rows are zero.

The above explanation shows that *overlap* relation in $2D$ space is more complex than any other topological relation. In this case all the Allen relations coexist in different directions.

4   Experiments and Discussion

In the following set of examples the objects A (argument object) and B (reference object) are represented by light and dark grey colors respectively. A matrix of fuzzy topological and directional relations are computed. Figure (2(a)) shows that argument object A meets the reference object B in direction *East*, their topological and directional relations show that there exist a topological relation meet EC with a maximum degree in direction *East* along with other neighboring directions and *Disjoint* topological relation exists due to application of $1D$ Allen relations (figure 2(b)). Argument object A in figure 2(c) touches the

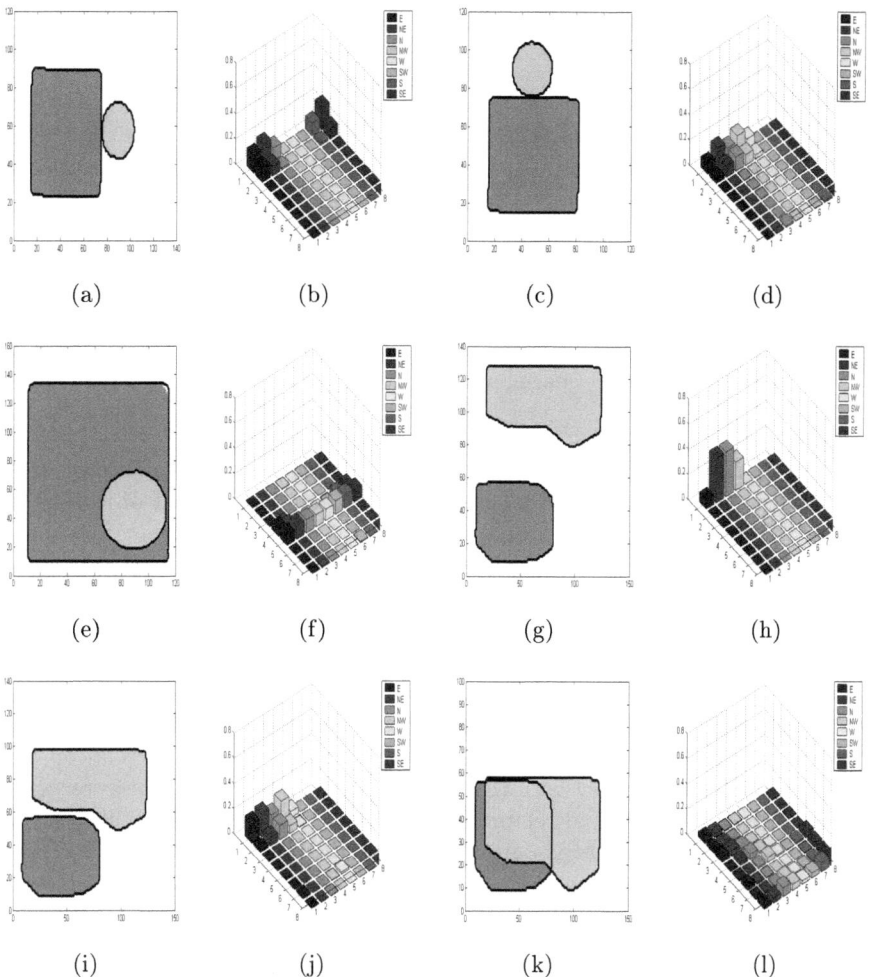

Fig. 2. Object pairs with meet topological relation and their directional relations

reference object from *North*, their relation matrix validates the said relation
(2(d)). In figure 2(e) argument object lies inside the reference object near the
boundary in the *East* and *South_ East* direction, their relations matrix (figure
2(f)) shows that the *TPP* topological relation exists with equal degree in the
East and *South_ East* direction. In figure 2(g), objects are disjoint and fuzzy
relations matrix shows that object lies in *North_ East, North, North_ West* to
the reference object. Directional components as shown in figure 2(h) specify the
object location. In figures 2(i), fuzzy topological relation *EC* exits due to fuzziness of Allen relations. Disjoint relation exist in directions *E,NE,N, NW and W*
with different degree due to fuzziness of directions. In figure 2(k) objects overlap
and a topological relation *PO* exists but existence of other relations like *D, EC*
represented in figure 2(j) express the complexity of *PO* relations.

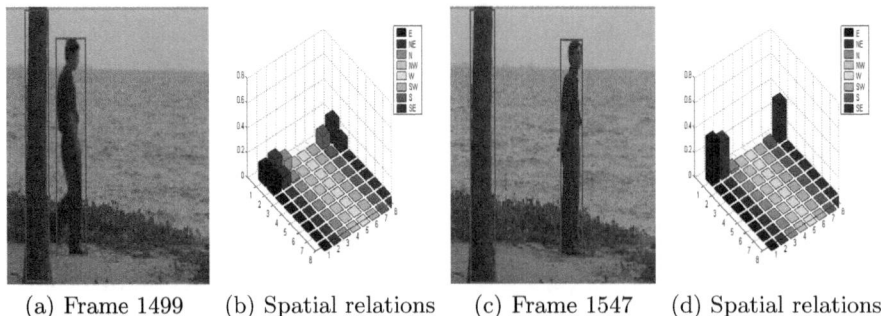

(a) Frame 1499   (b) Spatial relations   (c) Frame 1547   (d) Spatial relations

Fig. 3. Difference frames of image sequence "watersurface" and their spatial relations

In this example, the method is applied to a well known sequence of images "water surface sequence" [9] where a manual segmentation of objects is performed. The tree is taken as a reference object B while the shape of the person is taken as an argument object A. In figure 3(a) as the argument (person) object is very close to the reference object (tree). due to this closeness, there exist fuzzy meet (EC) relation in a certain directions along with the fuzzy disjoint relation in a specified directions. There exist number of directions because the object is very close and visual rang is too much large (results are shown in figure 3(b)). As the argument object walks away from the reference object (3(c)), their topological relations also change. Now only fuzzy disjoint topological relation exists and due to the distance between the objects, their visual rang also decreases and only E, NE, SE directional relations exist (figure 3(d)). In all the above examples, it is shown that the topological and directional relations can be successfully integrated in a single method. This method will be hopefully used for spatio-temporal reasoning where we need the topological and directional information at each step.

5   Conclusion

Spatial topological and directional relations are important to understand the scene configuration and spatio-temporal reasoning. Spatio-temporal information fusion is important to have a single method to understand the image configuration completely. In this paper, the key point is that different informations regarding the topological and directional relations are integrated through a single method. These relations are sensitive to the distance between the objects and cardinal directions. Due to the spatio-temporal nature it is possible to construct from the fuzzy Allen relations a set of spatio-temporal relations such as *Leave,Enter, Cross, Bypass* and others. This method could be used for spatio-temporal reasoning. Our future work will now in defining the spatio-temporal relations of the above mentioned classes between two moving spatial objects.

References

1. Bloch, I., Maitre, H.: Fuzzy distances and image processing. In: SAC 1995: Proceedings of the 1995 ACM Symposium on Applied Computing, pp. 570–574. ACM, New York (1995)
2. Clementini, E., Felice, P.D.: An algebraic model for spatial objects with indeterminate boundaries. In: Burrough, P., Frank, A. (eds.) Geographic Objects with Indeterminate, pp. 155–169. Taylor and Francis, London (1996)
3. Cohn, A.G., Gotts, N.M.: The 'egg-yolk' representation of regions with indeterminate boundaries. In: Burrough, P., Frank, A.M. (eds.) Proceedings of GISDATA Specialist Meeting on Geographical Objects with Undetermined Boundaries, pp. 171–187. Taylor and Francis, London (1996)
4. Du, S., Qin, Q., Wang, Q., Li, B.: Fuzzy description of topological relations i: A unified fuzzy 9-intersection model. ICNC (3), 1261–1273 (2005)
5. Egenhofer, M.J., Sharma, J., Mark, D.M.: A Critical Comparison of The 4-Intersection and 9-Intersection Models for Spatial Relations: Formal Analysis. Auto-Carto 11, 1–12 (1993)
6. Hudelot, C., Atif, J., Bloch, I.: Fuzzy Spatial Relation Ontology for Image Interpretation. Fuzzy Sets Syst. 159(15), 1929–1951 (2008)
7. Isabelle Bloch, A.R.: Directional Relative Position Between Objects in Image Processing: A Comparison Between Fuzzy Approaches. Pattern Recognition 36, 1563–1582 (2003)
8. Allen, J.F.: Maintaining Knowledge about Temporal Intervals. Communications of the ACM 26(11), 832–843 (1983)
9. Li, L., Huang, W., Gu, I.Y.H., Tian, Q.: Statistical modeling of complex backgrounds for foreground object detection. IEEE Transactions on Image Processing 13(11), 1459–1472 (2004)
10. Matsakis, P., Keller, J.M., Wendling, L.: F-Histograms and Fuzzy Directional Spatial Relations. In: Proceedings, LFA 1999 French-Speaking Conference on Fuzzy Logic and Its Applications, pp. 207–213 (1999)
11. Miyajima, K., Ralescu, A.: Spatial Organization in 2D Segmented Images: Representation and Recognition of Primitive Spatial Relations. Fuzzy Sets Syst. 65(2-3), 225–236 (1994)
12. Matsakis, P., Nikitenko, D.: Combined Extraction of Directional and Topological Relationship Information from 2D Concave Objects. In: Fuzzy Modeling with Spatial Information for Geographic Problems, pp. 15–40. Springer, New York (2005)
13. Randell, D., Cui, Z., Cohn, A.: A spatial logic based on regions and connection. In: Proc. 3rd Int. Conf. on Knowledge Representation and Reasoning, pp. 165–176. Morgan Kaufmann, San Mateo (1992)
14. Rosenfeld, A.: Fuzzy digital topology. Information and Control 40(1), 76–87 (1979)
15. Salamat, N., hadi Zahzah, E.: Spatial relations analysis by using fuzzy operators. In: Allen, G., Nabrzyski, J., Seidel, E., van Albada, G.D., Dongarra, J., Sloot, P.M.A. (eds.) Computational Science – ICCS 2009, Part 2. LNCS, vol. 5545, pp. 395–404. Springer, Heidelberg (2009)
16. Tang, X.: Spatial object model[l]ing in fuzzy topological spaces: with applications to land cover change. Ph.D. thesis, Enschede (2004), http://doc.utwente.nl/41448/

Reducing Artifacts in TMS-Evoked EEG

Juan José Fuertes[1], Carlos M. Travieso[2], A. Álvarez[2], M.A. Ferrer[2], and J.B. Alonso[2]

[1] Instituto Interuniversitario de Investigación en Bioingeniería y Tecnología Orientada al Ser Humano, Universidad Politécnica de Valencia
Camino de Vera s/n, 46022 Valencia, España
jjfuertes@labhuman.i3bh.es
[2] Dpto. de Señales y Comunicaciones, Universidad de Las Palmas de Gran Canaria
Centro Tecnológico para la Innovación en Comunicaciones
Campus de Tafira, 35017 Las Palmas de Gran Canaria, España
{ctravieso,mferrer,jalonso}@dsc.ulpgc.es

Abstract. Transcranial magnetic stimulation induces weak currents within the cranium to activate neuronal firing and its response is recorded using electroencephalography in order to study the brain directly. However, different artifacts contaminate the results. The goal of this study is to process these artifacts and reduce them digitally. Electromagnetic, blink and auditory artifacts are considered, and Signal-Space Projection, Independent Component Analysis and Wiener Filtering methods are used to reduce them. These last two produce a successful solution for electromagnetic artifacts. Regarding the other artifacts, processed with Signal-Space Projection, the method reduces the artifact but modifies the signal as well. Nonetheless, they are modified in an exactly known way and the vector used for the projection is conserved to be taken into account when analyzing the resulting signals. A system which combines the proposed methods would improve the quality of the information presented to physicians.

Keywords: Transcranial magnetic stimulation, electroencephalogram, artifact, electromagnetic, blink, auditory.

1 Introduction

Transcranial magnetic stimulation (TMS) may give new insights into the behavior of the human brain. Powerful magnetic pulses with a coil placed above the head of the subject let cortical areas be activated non-invasively [1, 2]. TMS, along with Navigated Brain Stimulation (NBS) and electroencephalography (EEG), has revealed itself as a powerful non-invasive tool in studies about the brain's excitation threshold [3] or the relation between cortical activity and movement [4]. Nevertheless, only the TMS-evoked brain response is desired. Any other signal corrupts the brain signal registered, complicating brain response analysis. Therefore, several methods used frequently to split up two signals [5-10] are considered in this work: Signal-Space Projection (SSP), Independent Component Analysis (ICA) and Wiener Filtering, in order to compare them and propose a novel system to reduce three different artifacts usually found in TMS-evoked responses: Electromagnetic artifact (EM artifact) [11], Blink artifact (B artifact) [13], and Auditory artifact (A artifact) [12].

M. Graña Romay et al. (Eds.): HAIS 2010, Part I, LNAI 6076, pp. 302–310, 2010.
© Springer-Verlag Berlin Heidelberg 2010

2 Measurements

The global experiment consisted of a set of 8 recordings with the goal of isolating each artifact thanks to the Nexstim eXimia NBS. The subject was a young healthy man (age 22, right handed) and he participated in the study after giving a written informed consent. The experimental protocol was approved by the Ethical Committee of the Helsinki University Central Hospital, where these data were obtained. The researcher used the Nexstim eXimia TMS stimulator and delivered single pulses using a focal mono-pulse coil. The subject was seated in a reclining chair wearing earplugs. MRI-based navigating system Nexstim eXimia NBS was used to target at the omega-shaped hand area on the left primary motor cortex, more specifically the representation area of APB (abductor pollicis brevis) muscle (right thumb abductor muscle). The electromyogram (EMG) of the muscle was registered to determine the motor threshold (MT, TMS intensity making 5 out of 10 motor evoked responses (MEP) greater than 50 µV). The TMS-compatible EEG equipment with a 60-electrode cap was used for recording TMS-evoked potentials and its associated artifacts [4]. The EEG, recorded from 100 ms pre- to 500 ms post-stimulus, was referenced to an additional electrode placed behind right ear, which is far away from the position of the coil (left hemisphere) when the desired location is stimulated. Simultaneously, an electrooculogram (EOG) was recorded to detect eye movements. One EOG electrode was placed above the right eye and the other one on the left side of the left eye in order to record both horizontal and vertical eye movements. Measurements 1-3 had the aim of showing EM artifact with no/little brain response ([3], analyzing the relation between brain response and intensity and show that the limit to elicit measurable EEG response is between 20% and 40% of MT). No electromagnetic artifact appeared until reaching 100% MT, having both artifact and brain signal together. Measurements 6 and 7 should contain only auditory artifact because the distance prevents the pulse from reaching the brain with enough strength (magnetic field decays rapidly when the distance from the coil is increased). Measurement 7 is intended to simulate also the sound transported through the bones as vibration goes through the plastic to the cranium while keeping the distance to weaken the brain stimulation. Recording 8 contains blinks without any other brain response (the subject is not performing any task but blinking and there is no TMS).

3 Methods

All the binary data acquired with the TMS-EEG equipment was read and stored in matrices in Matlab (The Mathworks Inc., Natick, Massachusetts, USA). At least, 50 pulses were averaged in every experiment. In the blink recording, the 19 blinks taken in experiment were averaged, extracting them by searching for the maximum point of each blink and then getting a window of 600 ms around it (300 ms before and 300 ms after). To present the EEG data clearly, it was low-pass filtered after all processing, so that the figures were easier to read while not interfering with the procedures. The filter used a 50th-order Hamming window and a cut-off frequency of 45 Hz. With the data acquired, the techniques to reduce the three artifacts were applied separately.

Signal-Space Projection (SSP) [5]

Considering a d-channel measurement and a matrix m containing the measured value of each channel at each instant of time. If we assume a certain number of signal sources with an associated fixed direction in the signal space, we can write:

$$m(t) = \sum_{i=1}^{M} a_i(t) \cdot s_i + n(t) \tag{1}$$

where $m(t)$ is the measured signal at t, a_i is the time-varying amplitude of a fixed component s_i, having M different components. This model also includes some noise $n(t)$, independently of the defined components. The direction in the signal space is, therefore, the relative strength of a signal from a given source in different channels. Using Signal-Space Projection, the aim is to separate the signal $m(t)$ into contributions of different sets of sources:

$$m(t) = s_\parallel(t) + s_\perp(t) + n(t) \tag{2}$$

The grade of success of SSP depends on SNR and the angles between the component vectors. We will consider $s_\parallel$ and $s_\perp$ perpendicular, so the accuracy of the method will depend on the accuracy of that affirmation.

In the current study, we are using SSP for reducing electromagnetic, blink and auditory artifacts separately. Hence, we are developing the equations in order to separate one source s_1 (that of the artifact being processed):

$$m(t) = a_1(t) \cdot s_1 + \sum_{i=2}^{M} a_i(t) \cdot s_i + n(t) \tag{3}$$

From (2) and (3):

$$s_\parallel = a_1(t) \cdot s_1 \tag{4.a} \qquad\qquad s_\perp = \sum_{i=2}^{M} a_i(t) \cdot s_i \tag{4.b}$$

Multiplying (3) by $s_1{}^T$, and considering the angle between $s_\parallel$ and $s_\perp$ 90° [5] (and therefore the angle between $s_1{}^T$, and $s_\perp$ 90° too):

$$a_1(t) = m(t) \cdot s_1{}^T \tag{5}$$

and from (2), ignoring noise:

$$s_\perp = m(t) - \left(m(t) \cdot s_1{}^T\right) \cdot s_1 \tag{6}$$

As the desired signal without a certain artifact is the one given by (6), we will need all the components of that equation. $m(t)$ is the measured signal with the d-channel EEG and s_1 must be estimated for each artifact. This can be done by carefully planning experiments where the artifacts can be measured alone, as done in 'measurements', and then considering:

$$\hat{s}_1 = \frac{m(t_1)}{\| m(t_1) \|} \tag{7}$$

being t_1 ideally the time when we have nothing but the artifact being extracted.

Finally, it must be remarked that the measuring accuracy of the artifact, and only the artifact, will also affect to the effectiveness of SSP. Moreover, if the artifact consists of several different directions at different proportions at different moments, t_l would not represent the whole artifact, resulting in more inaccuracy in this model.

Independent Component Analysis (ICA) [6-8]

The ICA model [8] assumes having d linear mixtures of signal components s_i, $x_1..x_d$, each of which has the form:

$$x = \sum_{i=1}^{d} a_i \cdot s_i \qquad (8)$$

where d is the number of channels, x the measured signal in one channel and a is a weighting coefficient. Using a vector-matrix notation, it can be rewritten as:

$$x = A \cdot s \qquad (9)$$

This equation (8) is a generative model; it describes how the data observed are generated by a process of mixing the components s_i through a mixing matrix A. Both mixing matrix A and components s are being estimated observing the vector x.

In order to achieve that goal, ICA needs some restrictions [7]. The components s_i must be statistically independent (s_i provides no information about s_j) and only one of them may follow a Gaussian distribution. These conditions are assumed to be fulfilled in our case of brain activity and artifacts (we are considering the brain responses and the artifacts to be non-Gaussian and independent from each other). The method will compute the inverse of A, then obtaining our components as follows:

$$s = A^{-1} \cdot x \qquad (10)$$

Before computing A^{-1}, usually denoted as W, the ICA algorithm used performs some pre-processing. First of all, the data is centered by subtracting the mean value (just for the computing phase, it will be added back at the end of the process). Then, whitening is carried out (turning the covariance matrix of x into an identity matrix). The dimension of the data is reduced before estimating the independent components relying on Principal Component Analysis. This part of the procedure must be handled manually and that will be further discussed in the following sections with the target of obtaining the number of independent components needed.

Once the data have been properly pre-processed, the core of ICA consists of measuring non-gaussianity. We compute $y = w^T \cdot x$ and then, its non-gaussianity will be measured. As the Central Limit Theorem tells that the sum of independent random variables tends towards a Gaussian distribution, w^T is changed until we maximize the non-gaussianity of y. When that point is reached, one independent component (y) and one row of W (w^T) are obtained and the subsequent analysis is constrained to the space that gives estimates uncorrelated with the previous ones. This corresponds to orthogonalization in a suitably transformed space like our whitened space. This process is repeated until we have all the independent components and the full W matrix. Although there are several ways to measure the non-gaussianity, in our case it is done by approximating the negentropy [6] (negentropy is based on the information-theoretic quantity of differential entropy).

This whole mathematical procedure is done by using Hyvärinen's fixed point algorithm [6] and our main concerns will be practical ones: deciding the number of independent components, interpreting the outcomes and identifying the components. A second step will be finding a way to make the extracted components useful. This last issue is accomplished with Wiener filtering, as it is described later.

Wiener Filtering [9, 10]

The so-called Wiener solution to design filters based on a desired output from a given input is widely known [9, 10], so it will be omitted here. These principles can be used for purposes like the one dealt in this study and shown in Fig. 1.

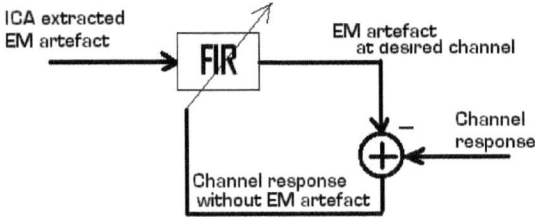

Fig. 1. FIR filter designed to reduce EM artifact using Wiener equations

4   Results

EM Artifact, SSP Approach - As told in the previous section, we need to discover the direction of the EM artifact in the signal space. There are two main features of this artifact: high amplitude and short duration. The former supports the assumption that if the direction of the artifact in the signal space is estimated at time when the artifact is strongest, the artifact will be so huge in comparison to the brain signal at that point of time that we may consider having only artifact. However, the second feature turns the method less useful, as it is not possible to choose a common point among all the channels where the artifact is maximal. Hence, the artifact will be reduced less and/or the brain signal will be distorted. The reason is that in one channel, the selected point will represent the EM artifact perfectly, but in some other channels the selected point will correspond to the brain signal and the EM artifact will be some samples before or some samples ahead, thus leading us to unsatisfactory results.

EM Artifact, ICA Approach - An Independent Component Analysis was carried out to separate the components of the registered EEG and isolate the EM artifact. Having 60 channels distributed across space makes ICA possible, but current understanding of brain signals may not be enough to identify the different independent components (ICs). Fortunately, the EM artifact has very well defined features (high frequency, large amplitude) which make it easy to be distinguished among the rest of the ICs.

With the EM artifact extracted, the next step consists of finding a way to take it out from each channel. For this purpose a Wiener filter is implemented. The scheme suggested in Fig. 1 is followed, so, our reference signal (input) is the ICA extracted EM artifact and our desired signal is the EEG signal in the channel we are processing. The output of the filter represents the EM artifact at the desired channel (since it is what input and desired signals have in common) and finally, the minimized error signal used to calculate the filter coefficients is the EEG signal in the processed channel with the EM artifact reduced. Each signal in the scheme is presented in Fig. 2 for a filter of order of 20. The outcome of ICA-Wiener (error signal) and the original signal (desired signal) are also shown low-pass filtered to facilitate comparison (in both cases a 50th-order Hamming window and a cut-off frequency of 45 Hz is used).

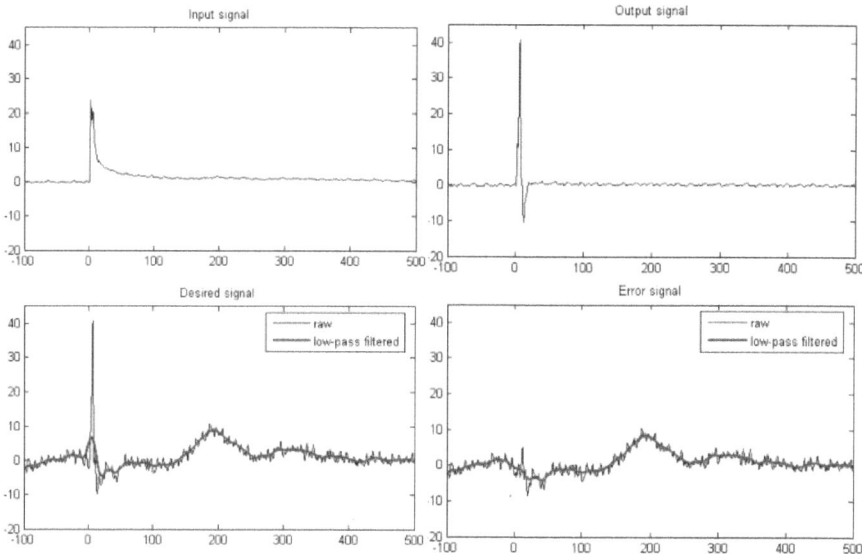

Fig. 2. Input signal (ICA extracted EM artifact); Desired signal (channel response); Output signal (EM artifact at desired channel) and error signal (cleaned channel response). Filter order M=20.

B Artifact, SSP Approach - The SSP method is applied to remove the B artifact [13]. The novelty here is having separate blink measurements (recording 8 of measurements). This allows us to estimate the blink artifact direction in the signal space and then use it to project the artifact away from the EEG signal. An artifact-direction analysis has been carried out to learn how the direction of the blink artifact vector in the signal space is changing in time during the blink. This reveals that the strongest influence of the blink is at the time when it peaks, the direction staying relatively constant in a window of 100 ms around the centre. It is chosen the direction vector measured at the peak time of the response to project the artifact away (Fig. 3).

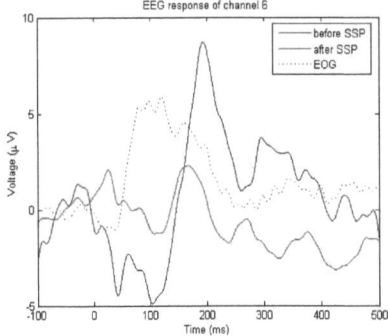
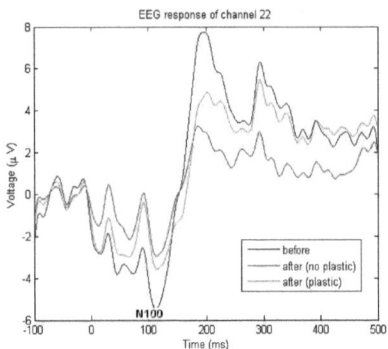

Fig. 3. Results of SSP projecting away the B artifact

Fig. 4. Application of SSP in the right temporal area

A Artifact, Direct Subtraction Approach - Before going to SSP, the feasibility of direct subtraction (subtracting recordings 6 and 7 from a TMS-EEG signal) was tested. The N100 response [4, 12], identified as the main consequence of the auditory artifact, is reduced in both cases; however, the rest of the waveforms are modified, especially the second one where the vibrations of the plastic distort them even more.

A Artifact, SSP Approach - SSP analysis has also been carried out. As done in the previous approach, recordings 6 and 7 are considered as auditory response. They are used for estimating the direction of the artifact in the signal space. To select the right moment of time to estimate this artifact, direction vectors have been calculated at each instant of time for both the plastic and the no-plastic cases. The sample at 100 ms has been chosen as the point to estimate the A artifact in the signal space in both cases aiming to reduce the effect of the A artifact on the N100. According to the results using SSP to reject this artifact at this point (Fig. 4), additional waveforms do not affect the method to the same great extent it does with direct subtraction.

4   Discussion and Conclusions

EM Artifact - Results achieved using SSP are poor when trying to reduce the EM artifact. The large amplitude and short duration characteristics cause problems in estimating the direction of the artifact in the signal space. On contrary, these features make it possible to be clearly identified with ICA. Wiener filtering makes good use of the ICA-extracted EM artifact to clean every channel from the EM artifact.

B Artifact - Notwithstanding the modification of the brain response, SSP reduce the B artifact, but it is impossible to determine whether the modification is due to the reduction of blink artifact or not and in what measure. The vector used to project the artifact is a key factor to the expert on this point, not only because it determines how the artifact has been projected away, but also tells how the non-artifact sources have been modified. This fact can be helpful to elucidate if the modification under discussion is due to the artifact reduction or to the after-effect caused to other sources.

A Artifact - The direct subtraction method modifies the brain waveform to an unacceptable level. Its results should not be trusted until deeper understanding of the effects of the auditory response is achieved to prevent information loss. SSP provides a more conservative approach, reducing only the contamination of the coil click regarding the N100 response.

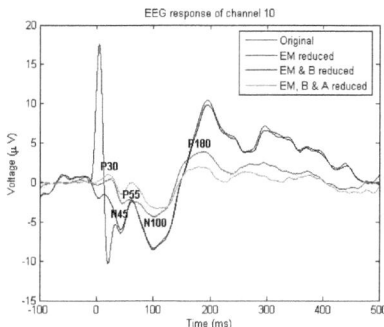

Fig. 5. Signal evolution after each step of the whole procedure

However, the auditory response has different directions at different instants of time and therefore, the whole auditory artifact is not removed.

In conclusion, there is little information and poor understanding regarding brain signals. Hence, among the methods studied, a criterion of minimal information loss must prevail. SSP provides a conservative approach. Moreover, keeping the vector used for projection makes the method reversible. When it is not applicable, the ICA-Wiener procedure proposed eradicates the EM artefact whereas other waveforms stay unmodified. It is easy to conclude that a system that combines the EM (ICA-Wiener), B (SSP) and A (SSP) artifact methods consecutively, would improve the quality of the information presented to physicians with TMS-EEG equipment (see Fig. 5).

Acknowledgments. This present work has been supported in part by private funds from Spanish Company, Telefónica, under the project called "Cátedra Teléfonica-ULPGC 2009"; and in part by TEC2009-14123-C04-01 from Spanish Government.

References

1. Barker, A.T., Jalinous, R., Freeston, I.L.: Non-invasive magnetic stimulation of human motor cortex. Lancet 1, 1106–1107 (1985)
2. Ilmoniemi, R.J.: Transcranial magnetic stimulation. Wiley Encyclopedia of Biomedical Engineering (2006)
3. Komssi, S., Savolainen, P., Heiskala, J., Kähkönen, S.: Excitation threshold of the motor cortex estimated with transcranial magnetic stimulation electroencephalography. NeuroReport 18(1), 13–16 (2007)
4. Nikulin, V.V., Kicic, D., Kähkönen, S., Ilmoniemi, R.J.: Modulation of electroencephalographic responses to transcranial magnetic stimulation: evidence for changes in cortical excitability related to movements. European Journal of Neuroscience 18(5), 1206–1212 (2003)

5. Uusitalo, M.A., Ilmoniemi, R.J.: Signal-space projection method for separating MEG or EEG into components. Med. & Biol. Eng. & Comput. 35(2), 135–140 (1997)
6. Hyvärinen, A., Oja, E.: Independent component analysis: algorithms and applications. Neuronal Networks 13(4-5), 411–430 (2000)
7. Zhukov, L., Weinstein, D., Johnson, C.: Independent component analysis for EEG source localization. IEEE Engineering in Medicine and Biology 19(3), 87–96 (2000)
8. Vigário, R., Särelä, J., Jousmäki, V., Hämäläinen, M., Oja, E.: Independent component approach to the analysis of EEG and MEG recordings. IEEE Transactions on Biomedical Engineering 47(5), 589–593 (2000)
9. Ferrer Ballester, M.A., Travieso González, C.M., Alonso Hernández, J.B.: Tratamiento digital de la señal: fundamentos y aplicaciones. ULPGC Editions (June 27, 2005)
10. Haykin, S.: Adaptive filter theory. Prentice-Hall, Inc., Upper Saddle River (1986)
11. Ilmoniemi, R.J., Karhu, J.: TMS and EEG: Methods and current advancements. In: Oxford handbook of Transcranial stimulation, February 2008. Oxford University Press, Oxford (2008)
12. Nikouline, V., Ruohonen, J., Ilmoniemi, R.J.: The role of the coil click in TMS assessed with simultaneous EEG. Clinical Neurophysiology 110(8), 1325–1328 (1999)
13. Huotilainen, M., Ilmoniemi, R.J., Tiitinen, H., Lavikainen, J., Alho, K., Kajola, M., Näätänen, R.: The projection method in removing eye-blink artifacts from multichannel MEG measurements. In: Biomagnetism: Fundamental Research and Clinical Applications. Elsevier Science, IOS Press (1995)

Model Driven Image Segmentation Using a Genetic Algorithm for Structured Data

Romain Raveaux and Guillaume Hillairet

L3I, University of La Rochelle, av M. Crépeau, 17042 La Rochelle Cedex 1, France
{romain.raveaux01,guillaume.hilairet01}@univ-lr.fr

Abstract. In this paper, a method, integrating efficiently a semantic approach into an image segmentation process, is proposed. A graph based representation is exploited to carry out this knowledge integration. Firstly, a watershed segmentation is roughly performed. From this raw partition into regions an adjacency graph is extracted. A model transformation turns this syntaxic structure into a semantic model. Then the consistence of the computer-generated model is compared to the user-defined model. A genetic algorithm optimizes the region merging mechanism to fit the ground-truth model. The efficiency of our system is assessed on real images.

1 Introduction

Image segmentation process requires a human judgment to control the quality of a partition into regions and to adjust algorithm parameters. This judgment can be considered as a semantic analysis. Introducing this analysis into a segmentation process must considerably improve the results. However, this integration is not a trivial task. The representation by graph formalism is a powerful tool since graphs can represent different points of view of a given image, from the region layout to knowledge configuration. Many studies have investigated the use of a semantic graph to describe objects contained into an image. Vertices of this graph are sub-parts of the considered object and the edges denote the spatial relationships between these sub-parts [1] [8] [3]. The scope of these approaches was reduced due to the main drawback that the semantic graph does not guide the segmentation process; this later is used as a final stage to bring sense to a heap of regions without feedback. Consequently, the results are highly influenced by the region found by the low level algorithms. Adjacency graphs are another type of representation involved in the segmentation tasks. This structure has been successfully chosen by many authors [7]. In these approaches, each node is a set of pixels and regions are merged according their number of pixels and their colour properties. This merging process can be controlled by several criteria, ie. Colour distances. This parsimonious merging should lead to a meaningful segmentation. The question is then to know how is it possible to adjust merging parameters automatically while keeping relevant semantic results. How to drive a segmentation process to suit a semantic model ? This is where the question turns to an optimization problem. A Genetic Algorithm is chosen to browse the search space. It aims to minimize the distance between the user-defined model graph and the semantic graph issued from a segmentation task. Although

M. Graña Romay et al. (Eds.): HAIS 2010, Part I, LNAI 6076, pp. 311–318, 2010.

adjacency graphs and semantic graphs are used for different levels of representation, their formalisms are similar. The main difference lies in the fact, that nodes of the adjacency graph represent regions while those of the semantic graph represent components of the semantic content. This formal proximity suggests that the combination of these two types of representation could be interesting. A simple idea is to apply a semantic judgment on the Region Adjacency Graph (RAG) obtained from low level processes, in our case a watershed algorithm [7]. This can be done through a model transformation which checks a feasible matching with a semantic graph. The rest of this paper is organized as follows. In section 2, the measurement between graphs choice is addressed. Then, the third section presents the genetic algorithm in use, and particularly the specific genetic operators involved. In four, image segmentation experiments are performed on synthetic and real images. Finally, a conclusion is given and future works are discussed in section 5.

1.1 Methodology

Model Driven Engineering is a well-suited candidate for image segmentation by providing a common framework for representing graph structures as models conforms to metamodels. In this approach, we consider image as a system which is represented by a model conforms to a metamodel call Region Adjacency Graph which defines basic constructs for image representation like Region and Pixel. Models conforms to the RAG metamodel represent the exact structure of the image under study. The segmentation process resulting in a semantic graph is done by model transformation. This latter is defined according the RAG metamodel and a Semantic metamodel representing image contents.

1.2 From Image to Semantic Graph

On a colour image, a watershed segmentation is applied. This morphological operator can be considered as a topographic region growing method. This first run aims to localize regions of interest but always creates an over-segmentation with many small areas. This problem is quite a good point for us, since this raw partition corresponds to a safe start to build a semantic segmentation. From that statement, a Region Adjacency Graph (RAG) is extracted. Each region represents a vertex in this graph. Then, edges are built using the following rule: two vertices are linked with an undirected and an unlabelled edge if one of the nodes is connected to the other node in the corresponding image. Finally, the RAG is turned to a semantic graph through the use of a model transformation. This dataflow process is illustrated in fig. 1.

1.3 From Syntaxic Structure to Semantic Graph: Model Transformation

This stage aims to transform a syntaxic representation (RAG) to a semantic graph under constraint of a metamodel. This metamodel contains a logical description: the vocabulary used to label each par of the image and how components have to be organized together. The rest of the paper will focus on a 'flower' description illustrated in fig 2(a).

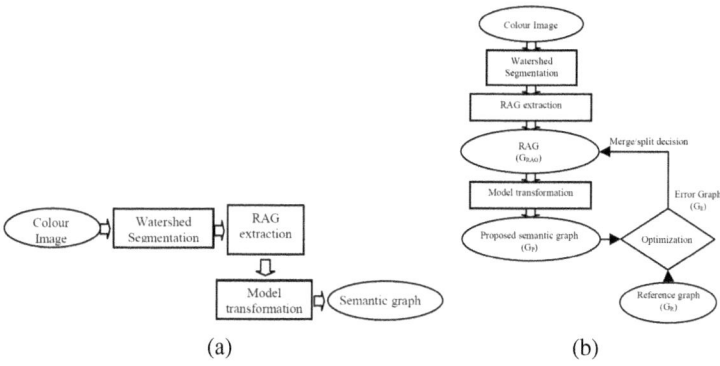

Fig. 1. (a) From image to graph; (b) Model Driven Optimization

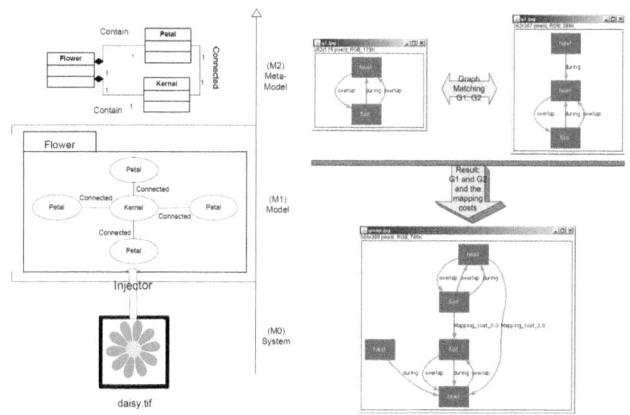

Fig. 2. (a)Logic of description:flower; (b)Probe matching : A case study

Tagging parts of an image is made through the use of a clustering algorithm, CLARA [4]. Regions are clustered into two groups according to their eccentricity. In mathematics, the eccentricity, denoted, is a parameter associated with every conic section. It can be thought of as a measure of how much the conic section deviates from being circular. In particular, the eccentricity of a circle is zero and the eccentricity of an (non-circle) ellipse is greater than zero but less than 1. According to this attribute, each region is tagged as circle or non-circle, and by extension, as 'kernel' or 'petal'. The eccentricity is a power full tool to discriminate 'petal' components from the 'kernel' element. The semantic graph is an undirected attributed graph. Each region represents an attributed vertex in this graph. Then, edges are built using the following rule: two vertices are linked with an undirected edge if one of the nodes is connected to the other node in the corresponding image. This transformation ensures a node to node mapping, a univalent matching with the RAG.

1.4   Model Driven Optimization

As stated in the introduction, now, the problem turns to an optimization question, how to converge to a segmentation that fits a given model? To reach this goal, two tools are needed. Firstly, a measure to quantify the suitability of a computer-generated model (GP), which is directly linked to the suitability of a given segmentation. This question is addressed in section 2.1. Secondly, an error graph expressed the unwanted components. This is built by error matching between GP and a reference model (GR). The way to construct such a dissimilarity graph (GE) is explained in section 2.2. This mechanism guides precisely the optimization to infer where the improvements have to be made. An overview of this optimization framework is presented in fig. 1(b).

2   Measure between Graphs

2.1   Dissimilarity between Graphs

Measures of dissimilarity between complex objects which have a structure (sets, lists, strings, ...) are based on the quantity of shared terms. To solve this problem, we choose an approximation of the well-known graph edit distance [2] called probe matching distance (PMD). This sub-optimal solution has the merit to be pretty accurate while keeping the time complexity quite low.

Probe definition. From the definition 1, probes of graph for the matching problem can be expressed as follow:

Let G be an attributed graph with edges labeled from the finite set $\{l1, l2, ..., a\}$. Let P be a set of probes extracted from G. There is a probe p associated to each vertex of the graph G. A probe (p) is defined as a pair $< Vr_i, H_i >$ where H_i is structure gathering the edges and their corresponding ending vertices from a root vertex (Vr_i). In such way, the neighborhood information of a given vertex is taken into account. A probe represents a local information, a "star" structure from a root node. The matching of these graph subparts should lead to a meaningfull graph matching approximation. The probe extraction is done by parsing the graph which is achievable in linear time through the joint use of the adjacency matrix.

Probe Matching. Let $G_1(V_1, E_1)$ and $G_2(V_2, E_2)$ be two attributed graphs. Without loss of generality, we assume that $| P_1 | \geq | P_2 |$. The complete bipartite graph $G_{em}(V_{em} = P1 \cup P2 \cup \triangle, P1 \times (P2 \cup \triangle))$, where $\triangle$ represents an empty dummy probe, is called the probe matching graph of $G1$ and $G2$. A probe matching between $G1$ and G_2 is defined as a maximal matching in G_{em}. Let there be a non-negative metric cost function $c : P_1 \times P_2 \to \Re_0^+$. We define the matching distance between G_1 and G_2, denoted by $PMD(G_1, G_2)$, as the cost of the minimum-weight probe matching between G_1 and G_2 with respect to the cost function c. This optimal probe assignment induces an univalent vertex mapping between G_1 and G_2, such as the function $f : V_1 \to V_2$ minimized the cost of probe matching. The approximation lies on the fact that the vertex mapping is not done considering the whole structure, but more likely subparts of it, subparts called probes. The node matching is only constraint by the assumption of "close" neiborghood imposed by the probe viewpoint of a vertex. Why such a restriction ? the mapping of two graphs when considering the entire structure is closely coupled with the maximum common subgraph search which is known to be a NP-Complete dilemma, more likely, this paper adopts a "Divide and Conquer strategy".

The matching distance can be calculated in $O(n^3)$ time in the worst case. To calculate the matching distance between two attributed graphs G_1 and G_2, a minimum-weight probe matching between the two graphs has to be determined. This is equivalent to determining a minimum-weight maximal matching in the probe matching graph of G_1 and G_2. To achieve this, the method of Kuhn [5] and Munkres [6] can be used. This algorithm, also known as the Hungarian method, has a worst case complexity of $O(n^3)$, where n is the number of probes in the larger one of the two graphs.

Cost function(c) for probe matching. Let p_1 and p_2 two probes. The cost function can be expressed as the sum of the edit operations to change a probe p_1 into a probe p_2. In the specific context of probes, the edit distance is reduced to its simple expression, a distance between two symbolic trees since a probe can be considered as a "star" data structure. Consequently, the set of edit paths transforming p_1 into p_2 is finite. When the graph edit distance is known to be NP-complete, its application to probes is tracktable in linear time in function of the probe cardinality $| p |$. A simple remark states the fact that since the edit distance is a metric our cost function c is obviously a metric too.

$$c(p_1, p_2) = d_{ed}(p_1, p_2) = \min_{(e_1,..,e_k) \in \gamma(p_1,p_2)} \sum_{i=1}^{k}(edit(e_i))$$

Where $\gamma(p_1, p_2)$ denotes the set of edit paths transforming p_1 into p_2, and $edit$ denotes the cost function measuring the strength $edit(e_i)$ of edit operation e_i. A simple application is depicted by the figure 2(b).

2.2   Inexact Graph Matching/Dissimilarity Graph

In order to express the topological dissimilarity between two graphs an inexact and fast graph matching is performed. Regarding, a given graph G2 and a reference graph G1, the error graph describes unmatched nodes of G2 related to G1. This can be expressed by the following notation: $G_E(G_2/G_1)$. From the bipartite graph, probes with an assignment cost greater than a given threshold are categorized as unmatched ($c(p_1, p_2) > \epsilon_p$). Unmatched nodes are considered to be part of the error graph. From that point, a relinking is done. If two vertices of G_E have common edges in G2, then these edges between the two given nodes are conserved in G_E.

3   Genetic Algorithm Dealing with Structural Data

Genetic Algorithms (GAs) are adaptive heuristic optimization algorithms based on the evolutionary ideas of natural selection and genetics. The basic concept of GAs is designed to simulate natural processes, necessary for evolution of artificial systems. They represent an intelligent exploitation of a random search within a defined search space to solve a problem. After a random initialization of a population of possible solutions, GA's are based on a sequential ordering of four main operators: selection, replication, crossover and mutation. In order to apply genetic algorithms to a given problem, three main stages are necessary: the coding of the problem solutions, the definition of the objective function which attributes a fitness to each individual, and the definition of the genetic operators which promote the exchange of genetic material between individuals. In most existing GA applications, a linear representation of individuals is used. Problem parameters are encoded through a binary or a real string. Crossover is then applied through a single-point or two-point based exchange of genes. Regarding mutations, it is applied through a random modification of a small number of genes chosen randomly.

The GA iterates in order to minimize the distance between the computer-generated model and the user-defined model. The stopping criterion is the generation number. In our context of optimization driven by model, each term of the genetic algorithm has to be redefined.

Individual and population definition: Each individual represents a hypothesis of segmentation. A feasible solution to the problem. An individual is a 3-tuple $I = (G_{RAG}, M_T, G_P)$. The RAG is extracted once during the initialization and modifications are applied thanks to the crossover and mutation operators. Hence, a population is defined as a set of size M, $\rho = \{I^i\}_{i=1}^M = \{(G_{RAG}^i, M_T, G_P^i)\}$

Fitness function: This function judges the quality of an individual. In our context, this means comparing G_P to G_R The graph probing is chosen to compute this dissimilarity measure, $d(I, G_R) = d(G_P, G_R)$.

Genetic operators: CrossOver: A given individual I1 exchanges its genetic material with I2 by calculating the dissimilarity graph $G_E(G_P^1/G_P^2)$. This error graph represents unmatched semantic components of the image. The nodes corresponding to these components have to be merged in the RAG. G_E drives the split and merge mechanism as stated in the algorithm 1. Finally, the semantic graph is generated by the model transformation. *Mutation:* The mutation operator randomly splits or merges a node of the RAG. Then the semantic graph is generated thanks to a model transformation. *Initialisation:* Each individual of the population is instanced as illustrated in fig. 3(c). In addition, a random number of mutations are performed on each graph.

Require: An Error graph G_E
Require: A Region Adjacency Graph G_{RAG}
Ensure: An adapted graphs
    Start
    for $i = 1$ TO NumberOfNodes in G_E **do**
        NE(i): the ith node.
        NRAG(i): getCorrespondingNodeInRAG(NE(i)).
        if coin flipping equal true **then**
            SplitNodeInRAG(NRAG(i))
        else
            MergeNodeInRAG(NRAG(i))
        end if
    end for
    return G_{RAG}
    End

Algorithm 1. Split and Merge scheme for graph data structure

4   Experimental Results

Protocol and Test: At the beginning, the user gives 2 inputs to the system. An image to be segmented and its corresponding graph model, fig 3.Then, the GA was set up according the following parameters: population size of 100 individuals, a cross-over rate of 0.8 and finally a number of generation equal to 100. This setting has been chosen after a comparative study. Since a high cross-over rate aims at focusing efforts on dissimilarities between individual pairs, we noticed that its impact can considerably change the corresponding children individuals while the mutaion operator is gently modifying the RAG structure.

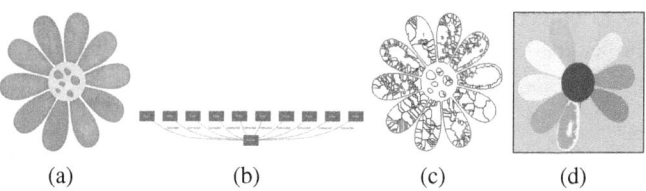

| (a) | (b) | (c) | (d) |

Fig. 3. (a) input image; (b) model graph; (c) Watershed basins-488 regions; (d) GA' best individual

Figure 3 denotes the raw regions given by the watershed algorithm and the segmentation outputted by the GA algorithm while fig. 4 depicts the GA evolution. The result is not perfectly segmented but at least it is close to the idea spread by the semantic model. Basically, the model graph is another way to express the user needs instead of asking insignificant numeric thresholds for instance. Two reasons can explain why the segmentation is not completely as expected. Firstly, as we said, the distance to compare 2 graphs is an approximation so it leads to some mistakes. Secondly, the model is too simple and not restrictive enough, hence, it will help to add some more structural relations, (contain, near,....).This could be done by constructing a neighbourhood graph during the model transformation to enrich the semantic graph (G_P).

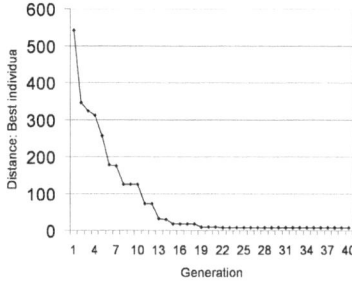

Fig. 4. The best individual: Distance to the model in function of the number of generations

5   Conclusion

In this paper, a model driven segmentation was presented. Basically, from a watershed segmentation a region adjacency graph is extracted and then exported to a semantic graph thanks to a model transformation. A Genetic Algorithm aims to minimize the distance between a computer-generated model and the user-defined model. This high level representation integrates a priori knowledge and represents an expression of the user needs. The preliminary results tend to show a reliable behaviour and a fast convergence of the whole system. The dissimilarity measure and the graph matching method are well-suited to deal with high dimension graphs. Ongoing studies are under investigation. A quantitative assessment will be performed on a tagged image sets and finally, an application to object extraction from colour cadastral maps is on the way, in the context of a project called ALPAGE (Diachronic analysis of Parisian urban space).

References

1. Bauckhage, C., Braun, E., Sagerer, G.: From image features to symbols and vice versa - using graphs to loop data- and model-driven processing in visual assembly recognition. IJPRAI 18(3), 497–517 (2004)
2. Bunke, H.: On a relation between graph edit distance and maximum common subgraph. Pattern Recogn. Lett. 18(9), 689–694 (1997)
3. Van Hentenryck, P., Deville, Y., Teng, C.-M.: A generic arc-consistency algorithm and its specializations. Artificial Intelligence 57(2-3), 291–321 (1992)
4. Kaufman, L., Rousseeuw, P.J.: Finding groups in data: an introduction to cluster analysis. Probability & Mathematical Statistics (1990), ISBN-10: 0
5. Kuhn, H.W.: The Hungarian method for the assignment problem. Naval Research Logistic Quarterly 2, 83–97 (1955)
6. Munkres, J.: Algorithms for the assignment and transportation problems. Journal of the Society of Industrial and Applied Mathematics 5(1), 32–38 (1957)
7. Saarinen, K.: Color image segmentation by a watershed algorithm and region adjacency graph processing, pp. 1021–1024 (1994)
8. Hode, Y.: Constraint satisfaction problem with bilevel constraint: application to interpretation of over-segmented images. Artificial Intelligence, 93 (June 1997)

Stamping Line Optimization Using Genetic Algorithms and Virtual 3D Line Simulation

Javier A. García-Sedano[1], Jon Alzola Bernardo[1], Asier González González[1],
Óscar Berasategui Ruiz de Gauna[2], and Rafael Yuguero González de Mendivil[2]

[1] Fundación LEIA - Technological Development Centre
C/ Leonardo Da Vinci, 11, 01510-Miñano, Álava
{javierg,asierg,jona}@leia.es
http://www.leia.es
[2] Sankyo Desarrollos Técnicos, S.L.
C/ Manisitu 5, Pab. A – Pol. Ind. Lurgorri, 01240 Alegría-Dulantzi, Álava
{obr,rafael.yuguero}@sankyo-sdt.com
http://www.sankyo-sdt.com

Abstract. This paper describes the use of a genetic algorithm (GA) in order to optimize the trajectory followed by industrial robots (IRs) in stamping lines. The objective is to generate valid paths or trajectories without collisions in order to minimize the cycle time required to complete all the operations in an individual stamping cell of the line. A commercial software tool is used to simulate the virtual trajectories and potential collisions, taking into account the specific geometries of the different parts involved: robot arms, columns, dies and manipulators. Then, a genetic algorithm is proposed to optimize trajectories. Both systems, the GA and the simulator, communicate as client - server in order to evaluate solutions proposed by the GA. The novelty of the idea is to consider the geometry of the specific components to adjust robot paths to optimize cycle time in a given stamping cell.

Keywords: Genetic Algorithm, Off-line Path Planning, Virtual Manufacturing.

1 Introduction

The process automation with industrial robots (IRs) and press machines is applied to a wide range of processes in different sectors like automotive, packaging and palletizing, metal transformation, foundry and forging, plastics and other manufacturing industries. Automation is achieved by means of robot and press programs, controlled from PLCs and robot control stations.

The optimization of the trajectories of IRs directly in the stamping cell is difficult and slow because collisions between components must be avoided. In recent years, different simulation software has appeared to solve this problem, allowing to simulate in Virtual Reality different robot-press programs before testing them in the physical environment. Simulating the behavior of IRs in a computer system is often referred as "off-line trajectory planning" [1, 2].

M. Graña Romay et al. (Eds.): HAIS 2010, Part I, LNAI 6076, pp. 319–326, 2010.

Different authors have tried to optimize robot off-line trajectory planning. Reference [3] presents a method, based in mathematical models, for computing the optimal motions of robot manipulators in the presence of moving obstacles. In reference [4], authors try to optimize trajectories and kinematics using Harmony Search Algorithm. References [5, 6] use two evolutionary multi-criteria algorithms, NSGA-II and MODE, to get optimal trajectory planning by minimizing travelling time, energy of the actuators and penalty for obstacle avoidance.

The objective of this paper is to describe a technique for finding optimal robot-press program solutions in a stamping line, automatically, by means of Genetic Algorithms (GAs) in connection to a virtual line simulator. In this work, Delmia V5 R18, from Dassault Systemes, has been the simulator chosen.

Most simulators, like Delmia [7], WorkSpace5 [8, 9] and RobotStudio [10] permit off-line programming and trajectory simulation but optimization must be manual. Parameters adjusting takes a long time, even being supported by simulation software, because task of searching optimal solutions is based on trial and error.

It exists software designed to optimize press lines, like StampWare RPS (Robot Press Synchronization) developed by ABB. This software tries to synchronize robots and presses in order to allow the robot to arrive inside the press precisely when it is opened enough. This software optimizes robots and press signals but it only takes into account the robots and presses without dies or claws.

The novelty of the technique presented in this paper is that this solution considers real processes, with their specific IRs, press machines, dies, workpieces and claws, and can be extended to different stamping processes provided that the specific line components are properly described and set in the simulator.

2 Description of the Problem

Nowadays, the optimization of paths is made by a human, who having the complete cell in the simulator changes the points of the trajectories himself. Then, he runs the simulation in order to get the cycle time. This operation is repeated several times until the worker thinks the path is good enough. This task is slow and repetitive. The idea presented in this article tries to optimize the paths of the robots automatically.

The chosen problem to be optimized is a stamping line that contains two IRs with their claws and a press machine with its pair of dies. The objective is to search the optimal trajectory for each IR without altering the behaviour of the press machine. Optimal trajectory planning is a function that involves minimum execution time and no risk of damage to the system. The model considers kinematic constraints such as velocities, accelerations and jerks limitation.

There are some steps that must be done manually, before starting the optimization process. Firstly, all the elements must be modelled in Delmia V5 except the two IRs that appear in the catalogue of Delmia. Secondly, all the elements must be assembled in the same model. Thirdly, the press machine movements are implemented by means of kinematic features of the software and finally different tags or points are added to specify the trajectories of IRs.

A trajectory of an IR is defined by a set of points called tags. The IR follows these tags. The initial and final tags are fixed. However, intermediate points or tags are changeable. These intermediate points must be changed manually or automatically, as it is proposed in this article, in order to optimize the trajectories.

3   Prototype Architecture

The trajectories of IRs are optimized using a genetic algorithm that incorporates information about the line simulation in the Delmia software. The link between the genetic algorithm and Delmia is achieved via Microsoft's Component Object Model (COM) interface. The client software is a program implementing the Genetic Algorithm and the server software in this communication is Delmia V5 with the stamping line process previously loaded.

The specific features of the GAs, process simulation software and communication link are described in this article. The following figure shows this communication.

Fig. 1. Communication between server (Delmia) and client (GA)

3.1   Genetic Algorithm Implemented Features

Individuals: An individual is a valid solution for the problem. In this case, the genome of each individual includes a matrix of the spatial coordinates and angles of each of the tag points as variables. The fitness function, in this case, is the "cycle time" in seconds.

Fitness/Cost Function: The fitness/cost function is the cycle time. In this problem, it represents a cost value of the individual, and the objective is to minimize it.

Constraints: The constraints, that each individual must satisfy, are the absence of collisions and unreachable points during the trajectory.

Initialization: Genetic Algorithms usually get a first population randomly, but in this case, it is not feasible in reasonable time. So, the first valid solution must be provided by a person, normally the line programmer.

Selection: The selection method used is the Roulette Wheel Selection [12]. This method, combined with a high probability of mutation, works efficiently in the problems studied.

Crossover and mutation operators: The crossover method and the mutation operator used are the uniform crossover [13] and uniform mutation, which change some genes randomly. The probability of using a mutation operator after crossover is 50 %. It has been chosen a high probability of mutation because in this problem any variation in a point of the trajectory can improve the cycle time, so it is needed a lot of changes in the genome and it is reached by having a high probability of mutation.

Replacement: The size of the population is fixed in 20 individuals and the Worst Among Most Similar Replacement (WAMS) [14, 15], has been chosen to replace the individuals in order to improve the population.

Stop criterion: Optimization stops when a number of generations has been reached, when the value of best cycle-time does not decrease over a number of generations, or when the execution time limit is surpassed.

3.2 Server-Client Communication

The communication between Delmia and the Genetic Algorithm has been achieved by COM interfacing technology. COM Automation allows users to build scripts in their applications to perform repetitive tasks or control one application from another [16]. The main advantage of using COM is the separation of interface from implementation.

Delmia has a Visual Basic editor in the main menu that allows communicating with an external program that has COM technology, so that Delmia can be driven from another program such as GA software.

3.3 Delmia Model

Delmia V5 is a virtual manufacturing tool that allows to define, plan, create, visualize and control production processes, among many other functionalities. It is possible to simulate a process in Delmia, and then translate IR tasks into IR controller-specific programming languages. The documentation of Delmia V5 R18 is available in [17].

Tags represent the points in the space that IRs' claws must pass through in their trajectories. Each tag has a position in the space defined by three dimensional space variables (x, y, z) and three angles (yaw, pitch, roll).

Trajectories defined are programmed in the Delmia virtual process, then they can be tested by performing a simulation, in order to get their cycle time while, simultaneously, possible collisions or unreachable points are checked. If all trajectories of IRs have been performed without incidents, the result is a correct simulation. If collisions have happened or unreachable points have been found along the simulation execution, then the result is a faulty simulation.

4 Prototype Working Schema

Firstly, the GA software must be executed. Secondly, a valid process model, without collisions or unreachable points, has to be ready in the Delmia Simulator. Thirdly, collision detection must be activated in "Analysis Configuration" mode. Finally, the GA software performs optimization, following these steps:

1. First simulation is performed and GA software creates its first individual genome with the matrix of tags of the initial solution. The cycle time is given by the simulator and it corresponds to the fitness value of the individual.

Repeat

2. Mutation operator is used to create a new genome.
3. Delmia simulates, automatically, the matrix of tags of the new genome.
    a. If the simulation is correct, a new individual is created with the genome and the cycle time as fitness value. This individual is inserted in the population.
    b. If the simulation has collisions or unreachable points the genome is discarded.

Until fill the population

Repeat

4. New genomes are generated using selection, crossover and mutation operators.
5. Delmia simulates, automatically, the matrix of tags of each new genome.

    a. If the simulation is correct, a new individual is created with the genome and the cycle time as fitness value. This individual can be inserted in the population using replacement operator.
    b. If the simulation has collisions or unreachable points the genome is discarded.

Until stop criterion is reached.

5 Description of the Real Application and Results

The real problem is to optimize the automation of a stamping line with six press machines and 7 IRs arranged in alignment. In order to test and compare the results obtained, the model has been simplified to a single cell consisting of two IRs and a machine press with a pair of dies. In this simplified process, the first IR drops the workpiece into the press machine, positioning it in the lower die and returns to its initial position. The press machine goes down, presses the workpiece and returns upwards. Then the second IR picks the pressed workpiece and takes it out from the press machine.

Three different models have been tested changing the type of die, claws and workpieces. However, the IRs and the press machine are the same in the three models.

Two approaches to optimize this type of problem are compared in the tests. The first approach is the manual method, in which a person (process designer) moves the tag points, simulates the process and searches new trajectories in order to minimize the cycle time. The second approach is minimizing the cycle time automatically by the working schema proposed in this paper. In both cases, the same valid initial solution is used to enable comparison of results.

Process models have 8 tags per robot, there are two robots and each tag has 6 variables (X, Y, Z, YAW, PITCH, ROLL), so the models have 96 input variables that can be changed modifying the trajectory and therefore the cycle time.

5.1 First Model

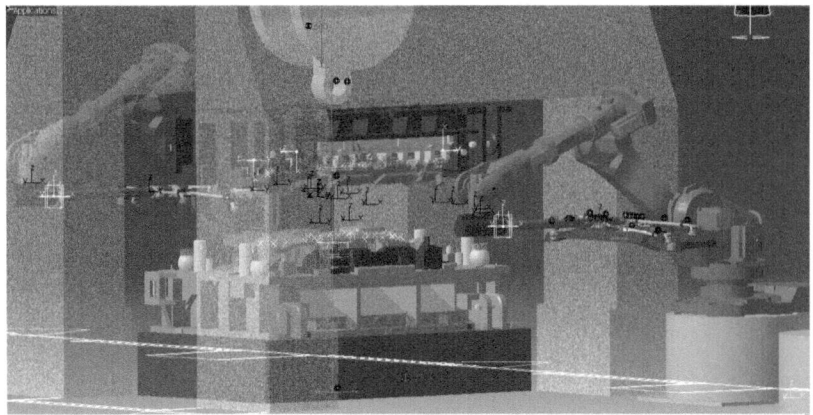

Fig. 2. First model. The two IRs, and the press machine with the pair of dies.

Table 1. Cycle times of the different solutions found for the first model

Solution	Time	Improvement
Initial valid solution	17.326 s	
Manual solution after two hours of work	16.853 s	0.473 s (2.5 %)
GA solution after two hours of automatic work	16.753 s	0.573 s (3.1 %)

5.2 Second Model

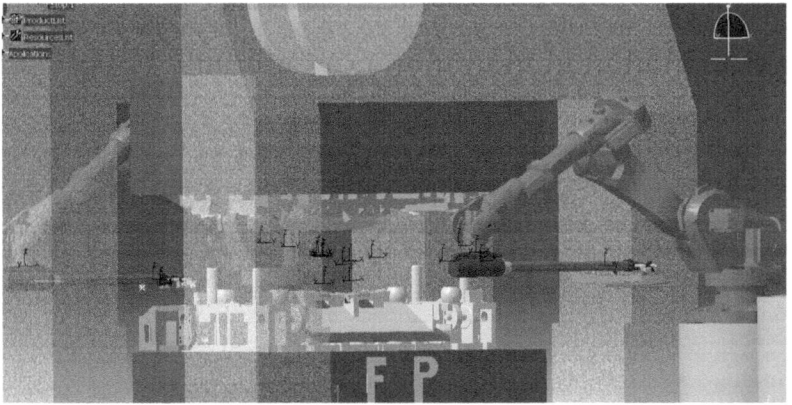

Fig. 3. Second model. The two IRs, and the press machine with the pair of dies.

Table 2. Cycle times of the different solutions found for the second model

Solution	Time	Improvement
Initial valid solution	17.918 s	
Manual solution after two hours of work	16.677 s	1.241 s (6.9 %)
GA solution after two hours of automatic work	16.527 s	1.391 s (7.8 %)

5.3 Third Model

Fig. 4. Third model. The two IRs, and the press machine with the pair of dies.

Table 3. The table shows the cycle time of the different solutions for the fist model

Solution	Time	Improvement
Initial valid solution	17.997 s	
Manual solution after two hours of work	17.032 s	0.965 s (5.4 %)
GA solution after two hours of automatic work	16.848 s	1.049 s (6.5 %)

6   Conclusions

This paper describes an approach to automate the calculation of optimal trajectories of IRs in stamping lines using a virtual simulation environment, which allows to simulate the process execution under near-real working conditions. This approach takes into account the real geometries of all the parts involved and the synchronisation between presses and IRs.

The time that human operator spends in the search process gives sense to the use of automatic optimization tools. A GA working together with the simulation software obtains better final solutions. The ideas presented in this paper could be used for different types of stamping processes, with different dies, robots and workpieces [18].

Acknowledgments

The authors gratefully appreciate the support given by the Basque Government under grant Gaitek 2009, OPCOT Project, with file number IG-2009/0000357.

References

1. Mitsi, S., Bouzakis, K.D., Mansour, G., Sagris, D., Maliaris, G.: Off-line programming of an industrial robot for manufacturing. International Journal of Advanced Manufacturing Technology 26, 262–267 (2005)
2. Zha, X.F., Du, H.: Generation and simulation of robot trajectories in a virtual CAD-based off-line programming environment. International Journal of Advanced Manufacturing Technology 17, 610–624 (2001)
3. Saramago, S.F.P., Junior, V.S.: Optimal trajectory planning of robot manipulators in the presence of moving obstacles. Mechanism and Machine Theory 35, 1079–1094 (2000)
4. Tangpattanakul, P., Artrit, P.: Minimum-Time Trajectory of Robot Manipulator Using Harmony Search Algorithm. IEEE Press, New York (2009)
5. Saravanan, R., Ramabalan, S.: Evolutionary minimum cost trajectory planning for industrial robots. Journal of Intelligent & Robotic Systems 52, 45–77 (2008)
6. Saravanan, R., Ramabalan, S., Balamurugan, C.: Evolutionary multi-criteria trajectory modeling of industrial robots in the presence of obstacles. Engineering Applications of Artificial Intelligence 22, 329–342 (2009)
7. Dassault Systemes: Delmia Documentation V5 R18,
   http://o1.cadfamily.com/delmia/online/DELMIA_default.htm
8. W. A. T. Solutions: Workspace 5 Robot Simulation and Off-Line Programming Software,
   http://www.workspace5.com
9. Johari, N.A.M., Haron, H., Jaya, A.S.M.: Robotic modeling and simulation of palletizer robot using Workspace5. In: Computer Graphics, Imaging and Visualisation: New Advances, pp. 217–222 (2007)
10. Connolly, C.: Technology and applications of ABB RobotStudio. Industrial Robot-an International Journal 36, 540–545 (2009)
11. ABB: El abc de industrial IT. ed: Revista ABB, pp. 6–13 (2002)
12. Kimura, S., Konagaya, A.: A Genetic Algorithm with Distance Independent Diversity Control for High Dimensional Function Optimization. Transactions of the Japanese Society for Artificial Intelligence 18, 193–202 (2003)
13. Michalewicz, Z.: Genetic Algorithms + Data Structures = Evolution Programs. 3rd rev. and extended ed., p. 387. Springer, Berlin (1996)
14. Syswerda, G.: Uniform Crossover in Genetic Algorithms. In: Proceedings of the Third International Conference on Genetic Algorithms, pp. 2–9. Morgan Kaufmann Publishers, San Francisco (1989)
15. Walter, C., Rao, V., Tom, S.: Multi-niche crowding in genetic algorithms and its application to the assembly of DNA restriction-fragments. Evolutionary Computation, 321–345 (1995)
16. Microsoft: Component Object Model technologies (COM),
    http://www.microsoft.com/com
17. Dassault Systemes, http://www.3ds.com
18. Graña, M., Torrealdea, F.J.: Hierarchically structured systems. European Journal of Operational Research 25, 20–26 (1986)

Evolutionary Industrial Physical Model Generation

Alberto Carrascal and Amaia Alberdi

Fundación Fatronik-Tecnalia, Paseo Mikeletegi 7,
Parque Tecnológico, 20009 Donostia, Spain

Abstract. Both complexity and lack of knowledge associated to physical processes makes physical models design an arduous task. Frequently, the only available information about the physical processes are the heuristic data obtained from experiments or at best a rough idea on what are the physical principles and laws that underlie considered physical processes. Then the problem is converted to find a mathematical expression which fits data. There exist traditional approaches to tackle the inductive model search process from data, such as regression, interpolation, finite element method, etc. Nevertheless, these methods either are only able to solve a reduced number of simple model typologies, or the given black-box solution does not contribute to clarify the analyzed physical process. In this paper a hybrid evolutionary approach to search complex physical models is proposed. Tests carried out on a real-world industrial physical process (abrasive water jet machining) demonstrate the validity of this approach.

Keywords: Evolutionary Computation, Genetic Programming, Genetic Algorithms, Symbolic Regression, Industrial Applications.

1 Introduction

In order to understand real-world complexity, science tries to formulate world by means of a mathematical language able to model each of the observed physical processes. Mathematical representation allows quantify magnitudes and establish relations between variables involved. Once the physical model is built, it can be employed to predict the system state in the future whenever the initial conditions are known.

There is no physic model construction methodology beyond the scientist intuition, experience and intelligence [1]. The more complex the physical process to describe is, the more difficult the construction process will be. Once a model is proposed, it has to be experimentally evaluated. When the obtained deviation between the model prediction and the experimental data is within reasonable error limits (arbitrarily determined), the model is considered valid. This inductive process assumes the model validity while there are no contradictory experimental cases found.

Other approach when building physical models consists of building process from data. When a model fits data it will be considered valid. There are several techniques based on this approach: regression, interpolation, finite element method, etc [2]. This approach can only be applied to simple physical process and frequently it provides black-box solutions that do not contribute to clarify the analyzed physical process.

M. Graña Romay et al. (Eds.): HAIS 2010, Part I, LNAI 6076, pp. 327–334, 2010.

Evolution-based algorithms have been considered to be the most flexible, efficient and robust of all optimization and search algorithms known to computer science. There are four main types of evolutionary algorithm currently in use: genetic programming (GP), genetic algorithm (GA), evolutionary programming (EP) and evolutionary strategies (ES). Besides, Memetic algorithm (MA) is a combination of GA and local search (LS) methods. These methods are now becoming widely used to solve a broad range of different problems [3].

Grammar-Guided Genetic Programming (GGGP) is an extension of traditional GP systems, conceived to always generate valid individuals (points or possible solutions that belong to the search space) [4]. To do so, GGGP employs a set of genetic programming operators such as grammar-based crossover operator (GBC), grammar-based mutation operator (GBM) and grammar-based initialization method (GBIM) [5]. Besides GGGP employs a context-free grammar (CFG) so that every individual in the population is a derivation tree that generates a sentence (solution) belonging to the language defined by the CFG [13]. A context-free grammar G comprises a 4-tuple G = (ΣN, ΣT, S, P) such as $\Sigma N \cap \Sigma T = \emptyset$; where ΣN is the alphabet of non-terminal symbols, ΣT is the alphabet of terminal symbols, S is the axiom of the grammar and P is the set of production rules, written in BNF (Backus-Naur Form).

The well known GA is an evolutionary algorithm which explores search spaces by maintaining a population of individual genotypes and applying them a set of genetic operators (selection, crossover, mutation, etc.). After phenotypes are obtained from genotypes they are evaluated and fitness values are assigned them. Typically phenotypes consist of collections of domain dependent parameters. Genotypes consist of coded versions of these parameters, represented as genes [6]. Real coded genes need specific genetic operators. Inspired by the mathematical morphology theory, MMX is a real coded crossover operator with a low computational cost, able to modify the exploration and exploitation capabilities dynamically depending on a genetic diversity measure. It has been demonstrated that obtains better results against other real coded crossover operators: RFX, BLX-α or GBX [7].

The use of a local search procedure generally improves the performance and the exploitation capabilities of the evolutionary algorithm, speeding up the convergence of the algorithm. One of the most common LS methods applies little random perturbations to each genotype gene [8].

In this paper a combined evolutionary approach is proposed as automatic physical models generator. By means of a grammar describing allowed mathematical expressions syntax, a GP algorithm will search into the physical models search space. The grammar will allow the definition of constants whose values will be determined by using a GA together with a LS method.

This approach has been applied to solve a real-world industrial case related to abrasive water jet (AWJ) machining. AWJ is an emerging technology and some important physical aspects of the AWJ milling process are still not well understood. A model that describes kerf profiles, generated during surface machining, has been automatically evolved by using this approach.

2 Evolutionary Physical Model Design

Physical model design can be considered as a symbolic regression problem. This kind of problems can be faced by combining genetic algorithms and genetic-programming paradigm [9].

The mathematical grammar defined in table 1 allows the creation of a great number of physical models. Thanks to both linear and non linear mathematic functions, a lot of physical processes can be modelled: kinematics, dynamics, thermodynamic, chemical models, etc.). Furthermore, by means of exponential functions a great number of simple linear differential equation solutions can be achieved.

Table 1. Simple math expressions grammar definition

$$P = \{ \ S ::= F \ \ ; F ::= + F \ F \ ; F ::= - F \ F \ ; F ::= * F \ F \ ;$$
$$F ::= \wedge F \ F \ ; F ::= e \ F \ ; F ::= k_i \ \ ; F ::= v_1 \ ; F ::= v_2 \ ; F ::= v_n \}$$
$$\Sigma_N = \{ \ S, F \} \ \Sigma_T = \{ \ +, -, *, e, \wedge, t, k_i, v_1, v_2, ..., v_n \}$$

The considered context-free grammar allows the definition of complex mathematical expressions. The number of constants is only limited by the maximum number of allowed derivations. t is the independent variable and n is the number of dependant variables v_n.

Figure 1 show the hybrid evolutionary system diagram composed of three modules: GP, GA and LS modules. GP module starts generating an initial mathematical expressions population (GBIM method). After each mathematical expression is evaluated, genetic programming operators (selection, GBC and GBM operators) are applied until the stop criterion is reached (typically model fits experimental data). A penalizing linear term, which is proportional to the mathematical expressions length, was added (Occam's razor principle). From a mathematical point of view, this term avoid obtaining complex interpolants.

GA module is called when each mathematical expression need to be evaluated. For this purpose a GA is executed with a population of real-coded individuals. Individual genes are formed with the mathematical expressions constants that need to be determined. After population random initialization each mathematical model is tested with available experimental data and a fitness value is obtained (absolute difference between experimental and predicted data). Then a set of genetic operators (roulette selection method, random mutation operator and MMX) is iteratively applied until an arbitrary number of iterations are reached.

Finally, an additional exploitation method is applied over GA descendants in the LS module. A traditional random best ascent LS method is employed. This step speeds up the convergence of the algorithm by adjusting the mathematical expressions constants values.

The evolutionary hybrid system outcome is a physical model in which all the constants have been solved. Together with the physical model, a measurement of the given solution validity is provided.

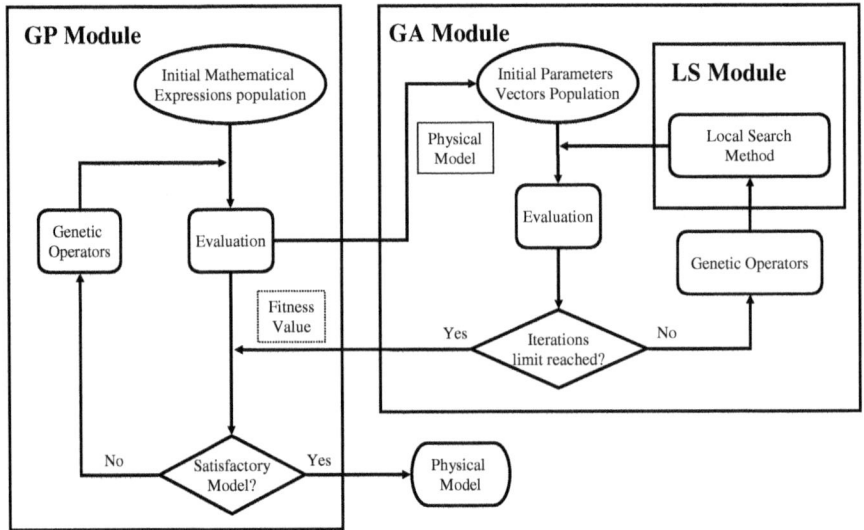

Fig. 1. Combined Evolutionary System proposed

3   Physical Models

The simple mathematical grammar defined in table 1 allows the creation of a great number of physical models. Thanks to both linear and non linear mathematic functions, a lot of physical processes can be modelled: kinematics, dynamics, thermodynamic, chemical models, etc.). Furthermore, by means of exponential functions a lot of simple linear differential equation solutions can be represented.

3.1   AWJ milling Industrial Scenario

Abrasive water jet (AWJ) machining is an emerging technology in evident growth since its first industrial application in 1983 [10]. The flexibility of the process brought a rapid spread in various fields, beyond the process of cutting all types of materials. The milling process using AWJ was first considered and mentioned by Hashish in 1987 [11].

AWJ consists on water pressurized at high hydrostatic pressure (up to 6000 bar) which is converted into kinetic energy and mixed with abrasive particles, forming a three-phase jet (air, water and abrasive) with very high velocity (300-1000 m/s) [12], able to erode the desired material. The low cost of the process along with the productivity, the flexibility and its ability to machine any kind of material without heat damage, convert the AWJ milling process into an opportunity to open new markets in the area of non-conventional machining.

The depth control is the key objective for the development of the AWJ milling, in order to obtain a desired depth with acceptable tolerance. However, the dependence of the machined depth with the traverse speed applied to the AWJ cutting head makes impossible to keep constant the depth of kerf profile during surface machining. In fact, due to the dynamic behaviour of the machine, the head suffers strong accelerations and decelerations at those points where the path direction changed. In these points, the jet impacts longer than in points where the traverse feed rate of the nozzle is constant. Consequently, milling by AWJ inevitably leads to a surface with a variable depth.

Furthermore, a large number of process parameters are involved in AWJ milling (Figure 2), and all of them have influences on the kerf, The fluctuation of the process parameters controlling the structure of the jet (the abrasive mass flow rate and the pressure), either the geometry of the abrasive particles, and the heterogeneity of the work material makes also the development difficult in this field. These variations inherent to the process are the origin of the stochastic nature of this technology [12-13].

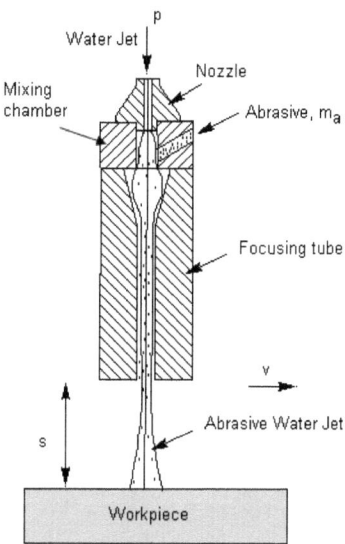

Fig. 2. Parameters involved in AWJ milling process

All these process characteristics make the AWJ milling a complex process control. Hence, modelling the AWJ process is an important tool to predict and control the geometry of the kerf profile.

The modelling of kerf profile should fulfil two important aspects: the first one is the kerf geometrical profile, and the other one is the dependence of the kerf profile on the AWJ process parameters.

In this work a hybrid evolutionary approach is used to model the kerf geometrical profile, in terms of two geometrical parameters: the maximum depth of cut (h_{max}) and the width at the half of the maximum depth (b_{05}). Figure 3 shows parameters used to define the kerf profile geometry.

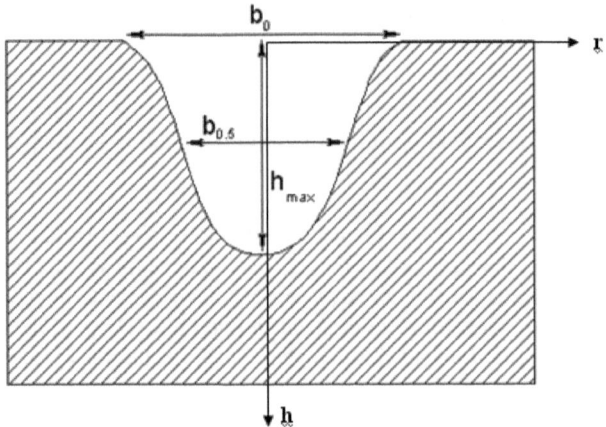

Fig. 3. Kerf profile geometry

3.2 AWJ Model Evolved

A total of 7 AWJ cutting process experiments were carried out with 7 different process conditions. For each condition, the width from the central axis of the kerf (r) was measured at 10 different depths (h). A total of 140 points was used to model the depth h in terms of r, h_{max} and b_{05}. The model to find $f(h_{max}, b_{0.5}, r)$ was evolved by means of a population of 100 GP individuals (experimentally chosen value) with a mutation probability equals to 0.03 (since genetic-programming crossover operator implements exploration capabilities, a higher mutation probability value is not needed).

A grammar including exponential, logarithmic, trigonometric and other mathematical functions was employed. The obtained expression after evolutionary system execution was the next:

$$f\left(h_{max}, b_{0.5}, r\right) = h_{max} - 1.18 h_{max} e^{-\left(\frac{53.33 + 0.44 b_{0.5}}{r}\right)^2}$$

This expression fits experimental data with minimum error (mean square error) for all the considered process conditions. The physical interpretation of this expression can be considered as a constant kerf deep close to the jet centre and as r increases, h decreases exponentially. It is thought that the shape of the kerf profile constitutes a print of the jet energy distribution shape, and consequently this expression represents also the jet energy distribution profile. Thus, it can be concluded that the energy has its maximum value and is constant in the center of the jet, and as r increases, the energy distribution falls exponentially, The center of the jet, where is located the converging part of the flow, is known as core, and the other part of the jet, where is located the diverging part of the jet, is known as the cover [14]. The figure 4 shows for each AWJ process condition how the model fits experimental data.

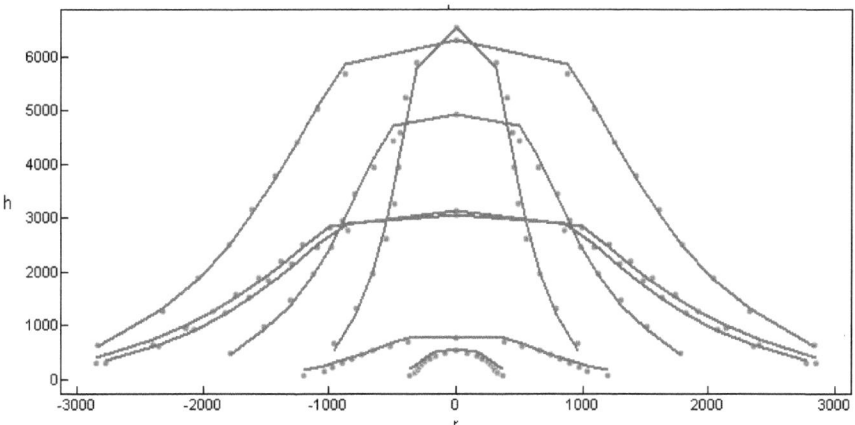

Fig. 4. Model fitting experimental data coming from different AWJ process conditions

4   Conclusions

A combined evolutionary system has been developed in order to tackle the physical model search problem. This evolutionary approach mixes Genetic Programming, Genetic Algorithms and Local Search techniques in order to obtain mathematical expressions which describe physical processes: the GP module generates individuals that codify well formed mathematical expressions, whilst GA and LS modules develop optimal parameter configurations for every generated individual. The system uses a basic mathematical context-free grammar that can be applied to model a great number of physical processes.

Experimental results have been retrieved from the application of the proposed system to a real world industrial scenario, with the goal of shaping the mathematical expression that models the kerf profiles of the AWJ milling process. These results show good performance of the system which has been able to predict the kerf geometry with a low mean square error. Moreover, the execution of the evolutionary system enhances the knowledge held about the physical model by providing meaningful information automatically extracted from the experiment data.

This is a very promising approach to assist scientists during investigation processes where an unknown physical process is involved. For this purpose, the mathematical grammar will be extended with more complex terms and the algorithm execution will be optimized.

References

1. Langley, P.: Elements of Machine Learning. Morgan Kaufmann, San Francisco (1995)
2. Meerschaert, M.M.: Mathematical Modeling. Academic Press, London (2007)
3. Dawkins, R.: Evolutionary Design By Computers. In: Bentley, P.J, ed. (1999)

4. Whigham, P.A.: Grammatically-based genetic programming. In: Rosca, J.P. (ed.) Proceedings of the Workshop on Genetic Programming: From Theory to Real-World Applications, Tahoe City, California, USA, pp. 33–41 (1995)
5. Couchet, J., Manrique, D., Rios, J., Rodríguez-Patón, A.: Crossover and mutation operators for grammar-guided genetic programming. Soft Comput. 11(10), 943–955 (2007)
6. Rusell, S., Norvig, P.: Artificial Intelligence. A Modern Approach. Prentice-Hall, Englewood Cliffs (2008)
7. Barrios, D., Carrascal, A., Manrique, D., Ríos, J.: Optimisation With Real-Coded Genetic Algorithms Based on Mathematical Morphology. Intern. J. Computer Math. 80(3), 275–293 (2003)
8. Selman, B., Kautz, H., Cohen, B.: Noise strategies for improving local search. In: Proceedings of the 12th National Conference on Artificial Intelligence, pp. 337–343 (1994)
9. Howard, L.M., D'Angelo, D.J.: The GA-P: A Genetic Algorithm and Genetic Programming Hybrid. IEEE Expert: Intelligent Systems and Their Applications 10(3), 11–15 (1995)
10. Öjmertz, K.M.C.: A study on Abrasive Waterjet Milling. PhD Thesis, Chalmers University of Technology, Göteborg, Sweden (1997)
11. Hashish, M.: Milling with abrasive waterjets: a preliminary investigation. In: Proceedings of the fourth U.S. Water Jet Conference, Berkeley, California, pp. 179–188 (1987)
12. Paul, S., Hoogstrate, A.M., van Luttervelt, C.A., Kals, H.J.J.: An experimental investigation of rectangular pocket milling with abrasive water jet. Journal of Materials Processing Technology 73, 179–188 (1998)
13. Öjmertz, K.M.C.: Abrasive Waterjet Milling - An Experimental Investigation. In: Proceedings of 7th American Water Jet Conference, Seattle, USA, pp. 777–791 (1993)
14. Hlaváč, L.M.: Investigation if the abrasive water jet trajectory curvature inside the kerf. Journal if Materials Processing Technology 209, 4154–4161 (2009)

Evolving Neural Networks with Maximum AUC for Imbalanced Data Classification

Xiaofen Lu[1], Ke Tang[1], and Xin Yao[1,2]

[1] Nature Inspired Computation and Applications Laboratory (NICAL),
School of Computer Science and Technology,
University of Science and Technology of China, Hefei, China, 230027
[2] The Center of Excellence for Research in Computational Intelligence and Applications
(CERCIA), School of Computer Science, The University of Birmingham,
B15 2TT Birmingham, U.K.
xiaofen@mail.ustc.edu.cn, ketang@ustc.edu.cn,
x.yao@cs.bham.ac.uk

Abstract. Real-world classification problems usually involve imbalanced data sets. In such cases, a classifier with high classification accuracy does not necessarily imply a good classification performance for all classes. The Area Under the ROC Curve (AUC) has been recognized as a more appropriate performance indicator in such cases. Quite a few methods have been developed to design classifiers with the maximum AUC. In the context of Neural Networks (NNs), however, it is usually an approximation of AUC rather than the exact AUC itself that is maximized, because AUC is non-differentiable and cannot be directly maximized by gradient-based methods. In this paper, we propose to use evolutionary algorithms to train NNs with the maximum AUC. The proposed method employs AUC as the objective function. An evolutionary algorithm, namely the Self-adaptive Differential Evolution with Neighborhood Search (SaNSDE) algorithm, is used to optimize the weights of NNs with respect to AUC. Empirical studies on 19 binary and multi-class imbalanced data sets show that the proposed evolutionary AUC maximization (EAM) method can train NN with larger AUC than existing methods.

Keywords: ROC, AUC, Class-imbalance Learning, Feed-forward Neural Networks, Evolutionary Algorithms, Differential Evolution.

1 Introduction

In the real world, a classification problem usually involves a data set with imbalanced distribution over different classes. That means, some classes may consist of abundant samples, while much less samples are available for the other classes. Such a scenario can often be found in medical diagnosis, fraud detection, etc. The large-size classes are referred to as the majority or common classes and the small-size classes are referred to as the minority or rare classes. When the data are imbalanced, the traditional performance measure for classifiers (e.g., classification accuracy) is not sufficient as it has bias against the rare classes [1, 2]. Since the construction of a classifier is usually guided by

M. Graña Romay et al. (Eds.): HAIS 2010, Part I, LNAI 6076, pp. 335–342, 2010.

some performance measure, alternatives to the classification accuracy are needed. In the literature, quite a few measures have been proposed for this purpose, including g-means, F-measure, the area under the Precision-Recall curve (PRC) and the area under the Receiver Operating Characteristic (ROC) curve (AUC in short). Among those measures, AUC might be the most commonly-used one, because ROC curves are insensitive to changes in the class distribution [3] and AUC does not bias against rare classes.

When employing AUC as the performance measure, one aims to seek a classifier with the largest AUC. In other words, training a classifier in this case can be formulated as an AUC maximization problem. Since AUC is believed to be a better performance measure than accuracy for imbalanced classification problems, many existing learning algorithms, such as decision trees [4], linear regression [5], SVM [6] and NNs [7], have been modified to deal with the new objective.

Unfortunately, the AUC is non-differentiable and discontinuous. For this reason, traditional learning algorithms that require derivative information of the objective function are no longer applicable. This makes it particularly difficult to train an NN with the maximized AUC. To address this problem, much effort has been devoted to either investigating the relationship between the existing differentiable performance measures (e.g. Mean Square Error (MSE)) and AUC [5, 8, 9] or inventing differentiable approximations of AUC [7, 10, 11]. The first type of work aims to find another differentiable measure that is consistent with AUC. The second type of work led to a few variants of AUC. These variants adopt either a sigmoid function [10] or a polynomial function [7, 11] to approximate AUC. Although these AUC variants have been partially validated by preliminary empirical studies, some recent research [12] revealed that none of them are as effective as AUC.

Motivated by the above considerations, we propose to train an NN using Evolutionary Algorithms (EAs) in this paper. Specifically, a recently proposed EA called Self-adaptive Differential Evolution with Neighborhood Search (SaNSDE) [13] is used to search for the optimal weights of the NN. Since EAs are direct search methods that do not require the objective function to be differentiable, they are capable of optimizing the weights with respect to AUC directly. Although EAs have been used to evolve the weights of NNs for a long time [14, 15, 16], this work is different from previous work in two aspects. First, a new EA, i.e., SaNSDE, is utilized to evolve an NN with the maximized AUC, while previous work focused on other objective functions such as MSE. Second, most existing learning algorithms for AUC maximization are only concerned with binary classification problems and little work has been done to extend them to multi-class cases, while both binary and multi-class problems are investigated in this work. The efficacy of our method is evaluated by comparing it to two well-known gradient-based NN training methods, one uses MSE as the objective function and the other employs a differentiable variant of AUC.

The rest of this paper is organized as follows: In section 2, we first give the detailed description of the AUC measure. Then, an approximation to the AUC (called AWMWS) and a multi-class extension of AUC are introduced. The AWMWS method is extended to multi-class problems as well. Section 3 details SaNSDE and presents the proposed Evolutionary AUC Maximization (EAM) method. Section 4 describes the experimental studies. Section 5 concludes the paper and discusses future work.

2 AUC: The Performance Measure

Given a data set, a sample can be identified as a tuple $(\mathbf{x}, c)$ where $\mathbf{x}$ represents the vector of features and c denotes which class this sample belongs to. When using an NN to classify samples, $\mathbf{x}$ is used as the input to the NN and the outputs of the NN can be easily transformed to some scores. Without loss of generality, we assume that a perfect classifier should assign larger scores to the minority samples than the majority samples. The sample is classified to the class corresponding to the largest score. The AUC of a classifier can be interpreted as the probability that the classifier assigns a randomly chosen minority sample a larger score than a randomly chosen majority sample [3]. Hence, given a finite set of samples, the AUC can be calculated as:

$$AUC = \frac{\sum_{i=0}^{m-1} \sum_{j=0}^{n-1} I(x_i, y_j)}{mn}. \tag{1}$$

where

$$I(x_i, y_j) = \begin{cases} 1, & x_i > y_j \\ 1/2, & x_i = y_j \\ 0, & \text{otherwise} \end{cases} \tag{2}$$

In the formula above, $\{x_0, x_1, ..., x_{m-1}\}$ represent the scores of all the m minority samples, and $\{y_0, y_1, ..., y_{n-1}\}$ are the scores of all the n majority samples.

2.1 An Approximation to the WMW Statistic

Since Eq. (1) is non-differentiable, it cannot be used as the objective function for gradient-based methods. Considering this, Yan et al. proposed an objective function by an approximation to the WMW statistic [7]. We call the objective function aAUC, and the method that minimizes aAUC by gradient-based method AWMWS. The aAUC is calculated as [7]:

$$aAUC = \sum_{i=0}^{m-1} \sum_{j=0}^{n-1} R(x_i, y_j). \tag{3}$$

where

$$R(x_i, y_j) = \begin{cases} (-(x_i - y_j - \gamma))^p, & x_i - y_j < r \\ 0, & \text{otherwise} \end{cases}. \tag{4}$$

In Eq. (4), $0 < \gamma \le 1$ and $p > 1$. According to [7], a value between 0.1 and 0.7 can be chosen for γ and $p = 2$ or 3 may lead to the best performance.

2.2 The mAUC

As AUC is a measure of discriminating a pair of classes, it is only applicable to binary class problems. Hand and Till [17] extended AUC to the multi-class problems. The proposed measure is called mAUC and can be calculated by Eq. (5):

$$mAUC = \frac{2}{|C|(|C|-1)} \sum_{(c_i, c_j) \in C} AUC(c_i, c_j). \tag{5}$$

where $|\mathbf{C}|$ is the number of classes. $AUC(c_i,c_j)$ is the AUC of the binary classification problem including only the c_i and c_j classes. All other details were summarized in [17].

Since mAUC is developed by decomposing a multi-class problem into a number of binary class sub-problems, it inherits all the characteristics of AUC. Therefore, the AWMWS measure introduced in the previous sub-section can be extended easily to multi-class cases as:

$$maAUC = \frac{2}{|\mathbf{C}|(|\mathbf{C}|-1)} \sum_{(c_i,c_j \in \mathbf{C})} aAUC(c_i,c_j). \qquad (6)$$

where $aAUC(c_i,c_j)$ is calculated according to Eq. (3) by taking the c_i as the positive class and c_j as the negative class.

3   EAM: The Training Method Based on SaNSDE

3.1   SaNSDE as the Global Optimizer

When the objective function is determined, an appropriate training algorithm is required. As mentioned before, direct AUC/mAUC maximization is considered in this paper. The weights of an NN are optimized by an EA named SaNSDE [13]. SaNSDE is an improved variant of Differential Evolution (DE) [18]. DE is a population-based stochastic search algorithm for solving optimization problems in a continuous space. It uses three reproductive strategies (i.e., mutation, crossover, and selection) to evolve the population until a stopping criterion is met. For the classical DE [18], it is often very hard to determine its control parameters because they are problem-dependent. In the new algorithm SaNSDE [13], a number of self-adaption strategies are utilized so that all the control parameters of DE can be determined automatically and appropriately during the search process. The efficacy of SaNSDE has been evaluated in [13] using 37 benchmark functions. It has been shown that SaNSDE has a significant advantage over other algorithms with respect to better adaptability and stronger search ability. Therefore, we will adopt it as the global optimizer to find the appropriate weights of an NN in the weight space when constructing classifiers by training the NN. Interested readers are referred to [13] for full details of SaNSDE.

3.2   Major Steps of EAM

When using SaNSDE to train an NN, we integrate all the weights which are involved in the input, hidden and output layers into a vector defined as:

$$\mathbf{W} = (w_1, w_2, ..., w_D). \qquad (7)$$

where D is the total number of weights of the NN. Correspondingly, the population on which SaNSDE works is denoted as $\mathbf{P}$:

$$\mathbf{P} = (\mathbf{W}_1, ..., \mathbf{W}_N). \qquad (8)$$

With the above definitions, SaNSDE directly searches for the optimal weights with respect to AUC and mAUC. Concretely, given a data set, the structure of the NN (i.e., the number of hidden neurons) is first determined. Then a population of weight vectors is randomly generated. After that, SaNSDE is applied to this population to search the weight vector with the maximum AUC/mAUC.

4 Experimental Studies

4.1 Experimental Setup

To evaluate the efficacy of the proposed method, experimental studies have been carried out to compare the EAM method with two well-known gradient-based training methods. One is the standard BP and the other is the AWMWS method, i.e., the BP variant using aAUC/maAUC as the objective function.

   Nineteen imbalanced data sets were used in the experiments. Eleven of them are binary class data sets and the others are multi-class data sets. All data sets were obtained from the UCI Machine Learning Repository [19]. All the data sets are imbalanced in the sense that each of them at least involves a class whose size is about twice of that of another class. To make a fair comparison, the number of hidden neurons of the NN was tuned using BP, and the same value was then used for all the methods. Furthermore, the control parameters of the EAM method were kept unchanged over all data sets unless noted otherwise. In this way, we can prevent the experiments from biasing towards any single method.

   There are two main parameters of SaNSDE that needs to be defined in advance. That is, the maximum generation number for evolution and the population size. For the binary data sets, the maximum generations of EAM was set to 5000. The population size was set to 100 for the *mfeate-mor* data set and 50 for the other data sets, and no other parameter is adjusted during evolution. For the multi-class data sets, the maximum generations of EAM was set to 5000 for the *balance* data set, 10000 for the *cmc* data set and 3000 for the other data sets. The population size was set to 100 for all data sets.

4.2 Experimental Results

For each data set, the experiment was conducted by applying 5-fold cross-validation for ten independent runs. Table 1 present the average AUC obtained on the 19 data sets. The standard deviations are also provided. We first employed the Friedman test, which was suggested in [20], to compare the general performance of the three methods on the 19 data sets. The null hypothesis that all the methods performed the same on average was rejected. Hence, a Bonferroni-Dunn posthoc-test was further carried out to compare EAM to the other two methods. It was observed that EAM significantly outperformed AWMWS, while the difference between EAM and BP is statistically insignificant. To evaluate the performance of EAM on each data set, Wilcoxon signed rank test (with a significance level 0.05) was employed to compare EAM with the other methods based on the results obtained in the 50 runs. From the last column of Table 1, it can be observed that the EAM significantly outperformed BP on 4 out of 11 binary data sets, while was inferior on only 1 data set. Similarly, the EAM was also significantly better than AWMWS on 4 out of 11 data sets, while was outperformed on only 1 data set. Among the 8 multi-class data sets, the EAM achieved better or comparable performance than BP on all data sets except for the *cmc* and *solarflare2* data sets. When compared to AWMWS, EAM is the clear winner again. It significantly outperformed AWMWS on 6 data sets and the two methods were comparable on the remaining two data sets.

Table 1. Average AUC of BP, AWMWS and EAM on the 19 data sets. The standard deviations on each data set are given in the parentheses. The results were obtained based on 10 independent runs of 5-fold cross-validation. The column Result shows the comparison results based on Wilcoxon test. The term "r1 - r2" means that the result between the EAM and BP is "r1" while the result between the EAM and AWMWS is "r2". "w", "l" and "d" denote the EAM is better than, worse than and comparable to the other method, respectively.

	Data Set	BP	AWMWS	EAM	Result
Binary class	abalone (7)	0.8614 (0.014)	0.8385 (0.116)	0.8601 (0.015)	d - d
	balance-scale (balance)	0.4200 (0.076)	0.8772 (0.151)	0.8789 (0.059)	w - w
	cmc (2)	0.7255 (0.033)	0.7073 (0.081)	0.7199 (0.035)	d - d
	haberman	0.6797 (0.067)	0.6889 (0.083)	0.7063 (0.082)	w - d
	housing ([20, 23])	0.7816 (0.060)	0.7676 (0.073)	0.7867 (0.044)	d - d
	mfeate-mor (10)	0.9181 (0.020)	0.8473 (0.100)	0.9225 (0.015)	w - w
	mfeate-zer (10)	0.9105 (0.017)	0.9231 (0.015)	0.9200 (0.018)	w - l
	ozone-onehr	0.9112 (0.043)	0.8915 (0.093)	0.8676 (0.055)	l - d
	pima	0.8389 (0.036)	0.7826 (0.146)	0.8350 (0.037)	d - w
	transfusion	0.7566 (0.041)	0.6099 (0.133)	0.7552 (0.044)	d - w
	wpbc	0.7795 (0.077)	0.7976 (0.073)	0.7887 (0.071)	d - d
Multi-class	abalone	0.7135 (0.022)	0.6704 (0.074)	0.7775 (0.016)	w - w
	balance	0.9273 (0.033)	0.9536 (0.042)	0.9563 (0.020)	w - w
	car	0.9728 (0.024)	0.8624 (0.098)	0.9677 (0.019)	d - w
	cmc	0.7309 (0.018)	0.7213 (0.018)	0.7140 (0.014)	l - d
	glass	0.7715 (0.046)	0.8177 (0.043)	0.8453 (0.032)	w - w
	page-blocks	0.9294 (0.031)	0.8824 (0.054)	0.9647 (0.019)	w - w
	solarflare2	0.8477 (0.017)	0.8250 (0.015)	0.8275 (0.011)	l - d
	soybean	0.8117 (0.033)	0.9723 (0.005)	0.9785 (0.006)	w - w

From the above comparisons, it can be seen that EAM is clearly better than AWMWS for both binary and multi-class data sets. Although the Bonferroni-Dunn posthoc-test failed to detect statistically significant difference between the performance of EAM and BP, EAM outperformed BP on majority of the 19 data sets. And thus the efficacy of EAM can be conservatively validated. The advantage of the EAM is more prominent on the multi-class data sets than on the binary data sets. One possible reason is that the objective function for multi-class problems (i.e., mAUC) is more complicated than that of binary problems, and thus approximating it using a differentiable function may change the landscape of the solution space significantly. In such a case, traditional gradient-based methods may be misguided to a wrong solution.

4.3 Further Analysis

As mentioned before, our method distinguishes from the compared methods in two aspects. One is the AUC objective function and the other is the utilization of SaNSDE as the search algorithm. To understand why our method has obtained better AUC, we have further combined SaNSDE with the objective functions and applied the resultant methods to selected data sets. Since the two resultant methods employ MSE and aAUC/maAUC as the objective functions, they are referred to as SaNSDE-MSE and SaNSDE-aAUC, respectively. For each method, four data sets were selected in such a way that two of them are binary and the others are multi-class ones. Due to the limit of the space, the detailed results of the additional experiments may not be presented in this paper. Instead, two main observations can be obtained from them. On one hand, the advantage of EAM is mainly due to the direct use of AUC/mAUC as the objective function for training. On the other hand, though SaNSDE performs well on most of the data sets, it is not a good optimizer for the *cmc* data set. This is reasonable since SaNSDE is a general optimization approach and was not specifically developed for NN training.

5 Conclusions and Discussions

In this paper, to tackle imbalanced classification problems, we propose the EAM that employs AUC as the objective function and uses SaNSDE to search for the best weights of NNs. Both binary and multi-class classification problems have been addressed. Empirical studies on 19 UCI data sets have demonstrated that the proposed method is superior to two existing methods, including the BP algorithm and a method using an approximation of AUC/mAUC as the objective function. Further analysis revealed that the success of the proposed method is mainly due to the direct optimization of AUC/mAUC, to which the traditional methods are inapplicable because the AUC is non-differentiable. Although the EAM has been shown to outperform other algorithms, there were a few data sets on which the EAM did not perform well. One direction for our future research is to develop more powerful search algorithms than SaNSDE for imbalanced classification problems.

Acknowledgments. This work was partially supported by a National Natural Science Foundation of China grant (No. 60802036).

References

1. Provost, F., Fawcett, T., Kohavi, R.: The case against accuracy estimation for comparing induction algorithms. In: 15th International Conference on Machine Learning, pp. 445–453. AAAI Press, Menlo Park (1998)
2. Weiss, G.M.: Mining with rarity: a unifying framework. ACM SIGKDD Explorations Newsletter 6(1), 7–19 (2004)
3. Fawcett, T.: An introduction to ROC analysis. Pattern Recognition Letters 27, 861–874 (2006)

4. Ferri, C., Flach, P., Hernández-Orallo, J.: Decision trees learning using the area under the ROC curve. In: 19th International Conference on Machine Learning, pp. 139–146. Morgan Kaufmann, San Francisco (2002)
5. Caruana, R., Niculescu-Mizil, A.: An empirical comparison of supervised learning algorithms. In: 23rd International Conference on Machine Learning, pp. 161–168. ACM Press, New York (2006)
6. Brefeld, U., Scheffer, T.: AUC maximizing support vector learning. In: Proc. ICML Workshop on ROC Analysis in Machine Learning (2005)
7. Yan, L., Dodier, R., Mozer, M.C., Wolniewicz, R.: Optimizing classifier performance via an approximation to the Wilcoxon-Mann-Whitney statistic. In: 20th International Conference on Machine Learning, vol. 20(2), pp. 848–855. AAAI Press, Menlo Park (2003)
8. Cortes, C., Mohri, M.: AUC optimization vs. error rate minimization. Advances in Neural Information Processing Systems 16, 313–320 (2004)
9. Huang, J., Ling, C., Zhang, H., Matwin, S.: Proper model selection with significance test. In: Daelemans, W., Goethals, B., Morik, K. (eds.) ECML PKDD 2008, Part I. LNCS (LNAI), vol. 5211, pp. 536–547. Springer, Heidelberg (2008)
10. Herschtal, A., Raskutti, B.: Optimizing area under the ROC curve using gradient descent. In: 21st International Conference on Machine Learning, vol. 69, pp. 49–56. ACM Press, New York (2004)
11. Calders, T., Jaroszewicz, S.: Efficient AUC optimization for classification. In: Kok, J.N., Koronacki, J., Lopez de Mantaras, R., Matwin, S., Mladenič, D., Skowron, A. (eds.) PKDD 2007. LNCS (LNAI), vol. 4702, pp. 42–53. Springer, Heidelberg (2007)
12. Vanderlooy, S., Hüllermeier, E.: A critical analysis of variants of the AUC. Machine Learning 72, 247–262 (2008)
13. Yang, Z., Tang, K., Yao, X.: Self-adaptive differential evolution with neighborhood search. In: Proceedings of the 2008 Congress on Evolutionary Computation, pp. 1110–1116 (2008)
14. Yao, X., Liu, Y.: A New Evolutionary System for Evolving Artificial Neural Networks. IEEE Transaction on Neural Networks 8(3), 694–713 (1997)
15. Hasheminia, H., Niaki, S.T.A.: A Hybrid Method of Neural Networks and Genetic Algorithm in Econometric Modeling and Analysis. Journal of Applied Science 8(16), 2825–2833 (2008)
16. Shanthi, D., Sahoo, G., Saravanan, N.: Evolving Connection Weights of Artificial Neural Networks Using Genetic Algorithm with Application to the Prediction of Stroke Disease. International Journal of Soft Computing 4(2), 95–102 (2009)
17. Hand, D.J., Till, R.J.: A Simple Generalisation of the Area Under the ROC Curve for Multiple Class Classification Problems. Machine Learning 45(2), 171–186 (2001)
18. Price, K., Storn, R., Lampinen, J.: Differential Evolution: A Practical Approach to Global Optimization. Springer, Berlin (2005)
19. Newman, D., Hettich, S., Blake, C., Merz, C.: UCI repository of machine learning databases (1998), http://archive.ics.uci.edu/ml/datasets.html
20. Demšar, J.: Statistical Comparisons of Classifiers over Multiple Data Sets. Journal of Machine Learning Research 7, 1–30 (2006)

A Neuro-genetic Control Scheme Application for Industrial R^3 Workspaces

E. Irigoyen, M. Larrea, J. Valera, V. Gómez, and F. Artaza⋆

Department of Systems Engineering and Automatic Control
Computational Intelligence Group & Intelligent Control Research Group
University of the Basque Country (UPV/EHU), ETSI, 48013 Bilbao
{eloy.irigoyen,m.larrea}@ehu.es

Abstract. This work presents a neuro-genetic control scheme for a R^3 workspace application. The solution is based on a Multi Objective Genetic Algorithm reference generator and an Adaptive Predictive Neural Network Controller. Crane position control is presented as an application of the proposed control scheme.

1 Introduction

Nowadays, our aggressive market requires more competitive, productive, reliable, and accurate industrial solutions. This implies a big effort from the technicians and researchers for solving more real-world complex problems. Among these problems is the industrial kinematic control (where it is necessary to manipulate raw materials, semi-finished and finished products), which has a wide number of goals to reach [11]. In sequential industrial processes, for transportation-handle-machining of materials and products into different manufacturing workplaces, it is more necessary than ever to obtain automated and enhanced solutions, based on new technologies such as Computational Intelligence.

This work presents a hybrid intelligent solution that solves movement problems in a R^3 workspace. This implies a complex calculation of a precise trajectory. It also solves accurate control action for precise and safe tracking operations.

Our solution implements a Multi Objective Genetic Algorithm (MOGA) in order to solve a non-linear and complex problem for calculating R^3 trajectories [14]. This solution takes into account requirements based on the workspace (non-allowed areas, points of pass, etc), and constraints on the basis of parameter values (max-min) to preserve the life of actuators and different pieces.

In addition, the tracking operation is made by an Adaptive-Predictive Neural Network (APNN) control system, which includes some intelligent strategies to achieve appropriately each target. This system contains two Recurrent Neural Networks (NNARX): The first one provides a non-linear process model to

⋆ This work comes under the framework of the ATICTA research project with reference SAIOTEK08 granted by Basque Government, and the BAIP2020 research project granted by CDTI of the Government of Spain, with permission of INGETEAM for paper publication.

M. Graña Romay et al. (Eds.): HAIS 2010, Part I, LNAI 6076, pp. 343–350, 2010.

estimate the process output and derivatives in time, and the second one is involved in the current action calculation in every sample time.

2 Adaptive Predictive Control Strategy

The Adaptive Predictive Control strategy has been selected for this work as a result of needs referring to the control strategy and the use of the NNs as Controllers and Identifiers. This strategy has been employed in several different works like [13][10].

The scheme used (Fig.1) has the following four basic blocks; a MOGA Reference Generator, an Identifier, a Controller and a nonlinear system to be controlled. Above these three elements the respective training algorithms can be found. The Identifier can provide an online identified model, which means the scheme has the capability to learn the system dynamics simultaneously to the nonlinear system evolution. The block "Adaptive Predictive Controller" has the duty to generate the control action for the nonlinear system calculated in a predefined prediction horizon. The block "MOGA Reference Generator" calculates a path to be tracked by the nonlinear system.

The Adaptive Predictive Controller performs a simulation of the entire loop and employs a replica of the nonlinear system provided by the NN Identifier in order to do so. This replica provides not only the nonlinear system output estimation ($\hat{y}$) but also the estimation of the identified system derivatives ($\frac{\partial \hat{y}_{k+1}}{\partial u_k}, \frac{\partial \hat{y}_{k+1}}{\partial y_k}, ...$). Those estimations are integrated in the training algorithm to be presented in the section (4.1). Once the training algorithm finalises its work, the NN Controller weight and bias are tuned to generate a control action that will be the output of the block.

One of the advantages that the Adaptive Predictive Control contributes is the capability to change the controller behaviour. This is positive when the nonlinear system to be controlled suffers a modification (e.g. deterioration, wear, slightly different parts, etc) and the nonlinear system model changes to a new operating regime, causing the Controller change too.

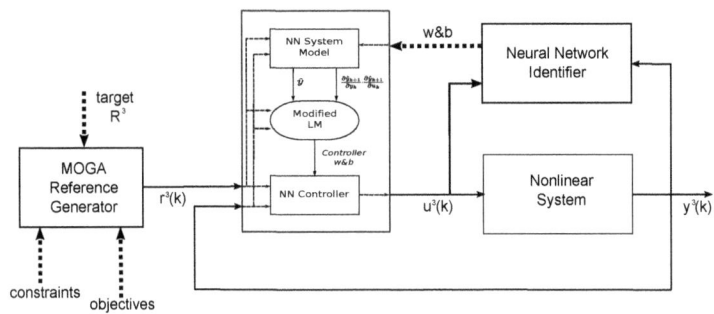

Fig. 1. Control Scheme

3 MOGA Reference Generator

Trajectory calculation in R^3 workspace is a complex optimization problem considering the multiple objectives, restrictions and constraint functions. Some important aspects have to be considered for an appropriate trajectory reference calculation: minimum process cycle time and distance travelled avoiding obstacles and non-allowed areas, minimum oscillation according to previous acceleration reference calculations, and reduction of mechanical elements wear in movement transition. Consequently, problem formulation is not so trivial, taking into account that some objectives are not differentiable, and gradient or higher derivatives information is not needed when searching for an optimal point. This kind of problem can be solved using Genetic Algorithm (GA) [2], in a Multi Objective Optimization strategy Valera et al [14].

The problem consists of calculating an optimal trajectory over an $OXYZ$ coordinate system. In industrial processes, the R^3 workspace usually has some restrictions, as in $0 \leq x(t) \leq X_{lim}$, $0 \leq y(t) \leq Y_{lim}$, and $0 \leq z(t) \leq Z_{lim}$. Thereby, a possible trajectory reference $r(t)$ is given by (eq.1).

$$r(t) = [x(t), y(t), z(t)] : \forall t \rightarrow [0, t_f] \tag{1}$$

This optimization problem has two main objectives to reach: minimize $r(t)$ length or travelled distance, and minimize the required path time. Furthermore, the trajectory has to satisfy the following constraints and restriction functions:

- Electromechanical component related constraints [12]: Speed $v(k)$ and Acceleration $a(k)$ on each axis or movement must not exceed the thresholds determined by the device manufacturers.
- Mechanical transmission elements and systems useful life: Acceleration or torque gradient $j(k)$ of each movement must not exceed a certain value to avoid so-called "impact torques" in mechanical transmission elements which cause jerky movements and vibrations reducing their useful life.
- Constraints related to no-allowed areas in the workspace: Being a new possible trajectory avoiding dangerous solutions. Any point of this trajectory cannot be included in the space defined by the constrained limited surface: $z = f_1(x, y)$, $y = f_2(x)$, and $z_p = f_3(x, y)$.

Furthermore, speed, acceleration and jerky movement constraint contribute to minimize sudden variations in the calculated control action. Obviously, at this

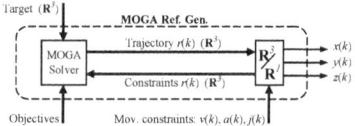

Fig. 2. MOGA Reference Generator

level, the effects due to external disturbance like gusts of wind are ignored. Disturbance will be taken into account in the position control loop context.

In order to have a smooth trajectory, a bounded acceleration reference and a bounded acceleration gradient [1], we divided the positioning time into six intervals taking into account the speed reference shown in Valera et al. [14].

To find three smooth position references ($x(k)$, $y(k)$, and $z(k)$), we used a non lineal search method based on a Multi Objective Genetic Algorithm (MOGA), resulting in a R^3 combined trajectory ($OXYZ$ workspace) that simultaneously minimizes the travelled distance, the time used, and the final position error. The objectives for MOGA execution can also be found in Valera et al. [14].

4   Neural Network Adaptive Predictive Control

In this section the one dimensional Adaptive Predictive Control will be introduced. In this strategy, the two NNs employed are MultiLayer Perceptrons (MLP), The MLP are known as Universal Approximators because of their capacity to approximate any function of interest (both linear or nonlinear) as well as its derivatives [7]. The latter one is of great importance in the implementation of the Identifier, since the derivatives that it provides will be integrated in the training algorithm. The topology of the two NNs is presented in Fig.3.

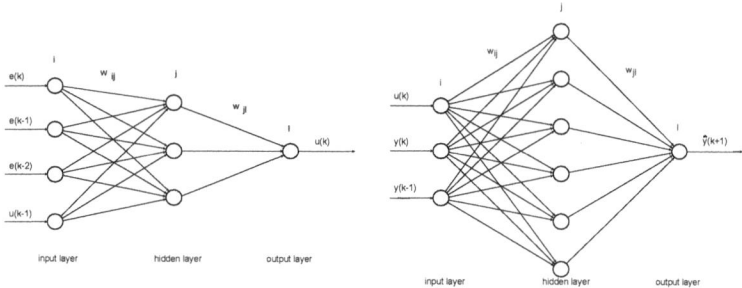

Fig. 3. a)NN Controller b)NN Identifier

The NN Controller (Fig.3a) is a NN AutoRegressive with eXogenous input (NNARX) that gives output feedback (control action).

The NN Identifier (Fig.3b) obtains the nonlinear system model based on the system input/output relation. Once the model is obtained, it can be used to emulate the nonlinear system behaviour and extract its derivatives. Both the NN Controller and the NN Identifier can be trained online or offline.

4.1   Neural Network Training

The NN Controller is trained in the"Adaptive Predictive Controller" block that can be seen in Fig.1. As mentioned, inside this block a simulation of the control loop is performed. This simulation enables the possibility to simulate the control loop evolution for a prediction horizon, and to simulate it for different control actions. The NN Controller needs to know, or estimate, the error produced on its output to be trained. As the desired control action (u) is unknown, the error produced on the output of the NN Controller is also unknown. The only known error is the one produced on the output of the nonlinear system $(y(k) - r(k)$ in Fig.1), which can be related to the NN Controller weight and bias through the NN System model. This way, the equation (eq.2)[8] can be used to train the NN Controller in a K prediction horizon.

$$\sum_{k=1}^{K} \frac{\partial E_k}{\partial w_{lij}} = \sum_{k=1}^{K} \sum_{k'=1}^{k} \sum_{k''=0}^{k'-1} \frac{\partial E_k}{\partial y_{k'}} \cdot \frac{\partial y_{k'}}{\partial u_{k''}} \cdot \frac{\partial u_{k''}}{\partial w_{lij}} \tag{2}$$

The equation (eq.2) is made up of three terms; the first one relates to the error committed in the control loop output to the nonlinear system output, the second one relates to the nonlinear system output to the control action, and finally, the third term relates to the control action to the NN Controller weights and biases. The first and the third terms are the known terms. The first is the one that depends on the used error function and the third is the one that can be calculated by backpropagation. The second term represents the model of the nonlinear system to be controlled. A general representation of a nonlinear system can be expressed in the following form (eq.3).

$$y(k') = M[y(k'-1), ..., y(k'-n), u(k'-1), ..., u(k'-m)] \tag{3}$$

Where n is the nonlinear system order that must satisfy $m \le n$. Deriving $y(k')$ from $u(k'')$ the unknown term $(\frac{\partial y_{k'}}{\partial u_{k''}})$ can be obtained. This term can in turn be decomposed in the following equation (eq. 4) [8].

$$\frac{\partial^{+} y_{k'}}{\partial u_{k''}} = \sum_{i=1}^{n} \frac{\partial y_{k'}}{\partial y_{k'-i}} \cdot \frac{\partial^{+} y_{k'-i}}{\partial u_{k''}} + \sum_{j=1}^{m} \frac{\partial y_{k'}}{\partial u_{k'-j}} \cdot \frac{\partial^{+} u_{k'-j}}{\partial u_{k''}} \tag{4}$$

Previous work [4][8] has shown that the reduction of the computational times can be achieved by neglecting some of these terms $(\frac{\partial u_{k'-j}}{\partial u_{k''}} = 0$ when $k' - j \ne k'')$. Neglecting these terms, the second term of the equation (eq.4) results in the following equation (eq.5).

$$\frac{\partial^{+} y_{k'}}{\partial u_{k''}} = \sum_{i=1}^{n} \frac{\partial y_{k'}}{\partial y_{k'-i}} \cdot \frac{\partial^{+} y_{k'-i}}{\partial u_{k''}} + \frac{\partial y_{k'}}{\partial u_{k''}} \tag{5}$$

Now the three terms of equation (eq.4) can be found. These three terms can be known on the basis of "NN System Model" input/output relations. The "Universal Approximator" property has been applied in [3] to obtain the derivatives of the identified system using the equation (eq.6) to do so, being the NN represented in Fig.3b.

$$\frac{\partial \hat{y}(k+1)}{\partial net\_input_p} = \sum_{1}^{j} w_{pj} o_j (1 - o_j) w_{j1} \tag{6}$$

Where p represents the NN input, j is the number of neurons in the hidden layer, w represents the weight that connects layers and o is the neuron output.

4.2   NN Controller Training Algorithm Modification

The LM algorithm calculates the update term for the weights and biases on the basis of the equation ΔW in [6]. The modification proposed, which includes the dynamics of the nonlinear system, affects the term on the output layer to be backpropagated (Δ^M presented in [6]).

$$\Delta^M = -\dot{F}^M(\underline{n}^M) \cdot \frac{\partial y_{k'}}{\partial u_{k''}} \qquad (7)$$

Applying this formula and following the development presented in [6] the dynamics of the nonlinear system and the ones of the NN Controller are backpropagated. Therefore all the jacobian terms are calculated so the weights adaptation term (ΔW) can be obtained. Finally we emphasise the different meaning of the term $e'(\underline{w})$ on the equation (eq.8) for this work. If the original work represented $e(\underline{w})$ as the error committed in the NN output, this work uses $e'(\underline{w})$ as the error committed in the output of the control loop.

$$\Delta W = \left[J^T(\underline{w}) \cdot J(\underline{w}) + \mu \cdot I \right]^{-1} \cdot J(\underline{w}) \cdot e'(\underline{w}) \qquad (8)$$

This equation is used in the same manner as the traditional LM algorithm in [6] does.

5   Application to Crane Position Control

The Adaptive Predictive Control strategy is applied in the control of a travelling crane. The load trajectory calculation in the R^3 workspace is a complex optimization problem considering the multiple objectives, restrictions and constraint functions. The nonlinear problem of the swinging angle control is considered as a good exercise for the proposed NN control system. The crane model used consists of a Matlab/ Simulink block provided by the company Inteco with the real model of the crane. See [11] for the mathematical model.

For an initial test it has been chosen to implement the x-axis control. Offline identification was carried out applying random entries (both positive and negative pulses inside the work range) to the NN identifier.

The information of the trajectory for the MOGA is the following; Initial Pos.$(0, 0, 0)$, Final Pos.$(30, 80, 10)$ with Crossing Point $(50, 50, 50)$cm. The constraints that the MOGA must respect in these 3 axes are; Max. Acceleration $5cm/s^2$, Max. Speed $10cm/s$ and Max. Jerk $0.5cm/s^3$. The objectives applied to the MOGA are; pass through the specified crossing point ($error < 0.5cm$), minimisation of the travel time required and minimisation of the distance travelled. The resultant trajectory is shown in Fig.4(a).

Fig.4(b) shows the control of the x-axis position, the first figure being the path generated by the MOGA and the tracking performed by the controller. The second and the third figures represent the control action generated and the swinging of the load.

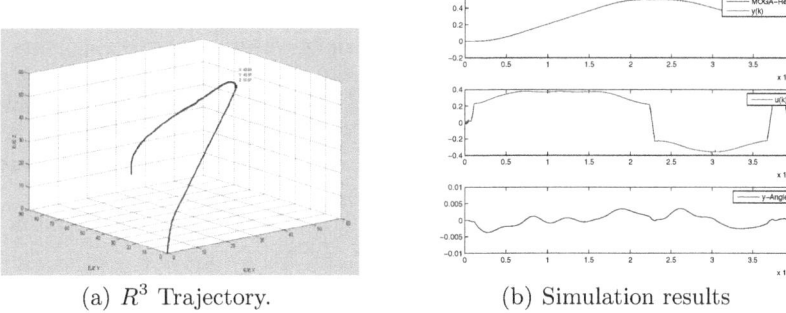

(a) R^3 Trajectory.   (b) Simulation results

Fig. 4. System response

6   Conclusions

This work tackles the problem of R^3 Multi Objective reference generation and the control of system under those circumstances. With an intelligent search algorithm based in MOGA the solution is stable, robust and it is a fast way to find optimal solutions when real-time requirements are not needed and when the problem involves many objectives.

Moreover, the present paper shows the use of NNs in an Adaptive Predictive Control strategy. The simulation results show a correct online adaptation of the NN controller and the validity of the modification made to the LM training algorithm. This modification allows the integration of the nonlinear system dynamic into the training algorithm, thus being able to train the NN Controller despite not knowing the nonlinear system. The NN Identifier estimates the dynamics of the nonlinear. The use of restrictions to control action has been tested on various works such as [9], where first order training algorithms are used. These restrictions may be of interest when implementing a Controller training that penalises abrupt changes in the control action.

Moreover, the present paper shows the use of NNs in an Adaptive Predictive Control strategy. The simulation results show a correct online adaptation of the NN controller and the validity of the modification made to the LM training algorithm. This modification allows the integration of the nonlinear system dynamic into the training algorithm, thus being able to train the NN Controller despite unknowing the nonlinear system. The dynamics of the nonlinear system are estimated by the NN Identifier. The use of restrictions to control action has been tested on various works such as [9], where first order training algorithms are used. These restrictions may be of interest when implementing a Controller training that penalises abrupt changes in the control action. We will also take into account hierachical issues [5].

References

1. Anand, V.B.: Computer Graphics and Geometric Modeling for Engineers. John Wiley & Sons, Inc., New York (1993)
2. Eiben, A.E., Smith, J.E.: Introduction to Evolutionary Computing. Springer, Heidelberg (2003)
3. Fujinaka, T., Kishida, Y., Yoshioka, M., Omatu, S.: Stabilization of double inverted pendulum with self-tuning neuro-pid. IJCNN 4, 345–348 (2000)
4. Galvan, J.B.: Tuning of optimal neural controllers. In: Proc. Int. Conf. on Engineering of Intelligent Systems, pp. 213–219 (1998)
5. Graña, M., Torrealdea, F.J.: Hierarchically structured systems. European Journal of Operational Research 25, 20–26 (1986)
6. Hagan, M.T., Menhaj, M.B.: Training feedforward networks with the marquardt algorithm. IEEE Transactions on Neural Networks 5(6), 989–993 (1994)
7. Hornik, K., Stinchcombe, M., White, H.: Universal approximation of an unknown mapping and its derivatives using multilayer feedforward networks. Neural Networks 3, 551–560 (1990)
8. Irigoyen, E., Galvan, J.B., Perez-Ilzarbe, M.J.: Neural networks for constrained optimal control of nonlinear systems. IJCNN 4, 299–304 (2000)
9. Irigoyen, E., Galvn, J.B., Prez-Ilzarbe, M.J.: A neuro predictive controller for constrained nonlinear systems. In: IASTED International Conference Artificial Intelligence and Applications (2003)
10. Lu, C.-H., Tsai, C.-C.: Adaptive predictive control with recurrent neural network for industrial processes: An application to temperature control of a variable-frequency oil-cooling machine. IEEE Transactions on Industrial Electronics 55(3), 1366–1375 (2008)
11. Pauluk, M., Korytowski, A., Turnau, A., Szymkat, M.: Time optimal control of 3d crane. In: Proceedings of the 7th Inter. Conference on Methods and Models in Automation and Robotics, pp. 927–936 (2001)
12. Suh, J.-H., Lee, J.-W., Lee, Y.-J., Lee, K.-S.: An automatic travel control of a container crane using neural network predictive pid control technique. International Journal of Precision Engineering and Manufacturing 7(1), 35–41 (2006)
13. Tan, K.K., Lee, T.H., Huang, S.N., Leu, F.M.: Adaptive-predictive control of a class of siso nonlinear systems. Dynamics and Control 11(2), 151–174 (2001)
14. Valera, J., Irigoyen, E., Gomez-Garay, V., Artaza, F.: Application of neuro-genetic techniques in solving industrial crane kinematic control problem. In: IEEE International Conference on Mechatronics, pp. 231–237 (2009)

Memetic Feature Selection: Benchmarking Hybridization Schemata

M.A. Esseghir[1,2], Gilles Goncalves[1], and Yahya Slimani[2]

[1] University of Lille Nord de France, F-59000 Lille,
Artois University, LGI2A Laboratory,
Technopark Futura,Béthune, 62400, France
[2] Tunis El-Manar University, Sciences Faculty of Tunis,
1060 Campus Universitaire

Abstract. Feature subset selection is an important preprocessing and guiding step for classification. The combinatorial nature of the problem have made the use of evolutionary and heuristic methods indispensble for the exploration of high dimensional problem search spaces. In this paper, a set of hybridization schemata of genetic algorithm with local search are investigated through a memetic framework. Empirical study compares and discusses the effectiveness of the proposed local search procedure as well as their components.

1 Introduction

Researchers in machine learning, data mining, pattern recognition and statistics have developed a number of methods for dimensionality reduction using usefulness and classifcation accuracy estimates for individual feature and subset assessment. In fact, feature selection (FS) tries to select the most relevant attributes from row data, and hence guide the construction of the final classification model or decision support system. From one hand, the majority, of learning scheme, are being relying on feature selection either as independent pre-processing technique or as an embedded stage within the learning process [3]. On the other hand, both feature selection and data mining techniques struggle to gain attended reliability, especially when they face high dimensional data [6]. As a result, some trends in FS have attempted to tackle this challenge by proposing hybrid approaches or models based on multiple criteria [3].

In this paper, we propose, a hybrid evolutionary approach for feature selection designed as a memetic model and we assess it through a set of variants involving different local search procedures. The main motivations for this proposal are two folds: (i) Both effective sequential search techniques [3] applying greedy descent methods and evolutionay approaches provide comparable results [3], hence, the combination might enhance and guide the search space exploration to suitable areas; (ii) Memetic approaches have shown their effectiveness in both search enhancement and diversification [4], with several hard optimization problems.

This paper is organized in six sections. Section 2 formalizes the feature selection problem and reviews representative approaches. Section 3 provide a brief

M. Graña Romay et al. (Eds.): HAIS 2010, Part I, LNAI 6076, pp. 351–358, 2010.

introduction of Memetic alhorithms as well as their components. Section 4 details the different variants of the memetic scheme. Section 5 compares and assesses memetic alternatives behaviors empirically. Finally, Section 6 concludes this paper and presents some directions of future research.

2   Feature Selection

Let D be a data set with F as a set of features such that $|N| = n$, and let X $(X \subseteq N)$ be a subset of N. Let $J(X)$ the function that assesses the relevance of the features subset X. The problem of feature selection states the selection of a subset Z such that:

$$J(Z) = max_{X \subseteq N} J(X) \qquad (1)$$

In other words, the retained feature subset should be compact and representative of the dataset or the underlying context. This might be done by both removing redundant, noisy and irrelevant attributes by keeping the minimal information loss. For a given dataset of n features, the exhaustive exploration requires the examination of $2^n - 1$ possible subsets. Consequently, the search through the feasible solutions search space is a np-hard combinatorial problem [6]. Numerous reference approaches have been proposed for the identification of features having the highest predictive power for a given target [5]. The representative approaches could be categorized in two classes: *filters* and *wrappers* [3].

Filters. Considered as the earliest approach to feature selection, filter methods discard irrelevant features, without any reference to a data mining technique, by applying independent search which is mainly based on the assessment of intrinsic attribute properties and their relationship with the data set class (*i.e.* Relief, Symmetrical uncertainty, *etc*, Pearson correlation) [6]. The main advantage of filter methods is their reduced computational complexity which is due to the *simple* independent criterion used for feature evaluation. Nevertheless, considering one feature at a time cripple the filter to cope with either redundant or interacting features.

Wrappers. When feature selection is based on a wrapper, subsets of attributes are evaluated with a classification algorithm. The exploration of such feasible solutions requires a heuristic search strategy. The wrapper methods often provide better results than filter ones because they consider a classifier within the evaluation process. Kohavi *et al.* [5] were the first to advocate the wrapper as a general framework for feature selection in machine learning. Numerous studies have used the above framework with different combinations of evaluation and search schema. Featured search technique are ranging from greedy sequential attribute selection methods (*i.e.* SFS, SBE, Floating search) [3] to randomized and stochastic methods (*i.e.* GRASP, TABU, Genetic Algorithms, *etc*) [3,8]. Hybrid approaches based on filter-wrapper combination include memetic techniques, ensemble and embedded methods [3,6,8].

3   Memetic Algorithms

Memetic Evolutionary Algorithms (MA) are a class of stochastic heuristics for a global optimization which combine the parallel global search ability of evolutionary algorithms (EA) with local search to improve individual solutions [4]. MA have proven its effectiveness across a wide range of problem domains and models for hybridizing EA with local search[4].Since EA are good at rapidly guiding the search to interesting areas, they are often less good at refining near optimal solutions. Such refinement could be achieved with local search, by moving the solutions to nearest local-optima. The rest of this section briefly overviews the EA used, followed by local search components description.

3.1   Genetic Algorithm as Evolutionary Scheme

Genetic Algorithm (GA) [2] is considered as one of the leading stochastic optimization scheme, reputed to be one of the more robust meta-heuristic dealing with *nb-hard* problems [4]. GA tries to make the analogy with the natural evolution using a set of concepts like selection, crossover, mutation, and reproduction in optimization processes. Algorithm 1 (*see Fig.* 1) details the basic steps of a commonly used GA in FS modeling. The process starts by the random generation of an initial population of solutions, also called chromosomes (Line 2). The population evolves during the search by keeping the fittest solutions. The evolution relies on an iterative process involving a set of stochastic operators (Line5-9), inspired from biological and genetic materials [2]. Siedlecki and Sklansky [7] was the first that have used GA as a feature subset selector. Several papers and comparative studies consider that wrappers based on GA are among the most interesting approaches for tackling high dimensional FS problems [3,7].

3.2   Local Search (LS)

Local search procedure is a search method that iteratively examines a set of solutions in the neighborhood of the current solution and replaces it with better neighbor if one exists. According to Krasnogor *et al.* [4], three components characterize the behavior of the local search procedure: (i) **Neighborhood generating function:** defines the set of solutions that could be reached by the application of the local search to a given solution. In addition, different neighborhood structures could be generated, from a given starting solution. The effectiveness of the local search depends, in a part, on the structure of the neighborhood. (ii) **Depth:** the LS depth (d) defines the nature of the local search, and how it will be applied. if $d = 1$, the LS is applied once, whereas with greater value of d the iterative process restarts with the best solution found. (iii) **Pivot rule:** defines the criteria of accepting an improving solution. Pivot rule could aggregate a set of criterion, particularly, in multi-objective optimization problems.

   In this paper, we investigate different concepts associated to LS components and their application to the FS problem.

Algorithm 1. Basic Genetic Algorithm	**Algorithm 2.** Iterative LS procedure
Input: $Size$: population size; Cla: Classifier; p_{mut}: mutation probability; p_{cross}: crossover probability $Maxgen$: Total number of iterations; D: Dataset **Output:** S' : Population of the last generation	**Input:** F: Initial Feature set C: Target class Attribute Cla: Classifier for solution evaluation S: Input Solution **Output:** S' : result of local search

	Algorithm 1		**Algorithm 2**
1	**begin**	1	**begin**
2	S_0=generateInitialSolutionSet($Size$)	2	$S1 \leftarrow S$, $S_{best} \leftarrow S1$
3	Population P=S, $P_{tmp}=\emptyset$; $i = 0$	3	Stop $\leftarrow false$
4	**while** $i< Maxgen$ **do**	4	**repeat**
5	P_{tmp}=Select (P)	5	$Sol_{list} \leftarrow NH(S1, F)$
6	Crossover(P_{tmp}, p_{cross})	6	$\forall X \in Sol_{list}, Evaluate(X, Cla)$
7	Mutate(P_{tmp}, p_{mut})	7	$S1 \leftarrow getBest(Sol_{list})$
8	Evaluate(P_{tmp}, Cla, D)	8	**if** $S1.fitness > S_{best}.fitness$ **then**
9	Replace(P_{tmp}, P)	9	$S_{best} \leftarrow S1$
10	$i = i + 1$	10	**else**
11	Return (S'=P)	11	Stop $\leftarrow true$
		12	**until** $(Stop = true)$;
		13	$S' \leftarrow S_{best}$
		14	Return (S')

Fig. 1. GA and LS pseudo-codes

4   Proposed Memetic Schemata

As the basic evolutionary genetic paradigm could be enhanced, with specific problem knowledge, the memetic scheme could be an attractive alternative, since it endows the basic evolutionary scheme with a local search. Besides, heuristics based on local search (TABU, GRASP) [8] pointed out the ability to provide comparable results to evolutionary algorithms.

In this paper, we focus on a set commonly used local search operators, and we try to deploy them within memetic schemata. The effectiveness of the operators will be assessed empirically. By doing so, we aim to give a coherent, and integrated view on the sweeted practices in terms of hybridization, with a memetic schemata providing various trade-offs between global and local search mechanisms. As introduced in the previous section, the proposed operators, use different design consideration in relation with the LS component and memetic integration.

Neighborhood structure. Two neighborhood structures are considered in this paper. The bit-Flip operator (BF), explores neighboring solutions by adding or removing one solution at a time. The BF neighborhood structure is formulated by equation 2.

$$NH_{BF}(S) = \{X | X = NH^+(S) \cup NH^-(S)\} \qquad (2)$$

where $NH^+(S)$ and $NH^-(S)$ denote respectively neighborhoods issued from the attribute addition or removal from the current solution.

$$NH^+(S) = \{X|X = S \cup \{f_i\}, \forall f_i \in F, f_i \notin X\} \tag{3}$$

$$NH^-(S) = \{X|X = S \setminus \{f_i\}, \forall f_i \in X\} \tag{4}$$

On the other hand, Attribute Flip operator (AF) constructs neighborhood using permutation between selected and non-selected features (*see eq.* 5). All combinations are considered.

$$NH_{AF}(S) = \{X|X = S \cup \{f_i\} \setminus \{f_j\}, \forall f_i \in X, \forall f_j \notin X\} \tag{5}$$

The two operators explore different region of the current solution neighborhood. There is no overlapping regions $(NH_{BF}(S) \cap NH_{AF}(S) = \emptyset)$ and the second neighborhood structure is much larger than the first which would require more computational time.

LS depth. The above presented neighborhood structure could be used in different ways within the local search operators. Here, we consider two application scenario: *sequential* and *iterative* LS. The sequential procedure, explores neighborhood and updates the current solution with the best solution found.The second procedure restarts the sequential procedure each time the current solution is improved. Consequently, the iterative procedure replaces the starting solution with a solution on a local minima. The pseudo-code of the iterative procedure is detailed by Algorithm 2 (*see Fig.* 1).

Hybridization. The local search could be applied to GA, at different level of the evolution process. The simplest way of integration, is to apply LS to the best solution at the end of each iteration. Furthermore, one can think to refine all the solutions at th end of each GA iteration. These two memetic schemata are applied with the above presented combination alternatives to the problem of Feature subset selection.

LS Computational Complexity. Table 1 compares the computational complexity of the proposed local search operators. The operators complexities depend on three factors: neighborhood structure, LS depth and the way of application (the number of the solutions to which it will be applied).

Table 1. Complexity of local search operators

LS-Operator		Order of Complexity	Parameters
SEQ	BitFlip(Best)	$\Theta(N)$	N: number of features
	AttribFlip(Best)	$\Theta(N^2)$	m : mating pool size
	BitFlip(all)	$\Theta(N.m)$	
	AttribFlip(all)	$\Theta(N^2.m)$	
Iterative	BitFlip(Best)	$\Theta(N.d)$	d: local search depth
	AttribFlip(Best)	$\Theta(N^2.d)$	
	BitFlip(all)	$\Theta(N.m.d)$	
	AttribFlip(all)	$\Theta(N^2.m.d)$	

5   Empirical Study

We empirically assess the behavior of the eight memetic schemata. They will also be, compared and ranked according to their respective improvement toward GA. Three UCI [1] benchmark datasets were used, in this study. During the search, fitness evaluation is based on error rate of the Naive Bayes (NB) classifier. Once the search terminated, the best solution is assessed with Artificial neural network (ANN) and NB [3] classifiers, using different data (validation stage).

Reported results include mean values, standard deviation, and statistical t-tests (improvement toward GA), of 20 trial runs per experiment. For each experiment we present best solution fitness (lowest error rate %), test accuracy on independent dataset, average runtime CPU, cardinality of best solution ($\#features$) and the gain Toward GA fitness. A ranking based on fitness is provided for each dataset. We note that the negative t-$test$ values correspond to improvement over the baseline method, and the confidence level of 99% requires absolute $t - value$ greater than 2.528 for 20 independent runs. Globally, we can point out, from the three Tables (2, 3, and 4), the superiority of memetic schemata over GA at the expense of computation cost resulting from additional evaluations. Another common point, is the highest and the lowest gain of memetic algorithms, the best improvements were obtained with the iterative AF operator applied to all the solutions at the end of each generation and the smallest ones were obtained by the non-iterative version of the BF operator

Table 2. Data set: SpamBase (57 Attrib.)

LS applied to GA		Measures	Fitness	VALIDATION ERROR%		CPU (s)	# Attrib.	# Eval	Gain%GA	RANK
				ANN	NB					
No LS (GA)		Mean:	9,32%	10,74%	7,81%	14774,13	15,04	1089		
		Sd:	0,95%	1,45%	1,10%	14759,99	3,15	0		
		t-test	0	0	0	0	0	-		
SEQ	BitFlip(Best)	Mean:	8,54%	11,10%	8,24%	35672,26	13,87	3089	8,37%	8
		Sd:	1,02%	2,04%	1,27%	36614,23	2,94	0		
		t-test	-18,92	3,71	4,95	22,08	-12,67	-	-	
	AttribFlip(Best)	Mean:	6,88%	9,61%	7,26%	32705,52	15,96	3089	26,18%	3
		Sd:	1,15%	2,25%	1,49%	28955,4	4,88	0		
		t-test	-37,43	-8,41	-5,85	18,74	5,31	-	-	
	BitFlip(all)	Mean:	8,19%	10,58%	8,23%	91471,7	15,45	11289	12,12%	6
		Sd:	0,98%	1,98%	1,50%	40881,06	3,2	0		
		t-test	-29,95	-1,7	7,22	31,64	1,49	-	-	
	AttribFlip(all)	Mean:	5,75%	8,95%	6,73%	95083,75	17,6	11289	38,30%	2
		Sd:	0,69%	1,93%	1,50%	45427,35	4,47	0		
		t-test	-73,7	-10,69	-23,21	44,9	85,05	-	-	
Iterative	BitFlip(Best)	Mean:	8,44%	9,98%	7,49%	36313,91	15,61	3171,17	9,44%	7
		Sd:	1,17%	1,75%	1,56%	34137,85	4,38	32,04		
		t-test	-20,55	-6,81	-4,72	54,25	8,08	-	-	
	AttribFlip(Best)	Mean:	7,01%	9,62%	7,27%	35944,87	14,87	3209,43	24,79%	4
		Sd:	1,01%	2,10%	1,44%	38229,41	3,63	33,37		
		t-test	-45,78	-11,65	-9,22	23,64	-3,54	-	-	
	BitFlip(all)	Mean:	7,93%	10,35%	7,70%	128806,75	15,35	14180,5	14,91%	5
		Sd:	0,93%	1,50%	1,18%	112289,05	3,1	418,7		
		t-test	-54,13	-3,5	-2,06	55,51	2,61	-	-	
	AttribFlip(all)	Mean:	5,52%	7,69%	6,30%	106967,85	17,6	12911	40,77%	1
		Sd:	0,49%	1,22%	1,31%	49985,26	2,91	137,52		
		t-test	-151,28	-31,84	-22,96	51,35	85,05	-	-	

Table 3. Data set: Colon cancer (2000 Attrib.)

LS applied to GA		Measures	Fitness	VALIDATION ERROR% ANN	NB	CPU (s)	# Attrib.	# Eval	Gain%GA	RANK
No LS (GA)		Mean:	6,52%	6,58%	12,19%	31079,73	23,18	3032		
		Sd:	2,92%	3,14%	4,41%	22980,17	7,45	0		
		t-test	0	0	0	0	0		-	
SEQ	BitFlip(Best)	Mean:	4,46%	6,28%	10,32%	38454,95	20,55	5032	31,60%	4
		Sd:	2,05%	2,97%	4,59%	30297,6	6,6	0	-	
		t-test	-20,87	-2,11	-7,8	5,73	-5,45		-	-
	AttribFlip(Best)	Mean:	4,64%	7,06%	10,06%	41058,14	21,41	5032	28,83%	5
		Sd:	2,25%	2,96%	3,23%	37162,49	8,55	0	-	
		t-test	-14,38	5,19	-15,01	7,69	-4,35		-	-
	BitFlip(all)	Mean:	4,78%	5,96%	11,49%	200004,95	22,05	13232	26,69%	6
		Sd:	2,96%	2,98%	2,96%	102160,5	6,34	0	-	
		t-test	-17,19	-5,06	-4,23	22,81	-3,15		-	-
	AttribFlip(all)	Mean:	3,59%	5,74%	11,49%	198320,55	22,05	13232	44,94%	2
		Sd:	1,62%	2,59%	3,12%	102691,3	6,78	0	-	
		t-test	-24,16	-4,14	-8,47	40,91	-3,15		-	-
Iterative	BitFlip(Best)	Mean:	5,58%	6,29%	11,47%	39703,43	20,91	5073,74	14,42%	7
		Sd:	2,25%	3,17%	4,39%	30596,31	7,36	30,84	-	
		t-test	-5,31	-1,42	-1,37	12,2	-3,23		-	-
	AttribFlip(Best)	Mean:	4,35%	6,94%	11,84%	39066,78	20,09	5068,09	33,28%	3
		Sd:	2,17%	2,81%	3,44%	31127,5	6,31	10,33	-	
		t-test	-15,9	2,48	-3,93	6,94	-6,98		-	-
	BitFlip(all)	Mean:	5,65%	7,02%	11,38%	249361,3	18,45	15199,5	13,34%	8
		Sd:	2,86%	3,59%	3,86%	142791,7	6,51	711,49	-	
		t-test	-4,35	1,71	-5,02	57,21	-12,59		-	-
	AttribFlip(all)	Mean:	2,83%	6,28%	9,89%	213912,1	20,2	13790	56,60%	1
		Sd:	1,88%	3,27%	3,86%	122469,18	7,03	66,38	-	
		t-test	-21,43	-1,33	-23,24	29,99	-6,06		-	-

Table 4. Data set: Arrhythmia (279 Attrib.)

LS applied to GA		Measures	Fitness	VALIDATION ERROR% ANN	NB	CPU (s)	# Attrib.	# Eval	Gain%GA	RANK
No LS (GA)		Mean:	17,14%	13,38%	17,33%	158683,53	85,79	1311		
		Sd:	0,90%	1,13%	1,31%	72380,76	17,63	0		
		t-test	0	0	0	0	0		-	
SEQ	BitFlip(Best)	Mean:	16,81%	13,86%	17,09%	490897,85	93,7	3311	1,93%	8
		Sd:	0,91%	1,11%	1,30%	222623,21	14,37	0	-	
		t-test	-23,47	6,69	-2	26,47	11,23		-	-
	AttribFlip(Best)	Mean:	15,52%	14,03%	17,29%	519275,2	92,25	3311	9,45%	3
		Sd:	1,08%	1,67%	1,59%	347110,37	46,42	0	-	
		t-test	-65,25	2,69	-0,42	17,8	2,1		-	-
	BitFlip(all)	Mean:	16,46%	14,02%	17,36%	1785624,68	82,74	11511	3,97%	6
		Sd:	1,24%	1,91%	1,75%	898120,57	20,56	0	-	
		t-test	-36,87	7,77	0,22	37,76	-3,46		-	-
	AttribFlip(all)	Mean:	14,76%	14,22%	16,83%	1892140,75	89,4	11511	13,89%	2
		Sd:	0,80%	2,25%	1,30%	1141857,26	42,76	0	-	
		t-test	-71,41	7,94	-5,5	33,02	11,46		-	-
Iterative	BitFlip(Best)	Mean:	16,80%	14,40%	16,59%	525793,95	91,2	3516	1,98%	7
		Sd:	0,91%	1,50%	1,67%	290212,63	26,49	55,2	-	
		t-test	-16,38	11,1	-8,17	43,48	5,22		-	-
	AttribFlip(Best)	Mean:	16,03%	14,16%	16,76%	468881,85	93,9	3512,5	6,48%	4
		Sd:	1,03%	1,78%	1,87%	315436,97	56,97	40,3	-	
		t-test	-26,71	5,14	-6,36	28,42	1,19		-	-
	BitFlip(all)	Mean:	16,29%	13,79%	16,67%	2591560,62	83,1	15471,95	4,96%	5
		Sd:	1,15%	1,50%	1,52%	1343356,45	22,25	600,1	-	
		t-test	-24,61	5,56	-7,31	51,56	-8,75		-	-
	AttribFlip(all)	Mean:	14,19%	14,91%	16,61%	1384673,95	51,65	13731,5	17,21%	1
		Sd:	0,92%	1,30%	1,38%	763942,71	32,57	272,29	-	
		t-test	-138,18	20,26	-7,89	172,14	-11,26		-	-

when it is only applied to the best solution. Such a result, could be explained by the computational complexity of respective local searches. Furthermore, when we compare resulting improvements over the three datasets, we can depict a remarkable enhancement of memetic schemata with colon cancer data set (Table 3). The results are interesting because it is the dataset with the largest search space ($2000attributes$). Such results are attractive and encouraging for tackling high dimensional search spaces and, particularly, genomic data. On the other hand, the memetic improvement are not proportional to operators computational complexity. In fact, some sequential LS operators are more interesting than some iterative ones. For example, sequential AF applied to all solutions is always ranked at the second position, and performing better than some iterative LS schemata. Finally, the top-3 operators, involve the same neighborhood structure: Attribute permutation (AF operator). Such neighborhood seems to be more adapted than the others for FS problem.

6   Conclusion

We compare and assess theoretical and empirical aspects of a set of hybrid schemata based on memetic algorithm for the problem of feature selection. Empirical study carried out some interesting local search components with a trade-off between computational complexity and enhancement of search quality. The behavioral study could be extended to heuristics mainly based on local search (*i.e.* Tabu search, GRASP, VNS: Variable Neighborhood Search) as well as EA with cooperating LS operators (*i.e.* "*multi-memes*" scheme).

References

1. Blake, C., Merz, C.: UCI repository of machine learning databases (1998), http://www.ics.uci.edu/~mlearn/MLRepository.html
2. Goldberg, D.E.: Genetic Algorithms in Search, Optimization and Machine Learning. Addison-Wesley Longman Publishing Co., Inc., Boston (1989)
3. Guyon, I., Gunn, S., Nikravesh, M., Zadeh, L.: Feature Extraction, Foundations and Applications. Series Studies in Fuzziness and Soft Computing. Springer, Heidelberg (2006)
4. Hart, W.E., Krasnogor, N., Smith, J.: Recent Advances in Memetic Algorithms. Studies in Fuzziness and Soft Computing. Springer, Heidelberg (2004)
5. Kohavi, R., John, G.H.: Wrappers for feature subset selection. Artificial Intelligence 97, 273–324 (1997)
6. Liu, H., Motoda, H.: Computational methods of feature selection. Chapman and Hall/CRC Editions (2008)
7. Siedlecki, W., Sklansky, J.: A note on genetic algorithms for large-scale feature selection. Pattern Recogn. Lett. 10(5), 335–347 (1989)
8. Yusta, S.C.: Different metaheuristic strategies to solve the feature selection problem. Pattern Recognition Letters 30(5), 525–534 (2009)

A Hybrid Cellular Genetic Algorithm for Multi-objective Crew Scheduling Problem

Fariborz Jolai* and Ghazal Assadipour

Department of Industrial Engineering, College of Engineering, University of Tehran,
P.O. Box 11155-45632, Tehran, Iran
Ph.: +98(021) 88021067; Fax: +98(021) 88013102
fjolai@ut.ac.ir, ghazal.assadipour@gmail.com

Abstract. Crew scheduling is one of the important problems of the airline industry. This problem aims to cover a number of flights by crew members, such that all the flights are covered. In a robust scheduling the assignment should be so that the total cost, delays, and unbalanced utilization are minimized. As the problem is *NP-hard* and the objectives are in conflict with each other, a multi-objective meta-heuristic called CellDE, which is a hybrid cellular genetic algorithm, is implemented as the optimization method. The proposed algorithm provides the decision maker with a set of non-dominated or Pareto-optimal solutions, and enables them to choose the best one according to their preferences. A set of problems of different sizes is generated and solved using the proposed algorithm. Evaluating the performance of the proposed algorithm, three metrics are suggested, and the diversity and the convergence of the achieved Pareto front are appraised. Finally a comparison is made between CellDE and PAES, another meta-heuristic algorithm. The results show the superiority of CellDE.

Keywords: CellDE, Crew scheduling problem, Multi-objective optimization, Pareto optimality, Performance metric.

1 Introduction

Robust scheduling of crews helps airline industries cover all flights on time with the minimum possible cost and unbalance utilization of their crews. Crew scheduling problem (CSP) is proved to be *NP-hard*, so it cannot be exactly solved in a reasonable computation time. To solve the problem, a genetic algorithm was applied in [1]. The schedule was shown by a flight graph, in which the nodes represent flights and the edges represent dependency constraints among the flights. Schaefer [2] studied the problem under uncertainty due to the short term disruptions. He then developed two algorithms to determine robust schedules, and calculated the operational performance by means of simulation. Another stochastic formulation of the CSP is suggested in Yen et al. [3], where disruptions arising from crew scheduling decisions are considered, and the delay effects are minimized. The problem then is solved implementing a branching algorithm. CSP is modeled as a multi-objective problem in Lee et al. [4]

---

* Corresponding author.

M. Graña Romay et al. (Eds.): HAIS 2010, Part I, LNAI 6076, pp. 359–367, 2010.

with the objectives of minimizing the percentage of late arrivals, and flight-time-credit (FTC). The problem then is solved implementing PAES.

In this paper we find the Pareto front for CSP using a multi-objective algorithm, and evaluate the performance using three different metrics. In contrast to other approaches, in which a single solution is offered to Decision Maker (DM), here we suggest different alternatives and give the DM the opportunity to choose the one which fits best according to his/her preferences. In the following section the problem is defined. Then section 3 describes the algorithm which is developed to produce the Pareto optima front. In section 4, three performance metrics are presented and a comparison between the Pareto sets achieved by the implemented CellDE and the PAES is made in section 5. Section 6 concludes our work.

2 Problem Definition

A rotation is a set of flights, which starts and ends at a same, base city. A crew can be assigned to one or several rotations, such that constraints are not violated. Normally, there is a rest time between two rotations, whose length depends on the flight time. If the rest time exceeds the normal time, the crew are underutilized, and if the rest time is shorter, the crew is over utilized, which both should be minimized. In addition, a flight is delayed if there is no available crew for allocation. As ordinarily the delay is of the greatest penalties, the delayed flight is done as soon as a crew is available, which it usually brings about the over utilization of the crew. Number of crews has a direct impact on other objectives, i.e. maximizing the number of crews, can minimize delay penalty, under and overutilization, but maximizes the cost. To represent the schedule, a graph is used which is similar to the one suggested in [1]. In this graph nodes represent the flights and edges represent that second flight leaves from the destination of the first flight. In contrast to [1], which assumes that the second flight leaves on time and after a predefined lag of time, we consider the probability of delay. Thus, three scenarios are possible: the second flight leaves on time after the pre specified lag of time, without any delay or overutilization, or it leaves on time before the rest time is finished, without delay but overutilization, or it leaves with delay and overutilization. Consider Table 1 for example.

Table 1. A sample schedule

Flight	Dep. city	Des. city	Dep. time	Arr. time
1	0	1	10:00	11:00
2	1	2	11:20	12:10
3	2	0	12:30	13:30
4	0	3	11:30	12:30
5	3	0	12:50	13:45

All flights might be covered by one crew, which results in at least 120 and 100 minutes of delay for flights 4 and 5 respectively, in addition to overutilization of the crew or, two crews, that one covers flights 1, 2 and 3, and the other covers 4 and 5. None of the mentioned cases is superior, as the first has less cost, and the second has less delay penalty and overutilization.

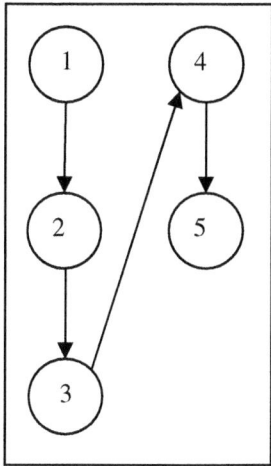

Fig. 1. Graph representation for the schedule in Table 1

3 Solution Procedure

Multi-objective algorithms provide a set of non-dominated solutions. A solution is non-dominated if there is no other feasible solution better in one objective but not worse at least in one other objective. As evolutionary algorithms (EAs) deal with sets of solutions, they have been reckoned among the best alternatives for multi-objective problems. The ability to handle complex problems and having features such as discontinuities, multimodality, disjoint feasible spaces and noisy function evaluations reinforces the potential effectiveness of EAs in multi-objective optimization [5]. To solve the problem, a hybrid multi-objective cellular genetic algorithm called CellDE, is implemented here. CellDE, developed by Durillo et al. [6] is a combination of MOCell, a multi-objective cellular genetic algorithm, and Generalized Differential Evolution 3, GDE3. It inherits good diversity from MOCell and convergence from GDE3 [6]. In the following, a brief description of cellular genetic algorithms, as the base of CellDE, Differential Evolution method, as the reproductive operator of CellDE, and PAES, as a base line approach, against which CellDE is compared, is brought.

3.1 Cellular GA

Cellular optimization models are structured EAs in which the population is decentralized. Using the concept of neighborhood, individuals only interact with their nearby individuals. Genetic operators perform the exploitation, while exploration is done by overlapped neighborhoods [7].

3.2 Differential Evolution

Differential Evolution is a parallel direct search method in which three parents collaborate to produce one offspring. By adding the weighted difference vector of two of the parents to the third one, a new individual is generated [8].

3.3 CellDE

Similar to other cellular genetic algorithms, after creation of an empty front, individuals are settled in a 2-dimensional toroidal grid. Then among the nearby neighbors of the current individual, two of them are chosen and the trio of parents is formed. The pseudo-code of the CellDE algorithm is illustrated in Fig. 2. In CellDE, one of the parents is the original individual, while in DE all three members are chosen among the neighbors of the current individual. The other two parents are chosen amongst eight neighbors of the current individual using the selection operator. The new offspring's vector is generated by adding a weighted difference vector between two of the parents to the third one (differentialEvolution function). If the original solution is dominated by the new individual, it will be replaced by the new one, but if both are non-dominated then the neighbor with worst crowding-distance is replaced (insert function). To compute the crowding-distance, all solutions are assigned a distance value. The boundary solutions (those which have the smallest or largest objective values), for each objective, are set to infinite value, while the others are set to the normalized difference in the objective values of two successive solutions.

In the next step, the offspring is added to the external archive (addToArchive function). Through a feedback mechanism implemented after each generation, some of the individuals in the population are selected by at random and replaced by a set of solutions in the archive (replaceIndividuals function).

3.3.1 Chromosome Representation
We used the direct coding to represent the chromosomes. As a consequence, the produced solutions are always feasible. Each chromosome's length is equal to the number of rotations and each allele's value is an integer limited to the maximum number of crews, which is equal to the number of rotations.

```
proc stepsUp (CellDE)                    //Algorithm parameters in 'CellDE'
population← randomPopulation ()          //Creates a random initial population
archive← createFront ()                    //Creates an empty Pareto front
while !terminationCondition() do
    for individuals← 1 to CellDE.populationSize do
        neighborhood← getNeighbors(population, position(individual));
        parent1← selection(neighborhood);
        parent2← selection(neighborhood);
        // parent1 and parent2 might be different
        while parent1=parent2 do
            parent2← selection(neighborhood);
        end while
        offspring← differentialEvolution(position(individual),
        position(individual),position(parent1), position(parent2));
        evaluateFitness(offsring);
        insert(position(individual), offspring, population);
        addToArchive(individual);
    end for
    population← replaceIndividuals(population, archive);
end while
end_proc stepsUp;
```

Fig. 2. The pseudo-code of the CellDE algorithm

3.3.2 Reproductive Operator

To produce new individuals, differential evolution operator is used. This operator uses two parameters of CR and F, where CR is the crossover constant and F is the mutation's scaling factor. The pseudo-code of producing new individuals is illustrated in Fig. 3.

An example is brought next. Consider the following three parents:

$$\begin{array}{ll} \text{Parent 1} & [5, 6, 7, 4, 9, 5] \\ \text{Parent 2} & [1, 4, 1, 2, 5, 3] \\ \text{Parent 3} & [3, 5, 1, 2, 1, 3] \end{array}$$

For $CR= 0.5$ and $F= 0.5$, and assuming all generated random values are less than CR, the offspring would be:

$$\text{Offspring} \quad [5, 6, 4, 3, 3, 4]$$

```
// r₁, r₂, r₃∈{1, 2,..., N}, randomly selected, except mutually different from i
proc differentialEvolution (i, r₁, r₂, r₃)
jrand= floor(randᵢ [0,1).D+1
for (j = 1; j ≤ D ; j = j+1) do
    if (randᵢ [0,1) < CR ∨ j = jrand) then
        u_{i[j],G}=x_{r3[i],G}+F.( x_{r1[i],G} - x_{r2[i],G})
    else
        u_{i[j],G}=x_{i[j],G}
    end if
end for
return u_{i,G}
end_proc differentialEvolution
```

Fig. 3. The pseudo-code of producing new individuals in DE

3.3.3 Parameterization

Other considerations for the implemented CellDE are the following:

- Population size: 100 individuals. For more information about the selection of the population size we refer the reader to [9].
- Neighborhood: individuals located at North, East, West, South, Northwest, Southwest, Northeast and Southeast of the current solution.
- Binary tournament selection: selects two individuals randomly. The one which is fitter is selected as a parent.
- Reproductive operator: differential evolution. Tests for real values in range [0, 1] lead to selection of 0.9 for CR and 0.9 for F. More explanation for the values of CR and F is presented in [10].
- Archive size: 100 individuals.
- Feedback: 20 individuals.
- Termination criteria: 25000 evaluations.

3.4 PAES

The Pareto archived evolution strategy (PAES), is a simple evolution scheme for multi-objective problems in which like most of other evolutionary algorithms, the parent individual is selected from a population, then applying the mutation operator, the new individual is generated. This algorithm enjoys an archive of non-dominated solutions. If the new solution is dominated by any member of the archive, it will be discarded; otherwise the dominated archive members will be removed. The archive implements an adaptive grid as a density estimator. If the archive is full when adding the new individual, a solution in the most populated area of the grid will be replaced. For more information we refer the reader to [11].

4 Performance Metric

Evaluating the performance of the developed algorithm, three metrics are implemented here. To calculate diversity and hyper volume, the Ideal and Nadir points should be calculated first. The vector which contains the best value of each objective in the objective space is considered as an Ideal point. The opposite of the Ideal point is the Nadir point, which contains the worst of objective values. In this problem, the Ideal point is a vector which contains the minimum possible cost and delay, and the unbalance utilization. A schedule has the minimum cost, when all the flights are covered by one crew, because additional cost to add a crew is of the greatest expense, and it has the minimum delay, when all the flights are covered by the maximum number of crews, i.e. when an exclusive crew is allocated to cover each rotation. The same can be said about unbalance utilization; a schedule has the minimum unbalance utilization when each crew covers only one rotation. In the following a brief description of each metric is brought.

4.1 Hypervolume Metric

Zitzler and Thiele [12] introduced a metric, called Hypervolume, which measures size of the space dominated by the Pareto front. Considering a cuboid between the Ideal and Nadir points, this indicator calculates fraction of the cuboid that is dominated by the obtained non-dominated solutions.

4.2 Spread Metric

Diversity metric of Δ was first introduced by Deb et al. [13] and computes the non-uniformity of spread through the Pareto front. It is defined as Equation (1).

$$\Delta = \frac{d_f + d_l + \sum\limits_{i=1}^{N-1} \left| d_i - \bar{d} \right|}{d_f + d_l + (N-1)\bar{d}} \tag{1}$$

where d_i is the Euclidean distance of two successive points, $\bar{d}$ is the average of distances and, d_f and d_l are the distances between bounding solutions. In well distributed fronts Δ is zero, because d_i is equal to $\bar{d}$ and $d_f = d_l = 0$, while in other cases Δ would be greater than zero.

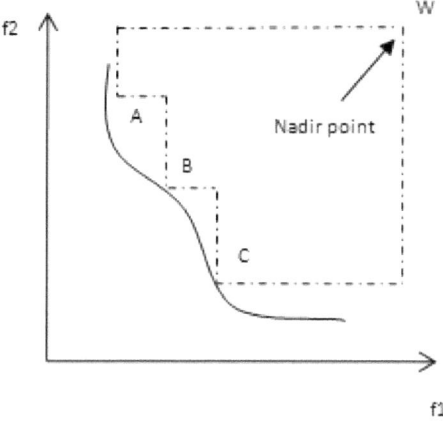

Fig. 4. A Hypervolume indicator in the two-objective case

4.3 Coverage Metric

Comparing two Pareto sets achieved by the implemented CellDE and the PAES, the coverage metric, firstly introduced in [12], is used (see Equation (2)). Zitzler and Thiele defined function $C(x', x'')$, where x' and x'' are two sets of decision vectors and it calculates the percent of points in x'' that are dominated by at least a point in x'.

$$C(X', X'') = \frac{\left|\{a'' \in X''; \exists a' \in X' : a' \geq a''\}\right|}{\left|X''\right|} \qquad (2)$$

5 Computational Experiments

The algorithm is tested with multiple problems of different size, and the solutions are compared with the results obtained by the PAES. Three types of problems, containing 30, 60 and 90 flights, are randomly generated. Each experiment is repeated 20 times in order to restrict the influence of random effects. The results of the implemented performance metrics are presented in Tables 4, 5 and 6.

Table 4. Mean and standard deviation of the Hypervolume metrics for the sample problems

#Flights	CellDE	PAES
30	0.805±0.011	0.617±0.031
60	0.794±0.006	0.661±0.016
90	0.722±0.004	0.526±0.012

Table 5. Mean and standard deviation of the Spread metrics for the sample problems

#Flights	CellDE	PAES
30	0.576±0.074	0.651±0.038
60	0.679±0.091	0.724±0.090
90	0.698±0.086	0.634±0.017

Table 6. Mean of the Coverage metric for the sample problems

#Flights	$C(x', x'')$	CellDE	PAES
30	CellDE	-	%31
	PAES	%11	-
60	CellDE	-	%28
	PAES	%8	-
90	CellDE	-	%30
	PAES	%8	-

Calculated values for all the metrics statistically prove our claim about superiority of the Pareto front achieved by the proposed algorithm. Regarding Table 4 about %77 of the space on average is dominated by CellDE, while this value is about %60 for PAES. According to Table 5 solutions achieved by CellDE are spread broadly and more uniformly through the Pareto front. In addition on average, %29.6 of solutions achieved by PAES is dominated by at least one solution obtained by CellDE, while the opposite is %9, according to Coverage metric presented in Table 6.

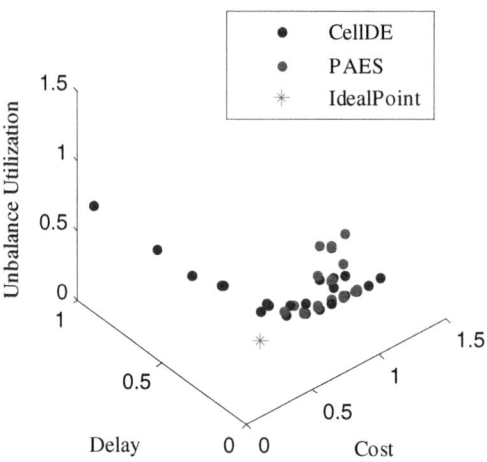

Fig. 5. Pareto fronts for the sample containing 30 flights

6 Conclusion

In this paper, a hybrid multi-objective cellular genetic algorithm, called CellDE, was implemented to solve the crew scheduling problem. A set of problems of different sizes was generated and solved using the proposed algorithm and another meta-heuristic called PAES. The Pareto solution set which is achieved by minimizing cost, delays and unbalanced utilization, gives the decision maker the opportunity to choose the best solution according to his/her preferences. Implementing three different metrics, the performance of the proposed algorithm was evaluated and the results showed acceptable convergence and diversity of the obtained Pareto front. Then a comparison was made between the obtained Pareto set and the one achieved using the PAES. The metrics showed a comparative superiority of CellDE over the existing PAES.

References

1. Ozdemir, H.T., Mohan, C.K.: Flight Graph Based Genetic Algorithm for Crew Scheduling in Airlines. Information Sciences 133, 165–173 (2001)
2. Schaefer, A.J., Johnson, E.L., Kleywegt, A.J., Nemhauser, G.L.: Airline Crew Scheduling Under Uncertainty. Technical Report TLI/LEC-01-01, Georgia Institute of Technology (2001)
3. Yen, J.W., Birge, J.R.: A Stochastic Programming Approach to the Airline Crew Scheduling Problem. Technical Report, Industrial Engineering and Management Sciences, Northwestern University (2003)
4. Lee, L.H., Lee, C.U., Tan, Y.P.: A Multi-objective Genetic Algorithm for Robust Flight Scheduling Using Simulation. European Journal of Operational Research 177, 1948–1968 (2006)
5. Fonseca, C.M., Fleming, P.J.: An Overview of Evolutionary Algorithms in Multi-objective Optimization. Evolutionary Computation 1, 1–16 (1995)
6. Durillo, J.J., Nebro, A.J., Luna, F., Alba, E.: Solving Three-Objective Optimization Problems Using a New Hybrid Cellular Genetic Algorithm, 661–670 (2008)
7. Nebro, A.J., Durillo, J.J., Luna, F., Dorronsoro, B., Alba, E.: Design Issues in a Multi-objective Cellular Genetic Algorithm. In: Obayashi, S., Deb, K., Poloni, C., Hiroyasu, T., Murata, T. (eds.) EMO 2007. LNCS, vol. 4403, pp. 126–140. Springer, Heidelberg (2007)
8. Storn, R., Price, K.: Differential Evolution - a Simple and Efficient Adaptive Scheme for Global Optimization over Continuous Spaces. Technical Report TR-95-012, Berkeley, CA (1995)
9. Neri, F., Tirronen, V.: On memetic differential evolution frameworks: a study of advantages and limitations in hybridization. In: Proceedings of the IEEE World Congress on Computational Intelligence, pp. 2135–2142 (2008)
10. Zielinski, K., Weitkemper, P., Laur, R., Kammeyer, K.D.: Parameter study for differential evolution using a power allocation problem including interference cancellation. In: Proceedings of the IEEE Congress on Evolutionary Computation, pp. 1857–1864 (2006)
11. Knowles, J., Corne, E.: The Pareto Archived Evolution Strategy: A New Baseline Algorithm for Multi-objective Optimization. IEEE Press on Evolutionary Computation, 9–105 (1999)
12. Zitzler, E., Thiele, L.: Multi-objective Evolutionary Algorithms: A Comparative Case Study and the Strength Pareto Approach. IEEE Transactions on Evolutionary Computation 3, 257–271 (1999)
13. Deb, K., Pratap, A., Agrawal, S., Meyarivan, T.: A Fast and Elitist Multi-objective Genetic Algorithm: NSGA II. IEEE Transactions on Evolutionary Computation 6, 182–197 (2002)

GENNET-Toolbox: An Evolving Genetic Algorithm for Neural Network Training

Vicente Gómez-Garay, Eloy Irigoyen, and Fernando Artaza

Automatic Control and System Engineering Department
University of the Basque Country, E.T.S.I., Bilbao, Spain
{vicente.gomez,eloy.irigoyen,fernando.artaza}@ehu.es

Abstract. Genetic Algorithms have been used from 1989 for both Neural Network training and design. Nevertheless, the use of a Genetic Algorithm for adjusting the Neural Network parameters can still be engaging. This work presents the study and validation of a different approach to this matter by introducing a Genetic Algorithm designed for Neural Network training. This algorithm features a mutation operator capable of working on three levels (network, neuron and layer) and with the mutation parameters encoded and evolving within each individual. We also explore the use of three types of hybridization: post-training, Lamarckian and Baldwinian. These proposes in combination with the algorithm, show for a fast and powerful tool for Neural Network training.

Keywords: Artificial Neural Networks, Genetic Algorithms, Training, Evolutionary Mutation, Hybridization.

1 Introduction

The process design of solutions based on Artificial Neural Networks (ANN's) needs a previous stage of selection: what kind of ANN has to use, which topology will be the best (neurons, functions, and interconnection), and how the ANN has to be training for tuning its parameters. This is due to the lack of a convenient methodology, with the dependency of a specific solution. When trying to select a topology, this issue falls into a multimodal, not differentiable, and infinite search space problem. Usually, the trial and error approach is selected by the users, therefore no guarantee of success.

Apart from topology selection, designers attempt to solve the problem of neural connection weights calculation. Most of the processed training algorithms are created based on descent gradient methodology, working on the goal to minimize the ANN output error. The local minima problem is one of the most typical in minimizing errors. The final solution depends heavily on the initial parameter values. In order to solve these problems Genetic Algorithms (GA's) [1], [2] appears as a high ability tool of global search that guides in searching into multidimensional spaces. Therefore, taking into account the GA's possibilities and the associated problem to the ANN's, interworking with both paradigms seems very convenient.

In this paper we present a slightly different approach, based on MATLAB GA Toolbox and a previous work [3], in order to solve the ANN training algorithm problems by

M. Graña Romay et al. (Eds.): HAIS 2010, Part I, LNAI 6076, pp. 368–375, 2010.

introducing a GA. This algorithm includes a mutation operator capable of working on three levels (network, neuron and layer) and with the mutation parameters encoded and evolving within each individual. The algorithm implemented is very robust against problems usually associated to ANN training. We will present the general structure of GENNET toolbox, in chapter 2. In chapter 3 we also explore the use of three types of hybridization [4], [5]: post-training, Lamarckian and Baldwinian, which can perform a fast and powerful tool for ANN training. Finally, in chapter 4, we test the algorithm solving several ANN training problems, and comparing the results into well-known classical methods.

2 GENNET Toolbox

GENNET toolbox can be executed in ©Matlab 2008a. GENNET includes a GUI for parameter configuration and running, in order to train an ANN based on GA methodology. Initially, this tool trains Multi-Layer Perceptron (MLP) ANN's from a target set, by MATLAB (The MathWorks, Inc.).

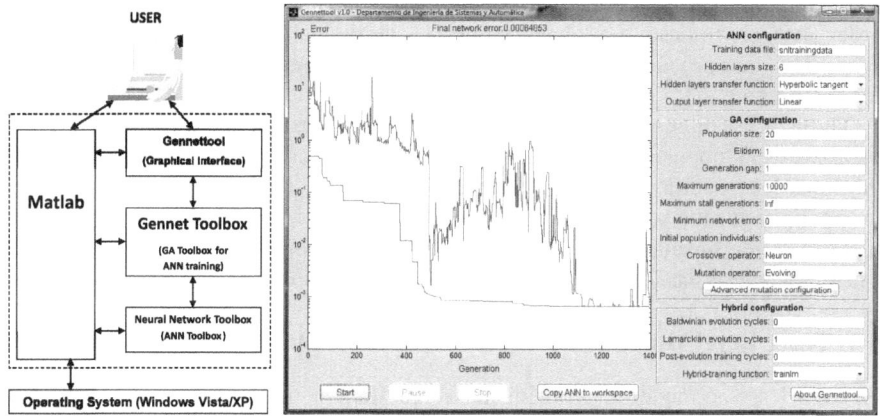

Fig. 1. GENNET toolbox – Workplace context and Graphical Interface

GENNET provides to the users a wide number of parameters for configuration: hidden layer number; size of layers (number of neurons); transfer functions in each layer (hyperbolic tangent sigmoid, logarithmic sigmoid and linear); and the possibility to adapt the input and output layer to the problem to solve.

3 Especial Features of GENNET

The implemented AG in GENNET is focused on the ANN training problem where it is not necessary to employ all functionalities of an AG traditional tool, avoiding redundant calculation, as mentioned by Michalewicz [6].

Population initialization is a very relevant data for the ANN training by GA's. For that reason, it has been necessary the implementation of a specific utility in order to avoid the saturation neurons into the ANN, giving to the algorithm a high parameters variability. The user can introduce into the tool several typical parameters as a population size, the elitism, population replacement strategies, stopping criteria, etc. The algorithm carries out the parent selection by the rank scaling and a uniform stochastic selection mechanism (such as replacing individuals in each generation). The user has different crossover operators where conventional operators are included as one point crossover, as well as a neural crossover operator. Furthermore, adaptive mutation operators have been added, including Gaussian degreasing mutation, and evolutionary mutation coded into individuals which has a high number of parameters. Finally, the GA adds hybridization options, both during algorithm execution (Lamarckian and Baldwinian) and after running.

3.1 Neuronal Crossover Operator

Generally, in the training problem of ANN's by GA's, the crossover operator is quite inefficient because of the permutation problem. In one ANN, a broad genotype level representation can be found. The ANN has the same functionality, although neural order changes. In despite of changes into GA individual codification, the ANN is the same. This fact produces an inefficient crossover operator, however is very important for GA running [7].

Three different crossover operators have been implemented into GENNET. Two of them are very popular in GA field: one point crossover and uniform crossover. The third one is a specific operator focused on the problem: neural crossover. This operator interchanges the parent chromosome information (with 50% of probability), avoiding parameter mismatch of each neuron. The three operators are used separately. Thereby, the user has to choose the specific crossover operator each time.

3.2 Three Level Mutation Operators (Network, Neuron and Parameter)

Nevertheless, permutation problem makes inefficient the crossover operator. Thus, the proper functioning of the GA leans on the mutation operator. GA uses real codification. So, the most appropriated mutation is based on the addition of white-Gaussian noise to the individual chromosome. Moreover, apart from GA classical developing where mutation and crossover operator are independents, in GENNET the mutation operator works over all individuals generated by crossover strategy. This is because of the mutation parameter are integrated into the chromosome. The mutation with Gaussian noise added develops in three levels: network, neuron and parameter. In network level, the Gaussian noise is added to the parameters of the whole ANN. In neuron level, the mutation interacts with weights and bias of the neuron. Finally in parameter level, the noise is introduced into each parameter. The possibility of mutation evolution through the evolutionary process is also an interesting choice [8]. In the beginning of the process, the introduction of high mutation rates seems convenient, because these will allow exploring globally. In contrast, in the final stages lower mutation rates are required in order to improve the local search [6]. Allowing variation both in mutation rates and magnitude through new generations is a very interesting option into the ANN training problem. So, during the ANN training, weights tuning variations will be decreased in order to improve the results. Based on these approaches, two different mutation operator have been implemented which performs in all mutation levels. The user may choose separately one of both operators. The first one named Gaussian Decreasing Mutation (GDM) includes by a fixed scheme in each of the three mutation level, a Gaussian zero-mean noise and typical decreasing deviation into new generations.

Nevertheless, in the running process, the GA needs to toggle between high mutation rates which perform a global search in particular moments, and low rates which increase the local search. On this basis, a second Evolutionary Mutation (EM) operator has been created. Operator parameters are coded into the chromosome, being variables on time, and leaving to the GA to choose which are the most appropriated in each time. Figure 2 shows the used code where p is the mutation probability, m is the mutation magnitude, and r, n and p subscript letters are respectively the network level, neuron number and parameter.

3.3 Hybridization

The GA can train by itself any ANN, but is slow in comparing with the classical method of Descent Gradient. In specially, the algorithm is very slow when parameter tuning has to be accurate and the GA is performing a local search. Thus, the hybridization with classical training is very interesting, embracing both features, GA for global search, and local search with classical ones. Based on these points of views, three hybridization interesting techniques have been incorporated to the GENNET tool: Post-evolutionary, Lamarckian and Baldwinian [4], [5].

The post-evolutionary hybridization consists in completing the training performed by GA with a classical training in a specific number of epochs, using over the best individual solution. This method is very useful for refining neural network training, because of classical methods are more efficient in developing local search. The Lamarckian hybridization modifies the evaluation function in order to develop fixed epoch training with a classical algorithm, after evaluation of the individual [4]. In selecting the Baldwinian hybridization, the individual genotype is not modified as previous one, but the individual is involved in a learning process by training with descent gradient techniques.

4   Test Results

In this work, a set of tests have been carried out to compare GENNET toolbox performance with cross-referenced classical method training. The evaluation function used is the mean square error (MSE) of ANN outputs in respect to the desired outputs.

Three representative problems have been selected to test GENNET tool. The first one is breast cancer diagnosis where the application tries to detect benign or malignant tumors from a datasheet of the Dpt. of General Surgery of the University of Wisconsin [9].

The second problem is a functional approximation very used in researching too [10]. This one trains an ANN in order to reproduce the behavior of the chaotic temporal series of Mackie-Glass:

$$Y_t = Y_{t-1} + 10.5 \cdot \left[\frac{0.2 \cdot Y_{t-5}}{1 + (Y_{t-5})^{10}} - 0.1 \cdot Y_{t-1} \right] \qquad (1)$$

Finally, the third one is related with Control Theory. Specifically, this one is a non-linear control problem where two ANN are implemented as a neural controller and a neural identifier [11]. The neural identifier tries to reproduce the behavior of a non-linear system, as shown in (2), taking into account some unstable work-points.

$$y_{k+1} = K_1 \cdot u_k^{\,3} + \frac{K_2 \cdot y_k - K_3 \cdot y_{k-1}}{1 + K_4 \cdot y_k^{\,2}}, \qquad K_1 = 0.3; K_2 = 2.4; K_3 = 1.1; K_4 = 0.8 \qquad (2)$$

All these problems are compared with training of 7 different tests, in similar computational cost. Each test is running in 20 experiments in order to validate statistically the obtained results. The different configurations used in each experiment are compared in Table 1 and defined by:

C_1.- Classical algorithm: 1000 epochs with the Levenberg-Marquardt algorithm.

C_2.- GA pure: 2000 generations.

C_3.- GA hybrid post-evolutionary: 1800 generations + classical NN training algorithm during 100 epochs.

C_4.- GA Lamarckian: Lamarckian hybridization during 2 epochs and 400 generations.

C_5.- GA Lamarckian with post-evolutionary hybridization: Lamarckian hybridization during 2 epochs and 360 generations + classical NN training algorithm during 100 epochs.

C_6.- GA Baldwinian: Baldwinian hybridization during 2 epochs and 400 generations.

C_7.- GA Baldwinian with post-evolutionary hybridization: Baldwinian hybridization during 2 epochs and 360 generations + classical NN training algorithm during 100 epochs.

Table 1. Computational comparison for different configurations

Computational comparison					
Configurations		Indiv. Eval.	Individual training iterations	Post-evoluti. training iterations	Global Training iterations
C_1	Classic Algorithm: 1000 epochs / LM	1	1000	0	1000
C_2	GA – 2000 generations	2020	0	0	0
C_3	Hybrid GA – Post-evol.: 1800 g. + 100 e.	1820	0	100	100
C_4	GA Lam. – H. Lam.: 2 it. + 400 g.	402	2	0	804
C_5	GA Lam. – H. P-e.: 2 it. + 360 g. + 100 e.	362	2	100	824
C_6	GA Bald. – H. Bald.: 2 it. + 400 g.	420	2	0	840
C_7	GA Bald. – H. P-e.: 2 it. + 360 g. + 100 e.	380	2	100	860

Table 2. First problem: breast cancer diagnosis. Training and Validation values.

Conf.	Training results				Validation results			
	Best	Worst	η	σ	Best	Worst	η	σ
C_1	3,22E-13	0,154970	0,007894	0,034624	0,028303	0,180616	0,051577	0,030986
C_2	0,015769	0,060014	0,032403	0,011199	0,027942	0,090451	0,053064	0,016481
C_3	2,73E-13	0,020467	0,001315	0,004596	0,027776	0,063209	0,044163	0,00970
C_4	3,09E-11	0,011596	0,001452	0,003352	0,017266	0,056591	0,039754	0,009665
C_5	2,55E-12	0,008771	0,001169	0,002204	0,026038	0,07050	0,040807	0,008934
C_6	0,009715	0,025655	0,018356	0,004921	0,018252	0,054231	0,035087	0,007712
C_7	3,02E-13	0,005847	0,00043	0,001430	0,018635	0,056753	0,038487	0,01007

In respect to the first problem, obtained results show important differences between training and validation error (table 2). This probably means ANN has been overtraining. The worst results have been reached with the Levenberg-Marquardt algorithm, and with the GA pure. The results with GA are understandable because of 2000 generations are insufficient to obtain good results, but not in the case of the classical algorithm. The fact of obtaining the worst results with the classical one both in training and in typical deviation shows as a severe problem the local minimum situation. Best results are obtained with Lamarckian and Baldwinian hybridization, both in mean and in the best individual. The results with Baldwinian are slightly better than Lamarckian ones. This shows the robustness of the hybridization strategy, at least in the matching problem. Evaluating the results of the temporal series problem (table 3) shows a better performance of the classical algorithm in respect with the GA evolutionary. This was relatively expected for solving a functional approximation problem. In this problem, the possibility of appearing local minimum is highly reduced. Consequently, evolutionary GAs does not show advantage, being obtained best results with Descent Gradient techniques. When working with GA's, the post- evolutionary hybridization alternatives obtain better results than other ones without hybridization.

Table 3. Second problem: chaotic temporal series of Mackie-Glass. Training and Validation.

Conf.	Training results				Validation results			
	Best	Worst	η	σ	Best	Worst	η	σ
C_1	8,59E-06	0,016444	0,004006	0,006286	4,19E-05	0,043466	0,009871	0,014766
C_2	0,127702	0,213834	0,16220	0,02250	0,144790	0,254668	0,188347	0,028568
C_3	0,000209	0,053994	0,011800	0,011846	0,00038	0,104987	0,023135	0,023750
C_4	0,000323	0,106257	0,018166	0,026101	0,000619	0,178600	0,027546	0,041748
C_5	5,34E-05	0,023079	0,007885	0,008886	1,71E-04	0,132440	0,01976	0,030431
C_6	0,064247	0,118518	0,090686	0,015533	0,072453	0,152860	0,109300	0,021833
C_7	0,00014	0,018652	0,009747	0,00794	0,000289	0,041877	0,020927	0,017320

Table 4. Third problem: non-linear control problem. Training and Validation values.

Conf.	Training results				Validation results			
	Best	Worst	η	σ	Best	Worst	η	σ
C_1	0,000555	0,131543	0,022941	0,037819	0,001731	28,00865	1,832883	6,258940
C_2	0,33939	0,650634	0,485201	0,091436	0,482956	1,045188	0,716132	0,17110
C_3	0,000245	0,070381	0,009421	0,016263	0,001625	0,850996	0,070516	0,188787
C_4	0,000403	0,159182	0,021962	0,037472	0,001312	1,340799	0,144020	0,319937
C_5	0,000603	0,11320	0,012188	0,025619	0,001487	0,732906	0,089525	0,196451
C_6	0,155258	0,328142	0,233706	0,040322	0,336507	0,997356	0,582253	0,173005
C_7	0,000314	0,040234	0,009663	0,01167	0,001462	0,156441	0,043948	0,048899

The third problem shows that the classical algorithms have notable gaps in order to solve it (table 4). As this problem has bigger complexity than Mackie-Glass series, many local minimum appear. Then, a Multimodal Function has to be solved. In fact, some of the obtained results with the classical algorithm are highly poor.

In contrast, the GA Baldwinian with post-evolutionary hybridization shows the best results, beyond the GA with post-evolutionary hybridization. This shows a high robustness in both methods, especially in Baldwinian with post-evolutionary hybridization, solving in an appropriate way the local minimum problem. Moreover, satisfied results can be obtained combining GA evolution with a classical training.

5 Discussion

It has been possible to test and validate the GENNET toolbox potential in order to train Artificial Neural Networks by Genetic Algorithms. In worse situations, the results show that GENNET applies in a competitive way, opposite to classical methods. Furthermore, in some cases GENNET is more effective than classical ones. The third analyzed problem has clearly shown the advantage of this tool in order to solve complicated problems. This validation work has demonstrated to reach better solutions in complex problems when the time-saving is not so critical. The hybridization process has performed in a longer time consuming than the classical algorithms. In other hand, the overtraining appeared in the first problem shows the weakest point of this tool that actually does not exist any mechanism to detect it. This will be the issue of future research lines for achieving GENNET robustness.

Acknowledgments. Authors would like to thank to INGETEAM for providing the opportunity of paper publication, being into CENIT research project "Buque Autónomo Inteligente para la Pesca 2020", granted by CDTI of the Government of Spain, and to the Government of the Basque Country for funding this research by the grant SAIOTEK'08 "Aplicación de Técnicas Inteligentes en Controles Tecnológicos Avanzados".

References

1. Goldberg, D.E.: Genetic Algorithms in Search, Optimization and Machine Learning. Addison-Wesley Publishing Company, Reading (1989)
2. Holland, J.H.: Adaptation in Natural and Artificial Systems. MIT Press, Cambridge (1992)
3. Irigoyen, E., Gómez, V., Artaza, F., Osorio, X.: An Evolving Genetic Algorithm for Neural Network Training. In: Proc. International Conference on Engineering and Mathematics (2009)
4. Davis, L.: Handbook of Genetic Algorithms. Van Nostrand Reinhold (1991)
5. Hinton, G.E., Nolan, S.J.: How Learning Can Guide Evolution. Complex Systems I (1987)
6. Michalewicz, Z.: Genetic Algorithms + Data Structures = Evolution Programs. Springer, Heidelberg (1996)
7. Fogel, D.E.: Phenotypes, Genotypes, and Operators in Evolutionary Computation. In: Proc. IEEE Int. Conf. Evolutionary Computation (ICEC 1995), pp. 193–198 (1995)
8. Eiben, A.E., Smith, J.E.: Introduction to Evolutionary Computing. Springer, Heidelberg (2007)
9. Wolberg, W.H.: University of Wisconsin Hospitals, USA (1992)
10. Sexton, R.S., Dorsey, R.S., Johnson, J.D.: Toward, Global Optimization of Neural Networks: A Comparison of the Genetic Algorithm and Backpropagation. Decision Support Syst. 22(2), 171–185 (1998)
11. Irigoyen, E., Galván, J.B., Pérez-Ilzarbe, M.J.: A Neural Controller for Constrained Optimal Control of Nonlinear Systems. In: IASTED International Conference Artificial Intelligence and Applications, Spain (2003)
12. Graña, M., Torrealdea, F.J.: Hierarchically structured systems. European Journal of Operational Research 25, 20–26 (1986)

An Evolutionary Feature-Based Visual Attention Model Applied to Face Recognition

Roberto A. Vázquez[1], Humberto Sossa[2], and Beatriz A. Garro[2]

[1] Escuela de Ingeniería – Universidad La Salle
Benjamín Franklin 47 Col. Condesa CP 06140 México, D.F.
[2] Centro de Investigación en Computación – IPN
Av. Juan de Dios Batiz, esquina con Miguel de Othon de Mendizábal
Ciudad de México, 07738, México
ravem@ipn.mx, hsossa@cic.ipn.mx, bgarro1@ipn.mx

Abstract. Visual attention is a powerful mechanism that enables perception to focus on a small subset of the information picked up by our eyes. It is directly related to the accuracy of an object categorization task. In this paper we adopt those biological hypotheses and propose an evolutionary visual attention model applied to the face recognition problem. The model is composed by three levels: the attentive level that determines where to look by means of a retinal ganglion network simulated using a network of bi-stable neurons and controlled by an evolutionary process; the preprocessing level that analyses and process the information from the retinal ganglion network; and the associative level that uses a neural network to associate the visual stimuli with the face of a particular person. To test the accuracy of the model a benchmark of faces is used.

1 Introduction

Visual object recognition, particularly face recognition, is an extremely difficult computational problem. The main problem is that each face appears as an infinite number of different 2-D images onto the retina because the face could vary relative to the viewer in position, pose, lighting, gesture, aging and background. Progress in understanding the brain's solution to object recognition requires the construction of artificial recognition systems that ultimately aim to emulate our own visual abilities, often with biological inspiration [1].

Attention allows us to dynamically select and enhance the processing of stimuli and events that are most relevant at each moment [2]. Visual attention is a powerful mechanism that enables perception to focus on a small subset of the information picked up by our eyes [3]. Visual attention has become an important feature in image analysis processing. It aims at reducing the quantity of data and considering only relevant information [4]. The main idea to incorporate visual attention into a face recognition task is that not all parts of an image give us information and analyzing only the relevant part of the image in detail is sufficient for recognition and classification [5].

Several visual attention models have been proposed in the last years. For example in [6], the authors describe the essential features of computational model of selective attention. Chauvin et al. [7] proposed a model inspired by the retina and the primary

M. Graña Romay et al. (Eds.): HAIS 2010, Part I, LNAI 6076, pp. 378–386, 2010.
© Springer-Verlag Berlin Heidelberg 2010

visual cortex cell functionalities. In [8], the authors proposed an attention model based on visual static features but also on face and text detection.

Many psychophysical studies have demonstrated that feature-based attention improves detection or otherwise enhances behavioral performance across the visual field [9-10]. Recent evidence supports color feature, in particular, showing an advantage in recognition of objects, faces and natural scenes [11].

In this paper we adopt those biological hypotheses and propose an evolutionary color-feature-based visual attention model applied to the face recognition problem. The model is composed by three levels: attentive level, preprocessing level and associative level. The attentive level determines where to look by means of a retinal ganglion network simulated using a network of bi-stable neurons and controlled by an evolutionary process; instead of using a salient map, bottom-up or top-down approach, we propose to use an evolutionary technique based in a differential evolution algorithm. The preprocessing level analyses and processes the information from the retinal ganglion network. Finally, the associative level uses a neural network to associate the visual stimuli from the preprocessing level with the face of a particular person. In order to test the accuracy of the model a benchmark of faces was used.

2 Evolutionary Strategy: Differential Evolution

Evolutionary algorithms not only have been used to design artificial neural networks [12-13], but also to evolve structure-function mapping in cognitive neuroscience [14] and compartmental neuron models [15].

Differential evolution (DE) is a powerful and efficient technique for optimizing nonlinear and non-differentiable continuous space functions [16]. Differential Evolution (DE) is regarded as a perfected version of genetic algorithms for rapid numerical optimization. DE has a lower tendency to converge to local maxima with respect to the conventional GA model, because it simulates a simultaneous search in different areas of solution space. Moreover, it evolves populations with smaller number of individuals, and have a lower computation cost.

DE begins by generating a random population of candidate solutions in the form of numerical vectors. The first of these vectors is selected as the target vector. Next, DE builds a trial vector by executing the following sequence of steps:

```
1.  Randomly select two vectors from the current generation.
2.  Use these two vectors to compute a difference vector.
3.  Multiply the difference vector by weighting factor F.
4.  Form the new trial vector by adding the weighted difference vec-
    tor to a third vector randomly selected from the current popula-
    tion.
```

The trial vector replaces the target vector in the next generation if and only if the trial vector represents a better solution, as indicated by its measured cost value. DE repeats this process for each of the remaining vectors in the current generation. DE then replaces the current generation with the next generation, and continues the evolutionary process over many generations.

3 Description of the Proposed Visual Attention Model

The evolutionary feature-based visual attention model (EFVAM) proposed in this paper is composed of three levels: attentive level, preprocessing level and associative level. The attentive level determines where to look by means of a retinal ganglion network simulated using a network of bi-stable neurons and controlled by an evolutionary process. The preprocessing level analyses and processes the information from the retinal ganglion network. Finally, the associative level uses a neural network to associate the visual stimuli from the preprocessing level with the face of a particular person. A feedback between attentive level and associative level is linked by means of a differential evolution algorithm that controls the attentive level. Figure 1 shows a schematic representation of the proposed model.

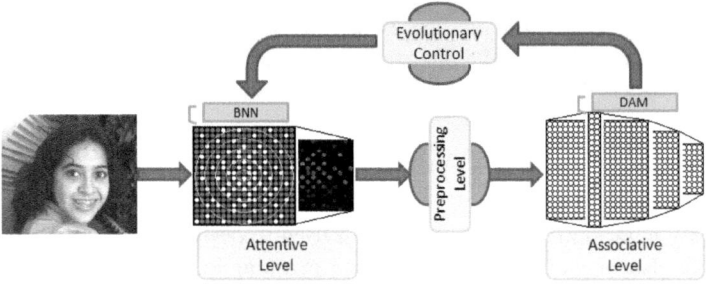

Fig. 1. Scheme of the proposed evolutionary feature-based visual attention model

It is important to point out that the evolutionary control will activate the bi-stable neurons which maximize the accuracy of the neural network used in the associative level during the process of recognition. Therefore, we can see the face recognition problem as a maximization problem where by means of a differential evolution algorithm it is determined where and what to see in order to maximize the accuracy of a neural network during a face recognition task.

3.1 Attentive Level

Visual attention is a mechanism that biolgical systems have to develop in order to reduce the large amount of visual information from a visual stimulus in order to efficiently perform a learning or recognition task.

A visual stimulus can be represented as a 2D image $f(i, j)$ composed by $m \times n$ pixels. This visual stimulus enters through the eyes and converges on the retinal ganglion cells which send the information to the visual cortex.

In order to simulate this retinal ganglion cells we used a 2 layer network, each layer composed by $m \times n$ bi-stable neurons (BNN). A neuron from the second layer receives the information from a neighborhood of neurons W, composed by $a \times b$ neurons, see Fig. 2.

Each neuron has two states: active and inactive. When the neuron receives an excitatory signal from the evolutionary control, the neuron is active and the information from the visual stimulus that converges on that neuron passes to the next level. On the contrary, the neuron is inactive if it receives an inhibitory signal. This mechanism selects the information that will be taken into account in the next levels; i.e., it determines where to look inside of the visual stimulus. The visual attention model will focused only in those pixels connected with the active neurons from first layer.

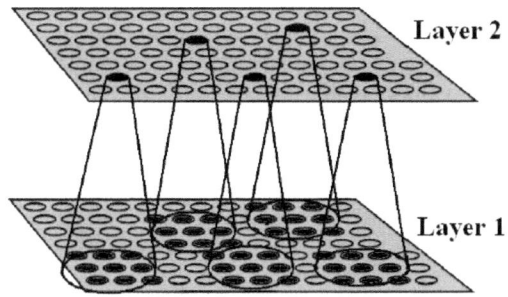

Fig. 2. Virtual retina composed by 2 layers. Each pixel from the visual stimulus directly converges on each neuron of the first layer. Note how second layer receives information from a neighborhood of neurons from the first layer.

Let $f(i, j)$ a visual stimulus and $y^l(i, j)$ the output of neuron (i, j) which belongs to l-th layer. The output of neurons which belongs to the second layer is given by:

$$y^2(i, j) = s(i, j) \cdot \left[\frac{1}{a \times b} \sum_{(i,j) \in W} y^1(i, j) \right] \qquad (1.1)$$

where $y^1(i, j) = f(i, j)$, a and b is the number of neurons that belongs to the neighborhood W of dimension $a \times b$ and $s(i, j)$ is the inhibitory/excitatory signal sent by the evolutionary control.

This level combined with the evolutionary control allows to determining which information from the visual stimulus will be used to learn and recognize a face. In other words, determine what to see from a face in order to be recognized.

3.2 Preprocessing Level

This level allows us to preprocess the information passed from the attentive level that will be used in the associative level. Although this level could be seen as a part of the attentive level due to determine what to see from the visual stimulus, we decided to present it separated of the attentive level.

This preprocessing level can also modify the behavior of the bi-stable neurons, in the sense of the neurons only allows to pass the low frequencies of the visual stimulus or the high frequencies, or to apply a Gabor filter to the information, etc. However, in this paper our efforts are centered only on the attentive and associative level.

3.3 Associative Level

At this level we associated the visual stimulus information with the desired information. In the context of face recognition, we can associate, for example, a face of a person with his name, then during the recognition process, when the model is stimulated using a face of a particular person, the associative model will respond with the name of the person; this is call hetero-associative model. Furthermore, we can associate the face of a person with the same face, and then during the recognition process the model will not respond with the name of the person but recalling the face of the person.

Some important to mention is that at this level we can use any neural network. However, we decided to use a dynamic associative model (DAM) [18], which changes their synapse connection strengths according to a visual stimulus, to simulate the hierarchically cortical regions consisting at least of V1, V2, V4, posterior inferior temporal cortex, inferior temporal cortex, and anterior temporal cortical areas [19] during the process of learning and recognition of faces.

3.4 Evolutionary Control

As we already said, the evolutionary control combined with the attentive level allows us determine which information from the visual stimulus will be used to learn and recognize a face. Based on the algorithm described in section 2, a set of active neurons is determined. For that reason, each individual from the population will codify the set of active neurons from the network of bi-stable neurons in terms of its position. Remember that the network of bi-stable neurons is a matrix of $m \times n$ neurons directly connected to each pixel from the visual stimulus. In other words, an individual is composed by the coordinate position (i, j) of each active neuron.

The evaluation function or fitness function is computed in terms of the DAM and the selected active neurons. First of all, the DAM is trained using a set of training faces and the information provided by the selected active neurons; after that, the accuracy of the DAM is evaluated using a set of validating faces.

Through each generation we expect to maximize the accuracy of the associative model in terms of the selected active neurons. At the end of this evolutionary learning process, we expect to obtain the set positions (i, j) of active neurons which maximize the accuracy of the DAM.

4 Experimental Results

To test the efficiency of the proposed method we have used the benchmark of faces given in [20]. This database contains twenty photos of fifteen different people. Each photo is in colour and size of 180×200 pixels, some examples of this set of images are shown in Fig. 3. Furthermore, people in images appear with different facial expressions that nowadays is still a challenging problem, in face recognition. Due to the level of complexity of this benchmark, we decided to use it to test the accuracy of the proposed method.

Fig. 3. Some of the image used to train and test the proposed model

The database was divided into three sets of images. First photo of each person (15 in total) was used to train the DAMs. The remaining 285 photos (19 for each person) were divided in two sets: validation test and testing set. While the training and validation sets were used to find the set of active neurons, the testing set was used to test the efficiency of the proposed method.

In the preprocessing, each RGB pixel (hexadecimal value) obtained from the active neurons was transformed into a decimal value. This information was used to train the DAM. The DAM was trained using the auto-associative version; this means that the model will recall the face of a person given a visual stimulus.

We performed eight experiments. In each experiment the number of desired active neurons was varied from 5 to 40 in steps of 5. The parameters for the DE algorithm were set to $NP = 10$, $MAXGEN = 100$, $CR = 0.5$ and $F = rand(0.3, 0.9)$.

Through the experiments, the evolutionary control was searching where to look (the most representative pixels) by means of activating or inactivating the neurons of the BNN. At the end of certain number of generations the evolutionary control found the set of active neurons which allows recognizing the faces belonging to the testing set.

Figure 4 shows how the accuracy of the model was increased through the time during the learning process. It is important to point out that from the 36000 neurons composing the BNN, at the end we used less than the 1% of all the neurons to perform a face recognition task.

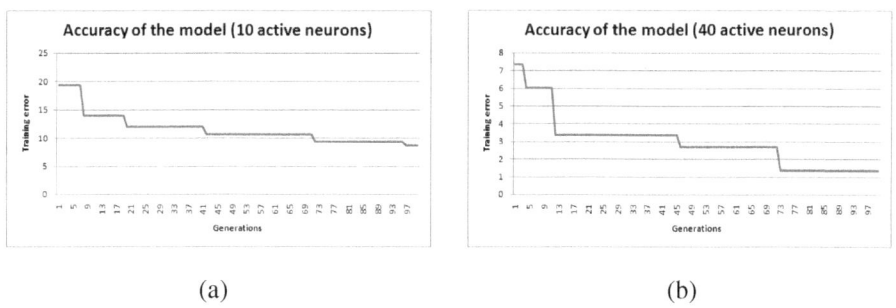

(a)   (b)

Fig. 4. Accuracy of the evolutionary feature-based visual attention model

These results were compared against the results provided by the infant vision model (RIVSM) described in [17] and [21-23]. As you can appreciate from Table 1, the results provided by the proposed method are better to those provided by the RIVSM. It is important to point out that only five active neurons were required to reach an error of 20% during the recognition process. This means that the model was able to find the most five representative pixel from the visual stimulus and this information passed through the five active neurons. It is important also to notice that by using only 40 active neurons the model was capable to correctly recognizing almost the 98% of the testing set faces. Notice also that although this model is perhaps not biologically plausible, it is capable to recognize faces even if they appear with different facial expressions.

Table 1. Comparison of the evolutionary feature-based visual attention model (EFVAM) against the infant vision system model (RIVSM)

	RIVSM		EFVAM		
Active Neurons from BNN	%Tr. Er.	%Te. Er.	%Tr. Er.	%Te. Er.	Gen.
5	0	47.4	11.3	20	100
10	0	32.2	8.6	16.6	100
15	0	22.3	5.3	12	100
20	0	17	3.3	11.3	100
25	0	17.3	2.6	10	100
30	0	14.2	3.3	10	100
35	0	12.6	1.3	6	100
40	0	12.1	1.3	2.6	100

Tr. Er = Training Error, Te. Er. = Testing Error.

5 Conclusions

In this paper we have proposed a new evolutionary feature-based visual attention model. This model is composed by three levels: attentive level, preprocessing level and associative level. The attentive level determines on where to look by means of a retinal ganglion network simulated using a network of bi-stable neurons and controlled by an evolutionary process. The preprocessing level analyses and processes the information from the retinal ganglion network. Finally, the associative level uses a neural network to associate the visual stimuli from the preprocessing level with the face of a particular person.

A feedback between attentive level and associative level is linked by means of a differential evolution algorithm that controls the attentive level. The evolutionary control determined the set of bi-stable neurons which maximize the accuracy of the neural network used in the associative level during the process of recognition.

Through several experiments, we have shown how the accuracy of the proposed method is increased through the evolutionary learning process using only less that the 1% of the information provided by the visual stimulus.

Acknowledgments. The authors thank the SIP-IPN under grant 20091421. H. Sossa thanks CINVESTAV-GDL for the support to do a sabbatical stay from December 1, 2009 to May 31, 2010. Authors also thank the European Union, the European Commission and CONACYT for the economical support. This paper has been prepared by economical support of the European Commission under grant FONCICYT 93829. The content of this paper is an exclusive responsibility of the CIC-IPN and it cannot be considered that it reflects the position of the European Union.

References

[1] Pinto, N., Cox, D.D., DiCarlo, J.J.: Why is real-world visual object recognition hard? PLos Comput. Biol. 4(1), e27, 151–156 (2008)

[2] Busse, L., et al.: The spread of attention across modalities and space in a multisensory object. PNAS 102(51), 18751–18756 (2005)

[3] Maunsell, J.H.R., Treue, S.: Feature-based attention in visual cortex. Trends in Neurosciences 29(6), 317–322 (2006)

[4] Guironnet, M., et al.: Static and dynamic feature-based visual attention model: comparison to human judgment. In: Proc. of EUSIPCO (2005)

[5] Salah, A.A., Alpaydin, E., Akarun, L.: A selective attention-based method for visual pattern recognition with application to handwritten digit recognition and face recognition. IEEE Trans. Pattern Anal. Mach. Intell. 24(3), 420–425 (2002)

[6] Itti, L., Koch, C.: Computational modeling of visual attention. Nature Reviews Neuroscience 2(3), 194–203 (2001)

[7] Chauvin, A., et al.: Natural scene perception: visual attractors and image processing. In: Connectionist Models of Cognition and Perception, 7th Neural Computation and Psychology Workshop, pp. 236–245. World Scientific Press, Singapore (2002)

[8] Chen, L.Q., et al.: Image adaptation based on attention model for small form factor devices. In: The 9th Inter. Conf. on Multimedia Modeling, pp. 483–490 (2003)

[9] Rossi, A.F., Paradiso, M.A.: Feature-specific effects of selective visual attention. Vision Res. 35, 621–634 (1995)

[10] Saenz, M., et al.: Global feature-based attention for motion and color. Vision Res. 43, 629–637 (2003)

[11] Martinovic, J., Gruber, T., Muller, M.: Coding of visual object features and feature conjunctions in the human brain. PLoS ONE 3(11), e3781, 1–10 (2008)

[12] Garro, B.A., Sossa, H., Vazquez, R.A.: Design of artificial neural networks using a modified particle swarm optimization algorithm. In: Proc. IEEE IJCNN (2009)

[13] Pavlidis, N.G., et al.: Spiking neural network training using evolutionary algorithms. In: Proc. IEEE IJCNN, pp. 2190–2194 (2005)

[14] Frias-Martinez, E., Gobet, F.: Automatic generation of cognitive theories using genetic programming. Minds and Machines 17(3), 287–309 (2007)

[15] Hendrickson, E., et al.: Converting a globus pallidus neuron model from 585 to 6 compartments using an evolutionary algorithm. J. BMC Neurosci. 8(suppl. 2), 122 (2007)

[16] Price, K., Storn, R.M., Lampinen, J.A.: Diffentential evolution: a practical approach to global optimization. Springer, Heidelberg (2005)

[17] Vazquez, R.A., Sossa, H., Garro, B.A.: The role of the infant vision system in 3D object recognition. In: Köppen, M., Kasabov, N., Coghill, G. (eds.) ICONIP 2008. LNCS, vol. 5507, pp. 800–807. Springer, Heidelberg (2009)

[18] Vazquez, R.A., Sossa, H.: A new associative model with dynamical synapses. Neural Processing Letters 28(3), 189–207 (2008)

[19] Rolls, E.T., Stringer, S.M.: Invariant visual object recognition: a model, with lighting invariance. Journal of Physiology-Paris 100, 43–62 (2007)

[20] Spacek, L.: Collection of facial images: Grimace (1996),
http://cswww.essex.ac.uk/mv/allfaces/grimace.html

[21] Vazquez, R.A., Sossa, H.: A computational approach for modeling the infant vision system in object and face recognition. J. BMC Neurosci. 8(suppl. 2), 204 (2007)

[22] Vazquez, R.A., Sossa, H., Garro, B.A.: Low frequency responses and random feature selection applied to face recognition. In: Kamel, M.S., Campilho, A. (eds.) ICIAR 2007. LNCS, vol. 4633, pp. 818–830. Springer, Heidelberg (2007)

[23] Vazquez, R.A., Sossa, H., Garro, B.A.: 3D Object recognition based on low frequency responses and random feature selection. In: Gelbukh, A., Kuri Morales, Á.F. (eds.) MICAI 2007. LNCS (LNAI), vol. 4827, pp. 694–704. Springer, Heidelberg (2007)

Efficient Plant Supervision Strategy Using NN Based Techniques

Ramon Ferreiro Garcia[1], Jose Luis Calvo Rolle[2], and Francisco Javier Perez Castelo[2]

[1] ETSNM, Dept. Industrial Eng. University of La Coruna
ferreiro@udc.es
[2] EUP, Dept. Industrial Eng. University of La Coruna
{jlcalvo,javierpc}@udc.es

Abstract. Most of non-linear type one and type two control systems suffers from lack of detectability when model based techniques are applied on FDI (fault detection and isolation) tasks. In general, all types of processes suffer from lack of detectability also due to the ambiguity to discriminate the process, sensors and actuators in order to isolate any given fault. This work deals with a strategy to detect and isolate faults which include massive neural networks based functional approximation procedures associated to recursive rule based techniques applied to a parity space approach.

Keywords: Backpropagation, Conjugate Gradient, Fault Detection, Fault Isolation, Neural Networks, Parity Space, Residual Generation.

1 Introduction

Safety in the process industry can be strongly related to the detection and isolation of the features indicative of changes in the sensors actuators or process performance. In using model-based approaches, when the models describing the process are accurate, the problem of fault detection may be solved by observer-type filters. These filters generate the so-called residuals computed from the inputs and outputs of the process. The generation of these residual signals is the first stage in the problem of FDI. To be useful in the FDI task, the residuals must be insensitive to modeling errors and highly sensitive to the faults under consideration. That way, the residuals are designed so that the effects of possible faults are enhanced, which in turn increases their detectability. The residuals must also respond quickly. The residuals are tested in order to detect the presence of faults. Various FDI methods have been previously reported, such as the papers of [1], [2], [3], [4], [5]. Among the classic books on the subject are those of [6], [7], [8].

1.1 Model Based Fault Detection Methods

Fault detection methods based on process and signal models include actuators, processes and sensors for which inputs and output variables must be precisely measured. Such methods deal mainly with parameter estimation, state observers and parity equation

M. Graña Romay et al. (Eds.): HAIS 2010, Part I, LNAI 6076, pp. 385–394, 2010.

methods. If measuring system fails, fault detection methods based on the use of input/output measurements yields ambiguous and/or erroneous results.

An intensive research on model based fault detection methods has been carried out during the last three decades. In this section a brief list on process model based fault detection methods is given:

1.- Fault detection with parameter estimation [4]

   -Equation error methods
   -Output error methods

2.- Fault detection with state-estimation.

   (a) Dedicated observers for multi-output processes.
   -State Observe, excited by one output [9].
   -Kalman filter, excited by all outputs [10], [1].
   -Bank of state observers, excited by all outputs [1].
   -Bank of state observers, excited by single outputs [3]
   -Bank of state observers, excited by all outputs except one [3].
   (b) Fault detection filters for multi-output processes [11].

3.- Fault detection with parity equations [2], [12], [13].

   (a) Output error methods.
   (b) Polynomial error methods.

4.- Fault detection using analytical redundancy [14].

   (a) Static analytical redundancy.
   (b) Dynamic analytical redundancy.

No general method exists for solving all FDI cases. Successful FDI applications are based on a combination of several methods. Practical FDI systems apply analytical redundancy using the so-called first-principles like action-reaction balances such as mass flow rate balance, energy flow rate balance, force/torque/power balances and commonly, the mathematical balance of any cause-effect equilibrium condition.

As stated before, diagnosing techniques previously mentioned, when applied to non-linear type one and type two processes, suffers from lack of detectability. With regard to residuals, they are the outcomes of consistency checks between the plant observations and a mathematical model. The three main ways to generate residuals are parameter estimation, observers and parity relations. For parameter estimation, the residuals are the difference between the nominal model parameters and the estimated model parameters. Derivations in the model parameters serve as the basis for detecting and isolating faults.

In most practical cases the process parameters are partially not known or not known at all. Such parameters can be determined with parameter estimation methods by measuring input and output signals if the basic model structure is known. There are two conventional approaches commonly used which are based on the minimization of equation error and output error. The first one is linear in the parameters and allows therefore direct estimation of the parameters (least squares) in non-recursive or recursive form. The second one needs numerical optimization methods and therefore iterative procedures, but may be more precise under the influence of process disturbances. The symptoms are deviation of the process parameters. As the process parameters depend on physically defined process coefficients, determination of changes usually allows deeper insight and makes fault diagnosis easier [2]. These conventional methods of parameter estimation usually need a process input excitation and are especially suitable for the detection of multiplicative faults. Parameter estimation requires an input/output correct measuring system. Some drawbacks of such methods are:

-the possibility of faulty measuring signals,
-unknown model structure and/or unknown model changes

1.2   Goals to Be Achieved

Afore-mentioned diagnosing techniques, when applied to non-linear type one and type two processes, suffer from lack of detectability. For this reason the work has been oriented towards functional approximation techniques using well known NN based modeling [15-19]. This research work is then focused on the problem of fault detection, fault isolation, and fault estimation by applying a parity space approach where plant modules models are achieved by steady state functional approximation techniques on the basis of backpropagation neural networks, and residual generation is achieved by comparing real-time measured data with real time data achieved from nominal NN based models. The tasks to be carried out consist in achieving a set of NN based steady state models of the plant modules to be used as a bank of observers. Models output are used as residual generators. Achieved residuals are evaluated by a set of rules that responsible for detect and isolate plant faults, which include actuator faults, process faults and sensor faults.

Subsequent sections are devoted to the description of the proposed alternative technique, resulting in an interesting complement or substitute to some conventional cited techniques.

2   Causality Based Approach

The relationship between cause and effect or a cause and effect relationship is defined as the principle of causality. The causality of two events describes to what extent one event is caused by the other. When there is open loop causality there is a measure of predictability of second event caused by the first event.

When there exists closed loop causality, such as in the case of a closed loop control system shown in figure 1, there is a measure of predictability between the two events where the first causes some effects on the second, and the second causes some effect on the first, and so on if a chained interdependent phenomenon is considered.

Functional approximation is currently the appropriate technique to describe nonlinear plant modules and devices such as actuators and/or sensors. Feedforward neural networks under backpropagation training strategies are effectively applied. The causality dependence of a feedback control loop is then described by means of the following NN based modeling functions, which are graphically represented by the block diagram of figure 1. The notation applied to the block diagram shown in figure 1 stands for SP = setpoint, e = control error, CV = control variable, MV = manipulated

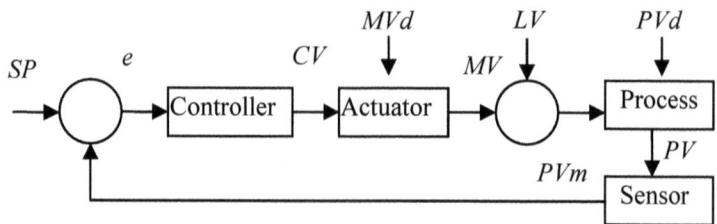

Fig. 1. Block diagram of the generic feedback control loop

variable, LV = Load variable, PV = process variable, PVm = measured process variable, MVd = disturbances to the manipulated variable and PVd = disturbances to the process variable.

The feedback control loop is modeled using the principle of causality by the proposed NN based functions described by equations (1), and (2), which are applicable to closed loop control systems under steady state conditions.

$$MV = f(CV, MVd).$$ (1)

$$PV = f(MV, PVd)$$ (2)

2.1 Relationship between Control Loop Variables under Causality Dependence

When a control loop is operating in absence of malfunctions or faults, it is assumed that under steady state conditions the control error should approach a negligible or null value. Under such situation it is considered also that certain error tolerance Te is assumed. Furthermore, the rate of change in the control error should not be greater than certain tolerance Tde. According described premises in order to schedule a recursive supervision task, a preliminary fault detection set of rules is scheduled. The proposed set of rules is described in table 1.

Table 1. The necessary set of rules to schedule a recursive supervision task

Premises	Conclusion
e <Te and de < Tde	SST
e > Te and de < Tde	ROI
e > Te and de > Tde and time duration > Time.MAX	ROI

The acronym SST in table 1 means a supervision starting task and ROI is a required operator intervention warning. Intervention request is not mandatory because the proposed supervision task is operating simultaneously in parallel with the plant SCADA.

In table 2 it is shown the sequence of rules to be processed after passing the consistence test carried out by the set of rules shown in table 1. Residuals are compared with a set of chosen tolerances, Ta, and Tp respectively for the actuator and process.

With regard to table 2, *MVm* and *PVm* are respectively actual measured manipulated variable and actual measured process variable, while *CVn* is the actual nominal control variable which coincides with the actual controller output.

Table 2. Residual based supervision task: Processed rules perform fault detection with inherent isolation and decision making tasks

Control loop device	Residual evaluation
Actuator test	IF abs(MV-MVm) < *Ta* THEN proceed, ELSE actuator fault
Process test	IF abs(PV-PVm) < *Tp* THEN proceed, ELSE fault due to process parameter changes assumed.
Sensor test	IF abs(PV-PVm) < *Ts* and process unchanged, THEN proceed, ELSE fault assumed due to sensor drift.

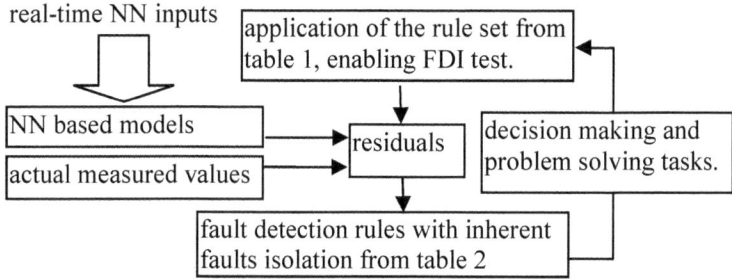

Fig. 2. A flowchart of the supervision strategy

A flowchart to schedule the supervision task is implemented as shown in figure 2. To generate residuals, the neural network based models output is compared with the real time measured variable. When the tolerances *Ta*, *Tp* or *Ts* are exceeded, then the conclusions given by the rules applied in table 2 are carried out.

2.2 Supervision Task Applied on the Level and Temperature Pilot Plant

In figure 3 it is depicted the scheme of the pilot plant where the test on the supervision task has been carried out.

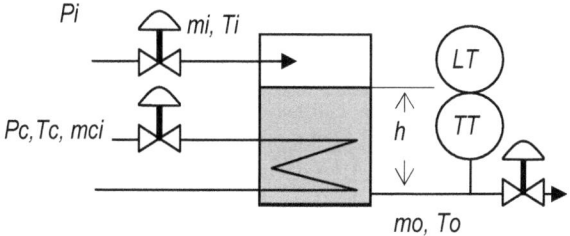

Fig. 3. Temperature and level process scheme

It consists of a heat exchanger submerged into the tank whose level and temperature is to be controlled and supervised. The layout of the pilot plant is shown in figure 4.

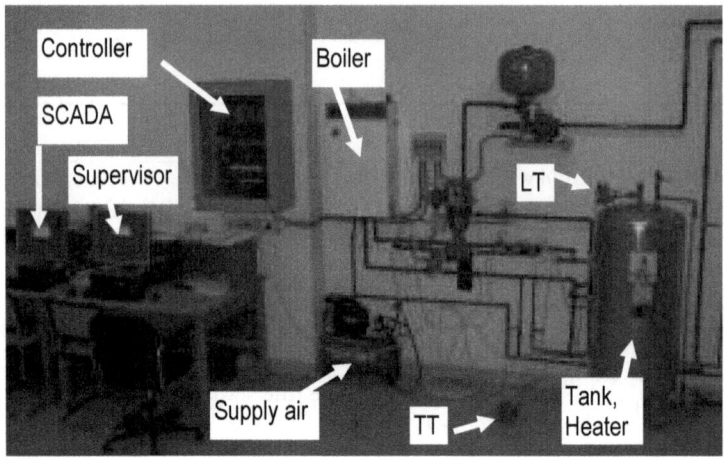

Fig. 4. Pilot plant layout

Table 3 shows the functional dependences associated with the researched pilot plant processes. It consists of level and temperature feedback control loops internally coupled.

Table 4 shows the NN based functions whose outputs are processed by the residual evaluation supervision block shown in figure 2. The residuals are evaluated according the rule base shown in table 2, previously validated by the conclusions of the rules of table 1.

Table 3. Inherent functional dependences on the pilot plant control loops

Feedback control loop variables	Tank level	Heat Exchanger
LV	f(mo)	f(Ti, mi, Tc)
MVd	f(Pi)	f(Pc)
PVd	f(h)	Heat losses

Table 4. The NN based models included in control loops supervision structure

NN based functions applied on pilot plant	Level control NN based models	Heat Exchanger control NN based models
MV = f(CV, MVd)	$mi=MV=$f(CV, Pi)	$mci=MV=$f(CV, Pc)
PV = f(MV, PVd)	$h=PV=$f(mi, mo)	$To=PV=$f(mci, mi, Ti, Tc)

2.3 Supervision Task Results

As shown in table 4, only two NN are required to detect and isolate faults per every feedback control loop. Since the *CV* is always deterministically known, the *MV* is well known if the disturbances are correctly measured. Such disturbances are not considered as faults because the controller output adjusts the *MV* to the required value also under such disturbances. Nevertheless, such supervision task is of great interest to detect just an unmeasured disturbance.

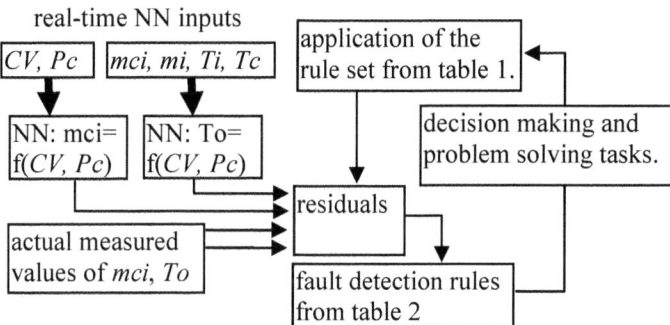

Fig. 5. The flowchart of the supervision strategy applied on the heat exchanger temperature control loop

With regard to the *MV* supervision task, a two input-one output backpropagation NN has been applied for every control loop. It consists in a feedforward Back propagation NN trained by the conjugate gradient algorithm of Fletcher and Rives. Training data is generated according to the functions described by expressions (1) and (2), into the ranges of interest of the inherent input variables. As shown in figure 5, the corresponding input/output set of variables applied in the training task for the heat exchanger system, are those shown in expressions (3) and (4) respectively.

$$mci = MV = f(CV, MVd) = f(CV, Pc) \cdot \tag{3}$$

$$To = PV = f(MV, PVd) = f(mci.mi, Ti, Tc) \tag{4}$$

With regard to the *PV or To* supervision task in the case of temperature control system, a four input-one output backpropagation NN has been applied as shown in figure 5. Training data is generated according the function $PV=To=f(mci, mi, Ti, Tc)$, into the ranges of interest of the inherent input variables under steady state conditions.

For the case of the temperature control system supervision task, the application of the described rules using the results of residuals evaluation yields the results shown in figure 6. According observed results in figure 6, a change in set point is applied at 300 sec. After 600 sec. a drift fault is observed in the *PV* sensor so that the *PVm* is deviated according to such drift value. The supervision system detects correctly such fault since the residual generator yields a clear evidence of the fault. In order to test the

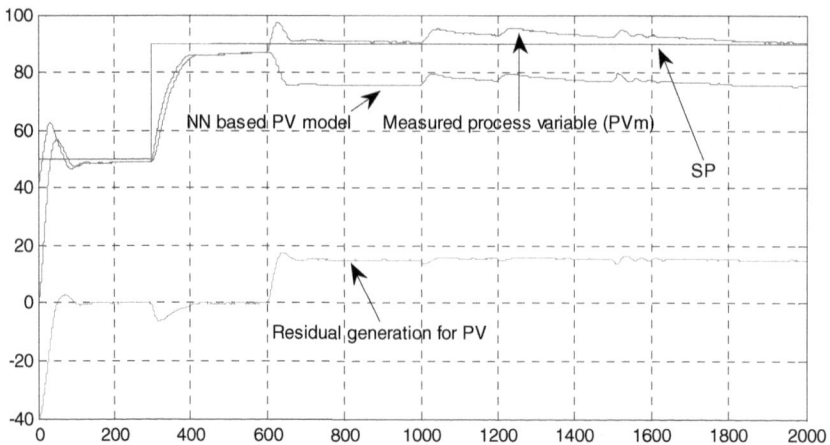

Fig. 6. Residual generation and fault isolation for temperature control system supervision task

robustness of the supervision method, heating process is disturbed. Results show that such fault detection method is not sensible to eventual process disturbances. As shown in the figure 6, at 1000, 1200, 1500 and 1800 sec., changes to the input flow rate, input flow temperature, supply pressure to the heating valve and supply temperature of the heating fluid are applied. The results show that the detection method is not sensible to such disturbances, and the sensor drift is correctly detected along the analyzed time horizon.

3   Conclusions

A supervision strategy focused on the detection and isolation of plant faults in closed loop control systems under steady state conditions, on the basis of causal NN based modeling techniques has been proposed and successfully applied.

Training data is accurately achieved since the plant model must be obtained under steady state conditions.

Results show that the detection of a drift fault associated to the process variable (temperature) measuring sensor has been successfully achieved under the condition of a correct measuring system.

The detection of a drift fault associated to the process variable (temperature) is not sensible to process disturbances. Such a characteristic is very interesting from the point of view of robustness and system reliability.

The fact of discarding the transient state as a portion of time in which a supervision task cannot be applied, allows us to ensure that such fault detection scheme is immune (not sensible) to the process disturbances.

This supervising system needs to be updated every time parameter changes are detected, by training the applied neural networks. This characteristic is a serious drawback since the plant must be forced to an off-line condition, which affects the productivity.

The most important disadvantage of the applied methodology is the impossibility to detect faults when the process is under transient state.

Acknowledgments. This work has been partially supported by the XUNTA DE GALICIA under the grant DPI 1 IN825N cod_web:772.

References

1. Willsky, A.S.: A survey of design methods for failure detection systems. Automatica 12, 601–611 (1976)
2. Isermann, R.: Process fault detection based on modeling and estimation methods - a survey. Automatica 20(4), 387–404 (1984)
3. Frank, P.M.: Fault Diagnosis in Dynamic systems via State Estimation - A Survey. In: Tzafestas, et al. (eds.) System Fault Diagnostics, Reliability and Related Knowledge-Based Approaches, vol. 1, pp. 35–98. D. Reidel Publíshing Company, Dordrecht (1987)
4. Gertler, J.J.: Survey of Model-Based Failure Detection and Isolation in Complex Plants. IEEE Control Systems Magazine 8(6), 3–11 (1988)
5. Patton, R.J., Chen, J.: A review of parity space approaches to fault diagnosis. In: IFAC Symposium SAFEPROCE5S 1991, Baden-Baden, Germany, vol. I, pp. 239–256 (1991) (preprints)
6. Himmelblau, D.M.: Fault detection and diagnosis in chemical and petrochemical processes. Elsevier, Amsterdam (1978)
7. Pau, L.F.: Failure Diagnosis and Performance Monitoring. Marcel Dekker, New York (1981)
8. Basseville, M.: Optimal Sensor Location for Detecting Changes in Dynamical Behaviour, Rapport de Recherche No. 498, INRIA (1986)
9. Clark, R.N.: A simplified instrument detection scheme. IEEE Trans. Aerospace Electron. Syst. 14, 558–563 (1978)
10. Mehra, R.K., Peschon, J.: An innovations approach to fault detection and diagnosis in dynamic systems. Automatica 7, 637–640, 316 (1971)
11. Beard, R.V.: Failure accommodation in linear systems through self-reorganization, Rept. MVT-71-1. Man Vehicle Laboratory, Cambridge, Massachusetts (1971)
12. Gertler, J.J.: Analytical Redundancy Methods in Fault Detection and Isolation - Survey and Synthesis. In: Preprints of the IFAC/IMACS-Symposium on Fault Detection, Supervision and Safety for Technical Processes, SAFEPROCESS 1991, Baden-Baden, FRG, September 10-13, vol. 1, pp. 9–21 (1991)
13. Patton, R.J., Chen, J.: A review of parity space approaches to fault diagnosis for aerospace systems. J. of Guidance Control Dynamics 17(2), 278–285 (1994)
14. Ragot, J., Maquin, D., Kratz, F.: Observability and redundancy decomposition application to diagnosis. In: Patton, R.J., Frank, P.M., Clark, R.N. (eds.) Issues of Fault Diagnosis for Dynamic Systems, ch. 3, pp. 52–85. Springer, London (2000)
15. Hong, S.J., May, G.S.: Neural Network-Based Real-Time Malfunction Diagnosis of Reactive Ion Etching Using In Situ Metrology Data. IEEE Transactions on Semiconductor Manufacturing 17(3), 408–421 (2004)
16. Rouhani, M., Soleymani, R.: Neural Networks based Diagnosis of heart arrhythmias using chaotic and nonlinear features of HRV signals. In: International Association of Computer Science and Information Technology - Spring Conference, pp. 545–549 (2009)

17. Ma, Y.-G., Ma, L.-Y., Ma, J.: RBF neural network based fault diagnosis for the thermody-namic system of a thermal power generating unit. In: Proceedings of the Fourth International Conference on Machine Learning and Cybernetics, Guangzhou, pp. 4738–4843 (2005)
18. Abe, Y., Konishi, M., Imai, J.: Neural network based diagnosis method for looper height controller of hot strip mills. In: Proceedings of the First International Conference on Innovative Computing, Information and Control (ICICIC 2006), 0-7695-2616-0/06 $20.00 © 2006. IEEE, Los Alamitos (2006)
19. Patan, K., Witczak, M., Korbicz, J.: Towards robustness in neural network based fault diagnosis. Int. J. Appl. Math. Computers. Sci. 18(4), 443–454 (2008)

FDI and Accommodation Using NN Based Techniques

Ramon Ferreiro Garcia, Alberto De Miguel Catoira, and Beatriz Ferreiro Sanz

ETSNM, Dept. Industrial Eng., University of La Coruna
ferreiro@udc.es

Abstract. Massive application of dynamic backpropagation neural networks is used on closed loop control FDI (fault detection and isolation) tasks. The process dynamics is mapped by means of a trained backpropagation NN to be applied on residual generation. Process supervision is then applied to discriminate faults on process sensors, and process plant parameters. A rule based expert system is used to implement the decision making task and the corresponding solution in terms of faults accommodation and/or reconfiguration. Results show an efficient and robust FDI system which could be used as the core of an SCADA or alternatively as a complement supervision tool operating in parallel with the SCADA when applied on a heat exchanger.

Keywords: Backpropagation, Conjugate gradient, Fault detection and isolation, Fault accommodation and reconfiguration, Neural Networks, Parity space, Residual evaluation.

1 Introduction

Among the most popular approaches to residual generation there is the model based concept. Generally, such approach is being currently realized using different kinds of modelling techniques, such as analytical, knowledge based and data based techniques according [1], [2], [6], [8], [9], [10], [20].

Analytical model based approaches are usually restricted to simpler linear and low order systems described by linear models. When there are no mathematical models of the diagnosed system or the complexity of a dynamic system increases and the task of modelling is very difficult to solve, analytical models cannot be applied or cannot give satisfactory results. In these cases experimental functional approximation or data based models, such as neural networks, fuzzy sets or their combination (neurofuzzy networks), can be considered [18].

With regard to FDI, robustness plays an important role. Model based fault diagnosis is built on a number of idealized assumptions. One of them is that the model of the system is a faithful replica of plant dynamics. Another one is that disturbances and noise acting upon the system are known. This is, obviously, not possible in practical engineering applications. The robustness problem in fault diagnosis is considered as an objective to the maximization of the detectability and isolability of faults and simultaneously the minimization of uncontrolled effects such as disturbances, noise, changes in sensors, actuators or process parameters, changes in inputs and/or the state, etc. [2]. With regard to fault diagnosis, robustness can be achieved by means of [2], [16]:

M. Graña Romay et al. (Eds.): HAIS 2010, Part I, LNAI 6076, pp. 395–404, 2010.

active approaches – based on generating residuals insensitive to model uncertainty and simultaneously sensitive to faults,

passive approaches – enhancing the robustness of the fault diagnosis system to the decision making task.

Active approaches to fault diagnosis are generally implemented by means of unknown input observers, robust parity equations or $H\infty$. However, in the case of models with uncertainty located in the parameters, perfect decoupling of residuals from uncertainties is limited by the number of available measurements [4]. An alternative solution consists in applying passive approaches, which propagate uncertainty into residuals. Robustness is then achieved through the use of adaptive thresholds. A practical limitation of passive approaches is that faults producing a residual deviation smaller than model uncertainty are not detected and consequently are missed.

Unfortunately, most of the existing approaches (both passive and active) were developed for linear systems as can be observed in the literature [1], [2], [6], [9], [19], [17].

Since most industrial FDI applications exhibit time varying, discontinuous and nonlinear behaviour, such characteristics have considerably limited their practical applications. Taking into consideration such a scenario, the main objective of this paper is to describe a neural network based passive approach that can be used for robust fault diagnosis of nonlinear systems.

In the approach presented in this work we tried to obtain a set of neural network based models that are best suited to a particular location of a generic closed loop control application. This results in a strategy with a relatively large robustness. A degraded performance of fault diagnosis constitutes a direct consequence of using poor modelling techniques, which it is avoided with this work. To settle such a problem within the framework of this work, it is proposed to use as the modelling strategy, the functional approximation technique based on feedforward neural networks trained under a back propagation algorithm, let's say the conjugate gradient.

The paper is organised as follows: Section 2 describes the technique to model the dynamic process including the associated the closed loop control devices. Section 3 presents an application of the described strategy to a pilot plant where a temperature control loop is associated to a heat exchanger. Finally, last section deals with a supervision task implementation and a brief discussion of results and conclusions on the contribution.

2 Neural Networks Based FDI

Artificial Neural Networks (ANNs) have been intensively studied and applied during the last three decades. As consequence they were successfully applied to dynamic system modelling and fault diagnosis [12], [3], [7], [9], [20], [14]. Neural networks (NN) constitute a serious alternative to the classical methods, because they can deal with very complex situations which could not be accurately described by means of deterministic algorithms. They are especially useful when there is no an analytical model of a process being considered. Commonly in such cases, the classical approaches, such as observers or parameter estimation methods, are not completely satisfactory or not at all useful. Functional approximation (FA) by means of neural networks provides excellent mathematical tools for dealing with nonlinear problems [5], [13].

FA based NN have an important property owing to which any nonlinear function can be approximated with an arbitrary accuracy using a neural network with a suitable architecture and weight parameters. For continuous mappings, one hidden layer based ANN is sufficient, but in other cases, two hidden layers should be implemented. ANNs considered as parallel data processing tools, are capable of learning functional dependencies of the data. This feature is extremely useful for solving various pattern recognition problems. Another attractive property is the self-learning ability. A neural network can extract the system features from historical training data using a learning algorithm, requiring little or no *a priori* knowledge about the process. This makes ANNs nonlinear modelling tools of a great flexibility.

Neural networks are also robust with respect to incorrect or missing data. Protective relaying based on ANNs is not affected by a change in the system operating conditions. FA based NN also have high computation rates, substantial input error tolerance and adaptive capability. These features allow applying neural networks effectively to the modelling and identification of complex nonlinear dynamic processes and fault diagnosis [11], [15].

2.1 Process Dynamics on the Basis of NN Based Models

It is well known that a state variable based model described under a phase variable technique can be represented by

$$\dot{x} = [A]x + [B]U$$
$$y = [C]x$$

(1)

where U is the control signal, y is the measured output, and the matrices A, B and C are parameters of the conventional nonlinear state space model.

Considering a general SISO process with accessible states, a backpropagation neural network based state space variable model, described under a phase variable technique, is represented by means of a nonlinear differential equation without a priori knowledge about plant parameters as follows:

$$D^N x = f(U, D^{N-1}x, \cdots D^0 x)$$

(2)

where eq. (2) is the highest order derivative of eq.(1), which yields the scheme depicted with figure 7.

The coefficients of the differential equation given in (2) are not known, and for observer implementation purposes don't need to be known because only the system dynamics must be mapped, if only the state variables are to be observed.

Consequently, the state space model can be reconstructed by means of the proposed backpropagation neural network based model under strict feedback form as shown in the scheme depicted with figure 2.

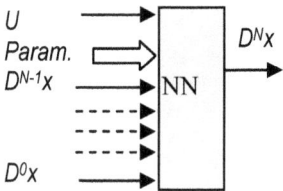

Fig. 1. Backpropagation neural network based structure

Conventionally, if the process parameters are known, either state observers or output observers can be applied. In the described case, if only the process dynamics is known, state observers are inherently achieved.

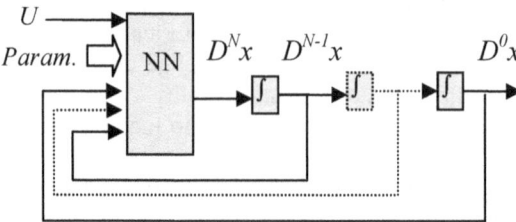

Fig. 2. Implementation of the dynamic neural network which includes input/output variables, internal state variables and process parameters

3   Supervision Applied Task on a Heat Exchanger Pilot Plant

The experimental validation of the proposed strategy has been implemented under a scheme shown in figure 3. In figure 3 it is depicted the scheme of the heating module of the supervised pilot plant where a heating fluid supplied under an input pressure Pc, input temperature Tc and mass flow rate mc is applied to the heat exchanger in order to heat a process flow rate mi, under a temperatures Ti and mass flow rate mi respectively, where M is the heat exchanger static mass.

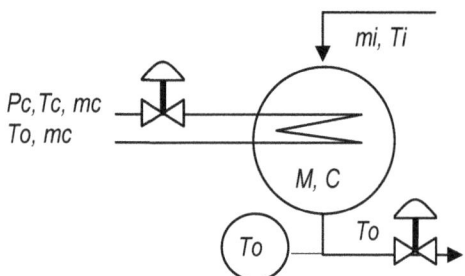

Fig. 3. The supervised heat exchanger process scheme

Table 1. The notation used in the heat exchanger NN based model

Process parameter	symbol
Heating fluid mass flow rate generated by the controller	mc
Heating fluid input temperature	Tc
Heating fluid input pressure	Pc
Heated fluid mass flow rate	mi
Heated fluid Inlet temperature	Ti
Heated fluid specific heat	C
Heated fluid temperature	To

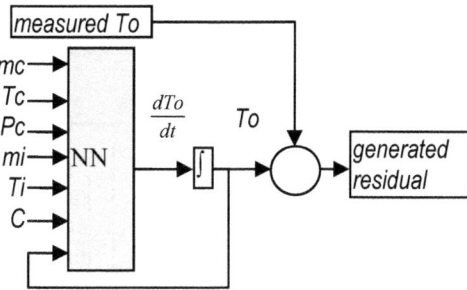

Fig. 4. The dynamic NN structure for residual generation applied on the supervised heat exchanger

The dynamic NN based model has the structure shown in figure 4. It consists in a backpropagation NN trained by the Fletcher-Reeves algorithm. The table 1 shows the set of input/output variables and the used notation.

The control objective consists in achieving an output temperature To in a finite time under common practical constraints and limitations.

The supervision objective consists in determine plant faults, performing plant accommodation tasks and subsequent control reconfiguration while achieving the desired control objective.

A flowchart of the supervision task is implemented according to the scheme shown in figure 5. To generate residuals, the neural network based model output To is compared with the real time measured process variable (measured To). When the maximum admitted tolerance Tol is exceeded, the conclusions given by the applied rules are carried out. A residual may exceed the limit value when changes in plant parameters, or sensor malfunction or both events are present. Because of the possibility of the occurrence of both events simultaneously, a rule based strategy to solve the given conflict must be applied. To enable the supervision task, the proposed strategy checks the changes in plant parameters by means of residuals evaluation at the first supervision step. If a residual exceed the maximum admitted tolerance Tol, then it is necessary to update the NN based model to the actual condition by applying a training session, and if residual persists then such symptom means that a fault in the measuring system is present. As consequence of the persistent residual due to the measuring system fault, a fault accommodation technique is to be applied based on the compensation of the estimated measuring signal drift error.

The trained NN based dynamic model must be initialized taking into account the actual real time measured output To. Consequently, the output of such dynamic model matches exactly the process output at the beginning of the supervision task.

Since the residual R is defined as (measured $To - To$), the accommodation technique is implemented under the following rule:

IF $R > Tol$ THEN feedback control signal is (measured $To - R$), and the closed loop control system is performing right.

NN RT inputs

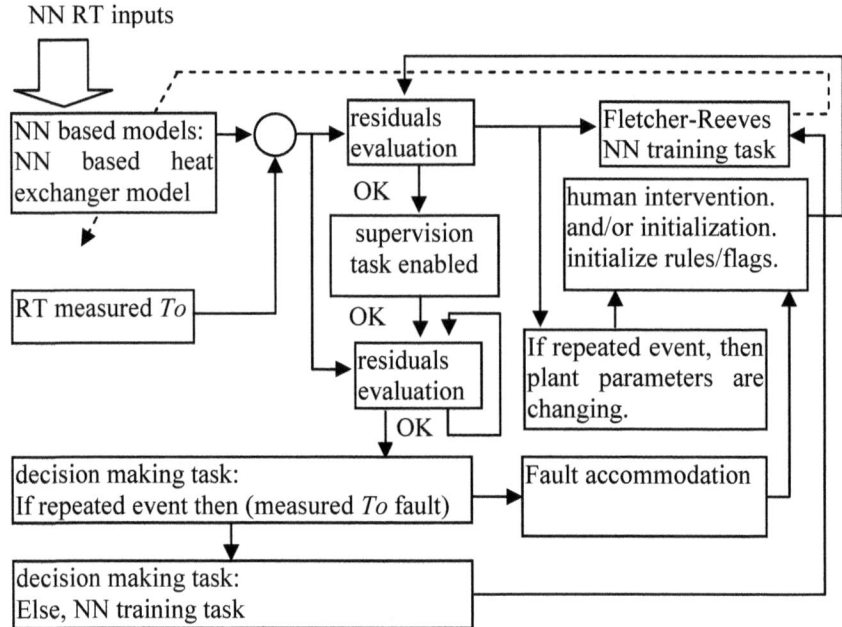

Fig. 5. A flowchart of the supervision scheduler implemented on the basis of a combination of dynamic NN based models with rule based logic. The scheduler is focused on the detection of plant parameters variation, and on process variable measuring system To.

The proof can be straightforward achieved as (measured $To - R$) = (measured To – (measured To-To)) = To. Such correction strategy ensures that the feedback signal is the true value even under process value sensor malfunction. Nevertheless, a fault due to the process value sensor is present. Consequently, according to the flow chart of figure 5, a human intervention is required or alternatively a system reconfiguration by means of physical redundancy.

4   Supervision Task Implementation

As described in the past section, a dynamic NN is responsible for generating an estimated response which is compared with the actual measured value to achieve a residual. As the residual exceed certain value, a flag is generated to activate the sequence described by means of the flowchart shown in figure 4. Extensive tests have been carried out to validate the proposed supervision strategy. In some of the tests some changes in parameters has been applied in order to detect the given plant changes. When a plant change is detected then, adaptation of the NN based model to the actual scenario is required before going on with the supervision task. Under such condition, two supervision tests are presented in figures 6 and 7.

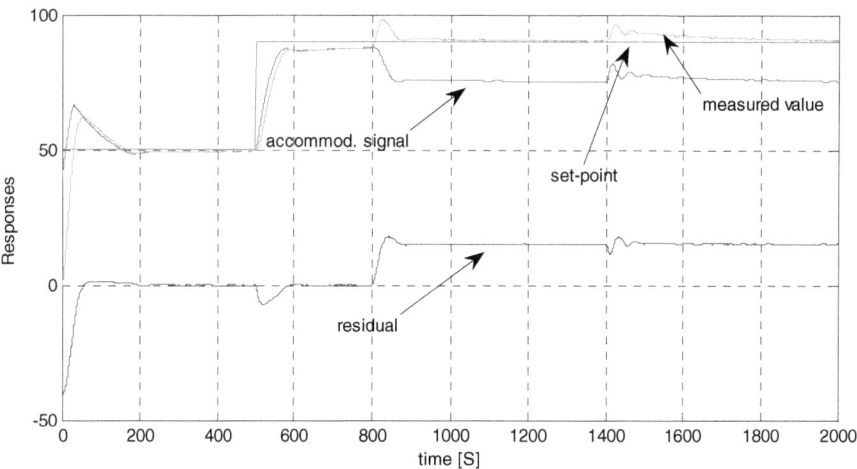

Fig. 6. The time responses of the supervisor operating in detection mode

In figure 6 it is shown the case where the heat exchanger is operating correctly before elapsed time reaches 800 sec. At this time a fault in the process variable sensor (drift fault type of 20% increase) has been intentionally applied. As consequence of the mentioned fault the following events has been generated and are shown in the time responses of the figure 6:

(a)   The feedback controller tray to avoid the control error and consequently the measured value reach the set-point value.

(b)   Nevertheless the supervision system has generated a relevant residual, which is responsible for advising of a problem that should be solved.

(c)   Since the decision making strategy is programmed to notify by means of a warning to the human operator and not to correct the fault in such a case, the supervision system finished the solving task. Under the present conditions, an alarm notifying the presence of a relevant residual is active.

Since the dynamic model has been initialized with the same value of the actual process output, the residual at the beginning of the supervision task must be negligible. To validate this condition, a single rule must be processed. If such values (NN based model output and actual process output) don't match, the supervision task is disabled and a training session must be considered before continuing. In figure 5 it is shown a flow diagram where such aspect is highlighted.

The same test has been repeated under the same process characteristics in order to validate the fault accommodation and reconfiguration strategy. Consequently the following events which are described in figure 7 occurred:

(d)   The feedback controller tray to avoid the control error as in the last case but the measured value doesn't reach the set-point value. This is due to the effect of signal accommodation to a value such that the process value is reaching the set-point value.

(e)   Nevertheless the supervision system has generated a relevant residual, which is responsible for notifying of the presence of a problem that has been eventually solved.

(f)   As the decision making strategy is programmed to notify an operator as well as to correct the fault in such a case, the supervision system finished the solving task successfully.

When elapsed running time reached 1400 sec., a disturbance entered the heating process, which can not be completely cancelled by the generated accommodation signal during a short period of time. This is due to the characteristics of the inherent process time constant and controller time lag. Nevertheless, after some characteristic time passed response became effective.

When more than a fault affects the system, the decision making rules cannot decide effectively on the isolation task due to the vagueness of the processed data. A technical solution presented by many authors consists of the application of redundancy.

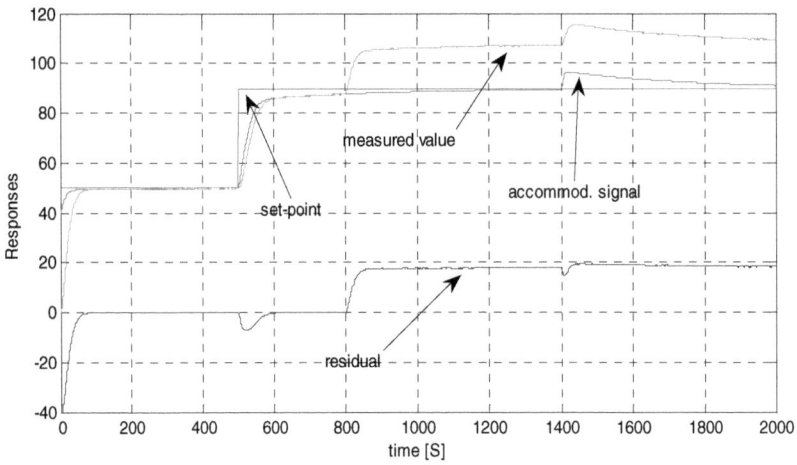

Fig. 7. The time response of the supervisor layout operating in fault accommodation mode

5   Conclusions

A supervision strategy to detect, isolate and accommodate faults in closed loop control systems on the basis of a dynamic NN based modeling technique has been implemented on a heat exchanger. A FDI strategy based on the combination of a rule based scheduler with a residual generator achieved by dynamic NN based models has been applied. A decision making strategy on the basis of system accommodation and control system reconfiguration has been successfully applied.

Results show that the detection of a fault due to a sensor drift as well as some process parameter variation may be efficiently detected and accommodated.

Since the NN based model must be initialized at the beginning of every supervision task, the initialization value must be measured from the actual real time value.

Such premise requires the condition of a correct measuring system at the starting instant.

The implemented supervising system needs to be updated when parameter changes have occurred by training the applied neural networks. This characteristic is a serious drawback since the plant must be forced to an off-line condition, which has a direct repercussion or influence on the system productivity.

Finally a relevant disadvantage of the applied methodology is the impossibility to isolate faults when more than a fault is affecting the plant due to the ambiguity of the processed data. A technical solution to such problem is the application of analytical and/or physical redundancy which will be analyzed in future works.

Acknowledgments. This work has been partially supported by the XUNTA DE GALICIA under the grant DPI 1 IN825N cod_web:772.

References

1. Blanke, M., Kinnaert, M., Lunze, J., Staroswiecki, M.: Diagnosis and Fault-Tolerant Control. Springer, New York (2003)
2. Chen, J., Patton, R.J.: Robust Model-Based Fault Diagnosis for Dynamic Systems. Kluwer, Berlin (1999)
3. Frank, P.M., Köppen-Seliger, B.: New developments using AI in fault diagnosis. Engineering Applications of Artificial Intelligence 10(1), 3–14 (1997)
4. Gertler, J.: Fault Detection and Diagnosis in Engineering Systems. Marcel Dekker, New York (1998)
5. Haykin, S.: Neural Networks. A Comprehensive Foundation, 2nd edn. Prentice-Hall, Englewood Cliffs (1999)
6. Iserman, R.: Fault Diagnosis Systems. In: An Introduction from Fault Detection to Fault Tolerance. Springer, New York (2006)
7. Köppen-Seliger, B., Frank, P.M.: Fuzzy logic and neural networks in fault detection. In: Jain, L., Martin, N. (eds.) Fusion of Neural Networks, Fuzzy Sets, and Genetic Algorithms, pp. 169–209. CRC Press, New York (1999)
8. Korbicz, J.: Fault detection using analytical and soft computing methods. Bulletin of the Polish Academy of Sciences:Technical Sciences 54(1), 75–88 (2006)
9. Korbicz, J., Kościelny, J., Kowalczuk, Z., Cholewa, W.: Fault Diagnosis. In: Models, Artificial Intelligence, Applications. Springer, Berlin (2004)
10. Korbicz, J., Patan, K., Kowal, M. (eds.): Fault Diagnosis and Fault Tolerant Control. Academic Publishing House EXIT, Warsaw (2007)
11. Marcu, T., Mirea, L., Frank, P.M.: Development of dynamical neural networks with application to observer based fault detection and isolation. International Journal of Applied Mathematics and Computer Science 9(3), 547–570 (1999)
12. Narendra, K.S., Parthasarathy, K.: Identification and control of dynamical systems using neural networks. IEEE Transactions on Neural Networks 1(1), 12–18 (1990)
13. Norgard, M., Ravn, O., Poulsen, N., Hansen, L.: Networks for Modelling and Control of Dynamic Systems. Springer, London (2000)
14. Patan, K., Korbicz, J., Głowacki, G.: DC motor fault diagnosis by means of artificial neural networks. In: Proceedings of the 4th International Conference on Informatics in Control, Automation and Robotics, ICINCO 2007, Angers, France. Published on CD-ROM (2007)

15. Patan, K., Parisini, T.: Identification of neural dynamic models for fault detection and isolation: The case of a real sugar evaporation process. Journal of Process Control 15(1), 67–79 (2005)
16. Puig, V., Stancu, A., Escobet, T., Nejjari, F., Quevedo, J., Patton, R.J.: Passive robust fault detection using interval observers: Application to the DAMADICS benchmark problem. Control Engineering Practice 14(6), 621–633 (2006)
17. Rodrigues, M., Theilliol, D., Aberkane, S., Sauter, D.: Fault tolerant control design for polytopic LPV systems. International Journal of Applied Mathematics and Computer Science 17(1), 27–37 (2007)
18. Rutkowski, L.: New Soft Computing Techniques for System Modelling, Pattern Classification and Image Processing. Springer, Berlin (2004)
19. Witczak, M.: Modelling and Estimation Strategies for Fault Diagnosis of Non-linear Systems. Springer, Berlin (2007)
20. Witczak, M., Korbicz, J., Mrugalski, M., Patton, R.J.: A GMDH neural network-based approach to robust fault diagnosis: Application to the DAMADICS benchmark problem. Control Engineering Practice 14(6), 671–683 (2006)

A Hybrid ACO Approach to the Matrix Bandwidth Minimization Problem

Camelia-M. Pintea[1], Gloria-Cerasela Crişan[2], and Camelia Chira[3]

[1] George Coşbuc N. College,
400083 Cluj-Napoca, Romania
cmpintea@yahoo.com
[2] Vasile Alecsandri University,
600115 Bacău, Romania
ceraselacrisan@ub.ro
[3] Babeş-Bolyai University,
400084 Cluj-Napoca, Romania
cchira@cs.ubbcluj.ro

Abstract. The evolution of the human society raises more and more difficult endeavors. For some of the real-life problems, the computing time-restriction enhances their complexity. The Matrix Bandwidth Minimization Problem (*MBMP*) seeks for a simultaneous permutation of the rows and the columns of a square matrix in order to keep its nonzero entries close to the main diagonal. The *MBMP* is a highly investigated $\mathcal{NP}$-complete problem, as it has broad applications in industry, logistics, artificial intelligence or information recovery. This paper describes a new attempt to use the Ant Colony Optimization framework in tackling *MBMP*. The introduced model is based on the hybridization of the Ant Colony System technique with new local search mechanisms. Computational experiments confirm a good performance of the proposed algorithm for the considered set of *MBMP* instances.

Keywords: Matrix Bandwidth Minimization Problem, Ant Colony Optimization.

1 Introduction

The tractability of (academic) Combinatorial Optimization Problems (*COP*s) is studied for more than fifty years [5]. As many of them are $\mathcal{NP}$, the researchers mainly use (meta)heuristic, approximation, or hybrid solving methods. The current real-life problems express some features that make the algorithm design a difficult task: parameter linkage, large number of constraints, high dimension, many locally optimal solutions, uncertainty or dynamicity. These characteristics lead to real need and permanent search for new frameworks able to provide better and better solutions.

The Matrix Bandwidth Minimization Problem (*MBMP*) considers a symmetric matrix and seeks for a permutation of its rows (and columns) that keeps the nonzero elements as close as possible to the main diagonal. The *MBMP* mainly arises in solving systems of linear equations, enabling broad practical applications in fields such as

M. Graña Romay et al. (Eds.): HAIS 2010, Part I, LNAI 6076, pp. 405–412, 2010.

engineering, physics, computer science and economics. The matrix bandwidth minimization problem has been shown to be $\mathcal{NP}$-complete [14].

The Ant Colony Optimization (*ACO*) metaheuristic studies artificial systems inspired by the behavior of real ant colonies and which are used to solve discrete optimization problems [8]. The *ACO* framework depicts a set of artificial ants that cooperate: each ant randomly constructs a solution, based on the expected quality of the available moves and on the previous collective good solutions. Many algorithms based on *ACO* use local search and problem-tailored procedures, which increase the quality of the solutions. *ACO* demonstrated a high flexibility and strength by solving with very good results either academic instances of many *COP*s, or real-life problems. Inspired by the real-world collective behavior of social insects, *ACO* algorithms have been successfully applied to a variety of combinatorial optimization problems ranging from quadratic assignment and scheduling to protein folding or vehicle routing.

It is proposed a new approach to address the matrix bandwidth minimization problem based on the hybridization of the Ant Colony System technique with new local search mechanisms. Two procedures aimed at reducing the maximal bandwidth are proposed for the solution's refinement during the local search stage. The resulting algorithms are engaged in a set of numerical experiments for solving several *MBMP* instances.

This paper is organized as follows: the investigated matrix bandwidth minimization problem is briefly presented in Section 2; the overview of the related work is in Section 3; the proposed algorithms are described in Section 4; the implementation and the numerical results are discussed in Section 5, and the last section describes the future development of our work.

2   The Matrix Bandwidth Minimization Problem

Given a square symmetric matrix A of order n, its bandwidth is $\beta = \max_{a_{ij} \neq 0} |i - j|$.

To solve the *MBMP* for A means to find a permutation π of the rows (and columns) of the matrix A, that minimizes the bandwidth of the resulted matrix.

Many algorithms for solving the *MBMP* use it's re-cast as a graph-theory problem. Starting from A, one can define the graph $G_A = (V, E)$ with $V = \{1, 2, ..., n\}$, and $E = \{(i, j) \ iff \ a_{ij} \neq 0\}$. This leads to the bandwidth of G_A $\beta = \max_{(i,j) \in E} |i - j|$. To solve the transformed problem means to find a permutation π of V that minimizes the graph bandwidth. In its graph-equivalent form, it is shown in [14] that the *MBMP* is $\mathcal{NP}$-complete.

Another research topic of interest refers to the investigation of the bandwidth-recognition: what is the structure of a graph that enables us to use fast algorithms in order to decide if its bandwidth has a specific value. For example, the bandwidth 2 is investigated in [2].

3   Related Work for MBMP

For specific graphs, one can find their bandwidth in polynomial time [8]. Approximation algorithms for general graphs are running in polylogarithmic time [1]. For some
particular graph structures, there are different approximation algorithms. For example,
a 3-approximation one for dense graphs presented in [7], or polynomial time $O(log$
$n)$-approximation algorithms for caterpillars is in [6].

Almost all heuristic algorithms designed for *MBMP* are level-based. To define a
level structure for a graph means to partition its vertices into levels $L_1, L_2,...L_k$, such
that:

- all vertices adjacent to vertices in level L_1 are in either level L_1; or L_2,
- all vertices adjacent to vertices in level L_k are in either level L_{k-1} or L_k,
- for $1 < i < k$, all vertices adjacent to vertices in level L_i are in either level L_{i-1}, L_i or
  L_{i+1}.

Some new approaches, using *GA* [16], *GRASP* [15], Tabu Search [11], or an innovative node-shift heuristic [11] constantly develop and expand the set of available algorithms for the *MBMP*. Based on *MBMP*, new problems were defined (for example,
the antibandwidth problem [9]).

Ant Colony System is a particular *ACO* heuristic that uses both local and global
pheromone updating rules, in order to favor exploration. The local rule is applied by
each ant during the solution construction; only the ant that finds the best tour is allowed to apply the global rule. In the *ACS* model, each ant generates a complete tour
(associated to a problem solution) by probabilistically choosing the next node based
on the cost and the amount of pheromone on the connecting edge (according to the
state transition rule) [3]. Stronger pheromone trails are preferred and the most
promising tours accumulate higher amounts of pheromone.

The existing hybrid *ACO* metaheuristic (with hill-climbing) approach for *MBMP* is
presented in [10]. The artificial ants are activated and coordinated by a queen that
also manages the common memory. A local search phase, hill climbing, is added to
the end of each ant process, before the ant's solution is sent to the queen process. At
each iteration, the queen updates the memory trail with the current global best solution, or the iteration best solution.

In the following, it is introduced a new hybrid ACO metaheuristic, using *Ant
Colony System* with new local procedures.

4   Proposed Model for Solving MBMP

In the proposed approach to address the *MBMP*, *Ant Colony System* is hybridized with
new local search mechanisms. The *ACS* frame used is based on the level structure
described by the Cuthill-McKee algorithm [4] resulting in the following main steps:

I.   the initial phase computes the current matrix bandwidth and sets the parameters
     values;
II. the construction phase starts by putting all the ants in the node from the first
     level, and repeatedly making pseudo-randomly choices from the available

neighbors. After each step, the local update rule is applied [3]. This second phase ends by the global pheromone update rule [3];

III. the final phase consists of writing the best solution.

These three phases are iteratively executed within a given number of iterations. A solution is a one-dimensional array that stores the permutation of $V = \{1, 2,..., n\}$. Furthermore, the integration of a local search phase within the proposed *ACS* approach to *MBMP* facilitates the refinement of ants' solutions.

The main scheme of the proposed model is given below:

```
Hybrid ACS model for solving MBMP
begin
I.  Initialization: computes the current matrix bandwidth;
initialize pheromone trails; sets the parameters values;
II. while (maximum number of iterations not reached) do
      Swap Procedure
      while (maximum number of ants not reached) do
         build a partial solution using ACS
            apply a local pheromone update rule
         Swap Procedure
         apply a global pheromone update rule
      end while
   end while
III. write the best solution
End
```

At first, all the trails are initialized with the same pheromone quantity (τ_0). After each partial solution, the trails (τ_{ij}) between two nodes i and j are modified using the *ACS* local($\tau_{ij} = (1-\rho)\tau_{ij} + \rho\tau_0$) and global($\tau_{ij} = (1-\rho)\tau_{ij} + \rho\Delta\tau_{ij}$) update pheromone rules. The rate evaporation is denoted by ρ and its value is between 0 and 1 and. $\Delta\tau_{ij}$ is the inverse of the already known best solution [3].

For the improvement of *ACS* solutions with a specific local search mechanism, it is introduced the **PSwap** procedure (given below) with the aim of reducing the maximal bandwidth. This procedure is used twice within the proposed hybrid model: at the beginning of the iteration and after each partial solution is built, in order to improve each ant's solution.

The hybrid *ACS* model based on **Swap Procedure**: **PSwap** as the local search stage is denoted *hACS*.

```
PSwap Procedure
find the maximum and minimum degrees
for all indices x with the maximum degree
  randomly select y, an unvisited node with a minimum degree
  SWAP(x,y)
end for
```

The second local mechanism `Swap Procedure` introduced is called **MPSwap** (see main scheme below) and extends the **PSwap** procedure in order to avoid stagnation.

The hybrid *ACS* model based on **MPSwap** as the local search stage is called Hybrid *MACS* (**hMACS**).

```
MPSwap Procedure
find the maximum and minimum degrees
for all indices x with the maximum degree
   select y, an unvisited node with a minimum degree such as
             the matrix bandwidth decreases
   SWAP(x,y)
end for
```

ACO-ACS, *hACS* and *MACS* approaches to the *MBMP* are further investigated in terms of solution quality and computation time.

5 Computational Experiments

The proposed algorithms were implemented in Java and ran on an AMD 2600 computer with 1024 MB memory and 1.9 GHz CPU clock. There are used nine simmetric Euclidean instances from Harwell-Boeing sparse matrix collection [13] as benchmarks (see Table 1).

The results are presented in Table 2. For each instance, both algorithms were executed 20 times; the average value is given in column *AVG* and the average execution time is depicted in the *AVGT* column. The best solution is reported in column *MIN*, and the number of times the best solution was reached is given in the column #.

The parameter values for all *ACS* implementations are: 10 ants, 10 iterations, $q_0 = 0.95$, $\alpha = 1$, $\beta = 2$, $\rho = 0.0001$, $\tau_0 = 0.1$.

Table 1. The benchmark instances from National Institute of Standards and Technology, Matrix Market, Harwell-Boeing sparse matrix collection *(MatrixMarket matrix coordinate pattern symmetric)[13]*

No	Instance	Euclidean Characteristics
1.	can___24	24 24 92
2.	can___61	61 61 309
3.	can___62	62 62 140
4.	can___73	73 73 225
5.	can___96	96 96 432
6.	can__187	187 187 839
7.	can__229	229 229 1003
8.	can__256	256 256 1586
9.	can__268	268 268 1675

Table 2. Exprimental results with *ACS, hACS* and *hMACS* on from Harwell-Boeing sparse matrix collection [13] from Table 1

No	Instance	ACS				hACS				hMACS			
		MIN	#	AVG	AVGT	MIN	#	AVG	AVGT	MIN	#	AVG	AVG T
1.	can___24	17	2	18.6	1.33	14	7	14.80	0.55	**11**	1	**12.6**	0.6
2.	can___61	47	1	49.8	2.23	43	8	43.60	1.22	**42**	6	**42.8**	1.18
3.	can___62	39	1	45.75	1.95	20	3	22.00	0.74	**12**	1	**16.35**	0.9
4.	can___73	37	6	38.1	1.69	28	1	31.30	1.15	**22**	1	**26.7**	1.3
5.	can___96	31	20	31	2.07	**17**	2	27.45	1.56	**17**	14	**19.7**	1.68
6.	can__187	63	20	63	3.2	63	20	63.00	4.52	**33**	4	**37.25**	5.2
7.	can__229	163	2	168.35	3.84	**120**	1	**131.25**	11.21	120	1	132.65	9.9
8.	can__256	241	1	249.45	5.02	**148**	1	**164.50**	44.48	189	1	197.45	26.05
9.	can__268	234	1	241.1	5.13	**165**	1	**193.80**	30.21	210	1	217.75	21.9

The *t-test* results are shown in Tables 3 and 4. The result of the paired t-test [17] performed for *ACS* and *hACS* is $t=2.51$. The probability of this result, assuming the null hypothesis, is for average values 0.037. The result of the paired t-test performed for *ACS* and *hMACS* (see Table 4) is t=4.41. The probability of this result, assuming the null hypothesis, is for average values 0.002. Both results are less than 0⊳05 indicating a significant statistic difference between the considered algorithms.

Table 3. T-test results for *ACS* and *hACS*

Alg.	Mean	95% confidence interval for Mean	Std. Dev.	Median	Avg.Absolute deviation from Median
ACS	101	29.20 thru 171.9	92.8	49.8	65.4
hACS	76.9	24.59 thru 129.1	68.0	43.6	50.8
ACS : hACS	23.7	1.901 thru 45.53	28.4	6.80	19.9

Table 4. T-test results for *ACS* and *hMACS*

Alg.	Mean	95% confidence interval for Mean	Std. Dev.	Median	Avg.Absolute deviation from Median
ACS	101	29.20 thru 171.9	92.8	49.8	65.4
hMACS	78.1	15.11 thru 141.2	82.0	37.2	57.3
ACS : hMACS	22.4	10.70 thru 34.17	15.3	23.3	11.9

The results show that the newly procedure **MPSwap** performs better on small instances, while **PSwap** is better on larger ones. The average execution time is better for the modified local search procedure. A balance between the quality of the solution and the time needed is also observed. There are no reported optimal or best-known solutions for these instances.

6 Conclusions and Future Work

This paper describes a hybrid heuristic method to solve the Matrix Bandwidth Minimization Problem, based on ACO framework and using two local search procedures. These two methods were tested on several benchmark instances, showing a balance between them: ACS is better for large instances and MACS performs better for smaller ones.

More investigations have to be made in order to study these two algorithms on all available problem instances from [13], and to highlight either some patterns in their behavior, or a quality bias.

Future work investigates new local search procedures (for example, inspired by the node-shift heuristic [11]), as well as the use a concurrent implementation on a coarse-grained parallel architecture.

Acknowledgments. This research is supported by the CNCSIS Grant ID 508, New Computational Paradigms for Dynamic Complex Problems, funded by the Ministry of Education, Research and Innovation, Romania.

References

1. Blum, A., Konjevod, G., Ravi, R., Vempala, S.: Semi-definite relaxations for minimum bandwith and other vertex-ordering problems. In: 30th ACM Symposium on Theory of Computing, pp. 284–293 (1998)
2. Caprara, A., Malucelli, F., Pretolani, D.: On bandwidth-2 graphs. Discrete Applied Mathematics 117(1-3), 1–13 (2002)
3. Dorigo, M., Stützle, T.: Ant Colony Optimization. MIT Press, Cambridge (2004)
4. George, A.: Computer implementation of the finite element method, STAN-CS-71-208. Computer Science Dept., Stanford Univ., Stanford (1971)
5. Graham, R.L.: Bounds for certain multiprocessing anomalies. Bell System Tech. J. 45, 1563–1581 (1966)
6. Haralambides, J., Makedon, F., Monien, B.: Bandwidth minimization: an approximation algorithm for caterpillars. Mathematical Systems Theory 24(3), 169–177 (1991)
7. Karpinski, M., Wirtgen, J., Zelikovsky, A.: An approximating algorithm for the bandwidth problem on dense graphs. Technical Report TR 97-017, ECCC (1997)
8. Kloks, T., Kratsch, D., Müller, H.: Bandwidth of chain graphs. Information Processing Letters 68(6), 313–315 (1998)
9. Leung, J.Y.-T., Vornberger, O., Witthoff, J.D.: On some variants of the bandwidth minimization problem. SIAM J. on Computing 13, 650–667 (1984)
10. Lim, A., Lin, J., Rodrigues, B., Xiao, F.: Ant Colony Optimization with hill climbing for the bandwidth minimization problem. Appl. Soft Comput. 6(2), 180–188 (2006)

11. Lim, A., Rodrigues, B., Xiao, F.: Heuristics for matrix bandwidth reduction. European J. of Oper. Res. 174(1), 69–91 (2006)
12. Martí, R., Laguna, M., Glover, F., Campos, V.: Reducing the bandwidth of a sparse matrix with Tabu Search. European J. of Oper. Res. 135(2), 211–220 (2001)
13. National Institute of Standards and Technology, Matrix Market, Harwell-Boeing sparse matrix collection,
    http://math.nist.gov/MatrixMarket/data/Harwell-Boeing/
14. Papadimitriou, C.H.: The NP-completeness of the bandwidth minimization problem. Computing 16(3), 263–270 (1976)
15. Piñana, E., Plana, I., Campos, V., Martí, R.: GRASP and Path Relinking for the matrix bandwidth minimization. European J. of Oper. Res. 153(1), 200–210 (2004)
16. Rodriguez-Tello, E., Jin-Kao, H., Torres-Jimenez, J.: An improved Simulated Annealing Algorithm for the matrix bandwidth minimization. European J. of Oper. Res. 185(3), 1319–1335 (2008)
17. http://www.physics.csbsju.edu/stats/t-test.html

Machine-Learning Based Co-adaptive Calibration: A Perspective to Fight BCI Illiteracy

Carmen Vidaurre[1], Claudia Sannelli[1], Klaus-Robert Müller[1,3], and Benjamin Blankertz[1,2,3]

[1] Berlin Institute of Technology, Computer Science Faculty, Machine Learning department,
Franklinstr. 28/29
10587 Berlin, Germany
[2] IDA group, FIRST, Fraunhofer Institute, Kekulestr. 7
12489 Berlin, Germany
[3] Bernstein Focus: Neurotechnology, Berlin, Germany
{carmen.vidaurre,claudia.sannelli,blanker}@cs.tu-berlin.de,
klaus-robert.mueller@tu-berlin.de

Abstract. "BCI illiteracy" is one of the biggest problems and challenges in BCI research. It means that BCI control cannot be achieved by a non-negligible number of subjects (estimated 20% to 25%). There are two main causes for BCI illiteracy in BCI users: either no SMR idle rhythm is observed over motor areas, or this idle rhythm is not attenuated during motor imagery, resulting in a classification performance lower than 70% (criterion level) already for offline calibration data. In a previous work of the same authors, the concept of machine learning based co-adaptive calibration was introduced. This new type of calibration provided substantially improved performance for a variety of users. Here, we use a similar approach and investigate to what extent co-adapting learning enables substantial BCI control for completely novice users and those who suffered from BCI illiteracy before.

1 Introduction

Brain-Computer Interface (BCI) systems aim to provide users control over a computer application by their brain activity (see [1,2,3,4,5]). In EEG-based BCIs, one of the biggest research challenges is to understand and solve the problem of "BCI Illiteracy", which means that BCI control cannot be achieved by a non-negligible number of users (estimated 20% to 25%), cf. ([6]). A screening study was conducted to observe BCI control in 80 participants. They performed motor imagery, firstly in a calibration (i.e. without feedback) measurement and then in a feedback measurement in which they could control a 1D cursor application. Coarsely, three categories of users were observed: participants for whom (I) a classifier could be successfully trained and who performed feedback with good accuracy; (II) a classifier could be successfully trained, but feedback did not work well. It is known that there are changes between the calibration and the feedback step that can affect the EEG signals, causing the feedback fail. In the screening study, the bias of the classifier was supervisedly updated using the first 20 feedback trials (as in [7]), but this strategy revealed not to be sufficient for some of

M. Graña Romay et al. (Eds.): HAIS 2010, Part I, LNAI 6076, pp. 413–420, 2010.

the participants; (III) no classifier with acceptable accuracy could be trained. Whereas participants of Cat. II had obviously difficulties with the transition between offline and online operation, users of Cat. III did not show the expected modulation of sensorimotor rhythms (SMRs): either no SMR idle rhythm was observed over motor areas, or this idle rhythm was not attenuated during motor imagery.

A previous work (cf. [8]) showed in a one session pilot study that co-adaptive calibration using machine-learning techniques can help users of Cat. II (2 participants) and Cat. III (3 participants) to achieve successful feedback. However in that pilot study, the number of participants was too low to conclude the success of the methods. In this study we focus in novice and Cat. III users (who suffer the most difficult to solve type of BCI illiteracy), and investigate to what extent co-adapting learning enables substantial BCI control for users whose separability could not be determined beforehand (with 4 novice volunteers and 10 Cat. III users).

2   Experimental Setup

The study consisted of a one-day session that immediately started with BCI feedback using a pre-trained subject-independent classifier, as in [8]. The classifiers and spatial filters were adapted to the specific brain signals of the user during the experimental session. Adaptation was performed in three levels but the feedback application stayed the same for the whole experiment.

All users performed 6 feedback runs. The first run consisted of 3 groups of 40 trials with a specific pair of classes (20 trials of each class, left-right, left-foot, right-foot). The total number of trials per class after the first run was 40. After this first run, two classes were selected and the rest of the runs consisted of 100 trials each, with 50 trials per class. The timing was as follows: at time 0, the cue was provided in the form of a small arrow over a cross placed in the middle of the screen, one second later (during the first run) or at the beginning of the most discriminative time window (rest of the runs), the cross started to move to provide feedback. Its speed was determined by the classification output (similar to [9,10]). The task of the participant was to use motor imagery to make the cursor move into a previously indicated target direction. The feedback lasted for 3 seconds and was followed by a short pause.

3   Methods

Fourteen participants took part in the study. Four of them were completely novice (naive users), so their Category could not be determined a priori, and ten belonged to Cat. III. The session immediately started with BCI feedback as in [8,11].

In order to choose the two classes to use (out of three: 'left', 'right' and 'foot' imagery movement), the first run presented four consecutive times ten trials for each class combination (five trials per class). A pretrained subject-independent classifier on simple features was used and adapted after each trial. The features were band-power estimates in alpha (8-15 Hz) and beta (16-35 Hz) bands, spatially filtered using small Laplacian derivations (cf. [12]) at C3, Cz, C4. The covariance matrix and pooled mean of the classifiers were updated once after each trial, see section 3.1.

After the first run, for each of the 3 possible class-combinations (left vs. right, left vs. foot, right vs. foot) the frequency band and the time interval where offline chosen. In addition, two optimum Laplacian channels per motor area where selected using a statistical criterion based in the 40 trials per class recorded in the first run, see section 3.2. Then, the classifier was trained on the resulting features and the best performing class combination was chosen. During the two following runs and after each trial, six Laplacian channels (2 per motor area) were on-line updated to provide flexibility with respect to the spatial location of the modulated brain activity. The classifier was retrained on the resulting band-power features (see section 3.2).

An off-line Common Spatial Pattern (CSP) analysis [13] of runs two and three followed. A classifier was then trained on the selected CSP features and used for the subsequent last three runs. Here, the pooled mean of the linear classifier was adapted after each trial [14], i.e. unsupervised adaptation was applied in order to assess a fair performance (see section 3.3).

Throughout the whole session, all classifiers were based on Linear Discriminant Analysis (LDA), which was regularized through shrinkage when the dimensionality of the features was too high (cf. [15,16]). During the adaptation, we used a specific variant of LDA. In LDA the covariance matrices of both classes are assumed to be equal (assumption of linear separability) and they are denoted by Σ here, then the sample means of the two classes are μ_1 and μ_2, and an arbitrary feature vector is x. We define:

$$D(x) = [b; w]^\top \cdot [1; x] \tag{1}$$

$$w = \Sigma^{-1} \cdot (\mu_2 - \mu_1) \tag{2}$$

$$b = -w^\top \cdot \mu \tag{3}$$

$$\mu = \frac{\mu_1 + \mu_2}{2} \tag{4}$$

where $D(x)$ is the difference in the distance of the feature vector x to the separating hyperplane, which is described by its normal vector w and bias b. Note that the covariance matrices and mean values used in this paper are sample covariance matrices and sample means, estimated from the data. In order to simplify the notation and the description of the methods, we will in the following use covariance matrix instead of sample covariance matrix and mean instead of sample mean. Usually, the covariance matrix used in Eq 2 is the class-average covariance matrix. But it can be shown that using the pooled covariance matrix (which can be estimated without using label information, just by aggregating the features of all classes) yields the same separating hyperplane. In this study we used the pooled covariance matrix in Eq. 2. Similarly, the class-average mean (calculated in Eq. 4) can be replaced by the pooled mean (average over all feature vectors of all classes). This implies that the bias of the separating hyperplane can be estimated (and adapted) in an unsupervised manner (without label information). The restriction of the method is to have an estimate of the prior probabilities of the 2 classes.

If LDA is to be used as a classifier, the observation x is classified as class 1 if $D(x)$ is less than 0, and otherwise as class 2. But in the cursor control application we use the classifier output $D(x)$ as real number to determine the speed of the cursor.

The next sections explain with some detail the methods used in the three levels of the experiment, including three on-line adaptation schemes: the first two are supervised, i.e., they require information about the class label (type of motor imagery task) of the past trial in order to update the classifier. The last method updates the classifier without knowing the task of the past trial (unsupervised adaptation).

3.1   Methods for Level 1 (Run 1)

The first run started with a pre-trained subject-independent classifier on simple features: band-power in alpha (8-15 Hz) and beta (16-35 Hz) frequency range and in 3 small Laplacian derivations at C3, Cz, C4. During these runs, the LDA classifier was adapted to the user after each trial. The inverse of the pooled covariance matrix (see Eq. 2) was updated for observation $x(t)$ using a recursive-least-square algorithm, (see [11] for more information):

$$\Sigma(t)^{-1} = \frac{1}{1 - UC} \left(\Sigma(t-1)^{-1} - \frac{v(t) \cdot v^\top(t)}{\frac{1-UC}{UC} + x^\top(t) \cdot v(t)} \right) \tag{5}$$

where $v(t) = \Sigma^{-1}(t-1) \cdot x(t)$. Note, the term $x^\top(t) \cdot v(t)$ is a scalar and no costly matrix inversion is needed. In Eq. 5, UC stands for update coefficient and is a small number between 0 and 1. For the present study, we chose $UC = 0.03$ based on a simulation using the data of the screening study. To estimate the class-specific adaptive mean $\mu_1(t)$ and $\mu_2(t)$ one can use an exponential moving average:

$$\mu_i(t) = (1 - UC) \cdot \mu_i(t-1) + UC \cdot x(t) \tag{6}$$

where i is the class of $x(t)$ and UC was chosen to be 0.05. Note that the class-mean estimation is done in a supervised manner.

3.2   Methods for Level 2 (Runs 2-3)

On the data of run 1, and for each of the three class combinations, a subject-specific narrow band was chosen automatically ([13]). For this frequency band six Laplacian channels were selected according to their discriminability, which was quantified by a robust variant of the Fisher score (mean replaced by median). The selection of the positions was constraint such that two positions have been selected from each of the areas over left hand, right hand and foot. Due to the dimensionality of the features compared to the number of trials, the estimation of the covariance matrix that is needed for LDA was corrected by shrinkage ([15,16]). A classifier was trained on the resulting log band-power features, and the class combination producing best performance was chosen to be used during feedback for the rest of the session.

For the subsequent 2 runs and after each trial, the position of the Laplacians was reselected based on robust Fisher score of the channels. The features were the log band-power of the selected channels. More specifically, the channel selection and the classifier were recalculated after each trial using up to the last 100 trials.

The repeatedly selected Laplacian channels was included in order to provide flexibility with respect to spatial location of modulated brain activity. During these two runs the adaptation to the user was done again in a supervised way.

3.3   Methods for Level 3 (Runs 4-6)

Finally for the last 3 runs, CSP filters were calculated on the data of runs 2 to 3 and a classifier was trained on the resulting log band-power features. The bias of the classifier in Eq. 3 was adapted by updating the pooled mean μ after each trial with $UC = 0.05$. The update rule for the pooled mean was analogue to Eq. 6, but without distinction by class labels. Note that this adaptation scheme is unsupervised. For more information about unsupervised methods, see [14].

4   Results

Figure 1 displays the grand average of the feedback performance within each run (bar, the dots are groups of 20 trials), according to the Category of the participants (novice, Cat. III who reached the level criterion and Cat. III who could not reach the level criterion).

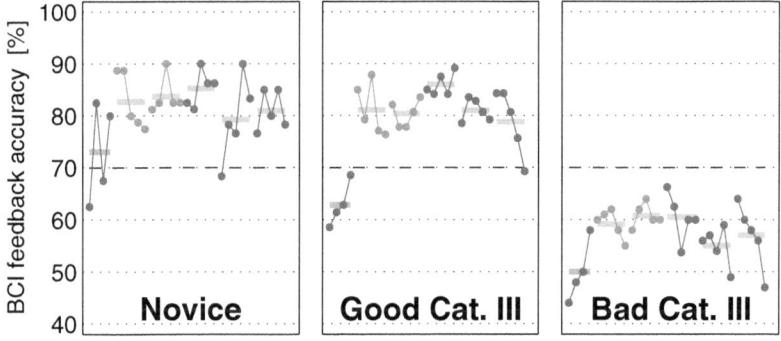

Fig. 1. Grand average of feedback performance within each run (horizontal bars and dots for each group of 20 trials) for novice participants (N=4), good performing Cat. III users (N=5) and bad performing Cat. III users (N=5). An accuracy of 70% is assumed to be a threshold required for BCI applications related to communication such as cursor control. Note that all runs of one volunteer have been recorded within one session.

All the runs of each volunteer have been recorded within just one experimental session. The goal of the study was to provide a proper training session that allowed an average performance of at least 70% of accuracy for two different types of users: completely novice (without any experience) and Cat. III (for whom no separability was possible before this experimental session). The level of 70% of accuracy was chosen according to [17], where 70% is assumed to be a threshold required for the control BCI applications related to communication, such as cursor control.

The session provided very good results for the four novice users, whose average performance was above 80% of accuracy during most of the experiment and always higher than 70 %, even during the first run. A significant hit rate increase is observed between

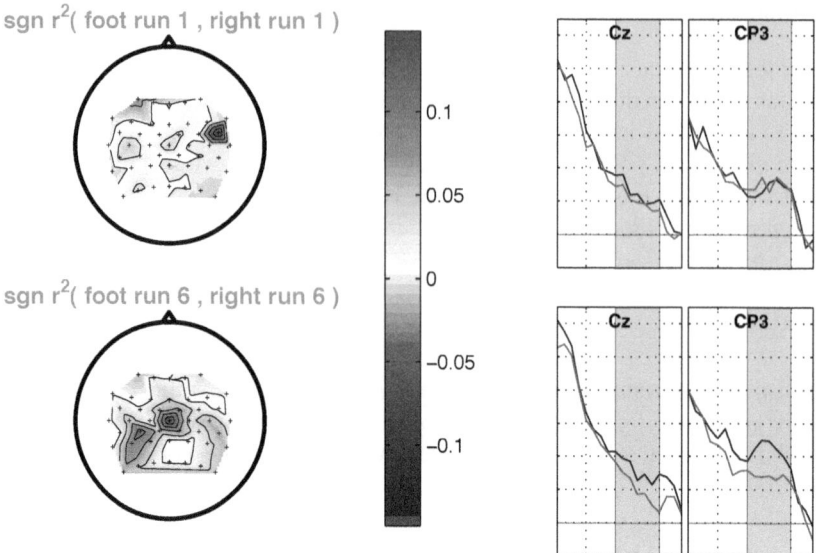

Fig. 2. Left top: r^2 of band power features during the first run. Right top: spectra of the two most discriminative channels at the beginning of the experiment. It corresponds to the picture on the Left top pattern. Left bottom: r^2 of band power features during the last run. Right bottom: spectra of the two most discriminative channels at the end of the experiment (run 6), they correspond to the Left bottom pattern. The classes used in the experiment were right hand and foot motor imagery. The band power was computed on the feedback band in the last 3 runs.

the first and the second runs, showing that the machine learning techniques we developed worked very effectively. During the last 3 runs, where unsupervised adaptation was applied, the performance of exhibited during previous runs was maintained.

Ten Cat. III users carried out the experimental session as well. Five of them reached the level criterion in the runs 2 or 3 and maintained it in the last three runs with unsupervised adaptation. For them, as for the novice users, machine learning techniques helped improving the performance, showing how advantageous they are. From the other five volunteers two of them were close to reach the criterion performance in the end of the experiment. Figure 2 shows how one of these participants could learn to modulate SMR rhythm. The performance of this user improved from 54% to 67% from the first to the last run, so we can hypothesize that further sessions could lead this subject to reach the criterion performance of 70%. The other 3 participants did unfortunately not improve during the session.

5   Conclusion

Machine Learning based BCIs use EEG features of larger complexity that can be fitted better to the individual characteristics of brain patterns of each user (see [9,13,18,1,19,20]). The down side of this approach is the need for an initial offline calibration. Furthermore, users are in a different mental state during offline calibration than during online feedback (cf. [7]), which renders the classifier that is optimized on the data of the calibration suboptimal and sometimes even non-functional for feedback (see [21,22] for a discussion of non-stationarities in BCI). Moreover, some users have difficulties to properly perform motor imagery for calibration due to the lack of feedback.

Here, we have presented a Machine Learning based brain-computer interfacing which overcomes these problems for a large percentage of users. It replaces the offline calibration by a "coadaptive calibration", in which the mental strategy of the user and the algorithm of the BCI system are jointly optimized. This approach leads completely novices users to achieve control of the system in just one session. In addition, at least a half of the Cat. III users, who could not gain BCI control in the classic Machine Learning approach, could achieve control within one session.

In short, machine learning based co-adaptive calibration is a promising new approach to broaden the applicability of BCI technology. From our results, at least the half of the users who suffered from BCI illiteracy before can now perform BCI experiments with a good level of control, and this within just one session. The question remains open whether operant conditioning or further sessions of co-adaptive calibration could provide BCI control to those users who remained without significant control in this study.

Acknowledgments. The studies were supported by TOBI FP7-224631, MU 987/3-1 and BFMBF 01GQ0850 and 01IB001A. This publication only reflects the authors' views.

References

1. Dornhege, G., del R. Millán, J., Hinterberger, T., McFarland, D., Müller, K.R. (eds.): Toward Brain-Computer Interfacing. MIT Press, Cambridge (2007)
2. Kübler, A., Kotchoubey, B., Kaiser, J., Wolpaw, J., Birbaumer, N.: Brain-computer communication: Unlocking the locked in. Psychol. Bull. 127(3), 358–375 (2001)
3. del R. Millán, J., Renkens, F., Mouriño, J., Gerstner, W.: Non-invasive brain-actuated control of a mobile robot by human EEG. IEEE Trans. Biomed. Eng. 51(6), 1026–1033 (2004)
4. Pfurtscheller, G., Neuper, C., Birbaumer, N.: Human Brain-Computer Interface. In: Riehle, A., Vaadia, E. (eds.) Motor Cortex in Voluntary Movements, pp. 367–401. CRC Press, New York (2005)
5. Wolpaw, J.R., Birbaumer, N., McFarland, D.J., Pfurtscheller, G., Vaughan, T.M.: Brain-computer interfaces for communication and control. Clin. Neurophysiol. 113(6), 767–791 (2002)
6. Dickhaus, T., Sannelli, C., Müller, K.R., Curio, G., Blankertz, B.: Predicting BCI performance to study BCI illiteracy. BMC Neuroscience 2009 10(Suppl. 1), 84 (2009) (in Press)
7. Shenoy, P., Krauledat, M., Blankertz, B., Rao, R.P.N., Müller, K.R.: Towards adaptive classification for BCI. J. Neural Eng. 3(1), 13–23 (2006)
8. Vidaurre, C., Blankertz, B.: Towards a cure for BCI illiteracy: Machine-learning based co-adaptive learning. Brain Topography (2009) (open access)
9. Blankertz, B., Dornhege, G., Krauledat, M., Müller, K.R., Curio, G.: The non-invasive Berlin Brain-Computer Interface: Fast acquisition of effective performance in untrained subjects. Neuroimage 37(2), 539–550 (2007)

10. Blankertz, B., Losch, F., Krauledat, M., Dornhege, G., Curio, G., Müller, K.R.: The Berlin Brain-Computer Interface: Accurate performance from first-session in BCI-naive subjects. IEEE Trans. Biomed. Eng. 55(10), 2452–2462 (2008)
11. Vidaurre, C., Schlögl, A., Cabeza, R., Scherer, R., Pfurtscheller, G.: A fully on-line adaptive BCI. IEEE Trans. Biomed. Eng. 53(6), 1214–1219 (2006)
12. McFarland, D.J., McCane, L.M., David, S.V., Wolpaw, J.R.: Spatial filter selection for EEG-based communication. Electroencephalogr Clin. Neurophysiol. 103, 386–394 (1997)
13. Blankertz, B., Tomioka, R., Lemm, S., Kawanabe, M., Müller, K.R.: Optimizing spatial filters for robust EEG single-trial analysis. IEEE Signal Process. Mag. 25(1), 41–56 (2008)
14. Vidaurre, C., Schlögl, A., Blankertz, B., Kawanabe, M., Müller, K.R.: Unsupervised adaptation of the LDA classifier for Brain-Computer Interfaces. In: Proceedings of the 4th International Brain-Computer Interface Workshop and Training Course 2008, pp. 122–127. Verlag der Technischen Universität Graz (2008)
15. Ledoit, O., Wolf, M.: A well-conditioned estimator for large-dimensional covariance matrices. J. Multivar Anal. 88, 365–411 (2004)
16. Vidaurre, C., Krämer, N., Blankertz, B., Schlögl, A.: Time domain parameters as a feature for eeg-based brain computer interfaces. Neural Networks 22, 1313–1319 (2009)
17. Kübler, A., Neumann, N., Wilhelm, B., Hinterberger, T., Birbaumer, N.: Predictability of brain-computer communication. Int. J. Psychophysiol. 18(2-3), 121–129 (2004)
18. Dornhege, G., Blankertz, B., Curio, G., Müller, K.R.: Boosting bit rates in non-invasive EEG single-trial classifications by feature combination and multi-class paradigms. IEEE Trans. Biomed. Eng. 51(6), 993–1002 (2004)
19. Müller, K.R., Anderson, C.W., Birch, G.E.: Linear and non-linear methods for brain-computer interfaces. IEEE Trans. Neural Syst. Rehabil. Eng. 11(2), 165–169 (2003)
20. Müller, K.R., Tangermann, M., Dornhege, G., Krauledat, M., Curio, G., Blankertz, B.: Machine learning for real-time single-trial EEG-analysis: From brain-computer interfacing to mental state monitoring. J. Neurosci. Methods 167(1), 82–90 (2008)
21. Sugiyama, M., Krauledat, M., Müller, K.R.: Covariate shift adaptation by importance weighted cross validation. Journal of Machine Learning Research 8, 1027–1061 (2007)
22. von Bünau, P., Meinecke, F.C., Király, F., Müller, K.R.: Finding stationary subspaces in multivariate time series. Physical Review Letters 103, 214101 (2009)

Analysing the Low Quality of the Data in Lighting Control Systems*

Jose R. Villar[1], Enrique de la Cal[1],
Javier Sedano[2], and Marco García-Tamargo[1]

[1] Computer Science Department, University of Oviedo, Campus de Viesques s/n
33204 Gijón (Spain)
{villarjose,delacal,marco}@uniovi.es
[2] Instituto Tecnológico de Castilla y León, Lopez Bravo 70, Pol. Ind. Villalonquéjar
09001 Burgos (Spain)
javier.sedano@itcl.es

Abstract. Energy efficiency represents one of the main challenges in the engineering field, i.e., by means of decreasing the energy consumption due to a better design minimising the energy losses. This is particularly true in real world processes in the industry or in business, where the elements involved generate data full of noise and biases. In other fields as lighting control systems, the emergence of new technologies, as the Ambient Intelligence can be, degrades the quality data introducing linguistic values. The presence of low quality data in Lighting Control Systems is introduced through an experimentation step, in order to realise the improvement in energy efficiency that its of managing could afford. In this contribution we propose, as a future work, the use of the novel genetic fuzzy system approach to obtain classifiers and models able to deal with the above mentioned problems.

1 Introduction

Energy Efficiency represents a big challange in different engineering fields as electric energy distribution [11], efficient design and operation [9], modeling and simulation [3], etc. In general, multi-agent architecture and the distribution among the intelligent devices of the control and the optimisation of the decisions may improve the energy efficiency [18]. In what follows, the field of lighting control systems will be analysed for the sake of simplicity, although the main conclusions can be extended to any other area.

In a lighting control system (see Fig. 1), the lighting system controller is the software responsible for co-ordinating the different islands and for integrating the information from the Building Management Systems (BMS). In each island, a controller establishes the operation conditions of all the controlled ballasts according to the sensor measurements and the operation conditions given by the lighting system controller.

---

* This research work is been funded by Gonzalez Soriano, S.A. by means of the the CN-08-028-IE07-60 FICYT research project and by Spanish M. of Science and Technology, under the grant TIN2008-06681-C06-04.

M. Graña Romay et al. (Eds.): HAIS 2010, Part I, LNAI 6076, pp. 421–428, 2010.

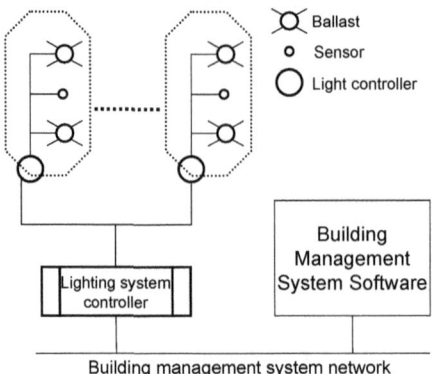

Fig. 1. The schema of a lighting control system. Each island includes a closed loop controller with the controlled gears, the luminosity sensors, the presence sensors, etc. The lighting system controller is the responsible of co-ordinating the islands.

The lighting control systems have been studied in depth: simulation issues [3], sensor processing and data improvement [4], the effect of daylight in the energy efficiency [7]. Moreover, the improvement in the energy efficiency and its measurement have been analysed in [7,9].

Nevertheless, the meta-information in the data gathered from processes is rarely used, and it is mainly related to non stochastic noise. This meta-information related with the low quality data can also be due to the precision of the sensors and to the emergence of new technologies such as Ambient Intelligence and the user profiles. In our opinion, the use of Genetic Fuzzy Systems (GFS) could improve the issues related with energy sharing and efficiency in distributed systems. We propose using the GFS able to deal with the meta-information to achieve better energy efficiency results.

In this research we show how the uncertainty in real world problems can be observed, specifically, in lighting systems. We propose the use of a novel method for learning GFS with low quality data for improving the energy efficiency in distributed systems taking advantage of the meta-data due to low quality data. The remainder of this manuscript is as follows. Firstly, a review of the literature concerned with considering the low quality data in modeling and in designing indexes is shown. Then, it will be shown the uncertainties in real world problems like the simulation of lighting control systems. Finally, some conclusions in how to manage such low quality data are presented.

2   Issues in Low Quality Data Management

The need for algorithms able to face low quality data is a well-known fact in the literature. Several studies have presented the decrease in the performance of crisp algorithms as uncertainty in data increases [5].

On the other hand, [10] analyses the complexity nature of the data sets in order to choose the better Fuzzy Rule Based System. Several measures are proposed to deal with the complexity of the data sets and the Ishibuchi fuzzy hybrid genetic machine learning method is used to test the validity of the measures. This research also concludes in the need to extend the proposed measures to deal with low quality data.

With low quality data we refer to the data sampled in presence of non stochastic noise or obtained with imprecise sensors. It is worth noting that all the sensors and industrial instrumentation can be regarded as low quality data. In our opinion, one of the most successful researches in soft computing dealing with low quality data is detailed in [2,13]. In these works the mathematical basis for designing vague data awareness genetic fuzzy systems -both classifiers and models- is shown. The low quality data are assumed as fuzzy data, where each $\alpha-$cut represents an interval value for each data.

Finally, it is worth pointing out that the fitness functions to train classifiers and models are also fuzzy valued functions when faced with low quality data. Hence the learning algorithms should be adapted to such fitness functions [16]. The ideas and principles previously shown have been used in several applications with low quality data, with both realistic and real world data sets. [14,15,19].

3 Low Quality Data in Lighting Systems and the Energy Efficiency

Lighting control systems aim to set the electric power consumption for the ballast in the installation so the luminance accomplishes with the regulations. In such systems, the luminance is measure through light sensors. Variables as the presence of inhabitants are also used in lighting control systems. Even though there are more variables, the relevance of the former is higher as it is used as the feedback in the lighting control loop. Nevertheless, the output of such sensors is highly dependant of the sunlight, the magnitude varies from one sensor to other, the repeatability is a compromise, etc. Consequently, the output of the sensors is usually filtered and then used as the feedback of the control loop, always as a crisp value.

Simulation of lighting systems has been widely studied, mainly to improve the energy efficiency [3,7]. A lighting system simulation needs to simulate the light measured in a room when a total electric power is applied for lighting. A simulation will use models to estimate the response of the light sensors. The main objective in simulation is to set and tune PID controllers for light control systems.

As before, the measurements from light sensors are considered crisp values, and so the inputs and the outputs of the light sensor models. To our knowledge, no model has been obtained including the meta-information due to low quality data and, thus, the effect of the daylight and other variables are introduced artificially -i.e., by considering such information within the input data set.

Let us consider one simple case. Let us suppose the simulation of the lighting system shown in Fig. 2, where there is a simple room with one light sensor installed and the light gears accomplishing the regulations. Where to fix the light sensor is of great significance as the shorter the distance from the light sensor to the windows the higher the daylight influence in the light measurements. On the other hand, the daylight should be estimated from the inner light sensors when no daylight sensors are available.

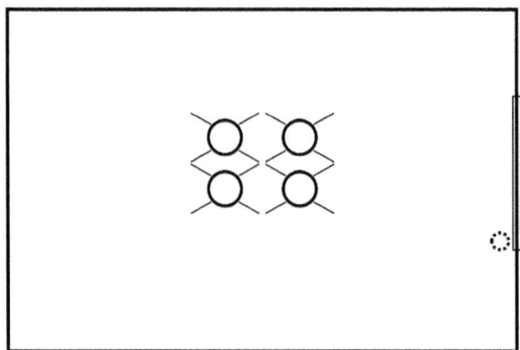

Fig. 2. The lighting system to simulate. Different places for the light sensor are proposed. The light measured will differ from one case to another.

Let us suppose the light sensor installed next to the window, with the light sensor being a LDR (light dependant resistor). Let us also consider a lighting control system that allows regulations on the electric power for lighting, so it is possible to introduce several steps, say 0%, 33%, 66% and 100% of the total power installed. Finally, there was a blind that could be opened or closed. In this scenario, several experiments were carried out. In all of them, the controlled variable was the percentage of electric power for lighting and the output from the light sensor (as a voltage value) was sampled.

The first experiment was the step response increasing and decreasing the controlled variable with the blind closed, measuring the light sensor output. This experiment was carried twice for each sensor, and repeated for five different sensors. In Fig. 3 the results are presented. As can be seen, the measurements are highly dependant of the sensor itself, but also the hysteresis behaviour can be perceived. In all the figures normalised values are presented for the sake of clearness.

Anyway, this is a measure linear with the resistance of the LDR, but what about the luminance? To calculate the lluminance $R = C_0 \cdot L^{-\gamma}$ applies, where R is the measured resistance, C_0 and γ are constants for each LDR. LDR's are characterised with a range of possible values of resistance for a luminance of 10 lux (R_{10}). In case of the ones used in the experiments, R_{10} varies from $[8, 20]k\Omega$ and γ is 0.85, typically. Thus, given a sensor, a minimum and a maximum of the luminance can be obtained if a resistance value is measure (see Fig. 4). And for the up/down step responses there is a wide margin of possible values of the luminance as shown in Fig. 5.

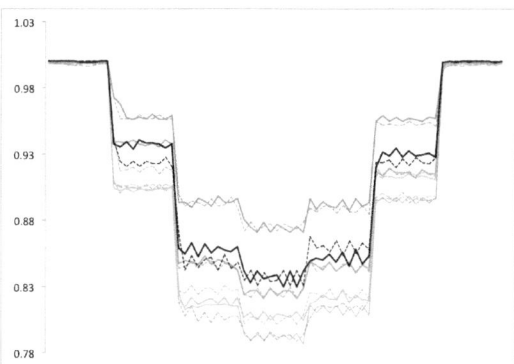

Fig. 3. The normalised output of the different light sensors. The up/down cycle was repeated twice for each one, so the dashed lines corresponds to the second run. Ten samples were consider for each step. No transient was considered, the sample rate was 1 sample/second.

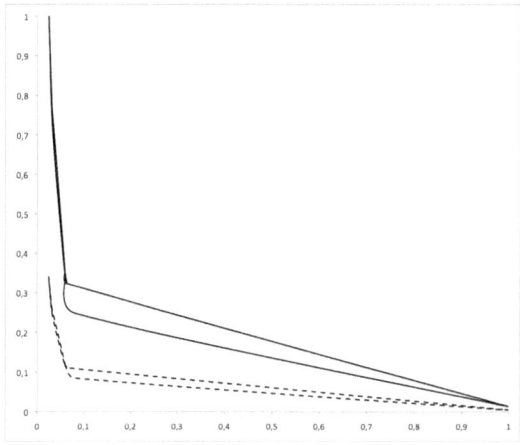

Fig. 4. The resistance against the luminance for the minimum and maximum bounds, both variables in percentage of their maximum value. A measurement of resistance corresponds with an interval of luminance. I.e., if $r = 0.6$ induces a luminance in the range $[\sim 0.04, \sim 0.15]\%$, where the hysteresis does not allow to establish the exact values of luminance.

The second experiment includes the opening of the blind. Three positions were consider: totally close, half open and totally open. With the same characteristics as in the first experiment, the step responses for the up/down sequence for one of the sensors is shown in Fig. 6 and Fig. 7.

As can be seen, there is an evidence that light controllers can not be optimum, thus the energy efficiency in lighting control systems can be improved if such low

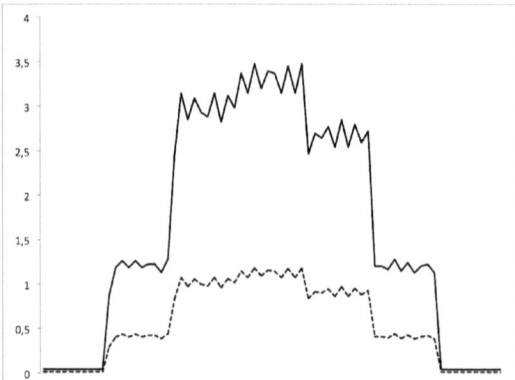

Fig. 5. The minimum and maximum values of luminance for the step responses. It can be seen that for the same power level different luminance values can be calculated using the sensor datasheet. Again, it can be seen the response lacks of hysteresis.

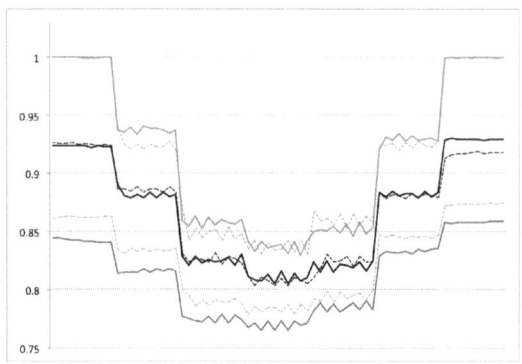

Fig. 6. The normalised output of the light sensors for different blind positions. The up/down cycle was reapeted twice for each one, so the dashed lines corresponds to the second run. Ten samples were consider for each step. No transient was considered, the sample rate was 1 sample/second.

quality data is considered. Specifically, the use of the methodology using classical control theory proposed by different authors as [3] may not be the best choose. In our opinion, the use of GFS to obtain models for simulation of lighting systems would help in the integration of the meta-information. The use of GFS allows determining behaviour laws and interpretability of the phenomena. Moreover, if low quality data is included in obtaining the models of the sensors the controllers would be robust to such variability.

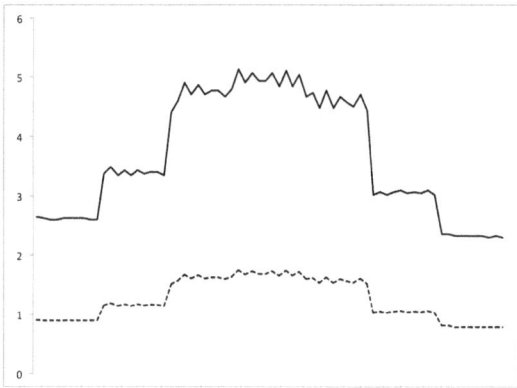

Fig. 7. The minimum and maximum values of luminance for the step responses when the blind is totally opened for a stormy weather day

4 Conclusions

Improving the energy efficiency represents a challenge in the real world applications, especially distributed systems within building management systems. The higher the human interaction in field the higher relevance of intelligent techniques that consider the meta-information and interpretability. Meta-information refers to the information that is present in a process but rarely considered, such as the data non-stochastic noise or the sensor precision and calibration, but also the ambiguity in the linguistic and crisp data. Meta-information can be presented as low quality data.

GFS have been found valid in energy efficiency, but have also been extended to manage interval and fuzzy data. Interval and fuzzy data are mechanisms to represent the low quality data. In this work the extended GFS to manage fuzzy data is proposed to be used in the energy efficiency improvement. To illustrate the idea, the uncertainty in the luminance measurements from light sensors is analysed. We expect that fuzzy data awareness GFS will outperform the modeling and simulation process, so better controllers can be obtained.

References

1. Bernal-Agustín, J.L., Dufo-López, R.: Techno-economical optimization of the production of hydrogen from PV-Wind systems connected to the electrical grid. Renewable Energy 35(4), 747–758 (2010)
2. Couso, I., Sánchez, L.: Higher order models for fuzzy random variables. Fuzzy Sets and Systems 159, 237–258 (2008)
3. de Keyser, R., Ionescu, C.: Modelling and simulation of a lighting control system. Simulation Modelling Practice and Theory (2009), doi:10.1016/j.simpat.2009.10.003

4. Doulos, L., Tsangrassoulis, A., Topalis, F.V.: The role of spectral response of photosensors in daylight responsive systems. Energy and Buildings 40(4), 588–599 (2008)
5. Folleco, A.A., Khoshgoftaar, T.M., Van Hulse, J., Napolitano, A.: Identifying Learners Robust to Low Quality Data. Informatica 33, 245–259 (2009)
6. Gligor, A., Grif, H., Oltean, S.: Considerations on an Intelligent Buildings Management System for an Optimized Energy Consumption. In: Proceedings of the IEEE Conference on Automation, Quality and Testing, Robotics (2006)
7. Hviid, C.A., Nielsen, T.R., Svendsen, S.: Simple tool to evaluate the impact of daylight on building energy consumption. Solar Energy (2009), doi:10.1016/j.solener.2008.03.001
8. Houwing, M., Ajah, A.N., Heijnen, P.W., Bouwmans, I., Herder, P.M.: Uncertainties in the design and operation of distributed energy resources: The case of micro-CHP systems. Energy 33(10), 1518–1536 (2008)
9. Li, D.H.W., Cheung, K.L., Wong, S.L., Lam, T.N.T.: An analysis of energy-efficient light fittings and lighting controls. Applied Energy 87(2), 558–567 (2010)
10. Luengo, J., Herrera, F.: Domains of competence of fuzzy rule based classification systems with data complexity measures: A case of study using a fuzzy hybrid genetic based machine learning method. Fuzzy Sets and Systems 161, 3–19 (2010)
11. Martín, J.A., Gil, A.J.: A new heuristic approach for distribution systems loss reduction. Electric Power Systems Research 78(11), 1953–1958 (2008)
12. Qiao, B., Liu, K., Guy, C.: A Multi-Agent System for Building Control. In: IAT 2006: Proceedings of the IEEE/WIC/ACM international conference on Intelligent Agent Technology, pp. 653–659. IEEE Computer Society, Los Alamitos (2006)
13. Sánchez, L., Couso, I.: Advocating the Use of Imprecisely Observed Data in Genetic Fuzzy Systems. IEEE Transactions on Fuzzy Systems 15(4), 551–562 (2007)
14. Sánchez, L., Otero, J.: Learning Fuzzy Linguistic Models from Low Quality Data by Genetic Algorithms. In: Proceedings of the IEEE Internacional Conference on Fuzzy Systems FUZZ-IEEE 2007 (2007)
15. Sánchez, L., Suárez, M.R., Villar, J.R., Couso, I.: Mutual Information-based Feature Selection and Fuzzy Discretization of Vague Data. Internacional Journal of Approximate Reasoning 49, 607–622 (2008)
16. Sánchez, L., Couso, I., Casillas, J.: Genetic Learning of Fuzzy Rules based on Low Quality Data. Fuzzy Sets and Systems (2009)
17. Villar, J.R., Pérez, R., de la Cal, E., Sedano, J.: Efficiency in Electrical Heating Systems: An MAS real World Application. In: Demazeau, Y., et al. (eds.) 7th International Conference on PAAMS 2009. AISC, vol. 55, pp. 460–469. Springer, Heidelberg (2009)
18. Villar, J.R., de la Cal, E., Sedano, J.: A fuzzy logic based efficient energy saving approach for domestic heating systems. Integrated Computer-Aided Engineering 16(2), 151–164 (2007)
19. Villar, J.R., Otero, A., Otero, J., Sánchez, L.: Taximeter verification with GPS and Soft Computing Techniques. SoftComputing 14(4), 405–418 (2010)

Type-1 Non-singleton Type-2 Takagi-Sugeno-Kang Fuzzy Logic Systems Using the Hybrid Mechanism Composed by a Kalman Type Filter and Back Propagation Methods

Gerardo M. Mendez[1], Angeles Hernández[2], Alberto Cavazos[3], and Marco-Tulio Mata-Jiménez[3]

[1] Instituto Tecnologico de Nuevo Leon, Department of Electrical and Electronics Engineering, Av. Eloy Cavazos 2001, Cd. Guadalupe, NL, CP 67170, Mexico
gmm_paper@yahoo.com.mx
[2] Instituto Tecnologico de Nuevo Leon, Department Bussineses Administration Sciences, Av. Eloy Cavazos 2001, Cd. Guadalupe, NL, CP 67170, Mexico
ahernandezr@yturria.com.mx
[3] Universidad Autónoma de Nuevo León, Av. Universidad S/N, 66450 San Nicolas de los Garza, NL, Mexico
acavazos@fime.uanl.mx

Abstract. This article presents a novel learning methodology based on the hybrid mechanism for training interval type-1 non-singleton type-2 Takagi-Sugeno-Kang fuzzy logic systems. As reported in the literature, the performance indexes of these hybrid models have proved to be better than the individual training mechanism when used alone. The proposed hybrid methodology was tested thru the modeling and prediction of the steel strip temperature at the descaler box entry as rolled in an industrial hot strip mill. Results show that the proposed method compensates better for uncertain measurements than previous type-2 Takagi-Sugeno-Kang hybrid learning or back propagation developments.

Keywords: IT2 TSK fuzzy logic systems, ANFIS, hybrid learning.

1 Introduction

In [1] both, one-pass and back-propagation (BP) methods are presented as interval type-2 (IT2) Mamdani Fuzzy Logic Systems (FLS) learning methods, but only BP is presented for IT2 Takagi-Sugeno-Kang (TSK) FLS systems. The one-pass method generates a set of IF-THEN rules by using the given training data one time, and combines the rules to construct the final FLS. When BP method is used in both Mamdani and TSK FLSs, none of antecedent and consequent parameters of the IT2 FLS is fixed at starting of training process; they are tuned using exclusively BP steepest descent method. In [1] hybrid learning algorithms, based on recursive parameter estimation methods such recursive least squares (RLS) or recursive Kalman type filter (REFIL) [2] are not presented as IT2 FLS learning mechanism.

M. Graña Romay et al. (Eds.): HAIS 2010, Part I, LNAI 6076, pp. 429–437, 2010.

The aim of this work is to present and discuss a BP-REFIL based hybrid-learning algorithm for antecedent and consequent parameters tuning during training process for interval type-1 non-singleton type-2 TSK FLS. Here such hybrid system will be abbreviated as IT2 NSFLS1 ANFIS after the Adaptive Neural Fuzzy Inference System which is a hybrid learning algorithm first introduced by J. S.-R. Jang [3] for TSK FLS, ANFIS will be described later. The abbreviation IT2 TSK NSFLS1 will be used for interval type-1 non-singleton type-2 TSK FLS systems with BP learning only. In this work IT2 NSFLS1 ANFIS will use training REFIL method for the forward pass while during the backward pass will use the BP method.

The hybrid algorithm for IT2 Mamdani FLS has been already presented elsewhere [2, 4-7] with three combinations of the learning method: RLS-BP, REFIL-BP and orthogonal least-squares-BP. The hybrid algorithm for singleton IT2 TSK SFLS (IT2 SFLS ANFIS) has been presented in [8, 9] with two combinations of the learning method: RLS-BP and REFIL-BP, whilst in [10, 11] the hybrid algorithm for IT2 NSFLS1 ANFIS has been presented only with the hybrid learning mechanism RLS-BP. Works on type-1 non-singleton IT2 TSK FLS using the REFIL-BP learning mechanisms have not been found in the literature.

In this work, the IT2 NSFLS1 ANFIS system with hybrid learning mechanism REFIL-BP has been developed and implemented for temperature prediction of the transfer bar at hot strip mill (HSM). In order to allow a straight comparison of performance, functionality and stability of the novel hybrid mechanism with previous work results the same data-set as in [7-10] was used. As mentioned, the intention of this paper is to present and discuss the hybrid-learning algorithm for antecedent and consequent parameters tuning during training process of IT2 NSFLS1 ANFIS with REFIL-BP hybrid mechanism, and to show its implementation in a real industrial application. Convergence and performance have been experimentally tested under the same conditions as previous works.

2 Proposed Methodology

Most of the HSM processes are highly uncertain, non-linear, time varying and non-stationary [2, 12], having very complex mathematical representations. IT2 NSFLS1 ANFIS takes easily the random and systematic components of type A or B standard uncertainty [13] of industrial measurements. The non-linearities are handled by FLS as identifiers and universal approximators of nonlinear dynamic systems [14-18]. Stationary and non-stationary additive noise is modeled as a Gaussian function centered at the measurement value [1].

The method IT2 SFLS ANFIS based on BP-RLS and BP-REFIL learning algorithm presented in [8, 9] and IT2 NSFLS1 ANFIS based on BP-RLS presented in [10. 11] has been used as a benchmark algorithm for parameter estimation or systems identification assessment [1]. However comparisons with BP only algorithms are also presented since this is a more standard method. As mentioned, works on IT2 NSFLS1 ANFIS approach has not been found in the literature.

2.1 Hybrid REFIL-BP Method in IT2 ANFIS Training

The IT2 TSK NSFLS1 (BP only) outputs are calculated during forward pass. During the backward pass, the error propagates backwards and the antecedent and consequent parameters are estimated using only the BP method.

The IT2 NSFLS1 ANFIS is trained using the hybrid mechanism, in this work it uses REFIL method during forward pass for tuning of consequent parameters as well as the BP method for tuning of antecedent parameters. It has the same training mechanism as the type-1 ANFIS [3, 19], using the RLS-BP hybrid combination.

The training method is presented as in [1]: Given N input-output training data pairs, the training algorithm for E training epochs, should minimize the error function:

$$e^{(t)} = \frac{1}{2}\left[f_{IT2-FLS}\left(\mathbf{x}^{(t)}\right) - y^{(t)}\right]^2 . \tag{1}$$

where e^t is the error function at time t, $f_{IT2-FLS}\left(\mathbf{x}^{(t)}\right)$ is the output of the IT2 FLS using the input vector $\mathbf{x}^{(t)}$ from the non-singleton type-1 input-output data pairs, and $y^{(t)}$ is the output from the non-singleton type-1 input-output data pairs.

3 Application to Transfer Bar Surface Temperature Prediction

3.1 Hot Strip Mill

The most critical process in the HSM is the Finishing Mill (FM). A model-based set-up system [20] calculates the FM initial working references needed to attain desired gauge, width and temperature at the FM exit stand. It takes as inputs: FM exit target gage, target width, target temperature, steel grade, hardness ratio from slab chemistry, load distribution, gauge offset, temperature offset, roll diameters, load distribution, transfer bar gauge, transfer bar width and bar entry temperature.

To calculate such working reference some rolling variables, as entry temperature, have to be known in advance. Therefore temperature, along with other variables, has to be predicted, and it is done from the Roughing Mill (RM) exit temperature, since this is the most reliable reading before the FM due to oxide layer formation [20]. According to the physical model existing in plant [20], the SB entry temperature is a function of the surface temperature measured at the exit of the RM (x_1), and the bar travelling time from the RM exit to the SB entry (x_2), being these the inputs to the IT2 NSF-1 ANFIS developed here to estimate the SB entry temperature (y).

3.2 Design of the IT2 NSFLS1 ANFIS

The architecture of the IT2 NSFLS1 ANFIS is established such that its parameters are continuously optimized. The number of rule-antecedents is fixed to two, one for the RM exit surface temperature (x_1), and one for transfer bar head traveling time (x_2). Each antecedent-input space is divided into three fuzzy sets (FSs); using all possible combination a total number of nine rules are formulated.

3.3 Input-Output Data Pairs

From an industrial HSM, noisy non-singleton type-1 input-output pairs of three different product types were collected and used as training and checking data. The inputs are the noisy measured RM exit surface temperature and the measured RM exit to SB entry transfer bar traveling time. The output is the noisy measured SB entry surface temperature.

3.4 Fuzzy Rule Base

The IT2 NSF1 ANFIS fuzzy rule base consists of a set of IF-THEN rules that represents the model of the system. The IT2 NSFLS1 ANFIS system has two inputs $x_1 \in X_1$, $x_2 \in X_2$ and one output $y \in Y$. The rule base has $M = 9$ rules of the form:

$$R^i : IF \quad x_1 \quad is \quad \tilde{F}_1^i \quad and \quad x_2 \quad is \quad \tilde{F}_2^i, \quad THEN \quad Y^i = C_0^i + C_1^i x_1 + C_2^i x_2 \tag{2}$$

where $\tilde{F}_1^i$ and $\tilde{F}_2^i$ are the antecedent's membership functions, Y^i the output of the ith rule is a fuzzy type-1 set, and the parameters C_j^i, with $i = 1,2,3,...,9$ and $j = 0,1,2$, are the consequent type-1 FSs.

3.5 Non-singleton Input Membership Functions

The primary MFs for each input of the IT2 NSFLS1 ANFIS are Gaussian functions of the form:

$$\mu_{X_k}(x_k) = \exp\left[-\frac{1}{2}\left[\frac{x_k - x_k'}{\sigma_k}\right]^2\right]. \tag{3}$$

where: $\sigma_k \in [\sigma_1, \sigma_2]$ $k=1,2$ (the number of type-1 non-singleton inputs), and $\mu_{Xk}(x_k)$ centered at the measured input $x_k = x'_k$.

3.6 Antecedent Membership Functions

The primary MFs for each antecedent $\tilde{F}_1^i$ and $\tilde{F}_2^i$ are FSs described by Gaussian functions with uncertain means:

$$\mu_k^i(x_k) = \exp\left[-\frac{1}{2}\left[\frac{x_k - m_k^i}{\sigma_k^i}\right]^2\right]. \tag{4}$$

where $m_k^i \in \left[m_{k1}^i, m_{k2}^i\right]$ is the uncertain mean, with $k = 1,2$ (the number of antecedents) and $i = 1,2,..9$ (the number of M rules), and σ_k^i is the standard deviation.

3.7 Consequent Membership Functions

Each consequent is an unnormalized interval type-2 TSK FLS with $Y^i = \left[y_l^i, y_r^i \right]$ where

$$y_l^i = \sum_{j=1}^{p} c_j^i x_j + c_0^i - \sum_{j=1}^{p} \left| x_j \right| s_j^i - s_0^i . \tag{5}$$

and

$$y_r^i = \sum_{j=1}^{p} c_j^i x_j + c_0^i + \sum_{j=1}^{p} \left| x_j \right| s_j^i + s_0^i . \tag{6}$$

both, are unnormalized type-1 TSK FLS, where c_j^i denotes the center (mean) of C_j^i as given in eq. (2) and s_j^i denotes the spread of C_j^i, with $i = 1,2,3,..,9$, $j = 0,1, \ldots$ p, and $p = 2$, the number of inputs variables.

4 Application Results

The IT2 NSFLS1 ANFIS system with hybrid REFIL-BP learning was trained and used to predict the SB entry temperature. Fifty epochs of training were run, one hundred and twenty six attempts of parameter tuning are performed, fourteen parameters per each one of the nine rules; using eighty seven, sixty eight and twenty eight input-output training data pairs per epoch, for type A, type B and type C products respectively. The parameters shown in Table 1 and Table 2 are for all the 9 rules.

Table 1. Gaussian's fuzzy set parameters from statistical analysis of x_1 input training data

m_{11}	m_{12}	σ_1
$^\circ C$	$^\circ C$	$^\circ C$
950	952	60
1016	1018	60
1080	1082	60

Table 2. Gaussian's fuzzy set parameters from statistical analysis of x_2 input training data

m_{21}	m_{22}	σ_2
s	s	s
32	34	10
42	44	10
56	58	10

The performance evaluation for the hybrid IT2 NSFLS1 ANFIS system was based on root mean-squared error (RMSE) criteria as in [1].

Fig. 1 shows the RMSEs of two non-hybrid IT2 TSK with BP learning only: IT2 TSK SFLS, and IT2 TSK NSFLS1 for type C products.

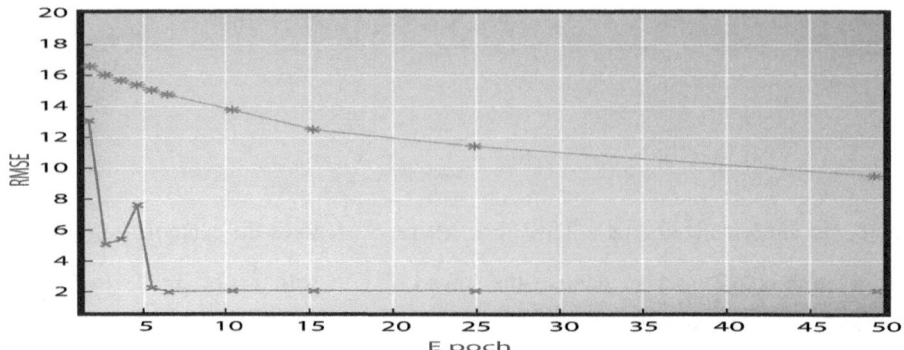

Fig. 1. (*) RMSE IT2 TSK SFLS (BP) (+) RMSE IT2 TSK NSFLS1 (BP)

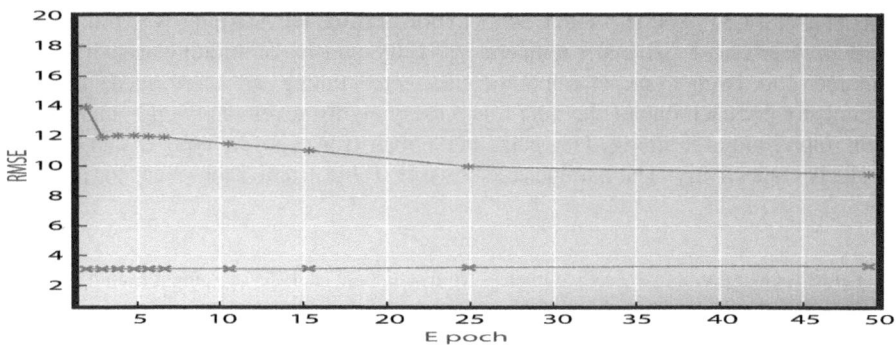

Fig. 2. (*) RMSE IT2 SFLS ANFIS (RLS-BP) (+) RMSE IT2 NSFLS1 ANFIS (RLS-BP)

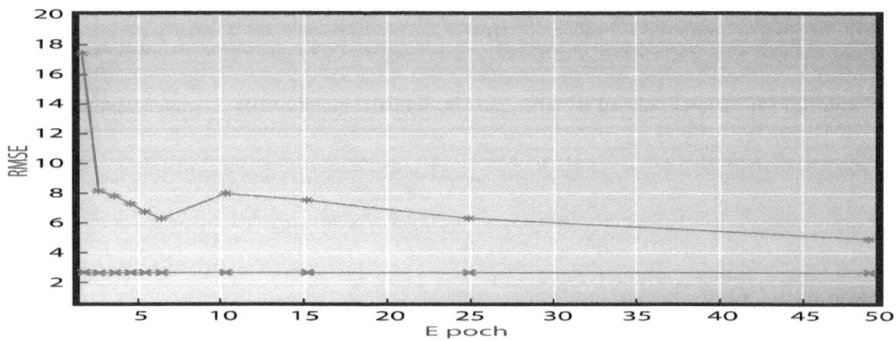

Fig. 3. (*) RMSE IT2 SFLS ANFIS (REFIL-BP) (+) RMSE IT2 NSFLS1 ANFIS (REFIL-BP)

Fig. 2 shows the RMSEs of two IT2 TSK ANFIS systems trained using the hybrid RLS-BP algorithm: IT2 SFLS ANFIS, and the IT2 NSFLS1 ANFIS. Fig. 2 also shows the results for type C products. Observe that from epoch 1 the IT2 NSFLS1 ANFIS has better performance than the IT2 SFLS ANFIS. At epoch 1, the RMSE of the IT2 SFLS ANFIS has a poor performance. At epoch 25, it reaches its minimum RMSE and is stable for the rest of the training epochs.

Fig. 3 shows the RMSEs of two IT2 TSK ANFIS systems trained using the proposed hybrid REFIL-BP algorithm, for type C products. For this experiment, the IT2 NSFLS1 ANFIS has better performance than IT2 SFLS ANFIS for the whole period of training. When compared to the IT2 TSK NSFLS1 (BP), and IT2 NSFLS1 ANFIS (RLS-BP) systems, the proposed hybrid approach IT2 NSFLS1 ANFIS (REFIL-BP) although was slightly over-performed after fifty epochs, it was proved to be better for temperature prediction in the first four epochs of training, an important characteristic for computational intelligent systems when there is a chance of only one epoch of training. However, it is required to emphasize that all IT2 ANFIS systems used are very sensitive to the values of learning parameter's gain.

Table 3 shows the RMSEs of six IT2 TSK systems for type C products using the same input-output data pair. The IT2 NSFLS1 ANFIS using the hybrid mechanism (REFIL-BP) shows the minimum prediction error in the testing phase.

Table 3. RMSEs of six IT2 TSK systems tested using the same input-otput data pair of type C materials

IT2 TSK FL system	Prediction error $^\circ C$
IT2 TSK SFLS (BP)	10.87
IT2 TSK NSFLS1 (BP)	3.26
IT2 SFLS ANFIS (RLS-BP)	8.71
IT2 NSFLS1 ANFIS (RLS-BP)	5.28
IT2 SFLS ANFIS (RLS-BP)	5.02
IT2 NSFLS1 ANFIS (RLS-BP)	3.25

5 Conclusions

An IT2 NSFLS1 ANFIS using the hybrid REFIL-BP training method was tested and compared for SB entry surface temperature prediction of the transfer bar. The antecedent MFs and consequent centroids of the IT2 NSFLS1 ANFIS absorbed the uncertainty introduced by all the factors: the antecedent and consequent initially values, the noisy temperature measurements, and the inaccurate traveling time estimation.

It has been shown that the proposed IT2 NSFLS1 ANFIS system can be applied in modeling of the steel coil temperature. It has also been envisaged its application in any uncertain and non-linear system prediction and control

The proposed hybrid IT2 NSFLS1 ANFIS (REFIL-BP) system has the best performance and stability for the first four epochs of training: an important characteristic for computational intelligent systems when there is a chance of only one epoch of training.

References

1. Mendel, J.M.: Uncertain Rule Based Fuzzy Logic Systems: Introduction and New Directions. Prentice-Hall, Upper Saddle River (2001)
2. Mendez, G.M., Cavazos, A., Soto, R., Leduc, L.: Entry Temperature Prediction of a Hot Strip Mill by Hybrid Learning Type-2 FLS. Jour. of Intell. and Fuz. Sys. 17, 583–596 (2006)
3. Jang, J.-S.R., Sun, C.-T.: Neuro-fuzzy Modeling and Control. The Proceedings of the IEEE 3, 378–406 (1995)
4. Mendez, G.M., Cavazos, A., Leduc, L., Soto, R.: Hot Strip Mill Temperature Prediction Using Hybrid Learning Interval Singleton Type-2 FLS. In: Proceedings of the IASTED International Conference on Modeling and Simulation, pp. 380–385 (2003)
5. Mendez, G.M., Cavazos, A., Leduc, L., Soto, R.: Modeling of a Hot Strip Mill Temperature Using Hybrid Learning for Interval Type-1 and Type-2 Non-singleton Type-2 FLS. In: Proceedings of the IASTED International Conference on Artificial Intelligence and Applications, pp. 529–533 (2003)
6. Mendez, G.M., Juarez, I.L.: Orthogonal-back Propagation Hybrid Learning Algorithm for Interval Type-1 Non-singleton Type-2 Fuzzy Logic Systems. WSEAS Trans. on Sys. 3-4, 212–218 (2005)
7. Mendez, G.M., De los Angeles Hernandez, M.: Hybrid Learning for Interval Type-2 Fuzzy Systems Based on Orthogonal Least-squares and Back-propagation Methods. Inf. Scien. 179, 2157–3146 (2009)
8. Mendez, G.M., Castillo, O.: Interval Type-2 TSK Fuzzy Logic Systems Using Hybrid Learning Algorithm. In: The IEEE international Conference on Fuzzy Systems, pp. 230–235 (2005)
9. Mendez, G.M., Juarez, I.L.: First-order Interval Type-2 TSK Fuzzy Logic Systems Using a Hybrid Learning Algorithm. WSEAS Trans. on Comp. 4, 378–384 (2005)
10. Mendez, G.M.: Interval Type-1 Non-singleton Type-2 TSK Fuzzy Logic Systems Using the Hybrid Training Method RLS-BP. In: Analysis and Design of Intelligent Systems Using Soft Computing Techniques, pp. 36–44. Springer, Heidelberg (2007)

11. Mendez, G.M., de los Angeles Hernandez, M.: Interval Type-2 ANFIS. In: Innovations in Hybrid Intelligent Systems, pp. 64–71. Springer, Heidelberg (2007)
12. Lee, D.Y., Cho, H.S.: Neural Network Approach to the Control of the Plate Width in Hot Plate Mills. International Joint Conference on Neural Networks 5, 3391–3396 (1999)
13. Taylor, B.N., Kuyatt, B.: Guidelines for Evaluating and Expressing the Uncertainty of NIST Measurement Results, NIST Technical Note 1297 (1994)
14. Wang, L.-X.: Fuzzy Systems are Universal Approximators. In: Proceedings of the IEEE Conf. on Fuzzy Systems, pp. 1163–1170 (1992)
15. Wang, L.-X., Mendel, J.M.: Back-propagation Fuzzy Systems as Nonlinear Dynamic System Identifiers. In: Proceedings of the IEEE Conf. on Fuzzy Systems, pp. 1409–1418 (1992)
16. Wang, L.-X.: Fuzzy Systems are Universal Approximators. In: Proceedings of the IEEE Conf. on Fuzzy Systems, San Diego, pp. 1163–1170 (1992)
17. Wang, L.-X.: A Course in Fuzzy Systems and Control. Prentice Hall PTR, Upper Saddle River (1997)
18. Liang, Q.J., Mendel, J.M.: Interval Type-2 Fuzzy Logic Systems: Theory and Design. Trans. Fuzzy Systems 8, 535–550 (2000)
19. Jang, J.-S.R., Sun, C.-T., Mizutani, E.: Neuro-fuzzy and Soft Computing: A Computational Approach to Learning and Machine Intelligence. Prentice-Hall, Upper Saddle River (1997)
20. GE Models, Users reference 1, Roanoke VA (1993)

An Hybrid Architecture Integrating Forward Rules with Fuzzy Ontological Reasoning

Stefano Bragaglia, Federico Chesani, Anna Ciampolini, Paola Mello,
Marco Montali, and Davide Sottara

University of Bologna, V.le Risorgimento 2 - Bologna, Italy
`name.surname@unibo.it`

Abstract. In recent years there has been a growing interest in the combination of rules and ontologies. Notably, many works have focused on the theoretical aspects of such integration, sometimes leading to concrete solutions. However, solutions proposed so far typically reason upon crisp concepts, while concrete domains require also fuzzy expressiveness.

In this work we combine mature technologies, namely the Drools business rule management system, the Pellet OWL Reasoner and the FuzzyDL system, to provide a unified framework for supporting fuzzy reasoning. After extending the Drools framework (language and engine) to support uncertainty reasoning upon rules, we have integrated it with custom operators that (*i*) exploit Pellet to perform ontological reasoning, and (*ii*) exploit FuzzyDL to support fuzzy ontological reasoning.

As a case study, we consider a decision-support system for the tourism domain, where ontologies are used to formally describe package tours, and rules are exploited to evaluate the consistency of such packages.

Topics: Fuzzy Reasoning, Rule-based Reasoning, Rules Integration with Ontologies, Decision Support Systems, eTourism.

1 Introduction

In the recent years there has been a growing interest in the combination of rules and ontologies. Notably, many works have focused on the theoretical aspects of such integration, sometimes leading to concrete solutions (e.g., [1,2,3,4,5,6]). However, solutions proposed so far typically reason upon crisp concepts, while concrete domains require also fuzzy expressiveness.

At the same time, some initiatives emerged in the last few years to implement fuzzy reasoning in both the context of ontology reasoning [7], and in the context of rule-based reasoning [8,9].

From a methodological viewpoint, the integration between the various forms of reasoning (ontological, rule-based and fuzzy-like) has been researched following two diverse approaches: *tight integration* vs. *loose integration*. The former aims to provide a single, comprehensive theoretical framework accounting for the various reasoning tasks (hence a unified language and semantics). The latter approach instead simply focuses on combining the different technologies available, to provide a functioning tool able to cope with the requirements.

M. Graña Romay et al. (Eds.): HAIS 2010, Part I, LNAI 6076, pp. 438–445, 2010.

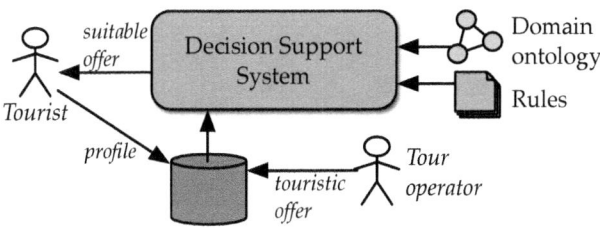

Fig. 1. Architecture of a touristic decision support system, combining ontologies with rules

In this work we focus on the integration of such diverse reasoning tasks, namely ontological, rule-base and fuzzy reasoning, following a *loose integration* approach. To this end, we have selected a set of mature technologies and, where necessary, we have properly extended them to achieve such integration.

As a case study, we consider a decision-support system (DSS) for the tourism domain, where ontologies are used to formally describe package tours, and rules are exploited to evaluate the consistency of such packages and their applicability to possible customers, as in Figure 1. The aim of our DSS is to support business tourism operators when evaluating which packages are suitable and consistent with possible customers. In this sense, the DSS helps to categorize both the customers (into a set of possible customer profiles) and the packages, and provides a matching degree between the profiles and the packages. In such scenario, two distinct kinds of knowledge come into play:

- *Ontological knowledge*, to model in a clear and unambiguous way the entities composing the tourism domain, as well as their relationships and categories.
- *(forward) Rules*, to formalize the "operational" knowledge exploited by the business operators when evaluating packages vs. customers.

For example, a rule would state that "*cultural* package tours should be preferably offered to *senior* customers". Here, the concepts of "cultural" and "senior" are examples of ontological knowledge. E.g., a senior customer could be defined as a customer whose age is higher than a certain threshold.

Moreover, notions like being "cultural" or "senior" are not crisp concepts. Tour operators implicitly interpret them as approximate concepts, which can assume several different degrees of truth. Using fuzzy reasoning, the classification of customers and offers, as well as their matching, becomes a graded matter of possibility instead of a definitive assignment. At the same time, for a given entity, the candidate classes can be ordered according to the degree of matching, so a "maximum-plausibility" classification can always be performed.

It is worth noting that fuzzy reasoning has, in this context, a twofold meaning. First of all, fuzzy ontological reasoning is needed to provide approximate reasoning at the concept level. Second, also the logical operators used inside the rules management system must be interpreted in a fuzzy manner, enabling the propagation of fuzzy truth values along the triggered rules.

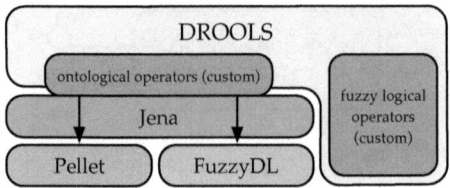

Fig. 2. The loosely coupled architecture of the system

2   Integrating Rules with Fuzzy Ontological Reasoning

Our DSS has been implemented adopting currently available technologies, preferring solutions that would offer more benefits in terms of interoperability, extensibility and support. Namely:

- *Drools Expert*[1] is a forward chaining inference rules engine based on an enhanced implementation of Charles Forgy's *Rete algorithm* [10].
- *Pellet*[2] is an OWL-DL Java-based reasoner which provides standard and advanced reasoning services for OWL ontologies.
- *Jena* and *JenaBean* are an open source Java-based framework for "semantic web" application [11].
- *FuzzyDL System* is a description logic reasoner that supports both Fuzzy Logic and fuzzy Rough Set reasoning [7].

Achieving a *loose integration* of the reasoning tools is a challenging task. Many issues are related on how interfacing the different tools, and how to provide "triggering mechanisms" from one tool to other's reasoning services. The former problem has been addressed by means of ontologies and Jena as a common representation framework. Ontologies provide explicit definitions of the concepts, while the Jena framework and its extension JenaBeans provide common APIs to access ontology files and binding of concepts to Java classes.

The latter issue, i.e. how to allow each tool to invoke reasoning services of other tools, has been addressed by choosing the Drools framework as base platform. In particular, Drools supports the definition of custom operators: we have implemented ontological operators that build the ontological inferred model and query it to evaluate some ontological operations. E.g., Drools can apply ontological queries by simply writing `Customer( this isA Single.class )` where the right operand is an ontological class defined as `Customer and (hasSpouse exactly 0) and (hasChild exactly 0)`. Drools supports fuzzy logic natively as a part of the experimental extension called Drools Chance [12] which enhance every formula by annotating it with a degree that models partial truth. Standard evaluators have been extended to return a real-valued degree instead of a boolean. A special class of fuzzy custom evaluator is formed by the *linguistic*

---

[1] http://www.jboss.org/drools/drools-expert.html
[2] http://clarkparsia.com/pellet

evaluators. Such evaluators are based on the concept of *fuzzy partition*: the numeric domain of a quantitative field X is partitioned using fuzzy sets [13]. Each fuzzy set S, labeled with a linguistic value is defined by its membership function $\mu_S : X \mapsto [0,1]$, which is a generalization of the concept of characteristic function. Thus, a fuzzy partition is a set of N fuzzy sets $S_{j:1..N}$ over X such that:

$$\forall x \in X : \left[\exists\, j^\star : \mu_{S_{j^\star}}(x) > 0 \land \sum_{k=1}^{N} \mu_{S_k}(x) = 1 \right]$$

For example, the domain of `age` could be partitioned in $\Phi_X = \{$young, mature, old$\}$. In Drools, a fuzzy predicate constraint can be applied simply by writing `Customer( age seems "young" )`. The custom meta-evaluator `seems` selects the fuzzy set corresponding to the label passed as right operand and uses it to compute the membership of a `Customer` in the set of young people.

If the atomic constraints have been combined in more complex formulas using logical connectives such as **and** or **or**, the degrees resulting from the evaluation are combined using the corresponding operators. Moreover, it is possible to choose the specific implementation of each operator using the attribute "`kind`" and choosing from a predefined set of values [12]. For example, the pattern `Customer( age Seems "young" or @[kind="Max"] "mature" )` instructs the engine to combine the two degrees by taking the maximum of the two.

Eventually, the degrees are combined until modus ponens is applied to compute the truth degree corresponding to an activation of a rule: this degree is available in the consequence part, so that the effects can be conditioned on its value. By default, a rule activates and fires only if the degree is strictly greater than 0, but even this behavior can be changed on a rule-by-rule basis.

3   Examples

In the context of a national project[3], we are investigating e-tourism applications, where customers register themselves on Internet sites to receive suggestions for their vacations. To this aim, they provide biographic information such as age, gender, marital status, number and age of children and how much they are willing to spend. On this base customers are classified in different profiles, such as *singles*, *couples*, *families* and *seniors*. Similarly, tour operators submit their offers to the same sites and their touristic products get organized in categories like *nature*, *culture*, *adventure*, *hedonism*, *wellness*, *shopping*, *sports*, *spirituality* and *festivals*. Once the classification stage has ended, the system tries to match customer profiles with categories of touristic packages suggesting the most suitable offers to each customer and providing the feedback for products to each tour operator (for example, the appeal of a product in terms of potential customers it can reach). The following examples illustrates some capabilities of our system.

---

[3] Italian MIUR PRIN 2007 project No. 20077WWCR8.

Example 1. Consider the rule below that suggests hedonistic nonadventurous products to families (static matching). It exploits the typical rule reasoning of Drools as well as Pellet's ontological reasoning and FuzzyDL's fuzzy reasoning.

```
rule "Family Customers"
  filter "0.75"
  when
      $parent : Customer ( this isA Married.class )
      exists Customer( age seems young, isChildOf == $parent)
      $offer : Offer ( this isA Hedonism.class
                       and not isA Adventure.class )
  then
      // Suggest $offer to $parent for her Family...
end
```

The custom operator **seems**, in fact, is actually an **is-a** operator with fuzzy expressiveness that exploits FuzzyDL to decide how much the age of a customer may be considered "young" discharging any result below the **filter** threshold (**young** is a fuzzy set with a left-shoulder function that returns 1 as degree of truth until ages of 10, a value that slowly decrease to 0 for ages between 10 and 16 and then always 0). The custom operator **isA** is instead a standard **is-a** operator whose evaluation is demanded to Pellet. In this case rightside operands should be existing ontological classes: **Married**, for example, is equivalent to **Customer and (hasSpouse exactly 1)**. Finally note that standard Drools predicates such as **isChildOf** are also mapped to ontological object properties.

Thus, an instance of **Customer** with a spouse and two children (4 and 2 years old) is correctly recognized as a **Family** while another one with a 18 years old daughter is not. Similarly a product involving the entrance in a water park, which is an **Hedonistic** offer, is suitably presented to the families but one with a rafting water park is not because it is also an **Adventure** offer.

Example 2. Consider a rule that dynamically discovers the associations between customers' profile and offers' categories and provides recommendations accordingly. This rule exploits operators similar to the ones seen in Example 1, but it is worth a mention for at least two reasons:

- <Profile, Category> couples are not hard-coded in rules, but rather evaluated by an external custom operator (**matches**);
- the fuzzy results computed by FuzzyDL can be understood by Drools and used in rules' consequents.

```
rule "Matching"
  when
      $pro : Profile ( )
      $cus : Customer ( this isA $pro )
      $cat : Category ( this matches $pro )
      $off : Offer ( this isA $cat )
```

```
then
    PriorityQueue queue = getQueue($cus);
    queue.insertOrd($off, drools.getConsequenceDegree());
end
```

In this case, the rule determines the `Profile` of and `Category` of any couple of `Customer`s and `Offer`s and then determining the strength of the association between them is demanded to `matches`. If we consider a family and a water park offer as in Example1, that couple will be evaluated as a good matching and it will produce the same results as before. On the other hand, if we consider a free-climbing offer that is an highly dangerous `Adventure` offer, the `matches` operator will likely report its association with a `Family` as less likely. By calling the `getConsequenceDegree()` method, Drools can handle the truth value being evaluated by the rule and also use it to sort offers for customers.

4 Related Works and Conclusions

Although many rule engines and ontology reasoners are currently available, only few of them support rules and DL reasoning at the same time. Jena, for example, includes a generic rule based inference engine that can easily cooperate with the supported reasoners. Hammurapi Rules[4] is another Java rule engine that leverages Java language semantics to express relationships between facts as ontologies do. Algernon[5] is an efficient and concise Protégé extension supporting both forward and backward chaining rules that stores and retrieves information in ontologies. Another solution is SweetRules[6], an integrated toolkit for semantic web revolving around RuleML and many other W3C standards that works with ontologies. Despite being remarkable, they are less easily customizable, less widespread than the components of our solution and also not supporting fuzzy reasoning.

This is mainly due to the general lack of fuzzy reasoners: even though a few are actually under development (such as DeLorean[7]), FuzzyDL system is the only mature Java-based solution we were able to find. Fuzzy logic is possibly the only type of non-boolean logic which has been integrated in mainstream, open source BRMS. Actually, there exist many tools supporting "fuzzy logic", but most of the times it must be understood as "fuzzy logic in a broad sense" [14]. Much fewer are the tools which intend fuzzy logic in the sense of a truth-functional, annotated many-valued logic. Nevertheless, two of the first and most important rule-based expert systems, Clips[8] and Jess[9], had a proper fuzzy extension (FuzzyClips[10] and FuzzyJess[11] respectively). Unfortunately, both projects are discontinued, and lack the full BRMS

---

[4] http://www.hammurapi.com/
[5] http://algernon-j.sourceforge.net/
[6] http://sweetrules.semwebcentral.org/
[7] http://webdiis.unizar.es/~fbobillo/delorean.php
[8] http://clipsrules.sourceforge.net/
[9] http://www.jessrules.com/
[10] http://www.nrc-cnrc.gc.ca/eng/projects/iit/fuzzy-reasoning.html
[11] http://www.csie.ntu.edu.tw/~sylee/courses/FuzzyJ/FuzzyJess.htm

capabilities offered by Drools. Other than that, an attempt to integrate logic programming and fuzzy logic has been made with FRIL [15], a prolog-like language and interpreter, but that project is currently inactive.

Concerning the problem of integrating semantic knowledge with other form of reasoning, a first approach is to exploit the common root of logic programming and description logics in first order logic by means of LP clauses. These problems have been addressed: that intersection has been named *DLP* (Description Logics Program) [2] and a method for translation has been proposed [3]. On these basis, dlpconvert [4], a tool that converts (the DLP fragment of) OWL ontologies to datalog clauses, has been developed. In [5] and [6], the authors propose techniques for reasoning on Description Logic with $\mathcal{SHOIN}$ and $\mathcal{SHIQ}$ expressiveness not based on the usual tableau algorithms but instead on bottom-up Datalog and Deductive Database inference, and top-down Prolog resolution respectively in order to deal with large data sets of individuals. Since Deductive Database deal natively with rules, extending the obtained reduction of the DL KB with a rule level appears straightforward by appending rules to the obtained KB [5]. The integration of rules and ontologies has been extensively studied in [16], where the full compatibility with OWL has been relaxed to introduce the Web Service Modeling Language, a language to be used in the WSMO framework. The MARS framework has been introduced in [17] as a framework focused on the rule layer of the Semantic Web cake. MARS follows a declarative style of modeling; its general language, however, is aimed at specifying rules for the semantic web, and it is not equipped with specific reasoning techniques for (semantic) web services.

To the best of our knowledge, our system is the first one that offer a "loose integration" of ontological, rule-based and fuzzy reasoning tools all together. It is build exploiting available technologies, starting form the Drools platform and building upon it to perform ontological and fuzzy reasoning. Currently, we are exploiting our system in the context of a national project to implement a Decision Support System for classifying customers profiles, touristic packages and the knowledge of professional operators. Future work will be devoted to investigate also the theoretical issues related to our integration, as well as extending our approach to support more ontological operators, since current implementation supports ontological isA (subClassOf and instanceOf ontological operators) and fuzzy seems (fuzzy ontological subClassOf and instanceOf). Further work will be devoted also to compare our integrated solution with other tools, taking into account both the expressivity as well as the performances.

Acknowledgements. This work has been partially supported by the Italian MIUR PRIN 2007 project No. 20077WWCR8.

References

1. Antoniou, G., Damásio, C., Grosof, B., Horrocks, I., Kifer, M., Maluszynski, J., Patel-Schneider, P.: Combining rules and ontologies: A survey. Reasoning on the Web with Rules and Semantics (2005)

2. Grosof, B., Horrocks, I., Volz, R.: Description logic programs: Combining logic programs with description logic. In: Proceedings of the 12th international conference on World Wide Web, pp. 48–57. ACM, New York (2003)
3. Hustadt, U., Motik, B., Sattler, U.: Reducing SHIQ- description logic to disjunctive datalog programs. In: Proc. KR, pp. 152–162 (2004)
4. Motik, B., Vrandečić, D., Hitzler, P., Studer, R.: Dlpconvert–converting OWL DLP statements to logic programs. In: European Semantic Web Conference 2005 Demos and Posters, Citeseer (2005)
5. Motik, B.: Reasoning in description logics using resolution and deductive databases. PhD theis, University Karlsruhe, Germany (2006)
6. Lukacsy, G., Szeredi, P., Kadar, B.: Prolog based description logic reasoning. In: Garcia de la Banda, M., Pontelli, E. (eds.) ICLP 2008. LNCS, vol. 5366, pp. 455–469. Springer, Heidelberg (2008)
7. Bobillo, F., Straccia, U.: FuzzyDL: An expressive fuzzy description logic reasoner. In: Proc. 2008 Intl. Conf. on Fuzzy Systems, FUZZ 2008 (2008)
8. Kochukuttan, H., Chandrasekaran, A.: Development of a Fuzzy Expert System for Power Quality Applications. In: Proceedings of the Twenty-Ninth Southeastern Symposium on System Theory, pp. 239–243 (1997)
9. Ozgur, N., Koyuncu, M., Yazici, A.: An intelligent fuzzy object-oriented database framework for video database applications. Fuzzy Sets and Systems 160(15), 2253–2274 (2009)
10. Forgy, C.: Rete: A fast algorithm for the many pattern/many object pattern match problem. Name: Artif. Intell. (1982)
11. Carroll, J., Dickinson, I., Dollin, C., Reynolds, D., Seaborne, A., Wilkinson, K.: Jena: implementing the semantic web recommendations. In: Proceedings of the 13th International World Wide Web Conference on Alternate Track Papers & Posters, pp. 74–83. ACM, New York (2004)
12. Mello, P., Proctor, M., Sottara, D.: A configurable RETE-OO engine for reasoning with different types of imperfect information. IEEE TKDE - Special Issue on Rule Representation, Interchange and Reasoning in Distributed, Heterogeneous Environments (2010) (in Press)
13. Zadeh, L.A.: The concept of a linguistic variable and its application to approximate reasoning - i. Inf. Sci. 8(3), 199–249 (1975)
14. Novk, V.: Abstract: Mathematical fuzzy logic in narrow and broader sense a unified concept
15. Baldwin, J., Martin, T., Pilsworth, B.: Fril-fuzzy and evidential reasoning in artificial intelligence. John Wiley & Sons, Inc., New York (1995)
16. de Bruijn, J.: Semantic Web Language Layering with Ontologies, Rules, and Meta-Modeling. PhD thesis, University of Innsbruck (2008)
17. Behrends, E., Fritzen, O., May, W., Schenk, F.: Embedding Event Algebras and Process for ECA Rules for the Semantic Web. Fundamenta Informaticae 82(3), 237–263 (2008)

Selecting Regions of Interest in SPECT Images Using Wilcoxon Test for the Diagnosis of Alzheimer's Disease

D. Salas-Gonzalez, J.M. Górriz, J. Ramírez, F. Segovia, R. Chaves,
M. López, I.A. Illán, and P. Padilla

Dpt. Signal Theory Networking and Communications,
ETSIIT 18071, Granada, Spain
dsalas@ugr.es
http://ugr.es/~dsalas

Abstract. This work presents a computer-aided diagnosis technique for improving the accuracy of the diagnosis of the Alzheimer's disease (AD). Some regions of the SPECT image discriminate more between healthy and AD patients than others, thus, it is important to design an automatic tool for selecting these regions. This work shows the performance of the Mann-Whitney-Wilcoxon U-test, a non-parametric technique which allows to select voxels of interest. Those voxels with higher U values are selected and their intensity values are used as input for a Support Vector Machine classifier with linear kernel. The proposed methodology yields an accuracy greater than 90% in the diagnosis of the AD and outperforms existing techniques including the voxel-as-features approach.

1 Introduction

Conventional evaluation of Single Photon Emission Computed Tomography scans often relies on manual reorientation, visual reading and semiquantitative analysis of certain regions of the brain. Therefore, a fully-automatic procedure to help clinicians in the Alzheimer's diagnosis is desirable. Distinguishing Alzheimer's disease remains a diagnostic challenge especially during the early stage of the disease. Furthermore, in this early stage, the disease offers better opportunities to be treated [1].

This work presents a computer aided diagnosis system for the detection of Alzheimer's disease using the Mann-Whitney-Wilcoxon test and Support Vector Machines (SVM) [2]. SVM is a powerful tool which has been recently used for classification of tomographic brain images [3,4,5,6,7,8]. The classification is performed by defining feature vectors and training a classifier with a given set of known training samples.

We measure the distance between voxels of the normal and AD images using Mann-Whitney-Wilcoxon test and we select the set of voxels which presents highest values. The intensity values of selected voxels are used as features for the linear SVM classifier.

M. Graña Romay et al. (Eds.): HAIS 2010, Part I, LNAI 6076, pp. 446–451, 2010.

This article is organized as follows: Section 2 presents the materials and methods used in this work: that is, the SPECT image acquisition and preprocessing and the statistical methods used to select voxels of interest in the brain images and the Support Vector classification procedure. In Section 3, we summarize the classification performance obtained in terms of the accuracy rate, sensibility and sensitivity. And finally, the conclusions are drawn in Section 4.

2   Material and Methods

2.1   SPECT Image Acquisition and Preprocessing

The patients were injected with a gamma emitting 99mTc-ECD radiopharmaceutical and the SPECT raw data was acquired by a three head gamma camera Picker Prism 3000. A total of 180 projections were taken for each patient with a 2-degree angular resolution. The images of the brain cross sections were reconstructed from the projection data using the Filtered Backprojection (FBP) algorithm in combination with a Butterworth noise removal filter [9,5].

The complexity of brain structures and the differences between brains of different subjects make necessary the normalization of the images with respect to a common template. This ensures that a given voxel in different images refers to the same anatomical position in the brain. In this work, the images have been initially normalized using a general affine model, with 12 parameters [10]. After the affine normalization, the resulting image is registered using a more complex non-rigid spatial transformation model. The deformations are parameterized by a linear combination of the lowest-frequency components of the three dimensional cosine transform bases [11]. A small-deformation approach is used, and regularization is by the bending energy of the displacement field. After that, we normalize the intensities of the SPECT images with respect to the maximum intensity.

2.2   Support Vector Machine with Linear Kernels

The images we work with belong to two different classes: normal and AD. SVM separate a given set of binary labeled training data with a hyper-plane that is maximally distant from the two classes (known as the maximal margin hyper-plane). In SVM-based pattern recognition, the objective is to build a function $f : R^N \rightarrow \pm 1$ using training data, that is, N-dimensional patterns $\mathbf{x}_i$ and class labels y_i:

$$(\mathbf{x}_1, y_1), (\mathbf{x}_2, y_2), ..., (\mathbf{x}_\ell, y_\ell) \in (R^N \times \pm 1), \qquad (1)$$

so that a classifier f is produced which maps an object x_i to its classification label y_i. The classifier f will correctly classify new examples $(\mathbf{x}, y)$.

2.3   Voxel Selection Using Mann-Whitney-Wilcoxon Test

We use the absolute value of the U-statistic of a two-sample unpaired Wilcoxon test to measure the voxel separability between classes. The Mann-Whitney U

test can be viewed as the nonparametric equivalent of Student's t-test. Mann-Whitney-Wilcoxon test is more robust to outliers in the data than the t-test and it is usually preferable when the data is not Gaussian [12].

First, all the observations are arranged into a single ranked series. We add up the ranks for the observations which came from sample 1. The statistic U is then given by:

$$U_1 = R_1 - \frac{n_1(n_1 + 1)}{2} \qquad (2)$$

where n_1 is the sample size for sample 1, and R_1 is the sum of the ranks in sample 1.

Analogously we make the same calculation for sample 2:

$$U_2 = R_2 - \frac{n_2(n_2 + 1)}{2} \qquad (3)$$

The distance U given by the Wilcoxon test is the smaller value of U_1 and U_2, $U = \min\{U_1, U_2\}$.

High values of the U-test denote voxels which are more separated between Normal and AD classes according to the Mann-Whitney-Wilcoxon test. We rank the U values in descending order and stack these values in a vector. ε voxels i which provide the greatest U-values are selected and used as input features of a support vector machine with linear kernel.

3   Results

The performance of the classification is tested on a set of 78 real SPECT images (41 normals and 37 AD) using the leave-one-out method: the classifier is trained with all but one images of the database. The remaining image, which is not used to define the classifier, is then categorized. In that way, all SPECT images are classified and the accuracy rate is computed from the number of correctly classified subjects.

Figure 1 shows the transaxial slices of the Mann-Whitney-Wilcoxon U image. In that case, U-values range from 0 to $+0.556$. Regions of interests are those which present higher values. Figure 2 shows the histogram with U-values. A mixture of two Gaussian components is also fitted to data. The plot shows that two Gaussian components are able to fit the histogram very accurately. Those voxels which present a U-value greater than 0.408, where $\mu = 0.408$ is the mean of the second Gaussian component, will be selected as feature vector for the SVM linear classifier. They are approximately the 2500 voxels with highest U-statistic values.

Figure 3 shows the correct rate obtained using the proposed methodology for varying ε values. We choose 25 ε values equally spaced from 100 to 2500. A correct rate greater than 90% is obtained for a wide range of ε values and best performance (92,3%) was obtained when $\varepsilon = 900$ and $\varepsilon = 1000$. The results outperform the accuracy rate obtained in [8], in which, using voxels as features, an accuracy rate of 84.8% and 89.9% was obtained using the nearest

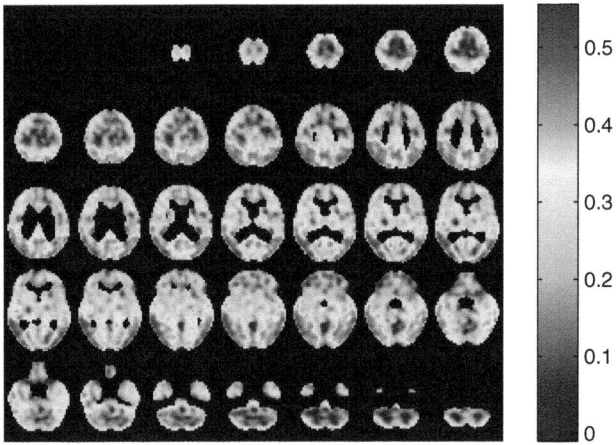

Fig. 1. Transaxial U-test brain image. Higher values denote regions of interests according to the Mann-Whitney-Wilcoxon test.

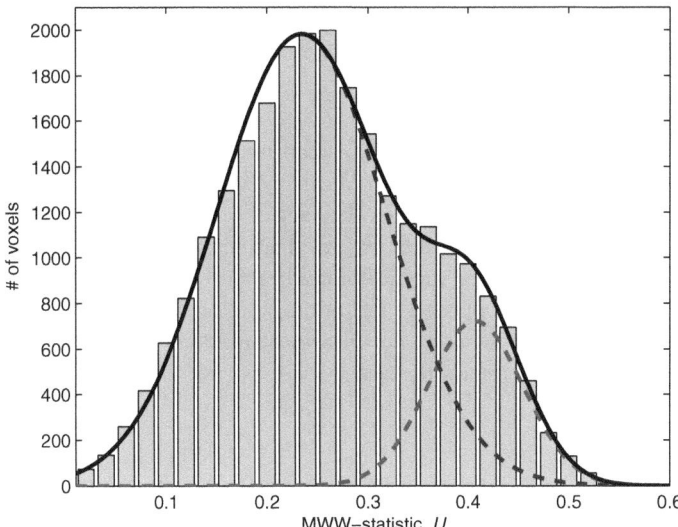

Fig. 2. Histogram with the U-values and two-component Gaussian mixture fit

mean classifier and Fisher Linear Discriminant ratio respectively. Specificity and sensitivity versus number of selected voxels ε are also plotted in Figure 3. The proposed methodology achieves higher values of sensitivity than specificity. Sensitivity ranges from 0.878 to 0.976 depending on the number of selected voxels ε while Specificity presents less variability, ranging from 0.865 to 0.892.

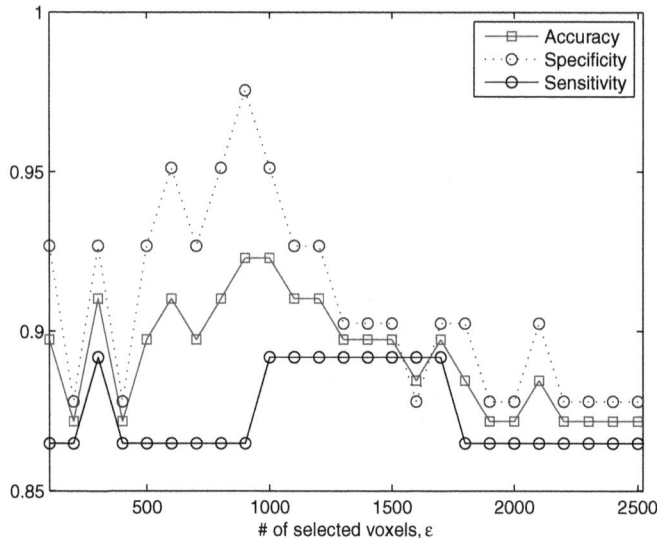

Fig. 3. Accuracy rate, specificity and sensitivity versus number of selected voxels ε

4   Conclusions

In this work, a criterion to select a set of discriminant voxels for the classification of SPECT brain images using the Mann-Whitney-Wilcoxon U-test is presented. After normalisation of the brain images, the set of voxels which presents higher U-value are selected. Selected voxels are used as features to a SVM classifier with linear kernel. The proposed methodology reaches an accuracy up to 92% in the classification task. The proposed methodology allows us to classify the brain images in normal and affected subjects in an automatic manner, with no prior knowledge about the Alzheimer's disease.

References

1. Johnson, E., Brookmeyer, R., Ziegler-Graham, K.: Modeling the effect of Alzheimer's disease on mortality. The International Journal of Biostatistics, Article 13, 3(1) (2007)
2. Vapnik, V.N.: Statistical Learning Theory. John Wiley and Sons, Inc., New York (1998)
3. Górriz, J.M., Lassl, A., Ramírez, J., Salas-Gonzalez, D., Puntonet, C.G., Lang, E.W.: Automatic selection of ROIs in functional imaging using Gaussian mixture models. Neuroscience letters 460(2), 108–111 (2009)
4. Ramírez, J., Górriz, J.M., Salas-Gonzalez, D., López, M., Álvarez, I., Gómez-Río, M.: Computer aided diagnosis of Alzheimer type dementia combining support vector machines and discriminant set of features. Information Sciences (2009) (in Press)

5. Ramírez, J., Górriz, J.M., Gómez-Río, M., Romero, A., Chaves, R., Lassl, A., Rodríguez, A., Puntonet, C.G., Theis, F., Lang, E.: Effective emission tomography image reconstruction algorithms for SPECT data. In: Bubak, M., van Albada, G.D., Dongarra, J., Sloot, P.M.A. (eds.) ICCS 2008, Part I. LNCS, vol. 5101, pp. 741–748. Springer, Heidelberg (2008)

6. Chaves, R., Ramírez, J., Górriz, J.M., Salas-Gonzalez, M.L.D., Álvarez, I., Segovia, F.: SVM-based computer aided diagnosis of the Alzheimer's disease using t-test NMSE feature selection with feature correlation weighting. Neuroscience Letters 461(1), 293–297 (2009)

7. Álvarez, I., Górriz, J.M., Ramírez, J., Salas-Gonzalez, D., López, M., Puntonet, C.G., Segovia, F.: Alzheimer's diagnosis using eigenbrains and support vector machines. IET Electronics Letters 45(7), 342–343 (2009)

8. Fung, G., Stoeckel, J.: SVM feature selection for classification of SPECT images of Alzheimer's disease using spatial information. Knowledge and Information Systems 11(2), 243–258 (2007)

9. Zhou, J., Luo, L.M.: Sequential weighted least squares algorithm for PET image reconstruction. Digital Signal Processing 16, 735–745 (2006)

10. Salas-Gonzalez, D., Górriz, J.M., Ramírez, J., Lassl, A., Puntonet, C.G.: Improved Gauss-Newton optimization methods in affine registration of SPECT brain images. IET Electronics Letters 44(22), 1291–1292 (2008)

11. Ashburner, J., Friston, K.J.: Nonlinear spatial normalization using basis functions. Human Brain Mapping 7(4), 254–266 (1999)

12. Wilcoxon, F.: Individual comparisons by ranking methods. Biometrics Bulletin 1(6), 80–83 (1945)

Effective Diagnosis of Alzheimer's Disease by Means of Association Rules

R. Chaves, J. Ramírez, J.M. Górriz, M. López,
D. Salas-Gonzalez, I. Illán, F. Segovia, and P. Padilla

University of Granada, Periodista Daniel Saucedo Aranda s/n,
18071, Granada (Spain)
{rosach,javierrp,gorriz,miriamlp
illan,dsalas,fsegovia,pablopadilla}@ugr.es
http://sipba.ugr.es/

Abstract. In this paper we present a novel classification method of SPECT images for the early diagnosis of the Alzheimer's disease (AD). The proposed method is based on Association Rules (ARs) aiming to discover interesting associations between attributes contained in the database. The system uses firstly voxel-as-features (VAF) and Activation Estimation (AE) to find tridimensional activated brain regions of interest (ROIs) for each patient. These ROIs act as inputs to secondly mining ARs between activated blocks for controls, with a specified minimum support and minimum confidence. ARs are mined in supervised mode, using information previously extracted from the most discriminant rules for centering interest in the relevant brain areas, reducing the computational requirement of the system. Finally classification process is performed depending on the number of previously mined rules verified by each subject, yielding an up to 95.87% classification accuracy, thus outperforming recent developed methods for AD diagnosis.

Keywords: SPECT Brain Imaging, Alzheimer's disease, Regions of Interest, Voxels as features, Association Rules, *Apriori* algorithm.

1   Introduction

Alzheimer's Disease (AD) is the most common cause of dementia in the elderly and affects approximately 30 million individuals worldwide [1]. Its prevalence is expected to triple over the next 50 years due to the growth of the older population. To date there is no single test or biomarker that can predict whether a particular person will develop the disease. With the advent of several effective treatments of AD symptoms, current consensus statements have emphasized the need for early recognition.

SPECT (Single Positron Emission Computed Tomography) is a widely used technique to study the functional properties of the brain [2]. After the reconstruction and a proper normalization of the SPECT raw data, taken with Tc-99m ethyl cysteinate dimer (ECD) as a tracer, one obtains an activation map displaying the local intensity of the regional cerebral blood flow (rCBF). Therefore,

M. Graña Romay et al. (Eds.): HAIS 2010, Part I, LNAI 6076, pp. 452–459, 2010.

this technique is particularly applicable for the diagnosis of neuro-degenerative diseases like AD. This functional modality has lower resolution and higher variability than others such as Positron Emission Tomography (PET), but the use of SPECT tracers is relatively cheap, and the longer half-life when compared to PET tracers make SPECT well suited, if not required, when biologically active radiopharmaceuticals have slow kinetics.

In order to improve the prediction accuracy (Acc) especially in the early stage of the disease, when the patient could benefit most from drugs and treatments, computer aided diagnosis (CAD) tools are desirable. At this stage in the development of CAD systems, the main goal is to reproduce the knowledge of medical experts in the evaluation of a complete image database, i.e. distinguishing AD patients from controls, thus errors from single observer evaluation are avoided achieving a method for assisting the identification of early signs of AD.

In the context of *supervised* multivariate approaches, the classification is usually done by defining feature vectors representing the different SPECT images and training a classifier with a given set of known samples [3]. After the training process, the classifier is used to distinguish between the brain images of normal and AD patients. The advantage of such a statistical learning approach is that no specific knowledge about the disease is necessary and the method is applicable for different types of brain diseases and brain imaging techniques. In this paper, each patient is represented by a feature vector containing the Regions of Interest (ROIs) selected using VAF (Voxels-as-features) [4] and a threshold based Activation Estimation (AE) similar to [5] which is currently a state-of-the-art approach to the meta-analysis of functional imaging data. ROIs selected are tridimensional blocks with a high concentration of activation coordinates [6] and are directly related to the perfusion level which varies widely between controls and AD in its three possible stages. Finally, relationships between ROIs using ARs are established to efficiently distinguish between AD and controls.

ARs have drawn researcher's attention in the past, enabling to find the associations and/or relationships among inputs items of any system in large databases and later eliminating some unnecessary inputs. ARs are typically used in market basket analysis, cross-marketing, catalog design, loss-leader analysis, store layout and customer buying pattern or the mining of data items [7]. The discovery of new and potentially important relationships between concepts in the biomedical field has focussed the attention of a lot of researchers in text mining [8]. The strengths of ARs are the capability to operate with large databases in an efficient way, while its execution time scales almost linearly with the size of the data. Nowadays its application to AD has not be widely explored, being this field the central goal of this work.

2   Matherial and Methods

2.1   Subjects and Preprocessing

Baseline SPECT data from 97 participants were collected from the Virgen de las Nieves hospital in Granada (Spain). The patients were injected with a gamma emitting ^{99m}Tc-ECD radiopharmeceutical and the SPECT raw data was acquired by a three head gamma camera Picker Prism 3000. A total of 180 projections were taken with a 2-degree angular resolution. The images of the brain cross sections were reconstructed from the projection data using the filtered backprojection (FBP) algorithm in combination with a Butterworth noise removal filter. The SPECT images are first spatially normalized using the SPM software, in order to ensure that voxels in different images refer to the same anatomical positions in the brain allowing us to compare the voxel intensities of different subjects. Then we normalize the intensities of the SPECT images with a method similar to [9]. After the spatial normalization, one obtains a $95 \times 69 \times 79$ voxel representation of each subject, where each voxel represents a brain volume of $2 \times 2 \times 2 \, \text{mm}^3$. The SPECT images were visually classified by experts of the Virgen de las Nieves hospital using 4 different labels to distinguish between different levels of the presence of typical characteristics for AD. The database consists of 43 NOR, 30 AD1, 20 AD2 and 4 AD3 patients.

2.2   Feature Extraction

In this article, we propose to apply a combination of VAF and threshold based AE for feature extraction. The former VAF is a way of including all the voxel intensities inside the brain as features, thus no explicit knowledge about the disease is needed, avoiding the inclusion of a priori information about the pathology into the system [10]. The latter AE leads to a reduced list of activation maxima containing only those which have one or more other maximums in their vicinity (activated voxels). In functional imaging, each voxel carries a grey level intensity $I(\mathbf{x}_j)$, which is related to the regional cerebral blood flow, glucose metabolism, etc. in the brain of a patient, depending on the image acquisition modality. In the first step (VAF), only those voxels with an intensity level above 50% of the maximum (i.e. considered as *relevant voxels*) defining a tridimensional mask were taken into account. Secondly, we parcel the resulting space into overlapped regions with size $(2v + 1) \times (2v + 1) \times (2v + 1)$ voxels centered at point with coordinates (x,y,z). These blocks are inside of the 3D mask and are considered to be part of the ROIs if the number of voxels included are above a threshold η that is tunned experimentally. If the activation threshold is decreased, more rules are mined and consequently more information to be processed, increasing the computational requirement. In order to achieve the best trade-off between computational time and processed information, a block of size $9 \times 9 \times 9$ is considered to be a ROI if a 90% of voxels inside of it are activated using the AE scheme. Figure 1 shows a contour representation of the brain and the location of the 3D ROIs centered at black points, which are used as inputs for the AR mining algorithm.

2.3   Mining Assocation Rules from SPECT Images

In data mining, AR learning is an effective method for discovering interesting relations between variables in large databases [11]. In this context, m binary attributes called items $I = i_1, i_2,...,i_m$ are extracted from a set of controls in a

SPECT database playing the role of activated brain regions or ROIs. Let $D = t_1$, $t_2,...,t_n$ be a set of transactions, where each transaction T is such that T $\subseteq$ I. We say that a transaction T supports an item x if $x \in I$ [7] and a set of items X in I, if X$\subseteq$T. An AR is defined as an implication of the form $X \Rightarrow Y$, where $X \subset I$, $Y \subset I$, and $X \cap Y = \emptyset$. It is said that the rule $X \Rightarrow Y$, which defines a relation between two activation regions defining a *normal* pattern, has support s if s% of the transactions in D contain $X \cup Y$ and a confidence c, if c% of the transactions in D that contain X also contain Y. Support and confidence do not measure association relationships but how-often patterns co-occur and only make sense in AR mining. The problem of AR mining is to generate all rules that have support and confidence greater than a minimum support (called *minsup*) and minimum confidence (called *minconf*) established by the user. If *minsup* and *minconf* values are increased, the number of rules mined is lower and vice-versa. Particularly, if minconf and minsup are chosen next to the maximum of 100%, the lowest number of ARs are extracted but the most relevant. The AR discovering has required the development of faster algorithms because users are more interested in some specific subsets of ARs. The fact of integrating the most relevant ARs as input into the mining algorithms, called supervised mode, can reduce significantly the execution time [7]. Moreover, supervised mode can be very useful in medical databases because we want to know how patterns existing in a SPECT database relate to a well-defined medical problem of diagnosis. The process of AR mining is based on the *Apriori* algorithm, which is a state of the art algorithm due to the rest of algorithms with the same goal are variation of this. *Apriori* works iteratively for finding all frequent sets and is described in [12]. Figure 2 shows transaxial, coronal and sagittal slices of a mean SPECT image illustrating the $4 \times 4 \times 4$ grid locations (crosses) and the activated regions involved in association rules (squares in white) in terms of antecendents and consequences. ARs were mined in supervised mode using a high *minsup* and *minconf* (98%) for mining rules which best discriminate AD subjects from normal subjects. Note that, temporoparietal brain regions, which correspond with the locations where first signs of AD are detected, are considered as activated ROIs by the algorithm.

3   Results

Several experiments were conducted to evaluate the combination of VAF and AE feature extraction aiming to posterior AR mining for brain image classification. The performance of the AR-based classifier was evaluated in depth as a tool for the early detection of the AD in terms of Accuracy(Acc), Sensitivity (Sen) and Specificity (Spe), which are estimed by the leave-one-out cross-validation. The experiments considered an increasing threshold for the number of verified ARs by the subject to be classified. Sen and Spe are defined as:

$$\text{Sensitivity} = \frac{TP}{TP+FN}; \quad \text{Specificity} = \frac{TN}{TN+FP}$$

respectively, where TP is the number of true positives: number of AD patients correctly classified; TN is the number of true negatives: number of controls

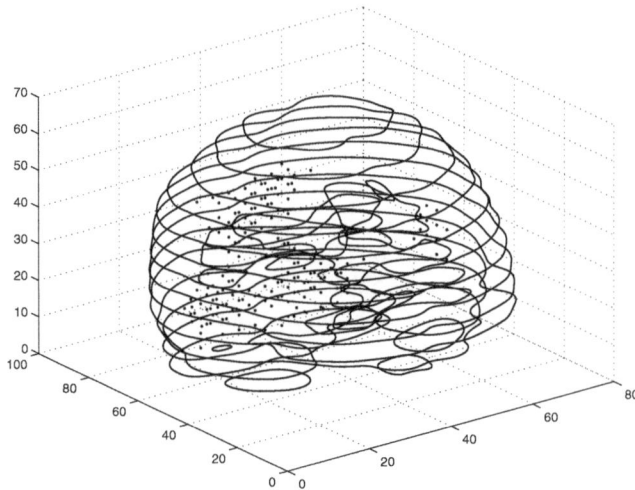

Fig. 1. Tridimensional ROIs centered at red points for a voxel size v=4, grid space=4 and activation threshold=650 of 729 voxels by block

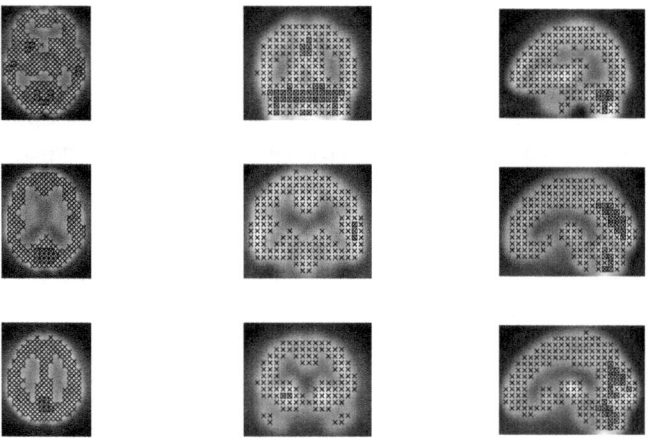

Fig. 2. Bidimensional activated ROIs from axial, sagittal and coronal axis obtained from ARs in supervised mode (2 of the most discriminant rules as input prior goals) with minsup and minconf of 98%

correctly classified; FP is the number of false positives: number of controls classified as AD patient; FN is the number of false negatives: number of AD patients classified as control.

Table 1. Number of ARs mined using different minsups and minconfs, differing between the use of supervised mode (2 of the most discriminant rules as prior goals) and unsupervised mode (no prior goals). Gain of velocity using supervised respectly to unsupervised mode and maximum Acc obtained in the classification process with both modes.

minsup, minconf	98%	95%	90%	85%	80%
supervised mode	183	314	419	506	596
unsupervised mode	33646	88347	152790	220660	295040
aceleration rate		183.85	281.35	364.65	436.08	495.033
accuracy		95.87	90.72	89.69	87.62	86.56

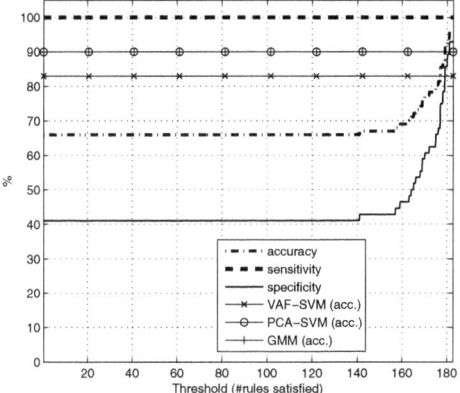

Fig. 3. Accuracy, Sensitivity and Specificity vs. Threshold for rules mined with minsup and minconf 98% and a voxel size v=4, grid space=4 and threshold=650 in supervised mode. Comparison to other recently reported methods.

The strategy to evaluate the method consists of differing, in terms of Acc, Sen, Spe and velocity of the CAD, the fact of using or not supervised mode, that is a subset of the most discriminant rules (obtained with minsup and minconf of 98%) as input in the AR mining. Results changing the number of rules in the subset, and the minsup and minconf are also analysed. First of all, the table 1 shows the set of mined rules obtained using the *Apriori* algorithm. In the first row, we show the results in supervised mode, showing the efficiency of the method when a subset of rules (2 rules as prior goals) related to relevant areas is used. A reduction in the number of ARs is achieved by limiting the number of rules that are used as inputs for the AR mining process. Moreover, such reduction of the computational cost of the CAD system, which is based on the verification of a reduced set of rules by each patient, have no impact on its Acc since non-informative or redundant rules are efficiently discarded by the proposed method. It can be observed that the number of rules extracted, when minsup and minconf are reduced, is higher. However, it may lead to an increase in the computational cost of the CAD system, and a penalty in the Acc rate because no-discriminant rules are being used too. For this reason, it is also shown that when minsup and minconf are lower than 85%, Acc is under the maximum raised by PCA-SVM classifier [13], and consequently results start not being interesting for a correct classification. In the second row, unsupervised mode (no prior goals) is used and in the third row the acceleration factor as a division between the supervised and unsupervised mode is shown. Observing table 1, we can conclude that using the algorithm of mining with a subset of relevant rules previously chosen, the results in terms of Acc (see fourth row in table 1) are the same but efficiency in terms of computer time is much better because attention is filtered in the most important regions of the brain. Furthermore, we obtain the same ROIs in both cases, that is, figures 1, 2 are equivalent for both supervised/non-supervised operation modes. Figure 3 shows that Acc, Sen and Spe converge to a peak maximum of 95.87%, 100% and 92.86%, respectively, when the threshold is set to about 183 rules verified. It can be concluded that the classification Acc improves when it is increased the threshold of verified rules by the subject. These results are in agreement with the expected behavior of the system since normal subjects are assumed to have a common SPECT image pattern and to verify most of the ARs mined.

4 Conclusions

ARs were investigated for SPECT images classification for the early AD's diagnosis, obtaining results of Acc of 95.87%, Sen of 100% and Spe of 92.86% and outperforming other recently reported methods including VAF, PCA in combination with a support vector machine (SVM) classifier [13], and the Gaussian mixture modeling (GMM) SVM classifier [14]. The fact of using a priori information on the AR mining is very positive in terms of improving the computational time of the AR extraction and the rest of checkings of the CAD system.

Acknowledgments

This work was partly supported by the MICINN under the PETRI DENCLASES (PET2006-0253), TEC2008-02113, NAPOLEON (TEC2007-68030-C02-01) and HD2008-0029 projects and the Consejería de Innovación, Ciencia y Empresa (Junta de Andalucía, Spain) under the Excellence Project (TIC-2566 and TIC-4530). We are grateful to M. Gómez-Río and coworkers from the "Virgen de las Nieves" hospital in Granada (Spain) for providing and classifying the SPECT images used in this work.

References

1. Petrella, J.R., Coleman, R.E., Doraiswamy, P.M.: Neuroimaging and early diagnosis of alzheimer's disease: A look to the future. Radiology 226, 315–336 (2003)
2. English, R.J., Childs, J. (eds.): SPECT: Single-Photon Emission Computed Tomography: A Primer. Society of Nuclear Medicine (1996)

3. Fung, G., Stoeckel, J.: SVM feature selection for classification of SPECT images of Alzheimer's disease using spatial information. Knowledge and Information Systems 11, 243–258 (2007)

4. Stoeckel, J., Malandain, G., Migneco, O., Koulibaly, P.M., Robert, P., Ayache, N., Darcourt, J.: Classification of SPECT images of normal subjects versus images of Alzheimer's disease patients. In: Niessen, W.J., Viergever, M.A. (eds.) MICCAI 2001. LNCS, vol. 2208, pp. 666–674. Springer, Heidelberg (2001)

5. Turkeltaub, P., Eden, G., Jones, K., Zeffiro, T.: Meta-analysis of the functional neuroanatomy of single-word reading: Method and validation. Neuroimage 16, 765–780 (2002)

6. Newman, J., von Cramon, D.Y., Lohmann, G.: Model-based clustering of meta-analytic functional imaging data. Human Brain Mapping 29, 177–192 (2008)

7. Skirant, R., Vu, Q., Agrawal, R.: Mining association rules with item constraints. In: Third International Conference on Knowledge Discovery and Data Mining, pp. 67–73 (1997)

8. Nearhos, J., Rothman, M., Viveros, M.: Applying data mining techniques to a health insurance information system. In: 22nd Int'l Conference on Very Large Databases, pp. 286–294 (1996)

9. Saxena, P., Pavel, D.G., Quintana, J.C., Horwitz, B.: An automatic threshold-based scaling method for enhancing the usefulness of Tc-HMPAO SPECT in the diagnosis of Alzheimer's disease. In: Wells, W.M., Colchester, A.C.F., Delp, S.L. (eds.) MICCAI 1998. LNCS, vol. 1496, pp. 623–630. Springer, Heidelberg (1998)

10. Stoeckel, J., Ayache, N., Malandain, G., Koulibaly, P.M., Ebmeier, K.P., Darcourt, J.: Automatic classification of SPECT images of Alzheimers disease patients and control subjects. In: Barillot, C., Haynor, D.R., Hellier, P. (eds.) MICCAI 2004. LNCS, vol. 3217, pp. 654–662. Springer, Heidelberg (2004)

11. Agrawal, R., Imielinski, T., Swami, A.: Mining association rules between sets of items in large databases. In: Proceedings of the ACM SIGMOID International Conference on the Management of Data, pp. 207–216 (1993)

12. Agrawal, R., Srikant, R.: Fast algorithms for mining association rules in large databases. In: Proceedings of the 20th International Conference on Very Large Databases, pp. 487–499 (1994)

13. Álvarez, I., Górriz, J.M., Ramírez, J., Salas-Gonzalez, D., López, M., Puntonet, C.G., Segovia, F.: Alzheimer's diagnosis using eigenbrains and support vector machines. IET Electronic Letters 45, 165–167 (2009)

14. Gorriz, J.M., Lassl, A., Ramirez, J., Salas-Gonzalez, D., Puntonet, C.G., Lang, E.: Automatic selection of rois in functional imaging using gaussian mixture models. Neuroscience Letters 460, 108–111 (2009)

Exploratory Matrix Factorization for PET Image Analysis

A. Kodewitz[1], I.R. Keck[1], A.M. Tomé[2], J.M. Górriz[3], and E.W. Lang[1]

[1] CIML Group/Biophysics, University of Regensburg, Germany
[2] IEETA/DETI, University of Aveiro, Portugal
[3] DSTNC, University of Granada, Spain

Abstract. Features are extracted from PET images employing exploratory matrix factorization techniques, here non-negative matrix factorization (NMF). Appropriate features are fed into classifiers such as support vector machine or random forest. An automatic classification is achieved with high classification rate and only few false negatives.

Keywords: exploratory matrix factorization, feature extraction, positron emission tomographic images.

1 Introduction

Today there are approximately 24 million people affected by dementia, and Alzheimer's disease is the most common cause of dementia. With the growth of the older population in developing countries, this number is expected to triple over the next 50 years, while the development of early diagnosis methods is still in its infancy. Dementias do not only affect the patient itself, but also his social environment. In many cases, relatives cannot handle daily live without external help. Hence, dementias also charge health care systems with huge amounts of money.

With positron emission tomography (PET) and single photon emission computed tomography (SPECT) nuclear medicine has imaging modalities providing functional information (blood flow, metabolic activity, etc.) which renders it possible to discover abnormalities, even before anatomic or structural alterations can be observed by other imaging techniques. However, discriminating age-related changes which are often seen in healthy aged people from changes caused by Alzheimer's disease is still a challenging task.

In the US, the Alzheimer's disease neuroimaging initiative (ADNI) collects data of patients affected by Alzheimer's decease (AD) or different kinds of dementia like mild cognitive impairment (MCI) and normal control group and is engaged in the development of early diagnosis and treatment of dementias. This includes diagnosis based on mental state exams (e.g. mini mental state exam (MMSE)), biomarkers, MRI and PET scans. With more than 200 Alzheimer's disease patients, 200 controls and 400 MCI patients, the ADNI database provides a fairly large data set for investigations. Following we will illustrate how EMF methods can be used to extract features from such image sets which can be used to train a classifier.

M. Graña Romay et al. (Eds.): HAIS 2010, Part I, LNAI 6076, pp. 460–467, 2010.

1.1 Data Sets

The ^{18}F-FDG PET data from 219 Alzheimer disease neuroimaging initiative (ADNI) participants, acquired with Siemens, General Electric and Philips PET scanners, were collected from the web site of the ADNI Laboratory on NeuroImaging (LONI, University of California, Los Angeles) [1] . The ADNI study has many inclusion and exclusion criteria for their participants. Many of them are related to general fitness, medication and former diseases that might influence the results. The same selection of images was also used for a classical statistical analysis [2], [3], [4], [5], [6], [7], [8].

The ADNI database provides several scans per patient. The first three scans are recorded in time intervals of 6 months and additional scans are registered in intervals of 12 months each. Due to the development of Alzheimer's disease, these time intervals lead to the acquisition of, on average, 3.9 scans per MCI patient. The latter are especially interesting when investigating the development of the disease. Fig. 1 shows the distribution of patients across the number of scans for all three disease types.

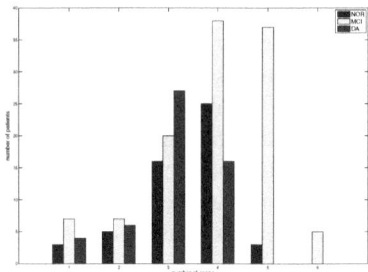

Fig. 1. Amount of scans per selected patient of the ADNI database

To select training subsets of all scans, two different procedures have been taken into account. Both procedures have in common that they select the scans at random, but while one procedure allows multiple inclusion of scans of one patient, the other one only allows one scan per patient. The second procedure avoids to obtain subsets that are very similar due to anatomical reasons. As preprocessing, pixels not belonging to the brain have been masked out. The mask has been generated by joining together all individual masks from all scans with the standard SPM brain mask. This reduces the amount of pixels from initially 517.845 pixels to 200.781 pixels. Further, all PET image intensities were normalized to the interval $[0, 1]$ using an average over the 2% highest intensities for normalization. Additionally, the 20% lowest intensities have been set to zero.

1.2 Learning Filters

Dealing with images, any NMF algorithm decomposes the $M \times N$ - dimensional matrix of images according to the above mentioned data model into an $M \times K$ - dimensional matrix of mixing coefficients and an $K \times N$ - dimensional matrix of filters or meta-images:

$$
\begin{pmatrix} \text{image 1} \\ \vdots \\ \text{image m} \\ \vdots \\ \text{image M} \end{pmatrix} = \begin{pmatrix} \text{mixing coefficients for image 1} \\ \vdots \\ \text{mixing coefficients for image m} \\ \vdots \\ \text{mixing coefficients for image M} \end{pmatrix} \cdot \begin{pmatrix} \text{meta image (filter) 1} \\ \vdots \\ \text{meta image (filter) 2} \\ \vdots \\ \text{meta image (filter) K} \end{pmatrix}
$$

with N the number of pixels, M the number of images and K the number of filters or meta-images. Using model order selection techniques [9] like Minimum Description Length (MDL) [10], [11], Akaike Information Criterion (AIC) [12], [13], Bayes Information Criterion (BIC) [14], [15] or evaluating the eigenvalue spectrum obtain through a PCA of the images, the optimal number K of relevant features for a binary classification of the images turned out to be $5 - 6$ features, hence meta-images. The first 5 PCA eigenimages already transport more than 99% of the variance of the data. For a three class classification (NOR - MCI - DA), $8 - 10$ features were estimated to be optimal but best results were achieved with 12 features instead.

Hence, the matrix factorization results in a filter matrix and a mixing matrix when dealing with images. The filter matrix learned from a training set of images can later be used to factorize a new image matrix. The mixing matrix obtained from a matrix factorization is used to train a classifier and new images can be classified by the mixing matrix resulting from their factorization using the learnt filter matrix. Restricting the filter matrix to only few components, one can extremely reduce the dimensionality of the problem. Finally filters, i.e. the meta images, themselves might provide information relevant for treatment or diagnosis of Alzheimer's disease, e.g. the regions in the brain which show metabolic changes first.

The EMF can be applied to all slices from the whole volume composed into one single image. Here all the information of the scans is used for classification. Problems of this approach are related with the huge amount of pixels, but also with many scans not imaging those parts of the brain which are related to Alzheimer's disease. Implementations of this approach are restricted by the number of scans due to limited storage capacity of the RAMs available in the computer. For diagnostic purposes, a relatively small amount of slices is enough. The computational benefit when taking only one slice is the immense reduction of pixels. The amount of different scans can be increased and a better generalization achieved. As Alzheimer's disease causes a degeneration of the temporal lobe, parietal lobe, and parts of the frontal cortex and cingulate gyrus, classification should be possible with many transversal slices. To avoid fluctuations, pixel-wise averaging neighboring slices is an appropriate solution.

Results were obtained with a training set of 60 images per class and a test set of 25 images per class. To select most informative slices, transversal slices have been chosen. Figure 2 shows in the left plot the classification rates of the three-class classification with feature extraction by NMF and classification by SVM. Slice 42 can be seen to provide the best classification performance and therefore was used further on. The corresponding MRI scan indicates that slice 42 encompasses all areas of the brain that are known to be affected by Alzheimer's disease, hence the maximal classification rate results from this slice. The correlation of the best matching column vector of matrix **M** with the design vector which represents the *a priori* diagnostic knowledge available allows one to estimate the number of filters to be extracted for good classification performance using a single filter only. Figure 3 shows a plot of the dependence of the correlation coefficient on the number of extracted components. The maximum of the graph appears with 6 images and stays almost constant for larger numbers of extracted features (filters, meta-images), especially in case of an NMF factorization. Note that best classification results were obtained with 12 extracted filters, however, using more than one filter as input to the classifier.

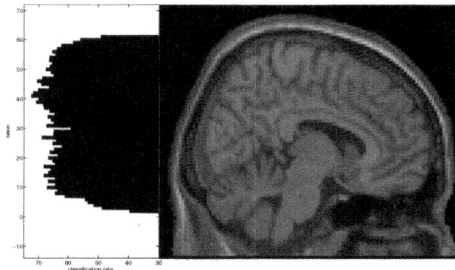

Fig. 2. *Left*: Classification rate depending on the selected transversal slice, *Right*: Transversal slice nr. 42 corresponding to a maximal classification rate

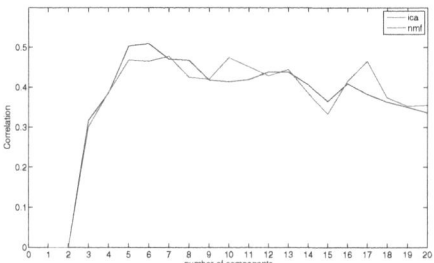

Fig. 3. Dependence of the correlation coefficient between the best matching column vector of matrix **M** and the design vector representing the *a priori* knowledge available. The graph can serve to estimate the number of filters or meta-images to be extracted for good classification results using only a single filter.

1.3   NMF Meta-images

The extracted features have been applied to a random forest classifier [16] to classify the meta-images according to the classes control group (NOR), mild cognitive impairment (MCI) and definitely Alzheimer (DA). The importance of the various features for the classification decision was measured using the Gini [17] index. As can be seen in figures 4 to 7 NMF learns parts based representations. The single meta-images of each figure are ordered by decreasing Gini importance beginning with the top left meta image. The images are adjusted with forehead to the right and the color scale is exactly the same for all images. There are interesting similarities to discover between the sets of

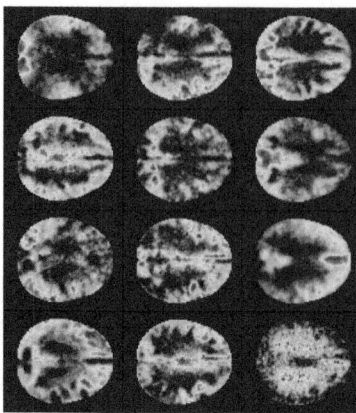

Fig. 4. Meta-images of binary classification NOR/DA ordered by decreasing Gini importance

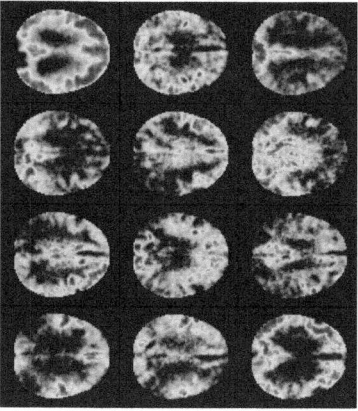

Fig. 5. Meta-images of binary classification MCI/DA ordered by decreasing Gini importance

meta-images. An exceptional similarity exists between the most important meta-image in figure 4 and for figures 5, 6 and 7 every second most important meta image. All these images show high intensity at the site of the occipital lobe, which is allocated in the back of the head and for parts of the parietal lobe, in the side area of the brain. The occipital lobe is known to be relatively unaffected by any dementia, not only by Alzheimer's disease.

All features have been classified using either a support vector machine (SVM) or a random forest (RF) classifier. All classification results are based on training sets of 60 images per class and testing sets of 25 images per class, drawn from all available whole brain scans. As stated before, an average of slice 42 and its nearest neighbors has been used for classification always. The number of extracted features has been 12 for both, binary and three class classification. As expected, the classification rate is considerably higher when classifying NOR against DA than when classifying MCI against DA or

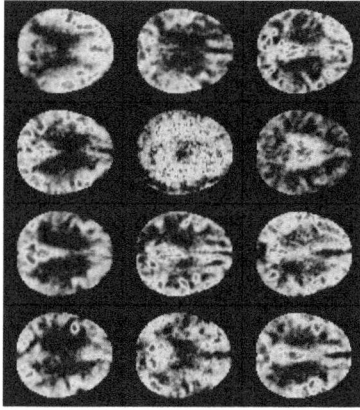

Fig. 6. Meta-images of binary classification NOR/MCI ordered by decreasing Gini importance

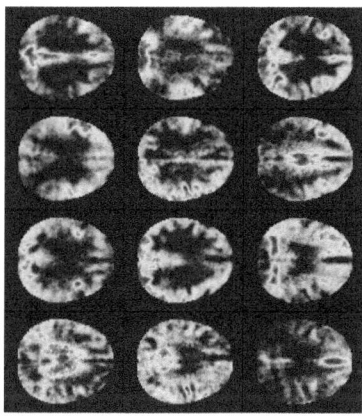

Fig. 7. Meta-images of classification NOR/MCI/DA ordered by decreasing Gini importance

Table 1. Results of a slice-wise NMF feature extraction and subsequent *left*: SVM or *right*: RF three class feature classification

actual	predicted by SVM			predicted by RF		
	NOR	MCI	DA	NOR	MCI	DA
NOR	74.4	20.3	5.3	74.1	19.4	6.5
MCI	16.7	64.4	18.9	19.5	60.1	20.4
DA	3.3	22.2	74.5	5.9	23.5	70.6
ACR	$(71 \pm 6)\%$			$(68 \pm 6)\%$		

Nor against MCI. This is because the decision is more gradual when MCI is involved than the hard binary decision in case NOR against DA. So it is not surprising that the classification rates decrease to about 70% in the three class classification applications.

Table 2. Results of a slice-wise NMF feature extraction and subsequent *top*: SVM or *bottom*: RF two class feature classification. Average classification rates (ACR) are given for all two class classification with either a support vector machine (SVM) or a random forest (RF) classifier.

actual	predicted by SVM		
	NOR MCI DA	NOR MCI DA	NOR MCI DA
NOR	91.3 8.7	74.7 25.3	
MCI		18.6 81.4	76.3 23.7
DA	6.2 93.8		20.2 81.4
ACR	$(92 \pm 4)\%$	$(78 \pm 7)\%$	$(78 \pm 5)\%$
actual	predicted by RF		
	NOR MCI DA	NOR MCI DA	NOR MCI DA
NOR	89.4 10.6	73.2 26.8	
MCI		27.3 78.4	76.7 23.3
DA	13.8 86.2		27.3 72.7
ACR	$(88 \pm 5)\%$	$75 \pm 6\%$	$75 \pm 6\%$

2 Conclusion

As expected, the classification of AD vs. NOR subjects provides best rates. Classification including MCI subjects definitely is the more challenging task, because the changes between as well normal and mild cognitive impairment and mild cognitive impairment and Alzheimer's disease are gradual.

Using a multi-level extraction by NMF the classification of MCI subjects might be improved, because the metabolic changes in the beginning of the disease are very small. Also comparing the results of mental state exams with an unsupervised classification might produce results that lead to an utility for early recognition of Alzheimer's disease.

An idea for further research is to divide the brain in several sub volumes train and classify on these volumes and in the end aggregate the classification result. This approach would provide lots of spacial information about the classification relevant brain areas and it would be easy to check a priori knowledge Alzheimer's disease.

References

1. Alzheimer's disease neuroimaging initiative
2. Ramírez, J., Górriz, J.M., Gómez-Rio, M., Romero, A., Chaves, R., Lassl, A., Rodríguez, A., Puntonet, C.G., Theis, F.J., Lang, E.W.: Effective emission tomography image reconstruction algorithms for spect data. In: Proc. ICCS 2008, pp. 741–748 (2008)
3. Ramírez, J., Chaves, R., Górriz, J.M., Álvarez, I., Salas-Gonzalez, D., López, M., Segovia, F.: Effective detection of the alzheimer disease by means of coronal nmse svm feature classification. In: Proc. ISNN 2009, pp. 337–344 (2009)
4. Ramírez, J., Chaves, R., Górriz, J.M., López, M., Salas-Gonzalez, D., Álvarez, I., Segovia, F.: Spect image classification techniques for computer aided diagnosis of the alzheimer disease. In: Cabestany, J., Sandoval, F., Prieto, A., Corchado, J.M. (eds.) IWANN 2009. LNCS, vol. 5517, pp. 941–948. Springer, Heidelberg (2009)

5. López, M., Ramírez, J., Górriz, J.M., Álvarez, I., Salas-Gonzalez, D., Segovia, F., Puntonet, C.G.: Automatic system for alzheimer's disease diagnosis using eigenbrains and bayesian classification rules. In: Cabestany, J., Sandoval, F., Prieto, A., Corchado, J.M. (eds.) IWANN 2009. LNCS, vol. 5517, pp. 949–956. Springer, Heidelberg (2009)
6. López, M., Ramírez, J., Górriz, J.M., Álvarez, I., Salas-Gonzalez, D., Segovia, F., Gómez-Rio, M.: Support vector machines and neural networks for the alzheimer's disease diagnosis using pca. In: Mira, J., Ferrández, J.M., Álvarez, J.R., de la Paz, F., Toledo, F.J. (eds.) IWINAC 2009. LNCS, vol. 5602, pp. 142–149. Springer, Heidelberg (2009)
7. Illán, I.A., Górriz, J.M., Ramírez, J., Salas-Gonzalez, D., Segovia, M.L.F., Puntonet, C.G.: ^{18}f-fdg pet imaging for computer aided alzheimer's diagnosis. NeuroImage (accepted 2010)
8. Górriz, J.M., Ramírez, J., Lassl, A., Álvarez, I., Segovia, F., Salas-Gonzalez, D., López, M.: Classification of spect images using clustering techniques revisited. In: Mira, J., Ferrández, J.M., Álvarez, J.R., de la Paz, F., Toledo, F.J. (eds.) IWINAC 2009. LNCS, vol. 5602, pp. 168–178. Springer, Heidelberg (2009)
9. Liddle, A.R.: Information criteria for astrophysical model selection. Monthly Notices of the Royal Astronomical Society: Letters 377(1), L74–L78 (2008)
10. Rissanen, J.: Modelling by shortest data description length. Automatica 14(5), 465–471 (1978)
11. Advances in Minimum Description Length: Theory and Applications. MIT Press, Cambridge (2004)
12. Akaike, H.: Information theory and an extension of the maximum likelihood principle. In: Proc. 2nd Int. Symp. Inforation Theory
13. Bozdogan, H.: Model selection and akaike's information criterion (aic): The general theory and its analytical extensions. Psychometrika 52, 345–370 (1987)
14. Schwarz, G.E.: Estimating the dimension of a model. Annals of Statistics 6, 461–464 (1978)
15. Liavas, A., Regalia, P.: On the behavior of information theoretic criteria for model order selection. IEEE Transactions on Signal Processing 49, 1689–1695 (2001)
16. Breiman, L.: Random forests. Random Forests 45 (2001)
17. Gini, C.: Measurement of inequality of income. Economic Journal 31, 124–126 (1921)

NMF-Based Analysis of SPECT Brain Images for the Diagnosis of Alzheimer's Disease

Pablo Padilla[1], Juan-Manuel Górriz[1], Javier Ramírez[1], Elmar Lang[2],
Rosa Chaves[1], Fermin Segovia[1], Ignacio Álvarez[1],
Diego Salas-González[1], and Miriam López[1]

[1] University of Granada, Periodista Daniel Saucedo Aranda S/N,
18071 Granada, Spain
[2] CIML Group, Biophysics, University of Regensburg,
D-93040 Regensburg, Germany,
{pablopadilla,gorriz,javierrp,rosach,fsegovia,
illan,dsalas,miriamlp}@ugr.es,
elmar.lang@biologie.uni-regensburg.de

Abstract. This paper offers a computer-aided diagnosis (CAD) technique for early diagnosis of Alzheimer's disease (AD) by means of single photon emission computed tomography (SPECT) image classification. The SPECT database for different patients is analyzed by applying the Fisher discriminant ratio (FDR) and non-negative matrix factorization (NMF) for the selection and extraction of the most significative features of each patient SPECT data, in order to reduce the large dimensionality of the input data and the problem of the curse of dimensionality, extracting score features. The NMF-transformed set of data, with reduced number of features, is classified by means of support vector machines (SVM) classification. The proposed NMF+SVM method yields up to 94% classification accuracy, thus becoming an accurate method for SPECT image classification. For the sake of completeness, comparison between conventional PCA+SVM method and the proposed method is also provided.

Keywords: Biomedical Engineering, Image Classification, Support Vector Machines (SVM), Non-Negative Matrix Factorization (NMF).

1 Introduction

Alzheimer's disease (AD) is the most common cause of dementia in the elderly and affects approximately 30 million individuals worldwide. With the growth of the older population in developed nations, the prevalence of AD is expected to triple over the next 50 years while its early diagnosis remains being a difficult task. Functional imaging modalities including single photon emission computed tomography (SPECT) and positron emission tomography (PET) are often used with the aim of achieving early diagnosis. The proper study of functional brain images in neurodegenerative diseases such as Alzheimer's Type Disease (ATD) is of great importance in early detection of brain anomalies and diseases, as they

M. Graña Romay et al. (Eds.): HAIS 2010, Part I, LNAI 6076, pp. 468–475, 2010.

provide valuable clinical information regarding regional cerebral blood flow or metabolic activity in the brain [1,2,3]. The evaluation of these images is usually done through visual ratings performed by experts and other subjective steps which are time-consuming and prone to error. To make reliable decisions about the presence of such abnormalities it is desirable to develop computer aided diagnosis (CAD) tools than can offer meaningful comparison in the functional brain image in contrast to normal cases (analysis of certain features in the image), regarding the appearance of the abnormalities. In this work, for early diagnosis of Alzheimer's disease, a non-negative matrix factorization (NMF) analysis approach is applied to a SPECT image database, in order to extract this meaningful information, and support vector machines (SVM) for classification.

1.1 SPECT Image Database

The proposed CAD techniques for Alzheimer's disease detection are evaluated by means of a SPECT image database that contains records for both: patients suffering Alzheimer's disease (AD) and healthy patients (NOR). This Baseline SPECT data from 97 participants was collected from the "Virgen de las Nieves" hospital in Granada (Spain). Each patient was injected with a gammaemitting technetium-99m labeled ethyl cysteinate dimer (^{99m}Tc-ECD) radiopharmaceutical and the SPECT scan was acquired by means of a 3-head gamma camera Picker Prism 3000. Brain perfusion images were reconstructed from projection data by filtered backprojection (FBP) in combination with a Butterworth noise filter [4].

SPECT images are spatially normalized [5], in order to ensure that a given voxel in different images refers to the same anatomical position. This process was done by using Statistical Parametric Mapping (SPM) [6] yielding normalized SPECT images. This step allows us to compare the voxel intensities of the brain images of different subjects. Then, the intensities of the SPECT images are normalized with the maximum intensity, which is computed for each image individually by referring each voxel to the highest voxel intensity. After the spatial normalization with SPM it is obtained a 95x69x79 voxel representation of each subject, where each voxel represents a brain volume of 2.18x2.18x3.56 mm. The SPECT images were labeled by experts of the "Virgen de las Nieves" hospital using 2 different labels: (NOR) for patients without any symptoms of AD, and (AD) for AD patients. The complete SPECT database consists of 97 patients: 41 NORMAL and 56 AD.

1.2 Non-negative Matrix Factorization for Feature Extraction

Non-negative matrix factorization (NMF) is a recently developed technique for finding parts-based, linear representations of non-negative data [7,8], being a useful decomposition tool for multivariate data. Given a non-negative data matrix A, NMF finds an approximate factorization $A \approx WH$ into non-negative matrices W and H. The non-negativity condition forces the representation to be purely additive (allowing no subtractions), in contrast to other existing linear representations such as principal component analysis (PCA) [9] or independent component analysis (ICA). PCA, ICA, vector quantization, and NMF can all be seen as matrix factorization, with different choices of objective function and/or constraints [10].

Formally, Non-negative matrix factorization is a linear, non-negative approximate data representation where the original database $A=[A_1, A_2, ..., A_M]$ (N by M elements), which consists of M measurements (profiles) of N non-negative scalar variables, is approximated by a non-negative matrix product, as given in 1.

$$A \approx WH \tag{1}$$

where the matrix $W=[W_1, W_2, ..., W_K]$ has dimension $N \times K$, and the matrix $H=[H_1, H_2, ..., H_M]$ has dimension $K \times M$. Thus matrix A is decomposed as offered in 2.

$$A_{nm} = \sum_{k=1}^{K} W_{nk} H_{km} \tag{2}$$

An appropriate decision on the value of k is critical in practice, but the choice of k is very often problem dependent. In most cases, however, k is usually chosen such that $k << min(M,N)$ in which case WH can be thought of as a compressed form of the data in A [11]. This property yields a reduced-variable matrix H that represents A in terms of W. After NMF factorization, the data contained in H (K by M elements) can be considered a transformed database with lower rank (k), than the original database A. Thus, a few variables are representing the data of each profile in the new representation.

Factorization Rule. Given the data matrix A, the optimal choice of matrices W and H are defined to be those nonnegative matrices that minimize the reconstruction error between A and WH. A variety of error functions (Err) have been proposed [7,8], some of the most useful are given below, in 3 and 4, and applied in this work [7].

$$Err_1 = \frac{1}{NM}\|A - WH\|^2 = \frac{1}{NM}\sum_{nm}(A_{nm}-(WH)_{nm})^2 \tag{3}$$

$$Err_2 = D(A||WH) = \sum_{nm}\left(A_{nm}\,log\frac{A_{nm}}{(WH)_{nm}}-A_{nm}+(WH)_{nm}\right) \tag{4}$$

where 3 is known as Frobenius norm (reduction of the Euclidean distance), and 4 as Kullback-Leibler divergence, among others. The NMF process is, thus, translated into an optimization problem, subject to minimization of Err, according to the one chosen.

Some NMF algorithms are proposed in [11]. There are different approaches for these algorithms [7]: with multiplicative update rule, with additive update rule or alternating least squares algorithms (ALS). Due to their fast convergence and lower iteration requirements, the last one is selected for NMF in this work.

1.3 Support Vector Machines for Classification

Support vector machines (SVM) is a widely used technique for pattern recognition and classification in a variety of applications for its ability for detecting patterns in experimental databases [2]. SVM techniques consist of two separate steps: first of all a given set of binary labeled training data is used for training; then new unlabeled data can be classified according to the learned behaviour. SVM separate a given set of binary labeled training data by means of a hyperplane that is maximally distant from the two possible classes (in our particular case, NOR an AD classes). The objective is to build a function f with the training data, as expressed in 5, able to properly classify new unclassified data.

$$f : R^N \rightarrow \{\pm 1\} \tag{5}$$

The training data is grouped in different profiles (p), each one containing N variables, together with their proper label (NOR or AD). Thus, the training database can be expressed as in 6.

$$S_p = [(x_1, x_2, ..., x_N), y]_p = [x, y]_p \tag{6}$$

where x_n are the variables of the profile p and y the corresponding label.

Linear discriminant functions define decision hyperplanes in the N-dimensional feature space:

$$g(x) = w^T x + w_0 \tag{7}$$

where w is the weight vector that is orthogonal to the decision hyperplane and w_0 is the threshold. The optimization task consists of finding the unknown parameters w_n, and w_0 that define the decision hyperplane. The hyperplane is not unique and the selection process focuses on maximizing the generalization performance of the classifier, that is, the ability of the classifier, designed using the training set, to operate satisfactorily with new data. Among the different design criteria, the maximal margin hyperplane is usually selected since it leaves the maximum margin of separation between the two classes [2].

When no linear separation of the training data is possible, SVM can work in combination with kernel techniques so that the hyperplane defining the SVM corresponds to a nonlinear decision boundary. According to [2], in this work 4 different kernels are applied: Linear, Quadratic, Radial Basis Function (RBF) and Polynomial.

1.4 Experiments

The normalized SPECT database is then selected as input data for the NMF plus SVM CAD tool. Each patient owns 95x69x79 voxels, which yields 517845 voxels per patient. In order to reduce the curse of dimensionality, the number of voxels results are downsampled by a factor of 0.5 (each couple of voxels are substituted by its average) and the most discriminant features are selected, with

Table 1. NMF+SVM results with four different kernels, applied to different number of NMF components (k)

k		2	3	4	5
Linear (%)	Acc	86,60	90,72	86,60	79,38
	Sens	89,29	94,64	89,29	78,57
	Spec	82,93	85,37	82,93	80,49
Quadratic (%)	Acc	85,57	84,54	83,51	83,51
	Sens	85,71	87,50	85,71	85,71
	Spec	85,37	80,49	80,49	80,49
RBF (%)	Acc	86,60	94,85	91,75	89,69
	Sens	89,29	96,43	96,43	96,43
	Spec	82,93	92,68	85,37	80,49
Polynomial (%)	Acc	82,47	85,57	86,60	86,60
	Sens	83,93	85,71	85,71	83,93
	Spec	80,49	85,37	87,80	90,24

the application of the Fisher discriminant ratio criterion, which is characterized by its separation ability as shown in [1,2]:

$$FDR = \frac{(\mu_1 - \mu_2)^2}{\sigma_1^2 + \sigma_2^2} \tag{8}$$

where μ_i and σ_i^2 denote the ith class mean value and variance of the input feature, respectively. The voxels that fatisfy a particular FDR threshold level are selected as discriminative features. The resulting reduced feature vectors obtained from the different patients, normalized and downsampled SPECT images are finally taken for classification.

Evaluation of CAD Tool. In order to evaluate the developed NMF plus SVM CAD tool, the success rate, sensitivity and specificity are obtained, these last two defined as in 9. These statistics are estimated by means of leave-one-out cross-validation.

$$Sensitivity(Sens) = \frac{TP}{TP + FN} \quad Specificity(Spec) = \frac{TN}{TN + FP} \tag{9}$$

where TP is the number of true positives (AD patients correctly classified); TN is the number of true negatives (NOR patients correctly classified); FP is the number of false positives (NOR classified as AD); FN is the number of false negatives (AD classified as NOR).

Results. In order to evaluate the proposed NMF+SVM method for functional brain image classification, a comparison between the proposed method and the equivalent PCA+SVM method is provided. Table 1 offers the NMF+SVM results in terms of accuracy (Acc), sensitivity (Sens) and specificity (Spec), for the four different SVM kernels.

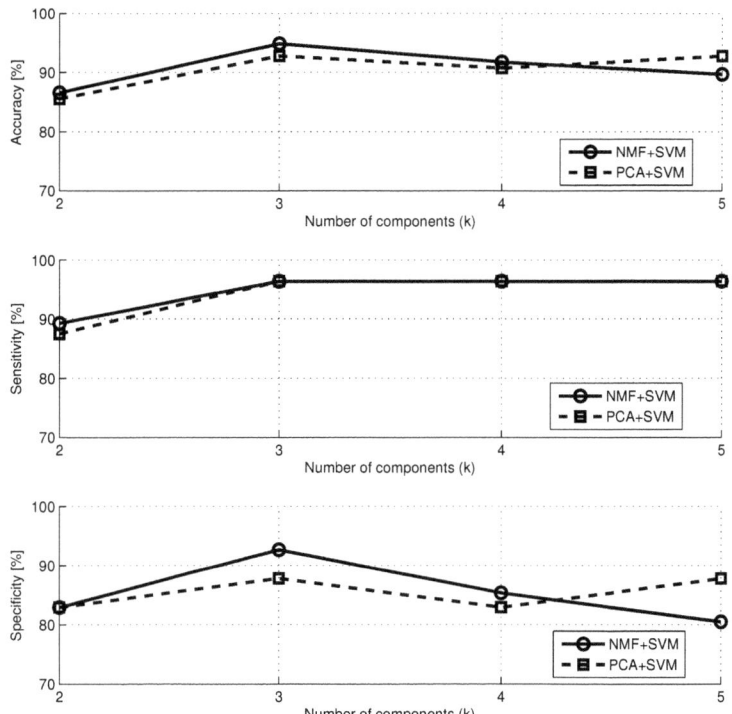

Fig. 1. Comparison between NMF+SVM and PCA+SVM techniques, for different k values

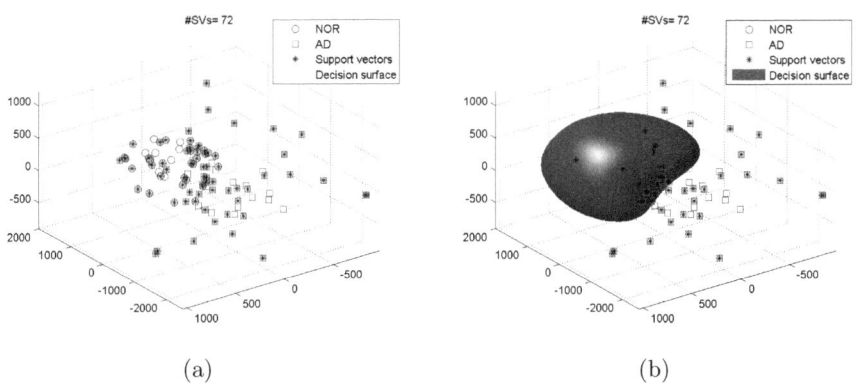

(a)   (b)

Fig. 2. SVM classifier using RBF kernel, for k=3. a)NOR patients, AD patients and Support vectors in the feature space. b) Decision surface

Comparison between the proposed NMF+SVM method and PCA+SVM approach with same features and parameters is offered in Fig. 1. In Fig. 2, the SVM decision hyperplane for the given database is shown.

1.5   Conclusion

A NMF+SVM analysis for functional brain images is applied for the proper classification of SPECT images and Alzheimer's disease detection. The proposed method is based on non-negative matrix factorization for selection and extraction of the SPECT image features of each patient of the database, considered as source data for further classification through a SVM-based method, considering different kernel functions. It was shown that the best results are obtained for a number of NMF components $k=3$. The method yielded up to 94% accuracy in classification and improves developed PCA+SVM methods for early Alzheimer's disease diagnosis. For the sake of completeness, results with PCA+SVM technique, with the same parameters, are offered. In these experiments NMF outperforms PCA as a feature extraction technique for the optimum number of components ($k=3$).

Acknowledgments. This work was partly supported by the MICINN of Spain under the PETRI DENCLASES (PET2006-0253), TEC2008-02113, NAPOLEON (TEC2007-68030-C02-01) and HD2008-0029 projects and the Consejería de Innovación, Ciencia y Empresa (Junta de Andalucía, Spain) under the Excellence Project TIC-02566.

References

1. Álvarez, I., Górriz, J.M., Ramírez, J., Salas, D., López, M., Puntonet, C.G., Segovia, F.: Alzheimer's diagnosis using eigenbrains and support vector machines. IET Electronic Letters 45, 165–167 (2009)
2. Ramírez, J., Górriz, J., Salas-Gonzalez, D., Romero, A., López, M., Álvarez, I., Gómez-Río, M.: Computer-aided diagnosis of alzheimer's type dementia combining support vector machines and discriminant set of features. Information Sciences (2009)
3. López, M., Ramírez, J., Górriz, J.M., Álvarez, I., Salas-Gonzalez, D., Segovia, F., Chaves, R.: Automatic tool for the alzheimer's disease diagnosis using pca and bayesian classification rules. IET Electronic Letters 45, 342–343 (2009)
4. Ramírez, J., Górriz, J.M., Gómez-Río, M., Romero, A., Lassl, A., Rodríguez, A., Puntonet, C.G., Theis, F., Lang, E.: Effective emission tomography image reconstruction algorithms for spect data. In: Bubak, M., van Albada, G.D., Dongarra, J., Sloot, P.M.A. (eds.) ICCS 2008, Part I. LNCS, vol. 5101, pp. 741–748. Springer, Heidelberg (2008)
5. Salas-González, D., Górriz, J.M., Ramírez, J., Lassl, A., Puntonet, C.G.: Improved Gauss-Newton optimization methods in affine registration of SPECT brain images. IET Electronics Letters 44, 1291–1292 (2008)
6. Friston, K.J., Ashburner, J., Kiebel, S.J., Nichols, T.E., Penny, W.D. (eds.): Statistical Parametric Mapping: The Analysis of Functional Brain Images. Academic Press, London (2007)
7. Lee, D.D., Seung, S.: Algorithms for non-negative matrix factorization. Advances in Neural Information Processing Systems 13, 556–562 (2001)

8. Paatero, P., Tapper, U.: Positive matrix factorization: A non-negative factor model with optimal utilization of error estimates of data values. Environmetrics 5, 111–126 (1994)
9. Turk, M., Pentland, A.: Eigenfaces for recognition. J. Cogn. Neuroscience 3, 71–86 (1991)
10. Lang, E., Schachtner, R., Lutter, D., Herold, D., Kodewitz, A., Blöchl, F., Theis, F.J., Keck, I.R., Górriz, J.M., Vilda, P.G., Tomé, A.M.: Exploratory Matrix Factorization Techniques for Large Scale Biomedical Data Sets. In: Recent Advances in Biomedical Signal Processing, Ed. Bentham (in press)
11. Berry, M.W., Browne, M., Langville, A.N., Pauca, V.P., Plemmons, R.J.: Algorithms and applications for approximate nonnegative matrix factorization. Computational Statistics and Data Analysis 52, 155–173 (2007)

Partial Least Squares for Feature Extraction of SPECT Images*

F. Segovia[1], J. Ramírez[1], J.M. Górriz[1], R. Chaves[1], D. Salas-Gonzalez[1],
M. López[1], I. Álvarez[1], P. Padilla[1], and C.G. Puntonet[2]

[1] Dept. of Signal Theory, Networking and Communications,
University of Granada, Spain
fsegovia@ugr.es
[2] Dept. of Computer Architecture and Computer Technology,
University of Granada, Spain

Abstract. Single Photon Emission Computed Tomography (SPECT) images are commonly used by physicians to assist the diagnosis of several diseases such as Alzheimer's disease (AD). The diagnosis process requires the visual evaluation of the image and usually entails time consuming and subjective steps. In this context, computer aided diagnosis (CAD) systems are desired. This work shows a complete CAD system that uses SPECT images for the automatic diagnosis of AD and combines of support vector machine (SVM) learning with a novel methodology for feature extraction based on the partial least squares (PLS) regression model. This methodology avoids the well-known small sample size problem that multivariate approaches suffer and yields peak accuracy rates of 95.9%. The results achieved are compared with the obtained ones by an PCA-based CAD system which is used as baseline.

1 Introduction

Functional neuroimaging (NI) has become a powerful tool in cognitive neuroscience, which enables us to investigate the relationship between particular cortical activations and cognitive tasks performed by a test subject or patient [1]. Single Photon Emission Computed Tomography (SPECT) is a noninvasive, functional imaging modality that can be used to analyze the regional cerebral blood flow (rCBF) in patients. This technique provides three-dimensional images with physiological functions contrary to other imaging modalities which produce images of anatomical structures. Thus, it is widely used in neurology to diagnose several dementias, such as AD [2,3].

Alzheimer's disease (AD) is the most common cause of dementia in the elderly that affects memory and cognitive functions and eventually causes the death.

---

* This work was partly supported by the MICINN under the PETRI DENCLASES (PET2006-0253), TEC2008-02113, NAPOLEON (TEC2007-68030-C02-01) and HD2008-0029 projects and the Consejería de Innovación, Ciencia y Empresa (Junta de Andalucía, Spain) under the Excellence Project (TIC-02566).

M. Graña Romay et al. (Eds.): HAIS 2010, Part I, LNAI 6076, pp. 476–483, 2010.

With the growth of the older population in developed nations, the prevalence of AD is expected to triple over the next 50 years [4]. AD diagnosis is traditionally performed by cognitive tests and the visual analysis of SPECT images of the brain what requires experimented clinicians and is prone to error. Thus, several CAD systems that use SPECT images of the brain to diagnose AD have been proposed in recent years [5,6,7,8].

This work shows a new way to perform feature extraction of SPECT images which allows addressing the small sample size problem [9] and thereby developing more effective CAD systems. In this sense, we have developed a CAD system for AD that use the mentioned feature extraction method. After a proper normalization of the SPECT raw data, we extract a reduced set of feature from the images according to an algorithm based on PLS regression model. Then, we use an SVM classifier to predict the class (AD or not AD) of the patient under study. The CAD system developed has been tested by means of a database with 97 SPECT images and the leave-one-out cross-validation technique yielding peak accuracy rates of 95.9%. These results outperform other recently developed AD CAD system.

This paper is organized as follows. Section 2 describes the procedure used for the feature extraction which is based on PLS. Section 3 shows a brief background on SVMs. The database description and the evaluation results appear in section 4. Finally conclusions are shown in section 5.

2   Feature Extraction

This section describes the feature extraction step for the CAD system. It is based on PLS but the images are reduced previously and only a set of voxels per image is selected by applying a mask. This initial reduction improves the classification results and reduces the computation effort.

2.1   Partial Least Squares

PLS [10] is a statistical method for modeling relations between sets of observed variables by means of latent variables. It comprises of regression and classification tasks as well as dimension reduction techniques and modeling tools. The underlying assumption of all PLS methods is that the observed data is generated by a system or process which is driven by a small number of latent (not directly observed or measured) variables. In its general form PLS creates orthogonal score vectors (also called latent vectors or components) by maximizing the covariance between different sets of variables. PLS can be naturally extended to regression problems. The predictor and predicted (response) variables are each considered as a block of variables. PLS then extracts the score vectors which serve as a new predictor representation and regresses the response variables on these new predictors. PLS can be also applied as a discrimination tool and dimension reduction method similar to Principal Component Analysis (PCA). After relevant latent vectors are extracted, an appropriate classifier can be applied.

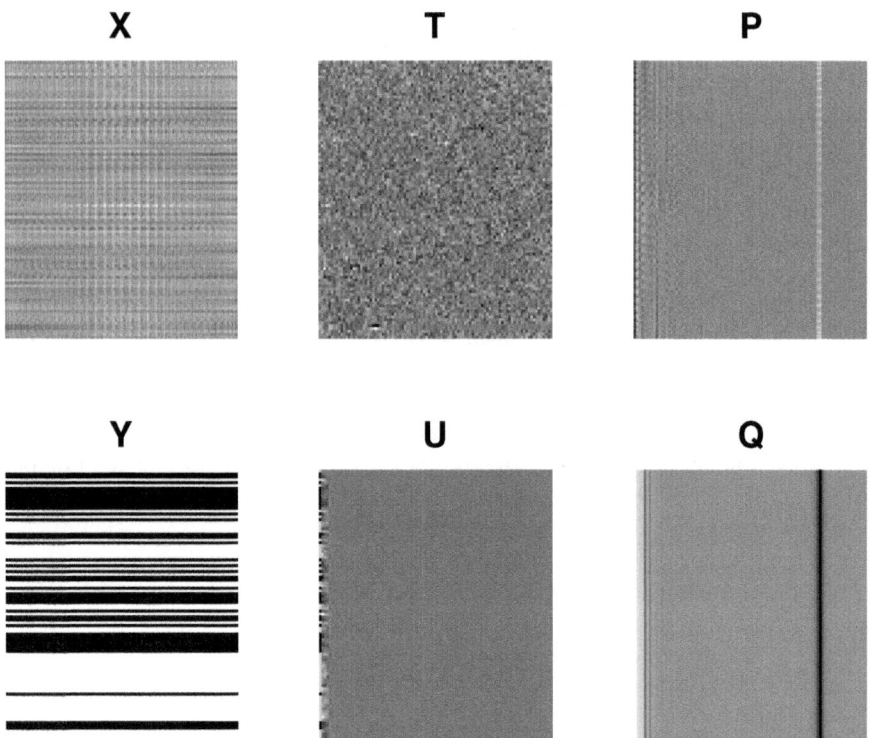

Fig. 1. Representation of the matrices involved in the PLS model for an Alzheimer's disease CAD system. X represent a selection of voxels of 97 SPECT images and Y contains the labels (control or AD) assigned to that images.

PLS is a linear algorithm for modeling the relation between two data sets $X \subset \mathbb{R}^N$ and $Y \subset \mathbb{R}^M$. After observing n data samples from each block of variables, PLS decomposes the $n \times N$ matrix of zero-mean variables $\mathbf{X}$ and the $n \times M$ matrix of zero-mean variables Y into the form

$$\mathbf{X} = \mathbf{T}\mathbf{P}^T + \mathbf{E}$$
$$\mathbf{Y} = \mathbf{U}\mathbf{Q}^T + \mathbf{F} \tag{1}$$

where the $\mathbf{T}$, $\mathbf{U}$ are $n \times p$ matrices of the p extracted score vectors (components, latent vectors), the $N \times p$ matrix $\mathbf{P}$ and the $M \times p$ matrix $\mathbf{Q}$ represent matrices of loadings and the $n \times N$ matrix $\mathbf{E}$ and the $n \times M$ matrix $\mathbf{F}$ are the matrices of residuals. PLS is implemented by means of nonlinear iterative partial least squares (NIPALS) algorithm [11]. Fig. 1 illustrates the feature extraction process and the matrices involved in PLS regression of $\mathbf{X}$ and $\mathbf{Y}$. It is shown how the PLS model accurately matches the given data by means of the extracted score vectors ($\mathbf{T}$ and $\mathbf{U}$) and loadings ($\mathbf{P}$ and $\mathbf{Q}$).

The difference between PLS and PCA is that the former creates orthogonal weight vectors by maximizing the covariance between elements in $\mathbf{X}$ and $\mathbf{Y}$. Thus, PLS not only considers the variance of the samples but also considers the class labels. Fisher Discriminant Analysis (FDA) is, in this way, similar to PLS. However, FDA has the limitation that after dimensionality reduction, there are only $c - 1$ meaningful latent variables, where c is the number of classes being considered. Additionally, when the number of features exceeds the number of samples, the covariance estimates when applying PCA do not have full rank and the weight vectors cannot be extracted.

2.2   Feature Extraction of SPECT Images

Once the SPECT images have been acquired, reconstructed and normalized, the first step consists of downsampling each of them with a factor of 2. Thus, we reduce the computation time without loss of information since marks of AD are not at voxel level but at higher structures level. Then we compute the average of all controls and define a binary mask by considering only those voxels with a mean intensity above 50% of the maximum intensity. Applying this mask to each image entails a significant reduction of the input space. Finally, score PLS vectors are extracted based on the regression model in equation 1 and we use them as features.

3   Background on SVM

Support Vector Machines (SVMs) have attracted recent attention from the pattern recognition community due to a number of theoretical and computational merits derived from the Statistical Learning Theory [12] developed by Vladimir Vapnik at AT&T.

SVM separates a set of binary labeled training data by means of a hyperplane (called maximal margin hyperplane) that is maximally distant from the two classes. The objective is to build a function $f : \mathbb{R}^N \to \pm 1$ using training data that is, N-dimensional patterns x_i and class labels y_i so that f will correctly classify new examples $(\mathbf{x}, \mathbf{y})$:

$$(x_1, y_1), (x_2, y_2), ..., (x_i, y_i) \in \mathbb{R}^N \times \pm 1 \tag{2}$$

Linear discrinant functions define decision hyperplanes in a multidimensional feature space:

$$g(\mathbf{x}) = \mathbf{w}^T \mathbf{x} + w_0 = 0, \tag{3}$$

where $\mathbf{w}$ is the weight vector that is orthogonal to the decision hyperplane and w_0 is the threshold. The optimization task consists of finding the unknown parameters $\mathbf{w}$ and w_0 that define the decision hyperplane. When no linear separation of the training data is possible, SVM can work effectively in combination with kernel techniques so that the hyperplane defining the SVM corresponds to a non-linear decision boundary in the input space. A kernel function is defined as:

$$\mathbf{K}(x_i, x_j) = \varphi(x_i)\varphi(x_j) \tag{4}$$

Kernel functions avoid having to work explicitly in feature space, thus the training algorithm only depends on the data through dot products in Euclidean space, i.e. on functions of the form $\varphi(x_i)\varphi(x_j)$.

4   Materials and Experiments

This section explains the experiments performed and shows the results obtained. In addition, the database of images used for the experiments and the preprocess step are described.

4.1   SPECT Image Database

The system proposed has been evaluated by means of a SPECT database which consists of 97 images collected from the "Virgen de las Nieves" hospital in Granada (Spain). The patients were injected with a gamma emitting ^{99m}Tc-ECD radiopharmeceutical and the SPECT raw data was acquired by a three head gamma camera Picker Prism 3000. A total of 180 projections were taken with a 2-degree angular resolution. The images of the brain cross sections were reconstructed from the projection data using the filtered backprojection (FBP) algorithm in combination with a Butterworth noise removal filter [13].

The SPECT images are then spatially normalized using the SPM software [14], in order to ensure that the voxels in different images refer to the same anatomical positions in the brain. This step allows us to compare the voxel intensities of the brain images of different subjects. Then we normalize the intensities of the SPECT images with the maximum intensity I_{max}, which is computed for each image individually by averaging over the 3% of the highest voxel intensities. After the spatial normalization with the SPM software one obtains a $95 \times 69 \times 79$ voxel representation of each subject, where each voxel represents a brain volume of $2.18 \times 2.18 \times 3.56\,\mathrm{mm}^3$. The SPECT images were visually classified by experts of the "Virgen de las Nieves" hospital using 4 different labels: *normal* (NOR) for patients without any symptoms of AD, and *possible AD* (AD1), *probable AD* (AD2) and *certain AD* (AD3) to distinguish between different levels of the presence of typical characteristics for AD. In total, the database consists of 41 NOR, 30 AD1, 22 AD2 and 4 AD3 patients. Table 1 shows other demographic details of the database.

4.2   Evaluation Experiments

Several experiments were conducted with the purpose of evaluating the CAD system which consists of the PLS-based feature extraction method described above and a SVM classifier with linear kernel. Moreover we performed similar experiments using a PCA approach in order to use its results as baseline. Both PCA and PLS attempt to reduce the input space and thereby they avoid the small sample size problem and improve the classification results.

After normalization, each SPECT image consists of 517845 voxels (see section 4.1) that results in an input space with 517845 dimensions. However before

Table 1. Demographic details of the dataset. AD 1 = possible AD, AD 2 = probable AD, AD 3 = certain AD. μ and σ stands for population mean and standard deviation respectively.

	#	Sex (%)		Age		
		M	F	μ	σ	range
NOR	41	73.17	26.83	71.51	7.99	46-85
AD1	30	36.67	63.33	65.86	13.36	23-81
AD2	22	54.55	45.45	67.22	8.25	46-86
AD3	4	0	100.00	76	9.90	69-83

Table 2. Maximum values of accuracy, sensitivity and specificity achieved by a PCA-based CAD system and other one based on the PLS regression model

	Accuracy	Sensitivity	Specificity
PCA	88.66%	87.50%	90.24%
PLS	95.88%	96.43%	95.12%

Fig. 2. Comparison between the accuracy rates achieved by the proposed CAD system and other one based on a PCA approach in function of the number of features used

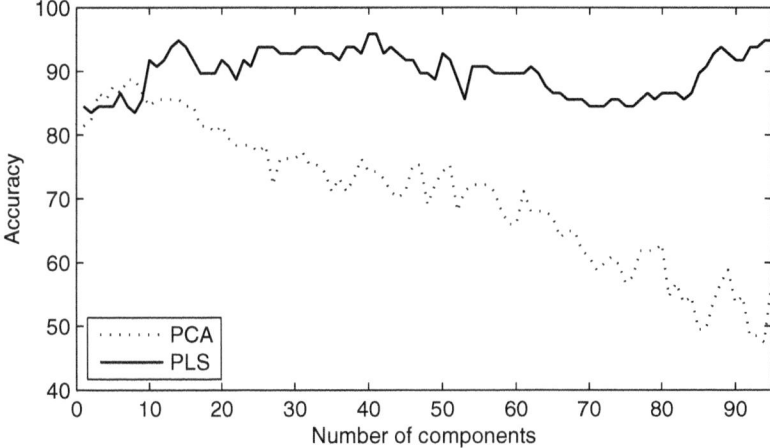

applying the PLS algorithm, images were reduced with a factor of 2 and then only most important voxels were selected by using a binary mask as it is described in section 2.2. Thus, initial number of features per image which was used as input for the PLS algorithm was 20638. Since, the database has 97 images and we used the leave-one-out technique to validate the CAD system, the final number of features per image was 95, i.e. the size of score vectors. However, a further reduction is possible by truncating these vectors. It is worth noting here that

PLS algorithm takes into account the image labels to extract score vectors and, in order to avoid biased results, we ran it once for each image using the 96 remaining images with their labels to extract weight matrix and from it we computed the score vector for the current image. In other words, we applied a leave-one-out methodology to the feature extraction method with the purpose of avoiding that the label of a given image is taken into account to compute its score vector.

Finally, the score vectors obtained are used as feature to train a SVM classifier. Fig. 2 shows accuracy rates yielded by the CAD system proposed in function of the number of features used and compare them with the obtained ones by a PCA-based CAD system. As it is shown, feature extraction based on the PLS regression model obtains higher rates of accuracy, sentivivity and specificity than a PCA approach and gets a peak of accuracy of 95.9%. Table 2 shows the maximum rates achieved by both systems. The sensitivity and specificity of each test is defined as:

$$\text{Sensitivity} = \frac{TP}{TP+FN}; \quad \text{Specificity} = \frac{TN}{TN+FP}$$

respectively, where TP is the number of true positives: number of AD patients correctly classified; TN is the number of true negatives: number of controls correctly classified; FP is the number of false positives: number of controls classified as AD patient; FN is the number of false negatives: number of AD patients classified as control.

5 Conclusions

In this work, we have shown a novel method for feature extraction of SPECT images based on the Partial Least Squares regression model. Firstly, we have reduced the dimension of the images by downsampling with a factor of 2 and we have applied a binary mask to select high-intensity voxels. Then, we have used the resulting voxels with a nonlinear iterative PLS algorithm, obtaining features as the score vectors. In order to test this method we have implemented a CAD system for Alzheimer's disease. The system has been validated by means of a SPECT database with 54 patients and 43 controls and the leave-one-out cross-validation technique. We have yielded peak values of accuracy= 95.9%, sensitivity= 96.4% and specificity= 95.1% that outperformed previous system based on Principal Component Analysis.

References

1. Friston, K., et al.: Statistical Parametric Mapping: The Analysis of Functional Brain Images. Academic Press, London (2007)
2. Illan, I.A.: Análisis en Componentes de Imágenes Funcionales para la Ayuda al Diagnóstico de la Enfermedad de Alzheimer. PhD thesis, Universidad de Granada (July 2009)

3. Górriz, J.M., Lassl, A., Ramírez, J., Salas-González, D., Puntonet, C.G., Lang, E.W.: Automatic selection of rois in functional imaging using gaussian mixture models. Neuroscience Letter 460(2), 108–111 (2009)
4. Brookmeyer, R., Johnson, E., Ziegler-Graham, K., Arrighi, H.: Forecasting the global burden of alzheimer's disease. Alzheimer's and Dementia 3(3), 186–191 (2007)
5. Stoeckel, J., Fung, G.: Svm feature selection for classification of spect images of alzheimer's disease using spatial information. In: Proc. of the Fifth International Conference on Data Mining, ICDM 2005 (2005)
6. Álvarez, I., Górriz, J.M., Ramírez, J., Salas-González, D., López, M., Puntonet, C.G., Segovia, F.: Alzheimer's diagnosis using eigenbrains and support vector machines. Electronics Letters 45(7), 342–343 (2009)
7. Ramírez, J., Górriz, J.M., Chaves, R., López, M., Salas-González, D., Álvarez, I., Segovia, F.: SPECT image classification using random forests. IET Electronics Letters 45(12), 604–605 (2009)
8. Chaves, R., Ramírez, J., Górriz, J.M., López, M., Salas-González, D., Álvarez, I., Segovia, F.: SVM-based computer aided diagnosis of the Alzheimer's disease using t-test NMSE feature selection with feature correlation weighting. Neuroscience Letters 461(3), 293–297 (2009)
9. Duin, R.P.W.: Classifiers in almost empty spaces. In: Proceedings 15th International Conference on Pattern Recognition, vol. 2, pp. 1–7. IEEE, Los Alamitos (2000)
10. Wold, S., Ruhe, H., Wold, H., Dunn III, W.J.: The collinearity problem in linear regression. the partial least squares (PLS) approach to generalized inverse. Journal of Scientific and Statistical Computations 5, 735–743 (1984)
11. Wold, H.: Path models with latent variables: The NIPALS approach. In: Quantitative Sociology: International perspectives on mathematical and statistical model building, pp. 307–357. Academic Press, London (1975)
12. Vapnik, V.N.: Statistical Learning Theory. John Wiley and Sons, Inc., New York (1998)
13. Ramírez, J., Górriz, J.M., Gómez-Río, M., Romero, A., Chaves, R., Lassl, A., Rodrguez, A., Puntonet, C.G., Theis, F., Lang, E.: Effective emission tomography image reconstruction algorithms for SPECT data. In: Bubak, M., van Albada, G.D., Dongarra, J., Sloot, P.M.A. (eds.) ICCS 2008, Part I. LNCS, vol. 5101, pp. 741–748. Springer, Heidelberg (2008)
14. Friston, K.J., Ashburner, J., Kiebel, S.J., Nichols, T.E., Penny, W.D.: Statistical Parametric Mapping: The Analysis of Functional Brain Images. Academic Press, London (2007)

Sensor Fusion Adaptive Filtering for Position Monitoring in Intense Activities

Alberto Olivares[1], J.M. Górriz[2], J. Ramírez[2], and Gonzalo Olivares[1]

[1] Dept. of Computer Architecture and Computer Technology, University of Granada, Spain
[2] Dept. of Signal Processing, Networking and Communications,
University of Granada, Spain
aolivares@atc.ugr.es, {gorriz,javierrp,gonzalo}@ugr.es

Abstract. Inertial sensors are widely used in body movement monitoring systems. Different factors derived from the sensors nature, such as the Angle Random Walk (ARW), and dynamic bias lead to erroneous measurements. Moreover, routines including intense exercises are subject to high dynamic accelerations that distort the angle measurement. Such negative effects can be reduced through the use of adaptive filtering based on sensor fusion concepts. Most existing published works use a Kalman filtering sensor fusion approach. Our aim is to perform a comparative study among different adaptive filters. Several Least Mean Squares (LMS) and Recursive Least Squares (RLS) filters variations are tested with the purpose of finding the best method leading to a more accurate angle measurement. An angle wander compensation and dynamic acceleration bursts filtering method has been developed by the implementing a sensor fusion approach based on LMS and RLS filters.

Keywords: Angle Measurement, Inertial Measurement Units, Sensor Fusion, Kalman Filter, RLS, LMS.

1 Introduction

Human body position monitoring is employed in many fields including entertainment industry, military, movement science, medical applications, etc. There exist several systems to monitor the movement being performed by a person, such as movement tracking cameras [1], and Inertial Measurement Units (IMUs) [2], [3]. Systems based on cameras are usually very accurate, however, their cost is very high and they are not suitable to be carried by the person under test, who has to move inside the area covered by the cameras. On the other hand, IMU based systems offer much more flexibility since they can be easily carried by the subject due to their low size. Moreover the cost of such a system is many times lower than a camera based system.

IMUs are typically composed by accelerometers, gyroscopes and occasionally magnetometers. Within the last decade the use of Microelectromechanic (MEM) sensors has been popularized mainly due to their low size and cost and their reasonable precision. Their market generalization has offered the possibility to develop low cost and low size Inertial Measurement Units (IMUs). However, MEM devices present a

M. Graña Romay et al. (Eds.): HAIS 2010, Part I, LNAI 6076, pp. 484–491, 2010.

set of negative factors that need to be treated to avoid a loss of precision in the measurements.

One of the main negative effects is the angle wander produced when the gyroscope signal is integrated. This wander is caused by two factors: the first is called Angle Random Walk and consists of random angle wander over time. It is produced when the small peaks which are present in the gyroscope output, due to thermal and electronic noise, are integrated. This effect will vary depending on the quality of the employed sensor. The second factor that contributes to the angle wander is caused by the progressive dynamic variation of the bias in the gyroscope output, mainly originated by the sensor self-heating. The presence of angle wander due to ARW and dynamic bias makes unfeasible the determination of the angle relying solely in the gyroscope.

Therefore, we need a sensor fusion strategy to compensate the negative effects of the angle wander. Sensor fusion is defined as the conjoint use of various sensors to improve the accuracy of the measurements under situations where a sensor is not behaving properly. In our case we have an accelerometer that will help to obtain better measurements.

Accelerometers also present noise in their output, but since we do not have to perform any integration to calculate the angle as it is obtained by the decomposition of the static gravity acceleration, no angle wander is produced. Why do not we always use the accelerometer to measure angles then? The answer depends on the situation in which the limb angles want to be measured. If the patient is moving its limbs slowly, the measured angle will be very accurate as the angle computation relies on static accelerations. By contrast, if the patient is carrying out a rather intense activity, the accelerometer will measure dynamic accelerations leading to totally erroneous measurements.

By using a sensor fusion based approach we will be able to reduce the angle drift in the gyroscope angle signal taking the accelerometer angle signal as a position reference that can be weighted through a variable trust parameter according to the degree of dynamic acceleration that we expect the accelerometer to measure.

Such a sensor fusion is usually done using a solution based on Kalman filtering [4], [5]. Most of the published works tend to use this kind of filters claiming they offer a better response than other solutions. To our knowledge, to this day, there are no published works showing a comparative study among other different adaptive filter sensor fusion approaches.

The goal of our work is to carry out a comparative study between various LMS and RLS filters and the already proposed Kalman filter approach.

This paper is divided as follows: Section 2 presents the sensor fusion approach based on the Kalman filter and the approach that will allow the use of different adaptive filters. Section 3 presents the obtained results on synthesized signals. Section 4 presents the obtained results on real signals registered by the IMU, and conclusions are drawn in Section 5.

2   Adaptive Filtering Sensor Fusion Approaches

As said in the introduction, angles are calculated using the information from acceleration and angular velocity sensed by accelerometers and gyroscopes.

To compute the angle using the accelerometer signal there is no need to perform any integration but just basic trigonometric relations. Since the signal is not integrated the random noise will not cause an angle wander as in the gyroscope case. Given that, the angle is computed by sensing the gravity acceleration, we will not be able to obtain a correct measurement when there are dynamic accelerations distorting the sensing of the gravity acceleration derived from intense activities. This fact prevents us from using only the accelerometer to measure the angle accurately as bursts of dynamic accelerations will drive the system to inaccurate performance.

We are forced to use a system that is robust under the presence of dynamic accelerations. If there was no bias drift the gyroscope angle signal would be very accurate since it does not have high amplitude noise components and is invulnerable to dynamic accelerations. If we manage to remove the bias in the gyroscope signal, we will have a good approximation of the position of the body.

In order to remove the bias we can just rely on the only available reference which is the accelerometer angle signal. Since this signal is erroneous under the presence of dynamic acceleration peaks we need a system that is able to decrease the impact of those peaks by filtering them. The proposed tools to perform this task by most authors are adaptive filters and more specifically the Kalman filter [6], [7].

2.1 Kalman filter Approach

The Kalman filter is an ideal solution to perform sensor fusion since it estimates a process based on an observation. The difference between the process estimation and the observation is weighted by a gain which depends on the measurement error covariance and the process error covariance.

The gyroscope signal is filtered based on the acceleration signal observations. We can tell the filter which signal to trust more by modifying the values of the filter parameters. When the measurement error covariance approaches zero, the acceleration signal is trusted more and more, while the predicted measurement is trusted less and less. On the other hand, as the a priori estimate error covariance approaches zero the acceleration signal is trusted less and less, while the predicted measurement using the gyroscope signal is trusted more and more.

This behavior allows us to tune the filter attending to the activity that is being monitored. When monitoring intense activities the accelerometer signal will be given a lower degree of trust to filter dynamic accelerations.

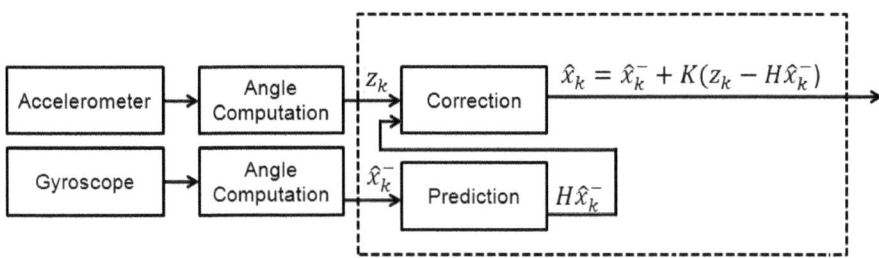

Fig. 1. Diagram of Kalman Filter Sensor Fusion Approach

Figure 1 depicts the diagram of the Kalman filter sensor fusion approach to remove dynamic bias and filter random noise and dynamic acceleration.

2.2 LMS/RLS Filter Sensor Fusion Approach

A similar approach is applied when using LMS and RLS adaptive filters. LMS and RLS filters are widely used to cancel undesired components in signals, such as noise and echo.

We will use the gyroscope signal as the input to be filtered and the accelerometer signal as the desired signal. This configuration will remove the gyroscope's dynamic bias while it will filter the accelerometer's noise, as resultant LMS and RLS filters will have low-pass nature in almost all configurations. The accuracy and convergence time will vary enormously depending on the filter parameters and the input signals nature as is later showed in section 3.

Many variations of LMS and RLS filters have been tested, more specifically, Normalized LMS (N-LMS) [8], Momentum Normalized LMS (MN-LMS) [9], standard RLS, Householder RLS (H-RLS) [10] and QR-decomposition-based RLS (QRD-RLS) [11].

Figure 2 shows the diagram of the developed LMS/RLS sensor fusion approach.

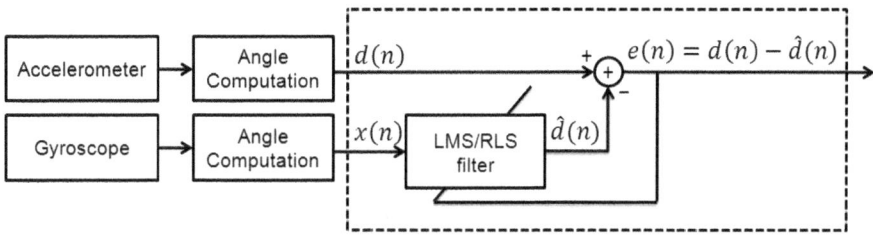

Fig. 2. Diagram of LMS/RLS Filter Sensor Fusion Approach

3 Application on Synthesized Signals

In order to perform a comparative study between the adaptive filters the Mean Squared Error (MSE) needs to be computed so we have an objective value reflecting the algorithms performance. To calculate the MSE we need to synthesize gyroscope and accelerometer angle signals. As the ideal unbiased gyroscope angle signal is unknown, we will synthesize it. The MSE of each of the filter outputs will be then obtained by applying the following expression:

$$MSE = \left[\alpha_{gu} - \hat{\alpha}_{gu} \right]^2 \tag{1}$$

where α_{gu} is the ideal unbiased gyroscope angle signal and $\hat{\alpha}_{gu}$ is the output of the adaptive filters.

Three signals are then synthesized: an accelerometer angle signal, an unbiased gyroscope signal and a biased gyroscope signal.

The unbiased gyroscope signal is synthesized by building a sinusoidal signal having an amplitude of ±180° with a sampling frequency of 50 Hz and a period of 2 seconds. The accelerometer signal is synthesized by adding two different random noises to the unbiased gyroscope signal. The first random noise is applied to simulate electronic noise and has a maximum amplitude of 10°. The second random noise is applied to simulate bursts of dynamic acceleration and has a maximum amplitude of 150°. The duration of the bursts is limited to 1 second. The biased gyroscope signal is built by adding a linear bias, having the same slope than real measured signals, to the unbiased gyroscope signal. All signals are 8 minutes long.

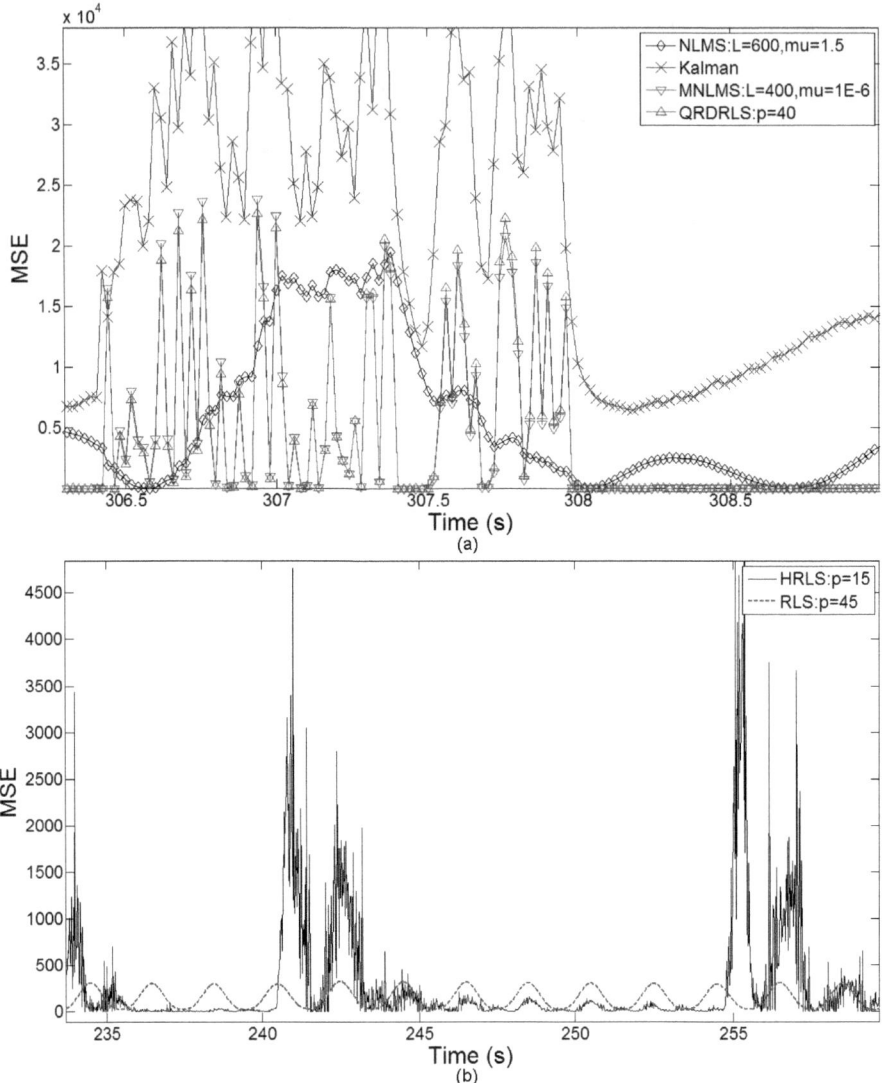

Fig. 3. MSE of different tested adaptive filters. NLMS, Kalman, MNLMS, QRDRLS (a), HRLS, RLS (b).

The biased gyroscope signal and the distorted accelerometer synthesized signals are used as inputs of the adaptive filters. To augment the precision of the executions the final MSE is calculated by averaging the MSE of 50 executions of each of the filter algorithms. New signals are synthesized at the beginning of every execution. The computed MSE is shown in figure 3.

Based on the simulation results the lowest MSE is obtained for the RLS filter having a filter size of 45 coefficients since it has the fastest convergence and is able to

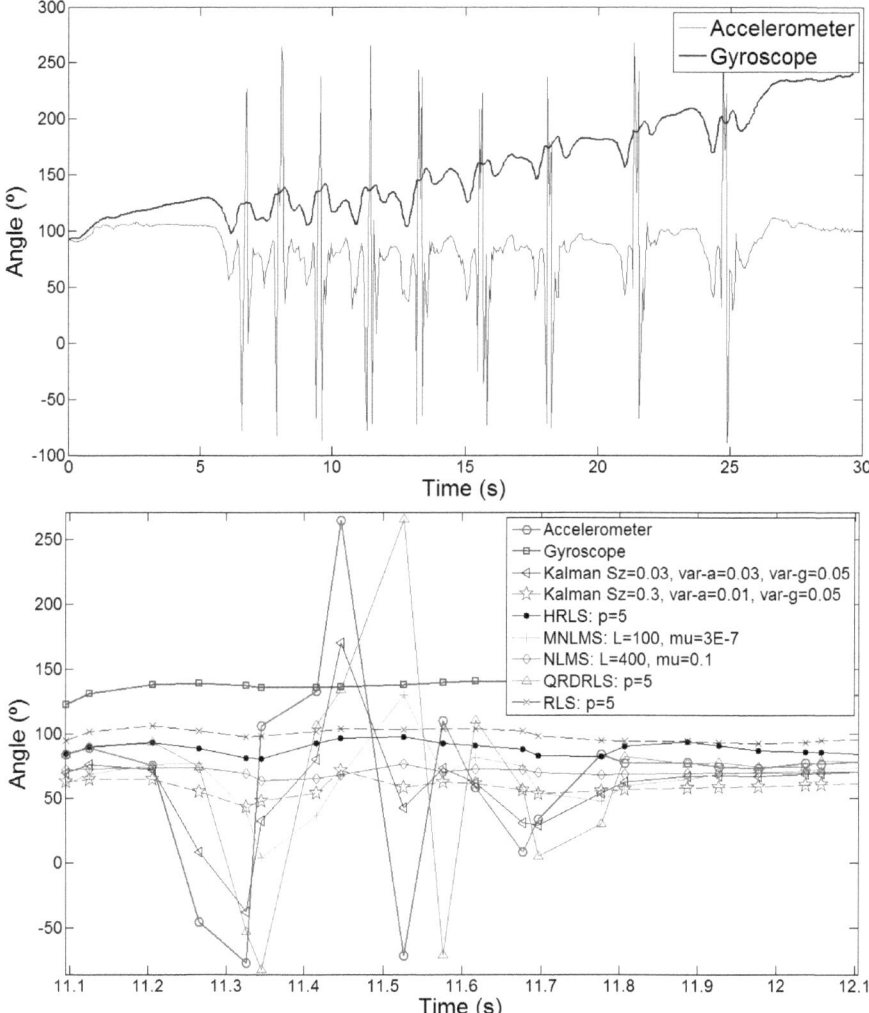

Fig. 4. Acceleration and gyroscope angle signals gathered during a vertical jump exercise (a). Output of different adaptive filters applied on the gathered signals (b). Sz=Observation signal noise covariance, var_a=Process noise covariance related to the acceleration signal, var_g:= Process noise covariance related to the gyroscope signal.

filter completely the dynamic acceleration peaks. NLMS is quite effective filtering the peaks but its large convergence time makes unfeasible its application in a real time application. On the other hand, QRDRLS and HRLS show a fast convergence but they are unable to filter the peaks.

Almost all the studied filters outperform Kalman filter in the theoretical simulations. This is due to the poor response offered by the Kalman filter when the dynamic bias value is rather large, and its inability to properly filter the undesired dynamic acceleration peaks without distorting the input signal. These results can be easily observed at a glance in figure 3.

In the following section the same adaptive filters are applied to real signals gathered by the IMU with the objective to confirm the results obtained in the theoretical simulations and determine any possible differences.

4 Application on Real Signals

After running theoretical simulations to obtain the MSE of each of the adaptive filters we can now apply them to real signals gathered from the accelerometer and gyroscope included inside the IMU. Many different exercises presenting bursts of dynamic acceleration were performed, such as running, jumping, falls, among others.

Figure 4 shows the acceleration and gyroscope angle signals gathered from an exercise composed of a series of vertical jumps having the IMU located on the subject's back. As in the theoretical simulations, RLS offers the best results as it completely filters the dynamic acceleration peaks in the accelerometer signal and removes the dynamic bias in the gyroscope signals. The rest of the adaptive filters behave in the same way it was commented in the previous section.

5 Conclusions

Following the results obtained in the theoretical simulations using synthesized signals and the results obtained by applying the adaptive filters to real signals, we can conclude that the standard RLS sensor fusion approach used to calculate the position angle, based on inertial signals, outperforms the existing Kalman filter approach. RLS has shown its superior capability of filtering large peaks of dynamic acceleration derived from intense activities that are present in the accelerometer angle signal and its good performance to remove the dynamic bias present in the gyroscope angle signal. Other filters such as QRDRLS and NLMS have revealed themselves to be unsuitable for this purpose as they do not filter peaks properly or converge too slowly. It is also very important to know the nature of the exercise to be performed to tune properly the filters as their performance will vary depending on the nature of the exercise.

References

[1] Vicon movement tracking cameras: http://www.vicon.com
[2] Xsens Inertial Measurement Units: http://www.xsens.com
[3] Memsense Inertial Measurement Units: http://www.memsense.com

 [4] Tao, Y., Hu, H.: A Novel Sensing and Data Fusion System for 3-D Arm Motion Track-
     ing in Telerehabilitation. IEEE Transactions on Instrumentation and Measurement 57(5),
     1029–1040 (2008)
 [5] Lim, Y.P., Brown, I.T.: Kalman Filtering of Inertial Sensors for Evaluation of Orthopae-
     dics Angles. In: ARATA 2008 Conference, Adelaide, Australia (2008)
 [6] Kalman, R.E.: A New Approach to Linear Filtering and Prediction Problems. Transaction
     of the ASME Journal of Basic Engineering, 35–45 (March 1960)
 [7] Welch, G., Bishop, G.: An introduction to the Kalman filter. In: Notes of ACM SIG-
     GRAPH tutorial on the Kalman filter (2001)
 [8] Widrow, B., Glover, J.R., Mccool, J.M., Kaunitz, J., Williams, C.S., Hean, R.H., Zeidler,
     J.R., Dong, E., Goodlin, R.C.: Adaptive noise cancelling: Principles and applications.
     Proc. IEEE 63(12), 1692–1716 (1975)
 [9] Douglas, S.C., Meng, T.H.Y.: Normalized data nonlinearities for LMS adaptation. IEEE
     Trans. Signal Process 42(6), 1352–1354 (1994)
[10] Rontogiannis, A.A., Theodoridis, S.: On inverse factorization adaptive least-squares
     algorithms. Signal Processing 52(1) (July 1996)
[11] Alexander, S.T., Ghirnikar, A.L.: A Method for Recursive Least Squares Filtering Based
     Upon an Inverse QR Decomposition. IEEE Transactions on Signal Processing 41(1),
     20–30 (1993)

Prediction of Bladder Cancer Recurrences Using Artificial Neural Networks

Ekaitz Zulueta Guerrero[1], Naiara Telleria Garay[2], Jose Manuel Lopez-Guede[1],
Borja Ayerdi Vilches[1], Eider Egilegor Iragorri[2], David Lecumberri Castaños[3],
Ana Belén de la Hoz Rastrollo[2], and Carlos Pertusa Peña[3]

[1] Dpto. de Ingeniería de Sistemas y Automática. Escuela Universitaria de Ingeniería,
Calle Nieves Cano 12, Vitoria-Gasteiz 01006, Álava (Spain)
[2] Dominion Pharmakine S.L., Parque Tecnológico de Bizkaia edificio 801A,
Derio 48160, Bizkaia (Spain)
[3] Servicio Urología, Hospital Cruces, Plaza Cruces s/n, Barakaldo 48903, Bizkaia (Spain)
ekaitz.zulueta@ehu.es

Abstract. Even if considerable advances have been made in the field of early
diagnosis, there is no simple, cheap and non-invasive method that can be applied to the clinical monitorisation of bladder cancer patients. Moreover, bladder cancer recurrences or the reappearance of the tumour after its surgical resection cannot be predicted in the current clinical setting. In this study, Artificial
Neural Networks (ANN) were used to assess how different combinations of
classical clinical parameters (stage-grade and age) and two urinary markers
(growth factor and pro-inflammatory mediator) could predict post surgical recurrences in bladder cancer patients. Different ANN methods, input parameter
combinations and recurrence related output variables were used and the resulting positive and negative prediction rates compared. MultiLayer Perceptron
(MLP) was selected as the most predictive model and urinary markers showed
the highest sensitivity, predicting correctly 50% of the patients that would recur
in a 2 year follow-up period.

Keywords: Artificial Neural Networks (ANN), Prediction, Bladder Cancer,
Recurrence.

1 Introduction

Bladder cancer remains a highly prevalent and lethal malignancy. Bladder cancer is
the fourth most common cancer in males and the ninth most common cancer in females, with 357,000 new cases and 145,000 deaths each year worldwide, and 107,400
new cases in Europe in 2006 [1], [2]. 90% of bladder cancers arise from the urothelium and are named Urothelial or Transitional Cell Carcinomas (TCC) [3].

Clinical prognosis of TCCs is predicted on the basis of tumour stage and grade [4].
Tumour stage represents the extension of the tumour (increasing from Ta to T4), and
classifies TCC in two main groups: Superficial, when the tumour is confined in the
urothelium (Ta, TIS and T1) and, Invasive, when the tumour has grown into deeper

M. Graña Romay et al. (Eds.): HAIS 2010, Part I, LNAI 6076, pp. 492–499, 2010.

muscular layers, fat or nearby organs (T2, T3 and T4) having a worse prognosis. TCC Histopathological grade refers to the decreasing differentiation degree of tumour cells from grade 1 to 3 (G1, G2, G3). Approximately 75% of bladder cancer patients present superficial lesion at diagnosis; 70% of this superficial TCCs recur into new superficial tumours and 15-25% of them will progress to invasive type TCC [5]. More precisely, after total endoscopic resection of the visible tumour, low grade papillary tumours (TaG1) show a 20% recurrence risk, while recurrence risk for higher stage and grade tumours increases to 40% and 90% at 1-2 years [6], [7].

Therefore, patients are checked regularly after tumour surgery in order to detect new recurrences as soon as possible. Currently, the standard methods include urine cytology together with cystoscopy. Urine cytology detects of tumour cells in urine, is non-invasive and easy to perform, but has a low sensitivity (66-79%) for detection of low grade tumours, giving frequent false negatives. Cystoscopy, based on the direct observation the bladder, remains the mainstay of diagnosis and surveillance; it is relatively sensitive and specific, but is expensive, invasive and uncomfortable for the patient [8]. Due to the high recurrence rate of bladder TCC and the need for lifelong surveillance, bladder cancer is one of the most expensive cancers to treat on a per patient basis.

In the last decade, many urinary biomarkers for bladder cancer have been identified in order supplement or replace cytology and cystoscopy. Ideally, such a marker would be office-based (point-of-service), rapid, cheap, and with high sensitivity and specificity. Currently, there are a few urine-based tests that are FDA-approved for bladder cancer surveillance, such as Bladder Tumour Antigen, ImmunoCyt, Nuclear Matrix Protein-22, and Fluorescent In Situ Hybridization (FISH). Unfortunately, none of the currently available urine marker tests is capable to warrant the substitution of the cystoscopic follow-up scheme [9].

Considering the lack of current clinical methods to predict disease recurrence, the integration of classical and non-invasive urine parameters using Artificial Neural Networks (ANN) was proposed as a promising strategy. ANN have been proposed as valuable instruments for the integration of heterogeneous data to build up clinically useful prediction models [10], [11]. In this study, ANN based mathematical models have been developed to predict bladder cancer recurrences. The ANN have been selected because is a very adaptative technique that take in accounts in a very easy way the new data in the future.

2 Methodology

2.1 Input Parameters in Disease Prediction

The role of growth factors (GF) and pro-inflammatory mediators (PF) in the aggressiveness and progression of cancer have been widely described, and are good candidate markers to predict bladder cancer recurrences. In the present study, clinical data (tumour stage-grade, patient age) from 145 patients diagnosed of TCC were available. Urine levels of GF and PF measured for 118 of the patients before tumour resection were available (GF1 and PF1), as well as the urine measurements of 63 of the patients 6 months after surgery (GF2 and PF2).

2.2 Output Variables to Be Predicted

The aim of the present study is to predict bladder cancer recurrences, that is, the patient relapsed or the tumour reappeared after complete surgical resection of the visible tumour. Recurrence has been considered through the use of 2 different output parameters:

Recurrence1 or tumour presence when the second urine sample is colleted 6 months after surgery, indicating an early relapse of the disease. The variable can take 3 different values: **1:** No relapse; **2:** Relapsed; **-1:** No available data.

Recurrence2 is the presence of a tumour recurrence in a 2 year follow-up period after initial tumour resection. This variable takes 2 possible values: -1: No recurrences; 1: Recurrence before 2 years after the initial resection of the tumour.

Table 1. Number of TCC cases for which data was available for ANN training

WITH DATA FOR OUTPUT VARIABLE	Recurrence1 (Recurrent / Non recurrent)	Recurrence2 (Recurrent / Non recurrent)
TOTAL	5 / 58	40 / 104
WITH INPUT PARAMETER DATA		
Age	5 / 30	28 / 69
Stage-Grade	5 / 58	33 / 46
GF1	5 / 58	31 / 85
PF1	5 / 48	30 / 75
GF2	5 / 57	20 / 33
PF2	5 / 48	23 / 39
WITH COMPLETE DATA	5 / 24	12 / 17

2.3 Artificial Neural Network (ANN) Architecture

The design of the prediction system was started using only a few data from the entire patient set available and proposing several different structures of artificial networks, and the structure giving the best predictions was selected. This was the Multi Layer Perceptron (MLP) with a Back Propagation learning algorithm, which is in accordance with the widespread use of MLP in supervised learning problems like the one under study, where patients would represent patterns and several input variables are considered with several possible outputs.

Besides the structure selection, different transfer functions were tested, including the logarithmic sigmoid function (logsig) and the hyperbolic tangent function (tagsig) for the hidden layers, and the linear transfer function for the output layer. We do not consider a hierarchical structure [12]

2.4 Multi Layer Perceptron (MLP) Design

In order to compare the prediction capacity of different input parameter combinations and select the most meaningful regarding early recurrences of bladder cancer, 5 different models of MLP artificial networks were designed to predict Recurrence1 or Recurrence2 as the output variable.

The characteristics and the inputs parameters are defined in Table 2. MLPA, for instance, was defined by 4 neurons in the unique hidden layer, the inputs parameters

Table 2. Main features and input parameters of the designed MLPs

	NEURONS IN INPUT LAYER	INPUT PARAME-TERS	HIDDEN LAYERS	HIDDEN LAYER NEURONS	OUTPUT LAYERS:VARIABLE
MLP21/MLPA	4	PF1, GF1, PF2, GF2		4	
MLP22/MLPB	5	PF1, GF1, PF2, GF2, AGE		5	1:
MLP23/MLPC	5	PF1, GF1, PF2, GF2, STAGE-GRADE	1	5	Recurrence1
MLP24/MLPD	6	PF1, GF1, PF2, GF2, AGE, STAGE-GRADE		6	/ Recurrence2
MLPE	2	AGE, STAGE-GRADE		2	

were {PF1, GF1, PF2, GF2} and the output layer had only one linear neuron that had to predict Recurrence1.

2.5 Training Options

For the training of the network, different options were considered, including the over training of the patterns with positive values for the output variable Recurrence1 (value of 2 representing presence of early recurrences). This aimed to compensate for the low number of cases available for this output variable value by giving greater importance them. Different learning schemas were also proposed, making learning session with subgroups of cases, and then trying to predict the left cases to see the prediction capacity achieved. To account for the very little presence of recurrent patients when Recurrence1 was considered, in each session different positive cases were selected as the validation data. Finally, different transfer functions were also tested for the hidden layer neurons.

3 Results

3.1 Phase I: Prediction of Early Recurrences (Recurrence1)

Recurrence1 was the output variable to be predicted in this first phase, with only 5 patients showing recurrences before 6 months after surgery (Recurrence1=2), a greater proportion of non recurrent patients (Recurrence1=1) and a high number of unknown data (Recurrence1=-1).

The learning ratio gives equal importance to all specific patterns and is a reasonable strategy only when the amount of cases associated to each possible value are similar, or when the prediction error for the fewer cases is not very high. But in the dataset under study, patients with an early relapse were scarce and very important for the efficiency of the prediction model. So, in this particular case, giving greater importance in the learning to these cases and over training the patients with positive values in Recurrence1 was well justified.

Due to the relatively low number of patients considered in the available dataset (maximum of 145 patients), a strategy of defining as many networks as patients minus

1 was followed. That is, the network was trained with all patients except for one, which was used as the validation patient, and the correct prediction ratio estimated. Similarly, training was performed for all 144 patients in the validation set, and the prediction rates attained calculated (Table 3). Total correct prediction rates were higher than 80% for most of the MLPs and reached up to 95% correct prediction rates of Recurrence1 for several of the training options and input parameters considered.

Table 3. Total prediction rates of early recurrences (output variable Recurrence1) obtained using different ANN models. Prediction rates above 95% are marked in bold.

TRAINING	TYPE A		TYPE B		TYPE C		TYPE D	
OVER TRAINING	YES		NO		YES		NO	
TRANSFER FUNCTION*	logsig				tagsig			
SOURCE DATA**	C	I	C	I	C	I	C	I
MLPA (PF1, GF1, PF2, GF2)	**95,23 %**	94,48 %	88,89 %	94,48 %	90,48 %	**95,17 %**	90,48 %	94,48 %
MLPB (PF1, GF1, PF2, GF2, AGE)	92,06 %	94,48 %	87,30 %	93,79 %	88,89 %	92,41 %	88,89 %	93,79 %
MLPC (PF1, GF1, PF2, GF2, STAGE-GRADE)	90,47 %	93,10 %	90,48 %	**95,17 %**	82,54 %	**95,86 %**	87,30 %	**95,17 %**
MLPD (PF1, GF1, PF2, GF2, AGE, STAGE-GRADE)	88,89 %	92,41 %	90,48 %	93,79 %	92,06 %	**95,17 %**	87,30 %	**95,86 %**
MLPE (AGE, STAGE-GRADE)	93,65 %	81,38 %	93,65 %	82,07 %	92,06 %	83,45 %	92,06 %	82,07 %

* Transfcer function: logsig=logarithmic sigmoid and tagsig= hyperbolic tangent
** Source data: C) Only patients with complete data considered; I) All available patients considered even if their data was incomplete.

3.2 Phase II: 2 Year Recurrence Prediction (Recurrence2)

In this phase, Recurrence2 was the output variable and there were not unknown values, with only 2 possible output values (1 or -1). This simplified the training of the neural networks. Besides, input parameters were normalized to values from 0 to 1.

Table 4. Total prediction rates of 2 year follow-up recurrences (output variable Recurrence2) using different ANN models

TRAINING	TYPE A	TYPE B	TYPE C	TYPE D
OVER TRAINING	YES	NO	YES	NO
TRANSFER FUNCTION	logsig		tagsig	
MLPA (PF1, GF1, PF2, GF2)	60,00 %	68,97 %	68,28 %	70,34 %
MLPB (PF1, GF1, PF2, GF2, AGE)	64,14 %	68,28 %	60,69 %	64,83 %
MLPC (PF1, GF1, PF2, GF2, STAGE-GRADE)	64,14 %	64,14 %	63,45 %	71,03 %
MLPD (PF1, GF1, PF2, GF2, AGE, STAGE-GRADE)	62,76 %	66,90 %	61,38 %	68,97 %
MLPE (AGE, STAGE-GRADE)	61,38 %	70,34 %	57,24 %	71,03 %

However, several patients showed one or more unknown input parameter. This fact explains the dramatic decrease of the prediction rates shown in Table 4, which were around 60-70% at best.

In this study, this problem was partially overcome by the introduction of a case filtering system that got rid of the incomplete data in a scalable manner. Filters were introduced to fix the maximum number of unknown data that could be accepted and define different training patient groups and data sets. As observed in table 5, the limit of only 1 unknown input value during the training increased total prediction rates of some of the parameter combinations and training options to above 85%.

When Filter 1 permitted the presence of 1 incomplete data per patient, MLPE got the highest prediction rate (90%) when Type A training was used, while MLPA (urinary markers) predicted correctly 81% of the cases with Type C training. Increasing further the number of incomplete data allowed (Filters 2 to 5) yielded a decreased prediction capacity of the models.

Table 5. Total prediction rates of 2 year follow-up recurrences (output variable Recurrence2) using different ANN models and input data filter levels. Prediction rates above 85% are marked in bold.

	FILTER 0	FILTER 1	FILTER 2	FILTER 3	FILTER 4	FILTER 5
Maximum number of unknown parameters	0	1	2	3	4	5
TRAINING	MLPA (PF1, GF1, PF2, GF2)					
Type A	72,41 %	79,25 %	79,10 %	71,15 %	72,50 %	60,00 %
Type B	72,41 %	79,25 %	77,61 %	70,19 %	68,33 %	68,28 %
Type C	79,31 %	81,13 %	76,12 %	75,96 %	71,67 %	68,97 %
Type D	72,41 %	77,36 %	77,61 %	69,23 %	68,33 %	70,34 %
TRAINING	MLPB (PF1, GF1, PF2, GF2, AGE)					
Type A	72,41 %	83,02 %	71,64 %	77,88 %	74,17 %	64,14 %
Type B	75,86 %	81,13 %	77,61 %	77,88 %	68,33 %	60,69 %
Type C	72,41 %	83,02 %	79,10 %	70,19 %	75,00 %	68,28 %
Type D	75,86 %	77,36 %	76,12 %	70,19 %	74,17 %	64,83 %
TRAINING	MLPC (PF1, GF1, PF2, GF2, STAGE-GRADE)					
Type A	72,41 %	**88,68 %**	77,61 %	69,23 %	66,67 %	64,14 %
Type B	68,97 %	**86,79 %**	79,10 %	77,88 %	65,00 %	63,45 %
Type C	82,76 %	83,02 %	80,60 %	78,85 %	68,33 %	64,14 %
Type D	75,86 %	83,02 %	77,61 %	66,35 %	65,00 %	71,03 %
TRAINING	MLPD (PF1, GF1, PF2, GF2, AGE, STAGE-GRADE)					
Type A	68,97 %	83,02 %	77,61 %	76,92 %	69,17 %	62,76 %
Type B	65,52 %	77,36 %	76,12 %	69,23 %	63,33 %	61,38 %
Type C	68,97 %	**86,79 %**	76,12 %	75,00 %	78,33 %	66,90 %
Type D	68,97 %	84,91 %	77,61 %	75,96 %	68,33 %	68,97 %
TRAINING	MLPE (AGE, STAGE-GRADE)					
Type A	**86,21 %**	**90,57 %**	80,60 %	76,92 %	76,67 %	61,38 %
Type B	82,76 %	**88,68 %**	70,15 %	70,19 %	71,67 %	57,24 %
Type C	**86,21 %**	**86,79 %**	82,09 %	78,85 %	79,17 %	70,34 %
Type D	68,97 %	**88,68 %**	68,66 %	71,15 %	70,00 %	71,03 %

Finally, the sensitivity and specificity of the trained networks to predict recurrences and lack of recurrences in a 2 year follow-up period (Recurrence2) respectively were further assessed. Figure 1 (left) shows that urinary parameters combined with stage-grade, as considered in MLPC, provided a considerable advantage to predict recurrences correctly, with sensitivities of 50% and 43% for filters 2 and 3 respectively. In contrast, the use of stage-grade and age alone, as in MLPE, was not able to predict recurrences at all under those filtering conditions, and only up to 13% sensitivity could be achieved with filter 4. In Figure 1 (right) it can be observed that both models, MLPC and MLPE, showed high specificity, which means they had a low risk of predicting a recurrence by error.

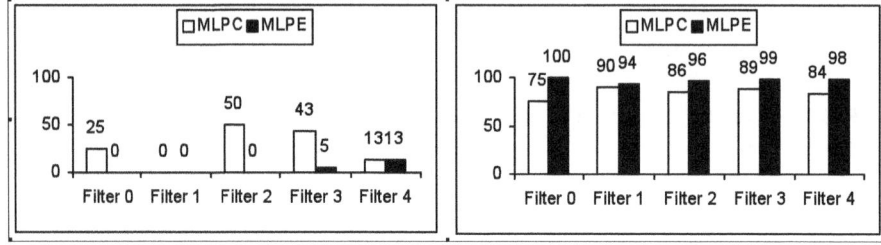

Fig. 1. Probability to predict recurrences and non-recurrences correctly: Left) Sensitivity or 1 minus probability of false negatives; Right) Specificity or 1 minus probability of false positives

4 Conclusions

This study has analysed the effect of data heterogeneity on ANN training, while bringing into the field of mathematical modelling the possibility to integrate parameters that are highly relevant to bladder cancer recurrences and that can be measured along time in non-invasive samples such as urine. In the case of early recurrences, urinary markers give slightly higher prediction rates than classical parameters (95% and 93% for MLPA and MLPE respectively for Recurrence1 prediction). In contrast, when data of recurrences occurring in a 2 year follow-up period (Recidivas2años) MLPE (stage-grade, age) predict 86-90% of the cases correctly, while MLPA (urinary markers) only gives the right answer for 79-81% of the patients (Filter 0-Filter 1 values). The combined use of urinary markers and stage-grade information in MLPC increase their prediction rate to 83% (Filters 0 and 1). Moreover, when sensitivity and specificity are considered separately rather than integrated in the overall prediction rate, urinary markers highlight very valuable information regarding their clinical use. The ANN designed using MLP for four urinary parameters plus stage-grade (MLPC) allowing a maximum of 2 unknown data in the training dataset (Filter 2) provide the chance to predict 50% of the patients that will recur in 2 years. This is currently impossible to predict using clinical data such as stage-grade and age, as demonstrated by the low sensitivity of MLPE. Moreover, the error rate or probability to tell a patient that he/she will recur when he/she will really not is kept at an acceptably low level of 14% (1-86%), while avoding unnecessary distress to 86% of the not recurring patients makes the prediction considerably secure.

In conclusion, urinary markers such as growth factors and pro-inflammatory mediators measured at different time points during bladder cancer follow-up, provide a unique means of predicting a considerable proportion of the patients that will recur after the initial resection of the tumour (50% sensitivity). They are highly complementary to the high specificity of stage-grade and age that allow the correct prediction of 94-100% of the patients that will not recur. In this study the use of ANNs has shown to be a valuable tool to discriminate which are the parameters that could be used as recurrence prediction biomarkers. The validation of such prediction models in larger data collections would provide the means of translating multiparametric data integration models into clinical practice with the final aim of reducing patient suffering and sanitary costs.

References

1. Parkin, M., Bray, F., Ferlay, J., Pisani, P.: Global Cancer Statistics 2002. CA Cancer J. Clin. 55, 74–108 (2005)
2. Ferlay, J., Autier, P., Boniol, M., Heanue, M., Colombet, M., Boyle, P.: Estimates of the cancer incidence and mortality in Europe in 2006. Ann. Oncol. 18(3), 581–592 (2007)
3. Johansson, S.L., Cohen, S.M.: Epidemiology and etiology of bladder cancer. Semin. Surg. Oncol. 13(5), 291–298 (1997)
4. Epstein, J.I., Amin, M.B., Reuter, V.R., Mostofi, F.K.: The World Health Organization/International Society of Urological Pathology consensus classification of urothelial (transitional cell) neoplasms of the urinary bladder. Bladder Consensus Conference Committee. Am. J. Surg. Pathol. 22(12), 1435–1448 (1998)
5. Kirkali, Z., Chan, T., Manoharan, M., Algaba, F., Busch, C., Cheng, L., Kiemeney, L., Kriegmair, M., Montironi, R., Murphy, W.M., Sesterhenn, I.A., Tachibana, M., Weider, J.: Bladder cancer: epidemiology, staging and grading, and diagnosis. Urology 66(6 Suppl. 1), 4–34 (2005)
6. Heney, N.M.: Natural history of superficial bladder cancer: prognostic features and long-term disease course. Urol. Clin. North Am. 19, 429–433 (1992)
7. Shelley, M., Mason, M.D., Kynaston, H.: Intravesical therapy for superficial bladder cancer: A systematic review of randomised trials and meta-analyses. Cancer Treat. Rev (2010) (in press), doi:10.1016/j.ctrv.2009.12.005
8. Sharma, S., Ksheersagar, P., Sharma, P.: Diagnosis and treatment of bladder cancer. Am. Fam. Physician 80(7), 717–723 (2009)
9. Herman, M.P., Svatek, R.S., Lotan, Y., Karakiewizc, P.I., Shariat, S.F.: Urine-based biomarkers for the early detection and surveillance of non-muscle invasive bladder cancer. Minerva Urol. Nefrol. 60(4), 217–235 (2008)
10. Agatonovic-Kustrin, S., Beresford, R.: Review, Basic concepts of artificial neural network (ANN) modelling and its application in pharmaceutical research. J. Pharm. Biomed. Anal. 22(5), 717–727 (2000)
11. Lin, C.C., Wang, Y.C., Chen, J.Y., Liou, Y.J., Bai, Y.M., Lai, I.C., Chen, T.T., Chiu, H.W., Li, Y.C.: Artificial neural network prediction of clozapine response with combined pharmacogenetic and clinical data Comput. Methods Programs Biomed. 91(2), 91–99 (2008)
12. Graña, M., Torrealdea, F.J.: Hierarchically structured systems. European Journal of Operational Research 25, 20–26 (1986)

Hybrid Decision Support System for Endovascular Aortic Aneurysm Repair Follow-Up

Jon Haitz Legarreta[1], Fernando Boto[1], Iván Macía[1,2], Josu Maiora[2],
Guillermo García[3], Céline Paloc[1], Manuel Graña[2], and Mariano de Blas[4]

[1] eHealth and Biomedical Applications Department, Vicomtech,
Mikeletegi Pasealekua, 57, Teknologi Parkea, 20009 Donostia-San Sebastián, Spain
jhlegarreta@vicomtech.org
[2] Computational Intelligence Group, UPV/EHU, Manuel Lardizabal Pasealekua, 1,
20018 Donostia-San Sebastián, Spain
[3] Industrial Processes Control Group, UPV/EHU, Europa Plaza, 1,
20018 Donostia-San Sebastián, Spain
[4] Angiology and Vascular Surgery and Interventional Radiology Service,
Hospital Donostia Ospitalea, Begiristain Doktorearen Pasealekua, 107-115
20014 Donostia-San Sebastián, Spain

Abstract. An Abdominal Aortic Aneurysm is an abnormal widening of the aortic vessel at abdominal level, and is usually diagnosed on the basis of radiological images. One of the techniques for Abdominal Aortic Aneurysm repair is Endovascular Repair. The long-term outcome of this surgery is usually difficult to predict in the absence of clearly visible signs, such as leaks, in the images. In this paper, we present a hybrid system that combines data extracted from radiological images and data extracted from the Electronic Patient Record in order to assess the evolution of the aneurysm after the intervention. The results show that the system proposed by this approach yields valuable qualitative and quantitative information for follow-up of Abdominal Aortic Aneurysm patients after Endovascular Repair.

Keywords: visual analytics, information fusion, data mining, medical imaging.

1 Introduction

An Abdominal Aortic Aneurysm (AAA) is a focal dilatation at some point of the abdominal section of the aorta. In the absence of any treatment, AAAs tend to grow until rupture. There are two main techniques for AAA reparation: Open Repair (OR), which is an invasive surgical procedure, and the Endovascular Aneurysm Repair (EVAR), which is a minimally invasive procedure where a stent graft is inserted using a catheter in order to exclude the bulge from the blood circulation. A positive evolution leads to the formation of a thrombus and a progressive reduction of the aneurysm size by re-absorption.

The EVAR technique requires a close follow-up in order to ensure that the exclusion of the aneurysm from the blood circulation is successful (the stent graft is stable

M. Graña Romay et al. (Eds.): HAIS 2010, Part I, LNAI 6076, pp. 500–507, 2010.

and it does not move from its fixation points). This should result in an absence of endoleaks (a leak of blood into or from the aneurysmatic bulge).

Nevertheless, it has been observed that some AAAs do not vary their size, and some even continue growing despite a successful surgery. A growth can be detected by the presence of endoleaks; other aneurysms do not present leaks, but continue growing (a phenomenon known as endotension). This poses a greater problem, since the cause of this undesired behavior remains unknown.

Previous works have shown that the sole information of the aneurysm diameter is not a good indicator of the evolution of the aneurysm [1][2]. Further morphometric parameters are needed to assess the aneurysm evolution, among which volume and stent graft migration can be mentioned.

One of the most valuable techniques used in the assessment of the evolution of aneurysms is Computerized Tomography Angiography (CTA). CTA acquisitions are performed one, two, and six months after the EVAR surgery. After, they are done yearly.

In collaboration with the Angiology and Vascular Surgery and the Interventional Radiology Services of Hospital Donostia Ospitalea, we have been working on a Clinical Decision Support (CDS) system for the aneurysm evolution assessment. Medical record data and quantitative data extracted from CTA image analysis have been selected in order to build such system.

1.1 Objectives

Currently, only the presence of endoleaks and the growth of the size of the aneurysm are taken into account to evaluate the state of the aneurysm. This work proposes to push further in the prediction of outcome of the EVAR technique.

The main goal of this work has been to develop an integrated hybrid platform which encompasses visualization tools, aneurysm morphometry information and aneurysm rupture risk prediction after EVAR procedure.

Semi-automated tools have been developed to segment different tissues of aneurysms, and image analysis techniques have been applied to extract relevant parameters. Also, we have developed a system to visualize the temporal evolution of the aneurysm by means of registration techniques. These tools provide a clear visual perception of what is happening over time, thus providing valuable diagnostic information.

This work combines the above information with information extracted from the Electronic Patient Record (EPR). A computational model is proposed from the fusion of these data.

2 System Overview

The system designed for this project reflects the stages involved in the diagnosis, treatment and follow-up of AAAs. The information system gathers the information related to all three pre-operative, intra-operative and post-operative follow-up stages, and performs analysis tasks in order to extract useful information for the medical team.

The system employs a hybrid data analysis approach to provide a Clinical Decision Support system; not only does the system analyze data selected from the Electronic Patient Record, but it also combines it with data obtained from the image analysis processes. The aim is to be able to characterize the behavior of the AAA as best as possible.

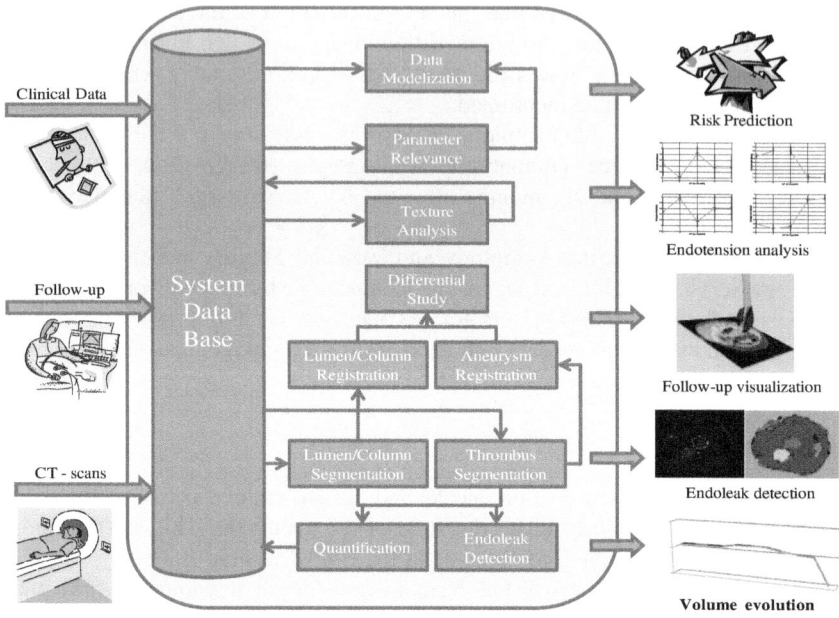

Fig. 1. EVAR patient screening system components

In fact, the underlying mechanism of AAAs that continue to grow with no apparent leak remains unknown. The system presented in this paper aims to help to discover these mechanisms.

The system is divided into five main subsystems:

– Segmentation
This subsystem performs the segmentation of the AAA. It is the basis for the registration and endoleak detection subsystems.
– Endoleak detection
An automated detection of Type II endoleaks is performed by this subsystem.
– Registration and Visualization
These tasks allow the physician to clearly visualize the evolution of the AAA of a patient over time.
– Texture Analysis
Texture analysis patterns are sought for aneurysm evolution after EVAR.

– Risk Prediction by *a priori* Knowledge

Statistical methods are applied in order to get a forecast of how a given AAA will evolve prior to surgery and after it.

2.1 System's Input Data

Patient selection was one of the first fundamental tasks to be done. The Angiology and Vascular Surgery and the Interventional Radiology Services of the Hospital Donostia Ospitalea have currently more than 300 patients that are screened since several years now.

Patients were split into three groups by the medical experts' team of the Services:

– Favorable evolution. The aneurysm of these patients shrinks over time.
– Unfavorable evolution with visible endoleaks. The aneurysm continues to grow due to visible leaks into or from the bulge.
– Unfavorable evolution without visible endoleaks. The aneurysm continues to grow without apparent leaks.

The medical experts' team identified and gathered variables that are related to the presence and evolution of AAAs [3]. All three phases are reflected: pre-operative, intra-operative and post-operative follow-up.

The identified parameters were structured together with the biomedical engineers, and corresponding data from the EPR of each selected patient was gathered and stored in a data base through a Web-based interface.

2.2 Segmentation

When doing the follow-up of an EVAR patient, one of the interests lies in knowing how its size evolves. An AAA is commonly composed by five different tissues: the aortic wall, blood, denaturalized blood (thrombus), calcifications and the stent graft. In this case, the segmentation subsystem is used to isolate the lumen (blood tissue) and the thrombus. The outer border, and thus, the size and shape of the AAA, are given by the thrombus. The thrombus is the tissue formed by the remaining blood between the stent graft and the aortic wall. It is formed in most non-shrinking AAAs.

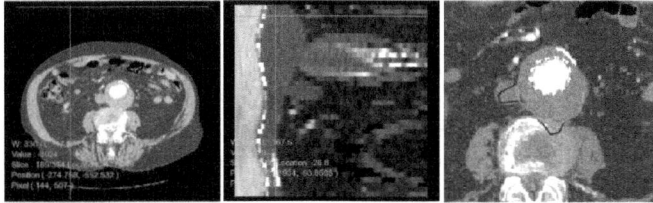

Fig. 2. Axial slice (left), corresponding polar representation (center) and segmentation result (right; initial estimation in blue and corrected in green)

The segmentation of the thrombus is not a trivial task. The poor contrast of denaturalized blood versus intensity values of surrounding tissues makes difficult to determine its boundaries.

Our approach is based on a 3D semi-automatic radial model [4]. As a first step, the segmentation of the lumen is performed based on a region growing algorithm. Based on the segmentation of the lumen, the 2D image moments give its centerline. This centerline serves as the reference for the radial model.

The proposed radial approach is based on a Connected Component (CC) analysis. Intensity and spatial-based coherence criteria are used on a row-by-row (RCC) and on a slice-by-slice (SCC) basis in order to filter adjacent tissues at different detail level, and to get the segmentation of the thrombus.

The output of the segmentation is used to extract morphometry measurements, and serves as endoleak detection and registration and visualization systems' input.

2.3 Endoleak Detection

Endoleaks represent the main known cause for aneurysmatic bulge growth after EVAR. Endoleaks are usually detected by visual inspection of CTA scans. However, it remains a time-consuming task. Their detection could be automated, and thus, contribute in saving time for the physicians. The aim is therefore to draw the attention of the physician over the cases where a leak is present, because this indicates that the bulge is still under stress, may continue to grow, and, at term, may rupture. Furthermore, an automatic processing can quantitatively characterize the leak.

The endoleak detection subsystem is designed to detect Type II endoleaks. A Type II endoleak appears as a result of a retrograde flow into the aneurysm through collateral aortic branch vessels (lumbar, testicular o inferior mesenteric). It is the most frequent type of endoleak.

The approach used by this subsystem is based on a Multilayer Perceptron (MLP) Artificial Neural Network (ANN) [5]. An ANN is a mathematical and computational model whose objective is data modeling or classification, by means of a learning process, and initially using a training and a test set.

Based on the output of the segmentation subsystem, the AAA is labeled using a Topological Grayscale Watershed Transform on a slice-by-slice basis. Previous to the watershed, the input AAA image is smoothed using a level-set modified curvature diffusion equation-based edge-preserving smoothing filter. A number of features for each Connected Component (CC) yielded are then calculated.

Type II endoleaks appear close to the thrombus boundary and perfusing inwards. Since the radius and shape of the thrombus and lumen, and the eccentricity of the lumen with respect to the thrombus, are not uniform, a normalization is needed. The use of a feature called Normalized Thrombus Distance (NTD) is proposed in this work. It is computed on the basis of Danielsson's Distance Maps.

A correlation analysis is then performed in order to reduce the complexity and to speed-up the computations. A reduced version of the feature vector is obtained.

The MLP takes the reduced version of the vector of features of each CC as its input and determines whether it is a Type II endoleak or not. The network is trained with manually classified CC feature vectors (as being Endoleaks or not).

2.4 Registration and Visualization

Registration is the process of transforming different datasets into the same coordinate-system. In this case, registration techniques are used to compare the evolution of the

AAA of a patient. The visualization of multiple segmented and registered AAAs gives a more accurate idea of their evolution as opposed to plain diameter and volume figures.

A sequence of rigid, deformable and affine registrations [6] is used to obtain the final result. All three stages run in 3D, and the aortic lumen is considered to be the non-moving structure, while the thrombus is considered to be the deformable object. The first step yields a rough alignment initialization using a rigid transformation. Then the result is refined with an affine transform, and its result is used as the bulk transform of a B-Spline deformable transform.

2.5 Texture Analysis

The texture analysis subsystem aims to yield information about the mechanism of growth of an AAA in the absence of leaks. The medical team hypothesized that subtle texture changes in the aneurysmatic sac, potentially detected by automatic processes, could provide with more information.

The subsystem uses a statistical texture analysis technique that uses the Gray Level Spatial Dependency Matrix (GLSDM) [7]. Based on the computed GLSDM, the subsystem evaluates several parameters, such as energy, correlation, entropy, or information correlation. The parameters that do not show coherent values are discarded.

As it has been already stated, patients were split into three groups: favorable evolution, unfavorable with leaks and unfavorable without endoleaks. The results of the analysis were evaluated against this classification. It is observed that patients with favorable evolution keep a similar pattern. However, current results do not yield any conclusion on the features of the unfavorable cases.

2.6 Risk Prediction by *a priori* Knowledge

The prediction subsystem aims to assist the physician in making decisions about the need of re-interventions in EVAR patients. The subsystem aims to yield an approximate mortality risk prediction, based on an *a priori* knowledge model. We hypothesize that the clinical information can be statistically modeled, first making a statistical variable selection, and then developing an Artificial Neural Network model for its ability to analyze nonlinear data [8][9].

The study can be made from two different points of view:

- Pre-operative evaluation: the statistical significance of certain intra-operative parameters can be estimated using the information from previous patients.
- Follow-up evaluation: this tool may provide additional information to the rupture risk prediction of a given EVAR patient. It takes into account past events' outcome and follow-up information of the current patient.

A very preliminary study has made in the first case to identify some parameters which take part in the first stages of the follow-up. We have detected that the sealing artery has a certain relationship with the success of the EVAR surgery, since it is statistically correlated to the evolution of the aneurysm.

A model based approach has been also carried out in order to extract more significant conclusions. We have detected some good results with a mixture model of a Naïve Bayes classifier with a 75% of the cases correctly classified in favorable and unfavorable evolution.

3 Results and Discussion

The data management or information system platform has been updated to reach 30 subjects. Based on data drawn from each of them and the corresponding CTs, a range of analysis has been applied to help predicting the outcome of an EVAR surgery.

The segmentation process is the first link of the chain. A radial based approach has been proposed. It has been observed that the algorithm gives, in general, satisfactory results. Furthermore, the computation speed is fast enough to make on-line segmentations. However, an underestimation of the thrombus radio is observed frequently. Its cause is under investigation. A higher degree of user intervention could be envisaged to make light corrections in the regions where the algorithm fails to yield good results. On the other hand, the curvature of the aortic vessel is not corrected. A curved reconstruction needs to be implemented in order introduce the fact that the aortic vessel is not normal to the axial plane. However, the segmentation process can automatically yield morphometric parameters, such as the maximal aneurysmatic diameter, the volume, etc.

It has been demonstrated that it is feasible to create a semi-automatic Type II endoleak detection system for AAAs. The system is based on the Connected Components analysis issued by the segmentation process, and applies geometric and image-based feature extraction techniques to obtain an input to the MLP Neural Network classifier. An average rate of 95% correctly classified labels was obtained for Type II endoleak detection.

The evolution that an AAA presents over time can be clearly seen thanks to the registration algorithm and the visualization tools developed. This subsystem enables the medical team to visualize a given AAA at different time lapses, and assess at first sight, whether the aneurysm has shrunk or continues to grow.

The texture analysis subsystem has proven a degree of liability for favorable evolution cases, but needs further investigation to conclude about unfavorable cases.

In addition, the multivariable analysis yields some interesting, but only preliminary, results. These results still lack of clinical significance, since at the time of the tests, the amount of complete test subjects was fairly low.

4 Conclusions and Future Work

We have developed a hybrid Clinical Decision Support System for the screening of Abdominal Aortic Aneurysms. This tool aims to help the Angiology and Vascular Surgery and the Interventional Radiology Services keep better track of AAA patients that undergo EVAR surgery, including tools that may predict the evolution of the patients.

The system needs further input data to assess its liability, but a first experience has shown that useful results may be drawn out of the work. It has not been possible to clearly state a model that truly indicates an unfavorable evolution or rupture risk yet. However, some trends have been identified.

The challenge lies now in validating the system, gathering as much evidence as possible from the widest range of subject patients.

Acknowledgements. This work is sponsored and partially financed by the Basque Government through the INTEK Program. We also thank the companies Bilbomatica and eMedica for their participation in this work.

References

1. Wever, J.J., Blankensteijn, J.D., Mali, W.P., Eikelboom, B.C.: Maximal Aneurysm Diameter Follow-up is Inadequate after Endovascular Abdominal Aortic Aneurysm Repair. Eur. J. Vasc. and Endovasc. Surg. 20(2), 177–182 (2000)
2. Lee, J.T., Aziz, I.N., Lee, J.T., Haukoos, J.S., Donayre, C.E., Walot, I., Kopchok, G.E., Lippmann, M., White, R.A.: Volume regression of abdominal aortic aneurysms and its relation to successful endoluminal exclusion. J. Vasc. Surg., 1254–1263 (2003)
3. Chaikof, E.L., Blankenstein, J.D., Harris, P.L., White, G.H., Zarins, C.K., Bernhard, V.M., et al.: Reporting standards for endovascular aortic aneurysm repair. J. Vasc. Surg. 35(5), 1048–1060 (2002)
4. Macía, I., Legarreta, J.H., Paloc, C., Graña, M., Maiora, J., García, G., de Blas, M.: Segmentation of Abdominal Aortic Aneurysms in CT Images using a Radial Model Approach. In: Corchado, E., Yin, H. (eds.) IDEAL 2009. LNCS, vol. 5788, pp. 664–671. Springer, Heidelberg (2009)
5. Macía, I., Graña, M., Paloc, C., Boto, F.: Neural Network-based Detection of Type II Endoleaks in Abdominal Aortic Aneurysms After Endovascular Repair. Int. J. of Neural Systems (submitted 2010)
6. Maiora, J., García, G., Macía, I., Legarreta, J.H., Paloc, C., de Blas, M., Graña, M.: Thrombus Change Detection after Endovascular Abdominal Aortic Aneurysm Repair. Int. J. of CARS (2010) (in press)
7. Haralick, R., Shanmugam, K., Dinstein, I.: Textural features for image classification. IEEE Transactions on Systems, Man, and Cybernetics SMC-3, 610–621 (1973)
8. Hadjianastassiou, V.J., Franco, L., Jerez, J.M., Evangelou, I.E., Goldhill, D.R., Tekkis, P.P., et al.: Optimal prediction of mortality after abdominal aortic aneurysm repair with statistical models. J. Vasc. Surg. 43(4), 467–473 (2006)
9. Turton, E.P.L., Scott, D.J.A., Delbridge, M., Snowden, S., Kester, R.C.: Ruptured Abdominal Aortic Aneurysm: a Novel Method of Outcome Prediction Using Neural Network Technology. Eur. J. Vasc. and Endovasc. Surg. 19(2), 184–189 (2000)

On the Design of a CADS for Shoulder Pain Pathology

K. López de Ipiña[1], M.C. Hernández[1], E. Martínez[2], and C. Vaquero[3]

[1] Grupo de Inteligencia Computacional
Universidad del País Vasco/Euskal Herriko Unibertsitatea
Plaza de Europa1, Donostia, 20008
{karmele.ipina,mamen.hernandez}@ehu.es
[2] Txagorritxu Hospital, Rehabilitation Service, Osakidetza, Basque Health Service
C/ José Atxotegi s/n. 01009 Vitoria-Gasteiz
elena.martinezgarcia@osakidetza.net
[3] Fundación LEIA CDT
Equipo de Seguridad Industrial P.T. Alava – C/ Leonardo Da Vinci,
11, 01510 Miñano (Álava) - Spain
celinav@leia.es

Abstract. A musculoskeletal disorder is a condition of the musculoskeletal system, which consists in part of it being injured continuously over time. Shoulder disorders are one of the most common musculoskeletal cases attended in primary health care services. Shoulder disorders cause pain and limit the ability to perform many routine activities, affecting about 15-25 % of the general population. Several clinical tests have been described to aid diagnosis of shoulder disorders. However, the current literature acknowledges a lack of concordance in clinical assessment, even among musculoskeletal specialists. We are working on the design of a Computer-Aided Decision Support (CADS) system for Shoulder Pain Pathology. The paper presents the results of our efforts to build a CADS system testing several classical classification paradigms, feature reduction methods (PCA) and K-means unsupervised clustering. The small database size imposes the use of robust covariance matrix estimation methods to improve the system performance. Finally, the system was evaluated by a medical specialist.

Keywords: Musculoskeletal disorders, Shoulder Pain, Computer-Aided Decision Support system, Machine Learning.

1 Introduction

A musculoskeletal disorder is a condition of continuous injure over time of a part of the musculoskeletal system. The disorder occurs when the body part is called to work harder, stretch farther, impact more directly or otherwise function at a greater stress level than it is prepared for. The immediate impact may be minute, but when it occurs repeatedly the accumulated trauma may cause damage [1,2,3]. As reported by recent assessments, especially those made by the Dublin Foundation for the Improvement of Living and Working conditions in its fourth report, Musculoskeletal disorders (MSDs)

M. Graña Romay et al. (Eds.): HAIS 2010, Part I, LNAI 6076, pp. 508–515, 2010.

are the most common work-related health problem in Europe, affecting to millions of workers. Across the EU27, 25% of workers complain of backache and 23% report muscular pains. MSDs are caused mainly by manual handling, heavy physical work, awkward and static postures, repetition of movements and vibration. Also, attention should be given to "lack of physical activities" during working time (derived from growing use of visual display units and of automated systems resulting in prolonged sitting at the work place) which has been identified by the European Agency for Safety and Health at Work as an emerging risk. As reported also by this Agency, the risk of MSDs can increase with the pace of work, low job satisfaction, high job demands, job stress and working in cold environments [1,2].

Shoulder Pain (SP) is one of the most frequent pathologies of the locomotor system, being nowadays the third reason of consultation in Primary Health care, and managing to affect 15-25 % of the adult population. Nevertheless, despite of this public impact in the literature, it can be appreciated a big disparity of criteria not only in the used terms but also in prediction factors, or in the used treatments. Several clinical tests (e.g. Hawkins, Neer, Yergason, Speed) have been described to aid diagnosis of shoulder disorders. However, research acknowledges a lack of concordance in clinical assessment, even among musculoskeletal specialists [3,4]. The test the developed for Duke's University of sports medicine, simplifies this differential diagnosis to four entities: impingement of the rotation cuff, frozen shoulder, instability glenohumeral and degenerative osteoarthritis. As there is no unanimity the reasons for shoulder pain. In this work, we have rejected those reasons that are diagnosed well by the causative mechanism, as fractures or luxations, or by the image as the degenerative osteoarthritis. Anyway, they are complex diagnoses and they are overlapped in numerous occasions [3,4,5].

In the near future, Computer-Aided Decision Support (CADS) applications for various diagnostic tasks will be developed and then implemented in clinical environments. To date, the majority of CADS applications focus on a limited number of important oncology tasks, mostly related to lung, breast, and colon cancers. Opportunities exist to expand the scope of CADS applications for organ systems and pathologies previously ignored. For example, new CADS applications for advanced musculoskeletal diagnosis could improve the accuracy and efficiency of human observers, potentially leading to improved patient care. An area of particular interest is orthopaedic imaging [6]. A common problem in medical decision support system design is the scarcity of data. That means that the algorithms must be built from small samples and some numerical problems may appear, namely the singularity of the covariance matrices, for methods using them. In this paper we apply robust covariance estimators developed in the area of remote sensing.

The next section presents the medical method and the database. Section 3 analyzed the classification methods and the robust covariance matrix estimation methods used to improve the system performance. Section 4 shows the experimentation with results that have been obtained from the classification systems applied to the database, results introducing the covariance matrix regularized methods and finally with K-means based clustering. Section 5 presents the discussion with the specialist evaluation and finally, some conclusions and future work are given in section 6.

2 Medical Method and Database

We have selected a sample of 200 patients directed to the Rehabilitation Service for SP. In the sample have been included those patients who after the valuation in consultation have been diagnosed of frozen shoulder, syndrome subacromial (impingement), and rotation cuff pathology. There have been excluded from the sample the fractures, the luxations, the above-mentioned pain and the degenerative osteoarthritis glenohumeral, because their diagnosis is mostly based on radiological information. In the first consultation, we realize the data collection that allows realize a more approximate diagnosis of the pain causes. The collected information is: age, sex, dominance of the arm, characteristics of the pain and its intensity by an analogical visual scale, received treatments, limitation of the mobility and its measure by goniometry, existence of previous history, type of work, sports activity. In the exploration the mobility has been gathered to articulate by goniometry, the muscular force, and diverse maneuvers for the exploration of the shoulder (empty can test, Hawkins-Kennedy, crossed adducing, apprehension test and subescapular test) [3,5].

These variables have been parameterized to be measured and analyzed in posterior studies. We have gathered some 50 patients diagnosed of syndrome subacromial, some 50 with frozen shoulder and some 50 with diagnosis of rotator cuff pathology. On the one hand, the database has been created with SP files from the Txagorritxu's Hospital consists of about 200 files catalogued in 4 different diagnoses: 1) Rotator Cuff Anomaly, 2) SubAcromial Syndrome, 3) frozen Shoulder and 4) Subacromial Syndrome and Rotator Cuff Anomaly. The obtained database is a database balanced for the four classes and labeled and codified in octal system as: 1, 2, 4 and 5. On the other hand files of not common analogous pathologies were also used obtaining 6 types of different diagnoses [7]. The database has been divided in two independent subsets, the first one for training and the other for test, constituted by 70 not diagnosed cases. The diagnoses fall into 6 classes. We have a set of training of about 100 samples, each having 30 features. Each of these features has been identified and the appropriate range has been assigned.

3 Methods

3.1 Classification and Clustering Methods

In order to develop the CADS system several classification methods have been tested: MLE (Maximum Likelihood Estimation), MDM (Minimum Distance to Means), FIS (Fisher's Linear Discriminant), QDF (Quadratic Discriminant Function), KNN (K-Nearest Neighbor), DT (Decision Trees). Also, two kinds of multi-class Support Vector Machines (SVM) have been used: SVM1: One-against-one decomposition, where the classification into nclass classes is decomposed into nrule = (nclass-1)*nclass/2 binary problems; SVM2: One-against-all decomposition, multi-class where the classification into nclass classes is decomposed to nclass binary problems. Moreover an unsupervised clustering using a K-means algorithm and Principal Component Analysis (PCA) have been also applied for feature space dimension reduction.

3.2 Regularized Covariance Matrix Estimation Methods

When covariance matrices used to build the discriminant functions for classification are singular it turns out impossible to compute the inverse matrix. In some cases, the covariance matrices of the classes are singular due to the small number of training samples. To deal with this problem, we must obtain non singular matrices whether using matrices with common covariance, if most of the classes have similar covariance matrices, or using diagonal matrices obtained from the covariance matrices of each class.

Given a sample set of vectors with p characteristics for which we know the total classification or a partial classification: $x_{ij} \in \mathcal{R}^p$ with $i \in \{1, ..., L\}$, being L the number of classes, and with $j \in \{1, ..., n_i\}$ where n_i is the sample size in the *i-th class*. This sample set is known as the *training* set. We consider that the distribution of the vectors in each class is given by a p-dimensional Gaussian distribution:

$$f\{x_{ij}|m_i, \Sigma_i\} = \frac{1}{\sqrt{(2\pi)^p \cdot |\Sigma_i|}} exp\left(-\frac{1}{2}(x_{ij} - m_i)^{\mathrm{T}} \cdot \Sigma_i^{-1} \cdot (x_{ij} - m_i)\right) \tag{1}$$

Where $i = 1, ..., L$, m_i is the mean of the *i-th* class and Σ_i its covariance matrix. For each class we calculate its average value from the training samples as (2) and and the corresponding covariance matrix is (3)

$$m_i = \frac{i}{n_i}\sum_{j=1}^{n_i} x_{ij} \quad (2) \quad \Sigma_i = \frac{1}{n_i - 1}\sum_{j=1}^{n_i}(x_{ij} - m_i) \cdot (x_{ij} - m_i)^{\mathrm{T}} \quad (3)$$

The common covariance matrix is the average of the covariance matrices:

$$S = \frac{1}{L}\sum_{i=1}^{L} \Sigma_i \tag{4}$$

The so-called *pooled* covariance matrix, or the weighted average matrix of the covariance matrices is given by the following expression:

$$S = \frac{1}{n - L}\sum_{i=1}^{L}(n_i - 1) \cdot \Sigma_i \qquad n = \sum_{i=1}^{L} n_i \tag{5}$$

where n denotes total number of pixels and n_i the pixel number for the *i*-th class.

Given a covariance matrix Σ_i we define the *trace matrix* of the diagonal matrix generates from the trace of that covariance matrix as (6) and given a covariance matrix Σ_i we define the *diagonal matrix of* the diagonal matrix of that covariance matrix as (7)

$$mTraza(\Sigma_i) = traza(\Sigma_i) \cdot I \quad (6) \quad mDiag(\Sigma_i) = diag(\Sigma_i) \cdot I \quad (7)$$

We will use several robust methods to estimate the covariance matrix: the Regularized Discriminant Analysis, RDA [8]; the LOOC estimation methods based on the search of the best parameters to maximize a function which depend on the mean and the covariance matrix of the training set; the Bayesian LOOC (BLOOC) method, an

Table 1. Regularized Methods to estimate the Covariance Matrix

Estimator	Covariance Matrix Estimation
RDA	$C_l^{RDA}(\lambda, \gamma) = (1 - \gamma) \cdot C_i(\lambda) + \dfrac{\gamma}{p} \cdot mTraza(C_l(\lambda))$
LOOC1	$C_i(\alpha_i) = \alpha_{i1} \cdot mDiag(\Sigma_i) + \alpha_{i2} \cdot \Sigma_i + \alpha_{i3} \cdot S + \alpha_{i4} \cdot mDiag(S)$
LOOC2	$C_i(\alpha_i) = \begin{cases} (1 - \alpha_i) \cdot mDiag(\Sigma_i) + \alpha_i \cdot \Sigma_i & 0 \le \alpha_i \le 1 \\ (2 - \alpha_i) \cdot \Sigma_i + (\alpha_i - 1) \cdot S & 1 \le \alpha_i \le 2 \\ (3 - \alpha_i) \cdot S + (\alpha_i - 2) \cdot mDi & 2 \le \alpha_i \le 3 \end{cases}$
BLOOC1	$C_i(\alpha_i) = \begin{cases} (1 - \alpha_i) \cdot \dfrac{mTraza(\Sigma_i)}{p} + \alpha_i \cdot \Sigma_i & 0 \le \alpha_i \le 1 \\ (2 - \alpha_i) \cdot \Sigma_i + (\alpha_i - 1) \cdot S_p(t) & 1 \le \alpha_i \le 2 \\ (3 - \alpha_i) \cdot S + (\alpha_i - 2) \cdot \dfrac{mTraza(\Sigma_i)}{p} & 2 \le \alpha_i \le 3 \end{cases}$
BLOOC2	$C_i(\alpha_i) = \begin{cases} (1 - \alpha_i) \cdot mDiag(\Sigma_i) + \alpha_i \cdot \Sigma_i & 0 \le \alpha_i \le 1 \\ (2 - \alpha_i) \cdot \Sigma_i + (\alpha_i - 1) \cdot S_p & 1 \le \alpha_i \le 2 \\ (3 - \alpha_i) \cdot S + (\alpha_i - 2) \cdot mDi & 2 \le \alpha_i \le 3 \end{cases}$
Mixed-LOOC1	$C_i(\alpha_i) = \alpha_{i1} \cdot \dfrac{mTraza(\Sigma_i)}{p} + \alpha_{i2} \cdot mDiag(\Sigma_i) + \alpha_{i3} \cdot \Sigma_i + \alpha_{i4} \cdot \dfrac{mTraza(S)}{p} + \alpha_{i5} \cdot mDiag(S) + \alpha_{i6} \cdot S$
Mixed-LOOC2	$C_i(\alpha_i) = \alpha_i \cdot A + (1 - \alpha_i) \cdot B$

extension of the RDA and LOOC methods [9,10,11]. Other variants of these methods used in this paper are summarized in Table 1.

4   Experimentation

4.1   Preliminary Experimentation

In order to set the baseline performance of the above enumerate classification methods we have been applied them directly on the data training set to build the classification system for the desired CADS. Figure 1a shows the values of accuracy for the selected methods. Results show a good performance for most methods obtaining the best accuracy for SVM2. It must also be highlighted that MLE and QDF obtain very poor results as figure 1a shows. The poor results, obtained by some of the algorithms come from the difficulty to calculate the covariance matrix due to the small size of the database.

4.2   Experimentation with Regularized Covariance Matrix Estimation Methods

The poor results of the previous experimentation is due to the fact that the covariance matrices used in the classification are singular and, therefore, it turns out impossible to find the inverse matrix. Following we will carry out a new experiment with several methods to regularize the covariance matrix estimation: MLE, FIS and QDF.

The robust covariance estimation methods tested are: LOOC estimation method, Bayesian LOOC estimation method (BLOOC) and mix-LOOC estimation method. In figure 1b it can see the values of accuracy for the selected methods. New methods improve the rates obtained in figure 1a.

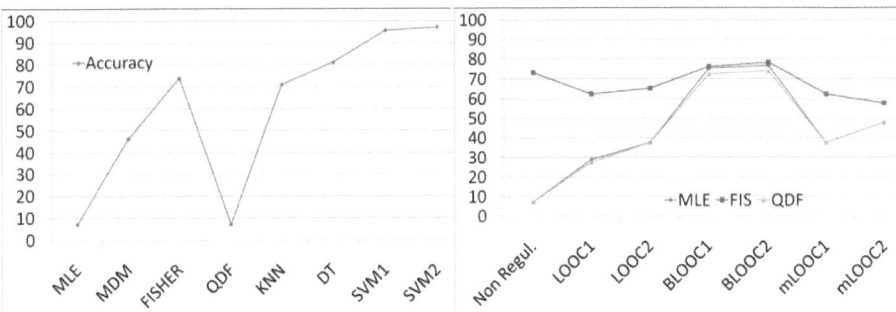

Fig. 1. (a) Accuracy for several training methods and (b) for the regularized Covariance Matrix estimation methods

4.3 Principal Component Analysis for Feature Selection

Several experiments with different number of Principal Components have been also carried out. In the experimentation regularized methods have been also introduce (figure 2). SVM1 and SVM2 obtain the best results in all cases and a high accuracy with more than 10 Principal Components. Regularized methods outperformer the results of MDM and KNN but they can not reach to DT and SVM methods.

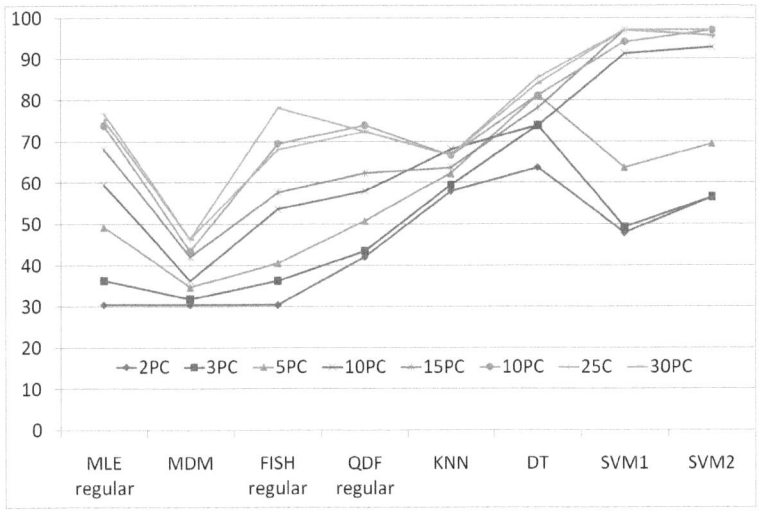

Fig. 2. Accuracy for all methods and different number of Principal Components

4.4 Unsupervised K-Means Clustering

In order to explore new possible diagnosis, unsupervised K-means clustering has been used to generate several partitions in the original training set: 4, 7, 10, 15, 20. A new experimentation has been carried out. The new unsupervised classifications obtain

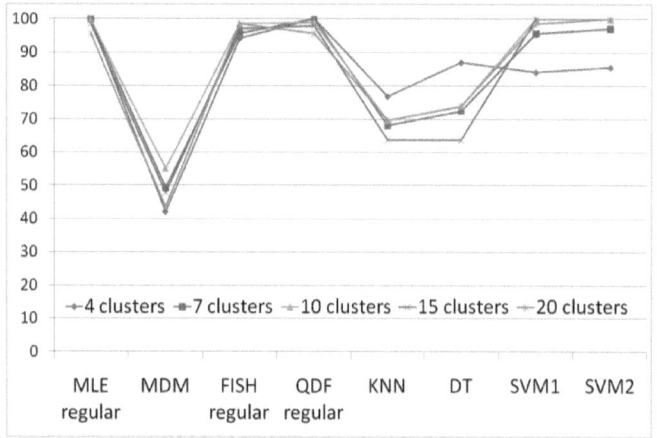

Fig. 3. Accuracy for unsupervised classification

best results in most cases. The results show (figure 3) that for 4 and 7 clusters classification regularized methods outperform SVM methods and for the rest of the classifications (10, 15 and 20 clusters) results are close to SVM. Finally the obtained information have been analyzes by the specialist suggesting new diagnosis strategies based on the information inferred from these results.

5   Discussion

A diagnosis evaluation was carried out with the developed system based on the classification optimum method. In this evaluation the independent test (70 cases) was used. The obtained results were supervised by the medical specialist who demonstrates a high degree of satisfaction not only with regard to the visual information provided by the automatic support system but also for the diagnosis results over the test cases. The system has obtained good performance in both supervised and unsupervised modes and results are very close to the diagnosis of the specialist. The specialist prefers in any case the results obtained in supervised mode but new encouraging strategies for the diagnosis have been proposed based on the results of the unsupervised mode.

6   Concluding Remarks

Shoulder disorders are one of the most common primary health care musculoskeletal presentations and affect to around 25% of the general population. Several clinical tests have been described to aid diagnosis of shoulder disorders. However, research acknowledges a lack of concordance in clinical assessment, even among musculoskeletal specialists. The work presents a Computer-Aided Decision Support (CADS) system for Shoulder Pain Pathology. The paper presents the development of the (CADS) system based on several classical classification paradigms. The poor results obtained in some cases due to the small database size suggest the use of covariance estimation methods. New methods improve considerably the system accuracy. The system obtains good performance in both supervised and unsupervised modes and results are very close to the diagnosis of the medical specialist. The specialist prefers in any case the results obtained in supervised mode but new encouraging strategies for the diagnosis have been proposed based on conclusions inferred from the results of the unsupervised mode. In future outlines, new covariance estimation methods will be developed and the system will be also improved with new unsupervised methods.

Acknowledgements. The reported work has received financial support from the Spanish Ministerio de Ciencia y Tecnología, IBEROEKA 2005 plan and the Spanish Ministerio de Ciencia y Tecnología, project TSI2006-14250-C02-01.

References

1. Gauthy, R.R.G.: Muskuloskeletal disorders. An ill-understood "pandemic". ETUI-REHS, Health and Safety Department, Brussels: ETUI-REHS, 54 p., 24 cm (2007); ISBN 978-2-87452-100-3; CDU 616.7 (2007)
2. European Agency for Safety and Health at Work. Work-related musculoskeletal disorders: Back to work report. Luxembourg, Office for Official Publications of the European Communities (2007)
3. Mitchell, C., Adebajo, A., Hay, E., Carr, A.: Shoulder pain: diagnosis and management in primary care. BM 331(7525), 1124-1128 (2005),
   http://www.bmj.com/cgi/content/full/331/7525/1124
4. Norlin, R.: Frozen shoulder: etiology, pathogenesis and natural course, October 13 (2005),
   http://www.shoulderdoc.co.uk
5. Ostor, A.j., Richards, C.A., Prevost, A.T., et al.: Diagnosis and relation to general health of shoulder disorders presenting to primary care Rheumatology (Oxford) 44(6), 800–805 (2005)
6. Huang, J.-Y., Kao, P.-F., Chen, Y.-S.: A Set of Image Processing Algorithms for Computer-Aided Diagnosis in Nuclear Medicine Whole Body Bone Scan Images. IEEE Transactions on Nuclear Science 54(3), 514–522 (2007)
7. López de Ipiña, K., Hernández, M., Graña, M., Martínez, E., Vaquero, C.: A Computer-Aided Decision Support system for Shoulder Pain Pathology. In: PAAMS 2010, SMC-Workshop-IEEE, Salamanca (2010)
8. Friedman, J.H.: Regularized discriminant analysis. Journal of the American Statistical Association 84, 165–175 (1989)
9. Hoffbeck, J.P., Landgrebe, D.: Covariance estimation and classification with limited training data. IEEE Transactions on Pattern Analysis and Machine Intelligence 18(7), 763–767 (1996)
10. Tadjudin, S., Landgrebe, D.: Classification of high dimensional data with limited training samples. Technical Report TRECE 98-8. School of Electrical and Computer Engineering, Purdue University, West Lafayette, Indiana (1998)
11. Tadjudin, S., Landgrebe, D.: Covariance Estimation with Limited Training Samples. IEEE Transaction on Geoscience and Remote Sensing 37 (2000)

Exploring Symmetry to Assist Alzheimer's Disease Diagnosis

I.A. Illán, J.M. Górriz, J. Ramírez, D. Salas-Gonzalez, M. López, P. Padilla,
R. Chaves, F. Segovia[1], and C.G. Puntonet[2]

[1] Dept. of Signal Theory, Networking and Communications
University of Granada, Spain
[2] Dept. of Computers Architecture and Technology
University of Granada, Spain

Abstract. Alzheimer's disease (AD) is a progressive neurodegenerative disorder first affecting memory functions and then gradually affecting all cognitive functions with behavioral impairments and eventually causing death. Functional brain imaging as Single-Photon Emission Computed Tomography (SPECT) is commonly used to guide the clinician's diagnosis. The essential left-right symmetry of human brains is shown to play a key role in coding and recognition. In the present work we explore the implications of this symmetry in AD diagnosis, showing that recognition may be enhanced when considering this latent symmetry.

1 Introduction

Distinguishing AD from other causes of dementia still remains a diagnostic challenge specially during the early stage of the disease that offers better opportunities to treat its symptoms. Thus, an accurate and early diagnosis of the AD by means of non-invasive methods, is of fundamental importance for the patients medical treatment. Nuclear imaging as SPECT is an example of non-invasive, three-dimensional functional imaging modality that provide clinical information regarding biochemical and physiologic processes in patients, and is frequently used as a diagnostic tool in addition to the clinical findings.

Many studies have examined the predictive abilities of nuclear imaging with respect to AD and other dementia illnesses. The evaluation of these images is usually done through visual assessments performed by experts[1]. However, computer aided diagnosis methods have not been widely used to assist the diagnosis, being Statistical Parametric Mapping (SPM) the most extended tool in the neuro-imaging community[2]. It consist of doing a voxelwise statistical test comparing the values of the image under study to the mean values of the group of normal images. Subsequently the significant voxels are inferred by using Random Field Theory [3]. This method fall into the category of unsupervised method, where at the end, an answer is given to the question of existence of differences between an image and a control group, and the location of them. On the other hand, supervised techniques try to give a final answer to the question

M. Graña Romay et al. (Eds.): HAIS 2010, Part I, LNAI 6076, pp. 516–523, 2010.

of diagnosis, by finding features that make possible the differentiation between groups, and then categorizing each subject.

The present approach lies in the category of supervised learning technique, through a multivariate pattern recognition system based on PCA. It is common that the number of patients in AD studies is small, suffering from the *curse of dimensionality* problem. This major problem, associated with pattern recognition systems, occurs when the number of available features for designing the classifier is very large compared with the number of available training examples. The importance of multivariate approaches is that the interactions among voxels and error effects are assessed statistically, while paying the price of losing capability of making statistical inferences about regionally specific changes. ManCova [4] or Principal Component Analysis (PCA) are examples of multivariate analysis that require more training examples than features and are not suitable for make any statistical inferences about the characterizations that obtain [2].

Other pattern recognition problems solved accurately by humans, as face recognition, provide compelling evidence for the modular character of recognition in support of the single "domain-specific" side in the cognitive science debate on whether mechanisms are specific or general. One consequence of these deliberations impacts on computer aided diagnosis debate on whether a brain image should be parsed or viewed holistically. There exist studies providing evidence that the human visual system chooses the holistic approach taken here [5, 6], as well as success in making use of symmetries for recognition [7], although there exist parsing approaches proven to be efficient. The proposed method, tested over SPECT, is developed by making use of the present left-right symmetry of the brain, with the final aim of reducing the subjectivity in visual assessments of these scans by clinicians, thus improving the accuracy of diagnosing Alzheimer's disease in its early stage.

2 Formulation

An image of a brain is represented by a scalar function $\mathbf{t}(\mathbf{x})$ of position $\mathbf{x} = (x, y, z)$, with the image centered on the midplane $x = 0$. We consider the possibility of extending the database to a ensemble of images $\mathbf{t}_n(x, y, z) \cup \mathbf{t}_n(-x, y, z)$, $n = 1, 2, ..., N$. The average brain image of the dataset is defined as:

$$\mathbf{t} = \frac{1}{2N} \sum_{n=1}^{N} \mathbf{t}_n(x, y, z) + \mathbf{t}_n(-x, y, z) \tag{1}$$

We will say that an image is even (in the midplane) if:

$$\mathbf{t}_n(x, y, z) = \mathbf{t}_n(-x, y, z) \tag{2}$$

and odd if

$$\mathbf{t}_n(x, y, z) = -\mathbf{t}_n(-x, y, z) \tag{3}$$

Following the approach in [8], we will try to represent each brain image by its eigenbrain expansion. We need firstly to extract the average of the image set to each brain image, producing a new set $\mathbf{p}_n = \mathbf{t}_n - \mathbf{t}$ more suitable for the PCA analysis. Consider each image as a M-dimensional vector, formed by the concatenation of all voxel values, the tridimensional pixel analogous. A PCA transformation is composed by M orthogonal vectors $\mathbf{u}_i$, such that

$$\lambda_i = \frac{1}{N} \sum_{n=1}^{N} (\mathbf{u}_i^T \mathbf{p}_n)^2 \tag{4}$$

is maximum, subject to the constrain

$$\mathbf{u}_i^T \mathbf{u}_j = \delta_{ij} \tag{5}$$

where δ_{ij} is the Kronecker delta. The resulting $\mathbf{u}_i$ and λ_i are the eigenvectors and eigenvalues respectively of the covariance matrix:

$$\mathbf{C} = \frac{1}{2N} \sum_{n=1}^{N} \mathbf{p}_n(x,y,z)\mathbf{p}_n(x',y',z') + \mathbf{p}_n(-x,y,z)\mathbf{p}_n(-x',y',z') \tag{6}$$

This orthogonal eigenvector basis $\{\mathbf{u}_i\}, i = 1, ..., M$ is formed of eigenbrains, called so because of its brain like appearance. Within this framework, the coefficients in the eigenbrain expansion are uncorrelated, and each eigenvalue represents the statistical variance of the corresponding coefficient in the expansion. As is directly verified, we can rewrite $\mathbf{C}$ as the sum of an even part $\mathbf{C}^r$ and an odd one $\mathbf{C}^\ell$:

$$\mathbf{C}^r = \frac{1}{4N} \sum_{n=1}^{N} (\mathbf{p}_n(x,y,z) + \mathbf{p}_n(-x,y,z))(\mathbf{p}_n(x,y,z) + \mathbf{p}_n(-x,y,z)) \tag{7}$$

$$\mathbf{C}^\ell = \frac{1}{4N} \sum_{n=1}^{N} (\mathbf{p}_n(x,y,z) - \mathbf{p}_n(-x,y,z))(\mathbf{p}_n(x,y,z) - \mathbf{p}_n(-x,y,z)) \tag{8}$$

that are orthogonal and that their eigenvectors are even and odd, respectively. In other words, the eigenspace of $\mathbf{C}$, $E(\mathbf{C})$ can be expressed as the direct sum of $E(\mathbf{C}^r)$ and $E(\mathbf{C}^\ell)$ (see [9]), i.e. :

$$E(\mathbf{C}) = E(\mathbf{C}^r) \oplus E(\mathbf{C}^\ell) \tag{9}$$

If we define

$$\mathbf{p}_n^r(x,y,z) = \mathbf{p}_n(x,y,z) + \mathbf{p}_n(-x,y,z) \tag{10}$$

and

$$\mathbf{p}_n^\ell(x,y,z) = \mathbf{p}_n(x,y,z) - \mathbf{p}_n(-x,y,z) \tag{11}$$

then it follows that we should consider the following two decoupled problems:

$$\mathbf{C}^r \mathbf{u}_i^r = \lambda_i \mathbf{u}_i^r \tag{12}$$

$$\mathbf{C}^\ell \mathbf{u}_j^\ell = \lambda_j \mathbf{u}_j^\ell \tag{13}$$

where:

$$\mathbf{C}^r = \frac{1}{4N} \sum_{n=1}^{N} \mathbf{p}_n^r(x,y,z)\mathbf{p}_n^r(x',y',z') \tag{14}$$

$$\mathbf{C}^\ell = \frac{1}{4N} \sum_{n=1}^{N} \mathbf{p}_n^\ell(x,y,z)\mathbf{p}_n^\ell(x',y',z') \tag{15}$$

taking into account that problems 12 13 are discrete problems in practice, since the position vector $\mathbf{x} = (x,y,z))$ takes only values at voxels.

We can view these two problems as equivalent to starting out with two separate ensembles $\mathbf{p}_n^r$ and $\mathbf{p}_n^\ell$, $n = 1, 2, ..., N$ consisting of even and odd images, and then proceeding with the two cases independently. To solve them, it is necessary to diagonalize two $M \times M$ covariance matrices, which for brain images would be approximately a $5 \cdot 10^5 \times 5 \cdot 10^5$ matrix. There are alternatives to deal with these problems, described in detail in [8, 10], resulting that it is only necessary to obtain $P \sim N << M$ eigenvectors. Once solved both eigenvector problems (12) (13), the general solution is obtained adding both eigenvector sets (see 9).

2.1   Classification

The post-processing ends with the training of a SVM with labelled data. The training data is obtained from the raw data as:

$$(x_k)_i = \mathbf{u}_k \mathbf{p}_i , \quad i = 1, ..., N \quad k = 1, 2, ..., P \tag{16}$$

These coefficients $(x_k)_i$ are the coordinates of the ith-brain image $\mathbf{t}_i$ in the subspace spanned by the eigenbrain images (for $\mathbf{p}_i$ being the full set $\{\mathbf{p}_i^r\} \cup \{\mathbf{p}_i^\ell\}$). We used this coordinates values $\mathbf{x}$ as N P-dimensional training vectors:

$$\mathbf{x}_i = [x_1, x_2, ..., x_P]_i, \quad i = 1, 2, ..., N \tag{17}$$

each of them with its corresponding class label $y_i \in \{\pm 1\}$.

SVM separate a given set of binary labeled training data with a hyperplane that is maximally distant from the two classes (known as the maximal margin hyper-plane). The objective is to build a function $f : R^P \longrightarrow \{\pm 1\}$ using training data that is, P-dimensional patterns $\mathbf{x}_i$ and class labels y_i:

$$(\mathbf{x}_1, y_1), (\mathbf{x}_2, y_2), ..., (\mathbf{x}_N, y_N) \in R^P \times \{\pm 1\}, \tag{18}$$

so that f will correctly classify new examples $(\mathbf{x}, y)$.

Linear discriminant functions define decision hypersurfaces or hyperplanes in a multidimensional feature space, that is:

$$f(\mathbf{x}) = \mathbf{w}^T \mathbf{x} + w_0 = 0, \tag{19}$$

where $\boldsymbol{w}$ is known as the weight vector and w_0 as the threshold. The weight vector $\mathbf{w}$ is orthogonal to the decision hyperplane and the optimization task consists of finding the unknown parameters w_i, $i = 1$, ..., K, defining the decision hyperplane.

Let $\mathbf{x}_i$, $i=1$, 2, ..., N, be the feature vectors of the training set, X. These belong to either of the two classes, ω_1 or ω_2. When no linear separation of the training data is possible, SVM can work effectively in combination with kernel techniques so that the hyperplane defining the SVM corresponds to a non-linear decision boundary in the input space. If the data is mapped to some other (possibly infinite dimensional) Euclidean space using a mapping $\Phi(\mathbf{x})$, the training algorithm only depends on the data through dot products in such an Euclidean space, i.e. on functions of the form $\Phi(\mathbf{x}_i) \cdot \Phi(\mathbf{x}_j)$. If a "kernel function" K is defined such that $K(\mathbf{x}_i, \mathbf{x}_j) = \Phi(\mathbf{x}_i) \cdot \Phi(\mathbf{x}_j)$, it is not necessary to know the Φ function during the training process. In the test phase, an SVM is used by computing dot products of a given test point $\mathbf{x}$ with $\mathbf{w}$, or more specifically by computing the sign of

$$f(\mathbf{x}) = \sum_{i=1}^{N_S} \alpha_i y_i \Phi(\mathbf{s}_i) \cdot \Phi(\mathbf{x}) + w_0 = \sum_{i=1}^{N_S} \alpha_i y_i K(\mathbf{s}_i, \mathbf{x}) + w_0, \qquad (20)$$

where $\mathbf{s}_i$ are the support vectors.

The SVM 'learns' from the labelled training data obtaining a hyperplane that separates the data into the two classes, maximizing the margin between them. Once it has been obtained, new samples with unknown labels can be categorized. A feature vector is obtained from the test image using eqs. (16) and (17), and it is classified according to its sign in eq. (20), once the hyperplane is determined. Also, samples with known labels may be used to test the reliability of the method, with some cross-validation strategy.

3   Experiments

The database consists of a set of 3D SPECT brain images produced with an injected gamma emitting ^{99m}Tc-ECD radiopharmeceutical and acquired by a three-head gamma camera Picker Prism 3000. Images of the brain cross sections are reconstructed from the projection data using the filtered backprojection (FBP) algorithm in combination with a Butterworth noise removal filter. The classification task is based on the assumption that the same position in the volume coordinate system within different images corresponds to the same anatomical position. The SPECT images are spatially normalized using the SPM software [2]. The preprocessing and spatial normalization procedure, described in detail in [11], is achieved using Affine and Non-linear spatial normalization [12], and essentially guarantees meaningful voxel-wise comparisons between images. For studying symmetry, it is crucial to fix correctly the symmetry plane with respect to both hemispheres. We undergo this problem by normalizing to a completely symmetric template. SPECT images consists of functional information and direct comparison of the voxel intensities, even different acquisitions of the same subject, is thus not possible without normalization of the intensities. Intensity level of the images is normalized to the maximum intensity, and consequently the basic assumptions are met.

The images were initially labelled by experienced physicians of the "Virgen de las Nieves" hospital (Granada, Spain), using 4 different labels: normal (NOR) for patients without any symptoms of AD and possible AD (AD-1), probable AD (AD-2) and certain AD (AD-3) to distinguish between different levels of the presence of typical characteristics for AD. In total, the database consists of $N = 97$ patients: 41 NOR, 30 AD1, 22 AD2 and 4 AD3. We considered the patient label positive when belonging to any of the AD classes, and negative otherwise.

Once the feature vectors were obtained using (16), a SVM was trained using 2 different kernels: linear and Radial Basis Function (RBF), and was tested using a leave-one-out cross-validation strategy. Representative eigenfunctions are shown in Fig. 2. The actual population contains 97 individuals, which exploiting the latent symmetry of brains (2), is doubled by including the midplane mirror brain images. The dichotomy of even or odd images in the midplane presented earlier is evident in Fig. 2, where odd eigenbrains appear first in the 7th and 9th place.

Figure 1 represents the scatter of training vectors using only the components of 16 correponding to the 7th and 9th eigenbrains, that is, the first two odd eigenbrains. Some correlation might be expected between them, while it is possible to identify only AD subjects with significative asymmetry in their patterns. However, despite this interesting fact being currently investigated, it is not a defining characteristic for the AD condition.

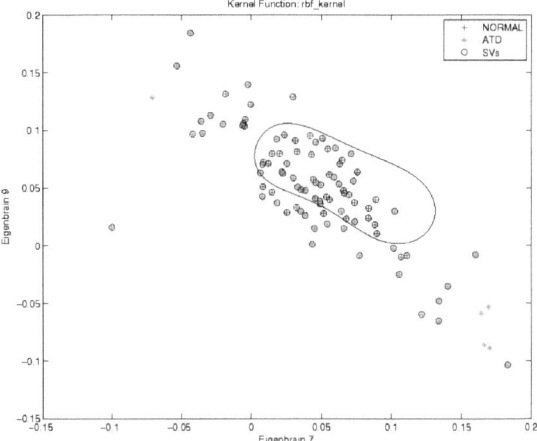

Fig. 1. Scatter plot of training vectors with odd parity

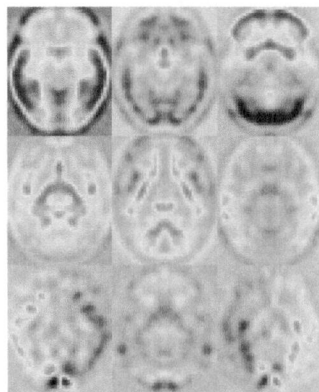

Fig. 2. Relevant transaxial slice of the first 9 eigenbrains, ordered by variance from top left to bottom right

4 Discussion

PCA applied to SPECT brain images is an effective way of extracting the relevant information for classification, besides its exploratory power. It is proven to be an opportune method of reducing the dimension of the feature space and selecting class-relevant features, and the final results show the success of this method when combined with kernel-SVM, as has been shown in the literature [8, 13]. When considering the enhanced set of images, we find that the first eigenbrains are even, thus explaining most of the variance. The optimum number of eigenbrains for classification has been proven to be below 10 [8, 13]. Considering all combinations of the first 10 eigenbrains (see table 1, where only the results for the more compelling combinations are reported), recognition rates are improved when removing those eigenbrains responsible for asymmetries, benefiting from the presence of latent symmetry.

Part of our discussion has centered around the notion of data extension using the natural symmetry of a pattern, separating them necessarily in even and odd. Patterns are now represented in terms of a basis possessing more structure, thus providing further characterization. Also, in hindsight, we can see that the

Table 1. Statistical performance measures in presence of absence of symmetry

	Parameter (%)	Kernel function	
		Linear	RBF
PCA	Accuracy	88.67	88.67
	Specificity	90.24	91.07
	Sensitivity	87.50	85.37
PCA symmetric	Accuracy	92.78	89.69
	Specificity	92.68	92.86
	Sensitivity	92.86	85.37

eigenpictures corresponding to the unextended ensemble are nearly even and odd as well, a rather surprising result. In light of this fact and the improved approximations, we view the modification as beneficial. The proposed work is tested on a real-life SPECT database with promising results, and can also be extended to other functional imaging modalities as PET or fMRI.

Acknowledgement

This work was partly supported by the MICINN under the PETRI DENCLASES (PET2006-0253), TEC2008-02113, TEC2007-68030-C02-01 and HD2008-0029 projects and the Consejería de Innovación, Ciencia y Empresa (Junta de Andalucía, Spain) under the Excellence Projects TIC-02566 and TIC-4530.

References

[1] Cummings, J.L., Vinters, H.V., Cole, G.M., Khachaturian, Z.S.: Alzheimer's disease: etiologies, pathophysiology, cognitive reserve, and treatment opportunities. Neurology 51(Suppl. 1), S2–S17 (1998)

[2] Friston, K., Ashburner, J., Kiebel, S., Nichols, T., Penny, W.: Statistical Parametric Mapping: The Analysis of Functional Brain Images. Academic Press, London (2007)

[3] Adler, R.: The Geometry of random fields. Wiley, New York (1981)

[4] Tabachnick, B.G., Fidell, L.S.: Computer-Assisted Reseach and Design Analysis. Pearson Education, London (2000)

[5] Tanaka, K., Saito, H., Fukada, Y., Moriya, M.: Coding visual images of objects in the inferotemporal cortex of the macaque monkey. J. Neurophysiol. 66(1), 170–189 (1991)

[6] Kanwisher, N.: NEUROSCIENCE: what's in a face? Science 311(5761), 617–618 (2006)

[7] Sirovich, L., Meytlis, M.: Symmetry, probability, and recognition in face space. Proceedings of the National Academy of Sciences 106(17), 6895–6899 (2009)

[8] Illán, I.A., Górriz, J.M., Ramírez, J., Salas-González, D., López, M., Puntonet, C.G., Segovia, F.: Alzheimer's diagnosis using eigenbrains and support vector machines. IET Electronics Letters 45(7), 342–343 (2009)

[9] Kirby, M., Sirovich, L.: Application of the Karhunen-Loeve procedure for the characterization of human faces. IEEE Trans. Pattern Anal. Mach. Intell. 12(1), 103–108 (1990)

[10] Turk, M., Pentland, A.: Eigenfaces for recognition. Journal of congnitive neuroscience 3(1), 71–86 (1991)

[11] Ramírez, J., Górriz, J.M., Romero, A., Lassl, A., Salas-Gonzalez, D., López, M., Alvarez, I., Gómez-Río, M., Rodríguez, A.: Computer aided diagnosis of alzheimer type dementia combining support vector machines and discriminant set of features. Accepted in Information Sciences (2008)

[12] Salas-González, D., Górriz, J.M., Ramírez, J., Lassl, A., Puntonet, C.G.: Improved gauss-newton optimization methods in affine registration of spect brain images. IET Electronics Letters 44(22), 1291–1292 (2008)

[13] López, M., Ramírez, J., Górriz, J.M., Salas-González, D., Illan, I.A., Segovia, F., Puntonet, C.G.: Automatic tool for the alzheimer's disease diagnosis using pca and bayesian classification rules. IET Electronics Letters 45(8), 389–391 (2009)

Thrombus Volume Change Visualization after Endovascular Abdominal Aortic Aneurysm Repair

Josu Maiora[1,4], Guillermo García[2], Iván Macía[3,4], Jon Haitz Legarreta[3],
Fernando Boto[3], Céline Paloc[3], Manuel Graña[4], and Javier Sanchez Abuín[5]

[1] Electronics and Telecomunications Department, [2] Engineering Systems and Automatic
Department, Technical University School, University of the Basque Country,
Donostia-San Sebastián, Spain
{j.maiora,g.garcia}@ehu.es
[3] eHealth and Biomedical Applications Department,
Vicomtech, Donostia-San Sebastián, Spain
{imacia,jhlegarreta,fboto,cpaloc}@vicomtech.org
[4] Computational Intelligence Group, Computer Science Faculty,
University of the Basque Country, Donostia-SanSebastián, Spain
manuel.grana@ehu.es
[5] Interventional Radiology Service, Donostia Hospital, Donostia-SanSebastián, Spain
javier.sanchezabuin@osakidetza.net

Abstract. A surgical technique currently used in the treatment of Abdominal
Aortic Aneurysms (AAA) is the Endovascular Aneurysm Repair (EVAR). This
minimally invasive procedure involves inserting a prosthesis in the aortic vessel
that excludes the aneurysm from the bloodstream. The stent, once in place acts
as a false lumen for the blood current to travel down, and not into the
surrounding aneurysm sac. This procedure, therefore, immediately takes the
pressure off the aneurysm, which thromboses itself after some time.
Nevertheless, in a long term perspective, different complications such as
prosthesis displacement or bloodstream leaks into or from the aneurysmatic
bulge (endoleaks) could appear causing a pressure elevation and, as a result,
increasing the danger of rupture. The purpose of this work is to explore the
application of image registration techniques to the visual detection of changes in
the thrombus in order to assess the evolution of the aneurysm. Prior to
registration, both the lumen and the thrombus are segmented.

1 Introduction

Abdominal Aortic Aneurysms (AAA) [1, 2] are a focal dilation in some point of the
abdominal section of the aorta. Several treatments exist today; one option is a
minimally invasive surgical procedure called Endovascular Aneurysm Repair
(EVAR) in which an endovascular prosthesis (endovascular graft) is inserted to
exclude the aneurysm from blood circulation [3].

The EVAR (Fig.1) requires a postoperative follow-up to ensure that the stent is
stable (absence of leakage, i.e.: blood flow within the aneurysm's sack). A reduction
in the size of the aneurysm ensures that exclusion has been effective [4, 5], while an

M. Graña Romay et al. (Eds.): HAIS 2010, Part I, LNAI 6076, pp. 524–531, 2010.
© Springer-Verlag Berlin Heidelberg 2010

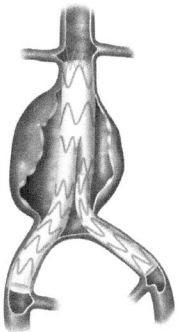

Fig. 1. Endovascular graft

The most widely used technique for EVAR monitoring is to obtain Computerized Tomography (CT) images of the abdominal region after an intravenous contrast agent has been injected. Such scans of the patient's abdominal area are available in the clinical routine as a set of 2D images whose visual analysis is time-consuming. The aim of our work is to make an automatic analysis of the AAA using digital image processing techniques, and yielding visual and quantitative information for monitoring and tracking of patients who underwent EVAR.

In our approach, first we estimate the rigid motion of the stent, as well as its deformation [6], and then we compute the spatial transformation of the segmented thrombus according to this estimation. Visual overlapping of such transformed data can help identifying deformation patterns having a high probability of dangerous progression of the aneurysm. The long term goal of our research is to make a prediction about future complications and disease progression. In the current state of the art of EVAR monitoring, the morphological changes and migration of the thrombus after EVAR are not studied in a systematic manner. The following are the main advances of our work concerning this state of the art:

- We use semi-automatic segmentation methods to segment the aneurysm lumen and thrombus. Using semi-automatic methods make the segmentation process less dependent on the intra-rater and intra-rater varibality, that have a proven intra-rater and interrater reliability and validity. A novel technique for thrombus segmentation, based on region growing algorithms, centerline extraction and radial functions, is used.
- Current registration methods used in EVAR monitoring are based in point set registration methods, which suffer from information loss. In our processing pipeline, registration is performed over binary images with much less information loss.

The processing pipeline is illustrated in figure 2. We compute the registration of the lumen of the last image to the target image. This registration allows aligning the two images to the same reference system. We compute a sequence of rigid, affine and deformable registrations, and then we apply the obtained lumen transformation to the thombus.

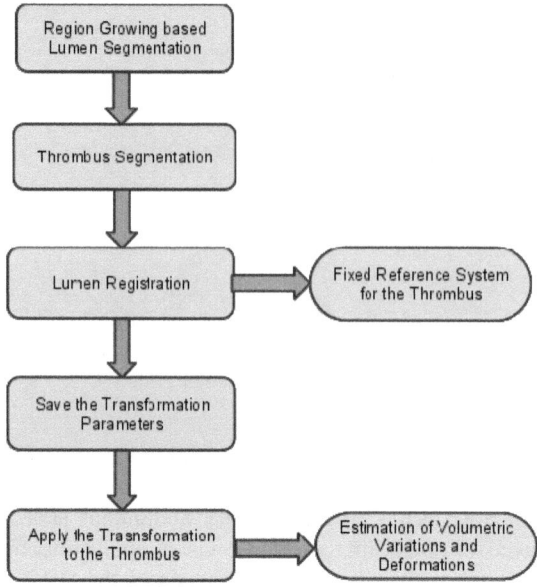

Fig. 2. Pipeline of the thrombus visual change detection process

2 Methods

We estimate the volumetric variations, as well as the deformations of the thrombus in a patient, (across different studies), registering the lumen of the aorta of the datasets to be compared, in order to place the respective thrombi in the same reference system, so that the comparison becomes meaningful. This registration is necessary because the relative position of the aorta varies from different studies of the same patient along time.

First, the lumen is segmented using a 3D region growing algorithm, followed by the calculation of the aorta centerline. The thrombus is segmented using a radial model approach [7]. After that, the registration of the lumen extracted from two datasets of the same patient obtained at different moments in time is computed and then, the obtained transformation is applied to the thrombus. Next, we proceed to describe each component of the system.

2.1 Image Segmentation

The first step in image analysis generally is to segment the image. Segmentation subdivides an image into its constituent parts or objects, which are defined as homogenous and disjoint regions (image segments) that are separated by boundaries. Independent of the segmentation technique, images usually need to be preprocessed for efficient segmentation[7].

Region Growing based Lumen Segmentation

Segmentation of the lumen is based on a 3D region-growing algorithm that needs an interactive selection of a seed voxel. First, the image is preprocessed to reduce noise and a Volume of Interest (VOI) is defined in order to reduce the data amount to be processed. The algorithm includes voxels whose intensity lies in the confidence interval of the intensity of the current segmented region in an iterative process that recomputes the region statistics at each iteration. The segmentation is smoothed by morphological closing of the resulting segmented region to fill possible small holes.

Centerline Extraction

The centerline approximates at each slice the centroid of the lumen region and is a good approximation for the morphological skeleton of the whole aorta. A single point on the center-line is obtained for every slice, since the aorta is almost normal to axial slices. The center-line determination is performed on a slice-by-slice basis using 2D image moments.

Thrombus Segmentation

We propose modeling the internal and external contours of the thrombus of the aneurysm as radial functions in cylindrical coordinates. At every slice, we choose the origin of these functions to be the centerline point of this slice. The segmentation procedure consists of calculating the internal and external radii at every point, which enclose the segmented region corresponding to the thrombus.

2.2 Image Registration

A spatial transformation maps each point in the 3D space to another point in the same space. Appropriate interpolator, cost/error function and an optimization methods are chosen to compute the optimal adjustment of the transformation parameters corresponding to a minimum of the cost function [8].

2.2.1 Lumen Registration

Our problem is an intra-subject and mono-modal registration, as it examines the same patient on different dates. A sequence of rigid, affine and deformable (B-splines) registrations is performed. The earliest CT volume is considered the target image and the others are registered according to it. A linear interpolator, Squared Intensity Differences and Mutual Information metrics and Regular Step Gradient Descent Optimizer are used to obtain the optimal transformation parameters.

Rigid Registration

First the two binary images corresponding to the patient's lumen are roughly aligned by using a transform initialization. Then the two images are registered using a rigid transformation. In three dimensions we have 6 degrees of freedom, which can be defined as translations in the x, y and z directions, and rotations α, β and γ around these three axes. From these unknowns we can construct a rigid body transformation matrix T_{rigid}. This transformation can be presented as a rotation R followed by a translation t that can be applied to any point x in the image domain.

$$T_{rigid}(x) = Rx + t$$

Affine Registration

The rigid transformation is used to initialize a registration with an affine transform of the lumen. While a rigid transformation preserves the distances between all points in the object transformed, an affine transformation preserves parallel lines. This model has 12 degrees of freedom and allows for scaling and shearing.

$$T(x,y,z) = \begin{pmatrix} x' \\ y' \\ z' \\ 1 \end{pmatrix} = \begin{pmatrix} a_{00} & a_{01} & a_{02} & a_{03} \\ a_{10} & a_{11} & a_{12} & a_{13} \\ a_{20} & a_{21} & a_{22} & a_{23} \\ 0 & 0 & 0 & 1 \end{pmatrix} \begin{pmatrix} x \\ y \\ z \\ 1 \end{pmatrix}$$

Deformable Registration

The warped image resulting from the affine registration is used as the initial image of a B-spline deformable transformation. Free Form Deformations (FFDs) based in locally controlled functions such as B-splines are a powerful tool for modelling 3D deformable objects. We use FFDs is to deform the lumen by manipulating an underlying mesh of control points. The resulting deformation controls the shape of the lumen and produces a smooth and continuous transformation. A spline-based FFD is defined on the image domain $\Omega = \{(x,y,z)|0 \le x < X, 0 \le y < Y, 0 \le z < Z\}$ where Φ denotes an $n_x \times n_y \times n_z$ mesh of control points $\phi_{i,j,k}$ with uniform spacing δ. In this case, the displacement field $\mathbf{u}$ defined by FFD can be expressed as the 3D tensor product of the 1D cubic B-splines:

$$\mathbf{u}(x,y,z) = \sum_{l=0}^{3} \sum_{m=0}^{3} \sum_{n=0}^{3} \theta(u)\theta(v)\theta(w)\phi_{i+l,j+m,k+n}$$

2.2.2 Evaluation of the Registration Quality

We use two similarity metrics: the sum of squared intensity differences (SSD) and mutual information (MI). These similarity metrics have each been used widely in the literature for non-rigid registration to measure the intensity agreement between a warped image and the target image. We briefly describe both distances in this section, following [9, 10].

SSD is suitable when the images have been acquired through similar sensors and thus are expected to present the same intensity range and distribution. For voxel locations x_A in image A, within an overlap domain $\Omega_{A,B}^T$, comprising N voxels:

$$SSD = \frac{1}{N} \sum_{x_A \in \Omega_{A,B}^T} |A(x_A) - B^T(x_A)|^2$$

where B^T is the transformed image.

Mutual information is a measure of how much information one random variable has about another. The information contributed by the images is simply the entropy of the portion of the image that overlaps with the other image volume, and the mutual information is a measure of the joint entropy with regard to the marginal entropies.

$$I(A,B) = H(A) + H(B) - H(A,B)$$

where $I(A,B)$ is the mutual information, $H(A)$ and $H(B)$ are the marginal entropies of the target and warped images and $H(A,B)$ is the joint entropy.

3 Results

We have tested the approach with 3 patients –with 5 datasets each– which have been treated with stent-graft devices. The CT image stacks consists of datasets obtained from a LightSpeed16 CT scanner (GE Medical Systems, Fairfield, CT, USA) with 512x512x354 voxel resolution and 0.725x0.725x0.8 mm. spatial resolution. The time elapsed between different studies of the same subject varies between 6 and 12 months.

We have computed the mean squares and mutual information similarity metrics for the evaluation of the registration. A decrease of both metric is observed in the consequent registration methods. Mutual information is reported as a negative number because it has been used as a cost function by the minimization algorithm.

Table 1. Similarity metric results of the sequence of registrations over one of the patient datasets. Image 2 is the target image for registration of images 3, 4 and 5.

Registered Studies		Metrics	
		Mean Squares	Mutual Information
2-3	Rigid	4,60E-01	-5,28E-06
	Affine	3,42E-01	-7,25E-06
	Deform. Coarse	3,05E-01	-8,35E-06
	Deform. Fine	2,88E-01	-9,24E-06
2-4	Rigid	4,94E-01	-4,96E-06
	Affine	2,97E-01	-7,91E-06
	Deform. Coarse	2,70E-01	-8,64E-06
	Deform. Fine	2,65E-01	-9,53E-06
2-5	Rigid	8,03E-01	-3,48E-06
	Affine	3,73E-01	-6,29E-06
	Deform. Coarse	3,19E-01	-7,27E-06
	Deform. Fine	2,88E-01	-8,96E-06

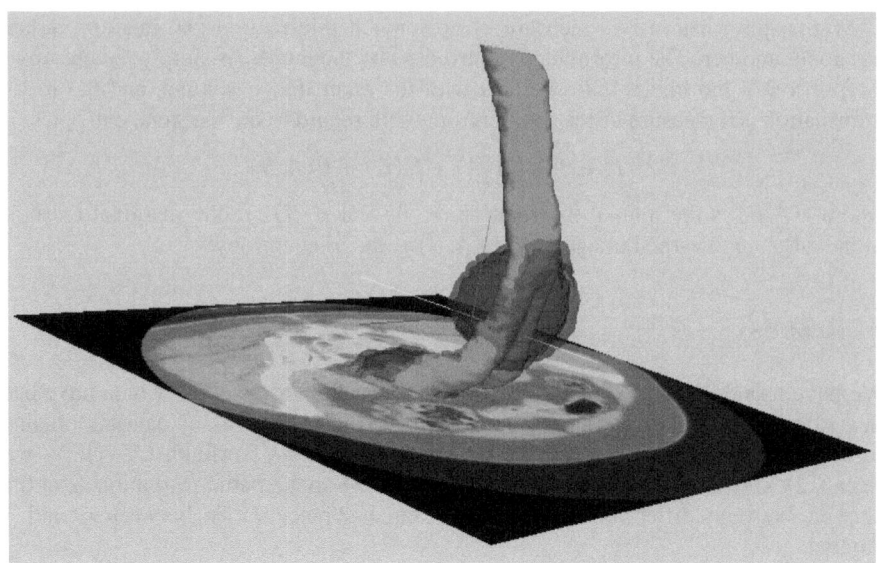

Fig. 3. Thrombus extracted for two instants in time (semi-transparent blue for the first one, semi-transparent red the second one), both registered to the lumen of the first instant in time. An increase in thrombus volume can be easily appreciated.

The segmented images are visualized in 3D together with a CT slice to have a referenced view. After the lumen is registered, volumetric changes and deformation of the thrombus from one point in time to the next can be visualized (Fig. 3).

4 Conclusion

We have developed a method that places the thrombi of different datasets of the same patient referenced to the lumen of the first dataset. The method allows detecting small changes in volume or deformation of the thrombus that may go unnoticed for radiologists while comparing individual slices of the same patient along time. With our method, any change in volume can be detected easily.

In the future, we expect to obtain quantitative values of the changes in the thrombus after registetration of images from different studies of the same patient. This could lead to a model that could predict the evolution of other patients and provide quantitative measurements for decision support. Support Vector Machines (SVM) will be used to determine if the evolution of the EVAR is positive or not.

References

1. Cronenwett, J., Krupski, W., Rutherford, R.: Abdominal aortic and iliac aneurysm. In: Vascular Surgery, Saunders, Philadelphia, pp. 1246–1280 (2000)
2. Rodin, M.B., Daviglus, M.L., Wong, G.C., Liu, K., Garside, D.B., Greenland, P., Stamler, J.: Middle age cardiovascular risk factors and abdominal aortic aneurysm in older age. Hypertension 42(1), 61–68 (2003)

3. Veith, F.J., Marin, M.L., Cynamon, J., Schonholz, C., Parodi, J.: 1992: Parodi, Montefiore, and the first abdominal aortic aneurysm stent graft in the United States. Annals of Vascular Surgery 19(5), 749–751 (2005)
4. Ellozy, S.H., Carroccio, A., Lookstein, R.A., Jacobs, T.S., Addis, M.D., Teodorescu, V.J., Marin, M.L.: Abdominal aortic aneurysm sac shrinkage after endovascular aneurysm repair: Correlation with chronic sac pressure measurement. Journal of Vascular Surgery 43(1), 2–6 (2006)
5. Dias, N.V., Ivancev, K., Malina, M., Resch, T., Lindblad, B., Sonesson, B.: Intra-aneurysm sac pressure measurements after endovascular aneurysm repair: Differences between shrinking, unchanged, and expanding aneurysms with and without endoleaks. Journal of Vascular Surgery 39(6), 1229–1235 (2004)
6. Mattes, J., Steingruber, I., Netzer, M., Fritscher, K., Kopf, H., Jaschke, W., Schubert, R.: Quantification of the migration and deformation of abdominal aortic aneurysm stent grafts - art. no. 61440V. In: Reinhardt, J.M., Pluim, J.P.W. (eds.) Medical Imaging 2006: Image Processing, Pts 1-3, p. V1440 (2006)
7. Garcia-Sebastian, M., Gonzalez, A.I., Grana, M.: An adaptive field rule for non-parametric MRI intensity inhomogeneity estimation algorithm. Neurocomputing 72(16-18), 3556–3569 (2009)
8. Macía, I., Legarreta, J.H., Paloc, C., Graña, M., Maiora, J., García, G., de Blas, M.: Segmentation of Abdominal Aortic Aneurysms in CT Images using a Radial Model Approach. In: Corchado, E., Yin, H. (eds.) IDEAL 2009. LNCS, vol. 5788, pp. 664–671. Springer, Heidelberg (2009)
9. Ibanez, L., Ng, L., Gee, J., Aylward, S.: Registration patterns: The generic framework for image registration of the insight toolkit. In: Proceedings of IEEE International Symposium on Biomedical Imaging (2002)
10. Yanovsky, I., Leow, A.D., Lee, S., Osher, S.J., Thompson, P.M.: Comparing registration methods for mapping brain change using tensor-based morphometry. Medical Image Analysis 13(5), 679–700 (2009)

Randomness and Fuzziness in Bayes Multistage Classifier

Robert Burduk

Department of Systems and Computer Networks, Wroclaw University of Technology,
Wybrzeze Wyspianskiego 27, 50-370 Wroclaw, Poland
robert.burduk@pwr.wroc.pl

Abstract. The paper considers the mixture of randomness and fuzziness in Bayes multistage classifier. Assuming that both the tree structure and the feature used at each non-terminal node have been specified, we present the probability of error. This model of classification is based on the fuzzy observations, the randomness of classes and the Bayes rule. The obtained error for fuzzy observations is compared with the case when observation are not fuzzy as a difference of errors. Additionally, the obtained results are compared with the bound on the probability of error based on information energy of fuzzy events.

1 Introduction

Many paper present the aspect of fuzzy and imprecise information in pattern recognition [3], [4], [11], [12], [13]. In the real-world recognition and classification problems we are faced with imprecise information that is connected with diverse facets of the human thinking. The origin of randomness and fuzziness sources is related to labels expressed in feature space as well as to labels of classes taken into account in classification procedures. There are many cases where the available information is a mixture of randomness and fuzziness. In [8] formulated the pattern recognition problem with fuzzy classes and fuzzy information and consider the following tree situations:

- fuzzy classes and exact information,
- exact classes and fuzzy information,
- fuzzy classes and fuzzy information.

The classification error is the ultimate measure of the classifier performance. Competing classifiers can also be evaluated based on their error probabilities. Several studies have previously described the Bayes probability of error for a single-stage classifier [1], [2], [14] and for a hierarchical classifier [5], [7].

In this paper, we consider the classification error problem. In our model of pattern recognition we use exact classes and fuzzy information of object features. We consider the problem of classification for the case in which the observations of the features are represented by the fuzzy sets. Additionally, the a priori probabilities of classes and class-conditional probability density functions

M. Graña Romay et al. (Eds.): HAIS 2010, Part I, LNAI 6076, pp. 532–539, 2010.

are random. For such assumptions we consider the global optimal strategy of multistage recognition task. The obtained error for fuzzy observations is compared with the case where observations are not fuzzy. The difference of errors for these two cases is the subject of this paper. Additionally, the obtained results are compared with the bound on the probability of error based on information energy of fuzzy events.

The contents of the work are as follows: Section 2 introduces the necessary background and describes the Bayes hierarchical classifier. In section 3, the introduction to fuzzy sets is presented. In section 4, we present the difference between the probability of misclassification for the fuzzy and crisp data in Bayes hierarchical classifier.

2   Bayes Hierarchical Classifier

In the paper [7], the Bayesian hierarchical classifier is presented. The synthesis of a multistage classifier is a complex problem. It involves specification of following components:

- the decision logic, i.e. hierarchical ordering of classes,
- the feature used at each stage of decision,
- the decision rules (strategy) for performing the classification.

This paper is devoted only to the last problem. This means that we will only consider the presentation of decision algorithms, assuming that both the tree structure and the feature used at each non-terminal node have been specified.

The procedure in the Bayesian hierarchical classifier consists of the following sequences of operations presented in Fig. 1. At the first stage, some specific features x_0 are measured. They are chosen from among all accessible features x, which describe the pattern that will be classified. These data constitute a basis for making a decision i_1. This decision, being the result of recognition at the first stage, defines a certain subset in the set of all classes and simultaneously

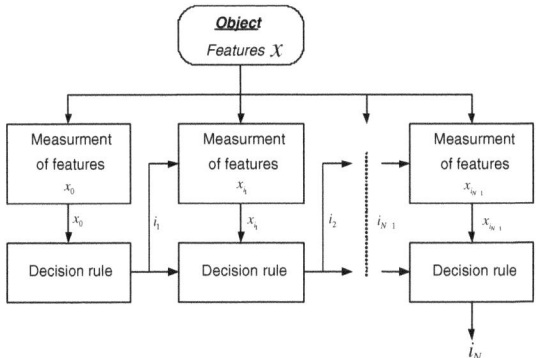

Fig. 1. Block diagram of the hierarchical classifier

indicates features x_{i_1} (from among x) which should be measured in order to make a decision at the next stage.

Now, at the second stage, features x_{i_1} are measured, which together with i_1 constitute a basis for making the next decision i_2. This decision, – like i_1 – indicates features x_{i_2} that are necessary to make the next decision (at the third stage, as in the previous stage) that in turn defines a certain subset of classes, not in the set of all classes, but in the subset indicated by the decision i_2, and so on. The whole procedure ends at the N-th stage, where the decision made i_N indicates a single class, which is the final result of multistage recognition.

2.1   Decision Problem Statement

Let us consider a pattern recognition problem, in which the number of classes equals M. Let us assume that the classes are organised in a $(N + 1)$ horizontal decision tree. Let us number all the nodes of the decision-tree constructed with consecutive numbers of $0, 1, 2, \ldots$, reserving 0 for the root-node, and let us assign numbers of classes from the $\mathcal{M} = \{1, 2, \ldots, M\}$ set to terminal nodes so that each of them can be labelled with the class number connected with that node. This allows us to introduce the following notation:

- $\mathcal{M}(n)$ – the set of nodes, whose distance from the root is n, $n = 0, 1, 2, \ldots, N$. In particular $\mathcal{M}(0) = \{0\}$, $\mathcal{M}(N) = \mathcal{M}$,
- $\overline{\mathcal{M}} = \bigcup\limits_{n=0}^{N-1} \mathcal{M}(n)$ – the set of internal nodes (non terminal),
- $\mathcal{M}_i \subseteq \mathcal{M}(N)$ – the set of class labels attainable from the i-th node ($i \in \overline{\mathcal{M}}$),
- $\mathcal{M}^i$ – the set of nodes of immediate descendant node i ($i \in \overline{\mathcal{M}}$),
- m_i – node of direct predecessor of the i-th node ($i \neq 0$),
- $s(i)$ – the set of nodes on the path from the root-node to the i-th node, $i \neq 0$.

We will continue to adopt the probabilistic model of the recognition problem, i.e. we will assume that the class label of the pattern being recognised $j_N \in \mathcal{M}(N)$ and its observed features x are the realizations of a couple of random variables $\boldsymbol{J}_N$ and $\boldsymbol{X}$. The complete probabilistic information denotes the knowledge of a priori probabilities of classes:

$$p(j_N) = P(J_N = j_N), \quad j_N \in \mathcal{M}(N) \tag{1}$$

and class-conditional probability density functions:

$$f_{j_N}(x) = f(x/j_N), \quad x \in X, \quad j_N \in \mathcal{M}(N) . \tag{2}$$

Let

$$x_i \in X_i \subseteq R^{d_i}, \quad d_i \leq d, \quad i \in \mathcal{M} \tag{3}$$

denote vector of features used at the i-th node, which have been selected from the vector x.

Our aim now is to calculate the so-called multistage recognition strategy $\pi_N = \{\Psi_i\}_{i \in \overline{\mathcal{M}}}$, that is the set of recognition algorithms in the form:

$$\Psi_i : X_i \rightarrow \mathcal{M}^i, \quad i \in \overline{\mathcal{M}} . \tag{4}$$

Formula (4) is a decision rule (recognition algorithm) used at the i-th node that maps observation subspace to the set of immediate descendant nodes of the i-th node. Analogically, decision rule (4) partitions observation subspace X_i into disjoint decision regions $D_{x_i}^k$, $k \in \mathcal{M}^i$, so that observation x_i is allocated to the node k if $k_i \in D_{x_i}^k$, namely:

$$D_{x_i}^k = \{x_i \in X_i : \Psi_i(x_i) = k\}, \ k \in \mathcal{M}^i, \quad i \in \overline{\mathcal{M}}. \tag{5}$$

Our aim is to minimise the expected risk function (expected loss function $L(I_N, J_N)$) denoted by:

$$R^*(\pi_N) = \min_{\pi_N} R(\pi_N) = \min_{\pi_N} E[L(I_N, J_N)]. \tag{6}$$

where π_N is the strategy of the decision tree classifier. The π_N is the set of classifying rules used at the particular node $\pi_N = \{\Psi_i\}_{i \in \overline{\mathcal{M}}}$.

Globally optimal strategy π_N^*. This strategy minimises the mean probability of misclassification on the whole multistage recognition process and leads to an optimal global decision strategy, whose recognition algorithm at the n-th stage is as follows:

$$\Psi_{i_n}^*(x_{i_n}) = i_{n+1} \quad \text{if} \tag{7}$$

$$i_{n+1} = \arg \max_{k \in \mathcal{M}^{i_n}} Pc(k)p(k)f_k(x_{i_n})$$

where $Pc(k)$ is the empirical probability of correct classification at the next stages if at the n-th stage decision i_{n+1} is made.

3   Basic Notions of Fuzzy Theory

Fuzzy number A is a fuzzy set defined on the set of real numbers $\mathbb{R}$ characterized by means of a membership function $\mu_A(x)$, $\mu_A : \mathbb{R} \rightarrow [0, 1]$. In this study, the special kinds of fuzzy numbers including triangular fuzzy numbers are employed. Triangular fuzzy numbers can be defined by a triplet $A = (a_1, a_2, a_3)$.

Fuzzy information $\mathcal{A}_k \in \Re^d$, $k = 1, ..., d$ (d is the dimension of the feature vector) is a set of fuzzy events $\mathcal{A}_k = \{A_k^1, A_k^2, ..., A_k^{n_k}\}$ characterized by membership functions

$$\mathcal{A}_k = \{\mu_{A_k^1}(x_k), \mu_{A_k^2}(x_k), ..., \mu_{A_k^{n_k}}(x_k)\}. \tag{8}$$

The value of index n_k defines the possible number of fuzzy events for x_k (for the k-th dimension of feature vector). In addition, assume that for each observation subspace x_k the set of all available fuzzy observations (8) satisfies the orthogonality constraint [8]:

$$\sum_{l=1}^{n_k} \mu_{A_k^l}(x_k) = 1. \tag{9}$$

The probability of fuzzy event is assumed in Zadeh's form [15]:

$$P(A) = \int_{\Re^d} \mu_A(x) f(x) dx. \tag{10}$$

The probability $P(A)$ of a fuzzy event A defined by (10) represents a crisp number in the interval $[0,1]$.

4 Global Optimal Strategy

The decision algorithms for the zero-one loss function in the case of the global optimal strategy of multistage recognition are as follows:

$$\Psi_{i_n}^*(A_{i_n}) = i_{n+1} \quad \text{if} \tag{11}$$

$$i_{n+1} = \arg \max_{k \in \mathcal{M}^{i_n}} \sum_{j_N \in \mathcal{M}_k} p(j_N) q^*(j_N/k, j_N) \int_{\Re^d} \mu_{A_{i_n}}(x_{i_n}) f_{j_N}(x_{i_n}) dx_{i_n}$$

for $i_n \in \mathcal{M}(n)$, $n = 0, 1, 2, \ldots, N-1$, where $q^*(j_N/i_{n+1}, j_N)$ denotes the probability of accurate object classification of the class j_N at further stages using π_N^* strategy rules on the condition that on the n-th stage the i_{n+1} decision has been made. The A_{i_n} denotes the fuzzy value of object feature observed in i_n node.

The probability of error $Pe(\pi_N^*)$ for crisp data and for globally optimal strategy π_N^* is represented by [7]:

$$Pe(\pi_N^*) = 1 - \sum_{j_N \in M(N)} p(j_N) \prod_{i_k \in s(j_N) - \{0\}} q(i_k/m_{i_k}, i_k). \tag{12}$$

Similarly, if (9) holds the probability of error $Pe(\pi_N^*)$ for fuzzy data and for globally optimal strategy π_N^* is as follows:

$$Pe_F(\pi_N^*) = 1 - \sum_{j_N \in M(N)} p(j_N) \prod_{i_k \in s(j_N) - \{0\}} q(i_k/m_{i_k}, i_k). \tag{13}$$

When we use fuzzy information on object features instead of exact information, we deteriorate the classification accuracy. The upper boundary of the difference between the probability of misclassification for the fuzzy $Pe(\pi_N^*)$ and crisp data $Pe(\pi_N^*)$ for the globally optimal strategy of multistage recognition π_N^* is as follows:

$$Pe_F(\pi_N^*) - Pe(\pi_N^*) \le \sum_{j_N \in M(N)} p(j_N) \sum_{i_k \in s(j_N) - \{0\}} \varepsilon_{m_{i_k}} \tag{14}$$

where

$$\varepsilon_i = \sum_{A_i \in X_i} \left| \int_{\Re^i} \mu_{A_i}(x_i) \max_{k \in \mathcal{M}^i} \{f_k(x_i)\} dx_i - \max_{k \in \mathcal{M}^i} \left\{ \int_{\Re^i} \mu_{A_i}(x_i) f_k(x_i) dx_i \right\} \right|.$$

4.1 Error Bounds in Terms of Information Energy

Some studies pertaining to bound on the probability of error in fuzzy concepts are presented in [10], [9]. They are based on information energy for fuzzy events. The marginal probability distribution on fuzzy information $\mathcal{A}$ of the fuzzy event A is given by:

$$P_m(A) = \int_{\Re^d} \mu_A(x)p(x)dx, \tag{15}$$

where $p(x)$ is the unconditional likelihood.

The conditional information energy (in node i_n) of $\mathcal{M}_{i_n}$ given by the fuzzy event A is as follows:

$$E_{i_n}(P(\mathcal{M}_{i_n}|A_{i_n})) = \sum_{k \in \mathcal{M}_{i_n}} (P(k|A_{i_n}))^2, \tag{16}$$

where $P(k|A_{i_n}) = \dfrac{P(k) \int_{\Re^d} \mu_{A_{i_n}}(x_{i_n})f_k(x_{i_n})dx_{i_n}}{P_{i_n}(A_{i_n})}$.

The conditional information energy (in node i_n) of $\mathcal{M}_{i_n}$ given the fuzzy information $\mathcal{A}_{i_n}$ is as follows:

$$E_{i_n}(\mathcal{A}_{i_n}, \mathcal{M}_{i_n}) = \sum_{A_{i_n} \in \mathcal{A}_{i_n}} E_{i_n}(P(\mathcal{M}_{i_n}|A_{i_n}))P_{i_n}(A_{i_n}). \tag{17}$$

For such a definition of conditional information energy, the upper and lower bounds on probability of error for fuzzy data in node i_n, similarly as in [9], are represented by:

$$\frac{1}{2}(1 - E_{i_n}(\mathcal{A}_{i_n}, \mathcal{M}_{i_n})) \le Pe_{i_n}(\Psi^*) \le (1 - E_{i_n}(\mathcal{A}_{i_n}, \mathcal{M}_{i_n})). \tag{18}$$

Hence, the upper boundary of the difference between the probability of misclassification for the fuzzy $Pe_F^{IE}(\pi_N^*)$ (in terms of information energy) and crisp data $Pe(\pi_N^*)$ for the globally optimal strategy of multistage recognition π_N^* is as follows:

$$Pe_F^{IE}(\pi_N^*) - Pe(\pi_N^*) \le \sum_{j_N \in \mathcal{M}(N)} p(j_N) \sum_{i_k \in s(j_N) - \{0\}} (1 - E_{m_{i_k}}(\mathcal{A}_{m_{i_k}}, \mathcal{M}_{m_{i_k}})). \tag{19}$$

5   Illustrative Example

Let us consider the two-stage binary classifier. Four classes have identical a priori probabilities that equal 0.25. We use 3-dimensional data $x = [x^{(1)}, x^{(2)}, x^{(3)}]$ where class-conditional probability density functions are normally distributed. For performing the classification at the root-node 0 the first coordinate was used, and components $x^{(2)}$ and $x^{(3)}$ were used at the nodes 5 and 6 respectively. In the data covariance matrices are equal for every class $\sum_{j_2} = 2I$, $j_2 \in \mathcal{M}(2)$,

Table 1. The difference between the probability of misclassification for global optimal strategy $Pe_F(\pi_N^*) - Pe(\pi_N^*)$ and the same difference in terms of information energy $Pe_F^{IE}(\pi_N^*) - Pe(\pi_N^*)$

| | | $\mu_1(x-k),$ | | $\mu_1(x-k),$ | | $k =$ | |
	0	0.25	0.5	0.75	1	1.25	1.5
$Pe_F^{IE}(\pi_N^*) - Pe(\pi_N^*)$	0.154	0.152	0.150	0.152	0.154	0.158	0.164
$Pe_F(\pi_N^*) - Pe(\pi_N^*)$	0.005	0.008	0.02	0.008	0.005	0.008	0.02

and the expected values are as follows: $\mu_1 = [0, 0, 0]$, $\mu_2 = [0, 4, 0]$, $\mu_3 = [4, 0, 0]$, $\mu_4 = [4, 0, 4]$. In experiments, the following sets of fuzzy numbers were used:

$$\mathcal{A}_1 = \mathcal{A}_2 = \mathcal{A}_3 = \{A^1 = (-\infty, 0, 1), \; A^2 = (0, 1, 2), \ldots, A^5 = (3, 4, \infty)\},$$

Tab. 1 shows the difference between the probability of misclassification for fuzzy and non fuzzy data in the globally optimal strategy of multistage classification $Pe_F(\pi_N^*) - Pe(\pi_N^*)$ calculated from (14) and the same difference in terms of information energy calculated from (19). The values for k are calculated for the translation of the class-conditional probability density functions by the value k. These results are calculated for full probabilistic information.

The obtained results show deterioration in the classification quality when we use fuzzy information on object features instead of exact information in Bayes hierarchical classifier. We have to notice that the difference in the misclassification for fuzzy and crisp data does not depend only on the fuzzy observations. The position of the class-conditional probability density in relation to the fuzzy features observed is the essential influence. The difference obtained $Pe_F(\pi_N^*) - Pe(\pi_N^*)$ on the probability of error is always tighter than the difference $Pe_F^{IE}(\pi_N^*) - Pe(\pi_N^*)$ based on information energy. This difference has the minimum in $k = 0.5$ but the difference $Pe_F(\pi_N^*) - Pe(\pi_N^*)$ is periodical. In this case, the period is equal to 1. This period is the half of the width of the fuzzy number. This is the observation which requires the analytic confirmation.

6   Conclusion

In the present paper, we have concentrated on the Bayes optimal classifier. Assuming a full probabilistic information, we have presented the difference between the probability of misclassification for fuzzy and crisp data in terms of information energy and exact difference of these probabilities of error. The illustrative example demonstrates that the position of the class-conditional probability density in relation to the fuzzy features observed is the essential influence for the difference $Pe_F(\pi_N^*) - Pe(\pi_N^*)$. This difference is periodical and is always tighter than the difference $Pe_F^{IF}(\pi_N^*) - Pe(\pi_N^*)$ based on information energy.

Acknowledgements. This research is supported in part by The Polish State Committee for Scientific Research under the grant which is realizing in years 2010–2013.

References

1. Antos, A., Devroye, L., Gyorfi, L.: Lower bounds for Bayes error estimation. IEEE Trans. Pattern Analysis and Machine Intelligence 21, 643–645 (1999)
2. Avi-Itzhak, H., Diep, T.: Arbitrarily tight upper and lower bounds on the bayesian probability of error. IEEE Trans. Pattern Analysis and Machine Intelligence 18, 89–91 (1996)
3. Burduk, R., Kurzyński, M.: Two-stage binary classifier with fuzzy-valued loss function. Pattern Analysis and Applications 9(4), 353–358 (2006)
4. Burduk, R.: Classification error in Bayes multistage recognition task with fuzzy observations. Pattern Analysis and Applications 13(1), 85–91 (2010)
5. Kulkarni, A.: On the mean accuracy of hierarchical classifiers. IEEE Transactions on Computers 27, 771–776 (1978)
6. Kuncheva, L.I.: Combining pattern classifier: Methods and Algorithms. John Wiley, New York (2004)
7. Kurzyński, M.: On the multistage Bayes classifier. Pattern Recognition 21, 355–365 (1988)
8. Okuda, T., Tanaka, H., Asai, K.: A formulation of fuzzy decision problems with fuzzy information using probability measures of fuzzy events. Information and Control 38, 135–147 (1978)
9. Pardo, J.A., Taneja, I.J.: On the Probability of Error in Fuzzy discrimination Problems. Kybernetes 21(6), 43–52 (1992)
10. Pardo, L., Menendez, M.L.: Some Bounds on Probability of Error in Fuzzy Discrimination Problems. European Journal of Operational Research 53, 362–370 (1991)
11. Pedrycz, W.: Fuzzy Sets in Pattern Recognition: Methodology and Methods. Pattern Recognition 23, 121–146 (1990)
12. Stańczyk, U.: Dominance-Based Rough Set Approach Employed in Search of Authorial Invariants. In: Advances in Intelligent and Soft Computing, vol. 57, pp. 293–301. Springer, Heidelberg (2009)
13. Supriya, K.D., Ranjit, B., Akhil, R.R.: An application of intuitionistic fuzzy sets in medical diagnosis. Fuzzy Sets and Systems 117(2), 209–213 (2001)
14. Woźniak, M.: Experiments on linear combiners. Advances in Soft Computing, vol. 47, pp. 445–452. Springer, Heidelberg (2008)
15. Zadeh, L.A.: Probability measures of fuzzy events. Journal of Mathematical Analysis and Applications 23, 421–427 (1968)

Multiple Classifier System with Radial Basis Weight Function

Konrad Jackowski

Department of Systems and Computer Networks, Wroclaw University of Technology,
Wybrzeze Wyspianskiego 27, 50-370 Wroclaw, Poland

Abstract. The paper presents novel algorithm of decision making in multiple classifier system (MCS), which response is based on weighted fusion of discriminating functions derived from a pool of elementary classifiers. Radial basis function model are used to establish the weights of the classifiers over a feature space. For best exploitation of knowledge collected by the classifiers parameters of the weight functions are set during learning process of the MCS that aims at minimizing misclassification rate of the MCS. Quality of the proposed radial basis function MCS (RB MCS) is verified in the set of experiments carried out on the set of benchmark datasets derived from UCI repository.

Keywords: pattern recognition, classifier fusion, multiple classifier system.

1 Introduction

The aim of classifier systems is to assign object being under recognition to one of predefined classes [1]. This task can be done by observation and analysis of the set of the object's features. There are plethora of available classification algorithms of different kind and features such as neural networks, linear or quadratic classifiers, algorithms that base on probability estimations to name just a few. Multiple classifier systems (MCSs) have been recently widely discussed as the proposition of possible way of improving classification accuracy by exploitation the knowledge collected by set of elementary classifier instead of one simple classifier [2]. There are number of important questions that have to be answered while building MCSs. The issue of selection classifiers that are to be used in the MCS to improve accuracy of the system is addressed by number of propositions aiming at ensuring possibly high diversity among the classifiers [3]. The other important question in this field is how to mix information derived from the classifiers in order to establish MCS's decision. In this regards MCSs algorithms can be divided into two main groups. The first one consists of algorithms fusing classifier responses [4], starting from simple majority voting [5], ending on its more sophisticated variant with classifier weighting. Nonetheless those methods of the fusion have some limitation [6]. The second group collects methods of the fusion of classifier discriminating function [6].

Regardless of the fussing type the next question arises, how to assess and utilize knowledge of each classifier. For example, simple selection algorithms neglect knowledge of all classifiers except the winner loosing some valuable information.

M. Graña Romay et al. (Eds.): HAIS 2010, Part I, LNAI 6076, pp. 540–547, 2010.

MCSs based on the voting incorporate response of all classifiers neglecting their competence or lack of competence. One possible way of diminishing aforementioned disadvantages is using a set of coefficients assigned to the classifiers that play role of weights controlling impact of the classifiers on MCS's decision. If the weights get different values depending on values of the object's attributes, MCS has even deeper control of the importance of the elementary classifiers that depends on their competence over a feature space.

Addressing that issue Jordan and Jacobs formulate proposition [7] that initiate researched stream called mixture of experts (ME). Originally proposed algorithm trained simultaneously set of expert networks together with the gate network that works as nonlinear, highly flexible weight function. Since then a lot of variants of ME have been proposed such as incorporating boosting algorithms [8] or clustering [9].

In the model of RB MCS presented in the paper Gaussian radial basis function that covers feature space is proposed to be used for calculating the weights. It the proposed approach it is assumed that classifiers that form MCS are granted they are not trained together with RB MCS. Their knowledge is fixed and the aim of RB MCS is to exploit that knowledge in the best way.

Radial basis function has been selected because it gains its maximum value at one point that can be considered as the point of highest competence of related classifier. There are two parameters of the function that control its shape over the feature space as the parameters are set separately for each classifier to estimate its competence. Learning process manipulate the set of that parameters, searching best estimation of classifiers' competences, in order to minimize misclassification rate of the MCS.

The learning process is treated as a compound optimization problem. Evolutionary algorithm is used to find the best possible configuration of the parameters giving the smallest number of misclassifications.

For the evaluation purposes of a performance of the proposed classifier model and learning algorithm results of set of experiments are provided. The experiments were carried out on the set of benchmark datasets derived from UCE repository are provided.

This paper has the following structure:

The model of the classification algorithm is presented in section 2. Section 3 defines optimization problem, while details of proposed learning algorithm are given in section 4. Details of experiments and the results are presented and discussed in section 5. The last section concludes the paper.

2   Model of the Classification Algorithm

The general purpose of classification algorithm is to assign the object to one of predefined classes by analysis of the set of features.

$$\Psi(x) = i, \tag{1}$$

where Ψ is the classifier,

$x = \left[x^{(1)}, ..., x^{(d)} \right]^T \in R^d$ is the feature vector, and

$i \in M = \{1, 2, ..., M\}$ is the class index returned by the classifier.

Let Π^{Ψ} denotes the set of elementary classifiers.

$$\Pi^{\Psi} = \{\Psi_1, \Psi_2, \ldots, \Psi_K\}, \tag{2}$$

where $\Psi_1, \Psi_2, \ldots, \Psi_K$ state for elementary classifiers in the pool, and K is the number of classifier in the pool

Each of them makes decision based on the values of set of discriminating functions.

$$F_k(i, x), \tag{3}$$

where k is the index of the classifier.

The discriminating function (3) can be regarded as a support given by the k-th classifier to the i-th class while classification object x.

As the one of the main assumptions in MCSs is that elementary classifiers differ in their competences over the feature space, one can introduce the competence function of k-th classifier φ_k. The higher result returned by the function the higher classifier competence is.

$$\Gamma^{\Psi} = \{\varphi_1(x), \varphi_2(x), \ldots, \varphi_K(x)\}, \tag{4}$$

where Γ^{Ψ} is the set of competence functions for each classifier in the pool respectively.

The decision of the proposed MCS incorporates the knowledge of elementary classifiers represented by discriminating functions weighted by their competence functions respectively.

$$\Psi(x) = \arg \max_{i=1}^{M} F(i, x), \tag{5}$$

where $F(i, x)$ is discriminating function of MCS.

$$F(i, x) = \sum_{k=1}^{K} \varphi_k(x) F_k(i, x) \tag{6}$$

2.1 The Competence Function

The following assumptions have to be taken into consideration while selecting the competence function of the classifier:

1. the function returns real positive values,
2. the function obtains its maximum at some points that is to become representation points of the classifier,
3. a value returned by the function decreases as the distance from the representation points increases.

Let us denotes the representation point of k-th classifier by C_k

$$C_k = \left[c_k^{(1)}, c_k^{(2)}, \ldots, c_k^{(d)} \right]^T \in R^d . \tag{7}$$

Now, set of all representation points related with the classifier in the poll is denoted by

$$C = \{ C_1, C_2, \ldots, C_K \} . \tag{8}$$

It has to be underlined here that only one competence area can be assigned to each classifier as the each representation point is assigned to only one classifier and the border between the areas results from comparison of the functions that have similar Gaussian shapes and gains their maximums at separate points.

Among many functions that met aforementioned conditions the Gaussian kernel function has been selected.

$$\varphi_k (x) = \exp\!\left(\beta_k \; d(x, C_k)^2 \right), \tag{9}$$

where d denotes Euclidean distance between two points, and

β_k is some real positive parameter assigned to the classifier that affects the shape of the function.

Selecting that model of competence function leads to the following form of RB MCS

$$\Psi(x) = \arg \max_{i=1}^{M} \left(\sum_{k=1}^{K} \exp\!\left(\beta_k \; d(x, C_k)^2 \right) F_k (i, x) \right), \tag{10}$$

3   Optimization Problem

Learning algorithm of the RB MCS aims at minimizing its misclassification rate. To achieve the goal a learning datasets can be used, i.e. the set of pairs consisting of feature vector and corresponding class index given by the expert and assumed to be real class number of the object.

$$DS = \{ (x_1, j_1), (x_2, j_2), \ldots, (x_N, j_N) \}, \tag{11}$$

where j_l is the class index of j-th element in the learning set.

According to formula (10) the misclassification rate of RB MCS can be obtained as follow

$$Q_e(\Psi) = \frac{1}{N} \sum_{n=1}^{N} L\!\left(\arg \max_{i=1}^{M} \left(\sum_{k=1}^{K} \exp\!\left(\beta_k \; d(x, C_k)^2 \right) F_k (i, x) \right), j_n \right) \tag{12}$$

where $L(i, j)$ is the loss function[1] that return one in the case of misclassification (i.e. $i \neq j$) and zero otherwise.

The learning algorithm is to search for the smallest misclassification rate by manipulating the set of parameters of the RB MCS model:

1. representation points C_k, and
2. parameters β_k.

4   Optimization Algorithm

Among many algorithms that can be selected for solving the optimization problem defined in section 3, a variant of evolutionary based algorithm has been choose.

The algorithm processes population of individuals that represents possible solution of the problem i.e. instances of the RB MCS with appropriately set parameters of the model according to formula (10). Individuals in the population are represented by their chromosomes that consist of two constituents representing aforementioned parameters.

Number of individuals in the population is a parameter of the algorithm and do not change during the optimization process. Initially individuals in the population consist of set of chromosomes generated randomly.

Two evolutionary operators that affect the population have been tailored to cope with the chromosome model given:

1   mutation operator that introduces small variation into randomly selected parameters in the chromosome;
2   crossover operator that generates two child chromosomes as a result of two point crossover of the parents' chromosomes.

It has to be underlined that two constituents of the chromosome play entirely different role in the classifier model and therefore they have to be processed separately, no data interchange are allowed between the two. That condition has to be especially fulfilled while building algorithm of crossover operators.

Table 1. Outline of proposed algorithm

Preliminary phase	
1	Setting up the parameters (of the model and the algorithm)
2	Generation of the population
3	Assessment of the population
Main phase (loop)	
4	Promoting the elite
5	Mutation
6	Crossover
7	Assessment of the population
8	Drawing members of the population
9	Assessment of the over training
10	Checking out exit condition
Ending phase	
11	Selecting the winner

The algorithm processes the population iteratively creating child population until one of stopping criteria is met:

- maximum number of iteration is reached,
- no change in quality of the best individual in the population is noted for a given number of subsequent iterations.

The next population consists of individuals that have been drawn from the parent population according to their fitness which is calculated according to formula 11. The smaller the misclassification rate of the individual the higher the probability of the promotion to the child population. The final solution of the problem is obtained by selection the individuals characterized by the smallest misclassification rate among the final population.

Table 1 presents the outline of the learning algorithm.

5 Experiments

Analysis of a performance of the RBF MCS were made in the set of experiments carried on benchmark datasets drown from the UCI repository. The main goal of the experiments was to verify if the RB MCS can effectively exploit local competences of the elementary classifier and create MCS with smaller misclassification rate. As the reference point we used classifiers in the pool, and MSC that make decision according to simple majority voting model.

To create the pool of elementary classifier nonlinear, multilayer neutral network trained according to back propagation algorithm were used. To ensure certain level of diversity of the pool [4,5] its elements were slightly undertrained.

Selection of fourth datasets that differ in: number of instances, number of attributes describing objects and number of classes aimed at assessing the performance of the RB MCS in different condition. Details of the experiments for the datasets are presented in Table 2.

Datasets were divided into three separated subsets:

- learning sets used for training elementary classifier in the pool (CL_LS),
- learning sets used for training RB MCS (RBF_MCS_LS),
- testing sets used for calculating resulting misclassification rate (TS).

Set up of all experiments were as follow:

- all experiments were carried out in Matlab environment using: PRtools toolbox [10], Matlab GA toolbox, and own software;
- in all experiments five neural networks with different (randomly selected) number of neurons in hidden layer were used as the classifiers in the pool,
- elementary classifier in the pool was trained only once,
- number of iteration of optimization algorithm was set to 30,
- number of population members was 35,
- each experiment was repeated 50 times.

Table 2. Details of datasets used in experiments

	Exp. 1	**Exp. 2**	**Exp. 3**	**Exp. 4**
Dataset name	Phoneme	Balance Scale	Cone Torus	ecoli
Number of classes	2	3	3	8
Number of attributes	5	4	2	7
Number of instances in CL_LS	1000	104	100	104
Number of instances in RBF_MCS_LS	1000	202	400	103
Number of instances in TS	2404	200	300	129
Number of classifier in pool	5	5	5	5

5.1 Results of Experiments

Results of the experiments are presented in figure 1. They consist of misclassification rate of the following classifiers:

- classifiers in the pool denoted by: Cl 1, Cl 2, Cl 3, Cl 4, Cl5,
- majority voting multiple classifier systems denoted by MV,
- proposed radial basis MCS denoted by RB MCS

Analysis of the results allow to notice following facts:

1. In all experiments RB MCSs outperform all elementary classifiers in the pool.
2. In all experiments RB MCSs outperforms MV classifiers.
3. In experiment 1, 3, and 4 MV did not managed to overcome the best of elementary classifier.

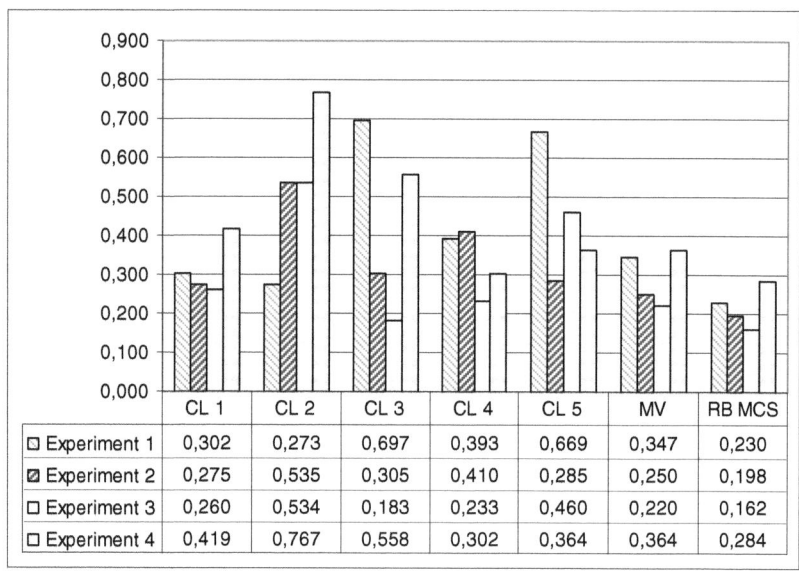

	CL 1	CL 2	CL 3	CL 4	CL 5	MV	RB MCS
□ Experiment 1	0,302	0,273	0,697	0,393	0,669	0,347	0,230
▨ Experiment 2	0,275	0,535	0,305	0,410	0,285	0,250	0,198
□ Experiment 3	0,260	0,534	0,183	0,233	0,460	0,220	0,162
□ Experiment 4	0,419	0,767	0,558	0,302	0,364	0,364	0,284

Fig. 1. Misclassification rate of the classifier in experiments 1, 2, 3,4

The facts show that using weight functions that cover feature space and control contribution of elementary classifier in MCS can significantly improve classification accuracy. It is so because correctly shaped weights can minimize influence on the classifier in the regions where they does not introduce any significant information. In opposite situation, when in some regions classifiers have huge competence their weights can be increased. Naturally radial basis representation of the weights is one of possible options, nonetheless the results prove that the proposition can be effectively exploit in fusing information in MCS.

Also effectiveness of the proposed learning algorithm have been positively verified. Evolutionary algorithms are strongly dependent on model of chromosome, implementation of evolutionary operators. The open question is if it is possible to tune the algorithm in order to improve the learning effectiveness even more.

6 Conclusion

The novel model of RB MCS was presented in the paper. Learning process that aims at minimizing misclassification rate searches for best set of parameters of the competence functions. Presented results of simulation performed on the exemplary datasets prove that algorithm is able to obtain results that outperform each classifier from the pool.

Acknowledgments. This research is supported in part by The Polish State Committee for Scientific Research under the grant which is realizing in years 2010-13.

References

1. Duda, R.O., Hart, P.E., Stork, D.G.: Pattern Classification. John Willey and Sons, New York (2001)
2. Jain, A.K., Duin, P.W., Mao, J.: Statistical Pattern Recognition: A Review. IEEE Trans. on PAMI 22(1), 4–37 (2000)
3. Krzanowski, W., Partrige, D.: Software Diversity: Practical Statistics for its Measurement and Exploatation, Raport University of Exeter, Department of Computer Science (1996)
4. Kuncheva, L.I.: Combining pattern classifiers: Methods and algorithms. Wiley Interscience, New Jersey (2004)
5. Ruta, D., Gabrys, B.: Classifier Selection for Majority Voting. Information Fusion 6, 63–81 (2005)
6. Duin, R.P.W.: The Combining Classifier: to Train or Not to Train? In: Proc. of the ICPR 2002, Quebec City (2002)
7. Jacobs, R.A., Jordan, M.I., Nowlan, S.J., Hinton, G.E.: Adaptive mixtures of local experts. Neural Computation 3, 79–87 (1991)
8. Avnimelech, R., Intrator, N.: Boosted mixture of experts: an ensemble learning scheme. Neural Comput., 483–497 (1999)
9. Tang, B., Heywood, M., Shepherd, M.: Input partitioning to mixture of experts. International Joint Conference on Neural Networks, 227–232 (2002)
10. Duin, R.P.W., Juszczak, P., Paclik, P., Pekalska, E., de Ridder, D., Tax, D.M.J.: PRTools4, A Matlab Toolbox for Pattern Recognition. Delft University of Technology, The Netherlands (2004)

Mixture of Random Prototype-Based Local Experts

Giuliano Armano and Nima Hatami

DIEE-Department of Electrical and Electronic Engineering,
University of Cagliari, Piazza D'Armi, I-09123 Cagliari, Italy
{armano,nima.hatami}@diee.unica.it

Abstract. The Mixture of Experts (ME) is one of the most popular ensemble methods used in pattern recognition and machine learning. This algorithm stochastically partitions the input space of the problem into a number of subspaces, experts becoming specialized on each subspace. The ME uses an expert called gating network to manage this process, which is trained together with the experts. In this paper, we propose a modified version of the ME algorithm which first partitions the original problem into centralized regions and then uses a simple distance-based gating function to specialize the expert networks. Each expert contributes to classify an input sample according to the distance between the input and a prototype embedded by the expert. As a result, an accurate classifier with shorter training time and smaller number of parameters is achieved. Experimental results on a binary toy problem and selected datasets from the UCI machine learning repository show the robustness of the proposed method compared to the standard ME model.

Keywords: Classifier ensembles, Mixture of Experts (ME), Neural Networks.

1 Introduction

Most real-world pattern recognition problems are too complicated for a single classifier to solve. Divide-and-conquer has proved to be efficient in many of these complex situations, using a combination of classifiers which have complementary properties. The issues are (i) how to divide the problem into simple subproblems, (ii) how to assign base classifiers to solve these subproblems, and (iii) how to obtain the final decision using the outputs of these base classifiers (experts).

Were it possible to naturally decompose the problem, then this could be done manually. However, in most real-world problems, we either know too little about the problem, or it is too complex to have a clear understanding of how to manually decompose it into subproblems. Thus, a method for automatically decomposing a complex problem into a set of overlapping or disjoint subproblems is desirable, assigning one or more experts to each subproblem. The remaining question is how to combine the outputs of these experts if the decomposition scheme is unknown a priori.

Jacobs et al. [1,2] have proposed an ensemble method based on the divide-and-conquer principle called mixture of experts (ME), in which a set of expert networks is trained together with a gate network. This tight coupling mechanism (i) encourages diversity between the single experts by automatically localizing them in different

M. Graña Romay et al. (Eds.): HAIS 2010, Part I, LNAI 6076, pp. 548–556, 2010.

regions of the input space and (ii) achieves good combination weights of the ensemble members by training the gate, which computes the dynamic weights together with the experts.

Since Jacobs' proposal in 1991, the ME model has been widely investigated. Waterhouse and Cook [3] and Avnimelech and Cook [4] proposed to combine ME with the boosting algorithm. Since boosting encourages classifiers to become experts on patterns that previous experts disagree on, it can be successfully used to split the data set into regions for the experts in the ME model, thus ensuring their localization. Tang et al. [5] tried to explicitly localize the experts by applying a cluster-based preprocessing step to partition the input space for the experts. They used self-organizing maps (SOM) to partition the input space according to the underlying probability distribution of the data. As a result, better generalization ability with more stability in parameter setting is achieved. Nevertheless, as they argue at the end of the paper, the proposed method has been designed for (and validated on) only binary and low dimensional problems. Won and Bone [6] used a mixture of radial basis function networks to partition the input space into statistically correlated regions and learn the local covariance model of the data in each region. Ebrahimpour et al. [7] proposed a view-independent face recognition system using ME by manual decomposition of the face view space into specific angles (views), an expert being specialized on each view. Nevertheless, the proposed method is only efficient in 2D face recognition and, as argued by the authors, extending this approach to other classification problems and applications could be challenging and not always possible.

Earlier works on the ME apply methods such as preprocessing to partition the input space or transform the input space into simpler and more separable spaces. An expert is then specialized on each subspace without altering the learning rules of standard ME. In any case, simultaneously training experts and gating network in the ME architecture to obtain sufficiently accurate classifiers with optimum parameters, continues to pose a research challenge.

The method proposed here randomly selects some prototype points from the input space and partitions this space according to nearest distance from these prototypes. This has permitted to adopt a weighting policy based on distances in both training and testing. In other words, instead of a complex gating network, which needs training process to adjust its weight parameters, the proposed gating function manages both training and testing using the same distance-based rules. Let us point out that, by removing the weight parameters from the gating networks, we limit the number of ME parameters, thereby simplifying the search and reducing the time required for training ME classifiers.

It is worth recalling that Puuronen et al. [8] and Tsymbal et al. [9] propose methods for the dynamic integration of classifiers based on the assumption that each base classifier is responsible for a subregion of the whole problem domain, without overlapping. These methods use an instance-based learning approach to collect information about the competence areas of the classifiers and apply a distance function to determine how close a new test sample is to each sample of the training set. The nearest sample or samples are used to determine the label of the test sample. Two main differences hold between the proposed method and the methods recalled above: First, their proposal applies only to the decision making step of bagging and boosting, without using any distance-based information during the training of base classifiers. On the contrary, our proposal uses distance-based information in both training (of base classifiers) and testing. Second, they elaborated a dynamic selection technique that estimates the local accuracy of base classifiers by analyzing the accuracy in the "neighborhood" of testing examples, whereas the proposed method weights base classifiers by simply measuring the distance of the test sample from the selected prototypes.

The rest of this paper is organized as follows: in section 2, we briefly recall the standard ME model for building classifiers. In Section 3 we introduce the proposed random prototype-based mixture of experts. Experimental results are reported and discussed in section 4. Section 5 concludes the paper and briefly outlines future research directions.

2   The Mixture of Experts Model

The adaptive mixture of local experts [1,2] is a learning procedure which achieves improved generalization performance by assigning different subtasks to different experts. Its basic idea consists of concurrently training several experts and a gating network. The gating function assigns a "probability" to each expert based on the current input. In the training phase, this value denotes the probability for a pattern to appear in an expert's training set. In the test step, it defines the relative contribution of each expert to the ensemble. The training step attempts to achieve two goals: for a given expert, find the optimal gating function. For a given gating function (network), train each expert to achieve maximal performance on the distribution assigned to it by the gating function. Accordingly, the accuracy of ME classifier is affected by the performance of both experts and gating networks. Resulting misclassifications in this model derive from two sources: (a) the gating network is unable to correctly estimate the probability for a given input sample and (b) local experts do not learn their subtask perfectly.

Let us consider the network shown in Fig. 1, known as an ME model with $N=3$ experts. The ith expert produces its output $o_i(x)$ as a generalized linear function of the input x:

$$o_i(x,W_i) = f(W_i x)$$

where W_i is the weight matrix of the ith expert and $f(.)$ is a predefined continuous nonlinearity. The gating network is also a generalized linear function, and its ith output, $g_i(x,V_i)$, is the multinomial logit or softmax function of the gating network's output, o_{g_i}.

$$g_i(x,V_i) = \frac{\exp(o_{g_i})}{\sum_{j=1}^{N} o_{g_j}} \quad i = 1,...,N$$

where V_i is the weight vector of the gating network. Hence, the overall output of the ME architecture, $o(x)$, is

$$o(x) = \sum_i g_i(x,V_i)o_i(x,W_i)$$

Two training procedures are suggested in the literature [1,10] for finding optimal weight parameters W_i and V_i. The first is the standard error back-propagation algorithm with gradient descent, whereas the second is based on the Expectation-Maximization (EM) method.

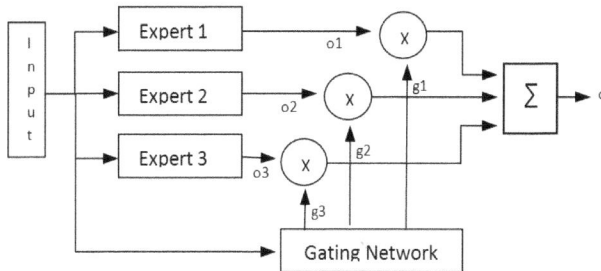

Fig. 1. Block diagram representing the mixture of experts (ME). The generic model shown here has three experts (N=3) and the gating network as a mediator for managing the process.

3   Mixture of Random Prototype-Based Local Experts

In this section, we illustrate the proposed mixture of random prototype-based experts with more detail. The key underlying idea is to randomly partition the input space of the problem into subspaces and then get each expert to specialize on each subspace by means of "soft" competitive learning. First of all, the input space is partitioned according to some prototypes randomly chosen from the training set, so that the input samples are weighted during the training and testing phases based on their distances from the selected prototypes. The main advantage of this method is that, instead of a complex gating network which must be trained concurrently with other experts, the generated gating function has no parameters (weights) to adjust –as it simply enforces a distance-based weighting policy. This modification improves three important aspects of the standard ME model. First, it reduces the training time by decreasing the number of parameters to be estimated. Secondly, as simple distance measures used by the gating function are more robust with respect to errors in determining the area of expertise of an expert, errors in the proposed ME model are mainly limited to the error made by the expert networks –thus improving the overall accuracy of the overall classifier. Lastly, the region of expertise for each expert in the standard ME model is nested, which makes the problem difficult to learn. In the proposed method, the area of expertise of each expert is more centralized, which makes the subproblem easier to learn. The latter property also makes the rules embedded by an expert easy to analyze, which is vital in some applications that need to have more information about the area of expertise of each expert.

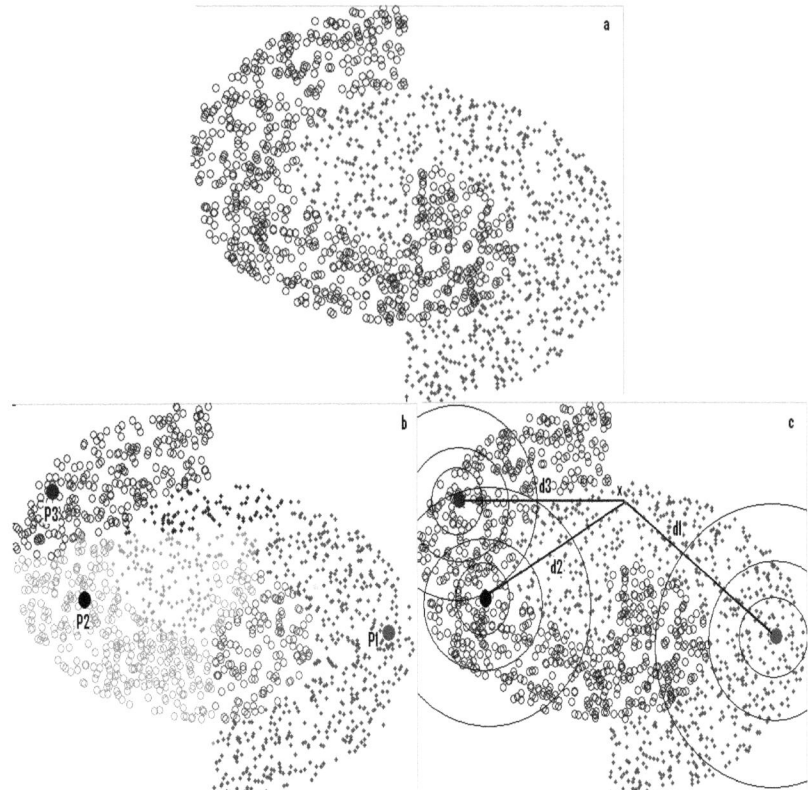

Fig. 2. Partitioning of a 2-class semantic classification problem using N=3 random prototypes (bold points denote prototypes selected from training data): a) original problem, b) partitioning into three disjoint regions based on the nearest distance from the prototypes, c) partitioning into three overlapping subspaces

For the sake of simplicity and ease of comprehension, we describe this approach for the synthetic two-class problem shown in Fig. 2.a. We used two different partitioning methods, i.e. disjoint and overlapping shown in Fig.2.b. and 2.c. respectively. In the case of disjoint partitioning, we first measure the distance between each training sample and the prototypes, and then assign a fixed value, η_j to the h_i of the expert proportional to these distances. h_i is an estimate of the "*a posteriori*" probability for the ith expert to generate the desired output o and used as the coefficient of the learning rate for updating the weight parameters of the expert. This means that the weights of the expert network whose prototype is nearest to the current input sample, will be updated more than those belonging to the other experts. Similarly, in the testing phase, the expert whose prototype is nearest to the input sample will contribute to a greater extent to the final output.

Mixture of Random Prototype – based Experts Algorithm

INITIALIZING:

- $P = \{p_i \in LS \,|\, i = 1, 2, ..., N\}$; LS = Learning Set, TS = Testting Set
- $\psi = \{\varepsilon_i \,|\, i = 1, 2, ..., N\}$
- strategy = $\{$static, dynamic$\}$
- $E = \{\eta_j \in (0,1) \,|\, j = 1, 2, ..., N\}$ such that:

$$\eta_k \leq \eta_{k+1}; k = 1, 2, ..., N - 1 \text{ and } |E| = \sum_j \eta_j = 1$$

TRAINING:

For each $x \in LS$ Do:

- $D(x) = \{d_i(x) \,|\, i = 1, 2, ..., N\}$ where

    $d_i(x) = \|x - p_i\|$ and $\|.\|$ is any distance metric (e.g. Euclidean)

- $H(x) = \{h_i(x) \,|\, i = 1, 2, ..., N\}$ where

    $h_i(x)$ represents the expected capacity of ε_i to deal with the given input x

    [strategy = static]: $h_i(x) = \eta_J$ where $J = Rank(\varepsilon_i, D(x))^*$

    [strategy = dynamic]: $h_i(x) = 1 - \dfrac{d_i}{|D(x)|}$ where $|D(x)| = \sum_j d_j(x)$

- update each expert ε_i ($i = 1, 2, ..., N$) according to the standard learning rule for ME

TESTING:

Given an $x \in TS$ Do:

- $D(x) = \{d_i(x) \,|\, i = 1, 2, ..., N\}$
- $G(x) = \{g_i(x) \,|\, i = 1, 2, ..., N\}$ where

    [strategy = static]: $g_i(x) = \eta_j$ where $j = Rank(\varepsilon_i, D(x))^*$

    [strategy = dynamic]: $g_i(x) = 1 - \dfrac{d_i}{|D(x)|}$ where $|D(x)| = \sum_j d_j(x)$

- calculate the overall output:

$$o_j(x) = \sum_{i=1}^{N} g_i(x).o(x, W_i)$$

- select the class label c_k such that

    $k = \arg \max_j (o_j(x))$

$^*j = Rank(\varepsilon_i, D(x))$ returns the rank of expert ε_i (i.e. a number in $[1, N]$) according to the distance $D(x)$ evaluated on the input x (the lovest the distance, the highest the ranking)

Fig. 3. Mixture of Random Prototype-based Experts Algorithm

Unlike disjoint partitioning, where the learning rate coefficients are the same for one partition and change sharply from one to another, in the overlapping method they change smoothly proportional to the distances. Similarly, the amount of d_i for the ith expert depends on how close the expert's prototype is to the current input sample d_i. In other words, in the disjoint learning, the amount of expertise and contribution of experts is fixed for each partition, whereas, in the overlapping learning, their expertise smoothly vary with the d_i distance from the prototypes embedded by the experts.

It is worth pointing out that the proposed method is general enough to be applied for building ME classifiers using both standard error back-propagation and EM learning rules. Fig.3 reports the algorithm for training and testing a mixture of random prototype-based experts, using both disjoint and overlapping partitioning rules for any chosen learning method.

4 Experimental Results

We used some of the UCI machine learning data sets [11] to check the validity of the proposed method. These data sets include real-world and synthetic problems, with variable characteristics, previously investigated by other researchers. Table 1 shows the selected datasets with more detail.

Table 1. The main characteristics of the selected UCI datasets

Problem	# Train	# Test	# Attributes	# Classes
Iris	150	-	4	3
Satimage	4435	2000	36	6
Pendigits	7494	3498	16	10
Letter	20000	-	16	26
Vowel	990	-	11	11
Segment	210	2100	19	7
Glass	214	-	9	7
Yeast	1484	-	8	10

We used 10-fold cross validation to ensure statistical significance while evaluating the accuracy of classifiers. To build the standard ME and the proposed random prototype-based ME models, we used a Multilayer perceptron (MLP) architecture with one hidden layer, trained with the back-propagation learning rule [12]. To determine the best value for the N number of partitions, which is equal to the number of experts, we varied it from 2 to 10 for each dataset. We also varied the number of hidden neurons in expert networks to experimentally find the optimal architecture of the MLP experts for each problem. The results of these experiments are shown in Table 2, which highlights that the proposed method outperforms the standard ME model for all selected datasets, no matter whether disjoint or overlapping partitions are adopted.

Table 2. The mean and standard deviation of accuracy of the ME vs. the proposed mixture of random prototype-based experts on the selected UCI datasets (in percentage)

	Iris	Sat.	Pen.	Lett.	Vow.	Seg.	Gla.	Yeast
Standard ME	87.7± 0.61	88.7± 1.05	88.0± 0.43	70.9± 0.93	61.1± 1.05	79.2± 0.95	72.3± 1.65	49.3± 2.01
Disjoint partition	88.2± 0.45	90.1± 0.83	89.0± 0.44	72.0± 0.80	62.9± 1.11	81.9± 0.79	74.8± 1.76	50.7± 1.96
Overlapping partition	88.5± 0.39	90.1± 0.79	89.2± 0.40	72.8± 0.95	63.4± 1.20	81.9± 0.83	75.5± 1.57	52.0± 1.95

The time required for training the different datasets is shown in Table 3 for further comparison. As shown here, the training time of the proposed method is considerably shorter than the standard version. Simulations are performed using an Intel CPU with 2.83GHz and 4GB RAM memory. Note that the results presented here which compare standard ME and the proposed method, use the same parameters and architecture.

Table 3. Training time of the ME vs. the proposed mixture of random prototype-based expert classifiers (seconds)

	Iris	Sat.	Pen.	Lett.	Vow.	Seg.	Gla.	Yeast
Standard ME	50	232	351	324	59	49	30	41
Proposed method	28	158	221	258	39	32	21	29

5 Conclusions and Future Directions

A modified version of the popular ME algorithm is presented here. Unlike the standard ME, which specializes expert networks on nested and stochastic regions of input space, the proposed method partitions the sample space into subspaces, based on similarities with randomly selected prototypes. This strategy enables to define a simple rule for the gating network for both training and testing. As shown by experimental results, despite its simplicity, the proposed method improves the accuracy of the standard ME model and reduces the training time.

Future work will focus on defining a procedure for automatically determining the number of optimal experts for each problem without resorting to complex preprocessing and time consuming methods. We also intend to investigate application of the proposed method to Hierarchical ME (HME) structure. Due to the randomness of the input space partitioning, improved diversity for the ME modules embedded by the HME structure is expected, thus improving the overall accuracy of the ensemble. Adaptation of this method to simple distance-based classifiers instead of neural networks could be another interesting future direction for reducing complexity and training time of the overall network while maintaining high accuracy.

We are currently making some experiments on heuristics able to help in the process of partitioning the input space instead of using random prototypes. Furthermore, as the proposed approach is not limited to neural networks, it would be interesting to investigate the behavior and performance of other learners in the proposed ME architecture.

References

1. Jacobs, R., Jordan, M., Barto, A.: Task decomposition through competition in a modular connectionist architecture: the what and where vision tasks. Tech rep. University of Massachusetts, Amherst, MA (1991)
2. Jacobs, R., Jordan, M., Nowlan, S., Hinton, G.: Adaptive mixtures of local experts. Neural Computation 3, 79–87 (1991)

3. Waterhouse, S., Cook, G.: Ensemble methods for phoneme classification. In: Mozer, M., Jordan, J., Petsche, T. (eds.) Advances in Neural Information Processing Systems, vol. 9, pp. 800–806. The MIT Press, Cambridge (1997)
4. Avnimelech, R., Intrator, N.: Boosted mixture of experts: an ensemble learning scheme. Neural Comput. 11(2), 483–497 (1999)
5. Tang, B., Heywood, M., Shepherd, M.: Input partitioning to mixture of experts. International Joint Conference on Neural Networks, 227–232 (2002)
6. Wan, E., Bone, D.: Interpolating earth-science data using RBF networks and mixtures of experts. In: NIPS, pp. 988–994 (1996)
7. Ebrahimpour, R., Kabir, E., Yousefi, M.R.: Teacher-directed learning in view-independent face recognition with mixture of experts using overlapping eigenspaces. Computer Vision and Image Understanding 111, 195–206 (2008)
8. Puuronen, S., Tsymbal, A., Terziyan, V.: Distance functions in dynamic integration of data mining techniques. In: Proceedings of SPIE Data mining and knowledge discovery: theory, tools and technology II, vol. 4057, pp. 22–32. SPIE, Bellingham (2000)
9. Tsymbal, A., Puuronen, S.: Bagging and boosting with dynamic integration of classifiers. In: Zighed, D.A., Komorowski, J., Żytkow, J.M. (eds.) PKDD 2000. LNCS (LNAI), vol. 1910, pp. 116–125. Springer, Heidelberg (2000)
10. Jordan, M.I., Jacobs, R.A.: Hierarchical mixtures of experts and the EM algorithm. Neural Comp. 6, 181–214 (1994)
11. Murphy, P.M., Aha, D.W.: UCI Repository of Machine Learning Databases, Dept. of Information and Computer Science, Univ. of California, Irvine (1994)
12. Haykin, S.: Neural Networks: A Comprehensive Foundation, 2nd edn. Prentice-Hall, Englewood Cliffs (1999)

Graph-Based Model-Selection Framework for Large Ensembles

Krisztian Buza, Alexandros Nanopoulos, and Lars Schmidt-Thieme

Information Systems and Machine Learning Lab (ISMLL)
Samelsonplatz 1, University of Hildesheim, D-31141 Hildesheim, Germany
{buza,nanopoulos,schmidt-thieme}@ismll.de

Abstract. The intuition behind ensembles is that different prediciton models compensate each other's errors if one combines them in an appropriate way. In case of large ensembles a lot of different prediction models are available. However, many of them may share similar error characteristics, which highly depress the compensation effect. Thus the selection of an appropriate subset of models is crucial. In this paper, we address this problem. As major contribution, for the case if a large number of models is present, we propose a graph-based framework for model selection while paying special attention to the interaction effect of models. In this framework, we introduce four ensemble techniques and compare them to the state-of-the-art in experiments on publicly available real-world data.

Keywords. Ensemble, model selection.

1 Introduction

For complex prediction problems the number of models used in an ensemble may have to be large (several hundreds). If many models are available for a task, they often deliver different predictions. Due to the variety of prediction models (SVMs, neural networks, decision trees, Bayesian models, etc.) and the differences in the underlying principles and techniques, one expects diverse error characteristics for the distinct models. Ensembles, also called blending or committee of experts, assumes that different models can compensate each other's errors and thus their right combination outperforms each individual model [3].

The aforementioned statement can be justified with the simple observation, that the average of the predictions of the models may outperform the best individual model. This is illustrated with an example in Tab. 1, which presents results of simple ensembles of 200 models contained in the AusDM-S dataset.[1] Combining all classifiers, however, may not be the best choice: many of the models may share similar error characteristics, that can highly depress the compensation effect. In particular, the average of the 10 individually best models' predictions outperforms the average of all the predictions. (See Table 1.) Instead, if one selects the 10 individually worst models, the average of their predictions perform much worse than the best model.

---

[1] We describe the dataset later.

M. Graña Romay et al. (Eds.): HAIS 2010, Part I, LNAI 6076, pp. 557–564, 2010.
© Springer-Verlag Berlin Heidelberg 2010

Table 1. Performance (Root Mean Squared Error) improvement w.r.t. best individual model using simple ensemble schemes on the AusDM-S dataset. (10 fold cross validation, averaged results, in each fold the best/worst model(s) were selected based on the performances on the train subset.)

Method	RMSE-improvement
Average over all models	2.40
Average over the best 10 models	8.72
Average over the worst 10 models	−20.84

We argue that different models have a high potential to compensate each other's errors, but the right selection of the models is important otherwise this compensation effect may be depressed. How much the compensation effect is depressed, also depends on how robust is the applied ensemble schema against overfitting. In case of well-regularized ensemble methods (like stacking with linear regression or SVMs) the depression of compensation is typically much lower. E.g. training a multivariate linear regression as meta-model on *all predictions* of AusDM-S is still worse than training it on the predictions of the *individually best 10 models* (RMSE-improvement: 8.58 vs. 9.42). Note, however that the selection of the 10 individually best models may be far from perfect: the potential power of an ensemble may be much higher than the quality we reach by combining the 10 individually best models. Thus, even in case of well-regularized models, the depression of compensation is an acute problem.

In this paper, we address this problem. As major contribution, we propose a new graph-based framework that is generic enough to describe a wide range of model selection strategies for ensembles varying from meta-filter to meta-wrapper methods.[2] In this framework, one can simply deploy our ensemble method, that successfully participated in the recent Ensembling Challenge at the Australian Data Mining Conference 2009. Using the framework, we propose 4 ensemble techniques: *Basic*, *EarlyStop*, *RegOpt* and *GraphOpt*. We evaluate these strategies in experiments on publicly available real-world data.

2   Related Work

Ensembles are frequently used to improve predictive models, see e.g. [8], [7], [6]. The theoretical background, especially some fundamental reasons, why ensembles work better than single models were discussed in [3].

Our focus in this paper is on a generic framework in order to describe *model selection strategies*. Such an approach can be based on the *stacking* schema [9] (also called *stacked generalization*[12]), in context of which, model selection is feature selection at the meta-level (and variable selection is feature selection at the elementary level), see Fig. 1. In the studied context, related work includes feature selection at the elementary level [5] [4]. Some more closely related works

---

[2] Filter (wrapper) methods score models without (with) involving the meta-model.

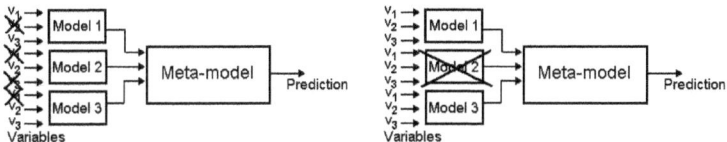

Fig. 1. Feature selection in ensembles: at the elementary level (variable selection, left) and at the meta-level (model selection, right)

study feature selection at the meta level, e.g. Bryll et al.[2] applies a ranking of models and selects the best models to participate in the ensemble. In our study, for comparison purposes, we use the schema of selecting the best models as baseline to evaluate our proposed approach.

Other, less closely related work includes Zhou et al.[14], who employed a genetic algorithm to find meta-level weights and selected models based on these weights. They found, that the ensemble of the selected models outperformed the ensemble of all of the models. Yang et al. [13] compared model selection and model weighting strategies for Ensembles of Naive-Bayes-extensions, called "Super-Parent-One-Dependence Estimators" (SPODE) [11]. All of these works focus on specific models: Zhou et al.[14] are concerned with neural networks, whereas Yang et al. focused on SPODE Ensembles[13]. In contrast to them, we develop a general framework, that operate with various models and meta-models. The model selection approach by Tsymbal et al.[10] is also essentially different from ours: they select (dynamically) those models that deliver the best predictions individually. In contrast, we view the task more globally by taking interactions of models into account and thus supporting less-greedy strategies. Bacauskiene et al. [1] applied genetic algorithm for finding the ensemble settings both at the elementary level (hyper-parameters and variable selection) and at the meta-level. However, due to their high computational cost, genetic algorithms are impractical in our case of having large number of models present.

Algorithm 1. Edge Score Function: edge_score

Require: Model m_j, Model m_k, data sample D, ErrorFunction $calc\_err$
Ensure: Edge weight of $\{m_j, m_k\}$

  1: $p_1 = m_j.\text{predict}(D)$, $p_2 = m_k.\text{predict}(D)$, $\forall x : p[x] = (p_1[x] + p_2[x])/2$
  2: **return** $calc\_err(p, D.\text{labels})$

---

3   Graph-Based Ensemble Framework

Given the prediction models $m_1, \ldots, m_N$, our goal is to find their best combination. As mentioned before, the key of our ensemble technique is the selection of models that compensate each other's errors. For this, we build a graph first, the *model-pair graph*, denoted as g in Alg. 2 (line 5). Each vertex corresponds to one of the models $m_1, \ldots, m_N$. The graph is complete (all vertices are connected).

Algorithm 2. Graph-based Ensemble Framework

Require: SubsetScoreFunction f, Predicate *examine*, ErrorFunction *calc_err*,
ModelType *meta_model_type*, Int n, Real ϵ, set of all models *MSet*, labelled data D
Ensure: Ensemble of selected models

1: data[ ] *splits* = split D into 10 partitions
2: **for** $i = 0; i < 10; i + +$ **do**
3:    data $D_A \leftarrow$ *splits*[i] $\cup \ldots \cup$ *splits*[$(i + 4)$ mod 10]
4:    data $D_B \leftarrow$ *splits*[$(i + 5)$ mod 10] $\cup \ldots \cup$ *splits*[$(i + 9)$ mod 10]
5:    $g \leftarrow$ build graph with edge scores calculated by Alg. 1 for all edges $\{ m_j, m_k \}$
6:    $M_i \leftarrow \emptyset$
7:    Let score$_{M_i}$ be the worst possible score
8:    $E(g) \leftarrow$ sort the edges of g according to their weights, begin with the best one
9:    **for all** edge $\{m_j, m_k\}$ in $E(g)$, process edges according to the order **do**
10:       **if** $(m_j \in M_i \wedge m_k \in M_i$ **then** proceed for the next edge
11:       **if** *examine*$(\{m_j, m_k\})$ **then**
12:          $M_i' \leftarrow M_i \cup \{m_j\} \cup \{m_k\}$
13:          score$_{M_i'} \leftarrow f(M_i', D_A, D_B, calc\_err, g)$
14:          **if** score$_{M_i'}$ better than score$_{M_i}$ at least by ϵ **then**
15:             $M_i \leftarrow M_i'$,   score$_{M_i} \leftarrow$ score$_{M_i'}$
16:          **end if**
17:       **end if**
18:    **end for**
19: **end for**
20: $M_{final} \leftarrow \{m \in MSet | m$ is included in at least n sets among $M_0 \ldots M_9\}$
21: $\mathcal{M} \leftarrow$ train a model of type *meta_model_type* over the prediction vectors of the
models in M_{final} using D
22: **return** $\mathcal{M}$

Edges of the graph are undirected and weighted, the weight of $\{m_j, m_k\}$ reflects
the mutual error compensation power of m_j and m_k. In Alg. 1 for each data
instance, we average the *predicitions* of the both regression models m_j and m_k
(line 1). This gives a new prediction vector p. Then the error of p is returned
(line 2), which is used as the weight of edge $\{m_j, m_k\}$.

Alg. 2 shows the pseudocode of our ensemble framework. This works with
various *error functions, subset score functions* and *meta model types*. The method
iterates over the edges of the graph (lines 9...18). To scale up the selection, one
can specify a predicate called *examine* that determines which edges should be
examined and which ones should be excluded. As we will see in section 4, the
specific choice of these parameters result in various ensemble methods having
the common characteristic, that they all exploit the error compensation effect.

While learning, we divide the train data into two disjoint subsets D_A and D_B
(lines 3 and 4)[3] and we build the model-pair graph (line 5). The division of the
train data is iteratively repeated in a round robin fashion (see line 2).

---

[3] This is a natural way to split because it allows effective learning of the selection
since it balances well between fitting and avoiding of overfitting.

We process the edges in order of their scores, beginning with the edge which corresponds to the best pair of models, see lines 6...18. (E.g. in case of RMSE smaller values indicate better predictions, so we process the edges in *ascending* order with respect to their weights.) M_i denotes a set of models, that are selected in the i-th iteration, $score_{M_i}$ denotes the score of M_i. This score reflects how good is the ensemble based on the models in M_i. When iterating over the edges of the model-pair graph, we try to improve $score_{M_i}$ by adding models to M_i.

In each iteration we select a set of models M_i. M_{final} denotes the set of such models that are contained at least n times among the selected models, i.e. improve at least n times by at least ϵ. Finally, we train a model $\mathcal{M}$ of type *meta_model_type* over the output of models in M_{final} using all training data instances. Then $\mathcal{M}$ can be used for the prediction task (for unlabelled data).

Note, that our framework operates fully at the meta level: the attributes of data instances are never accessed directly, only the prediction vectors that the models deliver for them. Also note, that the hyperparameters (ϵ and n) can be learned using a hold-out subset of the train data that is disjoint from D.

4 Ensemble Techniques

As we mentioned, the specific choice of the i) error function *calc_err*, ii) subset score function f, iii) *examine* predicate and iv) *meta_model_type* lead to different ensemble techniques. In all of our techniques the error function calculates RMSE (root mean squared error). As *meta_model_type* we chose multivariate linear regression. In the followings, we describe further characteristic settings of our ensemble techniques.

Basic. When searching for the appropriate subset of models M_i, we calculate the *component-wise average of prediction vectors* of models in M_i and based on that we score that subset of models M_i. We use f_{avg} (Alg. 3) as subset score function in Alg. 2 at line 13. The *examine* predicate is constant true.

EarlyStop. In order to save time we only examine the best N edges (w.r.t. their weights) of the model-pair graph. For this we use $examine_{topN}$ predicate that is true for the best N edges of the model-pair graph and false else. As subset score function, similar to the Basic technique, we chose f_{avg}.

RegOpt. Like in EarlyStop, we use the $examine_{topN}$ predicate. However, instead of f_{avg} we use multivariate linear regression to score the current model selection in each iteration (see f_{reg} in Alg. 4).

GraphOpt. This operates exclusively on the model-pair graph: we chose the f_{gopt} subset score function (Alg. 5) and the $examine_{topN}$ predicate. Function f_{gopt} calculates an average-like aggregation of the edge weights, but it gives priority to larger sets, as the sum of the weights is divided by a number that is larger than the number of edges (as we use RMSE as error measure, smaller numbers correspond better scores). If simply the average were calculated (without priorising large sets), the set M containing solely the vertices of the best edge (and no other vertices) would maximize the score function and that would not be capable to find model set having larger size than 2.

Algorithm 3. Score Average Prediction: f_{avg}

Require: Modelset M, Data samples D_A and D_B, ErrorFunction $calc\_err$, Graph g
1: **for** $\forall m_i \in M$ **do** $p_i = m_i.\text{predict}(D_B)$,
2: $\forall x : p[x] = (p_1[x] + \ldots + p_i[x] + \ldots)/M.\text{size}$ (predictions averaged *per* instance)
3: **return** $calc\_err(p, D_B.\text{labels})$

Algorithm 4. Score Model Set using Linear Regression: f_{reg}

Require: Modelset M, Data samples D_A and D_B, ErrorFunction $calc\_err$, Graph g
1: **for** $\forall m_i \in M$ **do** $p_i^A = m_i.\text{predict}(D_A)$,
2: **for** $\forall m_i \in M$ **do** $p_i^B = m_i.\text{predict}(D_B)$,
3: Train multivariate linear regression $\mathcal{L}$ using p_i^A as data and $D_A.\text{labels}$ as labels
4: $p = \mathcal{L}.\text{predict}(p_i^B)$
5: **return** $calc\_err(p, D_B.\text{labels})$

Basic examines $\mathcal{O}(N^2)$ edges (N is the number of models). As $examine_{\text{topN}}$ returns true for the most promising edges, we expect that EarlyStop does not lose much on quality against Basic, but the runtime is reduced by an order of magnitude, as EarlyStop examines only $\mathcal{O}(N)$ edges. We expect RegOpt to be slower than EarlyStop, because from the computational point of view, training a linear regression is more expensive then calculating an average. On the other hand, as f_{reg} is more sophisticated than f_{avg}, we expect quality improvement. RegOpt works in a meta-wrapper fashion, but filter methods, like GraphOpt, are expected to be faster, as they do not invoke the meta-model in the phase of model selection. Nevertheless, GraphOpt may produce worse results as only the information encoded in the model-pair graph is taken into account.

Note, that we expect well-performing ensemble techniques, if the score function f and the *meta_model_type* are chosen in a way that there is a natural correspondence between them, like in case of our ensemble techniques. Also note, that Alg. 3 and 4 are conceptual descriptions of the score functions: in the implementation, the base models are not invoked as many times as the score function is called, but their prediction vectors are pre-computed and stored in an array.

5   Evaluation

Datasets. We used the labelled datasets, namely *Small* (AusDM-S, 200 models, 15000 cases), *Medium* (AusDM-M, 250 models, 20000 cases) and *Large* (AusDM-L, 1151 models, 50000 cases) of the RMSE task of the Ensembling Challenge at the Australian Data Mining Conference 2009. These data sets are publicly available at http://www.tiberius.biz/ausdm09/. They contain the outputs of different prediction models for the same task, movie rating prediction. The prediction models were originally developed by different teams of the Netflix challenge. There the task was to predict how users rate movies on a 1 to 5 integer scale (5=best, 1=worst). In AusDM, however, both the predicted ratings and the target were multiplied by 1000 and rounded to an integer value.

Algorithm 5. Score Model Set using the Model-Pair Graph: f_{gopt}

Require: Modelset M, Data samples D_A and D_B, ErrorFunction $calc\_err$, Graph g
1: SumW $\leftarrow 0$
2: **for** $(\forall \{m_i, m_j\} \,|\, m_i, m_j \in M)$ **do** SumW $\leftarrow$ SumW $+ g$.edgeWeight($\{m_i, m_j\}$)
3: **return** $\frac{\text{SumW}}{(M.\text{size})^2 * \ln(M.\text{size})}$

Table 2. Performance of the baseline and our methods: root mean squared error
(RMSE) on test data averaged over 10 folds. The numbers in parenthesis indicate
in how many folds our method won against the baseline.

Method	AusDM-S	AusDM-M	AusDM-L
SVM-Stacking best 20 models	871.97	872.38	876.68
Basic	869.68 (9)	868.42 (10)	871.88 (10)
EarlyStop	869.79 (10)	868.59 (10)	872.61 (10)
RegOpt	868.81 (10)	867.88 (10)	871.41 (10)
GraphOpt	870.49 (7)	868.33 (10)	870.53 (10)

Experimental settings. We have examined several baselines, namely Tsymbal's method[10], as well as stacking of different number of best models with LinearRegression and SVM (this selection of the individually best models is in accordance with [2]). To keep comparison clear, we select as single baseline, the stacking of the individually best models with SVMs, because SVM is generally regarded as one of the best performing regression/classification methods.[4] We used the WEKA-implementations (http://www.cs.waikato.ac.nz/~ml/) of SVM (for the baseline) and Linear Regression (for RegOpt). We performed 10-fold-crossvalidation.[5] The hyperparameters of the SVM and our models (complexity constant C, exponent of the polynomial kernel e; and n, ϵ respectively) were searched on a hold-out subset of the train data.[6]

Results. The results on test data are summarized in Tab. 2. Similarly to [11] and [13], we report the number of folds where our method won against the baselines.

Discussion. All of our proposed techniques clearly (in the majority of folds) outperform the baselines. As expected, compared to *Basic*, *EarlyStop* lost almost nothing in terms of quality. *RegOpt* however outperformed not only *EarlyStop* but *Basic* as well. *GraphOpt*, that works according to the filter schema, could

---

[4] In our reported results, we used stacking of the 20 individually best models. The reason is two-fold: i) this number leads to very good performance for the baseline, and ii) ensures fair comparison of all examined methods by making them have approximately the same number of selected models.
[5] The internal data splitting in Alg. 2 is performed each time only on the current *training* data of the 10-fold-crossvalidation. In each round of the 10-fold-crossvalidation, Alg. 2 is executed according to which this internal splitting of the current training data is iteratively repeated several times in a round robin fashion.
[6] To simplify the reproduciblity, we report the found SVM-hyperparameters: $e = 2^0 = 1$ and $C = 2^{-5}$ (AusDM-S), $C = 2^{-3}$ (AusDM-M), $C = 2^{-8}$ (AusDM-L).

still outperform the baselines, but it did not clearly outperform *Basic*. Regarding runtimes, we observed *EarlyStop* to be 3.3-times faster than *Basic* on average, whereas *GraphOpt* was 1.65-times more performant than *Basic*, and *RegOpt* was 1.4-times faster than *Basic*. This is in accordance with our expectations.

6   Conclusion

We proposed a new graph-based ensemble framework that supports stacking-based ensemble with appropriate model selection in the case if large number of models are present. We put special focus on the selection of models that compensate each other's errors. Our experiments showed that our four techniques implemented in this framework outperforms the state-of-the-art technique.

Acknowledgements. This work was co-funded by the EC FP7 project My-Media under the grant agreement no. 215006. Contact: info@mymediaproject.org.

References

1. Bacauskiene, M., Verikas, A., Gelzinis, A., Valincius, D.: A feature selection technique for generation of classification committees and its application to categorization of laryngeal images. Pattern Recognition 42, 645–654 (2009)
2. Bryll, R., Gutierrez-Osuna, R., Quek, F.: Attribute bagging: improving accuracy of classifier ensembles by using random feature subsets. Pattern Recognition 36(6), 1291–1302 (2003)
3. Dietterich, T.G.: Ensemble methods in machine learning. In: Kittler, J., Roli, F. (eds.) MCS 2000. LNCS, vol. 1857, pp. 1–15. Springer, Heidelberg (2000)
4. Ho, T.K.: The random subspace method for constructing decision forests. IEEE Trans. Pattern Anal. Mach. Intell. 20(8), 832–844 (1998)
5. Li, G.-Z., Liu, T.-Y.: Feature selection for bagging of support vector machines. In: Yang, Q., Webb, G. (eds.) PRICAI 2006. LNCS (LNAI), vol. 4099, pp. 271–277. Springer, Heidelberg (2006)
6. Peng, Y.: A novel ensemble machine learning for robust microarray data classification. Computers in Biology and Medicine 36(6), 553–573 (2006)
7. Preisach, C., Schmidt-Thieme, L.: Ensembles of relational classifiers. Knowl. Inf. Syst. 14, 249–272 (2008)
8. Tan, A.C., Gilbert, D.: Ensemble machine learning on gene expression data for cancer classification (2003)
9. Ting, K.M., Witten, I.H.: Stacked generalization: when does it work? In: Int'l. Joint Conf. on Artificial Intelligence, pp. 866–871. Morgan Kaufmann, San Francisco (1997)
10. Tsymbal, A., Patterson, D.W., Puuronen, S.: Ensemble feature selection with simple bayesian classification. Inf. Fusion 4, 87–100 (2003)
11. Webb, G.I., Boughton, J.R., Wang, Z.: Not so naive bayes: Aggregating one-dependence estimators. Mach. Learn. 58(1), 5–24 (2005)
12. Wolpert, D.H.: Stacked generalization. Neural Networks 5, 241–259 (1992)
13. Yang, Y., et al.: To select or to weigh: A comparative study of linear combination schemes for superparent-one-dependence estimators. IEEE Trans. on Knowledge and Data Engineering 19, 1652–1665 (2007)
14. Zhou, Z.-H., Wu, J., Tang, W., Zhou, Z.h., Wu, J., Tang, W.: Ensembling neural networks: Many could be better than all. Artificial Intelligence 137(1-2), 239–263 (2002)

Rough Set-Based Analysis of Characteristic Features for ANN Classifier

Urszula Stańczyk

Institute of Informatics, Silesian University of Technology,
Akademicka 16, 44-100 Gliwice, Poland

Abstract. Selection of characteristic features for a classification task is always crucial to high recognition ratio, regardlessly of the particular processing technique applied. Most methodologies offer some inherent mechanisms of dimension reduction that lead to expression of available data in more succinct way, however, combining elements of distinctively different approaches to data analysis brings interesting conclusions as to the role of particular features and their influence on the power of the resulting classifier. The paper presents research on such fusion of processing techniques, namely employing rough set based analysis of features for ANN classifier within stylometric studies on writing styles.

Keywords: Feature Selection, Classifier, ANN, Rough Sets, Data Mining, Stylometry.

1 Introduction

To handle efficiently huge volumes of data automatically some dimension reduction is required, enabling to express the information in manageable portions. Therefore, the task of finding characteristic features that describe accessible data lays the foundation for classification and is as much important as the applied methodology for successful recognition. Features are not only task- and to some extent technique-dependent, as even within the same approach several distinct sets can be tried. The answer to the question how to find the best, that is leading to the highest correct classification ratio, is certainly not trivial if it exists at all. Instead of reaching for such an impossible goal the paper provides observations on fusion of two attitudes to data mining, namely rough sets and artificial neural networks, employed in feature selection for stylometric analysis of literary texts.

Stylometry belongs with information retrieval domain. By exploiting textual descriptors, which reveal quantitative properties of texts, it enables to characterise their individual literary styles and their authors to the point of being able to recognise them [6]. Thus stylometry brings study of writing styles, characterisation of authors, elements shared, and those unique which allow for authorship attribution. Yet with ever growing corpus of texts it is in bad need of an informed selection of features. This need is not answered positively within stylometry itself, rather being shifted to the phase of processing, with techniques applied typically coming either from statistics or artificial intelligence area.

M. Graña Romay et al. (Eds.): HAIS 2010, Part I, LNAI 6076, pp. 565–572, 2010.

Both connectionist approach of ANN and rule-based of rough sets possess inherent mechanisms of establishing significance of features describing the input data. In artificial neural networks this is obtained through the learning procedure, when there are found weights associated with all interconnections that express the degrees of influence of particular features on the final outcome. Rough set methodology determines relative reducts, which are such subsets of conditional attributes that keep intact the classification properties of the decision table [7]. With help of relative reducts there are constructed decision algorithms consisting of rules that specify conditions which must be met for each decision.

These two techniques can be used just by themselves for processing in stylometric tasks [4], [9], however, the combination of these approaches into one hybrid solution brings interesting, if somewhat surprising observations. In the past research [8] it was shown that relative reducts can be used in reduction of characteristic features for ANN-classifier, yet these reducts were applied within classical rough set approach [5] dealing only with abstract data, requiring discretisation of real values. Employing instead dominance-based rough set approach [11], with dominance substituting the indiscernibility relation, enables to analyse data with ordinal properties. This makes possible to handle real valued attributes and calculate reducts and decision algorithms for them. Both the numbers of reducts and decision rules are very high and their selection as much problematic as that in the primary problem of feature selection. Therefore, in the analysis there are employed frequency indicators based on occurrences of attributes within reducts and rules. It appears that contrary to natural, intuitive expectations, to some extent reducing these features that are used more often gives better results than when removing these that are used seldom.

2   Stylometry

Three main stylometric tasks involve such analysis of written texts that allows for author characterisation, comparison, and attribution. Historically they have been used for proving or disproving the authenticity of documents or settling the questions of dubious authorship.

Stylometry relies on numerical, quantifiable properties of texts which can only be exploited due to high computational powers of contemporary computers, while in the past it was forced to observe much more prone to imitation striking features of documents such as specific language. Descriptors that reflect subconsciously used elements of writing style are less likely to be falsified and thus allow to recognise individuality. Such textual markers that enable to settle the question of authorship form so-called author invariant and usually there are proposed lexical, syntactic, structural or content specific features. Lexical characteristics base on statistics such as usage frequency for words, syntactic descriptors reflect the structure of sentences as given by punctuation marks, structural markers define organisation of text into constructing elements such as headings or paragraphs, while content-specific features indicate words of certain meaning in the given context [6].

The choice of textual descriptors is one of crucial issues within stylometric analysis and corresponds to selection of characteristic features for classification.

3   ANN-Based Classification

Artificial neural networks constitute connectionist approach to classification problems and are generally considered to be efficient classifiers in cases when detection of rather subtle relations among characteristic features is needed. A specification of a network encompasses the number of neurons with their structure and organisation, neuron activation functions and offsets, weights of interconnections, and the network learning rule. The most popularly used type of a neural network employed in pattern classification tasks is Multilayer Perceptron, the feedforward network built from layers, possessing unidirectional weighted connections between neurons, with the sigmoid activation function

$$y(n) = \frac{1}{1 + e^{-\beta n}}, \qquad n = \mathbf{W} \cdot \mathbf{X} = \mathbf{W}^T \mathbf{X} = \sum_{j=0}^{J} w_j x_j \qquad (1)$$

n (net) being a scalar product of two vectors: weight $\mathbf{W}$ and input $\mathbf{X}$, and $j = 0$ reserved for offset t, by setting $x_0 = 1$ and $w_0 = -t$.

In popular classical backpropagation algorithm as a training rule the vector of weights $\mathbf{W}$ is modified accordingly to the descent direction of the gradient

$$\Delta \mathbf{W} = -\eta \nabla e(\mathbf{W}) = -\eta \nabla \left(\frac{1}{2} \sum_{m=1}^{M} \sum_{i=1}^{I} (d_i^m - y_i^m(\mathbf{W}))^2 \right) \qquad (2)$$

(η is the learning rate) of the error on the network output, which is a sum of errors for all M learning facts on all output neurons, each equal to the difference between the expected outcome d_i^m and the one generated by the network $y_i^m(\mathbf{W})$.

Characteristic features determine the number of input nodes whereas the number of outputs typically reflects the number of distinguished classes. The number of neurons in hidden layers influences the networks classification ability and accuracy, yet the one and only rule for it does not exist and when using some simulation software leaving its default settings is as good as employing one of indicators from the published works. This attitude was followed within the conducted research and California Scientific Braimaker software that was exploited proposes as many hidden neurons in a single layer as there are inputs when there are at least 10 of them, and exactly 10 for any number below 10.

4   Input Data

In experiments as the input data there were taken literary texts of two famous writers from XIXth century, Henry James and Thomas Hardy. The samples were created by computing characteristics for markers within 30 parts taken from 3

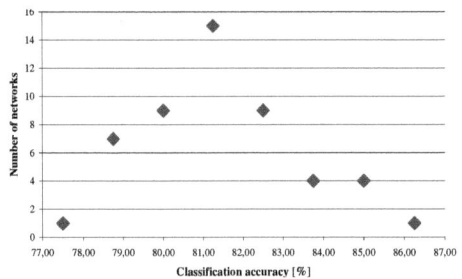

Fig. 1. Original network classification accuracy

novels for each writer for training and 8 parts from 5 novels for test, resulting in the total of 180 learning and 80 testing facts. The base set of descriptors allowing for author recognition consisted of 25 attributes and these were frequencies of usage for lexical and syntactic markers: but, and, not, in, with, on, at, of, this, as, that, what, from, by, for, to, if, a fullstop, a comma, a question mark, an exclamation mark, a semicolon, a colon, a bracket, a hyphen. Two outputs from the network corresponded to two authors distinguished.

As the initiation of interconnection weights at the learning phase plays an important role (depending on it the accuracy of the trained network can significantly vary), instead of a single training procedure there was applied multi-starting approach - for each network configuration the training was performed 50 times. Results for the base network are given in Fig. 1. The worst network (with the lowest accuracy) gave correct classification for 77.5%, the best (the highest accuracy) 86.25% and the average 81.25%.

Stylometric analysis cannot determine the importance of single features from the original set of 25 attributes and how disregarding some of them would influence the classifier performance. That is where the rough set based analysis comes into study - in the experiments some elements of rough set approach were employed to analysis of characteristic features. This led to observations how these attributes that are found the most or the least striking and significant within a rule-based methodology reflect on the performance of a connectionist classifier.

5   Rough Set-Based Feature Analysis

The first step in the rough set-based approach, invented by Z. Pawlak [5], is constructing a decision table that contains the whole available knowledge. Such table corresponds to the set of training samples for ANN, with columns of conditional attributes specifying characteristic features - inputs to the network, and values of the decision attribute being the expected classes of recognised objects.

To reduce dimensionality, rough set methodology determines relative reducts that are such subsets of conditional attributes that keep intact the classification properties of the decision table [7]. With the help of reducts there are constructed decision algorithms consisting of rules, each specifying conditions to be met for the decision to be applicable. When building decision algorithms there can be generated rules just providing a minimal cover of learning samples or all rules. In the latter case by some methodology an optimised classifier can be built, comprising selection of rules, basing for example on their support.

Since the classical rough set approach (CRSA) deals only with discrete data and the frequencies studied within the experiments are continuous values thus either there had to be applied some discretisation strategy by defining a discretisation factor, or modified indiscernibility relation applicable for continuous attributes [1], or there could be employed DRSA - the dominance-based rough set approach [3] integrating dominance relation with rough approximation, used in multicriteria decision support.

While the indiscernibility principle of the classical rough set approach says that if two objects x and y are indiscernible with respect to considered attributes then they should be classified to the same class, the *dominance principle* of the dominance-based rough set approach states that if x is as least as good as y with respect to the attributes, then x should be classified at least as good as y. That is why CRSA cannot deal with preference order in the value sets of attributes and it supports classification only when it is nominal, whereas DRSA has been proposed to deal with cases when the value sets of attributes are ordered [3,2].

6   Obtained Results

In the research there was assumed an arbitrary preference for all conditional attributes of "cost" type (the lower the better) and there were calculated all reducts (6664) and all rules (46191). The core (intersection of reducts) turned out to be empty, yet obviously some of features were exploited more often than others which led to observation of these frequencies of attributes for both reducts and constructed decision rules, as provided by Table 1a and Table 1b respectively.

The ordering of features presented in two tables was next used in tests with removing from the total set of 25 features of ANN-classifier those that were most frequently considered to be of importance within rough set methodology, those that were least often used, and when leaving those average.

For rule-based analysis of features removing either just the most (M1) or the least (L1) frequently employed attribute brought no significant change in the network performance. The same was true also for second step of reduction, as only 2 inputs (M2, L2) were reduced for rule- and 3 for reduct indicators (M1). The differences started to appear when the set was reduced below 20 attributes, with results for M4, L4 for rules and M2 for reducts, given in Fig. 2.

Fig. 2 indicates that much better results are obtained for removing the attributes more often used in decision rules rather than those employed seldom. Removing features most often used in reducts brings results somewhere in between the other two.

This observed trend shows alike progress in further reduction, as given in Fig. 3, where (Fig. 3b) there is also plotted performance for a network with inputs being neither the most, nor the least frequently used in rules. At the final

Table 1. Attribute occurrence indicators a) Reduct-based b) Rule-based

a)

M1	of	.	on						
	3478	3190	3083						
M2				,	not	;	in	by	this	at	L4
				2943	2778	2740	2726	2648	2585	2585	
M3				-	as	with	from	and	!	:	to	L3
				2035	2108	2161	2273	2324	2368	2384	2497	
		that	(	what	if	for	?				L2
		1343	1395	1415	1584	1609	1712				
	but										L1
	893										

b)

M1	of								
	13310								
M2		on							
		12921							
M3		to	this	,	.				
		11838	11426	11176	11004				
M4						!	:	not	in	L7
						10639	10326	10305	10240	
M5								;	at	L6
								9797	9082	
M6							with	as	by	L5
							8646	8471	8450	
M7				-	(	if	from	?	for	L4
				7996	7950	7691	7614	7468	7449	
		what	that							L3
		6172	6166							
	and									L2
	4172									
	but									L1
	3927									

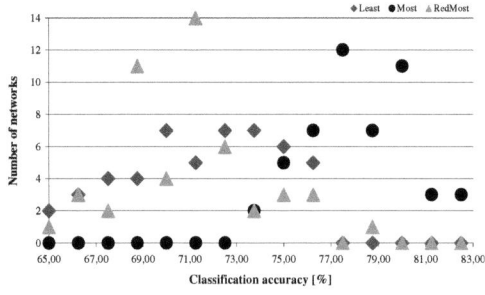

Fig. 2. Performance for networks with 15 inputs

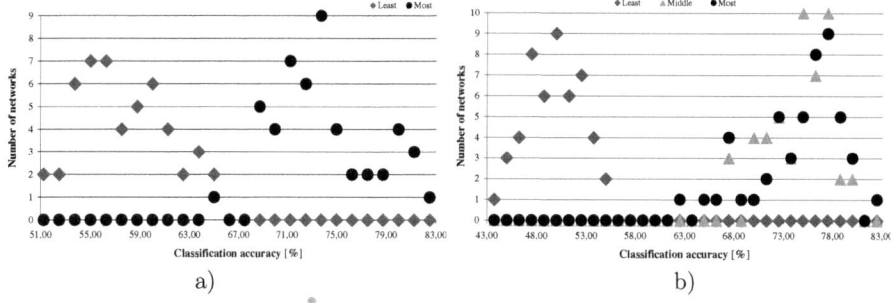

Fig. 3. Performance for networks with a) 12 or 13, b) 10 or 9 inputs

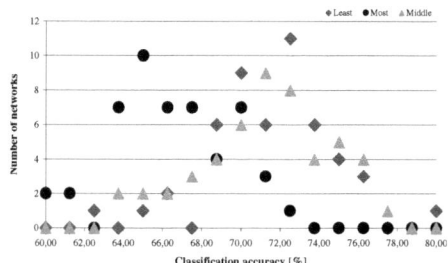

Fig. 4. Performance for networks with 10, 8 and 7 inputs

point of reduction, which means keeping just 6 most frequent attributes (L7) or 4 least frequent (M7), the recognition ratio in the former case falls to about 50% while for the latter it is still above 70%.

In reduction of inputs based on reduct indicators (Fig. 4) keeping seldom used attributes gives slightly worse classifications than for more frequent or average, yet this is also the network with just 7 inputs, the fewest out of this three.

7   Conclusions

The paper presents the analysis of characteristic features for ANN-classifier, based on elements of rough set approach, which results in a hybrid attitude to data mining. Computed relative reducts and decision rules indicate ordering of attributes based on usage frequency, reflecting their importance within the classification as perceived by the rule-based methodology. The ordering is then employed to reduce the set of base features by leaving either the most or the least frequently used attributes. Contrary to intuitive expectations the conducted research shows that the significance is to some extent reversed for the connectionist approach and the performance of the network with less often used attributes can be distinctively better than when these more exploited are kept. This detected trend requires verification by further studies involving other types of input data. Also combination of other processing techniques should be tried to check whether it is unique only for rough-neural solutions.

Acknowledgements. The software used to obtain frequencies for textual descriptors was implemented by Mr. P. Cichoñ in fulfilment of requirements for M.Sc. thesis, submitted at the Silesian University of Technology, Gliwice, Poland in 2003. 4eMka Software used in search for reducts and decision rules [3,2] is available at a website of Laboratory of Intelligent Decision Support Systems, Poznan University of Technology (http://www-idss.cs.put.poznan.pl/), Poland.

References

1. Cyran, K.A., Stanczyk, U.: Indiscernibility relation for continuous attributes: application in image recognition. In: Kryszkiewicz, M., Peters, J.F., Rybiński, H., Skowron, A. (eds.) RSEISP 2007. LNCS (LNAI), vol. 4585, pp. 726–735. Springer, Heidelberg (2007)
2. Greco, S., Matarazzo, B., Slowinski, R.: The use of rough sets and fuzzy sets in Multi Criteria Decision Making. In: Gal, T., Hanne, T., Stewart, T. (eds.) Advances in Multiple Criteria Decision Making, ch. 14, pp. 14.1–14.59. Kluwer Academic Publishers, Dordrecht (1999)
3. Greco, S., Matarazzo, B., Slowinski, R.: Dominance-based rough set approach as a proper way of handling graduality in rough set theory. In: Peters, J.F., Skowron, A., Marek, V.W., Orłowska, E., Słowiński, R., Ziarko, W.P. (eds.) Transactions on Rough Sets VII. LNCS, vol. 4400, pp. 36–52. Springer, Heidelberg (2007)
4. Matthews, R.A.J., Merriam, T.V.N.: Distinguishing literary styles using neural networks. In: Fiesler, E., Beale, R. (eds.) Handbook of neural computation, p. G8.1.1–6. Oxford University Press, Oxford (1997)
5. Pawlak, Z.: Rough sets and intelligent data analysis. Information Sciences 147, 1–12 (2002)
6. Peng, R.D., Hengartner, H.: Quantitative analysis of literary styles. The American Statistician 56(3), 15–38 (2002)
7. Shen, Q.: Rough feature selection for intelligent classifiers. In: Peters, J.F., Skowron, A., Marek, V.W., Orłowska, E., Słowiński, R., Ziarko, W.P. (eds.) Transactions on Rough Sets VII. LNCS, vol. 4400, pp. 244–255. Springer, Heidelberg (2007)
8. Stańczyk, U.: Relative reduct-based selection of features for ANN classifier. In: Cyran, K., et al. (eds.) Man-Machine Interactions. AISC, vol. 59, pp. 335–344. Springer, Heidelberg (2009)
9. Stańczyk, U., Cyran, K.A.: On employing elements of rough set theory to stylometric analysis of literary texts. International Journal on Applied Mathematics and Informatics 1(2), 159–166 (2007)
10. Stefanowski, J.: On combined classifiers, rule induction and rough sets. In: Peters, J.F., Skowron, A., Düntsch, I., Grzymała-Busse, J.W., Orłowska, E., Polkowski, L. (eds.) Transactions on Rough Sets VI. LNCS, vol. 4374, pp. 329–350. Springer, Heidelberg (2007)
11. Słowiński, R., Greco, S., Matarazzo, B.: Dominance-based rough set approach to reasoning about ordinal data. In: Kryszkiewicz, M., Peters, J.F., Rybiński, H., Skowron, A. (eds.) RSEISP 2007. LNCS (LNAI), vol. 4585, pp. 5–11. Springer, Heidelberg (2007)

Boosting Algorithm with Sequence-Loss Cost Function for Structured Prediction

Tomasz Kajdanowicz[1], Przemysław Kazienko[1], and Jan Kraszewski[2]

[1] Wrocław University of Technology, Wyb. Wyspiańskiego 27, 50-370 Wrocław, Poland
{tomasz.kajdanowicz,kazienko}@pwr.wroc.pl
[2] University of Wrocław, pl. Grunwaldzki 2/4, 50-384 Wrocław, Poland
jan.kraszewski@math.uni.wroc.pl

Abstract. The problem of sequence prediction i.e. annotating sequences appears in many problems across a variety of scientific disciplines, especially in computational biology, natural language processing, speech recognition, etc. The paper investigates a boosting approach to structured prediction, AdaBoost^{STRUCT}, based on proposed sequence-loss balancing function, combining advantages of boosting scheme with the efficiency of dynamic programming method. In the paper the method's formalism for modeling and predicting label sequences is introduced as well as examined, presenting its validity and competitiveness.

Keywords: boosting, structured prediction, structured learning, sequence prediction, ensemble method, classifier fusion, AdaBoost^{STRUCT}.

1 Introduction

Standard techniques of supervised learning aim to learn a function f that maps an input $x \in X$ to an output $y \in Y$. The goal of mapping is typically focused on binary classification $Y = \{-1,1\}$, multiclass classification $Y = \{1, ..., K\}$ or regression $Y = R$. An example of binary classification could be a problem of predicting whether the next day will or will not be rainy on the basis of historical weather data.

More sophisticated techniques allow solving prediction problems with more complex outputs. Such complex prediction problems are generally known as structured prediction algorithms or structured learning algorithms.

The definition of structured prediction derived from prior work that propose solutions for structured prediction problems, is not stated explicitly and is presented by means of examples while giving explanations and motivations [2, 9, 10, 13, 15]. Presented explanations describe among others the problems of sequence labeling, parsing, collective classification, bipartite matching.

On the other hand, according to definition in [3], it is assumed that a structured prediction problem D is a cost-sensitive classification problem, where Y has following structure: elements $y \in Y_T$ decompose into variable-length vectors $(y_1, y_2, ..., y_T)$, where vector notation is treated as useful encoding not only for sequence labeling problems.

Additionally, the algorithms realizing structured prediction make use of extended notion for feature input space. Besides, the algorithms may utilize the input data both

M. Graña Romay et al. (Eds.): HAIS 2010, Part I, LNAI 6076, pp. 573–580, 2010.

from the original input $x \in X$ and from the partially produced output $y \in Y$. This composition of x and y, i.e. (x, y) remains an input vector in Euclidean space, but now it also depends on the output achieved so far.

For instance, in the area of debt recovery sequence prediction [7, 8], an element in (x, y) might be the concatenation of business input information of particular debt with prediction output for the preceding period.

As the nature of structured prediction problems is complex, the majority of proposed algorithms is based on the well know binary classification adapted in the specific way [11]. The most natural adaptation is structured perceptron [2] that has minimal requirements on output space shape and is easy to implement. However, it provides somewhat poor generalization. Another solution are Max-margin Markov Nets that consider the structured prediction problem as a quadratic programming problem [13]. They are very useful, however, they perform very slow and are limited to Hamming loss function. Next, more flexible one, is an alternative adjustment of logistic regression to the structured outputs called Conditional Random Fields [9]. It provides probabilistic outputs and good generalization, but again it is relatively slow. Some other similar to Max-margin Markov Net technique, is Support Vector Machine for Interdependent and Structured Outputs (SVM^{STRUCT}) [15], which applies more loss functions.

The main goal of the paper is to develop a new boosting method for sequences, in which the boosting concept would be applied not independently to particular sequence items but the method would also respect prediction for the previous items obtained.

This paper is organized as follows: first, the nature of the structured prediction problem is described. Then, the details and formalism of Boosting algorithm based on sequence-loss balancing function is shown. Finally, an experiment on the real data classification task is employed to confirm the usefulness of the presented approach.

2 Problem Description

In the standard binary classification, boosting is the general machine learning concept that relies on the improvement of the final learning result by iteratively training a set of base classifiers on a weighted training set of data. Learning process results in a weighted linear combination of classifiers, trained at each iteration, forming the final classifier [5]. Boosting, making usage of base binary classifiers, while performing prediction of structures encoded in vectors, may be modified in two ways: the base classifiers will become able to predict whole structure or the boosting scheme will evaluate to be able to generalize structures [1]. Sequence labeling is a basic type of structured prediction because it is likely to be the simplest non-trivial structure. Formally, learning label sequences is a generalization to discover the discriminant function, mapping observations X to label sequences Y_T [4].

Considering the case, that an output vector $y \in Y_T$ can be produced by predicting each of y's components $y_1, y_2, ..., y_T$: $y = (y_1, y_2, ..., y_T)$ the boosting scheme may, in turn, be adapted to predict sequences, allowing dependent predictions. By treating predictions sequentially rather than independently [12], algorithms can focus on error minimization in prediction of large spans of the output. This may be done by the appropriate adjustment of the cost function.

A modified AdaBoost scheme with a sequence-loss balancing cost function, called AdaBoost^{STRUCT}, is introduced and formally presented in the next section of the paper.

3   AdaBoost^{STRUCT} Algorithm for Structured Prediction

Based on the most popular boosting algorithm, AdaBoost [6, 14], the modification to the cost function has been introduced. It is assumed that there is a binary sequence classification problem with $y_i^\mu \in \{-1,1\}$ for $i=1,2,\ldots,N$ and $\mu=1,2,\ldots,T$ (N – number of observations, T – length of sequence). The goal is to construct an T optimally designed linear combinations of K base classifiers of the form:

$$F^\mu(x) = \sum_{k=1}^{K} \alpha_k \phi(x, \theta_k) \tag{1}$$

where $F^\mu(x)$ is the combined, final classifier; $\Phi(x,\Theta_k)$ represents the kth base classifier, performing according to Θ parameters and returning a binary class label for each observation.; α_k is weight associated to the kth classifier.

Values of unknown parameters result from optimization for each sequence element being predicted, as follows:

$$arg \min_{\alpha_k, \theta_k, k:1,K} \sum_{i=1}^{N} exp\left(-y_i F^\mu(x_i)\right) \tag{2}$$

As the direct optimization of Eq. 2 is highly complex, a stage-wise suboptimal method is performed [14]. At each step optimization is carried out with respect to new parameter, leaving unchanged the previously optimized one. Therefore, let us define the result of the partial sum up to m terms (the mth partial sum):

$$F_m^\mu(x) = \sum_{k=1}^{m} \alpha_k \phi(x, \theta_k), \qquad m = 1, 2, \ldots, K \tag{3}$$

According to the definition from Eq. 3, the following recursion is a natural consequence:

$$F_m^\mu(x) = F_{m-1}^\mu(x) + \alpha_m \phi(x, \theta_m) \tag{4}$$

Due to assumption, that before calculating $F_m^{(\mu)}(x)$, the value of $F_{m-1}^{(\mu)}(x)$ has already been optimized in the previous step, the problem at step m is to compute:

$$(\alpha_m, \theta_m) = arg \min_{\alpha, \theta} J(\alpha, \theta) \tag{5}$$

where the sequence-loss balancing cost function J is defined as:

$$J(\alpha, \theta) = \sum_{i=1}^{N} exp\left(-y_i \left(\xi F_{m-1}(x_i) + (1-\xi)y_i \hat{R}^\mu(x_i) + \alpha\phi(x_i, \theta)\right)\right) \tag{6}$$

where $\hat{R}_m^\mu(x)$ is an impact function denoting the influence of the quality of preceding sequence labels prediction; the parameter $\xi \in \langle 0,1 \rangle$ allows controlling the influence of impact function in weights composition.

$\hat{R}_m^\mu(x)$ is applied in computation for current sequence position, as follows:

$$\hat{R}_m^\mu(x) = \sum_{i=1}^{m-1} \alpha_i R^\mu(x) \tag{7}$$

$$R^\mu(x) = \frac{\sum_{i=1}^T y \frac{F_i(x)}{\sum_{j=1}^K \alpha_j}}{T} \tag{8}$$

The impact function $\hat{R}_m^\mu(x)$, introduced in Eq. 7 and 8, measures the correctness of prediction for all preceding labels in sequence for each observation. This function is utilized in the cost function and it provides smaller error deviation for the whole sequence. The greater compliance between prediction and real value, the higher the function value is.

Considering α as a fixed constant, the cost function J may be optimized with respect to the base classifier $\phi(x_i, \theta)$ that is simplified to:

$$\theta = arg \min_\theta \sum_{i=1}^N w_i^{(m)} exp\left(-y_i \alpha \phi(x_i, \theta)\right) \tag{9}$$

where

$$w_i^{(m)} = exp\left(-y_i \left(\xi F_{m-1}(x_i) + (1-\xi) y_i \hat{R}^\mu(x)\right)\right) \tag{10}$$

As $w_i^{(m)}$ depends on neither α nor $\phi(x_i, \theta)$ for each x_i. $w_i^{(m)}$ it can be treated as a weight of sample observation x_i . Due to binary nature of the base classifier, minimization of θ is equivalent to:

$$\theta = arg \min_\theta \left\{ P_m = \sum_{i=1}^N w_i^{(m)} I\left(1 - y_i \phi(x_i, \theta)\right) \right\} \tag{11}$$

where

$$I(x) = \begin{cases} 0, if \ x = 0 \\ 1, if \ x > 0 \end{cases} \tag{12}$$

When the base classifier is computed at step m, we have:

$$\sum_{y_i \phi(x_i, \theta_m) < 0} w_i^{(m)} = P_m \tag{13}$$

$$\sum_{y_i \phi(x_i, \theta_m) > 0} w_i^{(m)} = 1 - P_m \tag{14}$$

and the optimum value of α_m results from:

$$\alpha_m = arg \min_\alpha \{exp(-\alpha)(1 - P_m) + exp(\alpha) P_m\} \tag{15}$$

The derivative of Eq. 15 with respect to α equaled to zero, results in:

$$\alpha_m = \frac{1}{2} \ln \frac{1 - P_m}{P_m} \tag{16}$$

Once the base classifier $\phi(x_i, \theta)$ and α_m are computed, the weights for step $m+1$ may be computed:

$$w_i^{(m+1)} = \frac{exp\left(-y_i\left(\xi F_m(x_i) + (1 - \xi)y_i \hat{R}_m^\mu(x)\right)\right)}{Z_m}$$

$$= \frac{w_i^{(m)} exp\left(-y_i \xi \alpha_m \phi(x_i, \theta_m) - (1 - \xi)\alpha_m R^\mu(x)\right)}{Z_m} \tag{17}$$

where Z_m is the normalizing factor:

$$Z_m = \sum_{i=1}^N w_i^{(m)} exp\left(-y_i \xi \alpha_m \phi(x_i, \theta_m) - (1 - \xi)\alpha_m R^\mu(x)\right) \tag{18}$$

The Eq. 17 was obtained according to following calculation:

$$w_i^{(m+1)} = \frac{exp\left(-y_i\left(\xi F_m(x_i) + (1-\xi)y_i \hat{R}_m^\mu(x)\right)\right)}{Z_m} =$$

$$\frac{exp\left(-y_i\left(\xi(F_{m-1}(x_i) + \alpha_m\phi(x_i,\theta_m)) + (1-\xi)y_i \hat{R}_m^\mu(x)\right)\right)}{Z_m} =$$

$$\frac{exp\left(-y_i\left(\xi F_{m-1}(x_i) + (1-\xi)y_i \hat{R}_{m-1}^\mu(x)\right) - y_i \xi \alpha_m\phi(x_i,\theta_m) - \left(-(1-\xi)\hat{R}_{m-1}^\mu(x) + (1-\xi)\hat{R}_m^\mu(x)\right)\right)}{Z_m} =$$

$$\frac{exp\left(-y_i\left(\xi F_{m-1}(x_i) - (1-\xi)y_i \hat{R}_{m-1}^\mu(x)\right)\right) exp\left(-y_i \xi \alpha_m\phi(x_i,\theta_m) - (1-\xi)\left(\hat{R}_m^\mu(x) - \hat{R}_{m-1}^\mu(x)\right)\right)}{Z_m} =$$

$$\frac{w_i^{(m)} exp\left(-y_i \xi \alpha_m\phi(x_i,\theta_m) - (1-\xi)\left(\left(\sum_{i=1}^m \alpha_i\right)R^\mu(x) - \left(\sum_{i=1}^{m-1}\alpha_i\right)R^\mu(x)\right)\right)}{Z_m} =$$

$$\frac{w_i^{(m)} exp\left(-y_i \xi \alpha_m\phi(x_i,\theta_m) - (1-\xi)\alpha_m R^\mu(x)\right)}{Z_m} \tag{19}$$

What is worth mentioning, the weight of the particular observation $w_i^{(m+1)}$ changes with respect to its value at the previous iteration step m. Simultaneously, the value of the impact function $\hat{R}_m^\mu(x)$ denoting the correctness in prediction of the preceding elements in the sequence changes as well.

The pseudo code of AdaBoost^{STRUCT} for sequence prediction is as follows:

```
For each sequence position (μ = 1 to T)
    Initialize wᵢ⁽¹⁾ = 1/N, m = 1

    While termination criterion is not met

            Compute θₘ and Pₘ (Eq. 11)

            Compute αₘ = ½ ln (1-Pₘ)/Pₘ
```

```
Set  Z_m = 0
For each observation (i = 1 to N)
    Compute  w_i^(m+1) = w_i^(m) exp(-y_i ξ α_m φ(x_i, θ_m) - (1 - ξ) α_m R^μ(x))
    Sum up  Z_m = Z_m + w_i^(m+1)
End For
For each observation (i = 1 to N)
    Normalize  w_i^(m+1) = w_i^(m+1) / Z_m
End For
Set  K = m, m = m + 1
End While
Calculate  f^μ(·) = sign(Σ_{k=1}^K α_k φ(·, θ_k))
End For
```

The typical termination criterion used in the above algorithm is the value of maximum K that denotes the number of base classifiers.

4 Experiments

To demonstrate the effectiveness and utility of the proposed approach, it was applied to the problem of financial sequence prediction [7]. The data set consisted of 4019 cases. Each case was described by the set of 20 input features and a sequence of 10 consecutive payments (was a payment in the month: 1, no payment: -1). The decision stump was utilized as the base classifier. The 10 fold cross-validation was applied. The model from the best fold was considered for the comparison.

Hence, the prediction accuracy for the labeled sequences of 10 positions long was examined in the experiment. During the experiment the ξ value was changed from 0.4 to 1 to observe how it infers the algorithm accuracy. Note that the value of $\xi = 1$

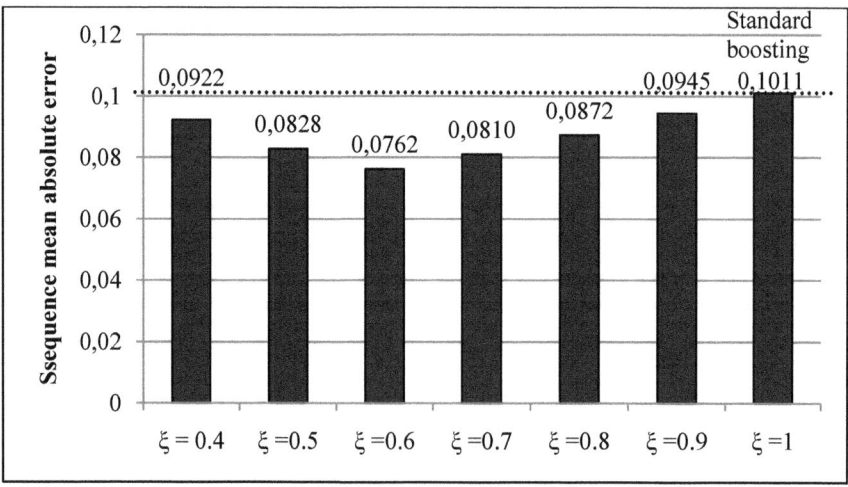

Fig. 1. Average absolute error for all sequence items with distinct ξ parameter, $\xi = 1$ denotes the standard boosting method

indicates the standard boosting approach, with no modification in the cost function (see Eq. 6), i.e. each item in the sequence is predicted independently using the standard AdaBoost algorithm.

As presented in Fig. 1 and Fig. 2, particular value of ξ parameter influences the prediction error. The mean absolute error reaches its smallest value for $\xi = 0.6$; it decreases by 24% for the whole sequence compared to the standard approach $\xi = 1$. In particular, this difference rises item by item, except the ninth item (Fig. 2). Obviously, there is no difference for the first item; the proposed algorithm AdaBoost^{STRUCT} does not make use of classification for the previous items. For the second item, the mean absolute error drops from 0.035 to 0.021 (-40%) while for the last one from 0.1026 to 0.0648 (-58%). It refers the highest difference between methods, i.e. for $\xi = 0.6$ and the standard boosting. The same error level at the first item for all ξ determines the maximum average difference in error between methods ($\xi = 0.6$ and $\xi = 1$) over all sequence items at the level of only -24%.

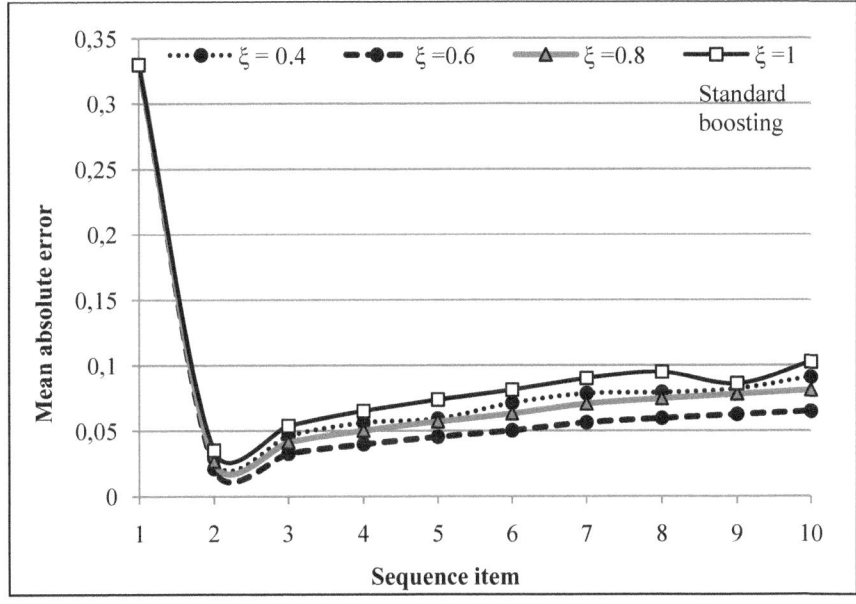

Fig. 2. Mean absolute error for each sequence item with 4 distinct values of ξ; the curve for $\xi = 1$ corresponds to the standard boosting method

5   Conclusions and Future Work

A new approach to formulation of boosting cost function for structure prediction is proposed in the paper. This function is used for the prediction of sequent class labels. It respects both the prediction error in the current sequence item and the average error in all other preceding items. This appears to provide an important contribution to learning of labeled sequences. The experiments have shown that the gain in accuracy is the highest for $\xi = 0.6$ and generally increases for the following items in the sequence.

More experiments on the proposed algorithm, especially in comparison to other known approaches to structured prediction problems as well as other data sets will be carried out in the future work. Additionally, some other interesting properties of the method, in particular immunity to overfitting or error bound will be extensively revised.

Acknowledgments. This work was supported by The Polish Ministry of Science and Higher Education, the development project, 2009-11.

References

1. Altun, Y., Hofmann, T., Johnson, M.: Discriminative Learning for Label Sequences via Boosting. In: Advances in Neural Information Processing Systems, vol. 15, pp. 1001–1008. MIT Press, Cambridge (2003)
2. Collins, M.: Discriminative training methods for hidden Markov models: Theory and experiments with perceptron algorithms. In: Conference on Empirical Methods in Natural Language Processing 2002, vol. 10, pp. 1–8 (2002)
3. Daume, H.: Practical Structured Learning Techniques for Natural Language Processing. Ph.D. thesis, University of Southern California, Los Angeles, CA, USA (2006)
4. Daume, H., Langford, J., Marcu, D.: Search-based structured prediction. Machine Learning 75, 297–325 (2009)
5. Freund, Y., Schapire, R.: A decision-theoretic generalization of on-line learning and an application to boosting. Journal of Computer and System Sciences 55, 119–139 (1997)
6. Friedman, J., Hastie, T., Tibshirani, R.: Additive logistic regression: a statistical view of boosting. The Annals of Statistics 28(2), 337–407 (2000)
7. Kajdanowicz, T., Kazienko, P.: Hybrid Repayment Prediction for Debt Portfolio. In: Nguyen, N.T., Kowalczyk, R., Chen, S.-M. (eds.) ICCCI 2009. LNCS (LNAI), vol. 5796, pp. 850–857. Springer, Heidelberg (2009)
8. Kajdanowicz, T., Kazienko, P.: Prediction of Sequential Values for Debt Recovery. In: Bayro-Corrochano, E., Eklundh, J.-O. (eds.) CIARP 2009. LNCS, vol. 5856, pp. 337–344. Springer, Heidelberg (2009)
9. Lafferty, J., McCallum, A., Pereira, F.: Conditional random fields: Probabilistic models for segmenting and labeling sequence data. In: International Conference on Machine Learning ICML 2001, pp. 282–289 (2001)
10. McCallum, A., Freitag, D., Pereira, F.: Maximum entropy Markov models for information extraction and segmentation. In: International Conference on Machine Learning ICML 2000, pp. 591–598 (2000)
11. Nguyen, N., Guo, Y.: Comparisons of Sequence Labeling Algorithms and Extensions. In: International Conference on Machine Learning ICML 2000, pp. 681–688 (2007)
12. Punyakanok, V., Roth, D.: The use of classifiers in sequential inference. In: Advances in Neural Information Processing Systems, vol. 13, pp. 995–1001. MIT Press, Cambridge (2001)
13. Taskar, B., Guestrin, C., Koller, D.: Max-margin Markov networks. In: Advances in Neural Information Processing Systems, vol. 16, pp. 25–32. MIT Press, Cambridge (2004)
14. Theodoris, S., Koutroumbas, K.: Pattern Recognition. Elsevier, Amsterdam (2009)
15. Tsochantaridis, I., Hofmann, T., Thorsten, J., Altun, Y.: Large margin methods for structured and interdependent output variables. Journal of Machine Learning Research 6, 1453–1484 (2005)

Application of Mixture of Experts to Construct Real Estate Appraisal Models

Magdalena Graczyk[1], Tadeusz Lasota[2], Zbigniew Telec[1], and Bogdan Trawiński[1]

[1] Wrocław University of Technology, Institute of Informatics,
Wybrzeże Wyspiańskiego 27, 50-370 Wrocław, Poland
[2] Wroclaw University of Environmental and Life Sciences, Dept. of Spatial Management
Ul. Norwida 25/27, 50-375 Wroclaw, Poland
mag.graczyk@gmail.com, tadeusz.lasota@wp.pl,
zbigniew.telec@pwr.wroc.pl, bogdan.trawinski@pwr.wroc.pl

Abstract. Several experiments were conducted in order to investigate the usefulness of mixture of experts (ME) approach to an online internet system assisting in real estate appraisal. All experiments were performed using 28 real-world datasets composed of data taken from a cadastral system and GIS data derived from a cadastral map. The analysis of the results was performed using recently proposed statistical methodology including nonparametric tests followed by post-hoc procedures designed especially for multiple 1×n and n×n comparisons. GLM (general linear model) architectures of mixture of experts achieved better results for ME with an adaptive variance parameter for each expert, whereas MLP (multilayer perceptron) architectures - for standard mixtures of experts.

Keywords: mixture of experts, statistical tests, real estate appraisal, MATLAB.

1 Introduction

Ensemble methods have been developed and applied to many areas for the last two decades. Ensembles combining diverse machine learning models have been theoretically and empirically proved to ensure significantly better performance than their single original models [12], [13], [17]. Although many multiple model creation techniques have been proposed [28], according to [26] five commonly used groups of them can be distinguished, namely bagging [3], boosting [25], AdaBoost [7], stacked generalization [29], and mixture of experts. The latter was devised by Jordan and Jacobs [14], [16] and then developed and extended by Avnimelech [2], Srivastava [30], Lima [21], and others.

The mixture of experts (ME) is a neural network architecture for supervised learning, which comprises a number of expert networks and a gating network (see Figure 1). Both expert and the gating networks are fed with the input vector x and the gating network produces one output per expert. The task of a gating network is to combine the various experts by assigning weights to individual networks, which are not constant but are functions of the input instances. The output of ME is the weighed sum of the expert outputs. The expectation-maximization (EM) algorithm is usually

M. Graña Romay et al. (Eds.): HAIS 2010, Part I, LNAI 6076, pp. 581–589, 2010.
© Springer-Verlag Berlin Heidelberg 2010

employed to learn the parameters of the ME architecture. Mixture of experts techniques have been applied to face [6], speech [15], handwriting [27] recognition, in molecular biology [4], and medicine [9], [11], [25].

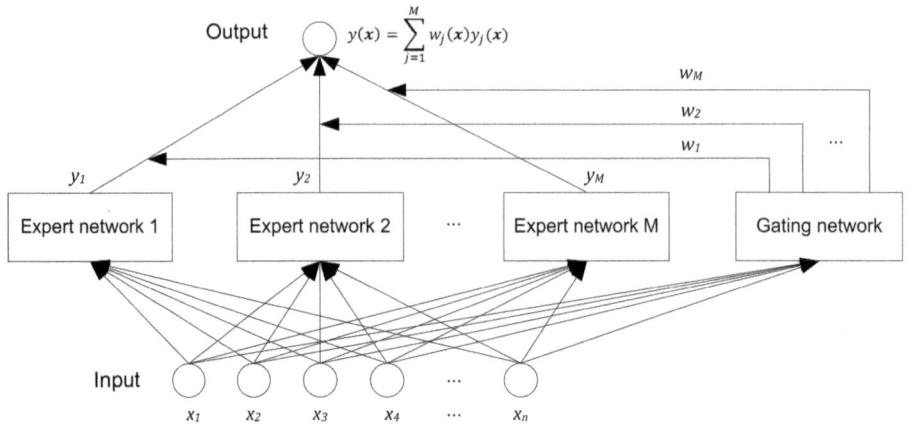

Fig. 1. General architecture of mixture of experts

So far the authors of the present paper have investigated several ensemble methods to construct regression models to assist with real estate appraisal: [10], [18], [19], [20]. In the current contribution is one step forward, we present our study on of mixture of experts applied to real-world cadastral data. The second goal of the paper was to investigate the potential of multiple comparison statistical procedures to analyse and select machine learning algorithms for real world application such as an internet system for real estate appraisal.

2 Plan of Experiments

The main goal of our study was to explore the potentiality of the ME models to be used in an online internet system assisting property valuation. The second goal was to investigate the usefulness of multiple comparison statistical procedures to analyse and select machine learning algorithms for real world application. For experiments we prepared a dataset obtained by combining cadastral data of residential premises, records of sales/purchase transactions, and GIS data derived from a cadastral map. Our resulting dataset covered the period of seven years from 1999 to 2005 and consisted of 3843 records with 6 input variables characterizing premises and the price of a transaction as the output. The features with their descriptive statistics are presented in Table 1.

In the next step we created all possible combinations of one-year datasets retaining chronological sequence of data. The list of so obtained 28 datasets which we used in our experiments is given in Table 2. All data were normalized using min-max technique. Having 28 datasets we were able to perform comparative analysis of ME algorithms using nonparametric tests followed by post hoc procedures designed for multiple comparisons.

Table 1. Features of residential premises supplemented with GIS data

Name	Max	Min	Avg	Std	Med	Description
Area	154.7	14.4	49.4	20.2	46.7	usable area of premises
Year	2004	1850	1946	34	1958	year of building construction
Storeys	12	1	6	2	5	no. of storeys in a building
Yc	49753	39809	44653	1708	44308	geodetic coordinate Yc (WE)
Centre	12396	20	2149	1196	1972	distance from the centre of a city
Shopping	3557	81	1022	526	1023	distance from the shopping centre
Price	540200	20500	107411	49185	95000	price of premises

Table 2. Data subsets comprising sales transactions ordered by date used in experiments

Dataset	# Inst	Dataset	# Inst	Dataset	# Inst	Dataset	# Inst
99	437	00	366	01-02	912	02-05	2049
99-00	803	00-01	808	01-03	1451	03	539
99-01	1245	00-02	1278	01-04	1960	03-04	1048
99-02	1715	00-03	1817	01-05	2491	03-05	1579
99-03	2254	00-04	2326	02	470	04	509
99-04	2763	00-05	2857	02-03	1009	04-05	1040
99-05	3294	01	442	02-04	1518	05	531

The experiments were conducted using MIXLAB – a matlab tool written by Perry Moerland dealing with the mixture of expert models [23]. 12 different ME architectures: six with GLM (general linear model) neural networks denoted by G01 to G06, and six with MLP (multilayer perceptron) neural networks denoted by M01 to M06 were employed. Two types of mixture of experts were used: a standard one and the other with an adaptive variance parameter for each expert [24]. Three optimisation routines for expectation maximisation algorithm were applied: scg – scaled conjugate gradient, qn – quasi-Newton, and cg – conjugate gradients. Each model was generated with six input variables, one output, and six experts. Datasets were randomly split into training sets containing 80% instances and test ones with remaining 20% instances. As fitness function the mean square error (MSE) was applied. Main parameters of the ME architectures used in experiments are listed in Table 3.

Table 3. Parameters of ME architectures used in experiments

Code	Network type	ME type	Optim. routine	No. of inputs	No. of outputs	No. of experts
G01/M01	GLM/MLP	standard	scg	6	1	6
G02/M02	GLM/MLP	standard	qn	6	1	6
G03/M03	GLM/MLP	standard	cg	6	1	6
G04/M04	GLM/MLP	variance	scg	6	1	6
G05/M05	GLM/MLP	variance	qn	6	1	6
G06/M06	GLM/MLP	variance	cg	6	1	6

In order to further evaluate the ME models, all 28 datasets were used to generate models using other experimental data mining system called KEEL *(Knowledge Extraction based on Evolutionary Learning)* [1]. The algorithms employed to carry out comparative experiments with the references to source articles are listed in Table 4, and details of the algorithms and references to source articles can be found on KEEL web site: www.keel.es. They were divided into two groups comprising deterministic and neural network techniques respectively. The algorithms were run in KEEL individually for each of 28 datasets using 10-fold cross validation (10cv) and the prediction accuracy was measured with the mean square error (MSE).

Table 4. Evolutionary fuzzy and deterministic KEEL algorithms used in study

Group	Code	KEEL name	Description
DET	SLR	Regr-LinearLMS	Statistical linear regression
	M5T	Regr-M5	Model tree which combines a decision tree model with statistical linear regression
	SVM	Regr-NU_SVR	Support vector machines for regression
ANN	MLP	Regr-MLPerceptron Conj-Grad	Multilayer perceptron for modeling
	RBF	Regr-RBFN	Radial basis function neural network for regression problems
	IRP	Regr-iRProp+	Multilayer perceptrons trained with the iRProp+ algorithm - resilient backpropagation algorithm

Several articles on the use of statistical tests in machine learning for comparisons of many algorithms over multiple datasets have been published recently [5],[8],[22]. Their authors argue that the commonly used paired tests i.e. parametric t-test and its nonparametric alternative Wilcoxon signed rank tests are not adequate when conducting multiple comparisons due to the so called multiplicity effect. They recommend following methodology. First of all the Friedman test or its more powerful derivative the Iman and Davenport test should be performed. Both tests can only inform the researcher about the presence of differences among all samples of results compared. After the null-hypotheses have been rejected he can proceed with the post-hoc procedures in order to find the particular pairs of algorithms which produce differences. The latter comprise Bonferroni-Dunn's, Holm's, and Hochberg's procedures in the case of 1×n comparisons and Nemenyi's, Shaffer's, and Bergmann-Hommel's procedures in the case of n×n comparisons.

3   Statistical Analysis of the Results of Experiments

Statistical analysis of the results of experiments was performed using a software available on the web page of Research Group "Soft Computing and Intelligent Information Systems" at the University of Granada (http://sci2s.ugr.es/sicidm). This JAVA program calculates multiple comparison procedures: Friedman, Iman-Davenport, Bonferroni-Dunn, Holm, Hochberg, and Shaffer tests as well as adjusted p-values. In all tables presented in this section the p-values less than $\alpha=0.05$, indicating that respective models differ significantly, were marked with italic font.

MSE values obtained for six ME architectures with GLM neural networks are shown in Table 5. The lowest median was obtained for G06 and G04 models, whereas the biggest values were achieved for G01. MSE values obtained for six ME architectures with MLP neural networks are shown in Table 6. The lowest median was obtained for M01 and M02 models, whereas the biggest values were achieved for M04.

Table 5. MSE values for ME models comprising GLM neural networks

Set	G01	G02	G03	G04	G05	G06
99	0.002319	0.002317	0.002322	0.002630	0.002127	0.002446
99-00	0.004945	0.004963	0.004949	0.004055	0.005349	0.004575
99-01	0.002706	0.002714	0.002703	0.002841	0.003427	0.007912
99-02	0.003091	0.003096	0.003091	0.002715	0.002857	0.003082
99-03	0.003968	0.003972	0.003967	0.003807	0.003752	0.003930
99-04	0.006073	0.006090	0.006101	0.005637	0.005175	0.005222
99-05	0.004725	0.004711	0.004720	0.004162	0.004380	0.004069
00	0.004684	0.004730	0.004673	0.005693	0.004377	0.008045
00-01	0.002557	0.002578	0.002553	0.002146	0.005484	0.002421
00-02	0.003136	0.003142	0.003144	0.002878	0.002896	0.002421
00-03	0.003782	0.003782	0.003789	0.003486	0.003519	0.002601
00-04	0.006112	0.006113	0.006098	0.005500	0.005459	0.005745
00-05	0.004277	0.004281	0.004287	0.003133	0.003543	0.003457
01	0.002283	0.002282	0.002279	0.001911	0.001847	0.001850
01-02	0.004121	0.003635	0.003616	0.004126	0.003195	0.003261
01-03	0.003631	0.003627	0.003635	0.003180	0.003267	0.003288
01-04	0.006042	0.006066	0.006071	0.005343	0.005686	0.005177
01-05	0.003493	0.003490	0.003498	0.002956	0.003011	0.002940
02	0.007008	0.006999	0.007006	0.007004	0.006060	0.006303
02-03	0.017061	0.003769	0.003782	0.003656	0.003471	0.003475
02-04	0.006364	0.002605	0.006354	0.005650	0.005301	0.005667
02-05	0.003316	0.006354	0.003315	0.002909	0.002715	0.002906
03	0.004101	0.004093	0.004096	0.004545	0.004771	0.005039
03-04	0.005318	0.005310	0.005302	0.004326	0.003662	0.003351
03-05	0.002700	0.002702	0.002699	0.002345	0.002410	0.002501
04	0.004878	0.004796	0.004869	0.001929	0.002737	0.003164
04-05	0.002441	0.002434	0.002443	0.001976	0.002044	0.002285
05	0.002522	0.002526	0.002499	0.001919	0.002070	0.001949
Median	**0.004035**	**0.003776**	**0.003780**	**0.003333**	**0.003495**	**0.003320**

Table 6. MSE values for ME models comprising MLP neural networks

Set	M01	M02	M03	M04	M05	M06
99	0.002352	0.002236	0.002188	0.003886	0.002837	0.003432
99-00	0.004950	0.003145	0.004821	0.002958	0.005606	0.003483
99-01	0.002956	0.002768	0.003003	0.004207	0.002698	0.003541
99-02	0.002753	0.002880	0.003007	0.003136	0.002839	0.003184
99-03	0.003837	0.003800	0.003810	0.003840	0.003900	0.003806
99-04	0.005217	0.005089	0.005277	0.005316	0.005358	0.005501
99-05	0.004343	0.004403	0.004240	0.004122	0.003095	0.004254
00	0.004999	0.004656	0.006939	0.004343	0.006040	0.005630
00-01	0.002425	0.002267	0.004025	0.002615	0.005153	0.002650
00-02	0.002981	0.002901	0.002955	0.003010	0.002896	0.002827
00-03	0.003581	0.003624	0.003671	0.003609	0.004271	0.003930
00-04	0.005469	0.005266	0.005497	0.005234	0.005690	0.004766
00-05	0.003195	0.003026	0.003206	0.003034	0.003039	0.003135
01	0.001957	0.001968	0.002280	0.004473	0.002622	0.002351
01-02	0.003127	0.003258	0.004262	0.003239	0.004739	0.003186
01-03	0.003174	0.003252	0.003233	0.003134	0.003445	0.003717
01-04	0.005179	0.004054	0.005141	0.004903	0.004925	0.004692
01-05	0.002962	0.003001	0.002988	0.002856	0.003038	0.002972
02	0.006756	0.006605	0.006939	0.006170	0.006611	0.005704
02-03	0.003535	0.003452	0.003572	0.003758	0.004166	0.003281
02-04	0.005518	0.005073	0.005475	0.004635	0.006304	0.005618
02-05	0.002996	0.003445	0.003015	0.002933	0.003399	0.003007
03	0.003813	0.004039	0.003949	0.004753	0.006654	0.005337
03-04	0.003500	0.003437	0.003835	0.005208	0.022165	0.004777
03-05	0.002535	0.002561	0.002551	0.002288	0.002452	0.002497
04	0.002239	0.001910	0.002949	0.002220	0.001714	0.002707
04-05	0.002151	0.002235	0.002143	0.002292	0.002316	0.002324
05	0.001720	0.001652	0.001703	0.001999	0.001926	0.001853
Median	**0.003185**	**0.003255**	**0.003622**	**0.003684**	**0.003673**	**0.003458**

Statistical tests adequate to multiple comparisons were performed for all 12 ME models altogether. The Friedman and Iman-Davenport tests were performed in respect of average ranks, which use χ^2 and F statistics, respectively. The calculated values of these statistics were 79.64 and 9.42, respectively, whereas the critical values at $\alpha=0.05$ are $\chi^2(11)=21.92$ and $F(11,297)=1.82$, what means that there are significant differences between some models. Average ranks of individual ME models are shown in Table 7, where the lower rank value the better model.

Table 7. Average rank positions of ME models comprising GLM and MLP neural networks

Rank	Model	Rank	Model	Rank	Model	Rank	Model
4.07	M02	5.07	G04	6.14	M03	8.98	G02
4.96	M01	5.43	M04	6.32	M06	9.13	G03
5.05	G05	5.79	G06	7.66	M05	9.39	G01

Thus, we were justified in proceeding to post-hoc procedures. In Table 8 adjusted p-values for Nemenyi, Holm, and Shaffer tests for n×n comparisons are shown for 20 pairs of models out of 66, where significant differences were noticed. Following main observations could be done: G01,G02, and G03 revealed significantly worse performance than any of first six models in the ranking. There are not significant differences among M01, M02, M03 and G04, G05, and G06 models.

Table 8. Adjusted p-values for n×n comparisons of ME algorithms with GLM and MLP over 28 datasets showing 20 hypotheses rejected out of 66

Alg vs Alg	pUnadj	pNeme	pHolm	pShaf
G01 vs M02	3.35E-08	2.21E-06	2.21E-06	2.21E-06
G03 vs M02	1.57E-07	1.04E-05	1.02E-05	8.63E-06
G02 vs M02	3.47E-07	2.29E-05	2.22E-05	1.91E-05
G01 vs M01	4.31E-06	0.000285	0.000272	0.000237
G01 vs G05	6.70E-06	0.000442	0.000415	0.000368
G01 vs G04	7.31E-06	0.000482	0.000446	0.000402
G03 vs M01	1.58E-05	0.001040	0.000946	0.000867
G03 vs G05	2.39E-05	0.001576	0.001409	0.001313
G03 vs G04	2.59E-05	0.001711	0.001504	0.001426
G02 vs M01	3.05E-05	0.002015	0.001740	0.001679
G01 vs M04	3.89E-05	0.002567	0.002178	0.002139
G02 vs G05	4.56E-05	0.003013	0.002511	0.002511
G02 vs G04	4.94E-05	0.003262	0.002669	0.002511
G03 vs M04	0.000125	0.008255	0.006629	0.005753
G01 vs G06	0.000182	0.011986	0.009444	0.008354
M02 vs M05	0.000195	0.012902	0.009970	0.008992
G02 vs M04	0.000226	0.014934	0.011314	0.010409
G03 vs G06	0.000530	0.034951	0.025948	0.024360
G01 vs M03	0.000744	0.049130	0.035731	0.034242
G02 vs G06	0.000910	0.060034	0.042751	0.041842

The performance of two best architectures of ME, namely GLM with an adaptive variance parameter for each expert (G04, G05, and G06 models) and MLP for standard mixtures of experts (M01, M02, and M03 models) were compared with single models generated by deterministic and neural algorithms implemented in KEEL. Statistical tests adequate to multiple comparisons were conducted altogether for 12 models comprising for six ME and KEEL ones. The Friedman and Iman-Davenport tests were performed in respect of average ranks, which use χ^2 and F statistics, respectively. The calculated values of these statistics were 180.43 and 38.19, respectively, whereas the critical values at α=0.05 are $\chi^2(11)$=21.92 and $F(11,297)$=1.82, what means that there are significant differences between some models. Average ranks of the models are shown in Table 9, where the lower rank value the better model. All ME models gained lower ranks than the KEEL ones. Nemenyi, Holm, and Shaffer tests for n×n comparisons indicated there were significant differences between all ME models and IRP, SLR, RBF, and M5T ones. In turn SVM and MLP models did not significantly differ from ME ones in any case but one: M02 versus MLP.

Table 9. Average rank positions of ME models versus KEEL ones

Rank	Model	Rank	Model	Rank	Model	Rank	Model
3.32	M02	4.11	M01	5.79	SVM	9.29	RBF
4.07	G04	4.82	M03	7.04	MLP	10.00	SLR
4.07	G05	5.00	G06	9.21	M5T	11.29	IRP

4   Conclusions and Future Work

Several experiments were conducted in order to investigate the usability of mixture of experts approach to an online internet system assisting with real estate appraisal. In the study 28 real-world datasets composed of data taken from a cadastral system, registry of property sales/purchase transaction and GIS data derived from a cadastral map were employed. The analysis of the results was performed using recently proposed statistical methodology including nonparametric tests followed by post-hoc procedures designed especially for multiple n×n comparisons. Following general conclusions could be drawn on the basis of the experiments: both GLM and MLP neural networks used in the ME architectures can lead to low values of prediction error. However, GLM architectures achieve better results for ME with an adaptive variance parameter for each expert, whereas MLP architectures for standard mixtures of experts. No significant differences were observed for various optimisation algorithms such as scaled conjugate gradient, quasi-Newton, and conjugate gradients. ME models outperformed significantly single models generated using deterministic and neural algorithms implemented in KEEL but SVM and MLP.

The investigation proved the usefulness and strength of multiple comparison statistical procedures to analyse and select machine learning algorithms for real estate appraisal. Further research is planning to conduct comparative experiments of mixture of experts and other commonly used ensemble techniques such as bagging, boosting, and stacking in the context of real estate appraisal.

References

1. Alcalá-Fdez, J., et al.: KEEL: A Software Tool to Assess Evolutionary Algorithms for Data Mining Problems. Soft Computing 13(3), 307–318 (2009)
2. Avnimelech, R., Intrator, N.: Boosted mixture of experts: An ensemble learning scheme. Neural Computation 11(2), 483–497 (1999)
3. Breiman, L.: Bagging Predictors. Machine Learning 24(2), 123–140 (1996)

4. Caragea, C., Sinapov, J., Dobbs, D., Honavar, V.: Mixture of experts models to exploit global sequence similarity on biomolecular sequence labeling. BMC Bioinformatics 10(Suppl. 4), S4 (2009)
5. Demšar, J.: Statistical comparisons of classifiers over multiple data sets. Journal of Machine Learning Research 7, 1–30 (2006)
6. Ebrahimpour, R., Kabir, E., Esteky, H., Yousefi, M.R.: View-independent face recognition with Mixture of Experts. Neurocomputing 71, 1103–1107 (2008)
7. Freund, Y., Schapire, R.E.: Decision-theoretic generalization of on-line learning and an application to boosting. J. Computer and System Sciences 55(1), 119–139 (1997)
8. García, S., Herrera, F.: An Extension on Statistical Comparisons of Classifiers over Multiple Data Sets for all Pairwise Comparisons. Journal of Machine Learning Research 9, 2677–2694 (2008)
9. Goodband, J.H., Haas, O.C.L., Mills, J.A.: A mixture of experts committee machine to design compensators for intensity modulated radiation therapy. Pattern Recog. 39, 1704–1714 (2006)
10. Graczyk, M., Lasota, T., Trawiński, B., Trawiński, K.: Comparison of Bagging, Boosting and Stacking Ensembles Applied to Real Estate Appraisal. In: Nguyen, N.T., Le, M.T., Świątek, J. (eds.) ACIIDS 2010, Part II. LNCS (LNAI), vol. 5991, pp. 340–350. Springer, Heidelberg (2010)
11. Güler, I., Übeyli, E.D.: A modified mixture of experts network structure for ECG beats classification with diverse features. Engineering Applications of Artificial Intelligence 18, 845–856 (2005)
12. Hansen, L., Salamon, P.: Neural network ensembles. IEEE Transactions on Pattern Analysis and Machine Intelligence 12(10), 993–1001 (1990)
13. Hashem, S.: Optimal linear combinations of neural networks. Neural Net. 10(4), 599–614 (1997)
14. Jacobs, R.A., Jordan, M.I., Nowlan, S.J., Hinton, G.E.: Adaptive mixtures of local experts. Neural Computation 3, 79–87 (1991)
15. Jianping, D., Bouchard, M., Yeap, T.H.: Linear Dynamic Models With Mixture of Experts Architecture for Recognition of Speech Under Additive Noise Conditions. IEEE Signal Processing Letters 13(9), 573–576 (2006)
16. Jordan, M.I., Jacobs, R.A.: Hierachical mixtures of experts and the EM algorithm. Neural Computation 6, 181–214 (1994)
17. Krogh, A., Vedelsby, J.: Neural network ensembles, cross validation, and active learning. In: Advances in Neural Inf. Proc. Systems, pp. 231–238. MIT Press, Cambridge (1995)
18. Krzystanek, M., Lasota, T., Telec, Z., Trawiński, B.: Analysis of Bagging Ensembles of Fuzzy Models for Premises Valuation. In: Nguyen, N.T., Le, M.T., Świątek, J. (eds.) ACIIDS 2010, Part II. LNCS (LNAI), vol. 5991, pp. 330–339. Springer, Heidelberg (2010)
19. Lasota, T., Telec, Z., Trawiński, B., Trawiński, K.: A Multi-agent System to Assist with Real Estate Appraisals using Bagging Ensembles. In: Nguyen, N.T., Kowalczyk, R., Chen, S.-M. (eds.) ICCCI 2009. LNCS (LNAI), vol. 5796, pp. 813–824. Springer, Heidelberg (2009)
20. Lasota, T., Telec, Z., Trawiński, B., Trawiński, K.: Exploration of Bagging Ensembles Comprising Genetic Fuzzy Models to Assist with Real Estate Appraisals. In: Corchado, E., Yin, H. (eds.) IDEAL 2009. LNCS, vol. 5788, pp. 554–561. Springer, Heidelberg (2009)
21. Lima, C.A.M., Coelho, A.L.V., Von Zuben, F.J.: Hybridizing mixtures of experts with support vector machines: Investigation into nonlinear dynamic systems identification. Information Sciences 177(10), 2049–2074 (2007)

22. Luengo, J., García, S., Herrera, F.: A Study on the Use of Statistical Tests for Experimentation with Neural Networks: Analysis of Parametric Test Conditions and Non-Parametric Tests. Expert Systems with Applications 36, 7798–7808 (2009)
23. Mitchell, H.B.: Multi-Sensor Fusion: An Introduction. Springer, Heidelberg (2007)
24. Moerland, P.: Some methods for training mixtures of experts, Technical Report IDIAP-Com 97-05, IDIAP Research Institute (1997)
25. Ng, S.K., McLachlan, G.J.: Extension of Mixture-of-experts networks for binary classification of hierachical data. Artificial Intelligence in Medicine 41, 51–67 (2007)
26. Polikar, R.: Ensemble Learning. Scholarpedia 4(1), 2776 (2009)
27. Rahman, A.F.R., Fairhurst, M.C.: A new hybrid approach in combining multiple experts to recognize handwritten numerals. Pattern Recognition Letters 18(8), 781–790 (1997)
28. Rokach, L.: Ensemble-based classifiers. Artificial Intelligence Review 33, 1–39 (2010)
29. Schapire, R.E.: The Strength of Weak Learnability. Machine Learning 5(2), 197–227 (1990)
30. Srivastava, A.N., Su, R., Weigend, A.S.: Data mining for features using scale-sensitive gated experts. IEEE Transactions on Pattern Analysis and Machine Intelligence 21, 1268–1279 (1999)
31. Wolpert, D.H.: Stacked Generalization. Neural Networks 5(2), 241–259 (1992)

Designing Fusers on the Basis of Discriminants – Evolutionary and Neural Methods of Training

Michal Wozniak and Marcin Zmyslony

Department of Systems and Computer Networks, Wroclaw University of Technology,
Wybrzeze Wyspianskiego 27, 50-370 Wroclaw, Poland
{Michal.Wozniak,Marcin.Zmyslony}@pwr.wroc.pl

Abstract. The combining approach to classification is nowadays one of the most promising directions in pattern recognition. There are many methods of decision-making that can be used by an ensemble of classifiers. The most popular methods have their origins in voting, where the decision of a common classifier is a combination of individual classifiers' outputs, i.e. class numbers or values of discriminants. This work focuses on the problem of fuser design. We propose to train a fusion block by algorithms that have their origin in neural and evolutionary approaches. As we have shown in previous works, we can produce better combining classifiers than *Oracle* can. Presented results of experiments confirm our previous observations.

Keywords: combining classifiers, evolutionary algorithms, neural networks, fuser design.

1 Introduction and Related Works

In the field of pattern recognition, the easiest way to get the result is by using an individual classifier. The problem is that real classification tasks involve a large number of classes and noisy inputs. For such tasks we need well-trained classifiers that can be experts in all areas of the problem. This is hard to get due to the complexity of the calculations. Perfect solutions are often difficult to achieve, because the design of a typical classifier is aimed to select the most valuable features and choose the best classification method from the set of available ones on the basis of their qualities. An alternative solution is to use multiple classifier systems (MCSs), which make decisions on the basis of the individual classifiers' outputs. The most popular way of combining the outputs of classifiers are voting methods, belief functions, statistical techniques and other integration schemes. [11]. The motivations of using MCSs are as follows:

- For a small sample, the selection of the worst classifier by e.g. averaging the individual classifiers [12].
- There is evidence that combining classifiers can improve the performance of the most successful ones and exploit unique classifier strengths.
- Many machine learning algorithms, like decision tree induction, are *de facto* heuristic search algorithms which do not guarantee that an optimal tree has been found. Exhaustive search i.e. testing the whole space of possible trees for the decision of the problem is impossible. The combining approach that starts the machine learning algorithm at different points is an attractive proposition.

M. Graña Romay et al. (Eds.): HAIS 2010, Part I, LNAI 6076, pp. 590–597, 2010.
© Springer-Verlag Berlin Heidelberg 2010

- A combined classifier could be used in a distributed environment, especially in the case that the database is partitioned for privacy reasons and in each node of the computer network only a final decision could be available.
- According to the „no free lunch theorem" there is not a single solution that can solve all problems, but classifiers do have different domains of competence [13].
  The typical architecture of MCSs is depicted in Fig.1.

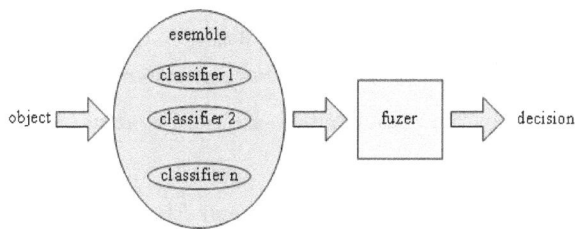

Fig. 1. Model of Multiple classifier system

There are a number of important issues to building the aforementioned MCSs, that can be grouped into three main problems:

- What is the topology of the MCSs.
- How to design the classifier ensemble,
- How to design the fuser.

There are several topologies of MCSs, but we assume parallel ones which are the most popular and intuitive. Therefore, let us focus on the last two issues. First, choosing classifiers from a pool of available ones. Apart from increasing the computational complexity, combining similar classifiers should not contribute to the system becoming constructed. Therefore, selecting members of the committee with different components seems interesting. Known works introduce different types of diversity measures which allow the possibility of a coincidental failure to be minimized. [1].

Another important issue is the choice of a collective decision making method. The first group of methods includes algorithms making fusion of classifiers on the level of their responses (discrete outputs) [2] and the second group of collective decision making methods is formed by the classifier fusion on the level of their discriminants (continuous outputs), the main form of which are the *posterior* probability estimators, referring to the probabilistic model of a pattern recognition task [3].

For making common decisions by the first group of classifiers, based on the types of outputs, we use following common classifier $\overline{\Psi}$:

$$\overline{\Psi} = \arg\max{}_{j \in M} \sum_{l=1}^{n} \delta\left(j, \Psi^{(l)}\right) w^{(l)} \Psi^{(l)} \tag{1}$$

where $w^{(l)}$ is the weight of the l-th classifier and

$$\delta(j,i) = \begin{cases} 0 & \text{if } i \neq j \\ 1 & \text{if } i = j \end{cases}. \tag{2}$$

Let us note that $w^{(l)}$ plays a key-role of the quality of the classifier $\Psi^{(l)}$. Much research has been done on how to set the weights, e.g. in [2] authors proposed to learn the fuser. Let us consider three possibilities possible weight set ups [6]:

- weights dependent on the classifier,
- weights dependent on the classifier and the class number,
- weights dependent on the features value, the classifier, and the class number.

The second group of classifiers make a decision on the basis of the values of discriminants. Let $F^{(l)}(i, x)$ mean such a function assigned to class i for a given value of x, which is used by the l-th classifier $\Psi^{(l)}$. A common classifier $\hat{\Psi}(x)$ looks as follows

$$\hat{\Psi}(x) = i \quad \text{if} \quad \hat{F}(i, x) = \max_{k \in M} \hat{F}(k, x), \tag{3}$$

where

$$\hat{F}(i, x) = \sum_{l=1}^{n} w^{(l,i)} F^{(l)}(i, x) \text{ and } \sum_{i=1}^{n} w^{(l,i)} = 1. \tag{4}$$

Let us consider four possible weights set ups for a fuser that is based on the values of the classifiers' discriminates:

- Weights dependent on the classifier
- Weights dependent on the classifier and the feature vector
- Weights dependent on the classifier and the class number
- Weights dependent on the classifier, the class number, and the feature vector

In this paper we will look at the case where weights are dependent on the classifier and the class number and will present an optimization problem that will return minimal misclassification results for fusion of the classifier. We will also present methods for solving such optimization problems using evolutionary algorithms (*GA*) and neural networks (*NN*).

2 Fuser Design

2.1 Optimization Problem

For the case described in point 1 an ensemble learning task leads to the problem of how to establish the following vector W

$$W = \left[W^{(1)}, W^{(2)}, ..., W^{(n)} \right] \tag{5}$$

which consists of weights assigned to each classifier (denoted as l) and each class number (denoted as i).

$$W^{(l)} = \left[w^{(l,i)}, w^{(l,i)}, ..., w^{(l,i)} \right]^T \tag{6}$$

We could formulate the following optimization problem. The weights should be established in such a way as to maximize the accuracy probability of the fuser:

$$\Phi(W) = 1 - P_e(W), \qquad (7)$$

where $P_e(W)$ is frequency of misclassification.

To show the limits of the classifier's committee quality we decided to use the *Oracle* classifier. This classifier is an abstract fusion model, where if the last value of the classifier recognizes the object correctly, then the committee of classifiers points to the correct class too. In literature a thesis that the Oracle classifier is an upper bound for the combined classification problem can be found [5], but it is possible to produce a better classifier than Oracle using some method of classifier fusion [6].

In order to solve the aforementioned optimization task, we could use one of a variety of widely used algorithms. In this work we have decided to engage in evolutionary algorithms [7] and neural networks.

2.2 Evolutionary Algorithms

We propose the following training algorithm whose idea is depicted in Fig.2.

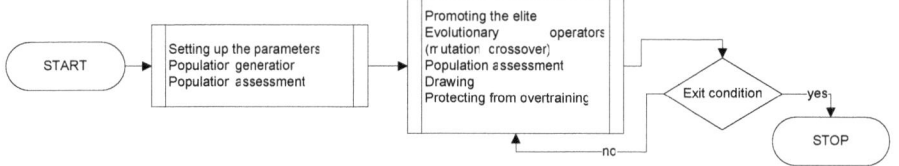

Fig. 2. Idea of optimization algorithm based on evolutionary approach

For each member of the population, a value of the fitness function is calculated according to (7). The learning set is exploited for that purpose.

A certain number of members that are characterized by the highest fitness are taken from the population. The elite is put into a descendant population, not being treated by mutation and crossover processes as well as selection procedure.

Mutation involves adding a vector of numbers randomly generated according to the normal density distribution (with mean equal to 0 and the standard deviation set to 1).

The crossover operator generates one offspring member on the basis of two parents according to the two-point crossover rule.

A selection of individuals from the population is formed by merging the descendant population with a set of individuals created by mutation and crossover. The probability of the selection of a particular individual is proportional to the value of its fitness, according to the roulette wheel selection rule.

A number of drawings are calculated so that some members of the new population will be the same as in the previous population, including the elite that has been previously promoted.

The main purpose of the overtraining assessment procedure is to break up the optimization process once it becomes likely that further learning can cause the loss of the generalization ability in favor of a too overfitting model to learning set samples. A validation set is used in order to calculate the fitness of the individuals in the same way as for the regular population assessment.

The procedure breaks the optimization process if deterioration of the result obtained by the best individual is observed in the course of the given number of subsequent learning cycles.

2.3 Neural Networks

Our second proposition of the training algorithm is based on the neural approach. Neural networks can be used to model complex relationships between inputs and outputs and of course to solve optimization problems. In our case we decided to use neural networks as a fuser where input values get discriminant functions denoted as F_l^i, where i is number of class to which the object belongs and l is the number of simple classifiers. The picture below presents such model.

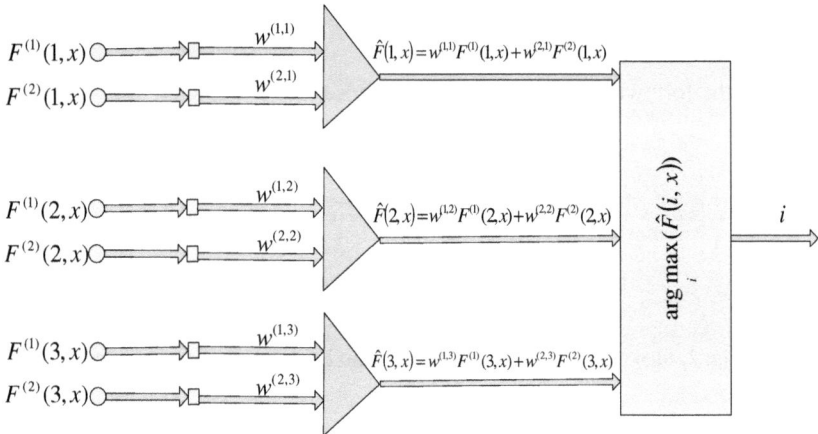

Fig. 3. Weights dependent on classifier and class number

3 Experiments

3.1 Set Up of Optimization Task

The aim of the experiments is to evaluate the performance of the discriminants's fuser based on weights dependent on classifier and class number.

All experiments were carried out in *Matlab* environment using dedicated software called *Genetic Algorithm Tool, PRTools* [4] and our own software.

For the purpose of this experiment, there were five neural networks prepared that could be treated as individual classifiers. To ensure the diversity of the simple classifiers, all were slightly undertrained (the training process was stopped early for each classifier).

The details of used neural nets are as follows:

- Five neurons in the hidden layer,
- sigmoidal transfer function,

- back propagation learning algorithm,
- number of neurons in last layer equals number of classes of given experiment.

Additionally the qualities of the classifiers mentioned above, were compared with the abstract fusion model called the *Oracle* classifier (which was described in section 2.1).

To evaluate the experiment we used five databases from UCI Machine Learning Repository [8], which are described in table 1.

Table 1. Databases' description

	Database	Number of		
		Attributes	classes	Examples
1	Glass_Identification	9	7	214
2	Letter_Recognition	16	26	20000
3	Haberman	3	2	306
4	Balance_scale	4	3	625
5	Ionosphere	34	2	351
6	Image_segmentation	19	7	2100

The set up of the experiments for each database was different, that is why there are only average values presented. For *GA* the mutation function was Gaussian, population size equals 300, 8 members of elite, the fraction of genes swapped between individuals equals 0.8 and 300 iterations.

For *NN* number of iterations to train equals 1500, number of units in each hidden layer equals 10 and the number of inputs equals the number of classes.

For each database the experiment was repeated ten times with:

- different parameter of population size for GA
- different epoch of learning for NN.

The best results obtained in those experiments are presented in table below with additional information about the result obtained by the *Oracle* classifier and the majority vote [9].

3.2 Results Evaluation

The results presented in Fig. 4 prove that genetic algorithms and neural networks are very good tools for solving optimization problems. As stated before, when weights depend on the classifier and the class number, it is possible to achieve results that are better than the *Oracle* classifier. The results obtained in these experiments show that for all of the database results using GA and NN were not equal. Because of this we are not able to judge which tool (*GA* or *NN*) gives the best results, because in both cases customizing parameters could always improve or make the final result worse. We should always remember that the tools that were used in our experiments are somehow black boxes and only appropriate settings of all the parameters can give the best results. One thing that we can confirm for *GA*, is that we get better results when we take more of the population into consideration and when the epoch of learning we establish for neural networks is higher.

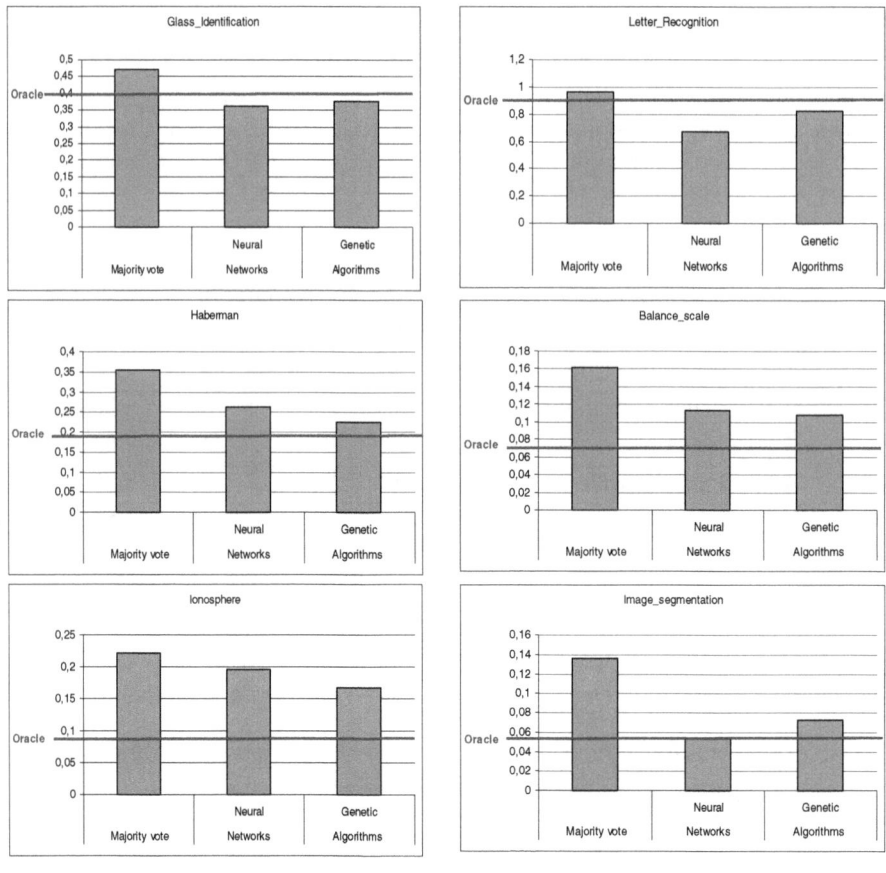

Fig. 4. Results obtained in experiments for majority vote, neural networks, genetic algorithms and the Oracle classifier

For the next step of our research we are going to carrying out more experiments where we are going to establish dependencies between the quality and the stability of classifiers and the set up of the optimizing algorithm.

4 Final Remarks

Some methods of classifier fusion were discussed in this paper and one of them was discussed on a real example.

Obtained results justify the use of the weighted combination and they are similar to what was published in [10]. Unfortunately, as it was stated, it is not possible to determine values of weights in the analytical way, therefore using heuristic methods of optimization (like evolutionary algorithms) seems to be a promising research direction.

Acknowledgments. This research is supported in part by European Union under European Social Fund and by The Polish State Committee for Scientific Research under the grant which is realizing in years 2010-13.

References

1. Kuncheva, L.I., Bezdek, J.C., Duin, R.P.W.: Decision templates for multiple classifier fusion: an experimental comparison. Pattern Recognition 34, 299–314 (2001)
2. Kuncheva, L.I.: Combining pattern classifiers: Methods and algorithms. Wiley, Chichester (2004)
3. Biggio, B., Fumera, G., Roli, F.: Bayesian Analysis of Linear Combiners. In: Haindl, M., Kittler, J., Roli, F. (eds.) MCS 2007. LNCS, vol. 4472, pp. 292–301. Springer, Heidelberg (2007)
4. Duin, R.P.W., et al.: PRTools4, A Matlab Toolbox for Pattern Recognition. Delft University of Technology, The Netherlands (2004)
5. Woods, K., Kegelmeyer, W.P.: Combination of multiple classifiers using local accuracy estimates. IEEE Transactions on PAMI 19(4), 405–410 (1997)
6. Woźniak, M., Jackowski, K.: Some remarks on chosen methods of classifier fusion based on weighted voting. In: Corchado, E., Wu, X., Oja, E., Herrero, Á., Baruque, B. (eds.) HAIS 2009. LNCS, vol. 5572, pp. 541–548. Springer, Heidelberg (2009)
7. Michalewicz, Z.: Genetics Algorithms + Data Structures = Evolutions Programs. Springer, Berlin (1996)
8. Asuncion, A., Newman, D.J.: UCI ML Repository, Irvine, CA: University of California, School of Information and Computer Science (2007),
   http://www.ics.uci.edu/~mlearn/MLRepository.html
9. Zmyślony, M., Woźniak, M.: Influence of fusion methods on quality of classification. Advanced Simulation of Systems, 117–120 (2010)
10. Kuncheva, L.I., Bezdek, J.C., Duin, R.P.W.: Decision templates for multiple classifier fusion: an experimental comparison. Pattern Recognition 34, 299–314 (2001)
11. Giacinto, G., Roli, F., Fumera, G.: Design of Effective Multiple Classifier Systems by Clustering of Classifiers. In: Proceedings of the 15th International Conference on Pattern Recognition (ICPR 2000), vol. 2, p. 2160 (2000)
12. Marcialis, G.L., Roli, F.: Fusion of Face Recognition Algorithms for Video-Based Surveillance Systems. In: Foresti, G.L., Regazzoni, C., Varshney, P. (eds.) Multisensor Surveillance Systems: The Fusion Perspective. Kluwer Academic Publishers, Dordrecht (2003)
13. Wolpert, D.H.: The supervised learning no-free-lunch theorems. In: Proceedings of the 6th Online World Conference on Soft Computing in Industrial Applications (2001)

Author Index